THE
AMERICAN LANGUAGE

An Inquiry into the Development
of English in the United States

BY
H. L. MENCKEN

SECOND EDITION
REVISED AND EXPANDED

LOS ANGELES :: CLAREMONT
COYOTE CANYON PRESS
2012

PUBLISHED BY
ALFRED A. KNOPF, INC.
1919

Revised Edition Published 1922

REISSUED BY COYOTE CANYON PRESS 2012

CONTENTS

	PAGE
PREFACE TO THE FIRST EDITION	vii
PREFACE TO THE REVISED EDITION	xi-xvii

I. INTRODUCTORY 1

   1. The Diverging Streams of English 1
   2. The Academic Attitude 5
   3. The View of Writing Men 12
   4. Foreign Observers 25
   5. The General Character of American English 28
   6. The Materials of the Inquiry 38

II. THE BEGINNINGS OF AMERICAN 45

   1. The First Differentiation 45
   2. Sources of Early Americanisms 51
   3. New Words of English Material 55
   4. Changed Meaning 62
   5. Archaic English Words 65
   6. Colonial Pronunciation 69

III. THE PERIOD OF GROWTH 74

   1. Character of the New Nation 74
   2. The Language in the Making 86
   3. The Expanding Vocabulary 91
   4. Loan-Words and Non-English Influences 100
   5. Pronunciation Before the Civil War 110

IV. AMERICAN AND ENGLISH TODAY 113

   1. The Two Vocabularies 113
   2. Differences in Usage 117
   3. Honorifics 137
   4. Euphemisms 143
   5. Expletives and Forbidden Words 148

V. INTERNATIONAL EXCHANGES 157

   1. Americanisms in England 157
   2. Briticisms in the United States 166

CONTENTS

		PAGE
VI.	TENDENCIES IN AMERICAN	173
	1. General Characters	173
	2. Lost Distinctions	178
	3. Processes of Word-Formation	183
	4. Foreign Influences Today	197
VII.	THE STANDARD AMERICAN PRONUNCIATION	206
	1. General Characters	206
	2. The Vowels	213
VIII.	AMERICAN SPELLING	221
	1. The Two Orthographies	221
	2. The Influence of Webster	228
	3. The Advance of American Spelling	235
	4. British Spelling in the United States	238
	5. Simplified Spelling	243
	6. The Treatment of Loan-Words	248
	7. Minor Differences	253
IX.	THE COMMON SPEECH	255
	1. Grammarians and Their Ways	255
	2. Spoken American As It Is	262
	3. The Verb	271
	4. The Pronoun	291
	5. The Adverb	304
	6. The Noun	308
	7. The Adjective	308
	8. The Double Negative	310
	9. Other Syntactical Peculiarities	313
	10. Vulgar Pronunciation	314
X.	PROPER NAMES IN AMERICA	321
	1. Surnames	321
	2. Given Names	338
	3. Geographical Names	343
	4. Street Names	357
XI.	AMERICAN SLANG	360
	1. Its Origin and Nature	360
	2. War Slang	368

CONTENTS v

	PAGE
XII. THE FUTURE OF THE LANGUAGE	372
1. English as a World Language	372
2. English or American?	382

APPENDICES

I. SPECIMENS OF THE AMERICAN VULGATE 388

   1. The Declaration of Independence in American . . . 388
   2. Baseball-American 392
   3. Ham-American 394
   4. Vers Américain 395

II. NON-ENGLISH DIALECTS IN AMERICA 397

   1. German 397
   2. French 400
   3. Spanish 402
   4. Yiddish 405
   5. Italian 408
   6. Dano-Norwegian 411
   7. Swedish 414
   8. Dutch 416
   9. Icelandic 419
  10. Greek 421
  11. The Slavic Languages 422

III. PROVERB AND PLATITUDE 422

BIBLIOGRAPHY 427

   1. General 425
   2. Dictionaries of Americanisms 432
   3. The Process of Language Growth 432
   4. Loan-Words 434
   5. Pronunciation 435
   6. Regional Variations 437

      a. General Discussions 437
      b. New England 437
      c. The Middle States 438
      d. The South 439
      e. The Middle West 440
      f. The Far West 441
      g. The Colonies 441
      h. Negro-English 441

CONTENTS

		PAGE
7.	Spelling	441
8.	Geographical Names	443
9.	Surnames and Given Names	446
10.	Non-English Languages in America	447
	a. German	447
	b. French	448
	c. Dano-Norwegian	449
	d. Dutch	450
	e. Swedish	450
	f. Spanish	450
	g. Icelandic	451
	h. Italian	451
	i. Yiddish	451
	j. Portuguese	452
	k. General	452
11.	Other Colonial Dialects of English	452
	a. Australian	452
	b. Beach-la-Mar	452
	c. South African	452
	d. Canadian	452
	e. East Indian	453
	f. Pidgin-English	453
12.	Slang	453
13.	Euphemisms, Nicknames, and Forbidden Words	455
14.	Rudimentary Speech	456
15.	The Future of the Language	456
16.	Bibliographies of American English	456

LIST OF WORDS AND PHRASES 458

GENERAL INDEX 483

PREFACE TO THE FIRST EDITION

The aim of this book is best exhibited by describing its origin. I am, and have been since early manhood, an editor of newspapers and books, and a critic of the last named. These occupations have forced me into a pretty wide familiarity with current literature, both periodical and within covers, and in particular into familiarity with the current literature of England and America. It was part of my daily work, for a number of years, to read the principal English newspapers and reviews; it has been part of my work, all the time, to read the more important English novels, essays, poetry and criticism. An American born and bred, I early noted, as everyone else in like case must note, certain salient differences between the English of England and the English of America as practically spoken and written—differences in vocabulary, in syntax, in the shade and habits of idiom, and even, coming to the common speech, in grammar. And I noted too, of course, partly during visits to England but more largely by a somewhat wide and intimate intercourse with English people in the United States, the obvious differences between English and American pronunciation and intonation.

Greatly interested in these differences—some of them so great that they led me to seek exchanges of light with Englishmen—I looked for some work that would describe and account for them with a show of completeness, and perhaps depict the process of their origin. I soon found that no such work existed, in either England or America—that the whole literature of the subject was astonishingly meagre and unsatisfactory. There were several dictionaries of Americanisms, true enough, but only one of them made any pretension to scientific method, and even that one was incomplete. The solitary general treatise on the American dialect, the work of a man foreign to both England and America in race and education, was more than 40 years old, and full of palpable errors. For the rest, there was only a fugitive and inconsequential literature—an almost useless mass of notes and essays, chiefly by the minor sort of pedagogues, seldom illuminating, save in small details, and often incredibly ignorant and inaccurate. On the large and important subject of American pronunciation, for example, I could find nothing save a few casual essays. On American spelling, with its wide and constantly visible divergences from English usages, there was little more. On American grammar there was nothing whatsoever. Worse, an important part of the poor literature that I unearthed was devoted to absurd efforts to prove that no such thing as an American variety of English existed—that the differences I constantly encountered in English and that my English friends encountered in American were chiefly imaginary, and to be explained away by denying them.

Still interested in the subject, and despairing of getting any illumination from such theoretical masters of it, I began a collection of materials for my own information and amusement, and gradually it took on a rather formidable bulk. My employment being made known by various articles in the newspapers and magazines, I began also to receive contributions from other persons of the same taste, both English and American, and gradually my collection fell into a certain order, and I saw the workings of general laws in what, at first, had appeared to be mere chaos. The present book then began to take form—its preparation a sort of recreation from other and far different labor. It is anything but an exhaustive treatise upon the subject; it is not even an exhaustive examination of the materials. All it pretends to do is to articulate some of those materials—to get some approach to order and coherence into them, and so pave the way for a better work by some more competent man. That work calls for the equipment of a first-rate philologist, which I am surely not. All I have done here is to stake out the field, sometimes borrowing suggestions from other inquirers and sometimes, as in the case of popular American grammar, attempting to run the lines myself.

That it should be regarded as an anti-social act to examine and exhibit the constantly growing differences between English and American, as certain American pedants argue sharply—this doctrine is quite beyond my understanding. All it indicates, stripped of sophistry, is a somewhat childish effort to gain the approval of Englishmen—a belated efflorescence of the colonial spirit, often commingled with fashionable aspiration. The plain fact is that the English themselves are not deceived, nor do they grant the approval so ardently sought for. On the contrary, they are keenly aware of the differences between the two dialects, and often discuss them, as the following pages show. Perhaps one dialect, in the long run, will defeat and absorb the other; if the two nations continue to be partners in great adventures it may very well happen. But even in that case, something may be accomplished by examining the differences which exist today. In some ways, as in intonation, English usage is plainly better than American. In others, as in spelling, American usage is as plainly better than English. But in order to develop usages that the people of both nations will accept it is necessary to study the differences now visible. This study thus shows a certain utility. But its chief excuse is its human interest, for it prods deeply into national idiosyncrasies and ways of mind, and that sort of prodding is always entertaining.

I am thus neither teacher, nor prophet, nor reformer, but merely inquirer. The exigencies of my vocation make me almost completely bilingual; moreover, I have a hand for a compromise dialect which embodies the common materials of both languages, and is thus free from offense on both sides of the water—as befits the editor of a magazine published in both countries. But that compromise dialect is the living speech of neither. What I have tried to do here is to make a first sketch of the living speech of these States. The work is confessedly incomplete, and in places very painfully so, but in such enterprises a man must put an arbitrary term to his labors, lest some mischance, after years of diligence, take him from them too suddenly for them to be closed, and his laborious accumulations, as Ernest Weekly says in his book on English surnames, be "doomed to the waste-basket by harassed executors."

If the opportunity offers in future I shall undoubtedly return to the subject. For one thing, I am eager to attempt a more scientific examination of the grammar of the American vulgar speech, here discussed briefly in Chapter VI.[1] For another thing, I hope to

[1] Now Chapter IX.

make further inquiries into the subject of American surnames of non-English origin. Various other fields invite. No historical study of American pronunciation exists; the influence of German, Irish-English, Yiddish and other such immigrant dialects upon American has never been fully investigated; there is no adequate treatise on American geographical names. Contributions of materials and suggestions for a possible revised edition of the present book will reach me if addressed to me in care of the publisher at 220 West Forty-second Street, New York. I shall also be very grateful for the correction of errors, some perhaps typographical, but others due to faulty information or mistaken judgment.

In conclusion, I borrow a plea in confession and avoidance from Ben Jonson's pioneer grammar of English, published in incomplete form after his death. "We have set down," he said, "that that in our judgment agreeth best with reason and good order. Which notwithstanding, if it seem to any to be too rough hewed, let him plane it out more smoothly, and I shall not only not envy it, but in the behalf of my country most heartily thank him for so great a benefit; hoping that I shall be thought sufficiently to have done my part if in tolling this bell I may draw others to a deeper consideration of the matter; for, touching myself, I must needs confess that after much painful churning this only would come which here we have devised." . MENCKEN.

Baltimore, January 1, 1919.

PREFACE TO THE REVISED EDITION

This edition has been greatly enlarged and thoroughly rewritten. Every chapter has been scrutinized for errors, and nearly every page shows changes. The corrections and suggestions that accumulated after the publication of the first edition—they came from all parts of the world, and from observers of the most various equipment and accuracy—were of such bulk that they almost alarmed me into abandoning the work altogether, but after due prayer I finally tackled them, and the result is now spread before the nobility and gentry. I thought it well, in a book opening so much new ground, to document liberally, that possible successors might be spared the tedious searches that I had to make myself. In the revision I have pursued the same plan, and I believe that all the useful material is now charted. Especially in the first chapter and in the chapters on Tendencies in American, American and English Today, American Spelling, and Proper Names in America there are summaries of much new matter, and somewhat elaborate references. The discussion of foreign languages in the United States, scarcely more than a footnote in the first edition, is now enlarged and put into an appendix. Another appendix offers some specimens of the American vulgate. The bibliography has been augmented, reorganized, and I hope, made more useful. Everywhere the text has been revised in the light of the criticism that has reached me.

Unluckily, the book does not contain all of the new matter that I hoped to get into it. For one thing, there is the "more scientific examination of the grammar of the American vulgar speech," spoken of in the preface to the first edition. It is not that I made no effort to carry out this promised inquiry; it is simply that I found it extending far beyond the limits of the time that I could give to it, and even further beyond the bounds of my philological equipment. The science of grammar, as it was taught and practised until a few years ago, had a very comfortable simplicity, for it dealt only with written languages, and what lay outside the printed page was conveniently neglected. But of late grammarians have been turning to spoken languages, and the result is a great increase in their difficulties. They must now deal, not with single words, but with whole phrases, many of which are not easily resolved into the words that originally made them. Worse, they must deal with phrases that no two individuals utter precisely alike. Thus grammar begins to ground itself on phonology, as it once grounded itself upon etymology, and the grammarian can no longer lock himself in his study with his books, but must go among men and women and listen attentively to what they say. The old-fashioned science of grammar was almost helpless in dealing with such a thing as the American vulgate; the new science, as I say, demands a wide and accurate knowledge in fields wherein my own knowledge is sadly imperfect. I have made various efforts to enlist professional philologists for the investigation, but with no success. From all that I have approached I have received far more courtesy than my amateurish inquiries deserved, and from many I have received very useful information and not a few acute suggestions. But the academic prudery that I spoke of in my first edition still flourishes. It would be regarded as *infra dig.*, I am told, for an American professor of English to concern himself too actively with the English spoken by nearly a hundred millions of his countrymen. He may, if he will, devote a lifetime to the English dialect of Norfolk or Dorset, but he may not waste his time and his dignity upon the dialect of his janitor, his barber and his trousers-presser. That dialect, it appears, does not belong to philology, but merely to humor. If it is to be investigated, then the work must be done by such wags as Ring W. Lardner and such dilettanti as I.

Thus the section on vulgar American, save for the introduction of new illustrative material, remains substantially as I originally wrote it. In the interval, of course, I have received contributions and criticisms from many correspondents, and some of them have suggested changes that I have adopted. But in the main the section is unchanged. So are the various historical discussions of American pronunciation. The meagre material that I made use of remains almost as meagre as it was then; the whole literature of the subject, in fact, is embraced in a few essays, chiefly by Dr. Charles H.

PREFACE TO THE REVISED EDITION

Grandgent. Why this inquiry, which demands the equipment of a competent phonologist, has not attracted more American scholars I do not know. It is certainly not open to objection on grounds of academic dignity. Nevertheless, it remains neglected, and so does the subject of American surnames. Practically all of the existing work upon American surnames, indeed, has been done by philological amateurs. As for geographical names, the material available is confined chiefly to incomplete and chaotic word-lists. Many of the etymologies currently accepted are clearly ridiculous, and many more have a dubious smack. There is certainly room here for a useful book. There is even more room in the field of loan-words. And quite as much in the field of artificial words, *e. g., kodak, crisco* and *postum,* though here Dr. Louise Pound and her pupils have done a great deal of careful and valuable work.

Since my first edition was published there have been various evidences of a renewed interest in the contemporary status and development of the language, both in the United States and in England. The Society for Pure English, organized in 1913 but paralyzed by the onset of the war, has resumed its functions, and, under the leadership of Dr. Robert Bridges, the Poet Laureate, is now showing an intelligent interest in the language that is in being, and a fine determination to rescue it from the outworn formulæ of the grammarians. At home the National Council of Teachers of English has begun to make propaganda for better instruction in the mother-tongue—though often without due discrimination, I fear, between what is in the books and what people actually speak—and a great many discussions of living philological questions, sometimes very penetrating, have appeared in the magazines and newspapers, and even in some of the more daring philological journals. The American Dialect Society continues its work, and still looks forward to the publication of its dictionary. *English,* the first English periodical devoted wholly to the mother-tongue, made its bow in March, 1919. Its prospectus announced that it would discuss, among other things, "American English, Americanisms, and Anglicisms in America," but this promise has not been fulfilled. *English* quickly degenerated, in fact, to what one correspondent denounced as "carping schoolmasterishness and conventional pedantry"; it is now no more than a sort of grammatical *Answers*. Mr. R. H. Thornton's revision and extension of his American Glossary remains unpublished, unfortunately, for lack of funds, and his materials have been turned over to the library of Harvard University. But Mr. Gilbert M. Tucker, a pioneer student of Americanisms, has published an important work, "American English," summarizing his observations over a period of forty years. Dr. George Philip Krapp has published an admirable study of the current standard pronunciation of English in America, and various other writers—for example, Mr. Ring W. Lardner and Mr. John V. A. Weaver—have made interesting contributions to American-English literature. All these new works are noticed in their proper places.

The first edition of this book was printed from type and limited in numbers deliberately—not, as some kind friends seem to suspect, because the publisher and I plotted to profiteer by putting up the price, but simply because I knew it to be full of imperfections and planned to submit a small edition to scholars and then prepare a revised edition for general circulation in the light of their criticism. The popular demand for the volume was a genuine surprise, and the whole edition was quickly sold out. Since then stray copies have brought large premiums in the second-hand book-shops—a consolation, perhaps, to original purchasers, but certainly no source of profit to either the publisher or me. The present edition will be electrotyped after the first printing has been run over and all errors of the press have been corrected, and is not limited in number; I do not plan to make any substantial changes in it for at least ten years. If it is reprinted in the interval, an effort, of course, will be made to correct all surviving errors; a great many will persist, I make no doubt. But I shall not rewrite the book until the investigations suggested in it have been carried out by competent hands—and this business, I fear, is not likely to be undertaken very soon. As before, I ask all readers who may observe omissions or inaccuracies to communicate with me in care of the publisher, or at my home, 1524 Hollins Street, Baltimore. In particular, I am eager to get more light upon the history of American pronunciation, upon the grammar and syntax of the vulgar speech, and upon the non-English languages spoken in the United States.

My debt to my many and far-flung correspondents is very heavy, and I have acknowledged it in various places in the text. But above all I owe thanks to Dr. Louise Pound, of the University of Nebraska, not only for the materials I have so lavishly borrowed from her, but also, and even more importantly, for her constant interest in the work and her generous toleration of my philological shortcomings. Various other scholars, notably Dr. Otto Jespersen, of Copenhagen, have volunteered very valuable encouragement. I regret that the appearance of my book caused Dr. Jespersen to postpone a work upon the same subject that he had long had in contemplation; I can only hope that he will return to it, for his great learning will make it of extraordinary utility. Among the many private friends and correspondents who have helped me over difficult places I owe most to Mrs. Harry C. Black of Baltimore, and Mr. H. W. Seaman, of New York, both English-born. Mrs. Black made parts of "English and American Today," especially in its first stages, almost her own, and Mr. Seaman prepared for me an exhaustive and extremely useful review and criticism of the whole book. Dr. W. W. Charters generously offered to place his unique collection of vulgar Americanisms at my disposal; Mr. Thornton and Mr. Tucker, the one the compiler of the best existing dictionary of Americanisms and the other the pioneer of their scientific study, both gave me much encouragement, though differing from some of my conclusions. The aid of Miss Marion L. Bloom, of Washington, has been peculiarly valuable. She pursued many investigations for me in the Library of Congress, and otherwise gave me intelligent assistance. Finally, I owe a special debt to my amanuensis, Miss Addie B. Deering, of Baltimore, whose extraordinary diligence and good sense rescued me more than once from the wild snarls of my own manuscript—a manuscript bristling with difficulties that she never failed to surmount.

The reviews of the first edition in philological periodicals were always friendly, and in many cases exhaustive and valuable. The notices in the lay press were extensive, but not often intelligent. The book appeared at a time when colonialism, revived by the war, was at its height, and so a number of newspaper reviewers were rather alarmed by its apparent tendency to defend American practise against English example. One such watchman went to the length of denouncing it as proof of a sinister effort, inspired by the Wilhelmstrasse, to introduce discord into the Anglo-American *entente*. This reviewer gave a final touch to his bill of complaint by accusing me of being a Jew. I remain unable to comprehend the relevancy of the charge, but hasten to give assurance that my earliest known ancestors were uncompromising Christians, and engaged gallantly in the *pogroms* of their time.

For all the changes made in the text, I am, of course, wholly responsible. In many cases, after inquiry, I have felt it necessary to reject the suggestions of correspondents; in other cases observers of equal authority have revealed such a conflict of opinion that I have had perforce to fall back upon my own judgment. This conflict has been especially noticeable in the field of current usages on the plane of educated speech. I observe that Englishmen, when they settle in the United States, quickly lose their sense of difference between the two dialects, and are thereafter apt to argue that every American locution they encounter has been borrowed from England. Various correspondents, for example, have sought to convince me that such typical American verbs as *to steam-roller* (in the political sense) and *to joy-ride* are actually English. Others have maintained that various well-known American spellings, lately begun to be imitated in England, originated there. In the face of such earnest assaults it becomes difficult to hold to the thesis that there is any American dialect at all, but nevertheless I have managed to do so. Here, fortunately, exact evidence is often procurable, for the locutions in question enter into the written speech. Whenever I have found a contemporary English journal referring to a given form as an Americanism I have thought it quite safe to accept that view of it. True enough, almost every imaginable Americanism is heard now and then in England. But when it seems strange to an active journalist, it is certainly not in common use.

Many American correspondents and reviewers have objected to this or that locution, particularly in the section on the vulgar speech, on the ground that it is a localism. Such objections, I believe, have been almost invariably based upon faulty observation. More than once, investigating a word or a phrase thus alleged to be confined to New England or the South or the far West, I have found it in Lardner or in the materials collected by Charters in Kansas City. The collections of the American Dialect Society dispose of most such criticisms. They show that what are accepted as localisms in Vermont or Connecticut are often also localisms in Texas or Nebraska—in brief, that the common speech of the different parts of the country differs a good deal less than superficial observers usually believe. A great many persons, I find, are strangely deaf to the dialect that they hear every day from humble lips. When their attention is called to a peculiar word or grammatical form they are first disposed to deny that it is used, and then to argue that it is a localism. Other earnest but useless criticisms have come to me from persons who have confused what I say about the vulgar speech with what I say about the speech of educated folk. More than one reviewer, in fact, has solemnly taken me to task for accusing *all* Americans of saying "I *seen*" and "if I *hadda went*." In part I must accept primary responsibility for this confusion. When I set out to write this book I soon found that I was dealing with two very distinct dialects, and that it was often difficult to keep the distinction between them clear. This difficulty still confronts me, and now and then, I fear, it has led me into obscurity. I say there are two dialects; an American scholar, whose suggestions have been most useful, argues that there are actually four: "a language of the intellectuals, another of the fairly educated (business men, Congressmen, etc.), another of the great American democracy, another of the poor trash." This scholar argues that I should compare the vulgar speech (which seems to me to be his third and fourth varieties), not with standard English, but with corresponding dialects of England. But that would obviously lead to confusion worse confounded. The only safe plan is to compare both varieties of American English with what is currently regarded as standard English. That is the method adopted by the students of the dialects of all other living languages. It has its disadvantages, but it at least avoids the necessity of stopping every few minutes to describe the standard. All my readers, I assume, know standard English.

H. L. M.

Baltimore, November 12, 1921.

I.

INTRODUCTORY

1.

The Diverging Streams of English

Thomas Jefferson, with his usual prevision, saw clearly more than a century ago that the American people, as they increased in numbers and in the diversity of their national interests and racial strains, would make changes in their mother tongue, as they had already made changes in the political institutions of their inheritance. "The new circumstances under which we are placed," he wrote to John Waldo from Monticello on August 16, 1813, "call for new words, new phrases, and for the transfer of old words to new objects. An American dialect will therefore be formed."

Nearly a quarter of a century before this, another great American, and one with an expertness in the matter that the too versatile Jefferson could not muster, had ventured upon a prophecy even more bold and specific. He was Noah Webster, then at the beginning of his stormy career as a lexicographer. In his little volume of "Dissertations on the English Language," printed in 1789 and dedicated to "His Excellency, Benjamin Franklin, Esq., LL.D., F.R.S., late President of the Commonwealth of Pennsylvania," Webster argued that the time for regarding English usage and submitting to English authority had already passed, and that "a future separation of the American tongue from the English" was "necessary and unavoidable." "Numerous local causes," he continued, "such as a new country, new associations of people, new combinations of ideas in arts and sciences, and some intercourse with tribes wholly unknown in Europe, will introduce new words into the American tongue. These causes will produce, in a course of time, a language in North America as different from the future language of England as the modern Dutch, Danish and Swedish are from the German, or from one another." [1]

Neither Jefferson nor Webster put a term upon his prophecy. They may have been thinking, one or both, of a remote era, not yet come to dawn, or they may have been thinking, with the facile imagination of those days, of a period even earlier than our own. In the latter case they allowed far too little (and particularly Webster) for factors that have worked powerfully against the influences they saw so clearly in operation about them. One of these factors, obviously, has been the vast improvement in communications across the ocean, a change scarcely in vision a century ago. It has brought New York relatively nearer to London today than it was to Boston, or even to Philadelphia, during Jefferson's presidency, and that greater proximity has produced a steady interchange of ideas, opinions, news and mere gossip. We latter-day Americans know a great deal more about the everyday affairs of England than the early Americans did, for we read more English books, and find more about the English in our newspapers, and meet more Englishmen, and go to England much oftener. The effects of this ceaseless traffic in ideas and impressions, so plainly visible in politics, in ethics and æsthetics, and even in the minutiæ of social intercourse, are also to be seen in the language. On the one hand there is a swift exchange of new inventions on both sides, so that many of our American neologisms quickly pass to London and the latest English fashions in pronunciation are almost instantaneously imitated, at least by a minority, in New York; and, on the other hand, the English, by so constantly having the floor, force upon us, out of their firmer resolution and certitude, and no less out of the authority that goes with their mere cultural seniority, a somewhat sneaking respect for their own greater conservatism of speech, so that our professors of the language, in the overwhelming main, combat all signs of differentiation with the utmost diligence, and safeguard the doctrine that the standards of English are the only reputable standards of American.

[1] Pp. 22-23.

INTRODUCTORY 3

This doctrine, of course, is not supported by the known laws of language, nor has it prevented the large divergences that we shall presently examine, but all the same it has worked steadily toward a highly artificial formalism, and as steadily against the investigation of the actual national speech. Such grammar, so-called, as is taught in our schools and colleges, is a grammar standing four-legged upon the theorizings and false inferences of English Latinists of a past generation,[2] eager only to break the wild tongue of Shakespeare to a rule; and its frank aim is to create in us a high respect for a book language which few of us ever actually speak and not many of us even learn to write. That language, elaborately artificial though it may be, undoubtedly has merits. It shows a sonority and a stateliness that you must go to the Latin of the Golden Age to match; its "highly charged and heavy-shotted" periods, in Matthew Arnold's phrase, serve admirably the obscurantist purposes of American pedagogy and of English parliamentary oratory and leader-writing; it is something for the literary artists of both countries to prove their skill upon by flouting it. But to the average American, bent upon expressing his ideas, not stupendously but merely clearly, it must always remain something vague and remote, like Greek history or the properties of the parabola, for he never speaks it or hears it spoken, and seldom encounters it in his everyday reading. If he learns to write it, which is not often, it is with a rather depressing sense of its artificiality. He may master it as a Korean, bred in the colloquial Onmun, may master the literary Korean-Chinese, but he never thinks in it or quite feels it.

This fact, I daresay, is largely responsible for the notorious failure of our schools and colleges to turn out pupils who can put their ideas into words with simplicity and intelligibility. What their professors try to teach is not their mother-tongue at all, but a dialect

[2] Most latter-day English grammarians, of course, (*e.g.* Sweet) ground their work upon the spoken language. But inasmuch as this obviously differs from American English, the American pedagogues remain faithful to the grammarians of the era before phonology became a science, and imitate them in most of their absurdities. For a discussion of the evil effects of this stupidity see O. Jespersen: Growth and Structure of the English Language, 3rd ed.; Leipzig, 1919, p. 125 *et seq.* See also The English Language in America, by Harry Morgan Ayres, in The Cambridge History of American Literature, vol. iv; New York, 1921.

that stands quite outside their common experience, and into which they have to translate their thoughts, consciously and painfully. Bad writing consists in making the attempt, and failing through lack of practise. Good writing consists, as in the case of Howells, in deliberately throwing overboard the principles so elaborately inculcated, or, as in the case of Lincoln, in standing unaware of them. Thus the study of the language he is supposed to use, to the average American, takes on a sort of bilingual character. On the one hand, he is grounded abominably in a grammar and syntax that have always been largely artificial, even in the country where they are supposed to prevail, and on the other hand he has to pick up the essentials of his actual speech as best he may. "Literary English," says Van Wyck Brooks,[3] "with us is a tradition, just as Anglo-Saxon law with us is a tradition. They persist, not as the normal expressions of a race, . . . but through prestige and precedent and the will and habit of a dominating class largely out of touch with a national fabric unconsciously taking form out of school." What thus goes on out of school does not interest most of the guardians of our linguistic morals. Now and then a Charters takes a somewhat alarmed peep into the materials of the vulgar speech, and now and then a Krapp investigates the pronunciation of actual Americans, but in the main there is little save a tedious repetition of nonsense. In no department are American universities weaker than in the department of English. The æsthetic opinion that they disseminate is flabby and childish, and their philological work in the national language is extraordinarily lacking in enterprise. No attempt to deduce the principles of vulgar American grammar from the everyday speech of the people has ever been made by an American philologist. There is no scientific study, general and comprehensive in scope, of the American vocabulary, or of the influences lying at the root of American word-formation. No professor, so far as I know, has ever deigned to give the same sober attention to the *sermo plebeius* of his country that his colleagues habitually give to the pronunciation of Latin, or to the irregular verbs in French.

[3] America's Coming of Age; New York, 1915, p. 15. See also the preface to Every-Day English, by Richard Grant White; Boston, 1881, p. xviii.

2.

The Academic Attitude

This neglect of the vulgate by those professionally trained to investigate it, and its disdainful dismissal when it is considered at all, are among the strangest phenomena of American scholarship. In all other countries the everyday speech of the common people, and even the grotesque dialects of remote yokels, have the constant attention of philologists, and the laws of their growth and variation are elaborately studied. In France, to name but one agency, there is the Société des Parlers de France, with its diligent inquiries into changing forms; moreover, the Académie itself is endlessly concerned with the subject, and is at great pains to observe and rate every fluctuation in popular usage.[4] There is, besides, a constant outpouring of books by private investigators, of which "Le Langage Populaire," by Henri Banche, is a good example.[5] In Germany, amid many other such works, there are the admirable grammars of the spoken speech by Dr. Otto Bremer. In Sweden there are several journals devoted to the study of the vulgate, and the government has granted a subvention of 7500 *kronen* a year to an organization of scholars called the Undersökningen av Svenska Folkmål, formed to investigate it systematically.[6] In Norway there is a widespread movement to overthrow the official Dano-Norwegian, and substitute a national language based upon the speech of the peasants.[7] In

---

[4] The common notion that the Académie combats changes is quite erroneous. In the preface to the first edition of its dictionary (1694) it disclaimed any purpose "to make new words and to reject others at its pleasure." In the preface to the second edition (1718) it confessed that "ignorance and corruption often introduce manners of writing" and that "convenience establishes them." In the preface to the third edition (1740) it admitted that it was "forced to admit changes which the public has made," and so on. Says D. M. Robertson, in A History of the French Academy (London, 1910): "The Academy repudiates any assumption of authority over the language with which the public in its own practise has not first clothed it. So much, indeed, does it confine itself to an interpretation merely of the laws of language that its decisions are sometimes contrary to its own judgment of what is either desirable or expedient."

[5] Paris, 1920.

[6] *Cf. Scandinavian Studies and Notes*, vol. iv, no. 3, Aug., 1917, p. 258.

[7] This movement won official recognition so long ago as 1885, when the Storthing passed the first of a series of acts designed to put the two languages on equal footing. Four years later, after a campaign going back to 1874, pro-

Spain the Real Academia Española de la Lengua is constantly at work upon its great Diccionario, Ortografía and Gramática, and revises them at frequent intervals, taking in all new words as they appear and all new forms of old ones. And in Latin-America, to come nearer to our own case, the native philologists have produced a copious literature on the matter closest at hand, and one finds in it excellent works upon the Portuguese dialect of Brazil, and the variations of Spanish in Mexico, the Argentine, Chili, Peru, Ecuador, Uruguay and even Honduras and Costa Rica.[8] But in the United States the business has attracted little attention and less talent. The only existing formal treatise upon the subject,[9] if the present work be excepted, was written by a Swede trained in Germany and is heavy with errors and omissions. And the only usable dictionary of Americanisms [10] was written in England, and is the work of an English-born lawyer.

I am not forgetting, of course, the early explorations of Noah Webster, of which much more anon, nor the labors of our later dictionary makers, nor the inquiries of the American Dialect Society,[11] nor even the occasional illuminations of such writers as Richard Grant White, Charles H. Grandgent, George Philip Krapp, Thomas S. Lounsbury and Brander Matthews. But all this preliminary work has left the main field almost uncharted. Webster,

vision was made for teaching the *landsmaal* in the schools for the training of primary teachers. In 1899 a professorship of the *landsmaal* was established in the University of Christiania. The school boards in the case of primary schools, and the pupils in the case of middle and high schools are now permitted to choose between the two languages, and the *landsmaal* has been given official status by the State Church. The chief impediment to its wider acceptance lies in the fact that it is not, as it stands, a natural language, but an artificial amalgamation of peasant dialects. It was devised in 1848-50 by Ivar Aasen. *Vide* The Language Question, London *Times*, Norwegian Supplement, May 18, 1914.

[8] A number of such works are listed in the Bibliography and in Part II, Section 3 of the Appendix. The late Ricardo Palma, director of the Biblioteca Nacional at Lima, was an ardent student of American-Spanish, and tried to induce the Academia to adopt a long list of terms used in the Spanish of South America.

[9] Maximilian Schele de Vere: Americanisms: The English of the New World; New York, 1872. Since this was written Gilbert M. Tucker has published his American English; New York, 1921.

[10] Richard H. Thornton: An American Glossary . . . 2 vols.; Phila. and London, 1912. Mr. Thornton returned to the United States after his dictionary was published.

[11] Organized Feb. 19, 1889, with Dr. J. J. Child, of Harvard, as its first president.

as we shall see, was far more a reformer of the American dialect than a student of it. He introduced radical changes into its spelling and pronunciation, but he showed little understanding of its direction and genius. One always sees in him, indeed, the teacher rather than the scientific inquirer; the ardor of his desire to expound and instruct was only matched by his infinite capacity for observing inaccurately, and his profound ignorance of elementary philological principles. In the preface to the first edition of his American Dictionary, published in 1828—the first in which he added the qualifying adjective to the title—he argued eloquently for the right of Americans to shape their own speech without regard to English precedents, but only a year before this he had told Captain Basil Hall [12] that he knew of but fifty genuine Americanisms—a truly staggering proof of his defective observation. Webster was the first American professional scholar, and despite his frequent engrossment in public concerns and his endless public controversies, there was always something sequestered and almost medieval about him. The American language that he described and argued for was seldom the actual tongue of the folks about him, but often a sort of Volapük made up of one part faulty reporting and nine parts academic theorizing. In only one department did he exert any lasting influence, and that was in the department of orthography. The fact that our spelling is simpler and usually more logical than the English we owe chiefly to him. But it is not to be forgotten that the majority of his innovations, even here, were not adopted, but rejected, nor is it to be forgotten that spelling is the least of all the factors that shape and condition a language.

The same caveat lies against the work of the later makers of dictionaries; they have often gone ahead of common usage in the matter of orthography, but they have hung back in the far more important matter of idiom. The defect in the work of the Dialect Society lies in a somewhat similar circumscription of activity. Its constitution, adopted in 1889, says that "its object is the investigation of the spoken English of the United States and Canada," but that investigation, so far, has got little beyond the accumulation of vocabularies of local dialects, such as they are.

[12] Author of the once famous Travels in North America; London, 1820.

Even in this department its work is very far from finished, and
Dictionary of Distinctively American Speech announced years
(and again in 1919) has not yet appeared. Until its collections
completed and synchronized, it will be impossible for its meml
to make any profitable inquiry into the general laws underly
the development of American, or even to attempt a classification
the materials common to the whole speech. The meagreness of
materials accumulated in the slow-moving volumes of *Dialect N*
shows clearly, indeed, how little the American philologist is in
ested in the language that falls upon his ears every hour of the d
And in *Modern Language Notes* that impression is reinforced,
its bulky volumes contain exhaustive studies of all the other liv
languages and dialects, but only an occasional essay upon Americ

Now add to this general indifference a persistent and often viol
effort to oppose any formal differentiation of English and Americ
initiated by English purists but heartily supported by various An
icans, and you come, perhaps, to some understanding of the unsa
factory state of the literature of the subject. The pioneer dict
ary of Americanisms, published in 1816 by John Pickering
Massachusetts lawyer,[13] was not only criticised unkindly; it
roundly denounced as something subtly impertinent and corrupti
and even Noah Webster took a formidable fling at it.[14] Most
the American philologists of the early days—Witherspoon, Wor
ter, Fowler, Cobb and their like—were uncompromising advoca
of conformity, and combated every indication of a national ir
pendence in speech with the utmost vigilance. One of their c
pany, true enough, stood out against the rest. He was George I
kins Marsh, and in his "Lectures on the English Language,"[15]
argued that "in point of naked syntactical accuracy, the Englisl
America is not at all inferior to that of England." But even Ma
expressed the hope that Americans would not, "with malice
pense, go about to republicanize our orthography and our syn
our grammars and our dictionaries, our nursery hymns (*sic*)

[13] A Vocabulary or Collection of Words and Phrases which Have Been
posed to be Peculiar to the United States of America; Boston, 1816.
[14] A Letter to the Hon. John Pickering on the Subject of His Vocabul
Boston, 1817.
[15] 4th ed., New York, 1870, p. 669.

r Bibles" to the point of actual separation.[16] Moreover, he was a
ilologist only by courtesy; the regularly ordained schoolmasters
ere all against him. The fear voiced by William C. Fowler, pro-
ssor of rhetoric at Amherst, that Americans might "break loose
om the laws of the English language" [17] altogether, was echoed by
e whole fraternity, and so the corrective bastinado was laid on.
owler, in fact, advocated heroic measures. He declared that all
mericanisms were "foreign words and should be so treated."
It remained, however, for two professors of a later day to launch
e doctrine that the independent growth of American was not only
imoral, but a sheer illusion. They were Richard Grant White, for
ng the leading American writer upon language questions, at least
 popular esteem, and Thomas S. Lounsbury, for thirty-five years
ofessor of the English language and literature in the Sheffield
ientific School at Yale, and an indefatigable controversialist.
oth men were of the utmost industry in research, and both had
ide audiences. White's "Words and Their Uses," published in
372, was a mine of erudition, and his "Everyday English," fol-
wing eight years later, was another. True enough, Fitzedward
all, the Anglo-Indian-American philologist, disposed of many of
s etymologies and otherwise did execution upon him [18] but in
e main his contentions held water. Lounsbury was also an adept
d favorite expositor. His attacks upon certain familiar pedantries
 the grammarians were penetrating and effective, and his two
oks, "The Standard of Usage in English" and "The Standard of
ronunciation in English," not to mention his excellent "History
 the English Language" and his numerous magazine articles,
owed a profound knowledge of the early development of the lan-
age, and an admirable spirit of free inquiry. But both of these
borious scholars, when they turned from English proper to Amer-

[16] *Op. cit.* p. 676.
[17] The English Language; New York, 1850; rev. ed., 1855. This was the first
merican text-book of English for use in colleges. Before its publication, ac-
rding to Fowler himself (rev. ed., p. xi), the language was studied only
uperficially" and "in the primary schools." He goes on: "Afterward, when
ler in the academy, during their preparation for college, our pupils perhaps
spised it, in comparison with the Latin and the Greek; and in the college
ey do not systematically study the language after they come to maturity."
[18] In Recent Exemplifications of False Philology; London, 1872.

ican English, displayed an unaccountable desire to deny its existence altogether, and to the support of that denial they brought a critical method that was anything but unprejudiced. White devoted not less than eight long articles in the *Atlantic Monthly* [19] to a review of the fourth edition of John Russell Bartlett's American Glossary [20] and when he came to the end he had disposed of nine-tenths of Bartlett's specimens and called into question the authenticity of at least half of what remained. And no wonder, for his method was simply that of erecting tests so difficult and so arbitrary that only the exceptional word or phrase could pass them, and then only by a sort of chance. "To stamp a word or a phrase as an Americanism," he said, "it is necessary to show that (1) it is of so-called 'American' origin—that is, that it first came into use in the United States of North America, or that (2) it has been adopted in those States from some language other than English, or has been kept in use there while it has *wholly* passed out of use in England." Going further, he argued that unless "the simple words in compound names" were used in America "in a sense different from that in which they are used in England" the compound itself could not be regarded as an Americanism. The absurdity of all this is apparent when it is remembered that one of his rules would bar out such obvious Americanisms as the use of *sick* in place of *ill*, of *molasses* for *treacle*, and of *fall* for *autumn*, for all of these words, while archaic in England, are by no means wholly extinct; and that another would dispose of that vast category of compounds which includes such unmistakably characteristic Americanisms as *joy-ride, rake-off, show-down, up-lift, out-house, rubber-neck, chair-warmer, fire-eater* and *back-talk*.

Lounsbury went even further. In the course of a series of articles in *Harper's Magazine*, in 1913,[21] he laid down the dogma that "cultivated speech . . . affords the only legitimate basis of comparison between the language as used in England and in America," and then went on:

[19] Americanisms, parts i-viii, April, May, July, Sept., Nov., 1878; Jan., March, May, 1879.
[20] A Glossary of Words and Phrases Usually Regarded as Peculiar to the United States, 4th ed.; Boston, 1877.
[21] Feb., March, June, July, Sept.

INTRODUCTORY

In the only really proper sense of the term, an Americanism is a word or phrase naturally used by an educated American which under similar conditions would not be used by an educated Englishman. The emphasis, it will be seen, lies in the word "educated."

This curious criticism, fantastic as it must have seemed to European philologists, was presently reinforced, for in his fourth article Lounsbury announced that his discussion was "restricted to the *written* speech of educated men." The result, of course, was a wholesale slaughter of Americanisms. If it was not possible to reject a word, like White, on the ground that some stray English poet or other had once used it, it was almost always possible to reject it on the ground that it was not admitted into the vocabulary of a college professor when he sat down to compose formal book-English. What remained was a small company, indeed—and almost the whole field of American idiom and American grammar, so full of interest for the less austere explorer, was closed without even a peek into it.

White and Lounsbury dominated the arena and fixed the fashion. The later national experts upon the national language, with a few somewhat timorous exceptions, pass over its peculiarities without noticing them. So far as I can discover, there is not a single treatise in type upon one of its most salient characters—the wide departure of some of its vowel sounds from those of orthodox English. Marsh, C. H. Grandgent, and Robert J. Menner have printed a number of valuable essays upon the subject, and George Philip Krapp has discussed the matter incidentally in "The Pronunciation of Standard English in America," but there is no work that co-ordinates these inquiries or that attempts otherwise to cover the field. When, in preparing materials for the following chapters, I sought to determine the history of the *a*-sound in America, I found it necessary to plow through scores of ancient spelling-books, and to make deductions, perhaps sometimes rather rash, from the works of Franklin, Webster and Cobb. Some time ago the National Council of Teachers of English appointed a Committee on American Speech and sought to let some light into the matter, but as yet its labors are barely begun and the publications of its members get little beyond preliminaries. Such an inquiry involves a laboriousness which should have attracted Lounsbury: he once counted the number of times the word *female* appears in "Vanity Fair." But you will find only a feeble dealing with the question in his book on pronunciation. Nor is there any adequate general work (for Schele de Vere's is full of errors and omissions) upon the influences felt by American through contact with the languages of our millions of immigrants, nor upon our peculiarly rich and characteristic slang.

Against all such enterprises, as I have said, academic opinion stands firmly. During the World War it seems to have taken on, if possible, an added firmness. Before the war, for example, Dr. Brander Matthews, of Columbia University, was a diligent collector of Americanisms, and often discussed them with much show of liking for them. He even used the term *Briticism* to designate an English locution rejected by 100% Americans. But during the war he appears to have succumbed to the propaganda for British-American unity launched by the eminent Anglo-Saxon idealist, Adolph S. Ochs, of the New York *Times*. I quote from one of his articles in the *Times:*

> We may rest assured that the superficial evidences of a tendency toward the differentiation of American-English and British-English are not so significant as they may appear to the unreflecting, and that the tendency itself will be powerless against the cohesive force of our common literature, the precious inheritance of both the English-speaking peoples. . . . So long as the novelists and the newspaper men on both sides of the ocean continue to eschew Briticisms and Americanisms, and so long as they indulge in these localisms only in quotation marks, there is no danger that English will ever halve itself into a British language and an American language.

3.

The View of Writing Men

Unluckily for Dr. Matthews, there is not the slightest sign that the novelists and newspaper men on the two sides of the ocean will ever bring themselves to such eschewing. On the contrary, they apparently delight in the use of the "localisms" he denounces, and the result is a growing difficulty of intercommunication. Americans, trained in book English and constantly reading English books and

INTRODUCTORY 13

journals, still make their way in British-English comfortably enough, though now and then, I daresay, an English novel daunts them. But the English have a great deal more difficulty with American, and devote a great deal of attention to its peculiarities—often with very ill grace. For a long while, as we shall see in the next chapter, they viewed its differentiation from standard English with frank indignation, and sought to put an end to the process by violent denunciation; even so late as the period of the Civil War their chief spokesman saw in every Americanism that quality of abhorrent barbarism which they looked upon as the salient mark of the American people. But in later years, despite a certain lingering waspishness, they have brought themselves to a more philosophical view, and the fact that American-English is definitely separating itself from British-English is now admitted as a matter of course. The Cambridge History of English Literature, for example, says that the two have become "notably dissimilar" in vocabulary, and that American is splitting off into a distinct dialect.[22] The Eleventh Edition of the Encyclopædia Britannica, going further, says that the two languages are already so far apart that "it is not uncommon to meet with [American] newspaper articles of which an untravelled Englishman would hardly be able to understand a sentence."[23] A great many other academic authorities, including A. H. Sayce and H. W. and F. G. Fowler, bear testimony to the same effect.

On turning to the men actually engaged in writing English, and particularly to those aspiring to an American audience, one finds nearly all of them adverting, at some time or other, to the growing difficulties of intercommunication. William Archer, Arnold Bennett, W. L. George, George Moore, H. G. Wells, Edgar Jepson, H. N. Brailsford, Sidney Low, J. C. Squire, the Chestertons and Kipling are some of those who have dealt with the matter, following Dickens, Ruskin, George Augusta Sala and others of an elder generation. Low, in an article in the *Westminster Gazette*[24] ironically headed "Ought American to be Taught in Our Schools?" has described how the latter-day British business man is "puzzled by his

[22] Vol. xiv, pp. 484-5; Cambridge, 1917.
[23] Vol. xxv, p. 209.
[24] July 18, 1913.

ignorance of colloquial American" and "painfully hampered" thereby in his handling of American trade. He continues:

> In the United States of North America the study of the English tongue forms part of the educational scheme. I gather this because I find that they have professors of the English language and literature there, and I note that in the schools there are certain hours allotted for "English" under instructors who specialize in that subject. This is quite right. English is still far from being a dead language, and our American kinsfolk are good enough to appreciate the fact.
>
> But I think we should return the compliment. We ought to learn the American language in our schools and colleges. At present it is strangely neglected by the educational authorities. They pay attention to linguistic attainments of many other kinds, but not to this. How many thousands of youths are at this moment engaged in puzzling their brains over Latin and Greek grammar only Whitehall knows. Every well-conducted seminary has some instructor who is under the delusion that he is teaching English boys and girls to speak French with a good Parisian accent. We teach German, Italian, even Spanish, Russian, modern Greek, Arabic, Hindustani. For a moderate fee you can acquire a passing acquaintance with any of these tongues at the Berlitz Institute and the Gouin Schools. But even in these polyglot establishments there is nobody to teach you American. I have never seen a grammar of it or a dictionary. I have searched in vain at the booksellers for "How to Learn American in Three Weeks" or some similar compendium. Nothing of the sort exists. The native speech of one hundred millions of civilized people is as grossly neglected by the publishers as it is by the schoolmasters. You can find means to learn Hausa or Swahili or Cape Dutch in London more easily than the expressive, if difficult, tongue which is spoken in the office, the bar-room, the tram-car, from the snows of Alaska to the mouths of the Mississippi, and is enshrined in a literature that is growing in volume and favor every day.

Low then quotes an extract from an American novel appearing serially in an English magazine—an extract including such Americanisms as *side-stepper, saltwater-taffy, Prince-Albert* (coat), *boob, bartender* and *kidding,* and many characteristically American extravagances of metaphor. It might be well argued, he goes on, that this strange dialect is as near to "the tongue that Shakespeare spoke" as "the dialect of Bayswater or Brixton," but that philological fact does not help to its understanding. "You might almost as well expect him [the British business man] to converse freely with a Portuguese railway porter because he tried to stumble through Cæsar when he was in the Upper Fourth at school."

Such a campaign of education is undertaken by the London news-

INTRODUCTORY 15

papers whenever a new American play of the racier sort, *e. g.,* Montague Glass' "Potash and Perlmutter" or Willard Mack's "Kick In," holds the boards in the West End. The legends shown in moving-pictures also keep the subject alive. Some time ago, in the London *Daily Mail,* W. G. Faulkner undertook an elaborate explanation of common American movie terms. Mr. Faulkner assumed that most of his readers would understand *sombrero, sidewalk, candy-store, freight-car, boost, elevator, boss, crook* and *fall* (for *autumn*) without help, but he found it necessary to define such commonplace Americanisms as *hoodlum, hobo, bunco-steerer, rubber-neck, drummer, sucker, dive* (in the sense of a thieves' resort), *clean-up, graft* and *to feature.* Curiously enough, he proved the reality of the difficulties he essayed to level by falling into error as to the meanings of some of the terms he listed, among them *dead-beat, flume, dub* and *stag.* Another English expositor, apparently following him, thought it necessary to add definitions of *hold-up, quitter, rube, shack, road-agent, cinch, live-wire* and *scab,*[25] but he, too, mistook the meaning of *dead-beat,* and in addition he misdefined *band-wagon* and substituted *get-out,* seemingly an invention of his own, for *get-away.* Faulkner seized the opportunity to read a homily upon the vulgarity and extravagance of the American language, and argued that the introduction of its coinages through the moving-picture theatre (*Anglais, cinema*) "cannot be regarded without serious misgivings, if only because it generates and encourages mental indiscipline so far as the choice of expressions is concerned." Such warnings are common in the English newspapers. Early in 1920 the London *Daily News* began a formal agitation of the subject, and laid particular stress upon the menace that American moving-pictures offered to the purity of the English learned and used by children. I quote from a characteristic contribution to the discussion:

I visited two picture theatres today for the express purpose of collecting slang phrases and of noticing the effect of the new language on the child as well as on the adult. What the villain said to the hero when the latter started

[25] Of the words cited as still unfamiliar in England, Thornton has traced *hobo* to 1891, *hold-up* and *bunco* to 1887, *dive* to 1882, *dead-beat* to 1877, *hoodlum* to 1872, *road-agent* to 1866, *stag* to 1856, *drummer* to 1836 and *flume* to 1792. All of them are probably older than these references indicate.

to argue with him was, "Cut out that *dope*," and a hundred piping voices repeated the injunction. The comic man announced his marriage to the Belle of Lumbertown by saying, "I'm *hitched*." . . .

The same writer protested bitterly against the intrusion of such commonplace Americanisms as *fire-water, daffy, forget it,* and *bootlegger.* The Associated Press, in reporting the protest, said:

> England is apprehensive lest the vocabularies of her youth become corrupted through incursions of American slang. Trans-Atlantic tourists in England note with interest the frequency with which resort is made to "Yankee talk" by British song and play writers seeking to enliven their productions. Bands and orchestras throughout the country when playing popular music play American selections almost exclusively. American songs monopolize the English music hall and musical comedy stage. It is the subtitle of the American moving picture film which, it is feared, constitutes the most menacing threat to the vaunted English purity of speech.[26]

But it is not only American slang that the English observe and object to; they also begin to find it difficult to comprehend American-English on higher planes. It was H. N. Brailsford who protested that many of the utterances of Dr. Woodrow Wilson, during and after the Versailles conference, were incomprehensible to Englishmen on linguistic grounds. "The irruption of Mr. Wilson upon our scene," he said,[27] "threatens to modify our terminology. If one knew the American language (as I do not)," and so on. At about the same time a leading English medical journal was protesting satirically against the Americanisms in an important American surgical monograph.[28] Some time before this, in the *New Witness,* the late Cecil Chesterton discussed the growing difficulty, for Englishmen, of understanding American newspapers. After quoting a characteristic headline he went on:

> I defy any ordinary Englishman to say that that is the English language or that he can find any intelligible meaning in it. Even a dictionary will be of no use to him. He must know the language colloquially or not at all. . . .

---

[26] Mail correspondence dated Jan. 22, 1920.
[27] London *Daily Herald,* Aug. 20, 1919.
[28] Review of Surgery, Gynecology and Obstetrics, by MacCarty and Connor, in the *Medical Press,* Sept. 17, 1919. "In the study of the terminology of diseases of the breast," says this review, "[the authors] suggest a scheme which seems simple, but unfortunately for British understanding it is written in American."

INTRODUCTORY 17

No doubt it is easier for an Englishman to understand American than it would be for a Frenchman to do the same, just as it is easier for a German to understand Dutch than it would be for a Spaniard. But it does not make the American language identical with the English.[29]

Chesterton, however, refrained from denouncing this lack of identity; on the contrary, he allowed certain merits to American. "I do not want anybody to suppose," he said, "that the American language is in any way inferior to ours. In some ways it has improved upon it in vigor and raciness. In other ways it adheres more closely to the English of the best period." Testimony to the same end was furnished before this by William Archer. "New words," he said, "are begotten by new conditions of life; and as American life is far more fertile of new conditions than ours, the tendency toward neologism cannot but be stronger in America than in England. America has enormously enriched the language, not only with new words, but (since the American mind is, on the whole, quicker and wittier than the English) with apt and luminous colloquial metaphors."[30] To which the Manchester *Guardian,* reviewing Henry G. Aikman's "Zell," added: "The writing is, frankly, not English but American, and it cannot be judged by our standards. Some of the sentences are simply appalling, from our point of view—but they serve their purpose. This prompts the interesting speculation whether it is not time that we gave up the pretense of a 'common language' and accepted the American on its own merits."

The list of such quotations might be indefinitely prolonged. There is scarcely an English book upon the United States or an English review of an American book which does not offer some discussion, more or less profound, of American peculiarities of speech, both as they are revealed in spoken discourse (particularly pronunciation and intonation) and as they show themselves in literature and in the newspapers, and to this discussion protest is often added, as it very often is by the reviews and newspapers. "The Americans," says a typical critic, "have so far progressed with their self-appointed task of creating an American language that much of their conversation is now incomprehensible to English people." "This amazing lack of a

[29] Summarized in *Literary Digest,* June 19, 1915.
[30] American Today, *Scribner's,* Feb., 1899.

sense of the beauty of words," says another,[31] "comes from the manner in which the language of the United States is spoken—that monotonous drone, generally nasal, or that monotonous nasal whine." English reviews of American books frequently refer in this way to the growing differences between the two dialects—in fact, it is rare for an English reviewer to refrain from noting and sneering at Americanisms. Even translations from foreign languages made by Americans are constantly under fire.[32]

But, now and then there appears a defender. One such is William Archer, already quoted, who lately protested eloquently against "pulling a wry face over American expressions, not because they are inherently bad, but simply because they are American." He continued:

> The vague and unformulated idea behind all such petty cavillings is that the English language is in danger of being corrupted by the importation of Americanisms and that it behooves us to establish a sort of quarantine in order to keep out the detrimental germs. This notion is simply one of the milder phases of the Great Stupidity. The current English of today owes a great deal to America, and though certain American writers carry to excess the cult of slang, that tendency is not in the least affecting serious American literature and journalism. Much of the best and purest English of our time has been, and is being, written in America. . . . If English journalists make a show of arrogant and self-righteous Briticism, it is quite possible that a certain class of American journalists may retaliate by setting afoot a deliberately anti-British movement and attempting (as an American has wittily put it) to "deserve well of mankind by making two languages grow where only one grew before."[33]

Another attorney for the defense is Richard Aldington, the poet. "Are Americans," he asks,[34] "to write the language they speak, which is slowly but inevitably separating itself from the language of England, or are they to write a devitalized idiom learned painfully from books or from a discreet frequentation of London literary cliques?" Now and then, says Mr. Aldington, "one encounters an American who speaks perfect standard [*i. e.*, British]

---

[31] Edgar Jepson, *Little Review*, Sept., 1918.
[32] For example, see the *Athenæum's* review of Barrett H. Clark's translation of Romain Rolland's *Danton*, April 4, 1919, p. 152. In the same way J. C. Squire protested bitterly because an American translator of the Journal of the Goncourts "spoke of a *pavement* as a *sidewalk*." See the *Literary Review* of the New York *Evening Post*, July 23, 1921.
[33] *Westminster Gazette*, reprinted in the *Literary Review* of the New York *Evening Post*, July 23, 1921.
[34] English and American, *Poetry: A Magazine of Verse*, May, 1920, p. 94.

English, but the great majority of Americans make no attempt to do so." He goes on:

> Language is made by the people; it is only fixed by writers and orators. When language, especially that of poetry, is too far removed from that of the people, it becomes conventional and hieratic, like church Latin; or languid and degenerate, like modern official French poetry. When language is conventionally used by writers it becomes burdened with *clichés* and dead phrases. If American soldiers, newspapers and popular novels are evidence, it is clear that the American people is evolving a new language, full of vigorous and racy expressions. In spite of the phenomenon of the "pure-English" American, mentioned above, I am compelled to believe that the majority of his countrymen use an idiom which differs considerably from that which he employs. Whitman wrote a language which is intelligible to all Englishmen (far more so than that of James); but it seems to us inaccurate, harsh and crude, for all its vigor and occasional rare beauty. The language of the American people— judging from a comparison between newspapers of the Civil War and of today —has altered considerably in fifty years, so that a modern Whitman would write a language almost needing a glossary for Englishmen. Contemporary American poets use this popular language merely for comic effect or for purposes of sentimentality; most of them, since they are cultivated and rather literary, are careful to use a speech which is as well understood here [in England] as in America. Yet even in their writings there is a conception of the language which differs from ours. Almost all the American poets in "The New Poetry" anthology seem to have a feeling for words which differs from that of the English. In the works of Miss Lowell, for example, there are few usages which an Englishman would not be prepared to defend; yet there is an Americanism in her language, indefinable but unmistakable. Miss Lowell will, I think, recognize this as one of the excellencies of her work; she is, however, too well versed in classic English literature to have any but a faint trace of the quality I am trying to describe. It is more marked in Mr. Carl Sandberg, and still more marked in American prose; for even American literary criticism is a little difficult to understand, and new novels are bewildering with vigorous but incomprehensible expressions. Englishmen of letters and literary journalists may publish their exhortations and practice their refinements; in vain—a vast and increasingly articulate part of the English-speaking and English-writing world will ignore them. Another century may see English broken into a number of dialects or even different languages, spoken in Canada, Australia, South Africa, the United States and England. The result may eventually be similar to the break-up of Latin. The triumph of any one of these languages will be partly a matter of commercial and military supremacy, and partly a matter of literary supremacy.

On the western shore of the Atlantic, despite the professors of English, there is equal evidence of a growing sense of difference. "The American," says George Ade, in his book of travel, "In Pastures New," "must go to England in order to learn for a dead certainty that he does not speak the English language. . . . This pitiful fact comes home to every American when he arrives in London—that there are two languages, the English and the American. One is correct; the other is incorrect. One is a pure and limpid stream; the other is a stagnant pool swarming with bacilli." [35] This was written in 1906. Twenty-five years earlier Mark Twain had made the same observation. "When I speak my native tongue in its utmost purity in England," he said, "an Englishman can't understand me at all." [36] The languages, continued Mark, "were identical several generations ago, but our changed conditions and the spread of our people far to the south and far to the west have made many alterations in our pronunciation, and have introduced new words among us and changed the meanings of old ones." Even before this the great humorist had marked and hailed these differences. Already in "Roughing It" he was celebrating "the vigorous new vernacular of the occidental plains and mountains," [37] and in all his writings, even the most serious, he deliberately engrafted its greater liberty and more fluent idiom upon the stem of English, and so lent the dignity of his high achievement to a dialect that was as unmistakably American as the point of view underlying it.

The same tendency is plainly visible in William Dean Howells. His novels are mines of American idiom, and his style shows an undeniable revolt against the trammels of English grammarians. In 1886 he made a plea in *Harper's* for a concerted effort to put American on its own legs. "If we bother ourselves," he said, "to write what the critics imagine to be 'English,' we shall be priggish and artificial, and still more so if we make our Americans talk 'English.' . . . On our lips our continental English will differ more and more from the insular English, and we believe that this is not deplorable but desirable." [38] Howells then proceeded to discuss the nature of the difference, and described it accurately as determined

[35] In Pastures New; New York, 1906, p. 6.
[36] Concerning the American Language, in The Stolen White Elephant; Boston, 1882. A footnote says that the essay is "part of a chapter crowded out of A Tramp Abroad." (Hartford, 1880.)
[37] Hartford, 1872, p. 45.
[38] The Editor's Study, *Harper's Magazine*, Jan., 1886.

by the greater rigidity and formality of the English of modern England. In American, he said, there was to be seen that easy looseness of phrase and gait which characterized the English of the Elizabethan era, and particularly the Elizabethan hospitality to changed meanings and bold metaphors. American, he argued, made new words much faster than English, and they were, in the main, words of much greater daring and savor.

Howells' position was supported by that of many other well-known American authors of his generation, including especially Lowell, Whitman and John Fiske. Fiske, always truculent, carried the war into Africa by making a bold attack upon Briticisms, and even upon English pronunciation and intonation. "The English," he said in 1873, "talk just like the Germans. So much guttural is very unpleasant, especially as half the time I can't understand them, and have to say, 'I beg your pardon?'"[39] In more recent days there have been many like defiances. Brander Matthews, as I have said, was an eager apologist for Americanisms until he joined the Ochs lodge of Anglo-Saxon brothers. Others in the forefront of the fray are Dr. Richard Burton and Rupert Hughes. "Who can doubt," says Dr. Burton, "that Mr. Mencken is right in speaking of the 'American language'? . . . One recalls the cowboy who made a trip to Paris and was asked by his bunkie on returning to the big plains, how he had got along with French; to which he answered: 'I got along fine, but the French had a hell of a time.' English has that sort of time in the United States, but the people are perfectly happy about it. Why worry? A few professors are hired, at very small pay, to do that, and the populace prefers to do its suffering vicariously. . . . When a mayor of a large western city says *has went* twice in a public speech, and a governor of a great eastern state in public utterances declares that 'it *ain't* in my heart to hurt any man,' it gives one a piquant sense of the democracy of language in these United States. . . . We get a charming picture of proletariat and pedants amiably exchanging idiom, while school larnin' goes glimmering, and go-as-you-please is the order of the day. Why bother about the form of sentences when vital questions are for settling, and when to make others understand your meaning is the main purpose of words? That, at least,

[39] J. S. Clarke's Life of Fiske, vol. i, p. 431.

appears to be the general view. No wonder Brander Matthews speaks of English as a grammarless tongue. America has done and is doing her full share to make it so." [40] Dr. Burton continues:

> The pundit, the pedant, and the professor who are fain to stem the turbid tide of popular vernacular may suffer pain; but they can have little influence on the situation. Even college-bred folk revert to type and use people's speech—when they are out from under the restraining, corrective monitions of academic haunts—in a way to shock, amuse, or encourage, according to the point of view. Artificial book-speech is struggled for in recitation halls; then forth issue the vital young, and just beyond the door real talk is heard once more: the words and sentences that come hot from the heart, eagerly from emotional reactions, spontaneously representing the feelings rather than a state of mind supposed to be proper. To see a pupil who on trial solemnly declares that two nouns call for a plural verb, hasten out into the happy sunshine and immediately begin to do what the race always has done—including truly idiomatic writers—namely, use a singular verb on all such occasions, is only depressing to those who place the letter before the spirit which is life.

Mr. Hughes is even more emphatic. There must be an end, he argues, to all weak submission to English precept and example. What is needed is "a new Declaration of Independence." Then he goes on: [41]

> Could anyone imagine an English author hesitating to use a word because of his concern as to the ability of American readers to understand it and approve it? The mere suggestion is fantastic. Yet it is the commonest thing imaginable for an American author to wonder if the word that interests him is good "English," or, as the dictionaries say, "colloquial U. S." The critics, like awe-inspiring and awe-inspired governesses, take pains to remind their pupils that Americanisms are not nice, and are not written by well-bred little writers. When you stop to think of it, isn't this monstrously absurd, contemptible, and servilely colonial? . . . Why should we fail to realize that all our arts must be American to be great? Why should we permit the survival of the curious notion that our language is a mere loan from England, like a copper kettle that we must keep scoured and return without a dent? Have we any less right to develop the language we brought away with us than they have who stayed behind?

Mr. Hughes, whose own novels are full of racy and effective Americanisms, describes some of his difficulties in England. "A London publisher," he says, "once wrote of a book of mine that it was bewil-

---

[40] English as She is Spoke, *Bookman*, July, 1920.
[41] Our Statish Language, *Harper's Magazine*, May, 1920, p. 846.

INTRODUCTORY

dering in its Americanism. He instanced, among others, the verb *tiptoed* as an amazing and incredible thing. *On tiptoe*, or *a-tiptoe*, he could well understand because he had seen it in print at home. But the well-recognized truth that our language is largely made up of interchangeable facts did not calm his dismay. We know what a *foot* is; therefore we can say 'she *footed* it gracefully,' or speak of *foot-troops* or *footers*. *To toe the mark* is a legitimate development from the noun *toe*. *Tiptoed* is a simple employment of the franchise of our language, a franchise that Shakespeare and countless others have taken full advantage of. In fact, Richardson used it in 'Clarissa Harlowe' as far back as 1747: 'Mabel *tiptoed* it to her door.' But even if he did not, why should not I?" Mr. Hughes is bitter against the "snobbery that divides our writers into two sharp classes—those who in their effort to write pure English strut pompously and uneasily in Piccadilly fashions, and those who in their effort to be true to their own environment seem to wear overalls and write with a nasal twang." Between the two extremes he evidently prefers the latter. "Americans who try to write like Englishmen," he says, "are not only committed to an unnatural pose, but doomed as well to failure, above all among the English; for the most likable thing about the English is their contempt for the hyphenated imitation Englishmen from the States, who only emphasize their nativity by their apish antics. The Americans who have triumphed among them have been, almost without exception, peculiarly American." Finally, he repeats his clarion call for a formal rebellion, saying:

> But let us sign a Declaration of Literary Independence and formally begin to write, not British, but Unitedstatish. For there is such a language, a brilliant, growing, glowing, vivacious, elastic language for which we have no specific name. We might call it Statesish, or for euphony condense it to Statish. But, whatever we call it, let us cease to consider it a vulgar dialect of English, to be used only with deprecation. Let us study it in its splendid efflorescence, be proud of it, and true to it. Let us put off livery, cease to be the butlers of another people's language, and try to be the masters and the creators of our own.

Meanwhile, various Americans imitate John Fiske by abandoning the defense for the attack. When, in 1919, a British literary paper [42] presumed to criticise the Americanisms in American advertisements, the editor of the Indianapolis *Star* replied with a vigorous denunciation of current Briticisms. "In British fiction," he said, "with the omission of a few writers rated as first class, badly constructed and even ungrammatical sentences are by no means uncommon, and even the books of the 'big' authors are not immune from criticism. As for slang, certain colloquialisms and peculiarities of English speech appear so frequently in even the pages of Wells and Galsworthy as to be irritating. *Right-o* is an example; *bloody* and *beastly*, as applied to commonplace happenings, are others; the use of *directly* with a meaning quite unlike our usage, and many more of their kind, jump at American readers from the pages of English novels, and are there usually without intent of the writers to put color or accuracy into their delineations, but merely as a part of their ordinary vocabulary and with unconsciousness of any differences between their own and American usages."

Other Americans remain less resolute, for example, Vincent O'Sullivan, whose English schooling may account for his sensitiveness. In America, he says in the London *New Witness*,[43] "the English literary tradition is dying fast, and the spoken, and to a considerable extent, the written language is drawing farther and farther away from English as it is used in England." He continues:

> To most English people, many pages of the published sermons of Billy Sunday, the evangelist, would be almost as unintelligible as a Welsh newspaper. But is American at its present point of development a language or a lingo? Professor Brander Matthews does not hesitate to liken it to Elizabethan English for its figurative vigour. American figures, however, are generally on a low level. When Bacon calls floods *great winding-sheets*, he is more impressive than when the Pennsylvania Railroad announces that there is a *wash-out* down 'round Harrisburg, Pa. It would, in fact, be impossible to express any grand or moving thought in American; humour, homely wisdom, yes; but not grandeur. Leaving aside the intellectual value of either, Bishop Latimer's sermons are in the plain language of his time, and they easily maintain themselves on heights that Billy Sunday never gets a clutch on, even for a moment. It is a fair claim that American is more vivid than English.

[42] *M. A. B.*, Nov., 1919, p. 288. The rejoinder is reprinted in the March, 1920, issue, p. 107.
[43] Sept. 12, 1919.

INTRODUCTORY 25

So much for the literati. The plain people of the two countries, whenever they come into contact, find it very difficult to exchange ideas. This was made distressingly apparent when American troops began to pour into France in 1917. Fraternizing with the British was impeded, not so much because of old animosities as because of the wide divergence in vocabulary and pronunciation between the doughboy and Tommy Atkins—a divergence interpreted by each as a sign of uncouthness in the other. The Y. M. C. A. made a characteristic effort to turn the resultant feeling of strangeness and homesickness among the Americans to account. In the Chicago *Tribune's* Paris edition of July 7, 1917, I find a large advertisement inviting them to make use of the Y. M. C. A. clubhouse in the Avenue Montaigne, "where *American* is spoken." At about the same time an enterprising London tobacconist, Peters by name, affixed a large sign bearing the legend *"American* spoken here" to the front of his shop, and soon he was imitated by various other London, Liverpool and Paris shop-keepers. Earlier in the war the *Illinoiser Staats-Zeitung,* no doubt seeking to keep the sense of difference alive, advertised that it would "publish articles daily in the *American* language."

4.

Foreign Observers

What English and American laymen have thus observed has not escaped the notice of Continental philologists. The first edition of Bartlett, published in 1848, brought forth a long and critical review in the *Archiv für das Studium der neueren Sprachen und Literaturen* by Prof. Felix Flügel,[44] and in the successive volumes of the *Archiv* there have been many valuable essays upon Americanisms, by such men as Herrig, Koehler and Kartzke. Various Dutch philologists, among them Barentz, Keijzer and Van der Voort, have also discussed the subject, and a study in French has been published by

[44] Die englische Sprache in Nordamerika, band iv, heft i; Braunschweig, 1848.

G. A. Barringer.[45] That, even to the lay Continental, American and English now differ considerably, is demonstrated by the fact that many of the popular German *Sprachführer* appear in separate editions, *Amerikanisch* and *Englisch*. This is true, for example, of the "Metoula-Sprachführer" [46] and of the "Polyglott Kuntze" books.[47] The American edition of the latter starts off with the doctrine that *"Jeder, der nach Nord-Amerika oder Australien will, muss Englisch können,"* but a great many of the words and phrases that appear in its examples would be unintelligible to most Englishmen—e. g., *free-lunch, real-estate agent, buckwheat, corn* (for *maize*), *conductor* and *popcorn*—and a number of others would suggest false meanings or otherwise puzzle—e. g., *saloon, wash-stand, water-pitcher* and *apple-pie*.[48] In the "Neokosmos Sprachführer durch England-Amerika" [49] there are many notes calling attention to differences between American and English usage, e. g., *baggage-luggage, car-carriage, conductor-guard*. The authors are also forced to enter into explanations of the functions of the *boots* in an English hotel and of the *clerk* in an American hotel, and they devote a whole section, now mainly archaic, to a discourse upon the nature and uses of such American beverages as *whiskey-sours, Martini-cocktails, silver-fizzes, John-Collinses,* and *ice-cream sodas*.[50] In other Continental works of the same sort there is a like differentiation between English and American. Baedeker follows suit. In his guide-book to the United States, prepared for Englishmen, he is at pains to explain the

[45] Étude sur l'Anglais Parlé aux États Unis (la Langue Américaine), *Actes de la Société Philologique de Paris*, March, 1874.
[46] Metoula-Sprachführer . . . Englisch von Karl Blattner; Ausgabe für Amerika; Berlin-Schöneberg, 1912.
[47] Polyglott Kuntze; Schnellste Erlernung jeder Sprache ohne Lehrer; Amerikanisch; Bonn a. Rh., n. d.
[48] Like the English expositors of American slang this German falls into several errors. For example, he gives *cock* for *rooster*, *boots* for *shoes*, *braces* for *suspenders* and *postman* for *letter-carrier*, and lists *ironmonger*, *joiner* and *linen-draper* as American terms. He also spells *wagon* in the English manner, with two *g*'s, and translates *schweinefüsse* as *pork-feet*. But he spells such words as *color* in the American manner and gives the pronunciation of *clerk* as the American *klörk*, not as the English *klark*.
[49] By Carlo di Domizio and Charles M. Smith; Munich, n. d.
[50] Like the Metoula expositor they make mistakes. Certainly no American bartender ever made a *Hock*-cup; he made a *Rhine-wine*-cup. They list several drinks that were certainly not known in America in the old days, e. g., the *knickebein* and the *white-lion*. They convert *julep* into *jules*—a foul blow, indeed!

meaning of various American words and phrases. Asiatics are equally observant of the fast-growing differences. In the first number of the *Moslem Sunrise*, a quarterly edited by Dr. Mufti Muhammad Sadig, there is an explanatory note, apparently for the guidance of East Indian Mohammedan missionaries in the United States, upon certain peculiarities of the American vocabulary.

All the Continental Europeans who discuss the matter seem to take it for granted that American and English are now definitely separated. When I was in Germany as a correspondent, in 1917, I met many German officers who spoke English fluently. Some had learned it in England and some in America, and I noted that they were fully conscious of the difference between the two dialects, and often referred to it. M. Clemenceau, who acquired a very fluent and idiomatic English during his early days in New York, is always at pains to inform those who compliment him upon it that it is not English at all, but American. The new interest in American literature in France, growing out of the establishment of a chair of American Literature and Civilization at the Sorbonne, with Charles Cestre as incumbent, has brought forth several articles upon the peculiarities of American in the French reviews. Early in May, 1920, in discussing "La Poésie américaine d'aujourd'hui" in *Les Marges,* Eugène Montfort argued that American showed every sign of being more vigorous than English, and would eventually take on complete autonomy. A philologist of Scandinavian extraction, Elias Molee, has gone so far as to argue that the acquisition of correct English, to a people grown so mongrel in blood as the Americans, has already become a useless burden. In place of it he proposes a mixed tongue, based on English, but admitting various elements from the other Germanic languages. His grammar, however, is so much more complex than that of English that most Americans would probably find his artificial "American" very difficult of acquirement. At all events it has made no progress.[51]

[51] Molee's notions are set forth in Plea for an American Language . . . ; Chicago, 1888; and Tutonish; Chicago, 1902. He announced the preparation of A Dictionary of the American Language in 1888, but so far as I know it has not been published. He was born in Wisconsin, of Norwegian parents, in 1845, and pursued linguistic studies at the University of Wisconsin, where he seems to have taken a Ph.B.

5.

The General Character of American English

The characters chiefly noted in American speech by all who have discussed it, are, first, its general uniformity throughout the country, so that dialects, properly speaking, are confined to recent immigrants, to the native whites of a few isolated areas and to the negroes of the South; and, secondly, its impatient disregard of rule and precedent, and hence its large capacity (distinctly greater than that of the English of England) for taking in new words and phrases and for manufacturing new locutions out of its own materials. The first of these characters has struck every observer, native and foreign. In place of the local dialects of other countries we have a general *Volkssprache* for the whole nation, and if it is conditioned at all it is only by minor differences in pronunciation and by the linguistic struggles of various groups of newcomers. "The speech of the United States," says Gilbert M. Tucker, "is quite unlike that of Great Britain in the important particular that here we have no dialects."[52] "We all," said Mr. Taft during his presidency, "speak the same language and have the same ideas." "Manners, morals and political views," said the New York *World*, commenting upon this dictum, "have all undergone a standardization which is one of the remarkable aspects of American evolution. Perhaps it is in the uniformity of language that this development has been most noteworthy. Outside of the Tennessee mountains and the back country of New England there is no true dialect."[53] "While we have or have had single counties as large as Great Britain," says another American observer, "and in some of our states England could be lost, there is practically no difference between the American spoken in our 4,039,000 square miles of territory, except as spoken by foreigners. We, assembled here, would be perfectly understood by delegates from Texas, Maine, Minnesota, Louisiana, or Alaska, from whatever walk of life they might come. We can go to any of the 75,000 postoffices

[52] American English, *North American Review*, Jan., 1883.
[53] Oct. 1, 1909.

INTRODUCTORY 29

in this country and be entirely sure we will be understood, whether we want to buy a stamp or borrow a match."[54] "From Portland, Maine, to Portland, Oregon," agrees an English critic, "no trace of a distinct dialect is to be found. The man from Maine, even though he may be of inferior education and limited capacity, can completely understand the man from Oregon."[55]

No other country can show such linguistic solidarity, nor any approach to it—not even Canada, for there a large part of the population resists learning English altogether. The Little Russian of the Ukraine is unintelligible to the citizen of Petrograd; the Northern Italian can scarcely follow a conversation in Sicilian; the Low German from Hamburg is a foreigner in Munich; the Breton flounders in Gascony. Even in the United Kingdom there are wide divergences.[56] "When we remember," says the New International Encyclopædia,[57] "that the dialects of the countries (sic) in England have marked differences—so marked, indeed, that it may be doubted whether a Lancashire miner and a Lincolnshire farmer could understand each other—we may well be proud that our vast country has, strictly speaking, only one language." This uniformity was noted by the earliest observers; Pickering called attention to it in the preface to his Vocabulary and ascribed it, no doubt accurately, to the restlessness of the Americans, their inheritance of the immigrant spirit, "the frequent removals of people from one part of our country to another." It is especially marked in vocabulary and grammatical forms—the foundation stones of a living speech. There may be slight differences in pronunciation and intonation—a Southern softness, a Yankee drawl, a Western burr—but in the words they use and the way they use them all Americans, even the least tutored, follow the same line. One observes, of course, a polite speech and a common speech. But the common speech is everywhere the same, and its uniform vagaries take the place of the dialectic variations of

[54] J. F. Healy, general manager of the Davis Colliery Co. at Elkins, W. Va., in a speech before the West Virginia Coal Mining Institute, at Wheeling, Dec., 1910; reprinted as The American Language; Pittsburgh, 1911.
[55] *Westminster Review*, July, 1888, p. 35.
[56] W. W. Skeat distinguishes no less than 9 dialects in Scotland, 3 in Ireland and 30 in England and Wales. *Vide* English Dialects from the Eighth Century to the Present Day; Cambridge, 1911, p. 107 *ff.*
[57] *Art.* Americanisms, 2nd ed.

other lands. A Boston street-car conductor could go to work in Chicago or San Francisco without running the slightest risk of misunderstanding his new fares. Once he had picked up half a dozen localisms, he would be, to all linguistic intents and purposes, fully naturalized.

Of the intrinsic differences that separate American from English the chief have their roots in the obvious disparity between the environment and traditions of the American people since the seventeenth century and those of the English. The latter have lived under a relatively stable social order, and it has impressed upon their souls their characteristic respect for what is customary and of good report. Until the Great War brought chaos to most of their institutions, their whole lives were regulated, perhaps more than those of any other people save the Spaniards, by a regard for precedent. The Americans, though partly of the same blood, have felt no such restraint, and acquired no such habit of conformity. On the contrary, they have plunged to the other extreme, for the conditions of life in their new country have put a high value upon the precisely opposite qualities of curiosity and daring, and so they have acquired that character of restlessness, that impatience of forms, that disdain of the dead hand, which now broadly marks them. From the first, says a recent literary historian, they have been "less phlegmatic, less conservative than the English. There were climatic influences, it may be; there was surely a spirit of intensity everywhere that made for short effort." [58] Thus, in the arts, and thus in business, in politics, in daily intercourse, in habits of mind and speech. The American is not, in truth, lacking in a capacity for discipline; he has it highly developed; he submits to leadership readily, and even to tyranny. But, by a curious twist, it is not the leadership that is old and decorous that fetches him, but the leadership that is new and extravagant. He will resist dictation out of the past, but he will follow a new messiah with almost Russian willingness, and into the wildest vagaries of economics, religion, morals and speech. A new fallacy in politics spreads faster in the United States than anywhere else on earth, and so does a new fashion in hats, or a new revelation

[58] F. L. Pattee: A History of American Literature Since 1870; New York, 1916. See also The American Novel, by Carl Van Doren; New York, 1921.

INTRODUCTORY 31

of God, or a new means of killing time, or a new shibboleth, or metaphor, or piece of slang.

Thus the American, on his linguistic side, likes to make his language as he goes along, and not all the hard work of his grammar teachers can hold the business back. A novelty loses nothing by the fact that it is a novelty; it rather gains something, and particularly if it meets the national fancy for the terse, the vivid, and, above all, the bold and imaginative. The characteristic American habit of reducing complex concepts to the starkest abbreviations was already noticeable in colonial times, and such highly typical Americanisms as *O. K., N. G.,* and *P. D. Q.,* have been traced back to the first days of the republic. Nor are the influences that shaped these early tendencies invisible today, for the country is still in process of growth, and no settled social order has yet descended upon it. Institution-making is yet going on, and so is language-making. In so modest an operation as that which has evolved *bunco* from *buncombe* and *bunk* from *bunco* there is evidence of a phenomenon which the philologist recognizes as belonging to the most youthful and lusty stages of speech. The American vulgate is not only constantly making new words, it is also deducing roots from them, and so giving proof, as Prof. Sayce says, that "the creative powers of language are even now not extinct."

But of more importance than its sheer inventions, if only because much more numerous, are its extensions of the vocabulary, both absolutely and in ready workableness, by the devices of rhetoric. The American, from the beginning, has been the most ardent of recorded rhetoricians. His politics bristles with pungent epithets; his whole history has been bedizened with tall talk; his fundamental institutions rest as much upon brilliant phrases as upon logical ideas. And in small things as in large he exercises continually an incomparable capacity for projecting hidden and often fantastic relationships into arresting parts of speech. Such a term as *rubber-neck* is almost a complete treatise on American psychology; it reveals the national habit of mind more clearly than any labored inquiry could ever reveal it. It has in it precisely the boldness and contempt for ordered forms that are so characteristically American, and it has too the grotesque humor of the country, and the delight in devastating opprobriums, and the acute feeling for the succinct and savory. The same qualities are in *rough-house, water-wagon, near-silk, has-been, lame-duck* and a thousand other such racy substantives, and in all the great stock of native verbs and adjectives. There is, indeed, but a shadowy boundary in these new coinages between the various parts of speech. *Corral*, borrowed from the Spanish, immediately becomes a verb and the father of an adjective. *Bust*, carved out of *burst*, erects itself into a noun. *Bum*, coming by way of an earlier *bummer* from the German *bummler*, becomes noun, adjective, verb and adverb. Verbs are fashioned out of substantives by the simple process of prefixing the preposition: *to engineer, to chink, to stump, to hog*. Others grow out of an intermediate adjective, as *to boom*. Others are made by torturing nouns with harsh affixes, as *to burglarize* and *to itemize*, or by groping for the root, as *to resurrect* and *to jell*. Yet others are changed from intransitive to transitive: a sleeping-car *sleeps* thirty passengers. So with the adjectives. They are made of substantives unchanged: *codfish, jitney*. Or by bold combinations: *down-and-out, up-state, flat-footed*. Or by shading down suffixes to a barbaric simplicity: *scary, classy, tasty*. Or by working over adverbs until they tremble on the brink between adverb and adjective: *right* and *near* are examples.

All of these processes, of course, are also to be observed in the English of England; in the days of its great Elizabethan growth they were in the lustiest possible being. They are, indeed, common to all languages; they keep language alive. But if you will put the English of today beside the American of today you will see at once how much more forcibly they are in operation in the latter than in the former. The standard southern dialect of English has been arrested in its growth by its purists and grammarians. It shows no living change in structure and syntax since the days of Anne, and very little modification in either pronunciation or vocabulary. Its tendency is to conserve that which is established; to say the new thing, as nearly as possible, in the old way; to combat all that expansive gusto which made for its pliancy and resilience in the days of Shakespeare. In place of the old loose-footedness there is set up a preciosity which, in one direction, takes the form of unyielding affectations in the spoken language, and in another form shows itself in

INTRODUCTORY 33

the heavy Johnsonese of current English writing—the Jargon denounced by Sir Arthur Quiller-Couch in his Cambridge lectures. This "infirmity of speech" Quiller-Couch finds "in parliamentary debates and in the newspapers"; . . . "it has become the medium through which Boards of Government, County Councils, Syndicates, Committees, Commercial Firms, express the processes as well as the conclusions of their thought, and so voice the reason of their being." Distinct from journalese, the two yet overlap, "and have a knack of assimilating each other's vices." [59]

American, despite the gallant efforts of the professors, has so far escaped any such suffocating formalization. We, too, of course, have our occasional practitioners of the authentic English Jargon; in the late Grover Cleveland we produced an acknowledged master of it. But in the main our faults in writing lie in precisely the opposite direction. That is to say, we incline toward a directness of statement which, at its greatest, lacks restraint and urbanity altogether, and toward a hospitality which often admits novelties for the mere sake of their novelty, and is quite uncritical of the difference between a genuine improvement in succinctness and clarity, and mere extravagant raciness. "The tendency," says one English observer, "is . . . to consider the speech of any man, as any man himself, as good as any other." [60] "All beauty and distinction," says another,[61] "are ruthlessly sacrificed to force." "The Americans, in a kind of artistic exuberance," says a third,[62] "are not afraid to

[59] *Cf.* the chapter, Interlude: On Jargon, in Quiller-Couch's On the Art of Writing; New York, 1916. Curiously enough, large parts of the learned critic's book are written in the very Jargon he attacks. See also ch. vi. of Growth and Structure of the English Language, by O. Jespersen, 3rd ed. rev.; Leipzig, 1919, especially pp. 143 *ff.* See also Official English, in *English*, March, 1919, p. 7; April, p. 45, and Aug., p. 135, and The Decay of Syntax, in the London *Times Literary Supplement*, May 8, 1919, p. 1.
[60] Alexander Francis: Americans: an Impression; New York, 1900.
[61] G. Lowes Dickinson, in the *English Review*, quoted by *Current Literature*, April, 1910.
[62] Frank Dilnot: The New America; New York, 1919, p. 25. The same author describes two tendencies in American, one toward the reinvigoration of English, the other toward its dilution and corruption. He regards the language as far more vivid and effective than the English of England. "Show me the alert Englishman," he says, "who will not find a stimulation in those nuggety word-groupings which are the commonplaces in good American conversation. They are like flashes of crystal. They come from all kinds of people—who are brilliantly innocent of enriching the language. . . . The written word in America follows generally along the lines of the spoken word. . . . In writing as well as

use words as we sometimes are in England." Moreover, this strong revolt against conventional bonds is by no means confined to the folk-speech, nor even to the loose conversational English of the upper classes; it also gets into more studied discourse, both spoken and written. I glance through the speeches of Dr. Woodrow Wilson, surely a conscientious purist and Anglomaniac if we have ever had one, and find, in a few moments, half a dozen locutions that an Englishman in like position would never dream of using, among them *we must get a move on*,[63] *hog* as a verb,[64] *gum-shoe* as an adjective with verbal overtones,[65] *onery* in place of *ordinary*,[66] and *that is going some*.[67] I turn to Dr. John Dewey, surely a most respectable pedagogue, and find him using *dope* for *opium*.[68]

From the earliest days, indeed, English critics have found this gipsy tendency in our most careful writing. They denounced it in Marshall, Cooper, Mark Twain, Poe, Lossing, Lowell and Holmes, and even in Hawthorne and Thoreau; and it was no less academic a work than W. C. Brownell's "French Traits" which brought forth, in a London literary journal, the dictum that "the language most depressing to the cultured Englishman is the language of the cultured American." Even "educated American English," agrees the chief of modern English grammarians, "is now almost entirely independent of British influence, and differs from it considerably, though as yet not enough to make the two dialects—American English and British English—mutually unintelligible."[69] Surely no English of position equal to Dr. Wilson's or Dr. Dewey's would venture upon such locutions as *dope* and *to hog*. One might conceivably think of George Saintsbury doing it—but Saintsbury is a privileged icono-

in speech there is a widespread range of what to an Englishman is looseness, occasionally slovenliness. . . . The American tongue, written or spoken, with its alteration from the English of England, is a potent and penetrating instrument, rich in new vibrations, full of joy as well as shocks for the unsuspecting visitor."

[63] Speech before the Chamber of Commerce Convention, Washington, Feb. 19, 1916.
[64] Speech at workingman's dinner, New York, Sept. 4, 1912.
[65] Wit and Wisdom of Woodrow Wilson, comp. by Richard Linthicum; New York, 1916, p. 54.
[66] Speech at Ridgewood, N. J., April 22, 1910.
[67] Wit and Wisdom . . . , p. 56.
[68] *New Republic*, Dec. 24, 1919, p. 116, col. 1.
[69] Henry Sweet: A New English Grammar, Logical and Historical, 2 parts; Oxford, 1900-03, part i, p. 224.

clast. Gilbert Murray would blush to death if merely accused of it falsely. When, on August 2, 1914, Sir Edward Grey ventured modestly to speak of "pressing the button in the interest of peace," the *New Age* denounced him for indulging in vulgarism, and, as one English correspondent writes to me, various other Britons saw in the locution "a sign of the impending fall of the Empire."

American thus shows its character in a constant experimentation, a wide hospitality to novelty, a steady reaching out for new and vivid forms. No other tongue of modern times admits foreign words and phrases more readily; none is more careless of precedents; none shows a greater fecundity and originality of fancy. It is producing new words every day, by trope, by agglutination, by the shedding of inflections, by the merging of parts of speech, and by sheer brilliance of imagination. It is full of what Bret Harte called the "sabre-cuts of Saxon"; it meets Montaigne's ideal of "a succulent and nervous speech, short and compact, not as much delicated and combed out as vehement and brusque, rather arbitrary than monotonous, not pedantic but soldierly, as Suetonius called Cæsar's Latin." One pictures the common materials of English dumped into a pot, exotic flavorings added, and the bubblings assiduously and expectantly skimmed. What is old and respected is already in decay the moment it comes into contact with what is new and vivid. "When we Americans are through with the English language," says Mr. Dooley, "it will look as if it had been run over by a musical comedy." Let American confront a novel problem alongside English, and immediately its superior imaginativeness and resourcefulness become obvious. *Movie* is better than *cinema;* and the English begin to admit the fact by adopting the word; it is not only better American, it is better English. *Bill-board* is better than *hoarding*. *Office-holder* is more honest, more picturesque, more thoroughly Anglo-Saxon than *public-servant*. *Stem-winder* somehow has more life in it, more fancy and vividness, than the literal *keyless-watch*. Turn to the terminology of railroading (itself, by the way, an Americanism): its creation fell upon the two peoples equally, but they tackled the job independently. The English, seeking a figure to denominate the wedge-shaped fender in front of a locomotive, called it a *plough;* the Americans, characteristically, gave it the far more pungent name of *cow-catcher*. So with the casting where two rails join. The English called it a *crossing-plate*. The Americans, more responsive to the suggestion in its shape, called it a *frog*.

This boldness of conceit, of course, makes for vulgarity. Unrestrained by any critical sense—and the critical sense of the professors counts for little, for they cry wolf too often—it flowers in such barbaric inventions as *tasty, alright, go-getter, he-man, go-aheadativeness, tony, semi-occasional, to fellowship* and *to doxologize*. Let it be admitted: American is not infrequently vulgar; the Americans, too, are vulgar (Bayard Taylor called them "Anglo-Saxons relapsed into semi-barbarism"); America itself is unutterably vulgar. But vulgarity, after all, means no more than a yielding to natural impulses in the face of conventional inhibitions, and that yielding to natural impulses is at the heart of all healthy language-making. The history of English, like the history of American and of every other living tongue, is a history of vulgarisms that, by their accurate meeting of real needs, have forced their way into sound usage, and even into the lifeless catalogues of the grammarians. The colonial pedants denounced *to advocate* as bitterly as they ever denounced *to compromit* or *to happify*, and all the English authorities gave them aid, but it forced itself into the American language despite them, and today it is even accepted as English and has got into the Concise Oxford Dictionary. *To donate*, so late as 1870, was dismissed by Richard Grant White as ignorant and abominable and to this day the more careful English will have none of it, but there is not an American dictionary that doesn't accept it, and surely no American writer would hesitate to use it.[70] *Reliable, gubernatorial, standpoint* and *scientist* have survived opposition of equal ferocity. The last-named was coined by William Whewell, an Englishman, in 1840, but was first adopted in America. Despite the fact that Fitzedward Hall and other eminent philologists used it and

[70] Despite this fact an academic and ineffective opposition to it still goes on. On the Style Sheet of the *Century Magazine* it is listed among the "words and phrases to be avoided." It was prohibited by the famous Index Expurgatorius prepared by William Cullen Bryant for the New York *Evening Post*, and his prohibition is still theoretically in force, but the word is now actually permitted by the *Post*. The Chicago *Daily News* Style Book, dated July 1, 1908, also bans it.

INTRODUCTORY 37

defended it, it aroused almost incredible opposition in England. So recently as 1890 it was denounced by the London *Daily News* as "an ignoble Americanism," and according to William Archer it was finally accepted by the English only "at the point of the bayonet." [71]

The purist performs a useful office in enforcing a certain logical regularity upon the process, and in our own case the omnipresent example of the greater conservatism of the English corrects our native tendency to go too fast, but the process itself is as inexorable in its workings as the precession of the equinoxes, and if we yield to it more eagerly than the English, it is only a proof, perhaps, that the future of what was once the Anglo-Saxon tongue lies on this side of the water. "The story of English grammar," says Murison, "is a story of simplification, of dispensing with grammatical forms." [72] And of the most copious and persistent enlargement of vocabulary and mutation of idiom ever recorded, perhaps, by descriptive philology. English now has the brakes on, but American continues to leap in the dark, and the prodigality of its movement is all the indication that is needed of its intrinsic health, its capacity to meet the ever-changing needs of a restless and emotional people, constantly fluent in racial composition, and disdainful of tradition. "Language," says Sayce, "is no artificial product, contained in books and dictionaries and governed by the strict rules of impersonal grammarians. It is the living expression of the mind and spirit of a people, ever changing and shifting, whose sole standard of correctness is custom and the common usage of the community. . . . The first lesson to be learned is that there is no intrinsic right or wrong in the use of language, no fixed rules such as are the delight of the teacher of Latin prose. What is right now will be wrong hereafter, what language rejected yesterday she accepts today." [73]

[71] *Scientist* is now in the Concise Oxford Dictionary and in Cassell's. So are *reliable*, *standpoint* and *gubernatorial*. But the *Century Magazine* still bans *standpoint* and the *Evening Post* (at least in theory) bans both *standpoint* and *reliable*. The Chicago *Daily News* accepts *standpoint*, but bans *reliable* and *gubernatorial*. All of these words, of course, are now almost as good as *ox* or *and*.
[72] Changes in the Language Since Shakespeare's Time, in Cambridge History of English Literature, vol. xiv, p. 491. See also Jespersen, *op. cit.*
[73] Introduction to the Science of Language, vol. ii, pp. 333-4.

6.

The Materials of the Inquiry

One familiar with the habits of pedagogues need not be told that, in their grudging discussions of American, they have spent most of their energies upon vain attempts to classify its materials. White and Lounsbury, as I have shown, carried the business to the limits of the preposterous; when they had finished identifying and cataloguing Americanisms there were no more Americanisms left to study. But among investigators of less learning there is a more spacious view of the problem, and the labored categories of White and Lounsbury are much extended. Pickering, the first to attempt a list of Americanisms, rehearsed their origin under the following headings:

1. "We have formed some new words."
2. "To some old ones, that are still in use in England, we have affixed new significations."
3. "Others, which have been long obsolete in England, are still retained in common use among us."

Bartlett, in the second edition of his dictionary, dated 1859, increased these classes to nine:

1. Archaisms, *i. e.*, old English words, obsolete, or nearly so, in England, but retained in use in this country.
2. English words used in a different sense from what they are in England. "These include many names of natural objects differently applied."
3. Words which have retained their original meaning in the United States, though not in England.
4. English provincialisms adopted into general use in America.
5. Newly coined words, which owe their origin to the productions or to the circumstances of the country.
6. Words borrowed from European languages, especially the French, Spanish, Dutch and German.
7. Indian words.
8. Negroisms.
9. Peculiarities of pronunciation.

Some time before this, but after the publication of Bartlett's first edition in 1848, William C. Fowler, professor of rhetoric at Am-

INTRODUCTORY 39

herst, devoted a brief chapter to "American Dialects" in his well-known work on English [74] and in it one finds the following formidable classification of Americanisms:

1. Words borrowed from other languages.
   a. Indian, as *Kennebec, Ohio, Tombigbee; sagamore, quahaug, succotash.*
   b. Dutch, as *boss, kruller, stoop.*
   c. German, as *spuke*(?), *sauerkraut.*
   d. French, as *bayou, cache, chute, crevasse, levee.*
   e. Spanish, as *calaboose, chapparal, hacienda, rancho, ranchero.*
   f. Negro, as *buckra.*
2. Words "introduced from the necessity of our situation, in order to express new ideas."
   a. Words "connected with and flowing from our political institutions," as *selectman, presidential, congressional, caucus, mass-meeting, lynch-law, help* (for *servants*).
   b. Words "connected with our ecclesiastical institutions," as *associational, consociational, to fellowship, to missionate.*
   c. Words "connected with a new country," as *lot, diggings, betterments, squatter.*
3. Miscellaneous Americanisms.
   a. Words and phrases become obsolete in England, as *talented, offset* (for *set-off*), *back and forth* (for *backward and forward*).
   b. Old words and phrases "which are now merely provincial in England," as *hub, whap* (?), *to wilt.*
   c. Nouns formed from verbs by adding the French suffix *-ment*, as *publishment, releasement, requirement.*
   d. Forms of words "which fill the gap or vacancy between two words which are approved," as *obligate* (between *oblige* and *obligation*) and *variate* (between *vary* and *variation*).
   e. "Certain compound terms for which the English have different compounds," as *bank-bill* (*bank-note*), *book-store* (*bookseller's shop*), *bottom-land* (*interval-land*), *clapboard* (*pale*), *sea-board* (*sea-shore*), *side-hill* (*hill-side*).
   f. "Certain colloquial phrases, apparently idiomatic, and very expressive," as *to cave in, to flare up, to flunk out, to fork over, to hold on, to let on, to stave off, to take on.*
   g. Intensives, "often a matter of mere temporary fashion," as *dreadful, might, plaguy, powerful.*
   h. "Certain verbs expressing one's state of mind, but partially or timidly," as *to allot upon* (for *to count upon*), *to calculate, to expect* (*to think* or *believe*), *to guess, to reckon.*
   i. "Certain adjectives, expressing not only quality, but one's subjective feelings in regard to it," as *clever, grand, green, likely, smart, ugly.*

[74] *Op. cit.*, pp. 119-28.

j. Abridgments, as *stage* (for *stage-coach*), *turnpike* (for *turnpike-road*), *spry* (for *sprightly*), *to conduct* (for *to conduct one's self*).

k. "Quaint or burlesque terms," as *to tote, to yank; humbug, loafer, muss, plunder* (for *baggage*), *rock* (for *stone*).

l. "Low expressions, mostly political," as *slangwhanger, loco foco, hunker; to get the hang of.*

m. "Ungrammatical expressions, disapproved by all," as *do don't, used to could, can't come it, Universal preacher* (for *Universalist*), *there's no two ways about it.*

Elwyn, in 1859, attempted no classification.[75] He confined his glossary to archaic English words surviving in America, and sought only to prove that they had come down "from our remotest ancestry" and were thus undeserving of the reviling lavished upon them by English critics. Schele de Vere, in 1872, followed Bartlett, and devoted himself largely to words borrowed from the Indian dialects, and from the French, Spanish and Dutch. But Farmer, in 1889,[76] ventured upon a new classification, prefacing it with the following definition:

An Americanism may be defined as a word or phrase, old or new, employed by general or respectable usage in America in a way not sanctioned by the best standards of the English language. As a matter of fact, however, the term has come to possess a wider meaning, and it is now applied not only to words and phrases which can be so described, but also to the new and legitimately born words adapted to the general needs and usages, to the survivals of an older form of English than that now current in the mother country, and to the racy, pungent vernacular of Western life.

He then proceeded to this classification:

1. Words and phrases of purely American derivation, embracing words originating in:
    a. Indian and aboriginal life.
    b. Pioneer and frontier life.
    c. The church.
    d. Politics.
    e. Trades of all kinds.
    f. Travel, afloat and ashore.
2. Words brought by colonists, including:
    a. The German element.
    b. The French.

[75] Alfred L. Elwyn, M.D.: Glossary of Supposed Americanisms . . .; Phila., 1859.
[76] John S. Farmer: Americanisms Old and New . . .; London, 1889.

INTRODUCTORY 41

    c. The Spanish.
    d. The Dutch.
    e. The negro.
    f. The Chinese.
3. Names of American things, embracing:
    a. Natural products.
    b. Manufactured articles.
4. Perverted English words.
5. Obsolete English words still in good use in America.
6. English words, American by inflection and modification.
7. Odd and ignorant popular phrases, proverbs, vulgarisms, and colloquialisms, cant and slang.
8. Individualisms.
9. Doubtful and miscellaneous.

Clapin, in 1902,[77] reduced these categories to four:

1. Genuine English words, obsolete or provincial in England, and universally used in the United States.
2. English words conveying, in the United States, a different meaning from that attached to them in England.
3. Words introduced from other languages than the English:—French, Dutch, Spanish, German, Indian, etc.
4. Americanisms proper, *i. e.*, words coined in the country, either representing some new idea or peculiar product.

Thornton, in 1912, substituted the following:

1. Forms of speech now obsolete or provincial in England, which survive in the United States, such as *allow, bureau, fall, gotten, guess, likely, professor, shoat.*
2. Words and phrases of distinctly American origin, such as *belittle, lengthy, lightning-rod, to darken one's doors, to bark up the wrong tree, to come out at the little end of the horn, blind tiger, cold snap, gay Quaker, gone coon, long sauce, pay dirt, small potatoes, some pumpkins.*
3. Nouns which indicate quadrupeds, birds, trees, articles of food, etc., that are distinctively American, such as *ground-hog, hang-bird, hominy, live-oak, locust, opossum, persimmon, pone, succotash, wampum, wigwam.*
4. Names of persons and classes of persons, and of places, such as *Buckeye, Cracker, Greaser, Hoosier, Old Bullion, Old Hickory,* the *Little Giant, Dixie, Gotham,* the *Bay State,* the *Monumental City.*
5. Words which have assumed a new meaning, such as *card, clever, fork, help, penny, plunder, raise, rock, sack, ticket, windfall.*

[77] Sylva Clapin: A New Dictionary of Americanisms, Being a Glossary of Words Supposed to be Peculiar to the United States and the Dominion of Canada; New York, 1902.

In addition, Thornton added a provisional class of "words and phrases of which I have found earlier examples in American than in English writers; . . . with the *caveat* that further research may reverse the claim"—a class offering specimens in *alarmist, capitalize, eruptiveness, horse of another colour (sic!), the jig's up, nameable, omnibus bill, propaganda* and *whitewash.*

Tucker, in 1921,[78] attempted to reduce all Americanisms to two grand divisions, as follows:

1. Words and phrases that originated in America and express something that the British have always expressed differently if they have mentioned it at all.
2. Words and phrases that would convey to a British ear a different meaning from that which they bear in this country.

To which he added seven categories of locutions *not* to be regarded as Americanisms, despite their inclusion in various previous lists, as follows:

1. Words and phrases stated by the previous compiler himself to be of foreign [*i. e.*, chiefly of English] origin, like Farmer's *hand-me-downs.*
2. Names of things exclusively American, but known abroad under the same name, such as *moccasin.*
3. Names of things invented in the United States, like *drawing-room car.*
4. Words used in this country in a sense hardly distinguishable from that they bear in England, like *force* for a gang of laborers.
5. Nonce words, like Mark Twain's *cavalieress.*
6. Perfectly regular and self-explanatory compounds, like *office-holder, planing-machine, ink-slinger* and *fly-time.*
7. Purely technical terms, such as those employed in baseball.

No more than a glance at these discordant classifications is needed to show that they hamper the inquiry by limiting its scope—not so much, to be sure, as the extravagant limitations of White and Lounsbury, but still very seriously. They leave out of account some of the most salient characters of a living language. Only Bartlett and Farmer establish a separate category of Americanisms produced by umlaut, by shading of consonants and by other phonological changes, though even Thornton, of course, is obliged to take notice of such forms as *bust* and *bile,* and even Tucker lists *buster.* None of them, however, goes into the matter at any length, nor even into the matter

[78] Gilbert M. Tucker: American English; New York, 1921.

INTRODUCTORY 43

of etymology. Bartlett's etymologies are scanty and often inaccurate; Schele de Vere's are sometimes quite fanciful; Thornton, Tucker and the rest scarcely offer any at all. It must be obvious that many of the words and phrases excluded by Tucker's *index expurgatorius* are quite genuine Americanisms. Why should he bar out such a word as *moccasin* on the ground that it is also used in England? So is *caucus,* and yet he includes it. He is also far too hostile to such characteristic American compounds as *office-holder, fly-time* and *parlor-car.*[79] True enough, their materials are good English, and they involve no change in the meaning of their component parts, but it must be plain that they were put together in the United States and that an Englishman always sees a certain strangeness in them. *Pay-dirt, panel-house, passage-way, patrolman, night-rider, low-down, know-nothing, hoe-cake* and *hog-wallow* are equally compounded of pure English metal, and yet he lists all of them. Again, he is too ready, it seems to me, to bar out archaisms, which constitute one of the most interesting and authentic of all the classes of Americanisms. It is idle to prove that Chaucer used *to guess.* The important thing is that the English abandoned it centuries ago, and that when they happen to use it today they are always conscious that it is an Americanism. *Baggage* is in Shakespeare, but it is not in the London *Times.* The *Times,* save when it wants to be American, uses *luggage,* as do the fashionable shop-keepers along Fifth avenue. Here Mr. Tucker allows his historical principles to run away with his judgment. His book represents the labor of nearly forty years and is full of shrewd observations and persuasive contentions, but it is sometimes excessively dogmatic.[80]

The most scientific and laborious of all these collections of Americanisms is Thornton's. It presents an enormous mass of quotations, and they are all very carefully dated, and it corrects most of the more

[79] He gives the term as *drawing-room car,* but obviously means *parlor-car.* The former is a Briticism borrowed in America.
[80] I detect a few rather astonishing errors. *P.D.Q.* is defined as an abbreviation of "pretty *deuced* quick," which it certainly is not. *Patent-outside* is substituted for *patent-inside. Passage* (of a bill in Congress) is listed as an Americanism; it is actually very good English and is used in England every day. *Standee* is defined as "standing place"; it really means one who stands. *Sundae* (the soda-fountain mess) is misspelled *sunday;* it was precisely the strange spelling that gave the term vogue. *Mucker,* a brilliant Briticism, almost unknown in America, is listed between *movie* and *muckraker.*

obvious errors in the work of earlier inquirers. But its very dependence upon quotations limits it chiefly to the written language, and so the enormously richer materials of the spoken language are passed over, and particularly the materials evolved during the past twenty years. One searches the two fat volumes in vain for such highly characteristic forms as *near-accident* and *buttinski,* the use of *sure* as an adverb, and the employment of *well* as a sort of general equivalent of the German *also.*

These grammatical and syntactical tendencies are beyond the scope of Thornton's investigation,[81] but it is plain that they must be prime concerns of any future student who essays to get at the inner spirit of the language. Its difference from standard English is not merely a difference in vocabulary, to be disposed of in an alphabetical list; it is, above all, a difference in pronunciation, in intonation, in conjugation and declension, in metaphor and idiom, in the whole fashion of using words. A page from one of Ring W. Lardner's baseball stories contains few words that are not in the English vocabulary, and yet the thoroughly American color of it cannot escape anyone who actually listens to the tongue spoken around him. Some of the elements which enter into that color will be considered in the following pages. The American vocabulary, of course, must be given first attention, for in it the earliest American divergences are embalmed and it tends to grow richer and freer year after year, but attention will also be paid to materials and ways of speech that are less obvious, and in particular to certain tendencies of the grammar of spoken American, hitherto not investigated.

[81] His two volumes, however, do not exhaust the materials gathered by him. He informed me in 1920 that he had enough matter collected to make three volumes. But his age—he was then beyond 75—dissuaded him from attempting to prepare it for the press, and so he planned to deposit it at Harvard University, for the use of some future philologist. In 1917 he appealed to various rich men for funds to complete and publish his work, but "to their lasting infamy, they were uniformly too unappreciative . . . to guarantee the success of this record of American self-expression." See his letter in *Dialect Notes,* vol. v, p. 43 (1919).

II.

THE BEGINNINGS OF AMERICAN

1.

The First Differentiation

William Gifford, the first editor of the *Quarterly Review,* is authority for the tale that a plan was set on foot during the Revolution for the abandonment of English as the national language of America, and the substitution of Hebrew in its place. An American chronicler, Charles Astor Bristed, makes the proposed tongue Greek, and reports that the change was rejected on the ground that "it would be more convenient for us to keep the language as it is, and make the English speak Greek." [1] The story, though it has the support of the editors of the Cambridge History of American Literature,[2] has an apocryphal smack; one suspects that the savagely anti-American Gifford invented it. But, true or false, it well indicates the temper of those times. The passion for complete political independence of England bred a general hostility to all English authority, whatever its character, and that hostility, in the direction of present concern to us, culminated in the revolutionary attitude of Noah Webster's "Dissertations on the English Language," printed in 1789. Webster harbored no fantastic notion of abandoning English altogether, but he was eager to set up American as a distinct and independent dialect. "Let us," he said, "seize the present moment, and establish a national language as well as a national government. . . .

[1] Bristed was a grandson of John Jacob Astor and was educated at Cambridge. He contributed an extremely sagacious essay on The English Language in America to a volume of Cambridge Essays published by a group of young men of the university; London, 1855. For Gifford see the *Quarterly,* Jan., 1814, p. 528.
[2] Vol. i, p. vi.

As an independent nation our honor requires us to have a system of our own, in language as well as government."

Long before this the challenge had been flung. Scarcely two years after the Declaration of Independence Franklin was instructed by Congress, on his appointment as minister to France, to employ "the language of the United States," not simply English, in all his "replies or answers" to the communications of the ministry of Louis XVI. And eight years before the Declaration Franklin himself had invented a new American alphabet and drawn up a characteristically American scheme of spelling reform, and had offered plenty of proof in it, perhaps unconsciously, that the standards of spelling and pronunciation in the New World had already diverged noticeably from those accepted on the other side of the ocean.[3] In acknowledging the dedication of Webster's "Dissertations" Franklin endorsed both his revolt against English domination and his forecast of widening differences in future, though protesting at the same time against certain Americanisms that have since come into good usage, and even migrated to England. Nor was this all. "A Scotchman of the name of Thornton," having settled in the new republic and embraced its *Kultur* with horrible fervor, proposed a new alphabet even more radical than Franklin's and, according to Gifford, was doubly honored by the American Philosophical Society for his project, first by being given its gold medal and secondly by having his paper printed in its *Transactions*. This new alphabet included *e*'s turned upside down and *i*'s with their dots underneath. "Di Amərikən languids," he argued, "uil dəs bi az distint az də gəvərnmənt, fri from aul foliz or ənfilosofikəl fasən."[4]

Franklin's protest to Webster was marked by his habitual mildness, but in other quarters dissent was voiced with far less urbanity. The growing independence of the colonial dialect, not only in its spoken form, but also in its most dignified written form, had begun, indeed, to attract the attention of purists in both England and America, and they sought to dispose of it in its infancy by *force majeure*. One of

[3] Scheme for a New Alphabet and a Reformed Mode of Spelling; Philadelphia, 1768.
[4] *Quarterly Review*, Jan., 1814, p. 529. The date of Thornton's project I have been unable to establish. Franklin wrote to Webster on Dec. 26, 1789. See Franklin's Works, ed. by A. F. Smythe; New York, 1905, vol. i, p. 40.

the first and most vigorous of the attacks upon it at home was delivered by John Witherspoon, a Scotch clergyman who came out in 1769 to be president of Princeton *in partibus infidelium*. This Witherspoon brought a Scotch hatred of the English with him, and at once became a leader of the party of independence; he signed the Declaration to the tune of much rhetoric, and was the only clergyman to sit in the Continental Congress. But in matters of learning he was orthodox to the point of immovability, and the strange locutions that he encountered on all sides aroused his pedagogic ire. "I have heard in this country," he wrote in 1781, "in the senate, at the bar, and from the pulpit, and see daily in dissertations from the press, errors in grammar, improprieties and vulgarisms which hardly any person of the same class in point of rank and literature would have fallen into in Great Britain." [5] It was Witherspoon who coined the word Americanism—and at once the English guardians of the sacred vessels began employing it as a general synonym for vulgarism and barbarism. Another learned immigrant, the Rev. Jonathan Boucher, soon joined him. This Boucher was a friend of Washington, but was driven back to England by his Loyalist sentiments. He took revenge by printing various charges against the Americans, among them that of "making all the haste they can to rid themselves of the [English] language." He was vigorously supported by many Englishmen, including Samuel Johnson, whose detestation of all things American is familiar to every reader of Boswell. Johnson's recognition of and aversion to Americanisms, in fact, long antedated the Revolution. When, in 1756, one Lewis Evans published a volume of "Geographical, Historical, Philosophical, and Mechanical Essays," with a map, the sage wrote of it: "The map is engraved with sufficient beauty, and the treatise written with such elegance as the subject admits, though not without some mixture of the American dialect; a trace of corruption to which every language widely diffused must always be exposed."

After the adoption of the Constitution nearly all the British reviews began to maintain an eager watchfulness for these abhorrent

[5] *The Druid*, No. 5; reprinted in Witherspoon's Collected Works, edited by Ashbel Green, vol. iv; New York, 1800-1.

inventions, and to denounce them, when found, with vast acerbity. The *Monthly Review* opened the new offensive in July, 1797, with an attack upon the American spelling in Webster's "Dissertations," and the *European Magazine and London Review* joined it a month later with a violent diatribe against Jefferson's Americanisms in his "Notes on Virginia." "For shame, Mr. Jefferson!" it roared. "Why, after trampling upon the honour of our country, and representing it as little better than a land of barbarism—why, we say, perpetually trample also upon the very grammar of our language, and make that appear as Gothic as, from your description, our manners are rude?—Freely, good sir, will we forgive all your attacks, impotent as they are illiberal, upon our *national character;* but for the future spare—O spare, we beseech you, our mother-tongue!" The *Edinburgh* joined the charge in October, 1804, with a patronizing article upon John Quincy Adams' "Letters on Silesia." "The style of Mr. Adams," it said, "is in general very tolerable English; which, for an American composition, is no moderate praise." The usual American book of the time, it went on, was full of "affectations and corruptions of phrase," and they were even to be found in "the enlightened state papers of the two great Presidents." The *Edinburgh* predicted that a "spurious dialect" would prevail, "even at the Court and in the Senate of the United States," and that the Americans would thus "lose the only badge that is still worn of our consanguinity." The appearance of the five volumes of Chief Justice Marshall's "Life of George Washington," from 1804 to 1807, brought forth corrective articles from the *British Critic,* the *Critical Review,* the *Annual,* the *Monthly,* and the *Eclectic.* The *Edinburgh,* in 1808, declared that the Americans made "it a point of conscience to have no aristocratical distinctions—even in their vocabulary." They thought, it went on, "one word as good as another, provided its meaning be as clear." The *Monthly Mirror,* in March of the same year, denounced "the corruptions and barbarities which are hourly obtaining in the speech of our trans-atlantic colonies (*sic*)," and reprinted with approbation a parody by some anonymous Englishman of the American style of the day. Here is an extract from it, with the words that the author regarded as Americanisms in italics:

In America authors are to be found who make use of new or obsolete words which no good writer in this country would employ; and were it not for my *destitution* of leisure, which obliges me to hasten the *occlusion* of these pages, as I *progress* I should *bottom* my assertation on instances from authors of the first *grade;* but were I to render my sketch *lengthy* I should *illy* answer the purpose which I have in view.

The *British Critic,* in April, 1808, admitted somewhat despairingly that the damage was already done—that "the common speech of the United States has departed very considerably from the standard adopted in England." The others, however, sought to stay the flood by invective against Marshall and, later, against his rival biographer, the Rev. Aaron Bancroft. The *Annual,* in 1808, pronounced its high curse and anathema upon "that torrent of barbarous phraseology" which was pouring across the Atlantic, and which threatened "to destroy the purity of the English language." [6] In Bancroft's "Life of George Washington" (1808), according to the *British Critic,* there were gross Americanisms, inordinately offensive to Englishmen, "at almost every page."

The Rev. Jeremy Belknap, long anticipating Elwyn, White and Lounsbury, tried to obtain a respite from this abuse by pointing out the obvious fact that many of the Americanisms under fire were merely survivors of an English that had become archaic in England, but this effort counted for little, for on the one hand the British purists enjoyed the chase too much to give it up, and on the other hand there began to dawn in America a new spirit of nationality, at first very faint, which viewed the differences objected to, not with shame, but with a fierce sort of pride. In the first volume of the *North American Review* William Ellery Channing spoke out boldly for "the American language and literature," [7] and a year later

[6] *Vide,* in addition to the citations in the text, the *British Critic,* Nov., 1793; Feb., 1810; the *Critical,* July, 1807; Sept., 1809; the *Monthly,* May, 1808; the *Eclectic,* Aug., 1813. For a laborious investigation of the whole question see British Criticisms of American Writings, 1783-1815, by William B. Cairns; Madison, Wis., 1918, pp. 20 et seq. Cairns says that the *Edinburgh,* the *Anti-Jacobin,* the *Quarterly,* and the *European Magazine and London Review* were especially virulent. He says that the *Monthly,* despite my quotations, was always "kindly toward America" and that the *Eclectic* was, "on the whole, fair." The *Literary Magazine and British Review* he describes as enthusiastically pro-American, but it lived only a short time.

[7] 1815, pp. 307-14; reprinted in his Remarks on National Literature; Boston, 1823.

Pickering published his defiant dictionary of "words and phrases which have been supposed to be peculiar to the United States."[8] This thin collection of 500 specimens sets off a dispute which yet rages on both sides of the Atlantic. Pickering, however, was undismayed. He had begun to notice the growing difference between the English and American vocabulary and pronunciation, he said, while living in London from 1799 to 1801, and he had made his collections with the utmost care, and after taking counsel with various prudent authorities, both English and American. Already in the first year of the century, he continued, the English had accused the people of the new republic of a deliberate "design to effect an entire change in the language," and while no such design was actually harbored, the facts were the facts, and he cited the current newspapers, the speeches from pulpit and rostrum, and Webster himself in support of them. This debate over Pickering's list, as I say, still continues. Lounsbury, entrenched behind his grotesque categories, once charged that four-fifths of the words in it had "no business to be there," and Gilbert M. Tucker[9] has argued that "not more than about fifty" of them were genuine Americanisms. But a careful study of the list, in comparison with the early quotations collected by Thornton, seems to indicate that both of these judgments, and many others no less, have done injustice to Pickering. He made the usual errors of the pioneer, but his sound contributions to the subject were anything but inconsiderable, and it is impossible to forget his diligence and his constant shrewdness. He established firmly the native origin of a number of words now in universal use in America—*e. g., backwoodsman, breadstuffs, caucus, clapboard, sleigh* and *squatter*—and of such familiar derivatives as *gubernatorial* and *dutiable*, and he worked out the genesis of not a few loan-words, including *prairie, scow, rapids, hominy* and *barbecue*. It was not until 1848, when the first edition of Bartlett appeared, that his work was supplanted.

[8] Pickering was a son of Col. Timothy Pickering, quartermaster-general of the Continental Army, and later Postmaster-General, Secretary of War, Secretary of State, Senator and Chief Justice of Massachusetts. The younger Pickering was born in 1777 and died in 1846. He was a famous linguist in his day and wrote a Greek lexicon and various works on the Indian languages. He was at one time in the diplomatic service, and was president of the American Academy of Sciences and first president of the American Oriental Society. There is a biography of him by his daughter, Mary Orne Pickering; Boston, 1887.

[9] American English, p. 53.

2.

Sources of Early Americanisms

The first genuine Americanisms were undoubtedly words borrowed bodily from the Indian dialects—words, in the main, indicating natural objects that had no counterparts in England. We find *opossum,* for example, in the form of *opasum,* in Captain John Smith's "Map of Virginia" (1612), and, in the form of *apossoun,* in a Virginia document two years older. *Moose* is almost as old. The word is borrowed from the Algonquin *musa,* and must have become familiar to the Pilgrim Fathers soon after their landing in 1620, for the woods of Massachusetts then swarmed with the huge animals and there was no English name to designate them. Again, there are *skunk* (from the Abenaki Indian *seganku*), *hickory, squash, caribou, pecan, scuppernong, paw-paw, raccoon, chinkapin, porgy, chipmunk, terrapin, menhaden, catalpa, persimmon* and *cougar.*[10] Of these, *hickory* and *terrapin* are to be found in Robert Beverley's "History and Present State of Virginia" (1705), and *squash, chinkapin* and *persimmon* are in documents of the preceding century. Many of these words, of course, were shortened or otherwise modified on being taken into colonial English. Thus, *chinkapin* was originally *checkinqumin,* and *squash* appears in early documents as *isquontersquash,* and *squantersquash.* But William Penn, in a letter dated August 16, 1683, used the latter in its present form. Its variations show a familiar effort to bring a new and strange word into harmony with the language—an effort arising from what philologists call the law of Hobson-Jobson. This name was given to it by Col. Henry Yule and A. C. Burnell, compilers of a standard dictionary of Anglo-Indian terms. They found that the British soldiers in India, hearing strange words from the lips of the natives, often converted them into English words of similar sound, though of widely different meaning. Thus the words *Hassan* and *Hosein,* frequently used by the Mohammedans of the country in their devotions, were

[10] *Cf.* Algonquin Words in American English, by Alex. F. Chamberlain, *Journal of American Folk-Lore,* vol. xv, p. 240. Chamberlain lists 132 words, but some are localisms and others are obsolete.

turned into *Hobson-Jobson*. The same process is constantly in operation elsewhere. By it the French *route de roi* has become *Rotten Row* in English, *écrevisse* has become *crayfish*, and the English *bowsprit* has become *beau pré* (= *beautiful meadow*) in French. No doubt *squash* originated in the same way. That *woodchuck* did so is practically certain. Its origin is to be sought, not in *wood* and *chuck*, but in the Cree word *otchock*, used by the Indians to designate the animal.

In addition to the names of natural objects, the early colonists, of course, took over a great many Indian place-names, and a number of words to designate Indian relations and artificial objects in Indian use. To the last division belong *hominy, pone, toboggan, canoe, pemmican, mackinaw, tapioca, moccasin, paw-paw, papoose, sachem, sagamore, tomahawk, wigwam, succotash* and *squaw*, all of which were in common circulation by the beginning of the eighteenth century. Finally, new words were made during the period by translating Indian terms, for example, *war-path, war-paint, pale-face, big-chief, medicine-man, pipe-of-peace* and *fire-water*. The total number of such borrowings, direct and indirect, was a good deal larger than now appears, for with the disappearance of the red man the use of loan-words from his dialects has decreased. In our own time such words as *papoose, sachem, tepee, wigwam* and *wampum* have begun to drop out of everyday use;[11] at an earlier period the language sloughed off *ocelot, manitee, calumet, supawn, samp* and *quahaug*, or began to degrade them to the estate of provincialisms.[12] A curious phenomenon is presented by the case of *maize*, which came into the

[11] A number of such Indian words are preserved in the nomenclature of Tammany Hall and in that of the Improved Order of Red Men, an organization with more than 500,000 members. The Red Men, borrowing from the Indians, thus name the months, in order: *Cold Moon, Snow, Worm, Plant, Flower, Hot, Buck, Sturgeon, Corn, Travelers', Beaver* and *Hunting*. They call their officers *incohonee, sachem, wampum-keeper*, etc. But such terms, of course, are not in general use.

[12] A long list of obsolete Americanisms, from Indian and other sources, is given by Clapin in his Dictionary. It is unfortunate that there is no dictionary of them on the plan of the New English Dictionary—that is, showing when they came in and when they went out. There is a constant loss in our own time. For example, the use of *cars* to designate railroad came in in the 40's, was universal during the Civil War (as a glance at any newspaper of the time will show), and then was abandoned. Today it survives only in the signs occasionally seen at railroad crossings: "Look Out for the *Cars*," *e. g.*, on the Long Island Railroad, and in the verb-phrase, *to change cars*. Again, there is *dude*, born, as Thornton shows, in 1883, and dead by 1895.

THE BEGINNINGS OF AMERICAN 53

colonial speech from some West Indian dialect, went over into orthodox English, and from English into French, German and other Continental languages, and was then abandoned by the colonists. We shall see other examples of that process later on.

Whether or not *Yankee* comes from an Indian dialect is still disputed. An early authority, John G. E. Heckwelder, argued that it was derived from an Indian mispronunciation of the word *English*. Certain later etymologists hold that it originated more probably in an Indian mishandling of the French word *Anglais*. Others derive it from the Scotch *yankie*, meaning a gigantic falsehood. Yet others derive it from the Dutch, and cite an alleged Dutch model for "Yankee Doodle," beginning *"Yanker didee doodle down."* Finally, Ernest Weekly, in his Etymological Dictionary,[13] makes the conjecture that it may be derived from the Dutch *Jan* (=*John*), possibly by back-formation from *Jan Kes* (=*John Cornelius*). Of these theories that of Heckwelder is the most plausible. But here, as in other directions, the investigation of American etymology remains sadly incomplete. An elaborate dictionary of words derived from the Indian languages, compiled by the late W. R. Gerard, is in the possession of the Smithsonian Institution, but on account of a shortage of funds it remains in manuscript.[14]

From the very earliest days of English colonization the language of the colonists also received accretions from the languages of the other colonizing nations. The French word *portage,* for example, was already in common use before the end of the seventeenth century, and soon after came *chowder, cache, caribou, voyageur,* and various words that, like the last-named, have since become localisms or disappeared altogether. Before 1750 *bureau,*[15] *gopher, batteau, bogus,* and *prairie* were added, and *caboose,* a word of Dutch origin, seems to have come in through the French. *Carry-all* is also French in origin, despite its English quality. It comes, by the law of Hobson-

---

[13] An Etymological Dictionary of Modern English; New York, 1921, p. 1651.
[14] I have examined this manuscript. It consists of a vast mass of notes, many of them almost undecipherable. Editing it for publication will be a colossal task.
[15] (a) A chest of drawers, (b) a government office. In both senses the word is rare in English, though its use by the French is familiar. In the United States its use in (b) has been extended, *e. g.,* in *employment-bureau.*

Jobson, from the French *carriole*. The contributions of the Dutch during the half century of their conflicts with the English included *cruller, cold-slaw, dominie* (for parson), *cookey, stoop, span* (of horses), *pit* (as in *peach-pit*), *waffle, hook* (a point of land), *scow, boss, smearcase* and *Santa Claus*.[16] Schele de Vere credits them with *hay-barrack*, a corruption of *hooiberg*. That they established the use of *bush* as a designation for back-country is very probable; the word has also got into South African English and has been borrowed by Australian English from American. In American it has produced a number of familiar derivatives, e. g., *bush-whacker* and *bush-town*. Barrère and Leland also credit the Dutch with *dander*, which is commonly assumed to be an American corruption of *dandruff*. They say that it is from the Dutch word *donder* (=*thunder*). *Op donderen*, in Dutch, means to burst into a sudden rage. The chief Spanish contributions to American were to come after the War of 1812, with the opening of the West, but *creole, calaboose, palmetto, peewee, key* (a small island), *quadroon, octoroon, barbecue, pickaninny* and *stampede* had already entered the language in colonial days. *Jerked beef* came from the Spanish *charqui* by the law of Hobson-Jobson. The Germans who arrived in Pennsylvania in 1682 also undoubtedly gave a few words to the language, though it is often difficult to distinguish their contributions from those of the Dutch. It seems very likely, however, that *sauerkraut*[17] and *noodle* are to be credited to them. Finally, the negro slaves brought in *gumbo, goober, juba* and *voodoo* (usually corrupted to *hoodoo*), and probably helped to corrupt a number of other loan-words, for example *banjo* and *breakdown*. *Banjo* seems to be derived from *bandore* or *bandurria*, modern French and Spanish forms of *tambour*, respectively. It may, however, be an actual negro word; there is a term of like meaning, *bania*, in Senegambian. Ware says that *breakdown*, designating a riotous negro dance, is a corruption of the French *rigadon*, but offers no evidence. The word, used in the American sense, is not in the English dictionaries. Bartlett listed it as an Americanism,

---

[16] From *Sint-Klaas*—*Saint Nicholas*. *Santa Claus* has also become familiar to the English, but the Oxford Dictionary still calls the name an Americanism.

[17] The spelling is variously *sauerkraut* (the correct German form), *sourkraut* and *sourkrout*.

but Thornton rejected it, apparently because, in the sense of a collapse, it has come into colloquial use in England. Its etymology is not given in the American dictionaries. It may be a compound regularly formed of English materials, like its brother, *hoedown*.

3.

New Words of English Material

But of far more importance than these borrowings was the great stock of new words that the colonists coined in English metal—words primarily demanded by the "new circumstances under which they were placed," but also indicative, in more than one case, of a delight in the business for its own sake. The American, even in the early eighteenth century, already showed many of the characteristics that were to set him off from the Englishman later on—his bold and somewhat grotesque imagination, his contempt for dignified authority, his lack of æsthetic sensitiveness, his extravagant humor. Among the first colonists there were many men of education, culture and gentle birth, but they were soon swamped by hordes of the ignorant and illiterate, and the latter, cut off from the corrective influence of books, soon laid their hands upon the language. It is impossible to imagine the austere Puritan divines of Massachusetts inventing such verbs as *to cowhide* and *to logroll*, or such adjectives as *no-account* and *stumped*, or such adverbs as *no-how* and *lickety-split*, or such substantives as *bull-frog, hog-wallow* and *hoe-cake;* but under their eyes there arose a contumacious proletariat which was quite capable of the business, and very eager for it. In Boston, so early as 1628, there was a definite class of blackguard roisterers, chiefly made up of sailors and artisans; in Virginia, nearly a decade earlier, John Pory, secretary to Governor Yeardley, lamented that "in these five months of my continuance here there have come at one time or another eleven sails of ships into this river, but fraighted more with ignorance than with any other marchansize." In particular, the generation born in the New World was uncouth and iconoclastic;[18]

[18] *Cf.* The Cambridge History of American Literature, vol. i, pp. 14 and 22.

the only world it knew was a rough world, and the virtues that environment engendered were not those of niceness, but those of enterprise and resourcefulness.

Upon men of this sort fell the task of bringing the wilderness to the ax and the plow, and with it went the task of inventing a vocabulary for the special needs of the great adventure. Out of their loutish ingenuity came a great number of picturesque names for natural objects, chiefly boldly descriptive compounds: *bull-frog, canvas-back, mud-hen, cat-bird, razor-back, garter-snake, ground-hog* and so on. And out of an inventiveness somewhat more urbane came such coinages as *live-oak, potato-bug, turkey-gobbler, sweet-potato, poke-weed, copper-head, eel-grass, reed-bird, egg-plant, blue-grass, pea-nut, pitch-pine, cling-stone* (peach), *moccasin-snake, June-bug, lightning-bug,* and *butter-nut. Live-oak* appears in a document of 1610; *bull-frog* was familiar to Beverley in 1705; so was *James-town weed* (later reduced to *Jimson weed,* as the English *hurtleberry* or *whortleberry* was reduced to *huckleberry*). These early Americans were not botanists. They were often ignorant of the names of the plants that they encountered, even when those plants already had English names, and so they exercised their fancy upon new ones. So arose *Johnny-jump-up* for the *Viola tricolor,* and *basswood* for the common European *linden* or *lime-tree* (*Tilia*), and *locust* for the *Robinia pseudacacia* and its allies. The *Jimson weed* itself was anything but a novelty, but the pioneers apparently did not recognize it as the *Datura stramonium,* and so we find Beverley reporting that "some Soldiers, eating it in a Salad, turn'd natural Fools upon it for several Days." The grosser features of the landscape got a lavish renaming, partly to distinguish new forms and partly out of an obvious desire to attain a more literal descriptiveness. I have mentioned *key* and *hook,* the one borrowed from the Spanish and the other from the Dutch. With them came *run, branch, fork, bluff* (noun), *neck, barrens, bottoms, watershed, foot-hill, water-gap, under-brush, bottom-land, clearing, notch, divide, knob, riffle, rolling-country* and *rapids,*[19] and the extension of *pond* from artificial pools

[19] The American origin of this last word has been disputed, but the weight of evidence seems to show that it was borrowed from the *rapides* of the French Canadians. It is familiar in the United States and Canada, but seldom met with in England.

THE BEGINNINGS OF AMERICAN 57

to small natural lakes, and of *creek* from small arms of the sea to shallow feeders of rivers. Such common English topographical terms as *downs, weald, wold, fen, bog, fell, chase, combe, dell, tarn, common, heath* and *moor* disappeared from the colonial tongue, save as fossilized in a few localisms and proper names.[20] So did *bracken*.

With the new landscape came an entirely new mode of life—new foods, new forms of habitation, new methods of agriculture, new kinds of hunting. A great swarm of neologisms thus arose, and, as in the previous case, they were chiefly compounds. *Back-country, back-woods, back-woodsman, back-settlers, back-settlements:* all these were in common use early in the eighteenth century. *Back-log* was used by Increase Mather in 1684. *Log-house* appears in the Maryland Archives for 1669.[21] *Hoe-cake, Johnny-cake, pan-fish, corn-dodger, roasting-ear, corn-crib, corn-cob* and *pop-corn* were all familiar before the Revolution. So were *pine-knot, snow-plow, cold-snap, land-slide, ash-can, bob-sled, apple-butter, salt-lick, prickly-heat, shell-road* and *cane-brake*. *Shingle* was a novelty in 1705, but one S. Symonds wrote to John Winthrop, of Ipswich, about a *clap-boarded* house in 1637. *Frame-house* seems to have come in with *shingle*. *Trail, half-breed, Indian-summer, Indian-giver,* and *Indian-file,* were obviously suggested by the Red Men.[22] *Statehouse* was borrowed, perhaps, from the Dutch. *Selectman* is first heard of in 1685, displacing the English *alderman*. *Mush* had displaced *porridge* by 1671. Soon afterwards *hay-stack* took the place of the English *hay-cock*, and such common English terms as *byre, mews, wier* and *wain* began to disappear. *Hired-man* is to be found in the Plymouth town records of 1737, and *hired-girl* followed soon after. So early as 1758, as we find by the diary of Nathaniel Ames, the second-year students at Harvard were already called *sophomores,* though for a while the spelling was often made *sophimores*. *Camp-meeting* was later; it did not appear until 1799. But *land-office* was familiar before 1700, and *side-walk, spelling-bee, bee-line, moss-*

---

[20] *E. g.,* Chevy *Chase,* Boston *Common,* the Back Bay *fens,* and *cranberry-bog.*
[21] *Log-cabin* came in later. Thornton's first quotation is dated 1818. The *Log-Cabin* campaign was in 1840.
[22] *Cf.* Memorials of the Indian, by Alex. F. Chamberlain, *Journal of American Folk-Lore,* April-June, 1902, p. 107.

back, crazy-quilt, mud-scow, stamping-ground and a hundred and one other such compounds were in daily use before the Revolution. After that great upheaval the new money of the confederation brought in a number of new words. In 1782 Gouverneur Morris proposed to the Continental Congress that the coins of the republic be called, in ascending order, *unit, penny-bill, dollar* and *crown.* Later Morris invented the word *cent,* substituting it for the English penny.[23] In 1785 Jefferson proposed *mill, cent, dime, dollar* and *eagle,* and this nomenclature was adopted.

Various nautical terms peculiar to America, or taken into English from American sources, came in during the eighteenth century, among them, *schooner, cat-boat* and *pungy,* not to recall *batteau* and *canoe.* According to a recent historian of the American merchant marine,[24] the first schooner ever seen was launched at Gloucester, Mass., in 1713. The word, it appears, was originally spelled *scooner. To scoon* was a verb borrowed by the New Englanders from some Scotch dialect, and meant to skim or skip across the water like a flat stone. As the first schooner left the ways and glided out into Gloucester harbor, an enraptured spectator shouted: "Oh, see how she scoons!" "A *scooner* let her be!" replied Captain Andrew Robinson, her builder—and all boats of her peculiar and novel fore-and-aft rig took the name thereafter. The Dutch mariners borrowed the term and changed the spelling, and this change was soon accepted in America.[25] The Scotch root came from the Norse *skunna,* to hasten, and there are analogues in Icelandic, Anglo-Saxon and Old High German. The origin of *cat-boat* and *pungy* I have been unable to determine. Perhaps the latter is related in some way to *pung,* a one-horse sled or wagon. *Pung* was once widely used in the United States, but of late it has sunk to the estate of a New England provincialism. Longfellow used it, and in 1857 a writer in the *Knickerbocker Magazine* reported that pungs filled Broadway, in New York, after a snow-storm.

Most of these new words, of course, produced derivatives, for example, *to shingle, to shuck* (*i. e., corn*), *to trail* and *to caucus.*

[23] Theodore Roosevelt: Gouverneur Morris; Boston, 1888, p. 104.
[24] William Brown Meloney: The Heritage of Tyre; New York, 1916, p. 15.
[25] The Germans have adopted the word, spelling it variously *schooner, schoner* and *schuner.*

Backwoods immediately begat *backwoodsman* and was itself turned into a common adjective. The colonists, indeed, showed a beautiful disregard for linguistic nicety. At an early date they shortened the English law-phrase, *to convey by deed,* to the simple verb, *to deed.* Pickering protested against this as a barbarism, and argued that no self-respecting law-writer would employ it, but all the same it was firmly entrenched in the common speech and it has remained there to this day. *To table,* for *to lay on the table,* came in at the same time, and so did various forms represented by *bindery,* for *bookbinder's shop.* *To tomahawk* appeared before 1650, and *to scalp* must have followed soon after. Within the next century and a half they were reinforced by many other such new verbs, and by such adjectives made of nouns as *no-account* and *one-horse,* and such nouns made of verbs as *carry-all* and *goner,* and such adverbs as *no-how.* In particular, the manufacture of new verbs went on at a rapid pace. In his letter to Webster in 1789 Franklin denounced *to advocate, to progress,* and *to oppose*—a vain enterprise, for all of them are now in perfectly good usage. *To advocate,* indeed, was used by Thomas Nashe in 1589, and by John Milton half a century later, but it seems to have been reinvented in America. In 1822 and again in 1838 Robert Southey, then poet laureate, led two belated attacks upon it, as a barbarous Americanism, but its obvious usefulness preserved it, and it remains in good usage on both sides of the Atlantic today—one of the earliest of the English borrowings from America. In the end, indeed, even so ardent a purist as Richard Grant White adopted it, as he did *to placate.*[26]

Webster, though he agreed with Franklin in opposing *to advocate,* gave his *imprimatur* to *to appreciate* (*i. e.,* to rise in value), and is credited by Sir Charles Lyell [27] with having himself invented *to demoralize.* He also approved *to obligate.* *To antagonize* seems to have been given currency by John Quincy Adams, *to immigrate* by John Marshall, *to eventuate* by Gouverneur Morris, and *to derange* by George Washington. Jefferson, always hospitable to new words, used *to belittle* in his "Notes on Virginia," and Thornton thinks

[26] *Vide* his preface to Every-Day English, pp. xxi and xv, respectively.
[27] *Vide* Lyell's Travels in North America; London, 1845.

that he coined it. Many new verbs were made by the simple process of prefixing the preposition to common nouns, *e. g., to clerk, to dicker, to dump, to negative, to blow* (*i. e.,* to bluster or boast), *to cord* (*i. e.,* wood), *to stump, to room* and *to shin.* Others were produced by phonological changes in verbs of the orthodox vocabulary, *e. g., to cavort* from *to curvet,* and *to snoop* from *to snook.* Others arose as metaphors, *e. g., to whitewash* (figuratively) and *to squat* (on unoccupied land). Others were made by hitching suffixes to nouns, or by groping for roots, *e. g., to deputize, to locate, to legislate, to infract, to compromit* and *to happify.* Yet others seem to have been produced by onomatopœia, *e. g., to fizzle,* or to have arisen by some other such spontaneous process, so far unintelligible, *e. g., to tote.* With them came an endless series of verb-phrases, *e. g., to draw a bead, to face the music, to darken one's doors, to take to the woods, to fly off the handle, to go on the war-path* and *to saw wood*—all obvious products of pioneer life. Many coinages of the pre-Revolutionary era later disappeared. Jefferson used *to ambition,* but it dropped out nevertheless. So did *conflagrative,* though a president of Yale gave it his *imprimatur.* So did *to compromit* (*i. e.,* to compromise), *to homologize* and *to happify.*[28] Fierce battles raged 'round some of these words, and they were all violently derided in England. Even so useful a verb as *to locate,* now in quite respectable usage, was denounced in the third volume of the *North American Review,* and other purists of the times tried to put down *to legislate.*

The young and tender adjectives had quite as hard a row to hoe, particularly *lengthy.* The *British Critic* attacked it in November, 1793, and it also had enemies at home, but John Adams had used it in his diary in 1759 and the authority of Jefferson and Hamilton was behind it, and so it survived. Years later James Russell Lowell spoke of it as "the excellent adjective,"[29] and boasted that American had given it to English. *Dutiable* also met with opposition, and moreover it had a rival, *customable;* but Marshall wrote it into his historic decisions, and thus it took root. The same

[28] Thornton's last example of the use of *to compromit* is dated 1842; of *to happify,* 1857, and of *to ambition,* 1861. *To happify* seems to have died in 1811.
[29] Pref. to the Biglow Papers, 2nd series, 1866.

anonymous watchman of the *North American Review* who protested against *to locate* pronounced his anathema upon "such barbarous terms as *presidential* and *congressional*," but the plain need for them kept them in the language. *Gubernatorial* had come in long before this, and is to be found in the New Jersey Archives of 1734. *Influential* was denounced by the Rev. Jonathan Boucher and by George Canning, who argued that *influent* was better, but it was ardently defended by William Pinkney, of Maryland, and gradually made its way. *Handy, kinky, law-abiding, chunky, solid* (in the sense of well-to-do), *evincive, complected, judgmatical, underpinned, blooded* and *cute* were also already secure in revolutionary days. So with many nouns. Jefferson used *breadstuffs* in his Report of the Secretary of State on Commercial Restrictions, December 16, 1793. *Balance,* in the sense of remainder, got into the debates of the First Congress. *Mileage* was used by Franklin in 1754, and is now sound English. *Elevator,* in the sense of a storage house for grain, was used by Jefferson and by others before him. *Draw,* for *drawbridge,* comes down from revolutionary days. So does *slip,* in the sense of a berth for vessels. So does *addition,* in the sense of a suburb. So, finally, does *darkey.*

The history of many of these Americanisms shows how vain is the effort of grammarians to combat the normal processes of language development. I have mentioned the early opposition to *dutiable, influential, presidential, lengthy, to locate, to oppose, to advocate, to legislate,* and *to progress. Bogus, reliable* and *standpoint* were attacked with the same academic ferocity. All of them are to be found in Bryant's *Index Expurgatorius*[30] (circa 1870), and *reliable* was denounced by Bishop Coxe as "that abominable barbarism" so late as 1886.[31] Edward S. Gould, another uncompromising purist, said of *standpoint* that it was "the bright particular star . . . of solemn philological blundering" and "the very counterpart of Dogberry's *non-com.*"[32] Gould also protested against *to jeopar-*

[30] Reprinted in Helpful Hints in Writing and Reading, comp. by Grenville Kleiser; New York, 1911, pp. 15-17.
[31] A. Cleveland Coxe: Americanisms in England, *Forum*, Oct., 1886.
[32] Edward S. Gould: Good English, or, Popular Errors in Language; New York, 1867, pp. 25-27. So recently as 1918 a reviewer denounced me for using it in a book and hinted that I had borrowed it from the German *standpunkt.*

dize, leniency and to *demean,* and Richard Grant White joined him in an onslaught upon *to donate.* But all of these words are in good use in the United States today, and some of them have gone over into English.[33]

4.

Changed Meanings

A number of the foregoing contributions to the American vocabulary, of course, were simply common English words with changed meanings. *To squat,* in the sense of to crouch, had been sound English for centuries; what the colonists did was to attach a figurative meaning to it, and then bring that figurative meaning into wider usage than the literal meaning. In a somewhat similar manner they changed the significance of *pond,* as I have pointed out. So, too, with *creek.* In English it designated (and still designates) a small inlet or arm of a large river or of the sea; in American, so early as 1674, it designated any small stream. Many other such changed meanings crept into American in the early days. A typical one was the use of *lot* to designate a *parcel* of land. Thornton says, perhaps inaccurately, that it originated in the fact that the land in New England was distributed by lot. Whatever the truth, *lot,* to this day, is in almost universal use in the United States, though rare in England. Our conveyancers, in describing real property, always speak of "all that *lot* or *parcel* of land." [34] Other examples of the application of old words to new purposes are afforded by *freshet, barn* and *team.* A *freshet,* in eighteenth century English, meant any stream of fresh water; the colonists made it signify an inundation. A *barn* was a house or shed for storing crops; in the colonies the word came to mean a place for keeping cattle also. A *team,* in English, was a pair of draft horses; in the colonies it came to mean both horses and vehicle.

[33] *Cf.* Chapter V, Section 1.
[34] *Lott* appears in the Connecticut Code of 1650. *Vide* the edition of Andrus; Hartford, 1822. On page 35 is "their landes, *lotts* and accommodations." On page 46 is "meadow and home *lotts.*"

THE BEGINNINGS OF AMERICAN 63

The process is even more clearly shown in the history of such words as *corn* and *shoe*. *Corn,* in orthodox English, means grain for human consumption, and especially wheat, *e. g.,* the *Corn* Laws. The earliest settlers, following this usage, gave the name of *Indian corn* to what the Spaniards, following the Indians themselves, had called *maiz*. The term appears in Bradford's "History of Plimouth Plantation" (1647) and in Mourt's "Relation" (1622). But gradually the adjective fell off, and by the middle of the eighteenth century *maize* was called simply *corn* and grains in general were called *breadstuffs*. Thomas Hutchinson, discoursing to George III in 1774, used *corn* in this restricted sense, speaking of "rye and *corn* mixed." "What corn?" asked George. "Indian corn," explained Hutchinson, "or, as it is called in authors, *maize*." [35] So with *shoe*. In English it meant (and still means) a topless article of footwear, but the colonists extended its meaning to varieties covering the ankle, thus displacing the English *boot,* which they reserved for foot coverings reaching at least to the knee. To designate the English *shoe* they began to use the word *slipper*. This distinction between English and American usage still prevails, despite the fashion which has lately sought to revive *boot* in the United States, and with it its derivatives, *boot-shop* and *boot-maker*.

Store, shop, lumber, pie, dry-goods, cracker, rock and *partridge* among nouns and *to haul, to jew, to notify* and *to heft* [36] among verbs offer further examples of changed meanings. Down to the middle of the eighteenth century *shop* continued to designate a retail establishment in America, as it does in England to this day. *Store* was applied only to a large establishment—one showing, in some measure, the character of a warehouse. But in 1774 a Boston young man was advertising in the *Massachusetts Spy* for "a *place* as a *clerk* in a *store*" (three Americanisms in a row!). Soon afterward *shop* began to acquire its special American meaning of a factory, *e. g., machine-shop*. Meanwhile *store* completely displaced *shop* in the English sense, and it remained for a late flowering of Anglomania, as in the case of *boot* and *shoe,* to restore, in a measure, the *status*

---

[35] *Vide* Hutchinson's Diary, vol. i, p. 171; London, 1883-6.
[36] A correspondent informs me that this verb occurs in the "testification" prefixed to the Book of Mormon.

quo ante. *Lumber,* in eighteenth century English, meant disused furniture, and this is its common meaning in England today, as is shown by *lumber-room.* But the colonists early employed it to designate cut timber, and that use of it is now universal in America. Its familiar derivatives, e. g., *lumber-yard, lumberman, lumberjack,* greatly reinforce this usage. *Dry-goods,* in England, means, "nonliquid goods, as corn" (*i. e.,* wheat); in the United States the term means "textile fabrics or wares." [37] The difference had appeared before 1725. *Rock,* in English, always means a large mass; in America it may mean a small stone, as in *rock-pile* and *to throw a rock.* The Puritans were putting *rocks* into the foundations of their meeting-houses so early as 1712.[38] *Cracker* began to be used for *biscuit* before the Revolution. *Tavern* displaced *inn* at the same time. As for *partridge,* it is cited by a late authority [39] as a salient example of changed meaning, along with *corn* and *store.* In England the term is applied only to the true partridge (*Perdix perdix*) and its nearly related varieties, but in the United States it is also used to designate the ruffed grouse (*Bonasa umbellus*), the common quail (*Colinus virginianus*) and various other tetraonoid birds. This confusion goes back to Colonial times. So with *rabbit.* Zoologically speaking, there are no native rabbits in the United States; they are all hares. But the early colonists, for some unknown reason, dropped the word *hare* out of their vocabulary, and it is rarely heard in American speech to this day. When it appears it is almost always applied to the so-called Belgian hare, which, curiously enough, is not a hare at all, but a true rabbit. *Bay* and *bayberry* have also acquired special American meanings. In England *bay* is used to designate the bay-tree (*Laurus nobilis*); in America it designates a shrub, the wax myrtle (*Myrica cerifera*). Both the tree and the shrub have berries. Those of the latter are used to make the well-known *bayberry* candles.

To haul, in English, means to move by force or violence; in the colonies it came to mean to transport in a vehicle, and this meaning

---

[37] The definitions are from the Concise Oxford Dictionary of Current English (1914) and the Standard Dictionary (1906) respectively.
[38] S. Sewall: Diary, April 14, 1712: "I lay'd a *Rock* in the Northeast corner of the Foundation of the Meeting-house."
[39] The Americans, . . . *art.* Americanisms; New York, 1903-6.

THE BEGINNINGS OF AMERICAN 65

survives in sound American. *To jew,* in English, means to cheat; the colonists made it mean to haggle, and devised *to jew down* to indicate an effort to work a reduction in price. *To heft,* in English, means to lift up; the early Americans made it mean to weigh by lifting, and kept the idea of weighing in its derivatives, *e. g., hefty.* Finally, there is the familiar American misuse of Miss or Mis' (pro *miz*) for Mrs. It was so widespread by 1790 that on November 17 of that year Webster solemnly denounced it in the *American Mercury.*

5.

Archaic English Words

Most of the colonists who lived along the American seaboard in 1750 were the descendants of immigrants who had come in fully a century before; after the first settlements there had been much less fresh immigration than many latter-day writers have assumed. According to Prescott F. Hall, "the population of New England . . . at the date of the Revolutionary War . . . was produced out of an immigration of about 20,000 persons *who arrived before 1640,*"[40] and we have Franklin's authority for the statement that the total population of the colonies in 1751, then about 1,000,000, had been produced from an original immigration of less than 80,000.[41] Even at that early day, indeed, the colonists had begun to feel that they were distinctly separated, in culture and customs, from the mother-country[42] and there were signs of the rise of a new native aristocracy, entirely distinct from the older aristocracy

[40] Immigration, 2nd ed.; New York, 1913, p. 4. Sir J. R. Seeley says, in The Expansion of England (2nd ed.; London, 1895, p. 84) that the emigration from England to New England, after the meeting of the Long Parliament (1640), was so slight for a full century that it barely balanced "the counter-movement of colonists quitting the colony." Richard Hildreth, in his History of the United States, vol. i, p. 267, says that the departures actually exceeded the arrivals. See also The Founding of New England, by James Truslow Adams; Boston, 1921, p. 221 *ff.*
[41] Works, ed. by Sparks: vol. ii, p. 319.
[42] *Cf.* Pehr Kalm: Travels into N. America, tr. by J. R. Forster, 3 vols.; London, 1770-71.

of the royal governors' courts.[43] The enormous difficulties of communication with England helped to foster this sense of separation. The round trip across the ocean occupied the better part of a year, and was hazardous and expensive; a colonist who had made it was a marked man—as Hawthorne said, "the *petit maître* of the colonies." Nor was there any very extensive exchange of ideas, for though most of the books read in the colonies came from England, the great majority of the colonists, down to the middle of the century, seem to have read little save the Bible and biblical commentaries, and in the native literature of the time one seldom comes upon any reference to the English authors who were glorifying the period of the Restoration and the reign of Anne. "No allusion to Shakespeare," says Bliss Perry,[44] "has been discovered in the colonial literature of the seventeenth century, and scarcely an allusion to the Puritan poet Milton." Benjamin Franklin's brother, James, had a copy of Shakespeare at the *New England Courant* office in Boston, but Benjamin himself seems to have made little use of it, for there is not a single quotation from or mention of the bard in all his voluminous works. "The Harvard College Library in 1723," says Perry, had nothing of Addison, Steele, Bolingbroke, Dryden, Pope, and Swift, and had only recently obtained copies of Milton and Shakespeare. . . . Franklin reprinted 'Pamela' and his Library Company of Philadelphia had two copies of 'Paradise Lost' for circulation in 1741, but there had been no copy of that work in the great library of Cotton Mather." Moreover, after 1760, the eyes of the colonists were upon France rather than upon England, and Rousseau, Montesquieu, Voltaire and the Encyclopedists began to be familiar names to thousands who were scarcely aware of Addison and Steele, or even of the great Elizabethans.[45]

The result of this isolation, on the one hand, was that proliferation

---

[43] Sydney George Fisher: The True Story of the American Revolution; Phila. and London, 1902, p. 27. See also John T. Morse's Life of Thomas Jefferson in the American Statesmen series (Boston and New York, 1898), p. 2. Morse points out that Washington, Jefferson and Madison belonged to this new aristocracy, not to the old one.
[44] The American Spirit in Literature; New Haven, 1918, p. 61.
[45] *Cf.* the Cambridge History of American Literature, vol. i, p. 119. Francis Jeffrey, writing on Franklin in the *Edinburgh Review* for July, 1806, hailed him as a prodigy who had arisen "in a society where there was no relish and no encouragement for literature."

THE BEGINNINGS OF AMERICAN 67

of the colonial speech which I have briefly reviewed, and on the other hand, the preservation of many words and phrases that gradually became obsolete in England. The Pilgrims of 1620 brought over with them the English of James I and the Authorized Version, and their descendants of a century later, inheriting it, allowed its fundamentals to be but little changed by the academic overhauling that the mother-tongue was put to during the early part of the eighteenth century. In part they were ignorant of this overhauling, and in part they were indifferent to it. Whenever the new usage differed from that of the Bible they were inclined to remain faithful to the Bible, not only because of its pious authority but also because of the superior pull of its imminent and constant presence. Thus when an artificial prudery in English ordered the abandonment of the Anglo-Saxon *sick* for the Old Norse *ill(r)*, the colonists refused to follow, for *sick* was in both the Old Testament and the New;[46] and that refusal remains in force to this day.

A very large number of words and phrases, many of them now exclusively American, are similar survivals from the English of the seventeenth century, long since obsolete or merely provincial in England. Among nouns Thornton notes *fox-fire, flap-jack, jeans, molasses, beef* (to designate the live animal), *chinch, cordwood, homespun, ice-cream, julep* and *swingle-tree;* Halliwell[47] adds *andiron, bay-window, cesspool, clodhopper, cross-purposes, greenhorn, loophole, ragamuffin* and *trash;* and other authorities cite *stock* (for cattle), *fall* (for autumn), *offal, din, underpinning* and *adze. Bub,* used in addressing a boy, is very old English, but survives only in American. *Flapjack* goes back to Piers Plowman, but has been obsolete in England for two centuries. *Muss,* in the sense of a row, is also obsolete over there, but it is to be found in "Anthony and Cleopatra." *Char,* as a noun, disappeared from English a long time ago, save in the compound, *charwoman,* but it survives in America

---
[46] Examples of its use in the American sense, considered vulgar and even indecent in England, are to be found in Gen. xlviii, 1; II Kings viii, 7; John xi, 1, and Acts ix, 37.
[47] J. O. Halliwell (Phillips): A Dictionary of Archaisms and Provincialisms, Containing Words now Obsolete in England All of Which are Familiar and in Common Use in America, 2nd ed.; London, 1850. See also Gilbert M. Tucker's American English; New York, 1921, p. 39 *ff.*

as *chore*. Among the verbs similarly preserved are *to whittle, to wilt* and *to approbate*. *To guess*, in the American sense of *to suppose*, is to be found in "Henry VI":

> Not all together; better far, I *guess*,
> That we do make our entrance several ways.

In "Measure for Measure" Escalus says "I *guess* not" to Angelo. The New English Dictionary offers examples much older—from Chaucer, Wycliffe and Gower. *To interview* is in Dekker. *To loan*, in the American sense of to lend, is in 34 and 35 Henry VIII, but it dropped out of use in England early in the eighteenth century, and all the leading dictionaries, both in English and American, now call it an Americanism.[48] *To fellowship*, once in good American use but now reduced to a provincialism, is in Chaucer. Even *to hustle*, it appears, is ancient. Among adjectives, *homely*, which means only homelike or unadorned in England, was used in its American sense of plain-featured by both Shakespeare and Milton. Other such survivors are *burly, catty-cornered, likely, deft, copious, scant* and *ornate*. Perhaps *clever* also belongs to this category, that is, in the American sense of amiable.

"Our ancestors," said James Russell Lowell, "unhappily could bring over no English better than Shakespeare's." Shakespeare died in 1616; the Pilgrims landed four years later; Jamestown was founded in 1607. As we have seen, the colonists, saving a few superior leaders, were men of small sensitiveness to the refinements of life and speech: soldiers of fortune, amateur theologians, younger sons, neighborhood "advanced thinkers," bankrupts, jobless workmen, decayed gentry, and other such fugitives from culture—in brief, Philistines of the sort who join tin-pot fraternal orders today, and march in parades, and whoop for the latest mountebanks in politics. There was thus a touch of rhetoric in Lowell's saying that they spoke the English of Shakespeare; as well argue that the London grocers of 1885 spoke the English of Pater. But in a larger sense he said truly, for these men at least brought with them the vocabulary of Shakespeare—or a part of it—even if the uses he made of it were

---

[48] An interesting discussion of this verb appeared in the *New York Sun*, Nov. 27, 1914.

THE BEGINNINGS OF AMERICAN 69

beyond their comprehension, and they also brought with them that sense of ease in the language, that fine contempt for formality, that bold experimentalizing in words, which were so peculiarly Elizabethan. There were no grammarians in that day; there were no purists that anyone listened to; it was a case of saying your say in the easiest and most satisfying way. In remote parts of the United States there are still direct and almost pure-blooded descendants of those seventeenth century colonists. Go among them, and you will hear more words from the Shakespearean vocabulary, still alive and in common service, than anywhere else in the world, and more of the loose and brilliant syntax of that time, and more of its gipsy phrases.[49]

6.

Colonial Pronunciation

The debate that long raged over the pronunciation of classical Latin exhibits the difficulty of determining with exactness the shades of sound in the speech of a people long departed from earth. The American colonists, of course, are much nearer to us than the Romans, and so we should have relatively little difficulty in determining just how they pronounced this or that word, but against the fact of their nearness stands the neglect of our phonologists. What Sweet did to clear up the history of English pronunciation,[50] and what Wilhelm Crossen did for Latin, no American philologian has yet thought to attempt for American. The literature is almost if not quite a blank. But here and there we may get a hint of the facts, and though the sum of them is not large, they at least serve to set at rest a number of popular errors.

One of these errors, chiefly prevalent in New England, is that the so-called Boston pronunciation, with its broad *a's,* comes down unbrokenly from the day of the first settlements, and that it is in consequence superior in authority to the pronunciation of the rest of the country, with its flat *a's.* A glance through Webster's "Dis-

[49] *Cf.* J. H. Combs: Old, Early and Elizabethan English in the Southern Mountains, *Dialect Notes,* vol. iv, pt. iv, pp. 283-97.
[50] Henry Sweet: A History of English Sounds; London, 1876; Oxford, 1888.

sertations" is sufficient to show that the flat *a* was in use in New England in 1789, for the pronunciation of such words as *wrath, bath* and *path*, as given by him, makes them rhyme with *hath*.[51] Moreover, he gives *aunt* the same *a*-sound. From other sources come indications that the *a* was likewise flattened in such words as *plant, basket, branch, dance, blast, command* and *castle*, and even in *balm* and *calm*. Changes in the sound of the letter have been going on in England ever since the Middle English period,[52] and according to Lounsbury,[53] they have moved toward the disappearance of the Continental *a*, "the fundamental vowel-tone of the human voice." Grandgent, another authority,[54] says that it became flattened "by the sixteenth century" and that "until 1780 or thereabouts the standard language had no broad *a*." Even in such words as *father, car* and *ask* the flat *a* was universally used. Sheridan, in the dictionary he published in 1780,[55] actually gave no *ah*-sound in his list of vowels. This habit of flatting the *a* had been brought over, of course, by the early colonists, and was as general in America, in the third quarter of the eighteenth century, as in England. Benjamin Franklin, when he wrote his "Scheme for a New Alphabet and a Reformed Mode of Spelling," in 1768, apparently had no suspicion that any other *a* was possible. But between 1780 and 1790, according to Grandgent, a sudden fashion for the broad *a* (not the *aw*-sound, as in *fall*, but the Continental sound as in *far*) arose in England,[56] and this fashion soon found servile imitation in Boston. But it was as much an affectation in those days as it is today, and Webster indicated the fact pretty plainly in his "Dissertations." How, despite his opposition, the broad *a* prevailed East of the Connecticut river, and how, in the end, he himself yielded to it, and even tried to force it upon the whole nation—this will be rehearsed in the next chapter.

[51] P. 124.
[52] *Cf.* Art. Changes in the Language Since Shakespeare's Time, by W. Murison, in The Cambridge History of English Literature, vol. xiv, p. 485.
[53] English Spelling and Spelling Reform; New York, 1909.
[54] C. H. Grandgent: Fashion and the Broad *A*, *Nation*, Jan. 7, 1915; reprinted in Old and New; Cambridge (Mass.), 1920, pp. 25-30.
[55] Thomas Sheridan: A Complete Dictionary of the English Language; London, 1780.
[56] It first appeared in Robert Nares' Elements of Orthography; London, 1784. In 1791 it received full approbation in John Walker's Critical Pronouncing Dictionary.

The colonists remained faithful much longer than the English to various other vowel-sounds that were facing change in the eighteenth century, for example, the long *e*-sound in *heard*. Webster says that the custom of rhyming *heard* with *bird* instead of with *feared* came in at the beginning of the Revolution. "To most people in this country," he adds, "the English pronunciation appears like affectation." He also argues for rhyming *deaf* with *leaf*, and protests against inserting a *y*-sound before the *u* in such words as *nature*. Franklin's authority stands behind *git* for *get*. This pronunciation, according to Menner,[57] was correct in seventeenth century England, and perhaps down to the middle of the next century. So was the use of the Continental *i*-sound in *oblige*, making it *obleege*. It is probable that the colonists clung to these disappearing usages much longer than the English. The latter, according to Webster, were unduly responsive to illogical fashions set by the exquisites of the court and by popular actors. He blames Garrick, in particular, for many extravagant innovations, most of them not followed in the colonies. But Garrick was surely not responsible for the use of a long *i*-sound in such words as *motive*, nor for the corruption of *mercy* to *marcy*. Webster denounced both of these pronunciations. The second he ascribed somewhat lamely to the fact that the letter *r* is called *ar*, and proposed to dispose of it by changing the *ar* to *er*.

As for the consonants, the colonists seem to have resisted valiantly that tendency to slide over them which arose in England after the Restoration. Franklin, in 1768, still retained the sound of *l* in such words as *would* and *should*, a usage not met with in England after the year 1700. In the same way, according to Menner, the *w* in *sword* was sounded in America "for some time after Englishmen had abandoned it." The sensitive ear of Henry James detected an unpleasant *r*-sound in the speech of Americans, long ago got rid of by the English, so late as 1905; he even charged that it was inserted gratuitously in innocent words.[58] The obvious slurring of the con-

[57] Robert J. Menner: The Pronunciation of English in America, *Atlantic Monthly*, March, 1915.
[58] The Question of Our Speech; Boston and New York, 1906, pp. 27-29. For a long and interesting discussion of the *r*-sound, see The Dog's Letter, in Grandgent's Old and New, *op. cit.*, p. 31.

sonants by Southerners is explained by a recent investigator [59] on the ground that it began in England during the reign of Charles II, and that most of the Southern colonists came to the New World at that time. The court of Charles, it is argued, was under French influence, due to the king's long residence in France and his marriage to Henrietta Marie. Charles "objected to the inharmonious contractions *willn't* (or *wolln't*) and *wasn't* and *weren't* . . . and set the fashion of using the softly euphonious *won't* and *wan't*, which are used in speaking to this day by the best class of Southerners." A more direct French influence upon Southern pronunciation is also pointed out. "With full knowledge of his *g's* and his *r's*, . . . [the Southerner] sees fit to glide over them, . . . and he carries over the consonant ending one word to the vowel beginning the next, just as the Frenchman does." The political importance of the South, in the years between the Mecklenburg Declaration and the adoption of the Constitution, tended to force its provincialisms upon the common language. Many of the acknowledged leaders of the nascent nation were Southerners, and their pronunciation, as well as their phrases, must have become familiar everywhere. Pickering gives us a hint, indeed, at the process whereby their usage influenced that of the rest of the people.[60]

The majority of Americans early dropped the initial *h*-sound in such words as *when* and *where*,[61] but so far as I can determine they never elided it at the beginning of other words, save in the case of *herb* and *humble*. This elision is commonly spoken of as a cockney vulgarism, but it has extended to the orthodox English speech. In *ostler* the initial *h* is openly left off; in *hotel* and *hospital* it is

[59] Elizabeth H. Hancock: Southern Speech, *Neale's Monthly*, Nov., 1913.
[60] *Vide* his remarks on *balance* in his Vocabulary. See also Marsh, p. 671.
[61] It is still supposed to be sounded in England, and its absence is often denounced as an American barbarism, but as a matter of fact few Englishmen actually sound it, save in the most formal discourse. Some time ago the English novelist, Archibald Marshall, published an article in a London newspaper arguing that it was a sheer physical impossibility to sound the *h* correctly. "You cannot pronounce *wh*," he said, "if you try. You have to turn it into *hw* to make it any different from *w*." Nevertheless, Mr. Marshall argued, with true English conservatism, that the effort should be made. "Most words of one syllable beginning with *wh*," he said, "and many of two syllables have a corresponding word, but of quite different meaning, beginning with *w* alone. *When-wen, whether-weather, while-wile, whither-wither, wheel-weal*. If there is a distinction ready to hand it is of advantage to make use of it." That is to say, to make use of *hwen, hwether, hwile, hwither* and *hweel*.

THE BEGINNINGS OF AMERICAN 73

sometimes not clearly sounded, even by careful Englishmen. Certain English words in *h,* in which the *h* is now sounded, betray its former silence by the fact that not *a* but *an* is still put before them. It is still good English usage to write *an hotel* and *an historical.*[62] The great authority of Webster was sufficient to establish the American pronunciation of *schedule*. In England the *sch* is always given the soft sound, but Webster decided for the hard sound, as in *scheme*. The variance persists to this day. The name of the last letter of the alphabet, which is always *zed* in English, is usually made *zee* in the United States. Thornton shows that this Americanism arose in the eighteenth century.

[62] An English correspondent sends me the following argument for *an* before *hotel*: "Personally, I cannot bring myself to write *a hotel* or *a historical* or indeed any combination wherein *a* is followed by an *h*-word not accented on the first syllable. My sense of euphony (and, I believe, the genius of the English language) requires something between the *a* and the *h*-sound in all such cases. Witness the absence of English words showing such a combination. I believe that all English words beginning with *a*, in which a syllable beginning with *h* follows, are dissyllables. That is to say, the *h*-syllable is accented. Witness *ahead, ahoy, ahem.*" *Cf.* Text, Type and Style, by George B. Ives; Boston, 1921, p. 269.

III.

THE PERIOD OF GROWTH

1.

Character of the New Nation

The English of the United States thus began to be recognizably differentiated from the English of England, both in vocabulary and in pronunciation, by the opening of the nineteenth century, but as yet its growth was hampered by two factors, the first being the lack of a national literature of any expanse and dignity and the second being an internal political disharmony which greatly conditioned and enfeebled the national consciousness. During the actual Revolution common aims and common dangers forced the Americans to show a united front, but once they had achieved political independence they developed conflicting interests, and out of those conflicting interests came suspicions and hatreds which came near wrecking the new confederation more than once. Politically, their worst weakness, perhaps, was an inability to detach themselves wholly from the struggle for domination then going on in Europe. The surviving Loyalists of the revolutionary era—estimated by some authorities to have constituted fully a third of the total population in 1776—were ardently in favor of England, and such patriots as Jefferson were as ardently in favor of France. This engrossment in the quarrels of foreign nations was what Washington warned against in his Farewell Address. It was at the bottom of such bitter animosities as that between Jefferson and Hamilton. It inspired and perhaps excused the pessimism of such men as Burr. Its net effect was to make it difficult for the people of the new nation to think of themselves, politically, as Americans. Their state of mind, vacillating, uncertain, alternately timorous and pugnacious, has been well described

THE PERIOD OF GROWTH 75

by Henry Cabot Lodge in his essay on "Colonialism in America."[1] Soon after the Treaty of Paris was signed, someone referred to the late struggle, in Franklin's hearing, as the War for Independence. "Say, rather, the War of the Revolution," said Franklin. "The War for Independence is yet to be fought."

"That struggle," adds Lossing, "occurred, and that independence was won, by the Americans in the War of 1812."[2] In the interval the new republic had passed through a period of *Sturm und Drang* whose gigantic perils and passions we have begun to forget—a period in which disaster ever menaced, and the foes within were no less bold and pertinacious than the foes without. Jefferson, perhaps, carried his fear of "monocrats" to the point of monomania, but under it there was undoubtedly a body of sound fact. The poor debtor class (including probably a majority of the veterans of the Revolution) had been fired by the facile doctrines of the French Revolution to demands which threatened the country with bankruptcy and anarchy, and the class of property-owners, in reaction, went far to the other extreme. On all sides, indeed, there flourished a strong British party, and particularly in New England, where the so-called codfish aristocracy (by no means extinct today) exhibited an undisguised Anglomania, and looked forward confidently to a *rapprochement* with the mother country.[3] This Anglomania showed itself, not only in ceaseless political agitation, but also in an elaborate imitation of English manners. We have already seen how it even extended to the pronunciation of the language.

In our own time, with the renewal of the centuries-old struggle for power in Europe, there has been a revival of the old itch to take a hand, with results almost as menacing to the unity and security of the Republic as those visible when Washington voiced his warning. But in his day he seems to have been heard and heeded, and so colonialism gradually died out. The first sign of the dawn of a new national order came with the election of Thomas

---
[1] In Studies in History; Boston, 1884.
[2] Benson J. Lossing: Our Country . . .; New York, 1879.
[3] The thing went, indeed, far beyond mere hope. In 1812 a conspiracy was unearthed to separate New England from the republic and make it an English colony. The chief conspirator was one John Henry, who acted under the instructions of Sir John Craig, Governor-General of Canada.

Jefferson to the Presidency in 1800. The issue in the campaign was a highly complex one, but under it lay a plain conflict between democratic independence and the European doctrine of dependence and authority; and with the Alien and Sedition Laws about his neck, so vividly reminiscent of the issues of the Revolution itself, Adams went down to defeat. Jefferson was violently anti-British and pro-French; he saw all the schemes of his political opponents, indeed, as English plots; he was the man who introduced the bugaboo into American politics. His first acts after his inauguration were to abolish all ceremonial at the court of the republic, and to abandon spoken discourses to Congress for written messages. That ceremonial, which grew up under Washington, was an imitation, he believed, of the formality of the abhorrent Court of St. James; as for the speeches to Congress, they were palpably modelled upon the speeches from the throne of the English kings.[4] Both reforms met with wide approval; the exactions of the English, particularly on the high seas, were beginning to break up the British party. But confidence in the solidarity and security of the new nation was still anything but universal. The surviving doubts, indeed, were strong enough to delay the ratification of the Twelfth Amendment to the Constitution, providing for more direct elections of President and Vice-President, until the end of 1804, and even then three of the five New England states rejected it,[5] and have never ratified it, in fact, to this day. Democracy was still experimental, doubtful, full of gun-powder. In so far as it had actually come into being, it had come as a boon conferred from above. Jefferson, its protagonist, was the hero of the populace, but he was not of the populace himself, nor did he ever quite trust it.

It was reserved for Andrew Jackson, a man genuinely of the people, to lead and visualize the rise of the lower orders. Jackson, in his way, was the archetype of the new American—ignorant, pushful, impatient of restraint and precedent, an iconoclast, a Philis-

[4] It is curious to note that the revival of the spoken message in our own time was made by a President whose foreign policy was chiefly marked by its violent Anglomania, *i. e.*, its colonialism. During his administration practically all of the ideas that entered into Jefferson's politics, from suspicion of England to free speech, were abandoned.
[5] Maine was not separated from Massachusetts until 1820.

tine, an Anglophobe in every fibre. He came from the extreme backwoods and his youth was passed, like that of Abraham Lincoln after him, amid surroundings but little removed from downright savagery.[6] Thousands of other young Americans of the same sort were growing up at the same time—youngsters filled with a vast impatience of all precedent and authority, revilers of all that had come down from an elder day, incorrigible libertarians. They swarmed across the mountains and down the great rivers, wrestling with the naked wilderness and setting up a casual, impromptu sort of civilization where the Indian still menaced. Schools were few and rudimentary; there was not the remotest approach to a cultivated society; any effort to mimic the amenities of the East, or of the mother country, in manner or even in speech, met with instant derision. It was in these surroundings and at this time that the thoroughgoing American of tradition was born; blatant, illogical, elate, "greeting the embarrassed gods" uproariously and matching "with Destiny for beers." Jackson was unmistakably of that company in his every instinct and idea, and it was his fate to give a new and unshakable confidence to its aspiration at the Battle of New Orleans. Thereafter all doubts began to die out; the new republic was turning out a success. And with success came a vast increase in the national egoism. The hordes of pioneers rolled down the western valleys and on to the great plains.[7] American began to stand for something quite new in the world—in government, in law, in public and private morals, in customs and habits of mind, in the minutiæ of social intercourse. And simultaneously the voice of America began to take on its characteristic twang, and the speech of America began to differentiate itself boldly and unmistakably from the speech of England. The average Philadelphian or Bostonian of 1790 had not the slightest difficulty in making himself understood by a visiting Englishman. But the average Ohio boatman of 1810 or plainsman of 1815 was already speaking a dialect that the Eng-

[6] *Vide* Andrew Jackson . . ., by William Graham Sumner; Boston, 1883, pp. 2-10.
[7] Indiana and Illinois were erected into territories during Jefferson's first term, and Michigan during his second term. Kentucky was admitted to the union in 1792, Tennessee in 1796, Ohio in 1803. Lewis and Clarke set out for the Pacific in 1804. The Louisiana Purchase was ratified in 1803, and Louisiana became a state in 1812.

lishman would have shrunk from as barbarous and unintelligible, and before long it began to leave its mark upon and to get direction and support from a distinctively national literature.

That literature, however, was very slow in coming to a dignified, confident and autonomous estate. Down to Jefferson's day it was almost wholly polemical, and hence lacking in the finer values; he himself, an insatiable propagandist and controversialist, was one of its chief ornaments. "The novelists and the historians, the essayists and the poets, whose names come to mind when American literature is mentioned," says a recent literary historian, "have all flourished since 1800."[8] Pickering, so late as 1816, said that "in this country we can hardly be said to have any authors by profession," and Justice Story, three years later, repeated the saying and sought to account for the fact. "So great," said Story, "is the call for talents of all sorts in the active use of professional and other business in America that few of our ablest men have leisure to devote exclusively to literature or the fine arts. . . . This obvious reason will explain why we have so few professional authors, and those not among our ablest men." All this was true, but a new day was dawning; Irving, in fact, had already published "Knickerbocker" and Bryant had printed "Thanatopsis." Difficulties of communication hampered the circulation of the few native books that were written. "It is much to be regretted," wrote Dr. David Ramsay, of Charleston, S. C., to Noah Webster in 1806, "that there is so little intercourse in a literary way between the states. As soon as a book of general utility comes out in any state it should be for sale in all of them." Ramsay asked for little; the most he could imagine was a sale of 2,000 copies for an American work in America. But even that was far beyond the possibilities of the time. Nor was there, indeed, much reading of English books; the Americans, as in colonial days, were faithful to a few sober works, and cared little for *belles lettres.* "There is at this moment," said an English observer in 1833,[9] "nothing in the United States worthy of the name of library. Not only is there an entire absence of learning, in the higher sense of the term, but an

---

[8] Barrett Wendell: A Literary History of America; New York, 1900.
[9] The anonymous author of Men and Manners in America; Edinburgh, 1833. See also Carl Van Doren's The American Novel; New York, 1921, ch. i.

THE PERIOD OF GROWTH 79

absolute want of the material from which alone learning can be extracted. At present an American might study every book within the limits of the Union, and still be regarded in many parts of Europe—especially in Germany—as a man comparatively ignorant. Why does a great nation thus voluntarily continue in a state of intellectual destitution so anomalous and humiliating?" According to this critic, the value of the books imported from Europe during the fiscal year 1829-30 for public institutions came to but $10,829.

But nevertheless English periodical literature seems to have been read, at least by the nascent *intelligentsia,* and its influence undoubtedly helped to keep the national literature imitative and timorous in those early and perilous days. "Before the Revolution," says Cairns,[10] "colonists of literary tastes prided themselves on reading the *Gentlemen's Magazine* or the *London Magazine,* and it is probable that the old tradition retained for these and similar publications many subscribers. . . . Letters from American readers appear occasionally in British magazines [of the period], and others imply the existence of a considerable American constituency. . . . It is certain, at all events, that the chief American [obviously a misprint for British] critical journals were received by American editors, and important criticisms of American writings were often reprinted in this country." The extraordinary animosity of the English and Scottish reviewers, then at the height of their pontifical authority, to all locutions that had an American smack was described in the last chapter; as everyone knows, that animosity extended to the content of American works as well as to the style. All things American, indeed, were under the ban in England after the War of 1812, and Sydney Smith's famous sneer—"In the four quarters of the globe, who reads an American book? or goes to an American play? or looks at an American picture or statue?"—was echoed and re-echoed in other planes. The Yankee, flushed with victory, became the pet abomination of the English, and the chief butt of the incomparable English talent for moral indignation. There was scarcely an issue of the *Quarterly Review,* the *Edinburgh,* the *Foreign Quarterly,* the *British Review* or *Blackwood's,* for a generation following 1812, in which he was not stupendously assaulted. Gifford, Sydney

[10] British Criticisms of American Writings, 1783-1815; p. 20.

Smith and the poet Southey became specialists in this business; it almost took on the character of a holy war; even such mild men as Wordsworth had a hand in it. It was argued that the Americans were rogues and swindlers, that they lived in filth and squalor, that they were boors in social intercourse, that they were poltroons and savages in war, that they were depraved and criminal, that they were wholly devoid of the remotest notion of decency or honor. "See what it is," said Southey in 1812, "to have a nation to take its place among civilized states before it has either gentlemen or scholars! They [the Americans] have in the course of twenty years acquired a distinct national character for low and lying knavery; and so well do they deserve it that no man ever had any dealings with them without having proofs of its truth." The *Quarterly,* summing up in January, 1814, accused them of a multitude of strange and hair-raising offenses: employing naked colored women to wait upon their tables; kidnapping Scotchmen, Irishmen, Welshmen and Hollanders and selling them into slavery; fighting one another incessantly under rules which made it "allowable to peel the skull, tear out the eyes, and smooth away the nose"; and so on, and so on. Various Americans, after a decade of this snorting, went to the defense of their countrymen, among them Irving, Cooper, Timothy Dwight, J. K. Paulding, John Neal, Edward Everett and Robert Walsh. Paulding, in "John Bull in America, or, the New Munchausen," published in 1825, attempted satire. Even a Briton, James Sterling, warned his fellow-Britons that, if they continued their intolerant abuse, they would "turn into bitterness the last drops of good-will toward England that exist in the United States." But the denunciation kept up year after year, and there was, indeed, no genuine relief until 1914, when the sudden prospect of disaster caused the English to change their tune, and even to find all their own great virtues in the degraded and disgusting Yankee, now so useful as a rescuer. This new enthusiasm for him was tried very severely by his slowness to come into the war, but in the main there was politeness for him so long as the emergency lasted, and all the British talent for horror and invective was concentrated, down to 1919 or thereabout, upon the Prussian.

How American-English appeared to an educated English visitor of

THE PERIOD OF GROWTH

Jackson's time is well indicated in the anonymous "Men and Manners in America" that I have already quoted. "The amount of bad grammar in circulation," said the author, "is very great; that of barbarisms [*i. e.*, Americanisms] enormous." Worse, these "barbarisms" were not confined to the ignorant, but came almost as copiously from the lips of the learned. "I do not now speak," explained the critic, "of the operative class, whose massacre of their mother-tongue, however inhuman, could excite no astonishment; but I allude to the great body of lawyers and traders; the men who crowd the exchange and the hotels; who are to be heard speaking in the courts, and are selected by their fellow-citizens to fill high and responsible offices. Even by this educated and respectable class, the commonest words are often so transmogrified as to be placed beyond recognition of an Englishman." He then went on to describe some of the prevalent "barbarisms":

> The word *does* is split into two syllables, and pronounced *do-es*. *Where*, for some incomprehensible reason, is converted into *whare*, *there* into *thare;* and I remember, on mentioning to an acquaintance that I had called on a gentleman of taste in the arts, he asked "whether he *shew* (showed) me his pictures." Such words as *oratory* and *dilatory* are pronounced with the penult syllable long and accented; *missionary* becomes *missionairy*, *angel*, *ángel*, *danger*, *dánger*, etc.
> But this is not all. The Americans have chosen arbitrarily to change the meaning of certain old and established English words, for reasons they cannot explain, and which I doubt much whether any European philologist could understand. The word *clever* affords a case in point. It has here no connexion with talent, and simply means pleasant and (or) amiable. Thus a good-natured blockhead in the American vernacular is a *clever* man, and having had this drilled into me, I foolishly imagined that all trouble with regard to this word, at least, was at an end. It was not long, however, before I heard of a gentleman having moved into a *clever* house, another succeeding to a *clever* sum of money, of a third embarking in a *clever* ship, and making a *clever* voyage, with a *clever* cargo; and of the sense attached to the word in these various combinations, I could gain nothing like a satisfactory explanation.
> The privilege of barbarizing the King's English is assumed by all ranks and conditions of men. Such words as *slick*, *kedge* and *boss*, it is true, are rarely used by the better orders; but they assume unlimited liberty in the use of *expect*, *reckon*, *guess* and *calculate*, and perpetrate other conversational anomalies with remorseless impunity.

This Briton, as usual, was as full of moral horror as of grammatical disgust, and put his denunciation upon the loftiest of grounds. "I will not go on with this unpleasant subject," he concluded, "nor should I have alluded to it, but I feel it something of a duty to express the natural feeling of an Englishman at finding the language of Shakespeare and Milton thus gratuitously degraded. Unless the present progress of change be arrested, by an increase of taste and judgment in the more educated classes, there can be no doubt that, in another century, the dialect of the Americans will become utterly unintelligible to an Englishman, and that the nation will be cut off from the advantages arising from their participation in British literature. If they contemplate such an event with complacency, let them go on and prosper; they have only to *progress* in their present course, and their grandchildren bid fair to speak a jargon as novel and peculiar as the most patriotic American linguist can desire."[11]

Such extravagant denunciations, in the long run, were bound to make Americans defiant, but while they were at their worst they produced a contrary effect. That is to say, they made all the American writers of a more delicate aspiration extremely self-conscious and diffident. The educated classes, even against their will, were daunted by the torrent of abuse; they could not help finding in it an occasional reasonableness, an accidental true hit. The result, despite the efforts of Channing, Knapp and other such valiant defenders of the native author, was uncertainty and skepticism in native criticism. "The first step of an American entering upon a literary career," says Lodge, writing of the first quarter of the century, "was to pretend to be an Englishman in order that he might win the approval, not of Englishmen, but of his own countrymen." Cooper, in his first novel, "Precaution," chose an English scene, imitated English models, and obviously hoped to placate the critics thereby. Irving, too, in his earliest work, showed a considerable discretion, and his "History of New York," as everyone knows, was first published anonymously. But this puerile spirit did not last long. The English onslaughts were altogether too vicious to be received lying down; their very fury demanded that they be met with a united and courageous front. Cooper, in his second novel, "The Spy," boldly chose an American setting and American characters, and though the influence of his wife,

[11] For further diatribes of the same sort, see As Others See Us, by John Graham Brooks; New York, 1908, ch. vii. Also, The Cambridge History of American Literature, vol. i, pp. 205-8.

who came of a Loyalist family, caused him to avoid any direct attack upon the English, he attacked them indirectly, and with great effect, by opposing an immediate and honorable success to their derisions. "The Spy" ran through three editions in four months; it was followed by his long line of thoroughly American novels; in 1834 he formally apologized to his countrymen for his early truancy in "Precaution." Irving, too, soon adopted a bolder tone, and despite his English predilections, he refused an offer of a hundred guineas for an article for the *Quarterly Review,* made by Gifford in 1828, on the ground that "the *Review* has been so persistently hostile to our country that I cannot draw a pen in its service."

The same year saw the publication of the first edition of Webster's American Dictionary of the English Language, and a year later followed Samuel L. Knapp's "Lectures on American Literature," the first history of the national letters ever attempted. Knapp, in his preface, thought it necessary to prove, first of all, that an American literature actually existed, and Webster, in his introduction, was properly apologetic, but there was no real need for timorousness in either case, for the American attitude toward the attack of the English was now definitely changing from uneasiness to defiance. The English critics, in fact, had overdone the thing, and though their clatter was to keep up for many years more, they no longer spread their old terror or had as much influence as of yore. Of a sudden, as if in answer to them, doubts turned to confidence, and then into the wildest sort of optimism, not only in politics and business, but also in what passed for the arts. Knapp boldly defied the English to produce a "tuneful sister" surpassing Mrs. Sigourney; more, he argued that the New World, if only by reason of its superior scenic grandeur, would eventually hatch a poetry surpassing even that of Greece and Rome. "What are the Tibers and Scamanders," he demanded, "measured by the Missouri and the Amazon? Or what the loveliness of Illysus or Avon by the Connecticut or the Potomack?"

In brief, the national feeling, long delayed at birth, finally leaped into being in amazing vigor. "One can get an idea of the strength of that feeling," says R. O. Williams, "by glancing at almost any book taken at random from the American publications of the period.

Belief in the grand future of the United States is the keynote of everything said and done. All things American are to be grand— our territory, population, products, wealth, science, art—but especially our political institutions and literature. The unbounded confidence in the material development of the country which now characterizes the extreme northwest of the United States prevailed as strongly throughout the eastern part of the Union during the first thirty years of the century; and over and above a belief in, and concern for, materialistic progress, there were enthusiastic anticipations of achievements in all the moral and intellectual fields of national greatness." [12] Nor was that vast optimism wholly without warrant. An American literature was actually coming into being, and with a wall of hatred and contempt shutting in England, the new American writers were beginning to turn to the Continent for inspiration and encouragement. Irving had already drunk at Spanish springs; Emerson and Bayard Taylor were to receive powerful impulses from Germany, following Ticknor, Bancroft and Everett before them; Bryant was destined to go back to the classics. Moreover, Cooper and John P. Kennedy had shown the way to native sources of literary material, and Longfellow was making ready to follow them; novels in imitation of English models were no longer heard of; the ground was preparing for "Uncle Tom's Cabin." Finally, Webster himself, as Williams demonstrated, worked better than he knew. His American Dictionary was not only thoroughly American: it was superior to any of the current dictionaries of the English, so much so that for a good many years it remained "a sort of mine for British lexicography to exploit."

Thus all hesitations disappeared, and there arose a national consciousness so soaring and so blatant that it began to dismiss all British usage and opinion as puerile and idiotic. William L. Marcy, when Secretary of State under Pierce (1853-57), issued a circular to all American diplomatic and consular officers, loftily bidding them employ only "the American language" in communicating with him. The legislature of Indiana, in an act approved February 15, 1838,

[12] Our Dictionaries and Other English Language Topics; New York, 1890, pp. 30-31.

THE PERIOD OF GROWTH 85

establishing the state university at Bloomington,[13] provided that it should instruct the youth of the new commonwealth (it had been admitted to the Union in 1816) "in the American, learned and foreign languages . . . and literature." Such grandiose pronunciamentos well indicate and explain the temper of the era.[14] It was a time of expansion and braggadocio. The new republic would not only produce a civilization and a literature of its own; it would show the way for all other civilizations and literatures. Rufus Wilmot Griswold, the enemy of Poe, rose from his decorous Baptist pew to protest that so much patriotism amounted to insularity and absurdity, but there seems to have been no one to second the motion. The debate upon the Oregon question gave a gaudy chance to the new breed of super-patriots, and they raged unchecked until the time of the Civil War. Thornton, in his Glossary, quotes a typical speech in Congress, the subject being the American eagle and the orator being the Hon. Samuel C. Pomeroy, of Kansas. I give a few strophes:

> The proudest bird upon the mountain is upon the American ensign, and not one feather shall fall from her plumage there. She is American in design, and an emblem of wildness and freedom. I say again, she has not perched herself upon American standards to die there. Our great western valleys were never scooped out for her burial place. Nor were the everlasting, untrodden mountains piled for her monument. Niagara shall not pour her endless waters for her requiem; nor shall our ten thousand rivers weep to the ocean in eternal tears. No, sir, no! Unnumbered voices shall come up from river, plain, and mountain, echoing the songs of our triumphant deliverance, wild lights from a thousand hill-tops will betoken the rising of the sun of freedom.

The vast shock of the Civil War, with its harsh disillusions, unhorsed the optimists for a space, and little was heard from them for some time thereafter. But while the Jackson influence survived and the West was being conquered, it was the unanimous conviction of all good Americans that "he who dallies is a dastard, and he who doubts is damned."

[13] It is curious to note that the center of population of the United States, according to the census of 1910, was "in southern Indiana, in the western part of Bloomington city, Monroe county." *Cf.* The Language We Use, by Alfred Z. Reed, *New York Sun*, March 13, 1918.
[14] Support also came from abroad. Czar Nicholas I, of Russia, smarting under his defeat in the Crimea, issued an order that his own state papers should be prepared in Russian and American—not English.

2.

The Language in the Making

All this jingoistic bombast, however, was directed toward defending, not so much the national vernacular as the national *belles lettres*. True enough, an English attack upon a definite American locution always brought out certain critical minute-men, but in the main they were anything but hospitable to the racy neologisms that kept crowding up from below, and most of them were eager to be accepted as masters of orthodox English and very sensitive to the charge that their writing was bestrewn with Americanisms. A glance through the native criticism of the time will show how ardently even the most uncompromising patriots imitated the Johnsonian jargon then fashionable in England. Fowler and Griswold followed pantingly in the footsteps of Macaulay; their prose is extraordinarily self-conscious, and one searches it in vain for any concession to colloquialism. Poe, the master of them all, achieved a style so ornate that many an English leader-writer must have studied it with envy. A few bolder spirits, as we have seen, spoke out for national freedom in language as well as in letters—among them, Channing—but in the main the Brahmins of the time were conservatives in this department and it is difficult to imagine Emerson or Irving or Bryant sanctioning the innovations later adopted so easily by Howells. Lowell and Walt Whitman, in fact, were the first men of letters, properly so called, to give specific assent to the great changes that were firmly fixed in the national speech during the half century between the War of 1812 and the Civil War. Lowell did so in his preface to the second series of "The Biglow Papers." Whitman made his declaration in "An American Primer." In discussing "Leaves of Grass," he said: "I sometimes think that the entire book is only a language experiment—that it is an attempt to give the spirit, the body and the man, new words, new potentialities of speech—an American, a cosmopolitan (for the best of America is the best cosmopolitanism) range of self-expression." And then: "The Americans are going to be the most fluent and melodious-voiced people in the world—and the most perfect users of words. The new world, the new times, the new

THE PERIOD OF GROWTH 87

people, the new vistas need a new tongue according—yes, what is more, they will have such a new tongue—will not be satisfied until it is evolved." [15] According to Louis Untermeyer, a diligent and enthusiastic Whitmanista, old Walt deserves to be called "the father of the American language." [16] He goes on:

> This, in spite of its grandiloquent sound, is what he truly was. When the rest of literary America was still indulging in the polite language of pulpits and the lifeless rhetoric of its libraries, Whitman not only sensed the richness and vigor of the casual word, the colloquial phrase—he championed the vitality of slang, the freshness of our quickly assimilated jargons, the indigenous beauty of vulgarisms. He even predicted that no future native literature could exist that neglected this racy speech, that the vernacular of people as opposed to the language of literati would form the living accents of the best poets to come. One has only to observe the contemporary works of Carl Sandburg, Robert Frost, James Oppenheim, Edgar Lee Masters, John Hall Wheelock, Vachel Lindsay and a dozen others to see how Whitman's prophecy has been fulfilled.
>
> Words, especially the neglected words regarded as too crude and literal for literature, fascinated Whitman. The idea of an enriched language was scarcely ever out of his mind. . . . This interest . . . grew to great proportions; it became almost an obsession.

Whitman himself spoke of "An American Primer" as "an attempt to describe the growth of an American English enjoying a distinct identity." He proposed an American dictionary containing the actual everyday vocabulary of the people. To quote him again:

> The Real Dictionary will give all words that exist in use, the bad words as well as any. The Real Grammar will be that which declares itself a nucleus of the spirit of the laws, with liberty to all to carry out the spirit of the laws; even by violating them, if necessary.
>
> Many of the slang words are our best; slang words among fighting men, gamblers, thieves, are powerful words. . . . Much of America is shown in these and in newspaper names, and in names of characteristic amusements and games. . . .
>
> Our tongue is full of strong words, native or adopted, to express the blood-born passion of the race for rudeness and resistance, as against mere polish. . . . These words are alive and sinewy—they walk, look, step with an air of command. . . .

[15] An American Primer was not printed until 1904, long after Whitman's death. As originally written in the 50's and 60's, it consisted of notes for a lecture. Among Whitman's papers, Horace Traubel found this alternative title: The Primer of Words: For American Young Men and Women, For Literati, Orators, Teachers, Judges, Presidents, etc.

[16] Whitman and the American Language, New York *Evening Post*, May 31, 1919.

> Ten thousand native idiomatic words are growing, or are already grown, out of which vast numbers could be used by American writers, with meaning and effect—words that would give that taste of identity and locality which is so dear in literature—words that would be welcomed by the nation, being of the national blood.

As everyone knows, Whitman delighted in filling his poetry and prose with such new words, among them, the verbs *to promulge, to eclaircise, to diminute, to imperturbe, to effuse* and *to inure,* the adjectives *ostent* and *adamic,* the adverb *affetuoso,* and the nouns *camerado, romanza, deliveress, literatus, acceptress* and *partiolist.* Many of his coinages were in Spanish metal; he believed that American should not be restricted to the materials of English. I have heard it argued that he introduced *finale* into everyday American; the evidence is dubious, but certainly the word is much oftener used in the United States than in England. Most of his coinages, alas, died with him, just as *ridiculosity* died with its inventor, Charles Sumner, who announced its invention to the Senate with great formality, and argued that it would be justified by the analogy of *curiosity.* But *These States* has survived.

Meanwhile, though conservatism lingered on the planes above Whitman, there was a wild and lawless development of the language on the planes below him, among the unfettered democrats of his adoration, and in the end the words and phrases thus brought to birth forced themselves into recognition, and profited by the literary declaration of independence of their very opponents. "The *jus et norma loquendi,*" says W. R. Morfill, the English philologist, "do not depend upon scholars." Particularly in a country where scholarship is still new and wholly cloistered, and the overwhelming majority of the people are engaged upon novel and highly exhilarating tasks, far away from schools and with a gigantic cockiness in their hearts. The remnants of the Puritan civilization had been wiped out by the rise of the proletariat under Jackson, and whatever was fine and sensitive in it had died with it. What remained of an urbane habit of mind and utterance began to be confined to the narrowing feudal areas of the south and to the still narrower refuge of the Boston Brahmins, now, for the first time, a definitely recognized caste of *intelligentsia,* self-charged with carrying the torch of culture

THE PERIOD OF GROWTH 89

through a new Dark Age. The typical American, in Paulding's satirical phrase, became "a bundling, gouging, impious" fellow, without either "morals, literature, religion or refinement." Next to the savage struggle for land and dollars, party politics was the chief concern of the people, and with the disappearance of the old leaders and the entrance of pushing upstarts from the backwoods, political controversy sank to an incredibly low level. Bartlett, in the introduction to the second edition of his Glossary, described the effect upon the language. First the enfranchised mob, whether in the city wards or along the western rivers, invented fantastic slang-words and turns of phrase; then they were "seized upon by stump-speakers at political meetings"; then they were heard in Congress; then they got into the newspapers; and finally they came into more or less good usage. Much contemporary evidence is to the same effect. Fowler, in listing "low expressions" in 1850, described them as "chiefly political." "The vernacular tongue of the country," said Daniel Webster, "has become greatly vitiated, depraved and corrupted by the style of the congressional debates." Thornton, in the appendix to his Glossary, gives some astounding specimens of congressional oratory between the 20's and 60's, and many more will reward the explorer who braves the files of the *Congressional Globe*. This flood of racy and unprecedented words and phrases beat upon and finally penetrated the retreat of the *literati*, but the purity of speech cultivated there had little compensatory influence upon the vulgate. The newspaper was enthroned, and *belles lettres* were cultivated almost in private, and as a mystery. It is probable, indeed, that "Uncle Tom's Cabin" and "Ten Nights in a Bar-room," both published in the early 50's, were the first contemporary native books, after Cooper's day, that the American people, as a people, ever read. Nor did the pulpit, now fast falling from its old high estate, lift a corrective voice. On the contrary, it joined the crowd, and Bartlett denounced it specifically for its bad example, and cited, among its crimes against the language, such inventions as *to doxologize* and *to funeralize*. To these novelties, apparently without any thought of their uncouthness, Fowler added *to missionate* and *consociational*.

As I say, the pressure from below broke down the defenses of the purists, and literally forced a new national idiom upon them. Pen in hand, they might still achieve laborious imitations of Johnson and Macaulay, but their mouths began to betray them. "When it comes to talking," wrote Charles Astor Bristed for Englishmen in 1855, "the most refined and best educated American, who has habitually resided in his own country, the very man who would write, on some serious topic, volumes in which no peculiarity could be detected, will, in half a dozen sentences, use at least as many words that cannot fail to strike the inexperienced Englishman who hears them for the first time." Bristed gave a specimen of the American of that time, calculated to flabbergast his inexperienced Englishman; you will find it in the volume of Cambridge Essays, already cited. His aim was to explain and defend Americanisms, and so shut off the storm of English reviling, and he succeeded in producing one of the most thoughtful and persuasive essays on the subject ever written. But his purpose failed and the attack kept up, and eight years afterward the Very Rev. Henry Alford, D.D., dean of Canterbury, led a famous assault. "Look at those phrases," he said, "which so amuse us in their speech and books; at their reckless exaggeration and contempt for congruity; and then compare the character and history of the nation—its blunted sense of moral obligation and duty to man; its open disregard of conventional right where aggrandisement is to be obtained; and I may now say, its reckless and fruitless maintenance of the most cruel and unprincipled war in the history of the world." [17] In his American edition of 1866 Dr. Alford withdrew this reference to the Civil War and somewhat ameliorated his indignation otherwise, but he clung to the main counts in his indictment, and most Englishmen, I daresay, still give them a certain support. The American is no longer a "vain, egotistical, insolent, rodomontade sort of fellow"; America is no longer the "brigand confederation" of the *Foreign Quarterly* or "the loathsome creature, . . . maimed and lame, full of sores and ulcers" of Dickens; but the Americanism is yet regarded with a bilious eye, and pounced upon viciously when found. Even the friendliest English critics seem to be daunted by the gargantuan copiousness of American inventions in speech. Their position, perhaps, was well stated by Capt. Basil Hall, author of the

[17] A Plea for the Queen's English; London, 1863; 2nd ed., 1864; American ed., New York, 1866.

THE PERIOD OF GROWTH 91

celebrated "Travels in North America," in 1827. When he argued that "surely such innovations are to be deprecated," an American asked him this question: "If a word becomes universally current in America, why should it not take its station in the language?" "Because," replied Hall in all seriousness, "there are words enough in our language already."

3.

The Expanding Vocabulary

A glance at some of the characteristic coinages of the time, as they are revealed in the *Congressional Globe,* in contemporary newspapers and political tracts, and in that grotesque small literature of humor which began with Judge Thomas C. Haliburton's "Sam Slick" in 1835, is almost enough to make one sympathize with Dean Alford. Bartlett quotes *to doxologize* from the *Christian Disciple,* a quite reputable religious paper of the 40's. *To citizenize* was used and explained by Senator Young, of Illinois, in the Senate on February 1, 1841, and he gave Noah Webster as authority for it. *To funeralize* and *to missionate,* along with *consociational,* were contributions of the backwoods pulpit; perhaps it also produced *hell-roaring* and *hellion,* the latter of which was a favorite of the Mormons and even got into a sermon by Henry Ward Beecher. *To deacon,* a verb of decent mien in colonial days, signifying to read a hymn line by line, responded to the rough humor of the time, and began to mean to swindle or adulterate, *e. g.,* to put the largest berries at the top of the box, to extend one's fences *sub rosa,* or to mix sand with sugar. A great rage for extending the vocabulary by the use of suffixes seized upon the corn-fed etymologists, and they produced a formidable new vocabulary in *-ize, -ate, -ify, -acy, -ous* and *-ment.* Such inventions as *to obligate, to concertize, to questionize, retiracy, savagerous, coatee* (a sort of diminutive for *coat*) and *citified* appeared in the popular vocabulary and even got into more or less good usage. Fowler, in 1850, cited *publishment* and *releasement* with no apparent thought that they were uncouth. And at the same time many verbs were made by the simple process of back formation, as, *to resurrect, to excurt, to resolute, to burgle* [18] and *to enthuse*.[19]

Some of these inventions, after flourishing for a generation or more, were retired with blushes during the period of æsthetic consciousness following the Civil War, but a large number have survived to our own day, and are in good usage. Not even the most bilious purist would think of objecting to *to affiliate, to endorse, to collide, to jeopardize, to predicate, to progress, to itemize, to resurrect* or *to Americanize* today, and yet all of them gave grief to the judicious when they first appeared in the debates of Congress, brought there by statesmen from the backwoods. Nor to such simpler verbs of the period as *to corner* (*i. e.,* the market), *to boss* and *to lynch*.[20] Nor perhaps to *to boom, to boost, to kick* (in the sense of to protest), *to coast* (on a sled), *to engineer, to chink* (*i. e.,* logs), *to feaze, to splurge, to bulldoze, to aggravate* (in the sense of to anger), *to yank* and *to crawfish*. These verbs have entered into the very fibre of the American vulgate, and so have many nouns derived from them, *e. g., boomer, boom-town, bouncer, kicker, kick, splurge, roller-coaster*. A few of them, *e. g., to collide* and *to feaze*, were archaic English terms brought to new birth; a few others, *e. g., to holler* [21] and *to muss*, were obviously mere corruptions. But a good many others, *e. g., to bulldoze, to hornswoggle* and *to scoot*, were genuine inventions, and redolent of the soil.

With the new verbs came a great swarm of verb-phrases, some of

[18] J. R. Ware, in Passing English of the Victorian Era, says that *to burgle* was introduced to London by W. S. Gilbert in The Pirates of Penzance (April 3, 1880). It was used in America 30 years before.

[19] This process, of course, is philologically respectable, however uncouth its occasional products may be. By it we have acquired many every-day words, among them, *to accept* (from *acceptum*), *to exact* (from *exactum*), *to darkle* (from *darkling*), and *pea* (from *pease = pois*).

[20] All authorities save one seem to agree that this verb is a pure Americanism, and that it is derived from the name of Charles Lynch, a Virginia justice of the peace, who jailed many Loyalists in 1780 without warrant in law. The dissentient, Bristed, says that *to linch* is in various northern English dialects, and means to beat or maltreat.

[21] The correct form of this appears to be *halloo* or *holloa*, but in America it is pronounced *holler* and usually represented in print by *hollo* or *hollow*. I have often encountered *holloed* in the past tense. But the Public Printer frankly accepts *holler*. Vide the *Congressional Record*, May 12, 1917, p. 2309. The word, in the form of *hollering*, is here credited to "Hon." John L. Burnett, of Alabama. There can be no doubt that the hon. gentleman said *hollering*, and not *holloaing*, or *holloeing*, or *hollowing*, or *hallooing*. *Hello* is apparently a variation of the same word.

THE PERIOD OF GROWTH 93

them short and pithy and others extraordinarily elaborate, but all showing the true national talent for condensing a complex thought, and often a whole series of thoughts, into a vivid and arresting image. Of the first class are *to fill the bill, to fizzle out, to make tracks, to peter out, to plank down, to go back on, to keep tab, to light out* and *to back water.* Side by side with them we have inherited such common coins of speech as *to make the fur fly, to cut a swath, to know him like a book, to keep a stiff upper lip, to cap the climax, to handle without gloves, to freeze on to, to go it blind, to pull wool over his eyes, to have the floor, to know the ropes, to get solid with, to spread one's self, to run into the ground, to dodge the issue, to paint the town red, to take a back seat* and *to get ahead of.* These are so familiar that we use them and hear them without thought; they seem as authentically parts of the English idiom as *to be left at the post.* And yet, as the labors of Thornton have demonstrated, all of them are of American nativity, and the circumstances surrounding the origin of some of them have been accurately determined. Many others are palpably the products of the great movement toward the West, for example, *to pan out, to strike it rich, to jump* or *enter a claim, to pull up stakes, to rope in, to die with one's boots on, to get the deadwood on, to get the drop, to back and fill, to do a land-office business* and *to get the bulge on.* And in many others the authentic American is no less plain, for example, in *to kick the bucket, to put a bug in his ear, to see the elephant, to crack up, to do up brown, to bark up the wrong tree, to jump on with both feet, to go the whole hog, to make a kick, to buck the tiger, to let it slide* and *to come out at the little end of the horn. To play possum* belongs to this list. To it Thornton adds *to knock into a cocked hat,* despite its English sound, and *to have an ax to grind. To go for,* both in the sense of belligerency and in that of partisanship, is also American, and so is *to go through* (*i. e.,* to plunder).

Of adjectives the list is scarcely less long. Among the coinages of the first half of the century that are in good use today are *non-committal, highfalutin, well-posted, down-town, two-fer, played-out, flat-footed, whole-souled* and *true-blue.* The first appears in a Senate debate of 1841; *highfalutin* in a political speech of the same decade. Both are useful words; it is impossible, not employing them, to convey the ideas behind them without circumlocution. The use of *slim* in the sense of meagre, as in *slim chance, slim attendance* and *slim support,* goes back still further. The English use *small* in place of it. Other, and less respectable contributions of the time are *brash, bogus, brainy, peart, locoe*(d)*, pesky, picayune, scary, well-heeled, hardshell* (e. g., Baptist), *low-flung, codfish* (to indicate opprobrium) and *go-to-meeting.* The use of *plumb* as an adjective, as in *plumb crazy,* is an English archaism that was revived in the United States in the early years of the century. In the more orthodox adverbial form of *plump* it still survives, for example, in "she fell *plump* into his arms." But this last is also good English.

The characteristic American substitution of *mad* for *angry* goes back to the eighteenth century, and perhaps denotes the survival of an English provincialism. Witherspoon noticed it and denounced it in 1781, and in 1816 Pickering called it "low" and said that it was not used "except in very familiar conversation." But it got into much better odor soon afterward, and by 1840 it passed unchallenged. Its use is one of the peculiarities that Englishmen most quickly notice in American colloquial speech today. In formal written discourse it is less often encountered, probably because the English marking of it has so conspicuously singled it out. But it is constantly met with in the newspapers and in the *Congressional Record,* and it is not infrequently used by such writers as Howells and Dreiser. In the familiar simile, *as mad as a hornet,* it is used in the American sense. But *as mad as a March hare* is English, and connotes insanity, not mere anger. The English meaning of the word is preserved in *mad-house* and *mad-dog,* but I have often noticed that American rustics, employing the latter term, derive from it a vague notion, not that the dog is demented, but that it is in a simple fury. From this notion, perhaps, comes the popular belief that dogs may be thrown into hydrophobia by teasing and badgering them.

It was not, however, among the verbs and adjectives that the American word-coiners of the first half of the century achieved their gaudiest innovations, but among the substantives. Here they had temptation and excuse in plenty, for innumerable new objects and relations demanded names, and here they exercised their fancy with-

THE PERIOD OF GROWTH 95

out restraint. Setting aside loan words, which will be considered later, three main varieties of new nouns were thus produced. The first consisted of English words rescued from obsolescence or changed in meaning, the second of compounds manufactured of the common materials of the mother-tongue, and the third of entirely new inventions. Of the first class, good specimens are *deck* (of cards), *gulch*, *gully* and *billion*, the first three old English words restored to usage in America and the last a sound English word changed in meaning. Of the second class, examples are offered by *gum-shoe, mortgage-shark, carpet-bagger, cut-off, mass-meeting, dead-beat, dug-out, shot-gun, stag-party, wheat-pit, horse-sense, chipped-beef, oyster-supper, buzz-saw, chain-gang* and *hell-box*. And of the third there are instances in *buncombe, greaser, conniption, bloomer, campus, galoot, maverick, roustabout, bugaboo* and *blizzard*.

Of these coinages perhaps those of the second class are most numerous and characteristic. In them American exhibits one of its most marked tendencies: a habit of achieving short cuts in speech by a process of agglutination. Why explain laboriously, as an Englishman might, that the notes of a new bank (in a day of innumerable new banks) are insufficiently secure? Call them *wild-cat* notes and have done! Why describe a gigantic rain storm with the lame adjectives of everyday? Call it a *cloud-burst* and immediately a vivid picture of it is conjured up. *Rough-neck* is a capital word; it is more apposite and savory than the English *navvy*, and it is overwhelmingly more American.[22] *Square-meal* is another. *Fire-eater* is yet another. And the same instinct for the terse, the eloquent and the picturesque is in *boiled-shirt, blow-out, big-bug, claim-jumper, spread-eagle, come-down, back-number, claw-hammer* (coat), *bottom-dollar, poppy-cock, cold-snap, back-talk, back-taxes, calamity-howler, fire-bug, grab-bag, grip-sack, grub-stake, pay-dirt, tender-foot, stocking-feet, ticket-scalper, store-clothes, small-potatoes, cake-walk, prairie-schooner, round-up, snake-fence, flat-boat, under-the-weather, on-the-hoof,* and *jumping-off-place*. These compounds (there must be thousands of them) have been largely responsible for giving the language its characteristic tang and color. Such specimens as *bell-*

---

[22] *Rough-neck* is often cited, in discussions of slang, as a latter-day invention, but Thornton shows that it was used in Texas in 1836.

96   THE AMERICAN LANGUAGE

hop, semi-occasional, chair-warmer and *down-and-out* are as distinctively American as baseball or the quick-lunch.

The spirit of the language appears scarcely less clearly in some of the coinages of the other classes. There are, for example, the English words that have been extended or restricted in meaning, *e. g., docket* (for court calendar), *betterment* (for improvement to property), *collateral* (for security), *crank* (for fanatic), *jumper* (for tunic), *tickler* (for memorandum or reminder),[23] *carnival* (in such phrases as *carnival of crime*), *scrape* (for fight or difficulty),[24] *flurry* (of snow, or in the market), *suspenders, diggings* (for habitation) and *range*. Again, there are the new assemblings of English materials, *e. g., doggery, rowdy, teetotaler, goatee, tony* and *cussedness*. Yet again, there are the purely artificial words, *e. g., sockdolager, hunky-dory, scalawag, guyascutis, spondulix, slumgullion, rambunctious, scrumptious, to skedaddle, to absquatulate* and *to exfluncticate*.[25] In the use of the last-named coinages fashions change. In the 40's *to absquatulate* was in good usage, but it has since disappeared. Most of the other inventions of the time, however, have to some extent survived, and it would be difficult to find an American of today who did not know the meaning of *scalawag* and *rambunctious* and who did not occasionally use them. A whole series of artificial American words groups itself around the prefix *ker*, for example, *ker-flop, ker-splash, ker-thump, ker-bang, ker-plunk, ker-slam* and *ker-flummux*. This prefix and its onomatopœic daughters have been borrowed by the English, but Thornton and Ware agree that it is American. Several of my correspondents suggest that it may have been suggested by the German prefix *ge-*—that it may represent a humorous attempt to make German words by analogy, *e. g., geflop, gesplash*, etc. I pass on this guess for what it is worth. Certainly such American-German words must have been manufactured frequently by the earliest "Dutch" comedians, and it is quite possible that some of them got into the language, and that the *ge-* was subsequently changed to *ker-*.

[23] This use goes back to 1839.
[24] Thornton gives an example dated 1812. Of late the word has lost its final *e* and shortened its vowel, becoming *scrap*.
[25] *Cf.* Terms of Approbation and Eulogy, by Elsie L. Warnock, *Dialect Notes*, vol. iv, part 1, 1913. Among the curious recent coinages cited by Miss Warnock are *scallywampus, supergobosnoptious, hyperfirmatious*, and *scrumdifferous*.

THE PERIOD OF GROWTH 97

In the first chapter I mentioned the superior imaginativeness revealed by Americans in meeting linguistic emergencies, whereby, for example, in seeking names for new objects introduced by the building of railroads, they surpassed the English *plough* and *crossing-plate* with *cow-catcher* and *frog*. That was in the 30's. Already at that day the two languages were so differentiated that they produced wholly distinct railroad nomenclatures. Such commonplace American terms as *box-car, caboose* and *air-line* are unknown in England. So are *freight-car, flagman, towerman, switch, switching-engine, switch-yard, switchman, track-walker, engineer, baggage-room, baggage-check, baggage-smasher, accommodation-train, baggage-master, conductor, express-car, flat-car, hand-car, way-bill, expressman, express-office, fast-freight, wrecking-crew, jerk-water, commutation-ticket, commuter, round-trip, mileage-book, ticket-scalper, depot, limited, hot-box, iron-horse, stop-over, tie, rail, fish-plate, run, train-boy, chair-car, club-car, diner, sleeper, bumpers, mail-clerk, passenger-coach, day-coach, railroad-man, ticket-office, truck* and *right-of-way*, not to mention the verbs, *to flag, to express, to dead-head, to sideswipe, to stop-over, to fire* (i. e., a locomotive), *to switch, to sidetrack, to railroad, to commute, to telescope* and *to clear the track*. These terms are in constant use in America; their meaning is familiar to all Americans; many of them have given the language everyday figures of speech.[26] But the majority of them would puzzle an Englishman, just as the English *luggage-van, permanent-way, goods-waggon, guard, carrier, booking-office, railway-rug, R. S. O.* (railway sub-office), *tripper, line, points, shunt, metals* and *bogie* would puzzle the average untraveled American.

In two other familiar fields very considerable differences between English and American are visible; in both fields they go back to the era before the Civil War. They are politics and that department of social intercourse which has to do with drinking. Many characteristic American political terms originated in revolutionary days and have passed over into English. Of such sort are *caucus* and *mileage*. But the majority of those in common use today were coined during the extraordinarily exciting campaigns following the defeat of Adams

---

[26] *E. g., single-track mind, to jump the rails, to collide head-on, broad-gauge man, to walk the ties, blind-baggage, underground-railroad, tank-town.*

by Jefferson. Charles Ledyard Norton has devoted a whole book to their etymology and meaning;[27] the number is far too large for a list of them to be attempted here. But a few characteristic specimens may be recalled, for example, the simple agglutinates: *omnibus-bill, banner-state, favorite-son, anxious-bench, gag-rule, executive-session, mass-meeting, office-seeker* and *straight-ticket;* the humorous metaphors: *pork-barrel, pie-counter, wire-puller, land-slide, carpet-bagger, lame-duck* and *on the fence;* the old words put to new uses: *plank, pull, platform, machine, precinct, slate, primary, floater, repeater, bolter, stalwart, filibuster, regular* and *fences;* the new coinages: *gerrymander, heeler, buncombe, roorback, mugwump* and *to bulldoze;* the new derivatives: *abolitionist, candidacy, boss-rule, per-diem, to lobby* and *boodler;* and the almost innumerable verbs and verb-phrases: *to knife, to split a ticket, to go up Salt River, to bolt, to eat crow, to boodle, to divvy, to grab* and *to run.* An English candidate never *runs;* he *stands.* To *run,* according to Thornton, was already used in America in 1789; it was universal by 1820. *Platform* came in at the same time. *Machine* was first applied to a political organization by Aaron Burr. The use of *mugwump* is commonly thought to have originated in the Blaine campaign of 1884, but it really goes back to the 30's. *Anxious-bench* (or *anxious-seat*) at first designated only the place occupied by the penitent at revivals, but was used in its present political sense in Congress so early as 1842. *Banner-state* appears in *Niles' Register* for December 5, 1840. *Favorite-son* appears in an ode addressed to Washington on his visit to Portsmouth, N. H., in 1789, but it did not acquire its present ironical sense until it was applied to Martin Van Buren. Thornton has traced *bolter* to 1812, *filibuster* to 1863, *roorback* to 1844, and *split-ticket* to 1842. *Regularity* was an issue in Tammany Hall in 1822.[28] There were *primaries* in New York city in 1827, and hundreds of *repeaters* voted. In 1829 there were *lobby-agents* at Albany, and they soon became *lobbyists;* in 1832 *lobbying* had already extended to Washington. All of these terms are now as firmly imbedded in the American vocabulary as *election* or *congressman.*

[27] Political Americanisms . . .: New York and London, 1890.
[28] Gustavus Myers: The History of Tammany Hall; 2nd ed.; New York, 1917, ch. viii.

THE PERIOD OF GROWTH 99

In the department of conviviality the imaginativeness of Americans was shown both in the invention and in the naming of new and often highly complex beverages. So vast was the production of novelties in the days before Prohibition, in fact, that England borrowed many of them and their names with them. And not only England: one buys *cocktails* and *gin-fizzes* to this day in "American bars" that stretch from Paris to Yokohama. *Cocktail, stone-fence* and *sherry-cobbler* were mentioned by Irving in 1809;[29] by Thackeray's time they were already well-known in England. Thornton traces the *sling* to 1788, and the *stinkibus* and *anti-fogmatic,* both now extinct, to the same year. The origin of the *rickey, fizz, sour, cooler, skin, shrub* and *smash,* and of such curious American drinks as the *horse's neck, Mamie Taylor, Tom-and-Jerry, Tom-Collins, John-Collins, bishop, stone-wall, gin-fix, brandy-champarelle, golden-slipper, hari-kari, locomotive, whiskey-daisy, blue-blazer, black-stripe, white-plush* and *brandy-crusta* remains to be established; the historians of alcoholism, like the philologists, have neglected them.[30] But the essentially American character of most of them is obvious, despite the fact that a number have gone over into English. The English, in naming their drinks, commonly display a far more limited imagination. Seeking a name, for example, for a mixture of whiskey and soda-water, the best they could achieve was *whiskey-and-soda.* The Americans, introduced to the same drink, at once gave it the far more original name of *high-ball.* So with *ginger-ale* and *ginger-pop.*[31] So with *minerals* and *soft-drinks.* Other characteristic Americanisms (a few

[29] Knickerbocker's History of New York; New York, 1809, p. 241.

[30] Extensive lists of such drinks, with their ingredients, are to be found in The Hoffman House Bartender's Guide, by Charles Mahoney, 4th ed.; New York, 1916; in The Barkeeper's Manual, by Raymond E. Sullivan, 4th ed.; Baltimore, n.d., and in Wehman Brothers' Bartenders' Guide; New York, 1912. An early list, from the Lancaster (Pa.) *Journal* of Jan. 26, 1821, is quoted by Thornton, vol. ii, p. 985. The treatise by Prof. Sullivan (whose great talents I often enjoyed at the Belvedere Hotel in Baltimore before the Methodist hellenium) is particularly interesting. The sale of all such books, I believe, is now prohibited, but they may be consulted by scholars in the Library of Congress.

[31] An English correspondent writes: "Did the Americans invent *ginger-ale* and *ginger-pop?* Then why don't they make some that is drinkable? Do you know of a decent unimported dry ginger? *Ginger-pop,* in England, is *ginger-beer,* an article rarely seen in America. *Stone-ginger* is the only temperance drink worth a damn, perhaps because, properly made, it contains a certain amount of alcohol. It is brewed, not charged with CO_2. Where in America can I buy *stone-ginger;* that is to say, *ginger-beer* from a brewery, sold in stone bottles? We say *pop* in England, but not *ginger-pop.*"

of them borrowed by the English) are *red-eye, corn-juice, eye-opener, forty-rod, squirrel-whiskey, phlegm-cutter, moon-shine, hard-cider, apple-jack* and *corpse-reviver*, and the auxiliary drinking terms, *speak-easy, boot-legger, sample-room, blind-pig, barrel-house, bouncer, bung-starter, dive, doggery, schooner, moonshine, shell, stick, duck, straight, hooch, saloon, finger* and *chaser*. Thornton shows that *jag, bust, bat* and *to crook the elbow* are also Americanisms. So are *bartender* and *saloon-keeper*. To them might be added a long list of common American synonyms for *drunk*, for example, *piffled, pifflicated, awry-eyed, tanked, snooted, stewed, ossified, slopped, fiddled, edged, loaded, het-up, frazzled, jugged, soused, jiggered, corned, jagged* and *bunned*. Farmer and Henley list *corned* and *jagged* among English synonyms, but the former is probably an Americanism derived from *corn-whiskey* or *corn-juice,* and Thornton says that the latter originated on this side of the Atlantic also.

4.

Loan-Words and Non-English Influences

The Indians of the new West, it would seem, had little to add to the contributions already made to the American vocabulary by the Algonquins of the Northwest. The American people, by the beginning of the second quarter of the nineteenth century, knew almost all they were destined to know of the aborigines, and they had names for all the new objects thus brought to their notice and for most of the red man's peculiar ceremonials. A few translated Indian terms, *e. g., squaw-man, Great White Father, Father of Waters,* and *happy-hunting ground,* represent the meagre fresh stock that the western pioneers got from him. Of more importance was the suggestive and indirect effect of his polysynthetic dialects, and particularly of his vivid proper names, *e. g., Rain-in-the-Face, Young-Man-Afraid-of-His-Wife* and *Voice-Like-Thunder.* These names, and other word-phrases like them, made an instant appeal to American humor, and were extensively imitated in popular slang. One of the surviving

THE PERIOD OF GROWTH 101

coinages of that era is *Old-Stick-in-the-Mud,* which Farmer and Henley note as having reached England by 1823. Contact with the French in Louisiana and along the Canadian border, and with the Spanish in Texas and further West, brought many more new words. From the Canadian French, as we have already seen, *prairie, batteau, portage* and *rapids* had been borrowed during colonial days. To these French contributions *bayou, picayune, levee, chute, butte, crevasse* and *lagniappe* were now added, and probably also *shanty* and *canuck.* The use of *brave* to designate an Indian warrior, almost universal until the close of the Indian wars, was also of French origin. From the Spanish, once the Mississippi was crossed, and particularly after the Mexican war, there came a swarm of novelties, many of which have remained firmly imbedded in the language. Among them were numerous names of strange objects: *lariat, lasso, ranch, loco* (weed), *mustang, sombrero, canyon, desperado, poncho, chapparal, corral, broncho, plaza, peon, cayuse, burro, mesa, tornado, presidio, sierra* and *adobe.* To them, as soon as gold was discovered, were added *bonanza, eldorado, placer* and *vigilante. Cinch* was borrowed from the Spanish *cincha* in the early Texas days, though its figurative use did not come in until much later. *Ante,* the poker term, though the etymologists point out its obvious origin in the Latin, probably came into American from the Spanish. Thornton's first example of its use in its current sense is dated 1857, but Bartlett reported it in the form of *anti* in 1848. *Coyote* came from the Mexican dialect of Spanish; its first parent was the Aztec *coyotl. Tamale* had a similar origin, and so did *frijole* and *tomato.* None of these is good Spanish.[32] As usual, derivatives quickly followed the new-comers, among them *peonage, broncho-buster, hot-tamale, ranchman* and *ranch-house,* and such verbs as *to ranch, to lasso, to corral, to ante up* and *to cinch. To vamose* (from the Spanish *vamos,* let us go), came in at the same time. So did *sabe.* So did *gazabo* in the American sense.

This was also the period of the first great immigrations, and the American people now came into contact, on a large scale, with peoples

[32] Many such words are listed in Félix Ramos y Duarte's Diccionario de Mejicanismos, 2nd ed., Mexico City, 1898; and in Miguel de Toro y Gisbert's Americanismos; Paris, n. d.

of divergent race, particularly Germans, Irish Catholics from the South of Ireland (the Irish of colonial days "were descendants of Cromwell's army, and came from the North of Ireland"),[33] and, on the Pacific Coast, Chinese. So early as the 20's the immigration to the United States reached 25,000 in a year; in 1824 the Legislature of New York, in alarm, passed a restrictive act.[34] The Know-Nothing movement of the 50's need not concern us here. Suffice it to recall that the immigration of 1845 passed the 100,000 mark, and that that of 1854 came within sight of 500,000. These new Americans, most of them Germans and Irish, did not all remain in the East; a great many spread through the West and Southwest with the other pioneers. Their effect upon the language was a great deal more profound than most of us think. The Irish, speaking the English of Cromwell's time, greatly reinforced its usages in the United States, where it was beginning to yield to the schoolmasters, who were inclined to follow contemporary English precept and practice. "The influence of Irish-English," writes an English correspondent, "is still plainly visible all over the United States. About nine years ago, before I had seen America, a relative of mine came home after twelve years' farming in North Dakota, and I was struck by the resemblance between his speech and that of the Irish drovers who brought cattle to Norwich market." [35] We shall see various indications of the Irish influence later on, not only on the vocabulary, but also upon pronunciation and idiom. The Germans also left indelible marks upon American, and particularly upon the spoken American of the common people. The everyday vocabulary is full of German words.

[33] Prescott F. Hall: Immigration. . . .; New York, 1913, p. 5.
[34] Most of the provisions of this act, however, were later declared unconstitutional. Several subsequent acts met the same fate.
[35] This same correspondent adds: "I find very little trace of Scotch on this continent. One might expect to find it in Toronto, the Presbyterian Lhassa, where slot machines are removed from the streets on Sunday, but the speech of Toronto is actually not distinguishable from that of Buffalo. That is to say, it is quite Irish. The Scotch are not tenacious of their dialect, in spite of the fuss they make about it. It disappears in the second generation. I have met Prince Edward Islanders who speak Gaelic and American, but not Scotch. The affinity between Scotch and French, by the way, is noticeable nowhere more than in the Province of Quebec, where I have met Macdonalds who couldn't speak English. The Scotch surrender their speech customs more readily than the English, and the Irish, it seems to me, are most tenacious of all."

THE PERIOD OF GROWTH

Sauerkraut and *noodle,* as we have seen, came in during the colonial period, apparently through the so-called Pennsylvania Dutch, *i. e.,* a mixture, much debased, of the German dialects of Switzerland, Suabia and the Palatinate. The later immigrants contributed *pretzel, pumpernickel, hausfrau, lager-beer, pinocle, wienerwurst* (often reduced to *wiener* or *wienie*), *frankfurter, bock-beer, schnitzel, leberwurst* (sometimes half translated as *liverwurst*), *blutwurst, rathskeller, schweizer* (cheese), *delicatessen, hamburger* (*i. e.,* steak), *kindergarten* and *katzenjammer.*[36] From them, in all probability, there also came two very familiar Americanisms, *loafer* and *bum.* The former, according to the Standard Dictionary, is derived from the German *laufen;* another authority says that it originated in a German mispronunciation of *lover, i. e.,* as *lofer.*[37] Thornton shows that the word was already in common use in 1835. *Bum* was originally *bummer,* and apparently derives from the German *bummler.*[38] Both words have produced derivatives: *loaf* (noun), *to loaf, corner-loafer, common-loafer, to bum, bum* (adj.) and *bummery,* not to mention *on the bum. Loafer* has migrated to England, but *bum* is still unknown there in the American sense. In England, indeed,

---

[36] The majority of these words, it will be noted, relate to eating and drinking. They mirror the profound effect of German immigration upon American drinking habits and the American cuisine. In July, 1921, despite the current prejudice against all things German, I found *sour-braten* on the bill-of-fare at Delmonico's in New York, and, more surprising still, "*braten* with potato-salad." It is a fact often observed that loan-words, at least in modern times, seldom represent the higher aspirations of the creditor nation. French and German have borrowed from English, not words of lofty significance, but such terms as *beefsteak, roast-beef, pudding, grog, jockey, tourist, sport, five-o'clock tea, cocktail* and *sweepstakes,* and from American such terms as *tango, foxtrot, one-step* and *canoe* (often spelled *kanu*). "The contributions of England to European civilization, as tested by the English words in Continental languages," says L. P. Smith, "are not, generally, of a kind to cause much national self-congratulation." See also The English Element in Foreign Language, by the same author, in *English,* March, 1919, p. 15 *et seq.* Nor would a German, I daresay, be very proud of the German contributions to American.
[37] *Vide* a paragraph in *Notes and Queries,* quoted by Thornton.
[38] Thornton offers examples of this form ranging from 1856 to 1885. During the Civil War the word acquired the special meaning of looter. The Southerners thus applied it to Sherman's men. *Vide* Southern Historical Society Papers, vol. xii, p. 428; Richmond, 1884. Here is a popular rhyme that survived until the early 90's:
        Isidor, psht, psht!
        Vatch de shtore, psht, psht!
        Vhile I ketch de *bummer*
        Vhat shtole de suit of clothes!
Bummel-zug is common German slang for slow train.

bum is used to designate an unmentionable part of the body and is thus not employed in polite discourse.

Another example of debased German is offered by the American *Kriss Kringle*. It is from *Christkindlein,* or *Christkind'l,* and properly designates, of course, not the patron saint of Christmas, but the child in the manger. A German friend tells me that the form *Kriss Kringle,* which is that given in the Standard Dictionary, and the form *Krisking'l,* which is that most commonly used in the United States, are both quite unknown in Germany. Here, obviously, we have an example of a loan-word in decay. Whole phrases have gone through the same process, for example, *nix come erous* (from *nichts kommt heraus*) and *'rous mit 'im* (from *heraus mit ihm*). These phrases, like *wie geht's* and *ganz gut,* are familiar to practically all Americans, no matter how complete their ignorance of correct German. So are such slang phrases, obviously suggested by German, as *ach Louie* and *on the Fritz.* So is the use of *dumb* for *stupid,* a borrowing from the German *dumm.* Most of them know, too, the meaning of *gesundheit, kümmel, seidel, wanderlust, stein, speck, männerchor, schützenfest, sängerfest, turn-verein, hoch, yodel, zwieback* and *zwei* (as in *zwei bier*). I have found *snitz* (=*schnitz*) in *Town Topics*.[39] *Prosit* is in all American dictionaries.[40] *Bower,* as used in cards, is an Americanism derived from the German *bauer,* meaning the jack. The exclamation, *ouch!* is classed as an Americanism by Thornton, and he gives an example dated 1837. The New English Dictionary refers it to the German *autsch,* and Thornton says that "it may have come across with the Dunkers or the Mennonites." *Ouch* is not heard in English, save in the sense of a clasp or buckle set with precious stones (=OF *nouche*), and even in that sense it is archaic. *Shyster* is very probably German also; Thornton has traced it back to the 50's.[41] *Rum-dumb* is grounded upon the

---

[39] Jan. 24, 1918, p. 4.
[40] Nevertheless, when I once put it into a night-letter a Western Union office refused to accept it, the rules requiring all night-letters to be in "plain English." Meanwhile, the English have borrowed it from American, and it is actually in the Oxford Dictionary. It is German student Latin.
[41] The word is not in the Oxford Dictionary, but Cassell gives it and says that it is German and an Americanism. The Standard Dictionary does not give its etymology. Thornton's first example, dated 1856, shows a variant spelling, *shuyster,* thus indicating that it was then recent. All subsequent examples show the present spelling. It is to be noted that the suffix *-ster* is not uncommon in English, and that it usually carries a deprecatory significance.

meaning of *dumb* borrowed from the German; it is not listed in the English slang dictionaries.[42] Bristed says that the American meaning of *wagon*, which indicates almost any four-wheeled, horse-drawn vehicle in this country but only the very heaviest in England, was probably influenced by the German *wagen*. He also says that the American use of *hold on* for *stop* was suggested by the German *halt an*, and White says that the substitution of *standpoint* for *point of view*, long opposed by all purists, was first made by an American professor who sought "an Anglicized form" of the German *standpunkt*. The same German influence may be behind the general facility with which American forms compound nouns. In most other languages, for example, Latin and French, the process is rare, and even English lags far behind American. But in German it is almost unrestricted. "It is," says L. P. Smith, "a great step in advance toward that ideal language in which meaning is expressed, not by terminations, but by the simple method of word position."

The immigrants from the South of Ireland, during the period under review, exerted an influence upon the language that was vastly greater than that of the Germans, both directly and indirectly, but their contributions to the actual vocabulary were probably less. They gave American, indeed, relatively few new words; perhaps *shillelah, colleen, spalpeen, smithereens* and *poteen* exhaust the unmistakably Gaelic list. *Lallapalooza* is also probably an Irish loan-word, though it is not Gaelic. It apparently comes from *allay-foozee*, a Mayo provincialism, signifying a sturdy fellow. *Allay-foozee*, in its turn, comes from the French *allez-fusil*, meaning "Forward the muskets!"—a memory, according to P. W. Joyce,[43] of the French landing at Killala in 1798. Such phrases as *Erin go bragh* and such expletives as *begob* and *begorry* may perhaps be added: they have got into American, though they are surely not distinctive Americanisms. But of far more importance, in the days of the great immigrations, than these few contributions to the vocabulary were certain speech

[42] *Dumb-head*, obviously from the German *dummkopf*, appears in a list of Kansas words collected by Judge J. S. Ruppenthal, of Russell, Kansas. (*Dialect Notes*, vol. iv, pt. v, 1916, p. 322.) It is also noted in Nebraska and the Western Reserve, and is very common in Pennsylvania. *Uhrgucker* (= *uhr-gucken*) is also on the Kansas list of Judge Ruppenthal.

[43] English As We Speak It in Ireland, 2nd ed.; London and Dublin, 1910, pp. 179-180.

habits that the Irish brought with them—habits of pronunciation, of syntax and even of grammar. These habits were, in part, the fruit of efforts to translate the idioms of Gaelic into English, and in part, as we have seen, survivals from the English of the age of James I. The latter, preserved by Irish conservatism in speech [44] came into contact in America with habits surviving, with more or less change, from the same time, and so gave those American habits an unmistakable reinforcement. The Yankees had lived down such Jacobean pronunciations as *tay* for *tea* and *desave* for *deceive,* and these forms, on Irish lips, struck them as uncouth and absurd, but they still cling, in their common speech, to such forms as *h'ist* for *hoist, bile* for *boil, chaw* for *chew, jine* for *join,*[45] *sass* for *sauce, heighth* for *height, rench* for *rinse* and *lep* for *leaped,* and the employment of precisely the same forms by the thousands of Irish immigrants who spread through the country undoubtedly gave them support, and so protected them, in a measure, from the assault of the purists. And the same support was given to *drownded* for *drowned, oncet* for *once, ketch* for *catch, ag'in* for *against* and *onery* for *ordinary.* Grandgent shows that the so-called Irish *oi*-sound in *jine* and *bile* was still regarded as correct in the United States so late as 1822, though certain New England grammarians, eager to establish the more recent English usage, had protested against it before the end of the eighteenth century.[46] The Irish who came in in the 30's joined the populace in the war upon the reform, and to this day some of the old forms survive. Certainly it would sound strange to hear an American farmer command his mare to *hoist* her hoof; he would invariably use *hist,* just as he would use *rench* for *rinse.*

[44] "Our people," says Dr. Joyce, "are very conservative in retaining old customs and forms of speech. Many words accordingly that are discarded as old-fashioned—or dead and gone—in England, are still flourishing—alive and well, in Ireland. [They represent] . . . the classical English of Shakespeare's time." Pp. 6-7.

[45] Pope rhymed *join* with *mine, divine* and *line;* Dryden rhymed *toil* with *smile.* William Kenrick, in 1773, seems to have been the first English lexicographer to denounce this pronunciation. *Tay* survived in England until the second half of the eighteenth century. Then it fell into disrepute, and certain purists, among them Lord Chesterfield, attempted to change the *ea*-sound to *ee* in all words, including even *great. Cf.* the remarks under *boil* in A Desk-Book of Twenty-five Thousand Words Frequently Mispronounced, by Frank H. Vizetelly; New York, 1917. Also, The Standard of Pronunciation in English, by T. S. Lounsbury; New York, 1904, pp. 98-103.

[46] Old and New, p. 127.

THE PERIOD OF GROWTH

Certain usages of Gaelic, carried over into the English of Ireland, fell upon fertile soil in America. One was the employment of the definite article before nouns, as in French and German. An Irishman does not say "I am good at Latin," but "I am good at *the* Latin." In the same way an American does not say "I had measles," but "I had *the* measles." There is, again, the use of the prefix *a* before various adjectives and gerunds, as in *a-going* and *a-riding*. This usage, of course, is native to English, as *aboard* and *afoot* demonstrate, but it is much more common in the Irish dialect, on account of the influence of the parallel Gaelic form, as in *a-n-aice=a-near*, and it is also much more common in American. There is, yet again, a use of intensifying suffixes, often set down as characteristically American, which was probably borrowed from the Irish. Examples are *no-siree* and *yes-indeedy*, and the later *kiddo* and *skiddoo*. As Joyce shows, such suffixes, in Irish-English, tend to become whole phrases. The Irishman is almost incapable of saying plain yes or no; he must always add some extra and gratuitous asseveration.[47] The American is in like case. His speech bristles with intensives; *bet your life, not on your life, well I guess, and no mistake,* and so on. The Irish extravagance of speech struck a responsive chord in the American heart. The American borrowed, not only occasional words, but whole phrases, and some of them have become thoroughly naturalized. Joyce, indeed, shows the Irish origin of scores of locutions that are now often mistaken for native Americanisms, for example, *great shakes, dead* (as an intensive), *thank you kindly, to split one's sides* (*i. e.*, laughing), and *the tune the old cow died of*, not to mention many familiar similes and proverbs. Certain Irish pronunciations, Gaelic rather than archaic English, got into American during the nineteenth century. Among them, one recalls *bhoy*, which entered our political slang in the middle 40's and survived into our own time. Again, there is the very characteristic American word *ballyhoo*, signifying the harangue of a *ballyhoo-man*, or

---

[47] Amusing examples are to be found in Donlevy's Irish Catechism. To the question, "Is the Son God?" the answer is not simply "Yes," but "Yes, certainly He is." And to the question, "Will God reward the good and punish the wicked?" the answer is "Certainly; there is no doubt He will."

spieler [48] (that is, barker) before a cheap show, or, by metaphor, any noisy speech. It is from *Ballyhooly,* the name of a village in Cork, once notorious for its brawls. Finally, there is *shebang.* Schele de Vere derives it from the French *cabane,* but it seems rather more likely that it is from the Irish *shebeen.*

The propagation of Irishisms in the United States was helped, during many years, by the enormous popularity of various dramas of Irish peasant life, particularly those of Dion Boucicault. So recently as 1910 an investigation made by the *Dramatic Mirror* showed that some of his pieces, notably "Mavourneen," "The Colleen Bawn" and "The Shaugraun," were still among the favorites of popular audiences. Irish plays of that sort, at one time, were presented by dozens of companies, and a number of actors, among them Andrew Mack, Joe Murphy, Chauncey Olcott and Boucicault himself, made fortunes appearing in them. An influence also to be taken into account is that of Irish songs, once in great vogue. But such influences, like the larger matter of American borrowings from Anglo-Irish, remain to be investigated. So far as I have been able to discover, there is not a single article in print upon the subject. Here, as elsewhere, our philologists have wholly neglected a very interesting field of inquiry.

From other languages the borrowings during the period of growth were naturally less. Down to the last decades of the nineteenth century, the overwhelming majority of immigrants were either Germans or Irish; the Jews, Italians, Scandinavians, and Slavs were yet to come. But the first Chinese appeared in 1848, and soon their speech began to contribute its inevitable loan-words. These words, of course, were first adopted by the miners of the Pacific Coast, and a great many of them have remained California localisms, among them such verbs as *to yen* (to desire strongly, as a Chinaman desires opium) and *to flop-flop* (to lie down), and such nouns as *fun,* a measure of weight. But a number of others have got into the common speech of the whole country, *e. g., fan-tan, kow-tow, chop-suey, ginseng, joss, yok-a-mi* and *tong.* Contrary to the popular opinion, *dope* and *hop* are not from the Chinese. Neither, in fact, is an Americanism,

---

[48] *Spieler,* of course, is from the German *spiel.*

though the former has one meaning that is specially American, *i. e.,* that of information or formula, as in *racing-dope* and *to dope out.* Most etymologists derive the word from the Dutch *doop,* a sauce. In English, as in American, it signifies a thick liquid, and hence the viscous cooked opium. *Hop* is simply the common name of the *Humulus lupulus.* The belief that hops have a soporific effect is very ancient, and hop-pillows were brought to America by the first English colonists.

The derivation of *poker,* which came into American from California in the days of the gold rush, has puzzled etymologists. It is commonly derived from *primero,* the name of a somewhat similar game, popular in England in the sixteenth century, but the relation seems rather fanciful. It may possibly come, indirectly, from the Danish word *pokker,* signifying the devil. *Pokerish,* in the sense of alarming, was a common adjective in the United States before the Civil War; Thornton gives an example dated 1827. Schele de Vere says that *poker,* in the sense of a hobgoblin, was still in use in 1871, but he derives the name of the game from the French *poche* (=*pouche, pocket*). He seems to believe that the bank or pool, in the early days, was called the *poke.* Barrère and Leland, rejecting all these guesses, derive *poker* from the Yiddish *pochger,* which comes in turn from the verb *pochgen,* signifying to conceal winnings or losses. This *pochgen* is probably related to the German *pocher* (=*boaster, braggart*). There were a good many German Jews in California in the early days, and they were ardent gamblers. If Barrère and Leland are correct, then *poker* enjoys the honor of being the first loan-word taken into American from the Yiddish. But more likely it is from the German direct. "There is a little-known German card game," says a correspondent, "which goes by the name of *poch.* It resembles poker in a number of ways. Its name is derived from the fact that at one stage of the game the players in turn declare the state of their hands by either passing or opening. Those who pass, signify it by saying, 'Ich *poche,*' or 'Ich *poch.*' This is sometimes indicated realistically by knocking on the table with one's knuckles." I leave the problem to the etymologists of the future.

5.

Pronunciation Before the Civil War

Noah Webster, as we saw in the last chapter, sneered at the broad *a,* in 1789, as an Anglomaniac affectation. In the course of the next 25 years, however, he seems to have suffered a radical change of mind, for in "The American Spelling Book," published in 1817, he ordained it in *ask, last, mass, aunt, grass, glass* and their analogues, and in his 1829 revision he clung to this pronunciation, besides adding *master, pastor, amass, quaff, laugh, craft,* etc., and even *massive.* His authority was sufficient to safeguard the broad *a* in the speech of New England, and it has remained there ever since, though often showing considerable variations from the true English *a.* Between 1830 and 1850, according to Grandgent,[49] it ran riot through the speech of the region, and was even introduced into such words as *handsome, matter, apple, caterpiller, pantry, hammer, practical* and *satisfaction.* Oliver Wendell Holmes, in 1857, protested against it in "The Autocrat at the Breakfast Table," but the great majority of New England schoolmasters were with Webster, and so the protest went for naught. There is some difficulty, at this distance and in the absence of careful investigation, about determining just what sound the great lexicographer advocated. His rival, Worcester, in 1830, recommended a sound intermediate between *ah* and the flat *a.* "To pronounce the words *fast, last, glass, grass, dance,* etc.," he said, "with the proper sound of short *a,* as in *hat,* has the appearance of affectation; and to pronounce them with the full Italian sound of *a,* as in *part, father,* seems to border on vulgarism." Grandgent says that this compromise *a* never made much actual progress—that the New Englanders preferred the "Italian *a*" recommended by Webster, whatever it was. Apparently it was much nearer to the *a* in *father* than to the *a* in *all.* A quarter of a century after Webster's death, Richard Grant White distinguished clearly between these *a*'s, and denounced the former as "a British peculiarity." Frank H.

---

[49] Old and New, p. 139. The two essays in this book, Fashion and the Broad A, and New England Pronunciation, contain the best discussion of the subject that I have ever encountered.

THE PERIOD OF GROWTH 111

Vizetelly, writing in 1917, still noted the difference, particularly in such words as *daunt, saunter* and *laundry;* some Americans, pronouncing these words, use one *a,* and some use the other. At the present time, says Grandgent, "the broad *a* of New Englanders, Italiante though it be, is not so broad as that of Old England. . . . Our *grass* really lies between the *grahs* of a British lawn and the *grass* of the boundless prairies." In the cities, he adds, it has been "shaken by contact with the Irish," and is now restricted to "a few specific classes of words—especially those in which an *a* (sometimes an *au*) is followed by a final *r,* by an *r* that precedes another consonant, by an *m* written *lm,* or by the sound of *f, s,* or *th:* as *far, hard, balm, laugh, pass, rather, path.* In the first two categories, and in the word *father, ah* possesses nearly all the English-speaking territory; concerning the other classes there is a wide divergence, although flat *a* appears everywhere to be disappearing from words like *balm.* Yankeedom itself is divided over such combinations as *ant, can't, dance, example,* in which a nasal and another consonant follow the vowel; *aunt,* however, always has broad *a. Ah,* in this region, is best preserved in rural communities and among people of fashion, the latter being more or less under British influence."

But the imprimatur of the Yankee Johnson was not potent enough to establish the broad *a* outside New England. He himself, compromising in his old age, allowed the flat *a* in *stamp* and *vase.* His successor and rival, Lyman Cobb, decided for it in *pass, draft,* and *dance,* though he advocated the *ah*-sound in *laugh, path, daunt* and *saunter.* By 1850 the flat *a* was dominant everywhere west of the Berkshires and south of New Haven, save for what Grandgent calls "a little *ah*-spot in Virginia," and its sound had even got into such proper names as *Alabama* and *Lafayette.*[50] "In the United States beyond the Hudson—perhaps beyond the Connecticut," says Grandgent, "the flat *a* prevails before *f, s, th,* and *n.*"

Webster failed in a number of his other attempts to influence American pronunciation. His advocacy of *deef* for *deaf* had popular support while he lived, and he dredged up authority for it out of Chaucer and Sir William Temple, but the present pronunciation

[50] Richard Meade Bache denounced it, in *Lafayette,* during the 60's. *Vide* his Vulgarisms and Other Errors of Speech, 2nd ed., Philadelphia, 1869, p. 65.

gradually prevailed, though *deef* remains familiar in the common speech. Joseph E. Worcester and other rival lexicographers stood against many of his pronunciations, and he took the field against them in the prefaces to the successive editions of his spelling-books. Thus, in that to "The Elementary Spelling Book," dated 1829, he denounced the "affectation" of inserting a *y*-sound before the *u* in such words as *gradual* and *nature,* with its compensatory change of *d* into *dj* and of *t* into *ch.* The English lexicographer, John Walker, had argued for this "affectation" in 1791, but Webster's prestige, while he lived, remained so high in some quarters that he carried the day, and the older professors at Yale, it is said, continued to use *natur* down to 1839. He favored the pronunciation of *either* and *neither* as *ee-ther* and *nee-ther,* and so did most of the English authorities of his time. The original pronunciation of the first syllable, in England, probably made it rhyme with *bay,* but the *ee*-sound was firmly established by the end of the eighteenth century. Toward the middle of the following century, however, there arose a fashion of an *ai*-sound, and this affectation was borrowed by certain Americans. Gould, in the 50's, put the question, "Why do you say *i-ther* and *ni-ther?*" to various Americans. The reply he got was: "The words are so pronounced by the best-educated people in England." This imitation still prevails in the cities of the East. "All of us," says Lounsbury, "are privileged in these latter days frequently to witness painful struggles put forth to give to the first syllable of these words the sound of *i* by those who who have been brought up to give it the sound of *e.* There is apparently an impression on the part of some that such a pronunciation establishes on a firm foundation an otherwise doubtful social standing." [51] But the overwhelming majority of Americans continue to say *ee*-ther and not *eye*-ther. White and Vizetelly, like Lounsbury, argue that they are quite correct in so doing. The use of *eye*-ther, says White, is no more than "a copy of a second-rate British affectation."

[51] The Standard of Pronunciation in English, pp. 109-112.

IV.

AMERICAN AND ENGLISH TODAY

1.

The Two Vocabularies

By way of preliminary to an examination of the American of today, here is a list of terms in everyday use that differ in American and English:

American	*English*
ash-can	dust-bin
ash-cart	dust-cart
ashman	dustman
backyard	garden
baggage	luggage
baggage-car	luggage-van
ballast (railroad)	metal
barbershop	barber's-shop
bath-robe	dressing-gown
bath-tub	bath
beet	beet-root
bid (noun)	tender
bill-board	hoarding
boarder	paying-guest
boardwalk (seaside)	promenade
boot	high-boot
brakeman	brakesman
bumper (car)	buffer
bureau	chest of drawers
calendar (court)	cause-list
campaign (political)	canvass
can (noun)	tin
candy	sweets
cane	stick
canned-goods	tinned-goods
car (railroad)	carriage, van or waggon
checkers (game)	draughts
chicken-yard	fowl-run
chief-clerk	head-clerk
chief-of-police	chief-constable
city-editor	chief-reporter
city-ordinance	by-law
clipping (newspaper)	cutting
closed-season	close-season
coal	coals
coal-oil	paraffin

3

American	English
collar-button	stud
commission-merchant	factor, or commission-agent
commutation-ticket	season-ticket
conductor (of a train)	guard
corn	maize, or Indian corn
corner (of a street)	crossing
corn-meal	Indian meal
counterfeiter	coiner
cow-catcher	plough
cracker	biscuit
crazy-bone	funny-bone
cross-tie	sleeper
crystal (watch)	watch-glass
department-store	stores
derby (hat)	bowler
dime-novel	penny-dreadful
district (political)	division
druggist	chemist
drug-store	chemist's shop
drummer	bagman
dry-goods-store	draper's-shop
editorial (noun)	leader, or leading-article
elevator	lift
elevator-boy	lift-man
enlisted-man	private-soldier
excursionist	tripper
ferns	bracken
filing-cabinet	nest-of-drawers
fire-department	fire-brigade
fish-dealer	fishmonger
floor-walker	shop-walker
fraternal-order	friendly-society
freight	goods
freight-agent	goods-manager
freight-car	goods-waggon
freight-elevator	hoist
frog (railway)	crossing-plate
garters (men's)	sock-suspenders
gasoline	petrol
grade (railroad)	gradient
grain	corn
grain-broker	corn-factor
groceries	stores
hardware-dealer	ironmonger
headliner	topliner
hod-carrier	hodman
hog-pen	piggery
hood (automobile)	bonnet
hospital (private)	nursing-home
huckster	coster (monger)
hunting	shooting
Indian	Red Indian
Indian Summer	St. Martin's Summer
instalment-business	credit-trade
instalment-plan	hire-purchase plan
internal-revenue	inland-revenue
janitor	caretaker, or porter
laborer	navvy

AMERICAN AND ENGLISH TODAY

American	English
legal-holiday	bank-holiday
letter-box	pillar-box
letter-carrier	postman
locomotive engineer	engine-driver
long-distance-call	trunk-call
lumber	deals
lumber-yard	timber-yard
mad	angry
mantelpiece	chimney-piece
Methodist	Wesleyan
molasses	treacle
monkey-wrench	spanner
moving-picture-theatre	cinema, or picture-palace
necktie	tie
news-dealer	news-agent
newspaper-man	pressman, or journalist
notions	small-wares
oatmeal	porridge
officeholder	public-servant
orchestra (seats in a theatre)	stalls
outbuildings (farm)	offices
overcoat	great-coat
package	parcel
parlor	drawing-room
parlor-car	saloon-carriage
patrolman (police)	constable
pay-day	wage-day
peanut	monkey-nut
pen-point	nib
period (punctuation)	full-stop
pitcher	jug
plant (industrial)	works
poorhouse	workhouse
post-paid	post-free
potpie	pie
prepaid	carriage-paid
press (printing)	machine
program (of a meeting)	agenda
public-school	board-school
quotation-marks	inverted-commas
railroad	railway [1]
railroad-man	railway-servant
rails	line
rare (of meat)	underdone
receipts (in business)	takings
Rhine-wine	Hock
road-bed (railroad)	permanent-way
road-repairer	road-mender
roast	joint
roll (of films)	spool
roll-call	division
rooster	cock
round-trip-ticket	return-ticket
saleswoman	shop-assistant
saloon	public-house

[1] *Railway*, of course, is sometimes used in the United States. But all the English dictionaries call *railroad* an Americanism.

American	English
scarf-pin	tie-pin
scow	lighter
sewerage	drains
shirtwaist	blouse
shoe	boot
shoemaker	bootmaker
shoe-shine	boot-polish
shoestring	bootlace
shoe-tree	boot-tree
sick	ill
sidewalk	footpath, or pavement
silver (collectively)	plate
sled	sledge
sleigh	sledge
soft-drinks	minerals
smoking-room	smoke-room
spigot (or faucet)	tap
sponge (surgical)	wipe
stem-winder	keyless-watch
stockholder	shareholder
stocks	shares
store-fixtures	shop-fittings
street-cleaner	crossing-sweeper
street-railway	tramway
subway	tube, or underground
suspenders (men's)	braces
sweater	jersey
switch (noun, railway)	points
switch (verb, railway)	shunt
taxes (municipal)	rates
taxpayer (local)	ratepayer
tenderloin (of beef)	under-cut, or fillet
ten-pins	nine-pins
terminal (railroad)	terminus
thumb-tack	drawing-pin
ticket-office	booking-office
tinner	tinker
tin-roof	leads
track (railroad)	line
trained-nurse	hospital-nurse
transom (of door)	fanlight
trolley-car	tramcar
truck (vehicle)	lorry
truck (of a railroad car)	bogie
typewriter (operator)	typist
typhoid-fever	enteric
undershirt	vest
vaudeville-theatre	music-hall
vest	waistcoat
warden (of a prison)	governor
warehouse	stores
wash-rag	face-cloth
wash-stand	wash-hand-stand
waste-basket	waste-paper-basket
whippletree	splinter-bar
witness-stand	witness-box

AMERICAN AND ENGLISH TODAY

2.

Differences in Usage

The differences here listed, most of them between words in everyday employment, are but examples of a divergence in usage which extends to every department of daily life. In his business, in his journeys from his home to his office, in his dealings with his family and servants, in his sports and amusements, in his politics and even in his religion the American uses, not only words and phrases, but whole syntactical constructions, that are unintelligible to the Englishman, or intelligible only after laborious consideration. A familiar anecdote offers an example in miniature. It concerns a young American woman living in a region of prolific orchards who is asked by a visiting Englishman what the residents do with so much fruit. Her reply is a pun: "We eat all we can, and what we can't we can." This answer would mystify most Englishmen, for in the first place it involves the use of the flat American *a* in *can't* and in the second place it applies an unfamiliar name to the vessel that the Englishman knows as a *tin,* and then adds to the confusion by deriving a verb from the substantive. There are no such things as *canned-goods* in England; over there they are *tinned.* The *can* that holds them is a *tin; to can* them is *to tin* them. . . . And they are counted, not as *groceries,* but as *stores,* and advertised, not on *bill-boards* but on *hoardings.* And the cook who prepares them for the table is not *Nora* or *Maggie,* but *Cook,* and if she does other work in addition she is not a *girl for general housework,* but a *cook-general,* and not *help,* but a *servant.* And the boarder who eats them is often not a *boarder* at all, but a *paying-guest.* And the grave of the tin, once it is emptied, is not the *ash-can,* but the *dust-bin,* and the man who carries it away is not the *garbage-man* or the *ash-man* or the *white-wings,* but the *dustman.*

An Englishman, entering his home, does not walk in upon the *first floor,* but upon the *ground floor.* What he calls the *first floor* (or, more commonly, *first storey,* not forgetting the penultimate *e!*) is what we call the *second floor,* and so on up to the roof—which is covered not with *tin,* but with *slate, tiles* or *leads.* He does not *take* a paper; he *takes in* a paper. He does not ask his servant, "Is there any *mail* for me?" but "Are there any *letters* for me?" for *mail,* in the American sense, is a word that he seldom uses, save in such compounds as *mail-van, mail-train* and *mail-order.* He always speaks of it as *the post.* The man who brings it is not a *letter-carrier* but a *postman.* It is *posted,* not *mailed,* at a *pillar-box,* not at a *mail-box.* It never includes *postal-cards,* but only *post-cards,* never *money-orders,* but only *postal-orders* or *postoffice-orders.*[2] The Englishman dictates his answers, not to a *typewriter,* but to a *typist;* a *typewriter* is merely the machine. If he desires the recipient to call him by telephone he doesn't say, " *'phone me* at a quarter *of* eight," but "*ring me up* at a quarter *to* eight." And when the call comes he says "*are you there?*" When he gets home, he doesn't find his wife waiting for him in the *parlor* or *living-room,*[3] but in the *drawing-room* or in her *sitting-room,* and the tale of domestic disaster that she has to tell does not concern the *hired-girl* but the *scullery-maid.* He doesn't bring her a box of *candy,* but a box of *sweets.* He doesn't leave a *derby* hat in the hall, but a *bowler.* His wife doesn't wear *shirtwaists,* but *blouses.* When she buys one she doesn't say "*charge it,*" but "*put it down.*" When she orders a *tailor-made suit,* she calls it a *costume* or a *coat-and-skirt.* When she wants a *spool of thread* she asks for a *reel of cotton.*[4] Such things are bought, not in the *department-stores,* but at the *stores,* which are substantially the same thing. In these stores *calico* means a plain cotton cloth; in the United States it means a printed cotton cloth. Things bought on the instalment plan in England are said to be bought on the *hire-purchase* plan or system; the instalment business itself is the *credit-trade.* Goods ordered by *post* (not *mail*) on which the dealer pays the cost of transportation are said to be sent, not *postpaid* or *prepaid,* but *post-free* or *carriage-paid.*

An Englishman does not wear *suspenders,* but *braces. Suspenders* are his wife's garters; his own are *sock-suspenders.* The family does not seek sustenance in a *rare tenderloin* but in an *underdone undercut* or *fillet.* It does not eat *beets,* but *beet-roots.* The wine on the

[2] However, the English send *money-orders* abroad.
[3] It is possible that the American *living-room* was suggested by the German *wohnzimmer.*
[4] *Spool of thread* is Irish.

table, if white and German, is not *Rhine wine,* but *Hock.* Yellow turnips, in England, are called *Swedes,* and are regarded as fit food for cattle only; when rations were short there, in 1916, the *Saturday Review* made a solemn effort to convince its readers that they were good enough to go upon the table. The English, of late, have learned to eat another vegetable formerly resigned to the lower fauna, to wit, American sweet corn. But they are still having some difficulty about its name, for plain *corn* in England, as we have seen, means all the grains used by man. Some time ago, in the *Sketch,* one C. J. Clive, a gentleman farmer of Worcestershire, was advertising *sweet corn-cobs* as the "most delicious of all vegetables," and offering to sell them at 6s. 6d. a dozen, *carriage-paid. Chicory* is something else that the English are unfamiliar with; they always call it *endive.* By *chicken* they mean any fowl, however ancient. *Broilers* and *friers* are never heard of over there. Neither are *crawfish,* which are always *crayfish.*[5] The classes which, in America, eat *breakfast, dinner* and *supper,* have *breakfast, dinner* and *tea* in England; *supper* always means a meal eaten late in the evening. No Englishman ever wears a *frock-coat* or *Prince-Albert,* or lives in a *bungalow;* he wears a *morning-coat* and lives in a *villa* or *cottage.* His wife's maid, if she has one, is not *Ethel,* or *Maggie* but *Robinson,* and the nurse-maid who looks after his children is not *Lizzie* but *Nurse.*[6] So, by the way, is a trained nurse in a hospital, whose full style is not *Miss Jones,* but *Nurse Jones* or *Sister.* And the hospital itself, if private, is not a hospital at all, but a *nursing-home,* and its trained nurses are plain *nurses,* or *hospital nurses,* or maybe *nursing sisters.* And the white-clad young gentlemen who make love to them are not *studying medicine* but *walking the hospitals.* Similarly, an English law student does not *study* law, but *reads the law.*

If an English boy goes to a *public school,* it is not a sign that he is getting his education free, but that his father is paying a good round sum for it and is accepted as a gentleman. A *public school*

---

[5] The verb *to crawfish,* of course, is also unknown in England.
[6] The differences between the nursery vocabulary in English and American deserve investigation, but are beyond the jurisdiction of a celibate inquirer. I have been told by an Englishman that English babies do not say *choo-choo* to designate a railroad train, but *puff-puff.*

over there corresponds to our *prep school;* it is a place maintained chiefly by endowments, wherein boys of the upper classes are prepared for the universities. What we know as a *public school* is called a *board school* or *council school* in England, not because the pupils are boarded but because it is managed by a school board or county council. The boys in a public (*i. e.,* private) school are divided, not into *classes,* or *grades,* but into *forms,* which are numbered, the lowest being the *first form.* The benches they sit on are also called *forms.* An English boy whose father is unable to pay for his education goes first into a *babies' class* (a *kindergarten* is always a private school) in a *primary* or *infants'* school. He moves thence to *class one, class two, class three* and *class four,* and then into the *junior school* or *public elementary school,* where he enters the *first standard.* Until now boys and girls have sat together in class, but hereafter they are separated, the boy going to a boys' school and the girl to a girls'. He goes up a *standard* a year. At the *third* or *fourth standard,* for the first time, he is put under a male teacher. He reaches the *seventh standard,* if he is bright, at the age of 12, and then goes into what is known as the *ex-seventh.* If he stays at school after this he goes into the *ex-ex-seventh.* But many leave the public elementary school at the *ex-seventh* and go into the *secondary school,* which is what Americans call a *high-school.* "The lowest class in a secondary school," says an English correspondent, "is known as the *third form.* In this class the boy from the public elementary school meets boys from private preparatory schools, who usually have an advantage over him, being armed with the Greek alphabet, the first twenty pages of 'French Without Tears,' the fact that Balbus built a wall, and the fact that lines equal to the same line are equal to one another. But usually the public elementary school boy conquers these disabilities by the end of his first high-school year, and so wins a place in the *upper fourth form,* while his wealthier competitors grovel in the *lower fourth.* In schools where the fagging system prevails the fourth is the lowest form that is fagged. The *lower fifth* is the retreat of the unscholarly. The *sixth form* is the highest. Those who fail in their matriculation for universities or who wish to study for the civil

AMERICAN AND ENGLISH TODAY

service or pupil teachers' examinations go into a thing called the *remove*, which is less a class than a state of mind. Here are the Brahmins, the contemplative Olympians, the *prefects*, the *lab. monitors*. The term *public elementary school* is recent. It was invented when the old board school system was abolished about 1906. But the term *standard* is ancient." The principal of an English public (*i. e.*, private) school is a *head-master* or *head-mistress*, but in a council school he or she may be a *principal*. The lower pedagogues used to be *ushers*, but are now *assistant masters* (or *mistresses*). The titular head of a university is a *chancellor* or *rector*.[7] He is always some eminent public man, and a *vice-chancellor* or *vice-rector* performs his duties. The head of a mere college may be a *president, principal, master, warden, rector, dean* or *provost*.

At the universities the students are not divided into *freshmen, sophomores, juniors* and *seniors*, as with us, but are simply *first-year-men, second-year-men*, and so on, though a *first-year-man* is sometimes a *fresher*. Such distinctions, however, are not as important in England as in America; members of the university (they are called *members*, not *students*) do not flock together according to seniority, and there is no regulation forbidding an upper classman, or even a graduate, to be polite to a student just entered. An English university man does not *study;* he *reads*. He knows nothing of *frats, class-days, senior-proms* and such things; save at Cambridge and Dublin he does not even speak of a *commencement*. On the other hand his daily speech is full of terms unintelligible to an American student, for example, *wrangler, tripos, head, pass-degree* and *don*.

The upkeep of *council-schools* in England comes out of the *rates*, which are local taxes levied upon householders. For that reason an English municipal taxpayer is called a *ratepayer*. The functionaries who collect and spend money are not *office-holders*, but *public-servants*. The head of the local police is not a *chief of police*, but a *chief constable*. The fire department is the *fire brigade*. The

[7] This title has been borrowed by some of the American universities, *e. g.*, *Chancellor* Day of Syracuse. But the usual title remains *president*. On the Continent it is *rector*.

street-cleaner is a *crossing-sweeper*.[8] The parish *poorhouse* is a *workhouse*. If it is maintained by two or more parishes jointly it becomes a *union*. A pauper who accepts its hospitality is said to be *on the rates*. A policeman is a *bobby* familiarly and a *constable* officially. He is commonly mentioned in the newspapers, not by his name, but as *P. C. 643 A*—*i. e.*, Police Constable No. 643 of the A Division. The *fire-laddie*, the *ward executive*, the *wardman*, the *roundsman*, the *strong-arm squad*, the *third-degree*, and other such objects of American devotion are unknown in England. An English saloon-keeper is officially a *licensed victualler*. His saloon is a *public house*, or, colloquially, a *pub*. He does not sell beer by the *bucket* or *can* or *growler* or *schooner*, but by the *pint*. He and his brethren, taken together, are the *licensed trade*. His back-room is a *parlor*. If he has a few upholstered benches in his place he usually calls it a *lounge*. He employs no *bartenders*. *Barmaids* do the work, with maybe a *barman* to help.

The American language, as we have seen, has begun to take in the English *boot* and *shop*, and it is showing hospitality to *headmaster*, *haberdasher* and *week-end*, but *subaltern, civil servant, porridge, moor, draper, treacle, tram* and *mufti* are still rather strangers in the United States, as *bleachers, picayune, air-line, campus, chore, stogie* and *hoodoo* are in England. A *subaltern* is a commissioned officer in the army, under the rank of captain. A *civil servant* is a public servant in the national civil service; if he is of high rank, he is usually called a *permanent official*. *Porridge, moor, scullery, draper, treacle* and *tram*, though unfamiliar, still need no explanation. *Mufti* means ordinary male clothing; an army officer out of uniform (American: *in cits*, or *in citizen's clothes*) is said to be *in mufti*. To this officer a sack-suit or business-suit is a *lounge-suit*. He carries his clothes in a *box*. He does not *miss* a train; he *loses* it. He does not ask for a *round-trip* ticket, but for a *return* ticket. If he proposes to go to the theatre

---

[8] However, the *street-cleaner* is beginning to appear in some of the English cities. He is commonly employed by the Urban Sanitary Authority, and so the letters "U.S.A." appear upon his cart—a shock to visiting Americans. The old-time *crossing-sweeper* was a free lance. He had his pitch at a crossing, and kept it clean; his income came from the free-will offerings of passers-by. As the English cities grow cleaner and official street-cleaning departments are set up he tends to disappear.

he does not *reserve* or *engage* seats; he *books* them. If he sits downstairs, it is not in the *orchestra*, but in the *stalls*. If he likes vaudeville, he goes to a *music-hall*, where the *head-liners* are *top-liners*. If he has to stand in line, he does it, not in a *line*, but in a *queue*. If he goes to see a new play, he says that it has just been put *up*, not put *on*.

In England a corporation is a *public company* or *limited liability company*. The term *corporation*, over there, is commonly applied only to the mayor, aldermen and sheriffs of a city, as in *the London corporation*. An Englishman writes *Ltd.* after the name of a limited liability (what we would call incorporated) bank or trading company, as we write *Inc.* He calls its president its *chairman* or *managing director*. Its stockholders are its *shareholders*, and hold *shares* instead of *stock* in it. The place wherein such companies are floated and looted—the Wall Street of London—is called the *City*, with a capital *C*. Bankers, stock-jobbers, promoters, directors and other such leaders of its business are called *City* men. The financial editor of a newspaper is its *City* editor. Government bonds are *consols*, or *stocks*, or *the funds*.[9] *To have money in the stocks* is to own such bonds. An Englishman hasn't a *bank-account*, but a *banking-account*. He draws *cheques* (not *checks*), not on his *bank* but on the *bankers*.[10] In England there is a rigid distinction between a *broker* and a *stock-broker*. A *broker* means, not a dealer in securities, as in our *Wall Street broker*, but a dealer in secondhand furniture. *To have the brokers*[11] *in the house* means to be bankrupt, with one's very household goods in the hands of one's creditors. For a *City man* to swindle a competitor in England is not *to do him up* or *to do him*, but *to do him in*. When any English business man retires he does not actually *retire;* he *declines business*.[12]

Tariff reform, in England, does not mean a movement toward free trade, but one toward protection. The word *Government*,

[9] This form survives in the American term *city-stock*, meaning the bonds of a municipality. But state and federal securities are always called *bonds*.
[10] *Cf.* A Glossary of Colloquial Slang and Technical Terms in Use in the Stock Exchange and in the Money Market, by A. J. Wilson; London, 1895.
[11] Or *bailiffs*.
[12] This was formerly good American. *Vide* Rufus King: Life and Correspondence; New York, 1894-1900, vol. i, p. 132.

meaning what we call *the administration,* is always capitalized and plural, *e. g.,* "The Government *are* considering the advisability, etc." *Vestry, committee, council, ministry* and even *company* are also plural, though sometimes not capitalized. A member of Parliament does not *run* for re-election; he *stands.* He does not make a *campaign,* but a *canvass.*[13] He does not represent a *district,* but a *division* or *constituency.* He never makes a *stumping trip,* but always a *speaking tour.* When he looks after his fences he calls it *nursing the constituency.* At a political meeting (they are often rough in England) the bouncers are called *stewards;* the suffragettes used to delight in stabbing them with hatpins. A member of Parliament is not afflicted by the numerous bugaboos that menace an American congressman. He knows nothing of *lame ducks, pork barrels, gag-rule, junkets, pulls, gerrymanders, omnibus-bills, snakes, niggers in the woodpile, Salt river, crow, bosses, ward heelers, men higher up, silk-stockings, repeaters, steam-rollers, ballot-box stuffers* and *straight* and *split tickets* (he always calls them *ballots* or *voting papers).* He has never heard, save as a report of far-off heresies, of *direct primaries,* the *recall,* or the *initiative and referendum.* A *roll-call* in Parliament is a *division.* A member speaking is said to be *up* or *on his legs.* When the house adjourns it is said to *rise.* A member referring to another in the course of a debate does not say "the gentleman from Manchester," but "the *honorable* gentleman" (written *hon. gentleman*) or, if he happens to be a privy councillor, "the *right honorable* gentleman," or, if he is a member of one of the universities, or a member of one of the learned professions, "the *honorable and learned* gentleman." If the speaker refers to a member of his own party he may say "my honorable *friend."*

In the United States a *pressman* is a man who runs a printing press; in England he is a newspaper reporter, or, as the English usually say, a *journalist.*[14] This journalist works, not at *space*

---
[13] But he is *run* by his party organization. *Cf.* The Government of England, by A. Lawrence Lowell; New York, 1910, vol. ii, p. 29. *Canvass* was formerly good American. *Cf.* Autobiography of Martin Van Buren; Washington, 1920, p. 8.

[14] Until a few years ago no self-respecting American newspaper reporter would call himself a *journalist.* He always used *newspaper man,* and referred to his vocation, not as a profession, but as *the newspaper business.* This old prejudice, however, now seems to be breaking down. *Cf.* Don't Shy at Journalist, *The Editor and Publisher and Journalist,* June 27, 1914.

AMERICAN AND ENGLISH TODAY 125

rates, but at *lineage* rates. A printing press is a *machine*. An editorial in a newspaper is a *leading article* or *leader*. An editorial paragraph is a *leaderette, or par*. A newspaper clipping is a *cutting*. A pass to the theatre is an *order*. The room-clerk of a hotel is the *secretary*. A real-estate agent or dealer is an *estate-agent*. The English keep up most of the old distinctions between physicians and surgeons, barristers and solicitors. A *barrister* is greatly superior to a *solicitor*. He alone can address the higher courts and the parliamentary committees; a solicitor must keep to office work and the inferior courts. A man with a grievance goes first to his solicitor, who then *instructs* or *briefs* a barrister for him. If that barrister, in the course of the trial, wants certain evidence removed from the record, he moves that it be *struck out*, not *stricken out*, as an American lawyer would say. Only barristers may become judges. An English barrister, like his American brother, takes a *retainer* when he is engaged. But the rest of his fee does not wait upon the termination of the case: he expects and receives a *refresher* from time to time. A barrister is never admitted to the bar, but is always *called*. If he becomes a *King's Counsel*, or *K. C.* (a purely honorary appointment), he is said to have *taken silk*. In the United States a lawyer *tries* a case and the judge *hears* it; in England the judge *tries* it. In the United States the court *hands down* a decision; in England the court hands it *out*. In the United States a lawyer *probates* a will; in England he *proves* it, or has it *admitted to probate*.

The common objects and phenomena of nature are often differently named in England and America. As we saw in a previous chapter, such Americanisms as *creek* and *run*, for small streams, are practically unknown in England, and the English *moor* and *downs* early disappeared from American. The Englishman knows the meaning of *sound* (*e. g.*, Long Island *Sound*), but he nearly always uses *channel* in place of it. In the same way the American knows the meaning of the English *bog*, but rejects the English distinction between it and *swamp*, and almost always uses *swamp* or *marsh* (often elided to *ma'sh*). The Englishman seldom, if ever, describes a severe storm as a *hurricane*, a *cyclone*, a *tornado*, or a *blizzard*. He never uses *cold-snap*, *cloudburst* or *under the weather*.

He does not say that the temperature is 29 degrees (Fahrenheit) or that the thermometer or the mercury is at 29 degrees, but that there are *three degrees of frost*. He calls ice water *iced-water*. He knows nothing of *blue-grass* country or of the *pennyr'yal*.[15] What we call the *mining regions* he knows as the *black country*. He never, of course, uses *down-East* or *up-State*. Many of our names for common fauna and flora are unknown to him save as strange Americanisms, *e. g., terrapin, moose, June-bug, persimmon, gumbo, egg-plant, alfalfa, catnip, sweet-potato* and *yam*. Until lately he called the *grapefruit* a *shaddock*. He still calls the *rutabaga* a *mangel-wurzel*. He is familiar with many fish that we seldom see, *e. g.,* the *turbot*. He also knows the *hare,* which is seldom heard of in America. But he knows nothing of *devilled-crabs, crab-cocktails, seafood-dinners, clam-chowder* or *oyster-stews,* and he never goes to *oyster-suppers, clam-bakes* or *burgoo-picnics*. He doesn't buy *peanuts* when he goes to the circus. He calls them *monkeynuts,* and to eat them publicly is *infra dig*. The common American use of *peanut* as an adjective of disparagement, as in *peanut politics,* is incomprehensible to him.

In England a *hack* is not a public coach, but a horse let out at hire, or one of similar quality. A life insurance policy is usually not an insurance policy at all, but an *assurance policy*. What we call the normal income tax is the *ordinary* tax; what we call the surtax is the *supertax*.[16] An Englishman never lives *on* a street, but always *in* it.[17] He never lives in a *block* of houses, but in a *row;* it is never in a *section* of the city, but always in a *district*. The *business-blocks* that are so proudly exhibited in all small American towns are quite unknown to him. He often calls an office-building (his are always small) simply a *house, e. g.,* Carmelite *House*. Going home by train he always takes the *down-train,* no matter whether he be proceeding southward to Wimbleton, westward to Shepherd's Bush, northward to Tottenham or eastward to Noak's

---

[15] The herb, of course, is used in England. It is popularly regarded as an effective abortifacient.

[16] *Cf*. a speech of Senator La Follette, *Congressional Record*, Aug. 27, 1917, p. 6992.

[17] Of late *in* has come into use in America, but only in relation to minor streets. Thus a man may be said to live *in* Sixty-first street, but his office is *on* Broadway.

Hill. A train headed toward London is always an *up-train*, and the track it runs on is the *up-line*. *Eastbound* and *westbound* tracks and trains are unknown in England, and in general the Englishman has a much less keen sense of the points of the compass than the American. He knows the *East End* and the *West End*, but he never speaks of the *north-east corner* of two streets. When an Englishman boards a 'bus, in fact, it is not at a corner at all, but at a *crossing*, though he is familiar with such forms as Hyde Park *Corner*. The place he is bound for is not three *squares* or *blocks* away, but three *turnings*. *Square*, in England, always means a small park. A backyard is a *garden*. A subway is always a *tube*, or the *underground*. But an underground passage for pedestrians is a *subway*. English streets have no *sidewalks;* they always call them *pavements* or *footpaths* or simply *paths*. An automobile is always a *motor-car* or *motor*. *Auto* is almost unknown, and with it *to auto*. So is *machine*.

An Englishman always calls russet, yellow or tan shoes *brown shoes* (or, if they cover the ankle, *boots*). He calls a pocketbook a *purse*, and gives the name of pocketbook to what we call a *memorandum-book*. His walking stick is always a *stick*, never a *cane*. By *cord* he means something strong, almost what we call *twine;* a thin cord he always calls a *string;* his *twine* is the lightest sort of *string*. When he applies the adjective *homely* to a woman he means that she is simple and home-loving, not necessarily that she is plain. He uses *dessert*, not to indicate the whole last course at dinner, but to designate the fruit only; the rest is *ices* or *sweets*. He uses *vest*, not in place of *waistcoat*, but in place of *undershirt*. Similarly, he applies *pants*, not to his trousers, but to his drawers. An Englishman who inhabits bachelor quarters is said to live in *chambers;* if he has a flat he calls it a *flat*, and not an *apartment*, which term he reserves for a single room.[18] *Flat-houses* are often *mansions*. The janitor or superintendent thereof is a *care-taker* or *porter*. The scoundrels who snoop around in search of divorce evidence are not *private detectives*, but *private enquiry agents*.

[18] According to the New International Encyclopedia, 2nd ed. (*Art.* Apartment House), the term *flat* "is usually in the United States restricted to apartments in houses having no elevator or hall service." In New York such apartments are commonly called *walk-up-apartments* or *walk-ups*. Even with the qualification, *apartment* is felt to be better than *flat*.

The Englishman is naturally unfamiliar with baseball, and in consequence his language is bare of the countless phrases and metaphors that it has supplied to American. Many of these phrases and metaphors are in daily use among us, for example, *fan, rooter, bleachers, batting-average, double-header, grand-stand-play, Charley-horse, pennant-winner, gate-money, busher, minor-leaguer, glass-arm, to strike out, to foul, to be shut out, to play ball, on the bench, on to his curves* and *three strikes and out*. The national game of draw-poker has also greatly enriched American with terms that are either quite unknown to the Englishman, or known to him only as somewhat dubious Americanisms, among them, *cold-deck, kitty, full-house, jack-pot, four-flusher, ace-high, pot, penny-ante, divvy, a card up his sleeve, three-of-a-kind, to ante up, to stand pat, to call* (a *bluff*), *to pony up, to hold out, to cash in, to go it one better, to chip in* and *for keeps*. But the Englishman uses many more racing terms and metaphors than we do and he has got a good many phrases from other games, particularly cricket. The word *cricket* itself has a definite figurative meaning. It indicates, in general, good sportsmanship. To take unfair advantage of an opponent is not *cricket*. The sport of boating, so popular on the Thames, has also given colloquial English some familiar terms, almost unknown in the United States, e. g., *punt* and *weir*. Contrariwise, *pungy, batteau* and *scow* are unheard of in England, and *canoe* is not long emerged from the estate of an Americanism.[19] The game known as *ten-pins* in America is called *nine-pins* in England, and once had that name over here. The Puritans forbade it, and its devotees changed its name in order to evade the prohibition.[20] Finally, there is *soccer*, a form of football that is still relatively little known in the United States. What we call simply football is *Rugby* or *Rugger* to the Englishman. The word *soccer* is derived from *association;* the

---

[19] Canoeing was introduced into England by John MacGregor in 1866, and there is now a Royal Canoe Club. In America the canoe has been familiar from the earliest times, and in Mme. Sarah Kemble Knight's diary (1704) there is much mention of *cannoos*. The word itself is from an Indian dialect, probably the Haitian, and came into American through the Spanish, in which it survives as *canoa*.

[20] "An act was passed to prohibit playing *nine-pins;* as soon as the law was put in force, it was notified everywhere, '*Ten-pins played here.*'"—Capt. Marryat: Diary in America, vol. iii, p. 195.

AMERICAN AND ENGLISH TODAY 129

rules of the game were established by the London Football Association. *Soccer* is one of the relatively few English experiments in portmanteau words. Another is to be found in *Bakerloo,* the name of one of the London underground lines, from *Baker-street* and *Waterloo,* its termini.

But though the English talk of racing, football, cricket and golf a great deal, they have developed nothing comparable to the sporting argot used by all American sporting reporters. When, during the war, various American soldier nines played baseball in England, some of the English newspapers employed visiting American reporters to report the games, and the resultant emission of wild and woolly technicalities interested English readers much more than the games themselves. An English correspondent, greatly excited, sent me the following report from the *Times* of May 26, 1919:

> The pastime was featured by the heavy stick work of Wallace, former Harvard University man, who slammed out a three-bagger and a clean home-run in three trys with the willow. The brand of twirling for both teams was exceptionally good, and the fielding not at all bad considering the chances the A. E. F. boys have had to practise since crossing the deep to join the bigger game over here. For the first three frames both teams hung tough and allowed no scoring, and both Shawenecy and Thomas appeared to have everything necessary, with Shawenecy holding the edge. Fourth innings netted a brace for the home lads. Ives clouted one to centre and Richards let the sphere slip; Eagle watched four bad ones go by, and, after Ives was tagged trying to steal home, was pushed over for the first tally when Williams leaned against one for two sacks. Shawenecy went bad here and gave Storey a free ticket, and Wallace came through with a three station bingle that shoved Williams and Storey across. Brown ended the agony by missing three.
> In the sixth, Cambridge made an effort to close the gap when Shawenecy kissed the leather for a bingle. Richards picked a double, and Myers followed up with a safe swat which brought the count within one. Looked good for another after Myers swiped the second stop, but Thorngate and Hart both carved the breeze. Oxford wasn't going to let them feel too good about it though, so they slipped up a few more to convince the crowd it wasn't visitors' day. Eagle went to first on Myers' error. Gammell took a stroll, and both were forced at the third corner by Williams and Storey. Cobb Wallace stepped into a nice one for the washout drive and was well over the platter before the pill was relayed in. Shawenecy was here yanked to give Clarke a chance to use his slants, and after singling through second, Brown was nabbed off the first pillow.

Cambridge came back strong in the eighth when Shawenecy singled. Richards was given a lift by a muff on third, and both scored with the help of a two-timer from Myers and a nifty sacrifice by Thorngate, but the combined efforts of Hart and Beal could not push the anxious Myers over and scoring for the day was no more.

This jargon, as I say, flabbergasted England, but it would be hard to find an American who could not understand it. As a set-off to it—and to *nineteenth hole,* the one American contribution to the argot of golf, if *African golf* for craps be omitted—the English have an ecclesiastical vocabulary with which we are almost unacquainted, and it is in daily use, for the church bulks large in public affairs over there. Such terms as *vicar, canon, verger, prebendary, primate, curate, nonconformist, dissenter, convocation, minster, chapter, crypt, living, presentation, glebe, benefice, locum tenens, suffragan, almoner, dean* and *pluralist* are to be met with in the English newspapers constantly, but on this side of the water they are seldom encountered. Nor do we hear much of *matins, lauds, lay-readers, ritualism* and the *liturgy.* The English use of *holy orders* is also strange to us. They do not say that a young man is *studying for the ministry,* but that he is *reading for holy orders.* They do not say that he is *ordained,* but that he *takes orders.* Save he be in the United Free Church of Scotland, he is never a *minister,* though the term appears in the Book of Common Prayer; save he be a nonconformist, he is never a *pastor;* a clergyman of the Establishment is always either a *rector,* a *vicar* or a *curate,* and colloquially a *parson.*[21]

In American *chapel* simply means a small church, usually the

---

[21] I am informed by the Rev. W. G. Polack, of Evansville, Ind., that certain Lutherans in the United States, following German usage, employ *vicar* to designate "a theological student, not yet ordained, who is doing temporary supply-work in a mission congregation." The verb, *to vicar,* means to occupy such a pulpit. Mr. Polack is occupied with an interesting inquiry into the American ecclesiastical vocabulary. He believes that *mission-festival,* common in the Middle West, comes from the German *missionsfest.* So with *agenda,* used by some of the Lutheran churches to designate their Book of Common Prayer. He says that it is not the English term, but the German *agende.* He notes the use of *services* to indicate a single service (this is common throughout the United States); the decay of *reverend* to *revernor, reverner, revenor* or *revener;* the use of *confirmand* to designate a candidate for confirmation; the use of *to announce* to indicate notifying a pastor of an intention to partake of communion (Ger. *sich anmelden*); and the use of *confessional-address* (*beichtrede*). All these terms are used by English-speaking Lutherans.

branch of some larger one; in English it has acquired the special sense of a place of worship unconnected with the Establishment. Though three-fourths of the people of Ireland are Catholics (in Munster and Connaught, more than nine-tenths), and the Protestant Church of Ireland has been disestablished since 1871, a Catholic place of worship in that country is still a *chapel* and not a *church*.²² So is a Methodist wailing-place in England, however large it may be, though now and then *tabernacle* is substituted. *Chapel*, of course, is also used to designate a small church of the Establishment, as St. George's *Chapel*, Windsor. A Methodist, in Great Britain, is not ordinarily a *Methodist*, but a *Wesleyan*. Contrariwise, what the English call simply a *churchman* is an *Episcopalian* in the United States, what they call the Church (always capitalized!) is the *Protestant Episcopal* Church,²³ what they call a *Roman Catholic* is simply a *Catholic*, and what they call a *Jew* is usually softened (if he happens to be an advertiser) to a *Hebrew*. The English Jews have no such idiotic fear of the plain name as that which afflicts the more pushing and obnoxious of the race in America.²⁴ "News of *Jewry*" is a common headline in the London *Daily Telegraph*, which is owned by Lord Burnham, a Jew, and has had many Jews on its staff, including Judah P. Benjamin, the American. The American language, of course, knowns nothing of *dissenters*. Nor of such gladiators of dissent as the *Plymouth Brethren*, nor of the *nonconformist conscience*, though the United States suffers from it even more damnably than England. The English, to make it even, get on without *circuit-riders, holy-rollers, Dunkards, hard-shell Baptists, United Brethren, Seventh Day Adventists* and

²² "The term *chapel*," says Joyce, in English as We Speak It in Ireland, "has so ingrained itself in my mind that to this hour the word instinctively springs to my lips when I am about to mention a Catholic place of worship; and I always feel some sort of hesitation or reluctance in substituting the word *church*. I positively could not bring myself to say, 'Come, it is time now to set out for *church*.' It must be either *mass* or *chapel*."
²³ Certain dissenters, of late, show a disposition to borrow the American usage. Thus the *Christian World*, organ of the English Congregationalists, uses *Episcopal* to designate the Church of England.
²⁴ So long ago as the 70's certain Jews petitioned the publishers of Webster's and Worcester's dictionaries to omit their definitions of the verb *to jew*, and according to Richard Grant White, the publisher of Worcester's complied. Such a request, in England, would be greeted with derision.

other such American *feræ naturæ* and are born, live, die and go to heaven without the aid of either the *uplift* or the *chautauqua*.

In music the English cling to an archaic and unintelligible nomenclature, long since abandoned in America. Thus they call a double whole note a *breve*, a whole note a *semibreve*, a half note a *minim*, a quarter note a *crotchet*, an eighth note a *quaver*, a sixteenth note a *semi-quaver*, a thirty-second note a *demisemiquaver*, and a sixty-fourth note a *hemidemisemiquaver*, or *semidemisemiquaver*. If, by any chance, an English musician should write a one-hundred-and-twenty-eighth note he probably wouldn't know what to call it. This clumsy terminology goes back to the days of plain chant, with its *longa, brevis, semi-brevis, minima* and *semiminima*. The French and Italians cling to a system almost as confusing, but the Germans use *ganze, halbe, viertel, achtel*, etc. I have been unable to discover the beginning of the American system, but it would seem to be borrowed from the German. Since the earliest times a great many of the music teachers in the United States have been Germans, and some of the rest have had German training.

In the same way the English hold fast (though with a gradual slacking of the grip of late) to a clumsy and inaccurate method of designating the sizes of printers' types. In America the simple point system makes the business easy; a line of *14-point* type occupies exactly the vertical space of two lines of *7-point*. But the English still indicate differences in size by such arbitrary and confusing names as *brilliant, diamond, small pearl, pearl, ruby, ruby-nonpareil, nonpareil, minion-nonpareil, emerald, minion, brevier, bourgeois, long primer, small pica, pica, English, great primer* and *double pica*. They also cling to a fossil system of numerals in stating ages. Thus, an Englishman will say that he is *seven-and-forty*, not that he is *forty-seven*. This is probably a direct survival, preserved by more than a thousand years of English conservatism, of the Anglo-Saxon *seofan-and-feowertig*. He will also say that he weighs eleven *stone* instead of 154 pounds. A *stone* is 14 pounds, and it is always used in stating the heft of a man. He employs such designations of time as *fortnight* and *twelve-month* a great deal more than we do, and has certain special terms of which we know nothing, for example, *quarter-day, bank-holiday, long-vacation, Lady Day* and *Michaelmas. Per contra,* he knows nothing whatever of our *Thanksgiving, Arbor, Labor* and *Decoration Days* or of *legal holidays,* or of *Yom Kippur.* Finally, he always says "a quarter *to* nine," not "a quarter *of* nine." If it is 8.35 he usually says that it is *five-and-twenty minutes to nine.* But he never inverts any other number; it is *twenty-three minutes to* and *twenty-seven minutes past.* He rarely says *fifteen minutes to;* nearly always he uses *quarter to.* He never says *a quarter hour* or *a half hour;* he says *a quarter of an hour* and *half an hour.*

In English usage, to proceed, the word *directly* is always used to signify *immediately;* in American a contingency gets into it, and it may mean no more than *soon.* In England *quite* means "completely, wholly, entirely, altogether, to the utmost extent, nothing short of, in the fullest sense, positively, absolutely"; in America it is conditional, and means only nearly, approximately, substantially, as in "he sings *quite* well." An Englishman does not say "I will pay you *up*" for an injury, but "I will pay you *back.*" He doesn't look *up* a definition in a dictionary; he looks it *out.* He doesn't say, being ill, "I am *getting* on well," but "I am *going* on well." He doesn't use the American "different *from*" or "different *than*"; he uses "different *to.*" He never adds the pronoun in such locutions as "it hurts *me,*" but says simply, "it hurts." He never "*catches up* with you" on the street; he "catches *you up.*" He never says "are you *through?*" but "have you *finished?*" He never uses *to notify* as a transitive verb; an official act may be *notified,* but not a person. He never uses *gotten* as the perfect participle of *get;* he always uses plain *got.*[25] An English servant never washes the *dishes;* she always washes the *dinner* or *tea things.* She doesn't *live out,* but *goes into service.* Her beau is not her *fellow,* but her *young man.* She does not *keep company* with him but *walks out* with him. She is never *hired,* but always *engaged;* only inanimate things, such as a hall or cab, are *hired.* When her wages are increased she does not get a *raise,* but a *rise.* When her young man goes into the army he does not *join* it; he *joins up.*

That an Englishman always calls out "*I* say!" and not simply "say!" when he desires to attract a friend's attention or register

[25] But nevertheless he uses *begotten,* not *begot.*

a protestation of incredulity—this perhaps is too familiar to need notice. His *hear, hear!* and *oh, oh!* are also well known. He is much less prodigal with *good-bye* than the American; he uses *good-day* and *good-afternoon* far more often. A shop-assistant would never say *good-bye* to a customer. To an Englishman it would have a subtly offensive smack; *good-afternoon* would be more respectful. Various very common American phrases are quite unknown to him, for example, *over his signature, on time* and *planted to corn*. The first-named he never uses, and he has no equivalent for it; an Englishman who issues a signed statement simply makes it *in writing*. He knows nothing of our common terms of disparagement, such as *kike, wop, yap* and *rube*. His pet-name for a tiller of the soil is not *Rube* or *Cy*, but *Hodge*. When he goes gunning he does not call it *hunting*, but *shooting; hunting* is reserved for the chase of the fox. When he goes to a dentist he does not have his teeth *filled*, but *stopped*. He knows nothing of *European plan* hotels, or of *day-coaches*, or of *baggage-checks*.

An intelligent Englishwoman, coming to America to live, told me that the two things which most impeded her first communications with untraveled Americans, even above the gross differences between English and American pronunciation and intonation, were the complete absence of the general utility adjective *jolly* from the American vocabulary, and the puzzling omnipresence and versatility of the verb *to fix*. In English colloquial usage *jolly* means almost anything; it intensifies all other adjectives, even including *miserable* and *homesick*. An Englishman is *jolly bored, jolly* hungry or *jolly well* tired; his wife is *jolly* sensible; his dog is *jolly* keen; the prices he pays for things are *jolly dear* (never *steep* or *stiff* or *high:* all Americanisms). But he has no noun to match the American *proposition,* meaning proposal, business, affair, case, consideration, plan, theory, solution and what not: only the German *zug* can be ranged beside it.[26] And he has no verb in such wide

[26] This specimen is from the *Congressional Record* of Dec. 11, 1917: "I do not like to be butting into this *proposition,* but I looked upon this post-office business as a purely business *proposition.*" The speaker was "Hon." Homer P. Snyder, of New York. In the *Record* of Jan. 12, 1918, p. 8294, *proposition* is used as a synonym for state of affairs. See also a speech by Senator Norris on Feb. 21, 1921, *Congressional Record*, p. 3741 *et seq.* He uses *proposition* in five or six different senses. See also a speech by Senator Borah, *Congressional Record,* May 13, 1921, p. 1395, col. 1.

practise as *to fix*. In his speech it means only to make fast or to determine. In American it may mean to repair, as in "the plumber *fixed* the pipe"; to dress, as in "Mary *fixed* her hair"; to prepare, as in "the cook is *fixing* the gravy"; to bribe, as in "the judge was *fixed*"; to settle, as in "the quarrel was *fixed* up"; to heal, as in "the doctor *fixed* his boil"; to finish, as in "Murphy *fixed* Sweeney in the third round"; to be well-to-do, as in "John is well-*fixed*"; to arrange, as in "I *fixed* up the quarrel"; to be drunk, as in "the whiskey *fixed* him"; to punish, as in "I'll *fix* him"; and to correct, as in "he *fixed* my bad Latin." Moreover, it is used in all its English senses. An Englishman never goes to a dentist to have his teeth *fixed*. He does not *fix* the fire; he *makes it up*, or *mends* it. He is never *well-fixed*, either in money or by liquor.[27] The American use of *to run* is also unfamiliar to Englishmen. They never *run* a hotel, or a railroad; they always *keep* it or *manage* it.

The English use *quite* a great deal more than we do, and, as we have seen, in a different sense. *Quite rich*, in American, means tolerably rich, richer than most; *quite so*, in English, is identical in meaning with *exactly so*. In American *just* is almost equivalent to the English *quite*, as in *just lovely*. Thornton shows that this use of *just* goes back to 1794. The word is also used in place of *exactly* in other ways, as in *just in time, just how many* and *just what do you mean?* Two other adverbs, *right* and *good,* are used in American in senses strange to an Englishman. Thornton shows that the excessive use of *right,* as in *right away, right good* and *right now,* was already widespread in the United States early in the last century; his first example is dated 1818. He believes that the locution was "possibly imported from the southwest of Ireland." Whatever its origin, it quickly attracted the attention of English visitors. Dickens noted *right away* as an almost universal Americanism during his first American tour, in 1842, and poked fun at it in the second chapter of "American Notes." *Right* is used as a synonym for *directly,* as in *right away, right off, right now* and *right on time;*

[27] Already in 1855 Bristed was protesting that *to fix* was having "more than its legitimate share of work all over the Union." "In English conversation," he said, "the panegyrical adjective of all work is *nice;* in America it is *fine.*" This was before the adoption of *jolly* and its analogues, *ripping, stunning, rattling,* etc. Perhaps *to fix* was helped into American by the German word.

for *moderately*, as in *right well, right smart, right good* and *right often*, and in place of *precisely*, as in *right there*. Some time ago, in an article on Americanisms, an English critic called it "that most distinctively American word," and concocted the following dialogue to instruct the English in its use:

> How do I get to ——?
> Go *right* along, and take the first turning (*sic*) on the *right*, and you are *right* there.
> *Right?*
> *Right.*
> *Right!* [28]

But this Englishman failed in his attempt to write correct American, despite his fine pedagogical passion. No American would ever say "take the first turning"; he would say "turn at the first corner." As for *right away*, R. O. Williams argues that "so far as analogy can make good English, it is as good as one could choose." Nevertheless, the Concise Oxford Dictionary admits it only as an Americanism, and avoids all mention of the other American uses of *right*. *Good* is almost as protean. It is not only used as a general synonym for all adjectives and adverbs connoting satisfaction, as in *to feel good, to be treated good, to sleep good,* but also as a reinforcement to other adjectives and adverbs, as in "I hit him *good* and hard" and "I am *good* and tired." Of late *some* has come into wide use as an adjective-adverb of all work, indicating special excellence or high degree, as in *some girl, some sick, going some,* etc. It is still below the salt, but threatens to reach a more respectable position. One encounters it in the newspapers constantly and in the *Congressional Record*, and not long ago a writer in the *Atlantic Monthly* [29] hymned it ecstatically as *"some* word—a true super-word, in fact" and argued that it could be used "in a sense for which there is absolutely no synonym in the dictionary." It was used by the prim Emily Dickinson forty or more years ago.[30] It will concern us again in Chapter IX.

It would be easy to pile up words and phrases that are used in both America and England, but with different meanings. I have

---

[28] I Speak United States, *Saturday Review*, Sept. 22, 1894.
[29] Should Language Be Abolished? by Harold Goddard, July, 1918, p. 63.
[30] Quoted by Gamaliel Bradford in the *Atlantic Monthly*, Aug., 1919, p. 219.

AMERICAN AND ENGLISH TODAY

already alluded to *tariff-reform*. *Open-shop* is another. It means, in England, what an American *union man* (English: *trades-unionist*) calls a *closed-shop*. And *closed-shop*, in England, means what an American calls an *open-shop!* Finally, there is the verb-phrase, *to carry on*. In the United States it means to make a great pother; in England it means to persevere. . . . But the record must have an end.

3.

Honorifics

Among the honorifics in everyday use in England and the United States one finds many notable divergences between the two languages. On the one hand the English are almost as diligent as the Germans in bestowing titles of honor upon their men of mark, and on the other hand they are very careful to withhold such titles from men who do not legally bear them. In America every practitioner of any branch of the healing art, even a chiropodist or an osteopath, is a doctor *ipso facto*, but in England a good many surgeons lack the title and it is not common in the lesser ranks. Even physicians may not have it, but here there is a yielding of the usual meticulous exactness, and it is customary to address a physician in the second person as *Doctor*, though his card may show that he is only *Medicinæ Baccalaureus*, a degree quite unknown in America. Thus an Englishman, when he is ill, always sends for the *doctor*, as we do. But a surgeon is usually plain *Mr.*,[31] and prefers to be so called, even when he is an M. D. An English veterinarian or dentist or druggist or masseur is never *Dr.*

Nor *Professor*. In all save a few large cities of America every male pedagogue is a professor, and so is every band leader, dancing master and medical consultant. But in England the title is very

[31] In the Appendix to the Final Report of the Royal Commission on Venereal Diseases, London, 1916, p. iv, I find the following: "*Mr.* C. J. Symonds, F.R.C.S., M.D.; *Mr.* F. J. McCann, F.R.C.S., M.D.; *Mr.* A. F. Evans, F.R.C.S. *Mr.* Symonds is consulting surgeon to Guy's Hospital, *Mr.* McCann is an eminent London gynecologist, and *Mr.* Evans is a general surgeon in large practice. All would be called *Doctor* in the United States. See also Tract IV, of the Society for Pure English; Oxford, 1920, p. 33.

rigidly restricted to men who hold chairs in the universities, a necessarily small body. Even here a superior title always takes precedence. Thus, it used to be *Professor* Almroth Wright, but now it is always *Sir* Almroth Wright. Huxley was always called *Professor* Huxley until he was appointed to the Privy Council. This appointment gave him the right to have *Right Honourable* put before his name, and thereafter it was customary to call him simply *Mr.* Huxley, with the *Right Honourable,* so to speak, floating in the air. The combination, to an Englishman, was more flattering than *Professor,* for the English always esteem political dignities far more than the dignities of learning. This explains, perhaps, why their universities distribute so few honorary degrees. In the United States every respectable Protestant clergyman is a D. D., and it is almost impossible for a man to get into the papers without becoming an LL. D.,[32] but in England such honors are granted only grudgingly. So with military titles. To promote a war veteran from sergeant to colonel by acclamation, as is often done in the United States, is unknown over there. The English have nothing equivalent to the gaudy tin soldiers of our governors' staffs, nor to the bespangled colonels and generals of the Knights Templar and Patriarchs Militant, nor to the nondescript captains and majors of our country towns. An English railroad conductor (*railway guard*) is never *Captain,* as he often is in the United States. Nor are military titles used by the police. Nor is it the custom to make every newspaper editor a colonel, as is done south of the Potomac. (In parts of the South even an auctioneer is a colonel!) Nor is an attorney-general or consul-general or postmaster-general called *General.* Nor are the glories of public office, after they have officially come to an end, embalmed in such clumsy quasi-titles as *ex-United States Senator, ex-Judge of the Circuit Court of Appeals, ex-Federal Trade Commissioner* and *former Chief of the Fire Department.*

But perhaps the greatest difference between English and Amer-

[32] I have before me an invitation to a dinner given by the Society of Arts and Letters in New York. On the invitation committee are Charles M. Schwab, LL.D., Otto H. Kahn, LL.D., and Abram I. Elkus, LL.D. Billy Sunday, the evangelist, is a D.D. In the South every negro preacher is *ex officio* a D.D., and is commonly addressed as *Doctor.* This enables white Southerners to show a decent respect for his sacred office, and yet avoid the solecism of calling him *Mister.*

AMERICAN AND ENGLISH TODAY 139

ican usage is presented by *the Honorable*. In the United States the title is applied loosely to all public officials of apparent respectability, from senators and ambassadors to the mayors of fifth-rate cities and the members of state legislatures, and with some show of official sanction to many of them, especially congressmen. But it is questionable whether this application has any actual legal standing, save perhaps in the case of certain judges, who are referred to as *the Hon.* in their own court records. Even the President of the United States, by law, is not *the Honorable,* but simply *the President*. In the First Congress the matter of his title was exhaustively debated; some members wanted to call him *the Honorable* and others proposed *His Excellency* and even *His Highness*. But the two Houses finally decided that it was "not proper to annex any style or title other than that expressed by the Constitution." Congressmen themselves are not *Honorables*. True enough, the *Congressional Record,* in printing a set speech, calls it "Speech of *Hon.* John Jones" (without the *the* before the *Hon.*—a characteristic Americanism), but in reporting the ordinary remarks of a member it always calls him plain *Mr.* Nevertheless, a country congressman would be offended if his partisans, in announcing his appearance on the stump, did not prefix *Hon.* to his name. So would a state senator. So would a mayor or governor. I have seen the sergeant-at-arms of the United States Senate referred to as *Hon.* in the records of that body. More, it has been applied in the same place to Sam Gompers, the labor agitator. Yet more, the prefix is actually usurped by the Superintendent of State Prisons of New York.[33]

In England the thing is more carefully ordered, and bogus *Hons.* are unknown. The prefix is applied to both sexes and belongs by law, *inter alia,* to all present or past maids of honor, to all justices of the High Court during their term of office, to the Scotch Lords of Session, to the sons and daughters of viscounts and barons, to the younger sons and all daughters of earls, and to the members of the legislative and executive councils of the colonies. But *not* to

---

[33] See, for the sergeant-at-arms, the *Congressional Record,* May 16, 1918, p. 7147. For Gompers, the *Congressional Record,* July 19, 1919, p. 3017. For the superintendent of prisons his annual reports, printed at Sing Sing Prison. This perhaps is not the worst. I sometimes receive letters from a United States Senator. Almost invariably his secretary makes me *Hon.* on the envelope.

members of Parliament, though each is, in debate, an *hon. gentleman*. Even a member of the cabinet is not an *Hon.*, though he is a *Right Hon.* by virtue of membership in the Privy Council, of which the Cabinet is legally merely a committee. This last honorific belongs, not only to privy councillors, but also to all peers lower than marquesses (those above are *Most Hon.*), to Lord Mayors during their terms of office, to the Lord Advocate and to the Lord Provosts of Edinburgh and Glasgow. Moreover, a peeress whose husband is a *Right Hon.* is a *Right Hon.* herself.

The British colonies follow the jealous usage of the mother-country. Even in Canada the lawless American example is not imitated. I have before me a "Table of Titles to be Used in Canada," laid down by royal warrant, which lists those who are *Hons.* and those who are not *Hons.* in the utmost detail. Only privy councillors of Canada (not to be confused with imperial privy councillors) are permitted to retain the prefix after going out of office, though ancients who were legislative councillors at the time of the union, July 1, 1867, may still use it by a sort of courtesy, and former speakers of the Dominion Senate and House of Commons and various retired judges may do so on application to the King, countersigned by the governor-general. The following are lawfully *the Hon.*, but only during their tenure of office: the solicitor-general, the speaker of the House of Commons, the presidents and speakers of the provincial legislatures, members of the executive councils of the provinces, the chief justice, the judges of the Supreme Courts of Ontario, Nova Scotia, New Brunswick, British Columbia, Prince Edward Island, Saskatchewan and Alberta, the judges of the Courts of Appeal of Manitoba and British Columbia, the Chancery Court of Prince Edward Island, and the Circuit Court of Montreal—these, and no more. A lieutenant-governor of a province is not *the Hon.*, but *His Honor*. The governor-general is *His Excellency,* and so is his wife, but in practise they usually have superior honorifics, and do not forget to demand their use.

But though an Englishman, and, following him, a colonial, is thus very careful to restrict *the Hon.* to its proper uses, he always insists, when he serves without pay as an officer of any organization, upon indicating his volunteer character by writing *Hon.* meaning *honorary,* before the name of his office. If he leaves it off it is a sign that he is a hireling. Thus, the agent of the New Zealand government in London, a paid officer, is simply the *agent,* but the agents at Brisbane and Adelaide, in Australia, who serve for the glory of it, are *hon. agents.* In writing to a Briton of condition one must be careful to put *Esq.,* behind his name, and not *Mr.,* before it. The English make a clear distinction between the two forms. *Mr.,* on an envelope, indicates that the sender holds the receiver to be his inferior; one writes to *Mr.* John Jackson, one's green-grocer, but to James Thompson, *Esq.,* one's neighbor. Any man who is entitled to the *Esq.* is a *gentleman,* by which an Englishman means a man of sound connections and what is regarded as dignified occupation—in brief, of ponderable social position. Thus a dentist, a shop-keeper or a clerk can never be a gentleman in England, even by courtesy, and the qualifications of an author, a musical conductor, a physician, or even a member of Parliament have to be established. But though he is thus enormously watchful of masculine dignity, an Englishman is quite careless in the use of *lady.* He speaks glibly of *lady-clerks, lady-typists, lady-doctors* and *lady-inspectors.* In America there is a strong disposition to use the word less and less, as is revealed by the substitution of *saleswoman* and *salesgirl* for the *saleslady* of yesteryear. But in England *lady* is still invariably used instead of woman in such compounds as *lady-golfer, lady-secretary* and *lady-champion.* The *women's singles,* in English tennis, are always *ladies' singles; women's wear,* in English shops, is always *ladies' wear.* Perhaps the cause of this distinction between *lady* and *gentleman* has been explained by Price Collier in "England and the English." In England, according to Collier, the male is always first. His comfort goes before his wife's comfort, and maybe his dignity also. *Gentleman-clerk* or *gentleman-author* would make an Englishman howl, though he uses *gentleman-rider* and *gentleman-player* in place of our *amateur.* So would the growing American custom of designating successive members of a private family bearing the same given name by the numerals proper to royalty. John Smith *3rd* and William Simpson *4th* are gravely received at Harvard; at Oxford they would be ragged unmercifully.

An Englishman, in speaking or writing of public officials, avoids those long and clumsy combinations of title and name which figure so copiously in American newspapers. Such locutions as *Assistant-Secretary of the Interior* Jones, *Fourth Assistant Postmaster-General* Brown, *Inspector of Boilers* Smith, *Judge of the Appeal Tax Court* Robinson, *Chief Clerk of the Treasury* Williams and *Collaborating Epidermologist* White [34] are quite unknown to him. When he mentions a high official, such as the Secretary for Foreign Affairs, he does not think it necessary to add the man's name; he simply says "the Secretary for Foreign Affairs" or "the Foreign Secretary." And so with the Lord Chancellor, the Chief Justice, the Prime Minister, the Bishop of Carlisle, the Chief Rabbi, the First Lord (of the Admiralty), the Master of Pembroke (College), the Italian Ambassador, and so on. Certain ecclesiastical titles are sometimes coupled to surnames in the American manner, as in *Dean Stanley,* and *Canon Wilberforce,* but *Prime Minister Lloyd-George* would seem heavy and absurd. But in other directions the Englishman has certain clumsinesses of his own. Thus, in writing a letter to a relative stranger he sometimes begins it, not *My dear Mr. Jones* but *My dear John Joseph Jones.* He may even use such a form as *My dear Secretary of War* in place of the American *My dear Mr. Secretary.* In English usage, incidentally, *My dear* is more formal than *Dear.* In America this distinction tends to be lost, and such forms as *My dear John Joseph Jones* appear only as conscious imitations of English usage.

I have spoken of the American custom of dropping the definite article before *Hon.* It extends to *Rev.* and the like, and has the authority of very respectable usage behind it. The opening sentence of the *Congressional Record* is always: "The Chaplain, Rev. ———, D. D., offered the following prayer." When chaplains for the army or navy are confirmed by the Senate they always appear in the *Record* as *Revs.,* never as *the Revs.* I also find the honorific without the article in the New International Encyclopædia, in the *World* Almanac, and in a widely-popular American grammar-book.[35]

[34] I encountered this gem in *Public Health Reports,* a government publication, for April 26, 1918, p. 619.
[35] For the *Record* see any issue. For the New International Encyclopædia see the article on Brotherhood of Andrew and Philip. For the *World* Almanac see the ed. of 1921, p. 195. The grammar-book is Longman's Briefer Grammar;

AMERICAN AND ENGLISH TODAY 143

So long ago as 1867, Gould protested against this elision as barbarous and idiotic, and drew up the following *reductio ad absurdum:*

> At last annual meeting of Black Book Society, honorable John Smith took the chair, assisted by reverend John Brown and venerable John White. The office of secretary would have been filled by late John Green, but for his decease, which rendered him ineligible. His place was supplied by inevitable John Black. In the course of the evening eulogiums were pronounced on distinguished John Gray and notorious Joseph Brown. Marked compliment was also paid to able historian Joseph White, discriminating philosopher Joseph Green, and learned professor Joseph Black. But conspicuous speech of the evening was witty Joseph Gray's apostrophe to eminent astronomer Jacob Brown, subtle logician Jacob White, etc., etc.[36]

Richard Grant White, a year or two later, joined the attack in the New York *Galaxy*, and William Cullen Bryant included the omission of the article in his *Index Expurgatorius*, but these anathemas were as ineffective as Gould's irony. The more careful American journals, of course, incline to the *the*, and I note that it is specifically ordained on the Style-sheet of the *Century Magazine*, but the overwhelming majority of American newspapers get along without it, and I have often noticed its omission on the signboards at church entrances.[37] In England it is never omitted.[38]

4.

Euphemisms

But such euphemisms as *lady-clerk* are, after all, much rarer in English than in American usage. The Englishman seldom tries

---

New York, 1908, p. 160. The editor is George J. Smith, a member of the board of examiners of the New York City Department of Education.

[36] Edwin S. Gould: Good English; New York, 1867, pp. 56-57.

[37] Despite the example of Congress, however, the Department of State inserts the *the*. *Vide* the *Congressional Record*, May 4, 1918, p. 6552. But the War Department, the Treasury and the Post Office omit it. *Vide* the *Congressional Record*, May 11, 1918, p. 6895 and p. 6914 and May 14, p. 7004, respectively. So, it appears, does the White House. *Vide* the *Congressional Record*, May 10, 1918, p. 6838.

[38] I wrote this in 1918. In 1914 the Society for Pure English had been organized in England, with the Poet Laureate, Dr. Henry Bradley, A. J. Balfour, Edmund Gosse, George Saintsbury, and other eminent purists among its charter members. In October, 1919, it issued its first tract—and on page 12 I found *Rev., Very Rev.* and *Rt. Hon.* without the *the!*

to gloss menial occupations with sonorous names; on the contrary, he seems to delight in keeping their menial character plain. He says *servants*, not *help*. Even his railways and banks have *servants*; the chief trades-union of the English railroad men is the Amalgamated Society of Railway *Servants*. He uses *employé* in place of *clerk*, *workman* or *laborer* much less often than we do. True enough he often calls a boarder a *paying-guest*, but that is probably because even a lady may occasionally take one in. Just as he avoids calling a fast train the *limited*, the *flier* or the *cannon-ball*, so he never calls an undertaker a *funeral director* or *mortician*,[39] or a *dentist* a *dental surgeon* or *odontologist*, or a *real estate agent* a *realtor*, or a *press-agent* a *publicist*, or a *barber shop* (he always makes it *barber's shop*) a *tonsorial parlor*, or a common *public-house* a *café*, a *restaurant*, an *exchange*, a *buffet* or a *hotel*, or a *tradesman* a *storekeeper* or *merchant*, or a fresh-water *college* a *university*. A *university*, in England, always means a collection of colleges.[40] He avoids displacing terms of a disparaging or disagreeable significance with others less brutal, or thought to be less brutal, e. g., *ready-to-wear*, *ready-tailored*, or *ready-to-put-on* for *ready-made*, *used* or *slightly-used* for *second-hand*, *popular priced* for *cheap*,[41] *mahoganized* for *imitation mahogany*, *aisle manager* for *floor-walker* (he makes it *shop-walker*), *loan-office* for *pawn-shop*.[42] Also he is careful not to use such words as *rector*, *deacon* and *baccalaureate* in merely rhetorical senses.[43] Nor does he call *mutton lamb*, or *milk cream*. Nor does he use *cuspidor* for *spittoon*, or *B. V. D.'s* as a euphemism for *underwear*, or *butterine* for *oleomargarine*.

"Business titles," says W. L. George,[44] "are given in America

[39] In the 60's an undertaker was often called an *embalming surgeon* in America.
[40] In a list of American "universities" I find the Christian of Canton, Mo., with 125 students; the Lincoln, of Pennsylvania, with 184; the Southwestern Presbyterian, of Clarksville, Tenn., with 86; and the Newton Theological, with 77. Most of these, of course, are merely country high-schools.
[41] Compare the German *civile preise*.
[42] The Australians use the French *mont-de-piété*. Australian euphemisms deserve to be investigated. No doubt the presence of so many convicts among the early settlers caused a great number to be invented.
[43] The Rev. John C. Stephenson in the *New York Sun*, July 10, 1914; . . . "that empty courtesy of addressing every clergyman as *Doctor*. . . . And let us abolish the abuse of . . . *baccalaureate* sermons for sermons before graduating classes of high schools and the like."
[44] Hail, Columbia!; New York, 1921, pp. 92-3.

AMERICAN AND ENGLISH TODAY 145

more readily than in England. Men are distinguished by being called *president* of a corporation. I know one *president* whose staff consists of two typists. Many firms have four *vice-presidents*. Or there is a *press-representative,* or a *purchasing-agent*. In the magazines you seldom find merely an *editor;* the others need their share of honor, so they are *associate* (not *assistant*) *editors*. A dentist is called a *doctor*. The hotel valet is a *tailor*. Magistrates of police-courts are *judges* instead of merely *Mr*. I wandered into a university, knowing nobody, and casually asked for the *dean*. I was asked, 'Which *dean?*' In that building there were enough deans to stock all the English cathedrals. The master of a secret society is *royal supreme knight commander*. Perhaps I reached the extreme at a theatre in Boston, when I wanted something, I forget what, and was told that I must apply to the *chief of the ushers*. He was a mild little man, who had something to do with people getting into their seats, rather a come-down from the pomp and circumstance of his title. Growing interested, I examined my program, with the following result: It is not a large theatre, but it has a *press-representative,* a *treasurer* (box-office clerk), an *assistant treasurer* (box-office junior clerk), an *advertising-agent,* our old friend the *chief of the ushers,* a *stage-manager,* a *head-electrician,* a *master of properties* (in England called *props*), a *leader of the orchestra* (pity this—why not *president?*), and a *matron* (occupation unknown)." George might have unearthed some even stranger magnificoes in other play-houses. I once knew an ancient bill-sticker, attached permanently to a Baltimore theatre, who boasted the sonorous title of *chief lithographer*.

I have already spoken of the freer use of *Jew* in England. In American newspapers it seems likely to be displaced by *Hebrew,* largely through the influence of Jewish advertisers who, for some strange reason or other, look upon *Hebrew* as more flattering. The Jews in England—that is, those of enough public importance to make themselves heard—are in the main of considerable education, and so they are above any silly shrinking from the name of *Jew*. But in the United States there is a class of well-to-do commercial Jews of a peculiarly ignorant and obnoxious type—chiefly department-store owners, professional Jewish philanthropists, and their attendant rabbis, lawyers, doctors, and so on—and the great majority of newspapers are disposed to truckle to their every whim. Along about the year 1900 they began to protest against the use of the word *Jew* to differentiate Jewish law-breakers from the baptized, and, soon thereafter, to be on the safe side, the newspapers began to employ *Hebrew* whenever it was necessary to designate an institution or individual of the Chosen. Thus, one often encounters such absurdities as *Hebrew congregation, Hebrew rabbi* and *Hebrew holidays*. A few years ago a number of more cultured American Jews, alarmed by the imbecility into which the campaign was falling, issued a "Note on the Word *Jew*" for the guidance of newspapers. From this document I extract the following:

> 1. The words *Jew* and *Jewish* can never be objectionable when applied to the whole body of Israel, or to whole classes within that body, as, for instance, *Jewish young men*.
> 2. There can be no objection to the use of the words *Jew* and *Jewish* when contrast is being made with other religions: "*Jews* observe Passover and Christians Easter."
> 3. The application of the word *Jew* or *Jewish* to any individual is to be avoided unless from the context it is necessary to call attention to his religion; in other words, unless the facts have some relation to his being a Jew or to his Jewishness. . . . Thus, if a Jew is convicted of a crime he should not be called a *Jewish criminal;* and on the other hand, if a Jew makes a great scientific discovery he should not be called an eminent *Jewish scientist*.
> 4. The word *Jew* is a noun, and should never be used as an adjective or verb. To speak of *Jew girls* or *Jew stores* is both objectionable and vulgar. *Jewish* is the adjective. The use of *Jew* as a verb, in *to Jew down*, is a slang survival of the medieval term of opprobrium, and should be avoided altogether.
> 5. The word *Hebrew* should not be used instead of *Jew*. As a noun it connotes rather the Jewish people of the distant past, as *the ancient Hebrews*. As an adjective it has an historical rather than a religious connotation; one cannot say *the Hebrew religion*, but *the Jewish religion*.

Unfortunately this temperate and intelligent pronunciamento seems to have had but little effect. Potash and Perlmutter still insist that the papers they support refer to them as *Hebrews,* and the thing is docilely done. In the vaudeville journal, *Variety,* which is owned and edited by a Jew, *Hebrew* is invariably used. I have often observed references to *Hebrew comedians, Hebrew tragedians,* the *Hebrew drama,* the *Hebrew holidays* and even the *Hebrew church*. For an American newspaper to refer to *Jewry* would be almost as hazardous as for it to refer to the *ghetto*. When the New York papers desire to discuss the doings of the Jewish Socialists on the East Side, they are forced to retire behind *East side agitators* or *soap-boxers*. Years ago, being city editor of a newspaper in a large city, I employed a reporter to cover the picturesque and often strikingly dramatic life of the Russian and Polish Jews in its slums. He staggered along for two or three months, trying in vain to invent terms to designate them that would not offend the large Jewish advertisers. Finally, the business office bombarded me with so many complaints that I instructed him to abandon the Jews, and devote himself to the Italians and Bohemians, who were all poor and without influential compatriots uptown.

Save in this one particular I believe that the American newspapers have made appreciable progress toward the use of plain English in recent years. The gaudy style of a generation ago has perished, and with it have vanished its euphemisms—*casket* for *coffin,* *obsequies* for *funeral,* *nuptial ceremony* for *wedding,* *happy pair* for *bridal couple,* and *consigned to earth* for *buried.* A death notice offers an excellent test of a reporter; if he is an idiot he will invariably show it when he writes one. Save in the small towns and in some of the cities of the South—where an aged Methodist sister still "goes to her heavenly father" or "falls asleep in the arms of Jesus"—the newspapers of the Republic now deal with death in a simple and dignified manner. On account of their sharp differentiation between news and editorial opinion, they even avoid the "we regret to announce" with which all English journals begin their reports of eminent dissolutions. Nine-tenths of them are now content to open proceedings by saying baldly that "John Smith died yesterday." Nor do they slobber as they used to over weddings, balls, corner-stone layings and other such ceremonies.

The use of *Madame* as a special title of honor for old women of good position survived in the United States until the 70's. It distinguished the dowager Mrs. Smith from the wife of her eldest son; today the word *dowager,* imitating the English usage, is frequently employed in fashionable society.[45] *Madame* survives among the

---

[45] Mrs. Washington was often called *Lady* Washington during her life-time. But this title seems to have died with her.

colored folk, who almost always apply it to women singers of their race, and often to women hairdressers, dressmakers and milliners also. It is felt to be a shade more distinguished than *Miss* or *Mrs.*, and is applied to married and unmarried women indiscriminately.

5.

Expletives and Forbidden Words

When we come to words that, either intrinsically or by usage, are improper, a great many curious differences between English and American reveal themselves. The Englishman, on the whole, is more plain-spoken than the American, and such terms as *bitch, mare* and *in foal* do not commonly daunt him, largely, perhaps, because of his greater familiarity with country life; but he has a formidable index of his own, and it includes such essentially harmless words as *sick, stomach, bum* and *bug*. The English use of *ill* for *sick* I have already noticed, and the reasons for the English avoidance of *bum*. *Sick,* over there, means nauseated, and when an Englishman says that he was *sick* he means that he vomited, or, as an American would say, was *sick at the stomach*. The older (and still American) usage, however, survives in various compounds. *Sick-list,* for example, is official in the navy,[46] and *sick-leave* is known in the army, though it is more common to say of a soldier that he is *invalided home*. *Sick-room* and *sick-bed* are also in common use, and *sick-flag* is used in place of the American *quarantine-flag*. But an Englishman hesitates to mention his stomach in the presence of ladies, though he discourses freely about his liver. To avoid the necessity he employs such euphemisms as *Little Mary*. As for *bug*, he restricts its use very rigidly to the *Cimex lectularius*, or common bed-bug, and hence the word has highly impolite connotations. All other crawling things he calls *insects*. An American of my acquaintance once greatly offended an English friend by using *bug* for *insect*. The two were playing billiards one summer evening in the Englishman's house, and various flying things came through the window and alighted

[46] *Cf.* Dardanelles Commission Report; London, 1916, p. 56, § 47.

AMERICAN AND ENGLISH TODAY 149

on the cloth. The American, essaying a shot, remarked that he had killed a *bug* with his cue. To the Englishman this seemed a slanderous reflection upon the cleanliness of his house.[47]

The Victorian era saw a great growth of absurd euphemisms in England, including *second wing* for the leg of a fowl, but it was in America that the thing was carried farthest. Bartlett hints that *rooster* came into use in place of *cock* as a matter of delicacy, the latter word having acquired an indecent significance, and tells us that, at one time, even *bull* was banned as too vulgar for refined ears. In place of it the early purists used *cow-creature, male-cow* and even *gentleman-cow*.[48] *Bitch, ram, boar, stallion, buck* and *sow* went the same way, and there was a day when even *mare* was prohibited. Bache tells us that *pismire* was also banned, *antmire* being substituted for it. *To castrate* became *to alter*. In 1847 the word *chair* was actually barred out and *seat* was adopted in its place.[49] These were the palmy days of euphemism. The delicate *female* was guarded from all knowledge, and even from all suspicion, of evil. "To utter aloud in her presence the word *shirt*," says one historian, "was an open insult."[50] Mrs. Trollope, writing in 1832, tells of "a young German gentleman of perfectly good manners" who "offended one of the principal families . . . by having pronounced the word *corset* before the ladies of it."[51] The word *woman*, in those sensitive days, became a term of reproach, comparable to the German *mensch*: the uncouth *female* took its place.[52] In the same way the legs of the fair became *limbs* and their breasts *bosoms*, and *lady*

[47] Edgar Allan Poe's "The Gold *Bug*" is called "The Golden *Beetle*" in England. Twenty-five years ago an Englishman named *Buggey*, laboring under the odium attached to the name, had it changed to *Norfolk-Howard*, a compound made up of the title and family name of the Duke of Norfolk. The wits of London at once doubled his misery by adopting *Norfolk-Howard* as a euphemism for bed-bug.
[48] A recent example of the use of *male-cow* was quoted in the *Journal* of the American Medical Association, Nov. 17, 1917, advertising page 24.
[49] The New York *Organ* (a "family journal devoted to temperance, morality, education and general literature"), May 29, 1847. One of the editors of this delicate journal was T. S. Arthur, author of Ten Nights in a Bar-room.
[50] John Graham Brooks: As Others See Us; New York, 1908, p. 11.
[51] Domestic Manners of the Americans, 2 vols.; London, 1832; vol. i, p. 132.
[52] *Female*, of course, was epidemic in England too, but White says that it was "not a Briticism," and so early as 1839 the Legislature of Maryland expunged it from the title of a bill "to protect the reputation of unmarried *females*," substituting *women*, on the ground that *female* "was an Americanism in that application."

was substituted for *wife*. *Stomach*, under the ban in England, was transformed, by some unfathomable magic, into a euphemism denoting the whole region from the nipples to the pelvic arch. It was during this time that the newspapers invented such locutions as *interesting* (or *delicate*) *condition, criminal operation, house of ill* (or *questionable*) *repute, disorderly-house, sporting-house, statutory offense, fallen woman* and *criminal assault*. Servant girls ceased to be seduced, and began to be *betrayed*. Syphilis became transformed into *blood-poison, specific blood-poison* and *secret disease,* and it and gonorrhea into *social diseases*. Various French terms, *enceinte* and *accouchement* among them, were imported to conceal the fact that careless wives occasionally became pregnant and had lyings-in.

White, between 1867 and 1870, launched several attacks upon these ludicrous gossamers of speech, and particularly upon *enceinte, limb* and *female,* but only *female* succumbed. The passage of the Comstock Postal Act, in 1873, greatly stimulated the search for euphemisms. Once that amazing law was upon the statute-book and Comstock himself was given the inquisitorial powers of a post-office inspector, it became positively dangerous to print certain ancient and essentially decent English words. To this day the effects of that old reign of terror are still visible. We yet use *toilet, retiring-room* and *public comfort station* in place of better terms,[53] and such idiotic forms as *red-light district, disorderly-house, social disease* and *white slave* ostensibly conceal what every flapper is talking about. The word *cadet,* having a foreign smack and an innocent native meaning, is preferred to the more accurate *procurer;* even prostitutes shrink from the forthright *pimp,* and employ a characteristic American abbreviation, *P. I.*—a curious brother to *S. O. B.* and *2 o'clock.* Nevertheless, a movement toward honesty is getting on its legs. The vice crusaders, if they have accomplished nothing else, have at least forced many of the newspapers to use the honest terms, *syphilis, prostitute* and *venereal disease,* albeit somewhat gingerly. It is, perhaps, sig-

---

[53] The French *pissoir,* for instance, is still regarded as indecent in America, and is seldom used in England, but it has gone into most of the Continental languages, though the French themselves avoid it in print, and use the inane *Vespasien* in place of it. But all the Continental languages have their euphemisms. Most of them, for example, use *W. C.,* an abbreviation of the English *water-closet,* as a euphemism. The whole subject of national pruderies, in both act and speech, remains to be investigated.

nificant of the change going on that the New York *Evening Post* recently authorized its reporters to use *street-walker*.[54] But in certain quarters the change is viewed with alarm, and curious traces of the old prudery still survive. The Department of Health of New York City, in April, 1914, announced that its efforts to diminish venereal disease were much handicapped because "in most newspaper offices the words *syphilis* and *gonorrhea* are still tabooed, and without the use of these terms it is almost impossible to correctly state the problem." The Army Medical Corps, in the early part of 1918, encountered the same difficulty: most newspapers refused to print its bulletins regarding venereal disease in the army. One of the newspaper trade journals thereupon sought the opinions of editors upon the subject, and all of them save one declared against the use of the two words. One editor put the blame upon the Post-office, which still cherishes the Comstock tradition. Another reported that "at a recent conference of the Scripps Northwest League editors" it was decided that "the use of such terms as *gonorrhea, syphilis,* and even *venereal diseases* would not add to the tone of the papers, and that the term *vice diseases* can be readily substituted."[55] The Scripps papers are otherwise anything but distinguished for their "tone," but in this department they yield to the Puritan habit. They are not alone; even some of the New York papers remain squeamish. On April 29, 1919, for example, the New York *Tribune* printed an article quoting with approbation a declaration by Major W. A. Wilson, of the Division of Venereal Control in the Merchant Marine, that "the only way to carry on the campaign (*i. e.,* against venereal disease) is to look the evil squarely in the face and fight it openly," and yet the word *venereal* was carefully avoided throughout the article, save in the place where Major Wilson's office was mentioned. Whereupon a medical journal made the following comment:

The words "the only way to carry on the campaign is to look the evil squarely in the face and fight it openly" are true, but how has the *Tribune* met the situation? Its subhead speaks of *preventable disease;* in the first paragraph *social diseases* are mentioned; elsewhere it alludes to *certain dangerous diseases, com-*

[54] Even the Springfield *Republican,* the last stronghold of Puritan *Kultur,* printed the word on Oct. 11, 1917, in a review of New Adventures, by Michael Monahan.
[55] *Pep,* July, 1918, p. 8.

municable diseases and *diseases*, but nowhere in the entire article does it come out with the plain and precise designation of syphilis and gonorrhea as *venereal diseases*. The height of absurdity is reached in the *Tribune's* last paragraph. Presumably it wants to say that venereals are being kept in France until cured; but being too polite to say what it means, it makes a very sweeping statement indeed. Flat feet are a *preventable disease*, but the *Tribune* can hardly suppose that no soldier with flat feet is allowed to return home until he has been cured.[56]

Alas, even medical men yet show some of the old prudery. I am informed by Dr. Morris Fishbein, of the *Journal* of the American Medical Association, that not a few of them, in communications to their colleagues, still state the fact that a patient has syphilis by saying that he has a *specific stomach* or a *specific ulcer,* and that the *Journal* lately received a paper discussing the question, "Can a positive woman have a negative baby?"—*i.e.,* can a woman with a positive Wassermann, indicating syphilis, have a baby free from the disease? But a far more remarkable example of American prudery—this time among laymen—came to my notice in Philadelphia some years ago. A one-act play of mine, "The Artist," was presented at the Little Theatre there, and during its run, on February 26, 1916, the *Public Ledger* reprinted some of the dialogue. One of the characters in the piece is *A Virgin.* At every occurrence a change was made to *A Young Girl.* Apparently, even *virgin* is still regarded as too frank in Philadelphia.[57] Fifty years ago the word *decent* was indecent in the South: no respectable woman was supposed to have any notion of the difference between *decent* and *indecent.* To this day many essentially harmless words and phrases are avoided in conversation because they have acquired obscene significances. The adjective *knocked up,* so common in England, means pregnant in America, and is thus not used politely. American women use *unwell* in a certain indelicate significance, and hence avoid its use generally. In Kansas, I am informed, even *bag* is under the ban; when they hear it out there they always think of *scrotum.*[58]

[56] *Social Hygiene Bulletin,* May, 1919, p. 7.
[57] Perhaps the Quaker influence is to blame. At all events, Philadelphia is the most pecksniffian of American cities, and thus probably leads the world. Early in 1918, when a patriotic moving-picture entitled "To Hell with the Kaiser" was sent on tour under government patronage, the word *hell* was carefully toned down, on the Philadelphia billboards, to *h*——.
[58] I do not go into nursery euphemisms. They are very numerous, and deserve investigation. It is my observation that they differ considerably in different parts of the country.

AMERICAN AND ENGLISH TODAY 153

In their vocabularies of opprobrium and profanity English and Americans diverge sharply. The English *mucker, rotter* and *blighter* are practically unknown in America, and there are various American equivalents that are never heard in England. A *guy,* in the American vulgate, simply signifies a man; there is not necessarily any disparaging significance. But in English, high or low, it means one who is making a spectacle of himself. When G. K. Chesterton toured the United States, in 1920-21, "some reporter in the West referred to him as a *regular guy.* At first Mr. Chesterton was for going after the fellow with a stick. Certainly a topsy-turvy land, the United States, where you can't tell opprobrium from flattering compliment." [59] The American derivative verb, *to guy,* is unknown in English; its nearest equivalent is *to spoof,* which is used in the United States only as a conscious Briticism. The average American, I believe, has a larger profane vocabulary than the average Englishman, and swears rather more, but he attempts an amelioration of many of his oaths by softening them to forms with no apparent meaning. *Darn* (= *dern* = *durn*) for *damn* is apparently of English origin, but it is heard ten thousand times in America to once in England. So is *dog-gone.* Such euphemistic written forms as *damphool, helluva* and *damfino* are also far more common in this country.[60] *All-fired* for *hell-fired, gee-whiz* for *Jesus, tarnal* for *eternal, tarnation* for *damnation, cuss* for *curse, holy gee* for *holy Jesus, cussword* for *curse-word, goldarned* for *God-damned, by gosh* for *by God, great Scott* for *great God,* and *what'ell* for *what the hell* are all Americanisms; Thornton has traced *all-fired* to 1835, *tarnation* to 1801 and *tarnal* to 1790; Tucker says that *blankety* is also American. *By golly* has been found in England so early as 1843, but it probably originated in America; down to the Civil War it was the char-

[59] Murray Hill Bids Mr. Chesterton Goodby, *Bookman,* June 21, 1921, p. 309.
[60] Both of the great American telegraph companies have rules strictly forbidding the acceptance of telegrams containing profane words. Some time ago a telegram of mine containing the harmless adjective *damndest* was refused by both. I appealed to the higher authorities of the Western Union. After I had solemnly filed a brief in defense of the term, Mr. T. W. Carroll, general manager of the Eastern Division, as solemnly decided that the company "must take the position that, if there is any question or doubt on the subject, the safest plan is to request the sender to so modify his language as to make his message acceptable." In other words, any locution which happens to scratch the prudery of a telegraph clerk (however imbecile) must be omitted.

acteristic oath of the negro slaves. Such terms as *bonehead, pinhead* and *boob* have been invented, perhaps, to take the place of the English *ass,* which has a flavor of impropriety in America on account of its identity in sound with the American pronunciation of *arse.*[61] At an earlier day *ass* was always differentiated by making it *jackass.* Another word that is improper in America but not in England is *tart,* a clipped form of *sweetheart.* To a Londoner the word connotes sweetness, and so, if he be of the lower orders, he may apply it to his best girl. But to the American it signifies a prostitute, or, at all events, a woman of too ready an amiability. However, it is also of a disparaging significance in several of the English provincial dialects.

An English correspondent, resident in the United States for half a dozen years, tells me that many American expletives seem to him to be of Irish origin. *Son-of-a-bitch,* and its euphemistic American daughter, *son-of-a-gun,* are very seldom heard in England. "True oaths," says this correspondent, "are rather rare among the English. There are a number of ugly words, probably descendants of true religious oaths, and a few that are merely dirty, and beyond that practically nothing. Sound rather than significance, it appears, gives a word evil qualities. Men have been put in jail for using meaningless words. There is, however, the same tendency to euphemism as in America. Just as *God damn* becomes *gol darn* here, *Christ* becomes *crikey* there. *God damn* is rare in England, and Englishmen say 'I don't *care* a damn' much more often than 'I don't *give* a damn.' *Jesus* is never used as an oath, and I never met any of the charming ones beginning with 'Holy, jumping, bandy-legged, sacrificing . . .' until I came to America. A Trinity College man here tells me the Irish don't say *Jesus;* but he is the son of a schoolmaster. Without *Jesus* there could be no *bejabers.* In England, as I say, *damn* usually stands alone. *God damn* seemed as quaint as *egad* or *odsblood* when I heard it first. I had climbed into a hayloft without a ladder, and my dear father remarked that one of these days I would break my *God damned* neck. I think my father, too, realized the quaintness of the oath; usually he, like any

[61] *Cf.* R. M. Bache: Vulgarisms and Other Errors of Speech; Phila., 1869, p. 34 *ff.*

Englishman, would have said *bloody*. The word *Christer* has two meanings in England. It is used by printers to designate an exclamation point, and by other people in a sense which I can best explain by illustration. A Harvard professor, an Englishman, was discussing a certain English journalist then in this country, and he said to me: 'Oh, he's a simply fearful *Christer;* preaches in chapel every Sunday, and all that.' " *Dirt,* to designate earth, and *closet,* in the sense of a cupboard are seldom used by an Englishman. The former always suggests filth to him, and the latter has obtained the limited sense of *water-closet.*

But the most curious disparity between the profane vocabulary of the two tongues is presented by *bloody*. This word is entirely without improper significance in America, but in England it is regarded as the vilest of indecencies. The sensation produced in London when George Bernard Shaw put it into the mouth of a woman character in his play, "Pygmalion," will be remembered. "The interest in the first English performance," said the New York *Times*,[62] "centered in the heroine's utterance of this banned word. It was waited for with trembling, heard shudderingly, and presumably, when the shock subsided, interest dwindled." But in New York, of course, it failed to cause any stir. Just why it is regarded as profane and indecent by the English is one of the mysteries of the language. It came in during the latter half of the seventeenth century, and remained innocuous for 200 years. Then it suddenly acquired its present abhorrent significance. Two etymologies have been proposed for it. By the one it is held to be synonymous with "in the manner of a *blood*," *i. e.,* of a rich young roisterer; this would make *bloody drunk* equivalent to *as drunk as a lord.* The other derives it from *by our Lady.*[63] But both theories obviously fail to account for its present disrepute. *As drunk as a lord* would certainly not offend English susceptibilities, and neither would *by our Lady.* An Englishwoman once told me that it grated upon her ears because it somehow suggested catamenia; perhaps this affords a clue to the current aversion to it among the polite. It is

[a] April 14, 1914. In 1920 the English Licenser of Stage Plays ordered *bloody* expunged from a play dealing with labor. *Cf. English*, Oct., 1920, p. 403.
[63] Swift, in his Journal to Stella, says: "It grows *by 'r Lady* cold, and I have no waistcoat on."

used incessantly by the English lower classes; they have even invented an intensive, *bleeding*. So familiar has it become, in fact, that it is a mere counter-word, without intelligible significance. A familiar story illustrates this. Two Yorkshire miners are talking. "What do they mean," asks one, "by one man, one vote?" "Why," is the reply, "it means one bloody man, one bloody vote."

So far no work devoted wholly to the improper terms of English and American has been published, but this lack will soon be remedied by a compilation made by a Chicago journalist. It is entitled "The Slang of Venery and Its Analogues," and runs to two large volumes. A small edition, mimeographed for private circulation, was issued in 1916. I have examined this work and found it of great value.

V.

INTERNATIONAL EXCHANGES

1.

Americanisms in England

More than once, during the preceding chapters, we encountered Americanisms that had gone over into English, and English locutions that had begun to get a foothold in the United States. Such exchanges are made frequently and often very quickly, and though the guardians of English, as we saw in Chapter I, Section 3, still attack every new Americanism vigorously, even when, as in the case of *scientist,* it is obviously sound, or, as in the case of *joy-ride,* it is irresistibly picturesque, they are often routed by public pressure, and have to submit in the end with the best grace possible.

For example, consider *caucus.* It originated in Boston at some indeterminate time before 1750, and remained so peculiarly American for more than a century following that most of the English visitors before the Civil War remarked its use. But, according to J. Redding Ware,[1] it began to creep into English political slang about 1870, and in the 80's it was lifted to good usage by the late Joseph Chamberlain. Ware, writing in the first years of the present century, said that the word had become "very important" in England, but was "not admitted into dictionaries." But in the Concise Oxford Dictionary, dated 1914, and in Cassell's New English Dictionary, published five years later, it is given as a sound English word, though its American origin is noted. The English, however, use it in a sense that has become archaic in America, thus preserving an abandoned American meaning in the same way that many abandoned British meanings have been preserved on this side. In the

[1] Passing English of the Victorian Era; London, n. d., p. 68.

United States the word means, and has meant for years, a meeting of some division, large or small, of a political or legislative body for the purpose of agreeing upon a united course of action in the main assembly. In England it means the managing committee of a party or fraction—something corresponding to our national committee, or state central committee, or steering committee, or to the half-forgotten congressional caucuses of the 20's. It has a disparaging significance over there, almost equal to that of our words *organization* and *machine*. Moreover, it has given birth to two derivatives of like quality, both unknown in America—*caucusdom*, meaning machine control, and *caucuser*, meaning a machine politician.[2]

A good many other such Americanisms have got into good usage in England, and new ones are being exported constantly. Farmer describes the process of their introduction and assimilation. American books, newspapers and magazines, especially the last, circulate in England in large number, and some of their characteristic locutions strike the English fancy and are repeated in conversation. Then they get into print, and begin to take on respectability. "The phrase, 'as the Americans say,'" he continues, "might in some cases be ordered from the type foundry as a logotype, so frequently does it do introduction duty."[3] Ware shows another means of ingress: the argot of sailors. Many of the Americanisms he notes as having become naturalized in England, *e. g., boodle, boost* and *walk-out,* are credited to Liverpool as a sort of half-way station. Travel brings in still more: England swarms with Americans, and Englishmen themselves, visiting America, are struck by the new and racy phrases that they hear, and afterward take them home and try them on their friends. The English authors who burden every westbound ship, coming here to lecture, have especially sharp ears for

[2] The Concise Oxford Dictionary and Cassell, following the late J. H. Trumbull, the well-known authority on Indian languages, derive the word from the Algonquin *cau-cau-as-u* or *kaw-kaw-asu*, one who advises. But most other authorities, following Pickering, derive it from *caulkers*. The first caucuses, it would appear, were held in a caulkers' shop in Boston, and were called *caulkers' meetings*. The Rev. William Gordon, in his History of the Rise and Independence of the United States, Including the Late War, published in London in 1788, said that "more than fifty years ago Mr. Samuel Adams' father and twenty others, one or two from the north end of the town [Boston], where the ship business is carried on, used to meet, make a caucus and lay their plans for introducing certain persons into places of trust and power."

[3] Americanisms Old and New; p. vii.

such neologisms, and always use them when they get home—often, as we shall see, inaccurately. Dickens was the first of these visitors to carry back that sort of cargo; according to Bishop Coxe [4] he gave currency in England, in his "American Notes," to *reliable, influential, talented* and *lengthy*. Bristed, writing in 1855, said that *talented* was already firmly fixed in the English vocabulary by that time. All four words are in the Concise Oxford Dictionary, and only *lengthy* is noted as "originally an Americanism." Cassell lists them without any remark at all; they have been thoroughly assimilated. Finally, there is the influence of American plays and moving pictures. Hundreds of American films are shown in England every week, and the American words and phrases appearing in their titles, sub-titles and other explanatory legends thus become familiar to the English. "The patron of the picture palace," says W. G. Faulkner, in an article in the London *Daily Mail*, "learns to think of his railway station as a *depot;* he has alternatives to one of our newest words, *hooligan,* in *hoodlum* and *tough;* he watches a *dive,* which is a thieves' kitchen or a room in which bad characters meet, and whether the villain talks of *dough* or *sugar* he knows it is money to which he is referring. The musical ring of the word *tramp* gives way to the stodgy *hobo* or *dead-beat*. It may be that the plot reveals an attempt to deceive some simple-minded person. If it does, the innocent one is spoken of as a *sucker,* a *come-on,* a *boob,* or a *lobster* if he is stupid in the bargain."

Mr. Faulkner goes on to say that a great many other Americanisms are constantly employed by Englishmen "who have not been affected by the avalanche . . . which has come upon us through the picture palace." "Thus today," he says, "we hear people speak of the *fall* of the year, a *stunt* they have in hand, their desire to *boost* a particular business, a *peach* when they mean a pretty girl, a *scab*—a common term among strikers—the *glad-eye, junk* when they mean worthless material, their efforts *to make good,* the *elevator* in the hotel or office, the *boss* or manager, the *crook* or swindler; and they will tell you that they have the *goods*—that is, they possess the requisite qualities for a given position." The venerable Frederic Harri-

[4] A. Cleveland Coxe: Americanisms in England, *Forum*, Oct., 1886.

son, writing in the *Fortnightly Review* in the Spring of 1918, denounced this tendency with a vigor recalling the classical anathemas of Dean Alford and Sydney Smith.[5] "Stale American phrases, . . . " he said, "are infecting even our higher journalism and our parliamentary and platform oratory. . . . A statesman is now *out* for victory; he is *up against* pacificism. . . . He has *a card up his sleeve,* by which the enemy are at last to be *euchred.* Then a fierce fight in which hundreds of noble fellows are mangled or drowned is a *scrap.* . . . To criticise a politician is to call for his *scalp.* . . . The other fellow is beaten to a *frazzle."* And so on. "Bolshevism," concluded Harrison sadly, "is ruining language as well as society." Other watchmen have often sounded the same alarm, sometimes in very acrimonious terms. "Thou callest trousers *pants,"* roared Samuel Butler in his "Psalm to Montreal," "whereas I call them *trousers;* therefore thou art in hell-fire and may the Lord pity thee!"[6]

But though there are many such protests, the majority of Englishmen make borrowings from the tempting and ever-widening American vocabulary, and many of these loan-words take root, and are presently accepted as sound English, even by the most squeamish. The two Fowlers, in "The King's English," separate Americanisms from other current vulgarisms, but many of the latter on their list, in the sense indicated, are actually American in origin, though they do not seem to know it—for example, *to demean* and *to transpire.* More remarkable still, the Cambridge History of English Literature lists *backwoodsman, know-nothing* and *yellow-back* as English compounds, apparently in forgetfulness of their American origin, and adds *skunk, squaw* and *toboggan* as direct importations from the Indian tongues, without noting that they came through American, and remained definite Americanisms for a long while.[7] It even adds *musquash,* a popular name for the *Fiber zibethicus,* borrowed from the Algonquin *mushwessu* but long since degenerated to *muskrat* in America. *Musquash* has been in disuse in this country, indeed, since the middle of the last century, save as a stray localism,

---

[5] Reprinted, in part, in the New York *Sun,* May 12, 1918.
[6] The Note-Books of Samuel Butler; New York, 1917, p. 389.
[7] Vol. xiv, pp. 507, 512.

but the English have preserved it, and it appears in the Oxford Dictionary.[8] A few weeks in London or a month's study of the London newspapers will show a great many other American pollutions of the well of English. The argot of politics is full of them. Many beside *caucus* were introduced by Joseph Chamberlain, a politician skilled in American campaign methods and with an American wife to prompt him. He gave the English their first taste of *to belittle,* one of the inventions of Thomas Jefferson. *Graft* and *to graft* crossed the ocean in their nonage. *To bluff* has been well understood in English for 30 years. It is in Cassell's and the Oxford Dictionaries, and has been used by no less a magnifico than Sir Almroth Wright.[9] *To stump,* in the form of *stump-oratory,* is in Carlyle's "Latter-Day Pamphlets," published in 1850, and *caucus* appears in his "Frederick the Great,"[10] though, as we have seen on the authority of Ware, it did not come into general use in England until ten years later. *Buncombe* (usually spelled *bunkum*) is in all the later English dictionaries. *Gerrymander* is in H. G. Wells' "Outline of History."[11] In the London stock market and among English railroad men various characteristic Americanisms have got a foothold. The meaning of *bucket-shop* and *to water,* for example, is familiar to every London broker's clerk. English trains are now *telescoped* and carry *dead-heads,* and in 1913 a rival to the Amalgamated Order of Railway *Servants* was organized under the name of the National Union of *Railway Men.* The beginnings of a movement against the use of *servant* are visible in other directions, and the American *help* threatens to be substituted; at all events, *Help*

[8] In this connection it is curious to note that, though the raccoon is an animal quite unknown in England, there was, during the Great War, a destroyer called the *Raccoon* in the British Navy. This ship was lost with all hands off the Irish coast, Jan. 9, 1918.
[9] The Unexpurgated Case Against Woman Suffrage; London, 1913, p. 9. *To bluff* has also gone into other languages. During the Cuban revolution of March, 1917, the newspapers of Havana, objecting to the dispatches sent out by American correspondents, denounced the latter as *los blofistas*. It has also got into German, and has been used in a formal speech by Herr von Bethmann-Hollweg. Meanwhile, *to bluff* was once shouldered out in the country of its origin, at least temporarily, by a verb borrowed from the French, *to camouflage*. This first appeared in the Spring of 1917. It was, however, quickly done to death, and so *to bluff* was revived.
[10] Book iv, ch. iii. The first of the six volumes was published in 1858 and the last in 1865.
[11] Vol. i, p. 496; New York, 1920.

Wanted advertisements are now occasionally encountered in English newspapers. But it is American verbs that seem to find the way into English least difficult, particularly those compounded with prepositions and adverbs, such as *to pan out* and *to swear off*. Most of them, true enough, are still used as conscious Americanisms, but used they are, and with increasing frequency. The highly typical American verb *to loaf* is now naturalized, and Ware says that *The Loaferies* is one of the common nicknames of the Whitechapel workhouse. Both the Concise Oxford and Cassell list *to loaf* without mentioning its American origin. The former says that its etymology is "dubious" and the latter that it is "doubtful."

It is curious, reading the fulminations of American purists of the last generation, to note how many of the Americanisms they denounced have not only got into perfectly good usage at home but even broken down all guards across the ocean. *To placate* and *to antagonize* are examples. The Concise Oxford and Cassell distinguish between the English and American meanings of the latter: in England a man may antagonize only another man, in America he may antagonize a mere idea or thing. But, as the brothers Fowler show, even the English meaning is of American origin, and no doubt a few more years will see the verb completely naturalized in Britain. *To placate*, attacked vigorously by all native grammarians down to (but excepting) White, now has the authority of the *Spectator*, and is accepted by Cassell. *To donate* is still under the ban, but *to transpire* has been used by the London *Times*. Other old bugaboos that have been embraced are *gubernatorial, presidential* and *standpoint*. White labored long and valiantly to convince Americans that the adjective derived from *president* should be without the *i* before its last syllable, following the example of *incidental, regimental, monumental, governmental, oriental, experimental* and so on; but in vain, for *presidential* is now perfectly good English. *To demean* is still questioned by purists, but Cassell accepts it. English authors of the first rank have used it, and it will probably lose its dubious character very soon. *To engineer, to collide, to corner, to aggravate, to obligate,* and *to lynch* are in Cassell with no hint of their American origin, and so are *home-spun, out-house, cross-purposes, green-horn, blizzard, excursionist, wash-stand* and *wash-*

basin, though *wash-hand-stand* and *wash-hand-basin* are also given. *To boom, to boost* and *to boss* are listed as Americanisms; so are *highfalutin, skeedaddle* and *flat-footed.* But *to donate* and *to feature* are not there at all, and neither are *non-committal, bay-window, semi-occasional, square-meal, back-number, spondulix, back-yard, stag-party, derby* (hat) and *trained-nurse.* *Drug-store* is slowly making its way in England; the firm known as Botts Cash Chemists uses the term to designate its branches. But it is not yet listed by either Cassell or the Concise Oxford, though both give *druggist.* L. Pearsall Smith adds *platform* (political), *interview, faith-healing, co-education* and *cake-walk.*[12] Cassell says that *letter-carrier* is obsolete in England and that *pay-day* is used only on the Stock Exchange there. *Tenderfoot* is creeping in, though the English commonly mistake it for an Australianism; it is used by the English Boy Scouts just as our own Boy Scouts use it. *Scalawag,* characteristically, has got into English with an extra *l,* making it *scallawag.* *Rambunctious* is not in any of the new English dictionaries, but in Cassell I find *rumbustious,* probably its father.

It is easy to overestimate the importance of these exportations, and of the transient slang-phrases that go with them. It takes a long while for one of them to become thoroughly naturalized in England, and even then the business is commonly achieved only at the cost of a change in meaning or spelling. To the Englishman Americanisms continue to show an abhorrent quality, even after he has begun to use them; he never feels quite at ease in their use, and so he seldom uses them correctly. When, a few years ago, the English borrowed the highly characteristic American phrase, *I should worry* (probably borrowed by American, in turn, from the Yiddish), they changed it absurdly into *I should not worry.* In the same way they confused the two Americanisms, *gink* and *jinx,* and so produced the bastard *ginx.*[13] Perhaps their inability to understand the generality of Americanisms or to enter naturally into the spirit of the language helps to explain the common American notion that they are dull-pated

---

[12] *English,* Oct., 1919, p. 177. He also adds *table-turning* and *yellow-press.* The first is a characteristic modification of the American *table-tapping* and the latter of *yellow-journalism.* See also Words on Trial, by T. Michael Pope, *English,* Sept., 1919, pp. 150-1.
[13] *English,* Sept., 1919, p. 151.

and unable to appreciate a joke. Certain it is that very few of their authors, even after the most careful preparation, show any capacity for writing American in a realistic manner. A proof of it is offered by the English novelist, W. L. George, in a chapter entitled "Litany of the Novelist" in his book of criticism, "Literary Chapters." [14] George has been in the United States, knows many Americans, and is here addressing Americans and trying to help out their comprehension by a studied use of purely American phrases. One hears, not of the *East End,* but of the *East Side;* not of the *City,* but of *Wall Street;* not of *Belgravia* or the *West End,* but of *Fifth avenue;* not of *bowler* hats, but of *derbys;* not of idlers in *pubs,* but of *saloon loafers;* not of *pounds, shillings* and *pence,* but of *dollars* and *cents.* In brief, a gallant attempt upon a strange tongue, and by a writer of the utmost skill—but a hopeless failure none the less. In the midst of his best American, George drops into Briticism after Briticism, some of them quite as unintelligible to the average American reader as so many Gallicisms. On page after page they display the practical impossibility of the enterprise: *back-garden* for *back-yard, perambulator* for *baby-carriage, corn-market* for *grain-market, coal-owner* for *coal-operator, post* for *mail,* and so on. And to top them there are English terms that have no American equivalents at all, for example, *kitchen-fender.* In other chapters of the same book his blunders are even worse: *petrol* and *cruet* most certainly puzzle many of his American readers.

Nor is he alone. Every English author who attempts to render the speech of American characters makes a mess of it. H. G. Wells' American in "Mr. Britling Sees It Through" is only matched by G. K. Chesterton's in "Man Alive." Even Kipling, who submitted the manuscript of "Captain Courageous" to American friends for criticism, yet managed to make an American in it say "He's *by way of being* a fisherman now." The late Frank M. Bicknell once amassed some amusing examples of this unanimous failing.[15] Max Pemberton, in a short story dealing with an American girl's visit to England, makes her say: "I'm right glad. . . . You're as pale as spectres, I guess. . . . Fancy that, now! . . . You are my guest, I

[14] Boston, 1918, pp. 1-43.
[15] The Yankee in British Fiction, *Outlook,* Nov. 19, 1910.

reckon, . . . and here you are, my word!" C. J. Cutcliffe Hyne, in depicting a former American naval officer, makes him speak of *saloon-corner men* (*corner-loafers?*). E. W. Hornung, in one of his "Raffles" stories, introduces an American prize-fighter who goes to London and regales the populace with such things as these: "Blamed if our Bowery boys ain't cock-angels to scum like this. . . . By the holy tinker! . . . Blight and blister him! . . . I guess I'll punch his face into a jam pudding. . . . Say, sonny, I like you a lot, but I sha'n't like you if you're not a good boy." The American use of *way* and *away* seems to have daunted many of the authors quoted by Mr. Bicknell; several of them agree on forms that are certainly never heard in the United States. Thus H. B. Marriott Watson makes an American character say: "You ought to have done business with me *away* in Chicago," and Walter Frith makes another say: "He has gone *way* off to Holborn," "I stroll a block or two *way* down the Strand," "I'll drive him *way* down home by easy stages," and "He can pack his grip and be *way* off home."

Various other American critics have noted similar and even worse solecisms in the current English novels, and one of them, Miss Anna Branson Hillyard, once offered publicly in the *Athenæum* [16] to undertake the revision of English manuscripts for "fees carefully and inversely scaled by the consultant's importance." Miss Hillyard, in this article, cited a curious misunderstanding of American by the late Rupert Brooke. When Brooke was in the United States he sent a letter to the *Westminster Gazette* containing the phrase "You bet your——." The editor, unable to make anything of it, inserted the word *boots* in place of the dash. Brooke thereupon wrote a letter to a friend, Edward Marsh, complaining of this mauling of his Americanism, and Marsh afterward printed it in his memoir of the poet. Miss Hillyard says that she was long puzzled by this alleged Americanism, and wondered where Brooke had picked it up. Finally, "light dawned by way of a comic cartoon. It was the classic phrase, *you betcha* (accent heavily on the *bet*) which Brooke was spelling conventionally!" And, as Miss Hillyard shows, incorrectly, as usual, for *you betcha* is not a collision form of "you bet *your*" but a collision form of "you bet *you*"—an imitative second

[16] American Written Here, Dec. 19, 1919, p. 1362.

person of "I bet you," which in comic-cartoon circles is pronounced and spelled "I *betcha.*" [17]

I doubt that the war gave much new currency to Americanisms among the English. The fact is that the American and British troops were seldom on the best of terms, and so fraternized very little. Cassell's New English Dictionary, published in 1919, lists a number of words borrowed by the British from the Americans, among them *cold-feet, delicatessen, guy* (noun), *high-brow, hobo, jitney, hot-stuff, jazz, joy-ride, milk-shake, movies, pronto, tangle-foot, to make good, to hike,* and *to frazzle,* but not many of them were in general use. Cassell lists *chautauquan* but not *chautauqua,* and converts the American *dub* into *dud.* A correspondent who was an officer in the American army writes:

> I was with an American division brigaded with the British. The chief result seemed to be the adoption of a common unit of swearing, but probably even this had been arrived at independently. The passage of all the American troops that went through Liverpool, which was near-American before the war, didn't make much difference. I had to get some shoes while I was on furlough there after the armistice, and although I was in my American uniform, a fact that should have made the nature of the shoes demanded doubly sure, they brought out a pair of low shoes.

2.

Briticisms in the United States

Nor did the American troops pick up many Briticisms during their year and a half in France, save temporarily. In an exhaustive and valuable vocabulary of soldiers' slang compiled by E. A. Hecker and Edmund Wilson, Jr., I can find few words or phrases that seem to be certainly English in origin. *To carry on* retains in American its old American meaning of to raise a pother, despite its widespread use among the English in the sense of to be (in American) *on the job.* Even *to wangle,* perhaps the most popular of all the new verbs brought out of the war by the English, has never got a

---

[17] See also Novelists Far Afield, New York *Evening Post* (editorial), May 6, 1919.

INTERNATIONAL EXCHANGES 167

foothold in the United States, and would be unintelligible to nine Americans out of ten.

It is on far higher and less earthly planes that Briticisms make their entry into American, and are esteemed and cultivated. Because the United States has failed to develop a native aristocracy of settled position and authority, there is still an almost universal tendency here, among folk of social pretensions, to defer to English usage and opinion.[18] The English court, in fact, still remains the only fount of honor that such persons know, and its valuations of both men and customs take precedence of all native valuations. I can't imagine any fashionable American who would not be glad to accept even so curious an English aristocrat as Lord Reading or Lord Birkenhead at his face value, and to put him at table above a United States Senator. This emulation is visible in all the minutiæ of social intercourse in America—in the hours chosen for meals, in the style of personal correspondence, in wedding customs, in the ceremonials incidental to entertaining, and in countless other directions. It even extends to the use of the language.[19] We have seen how, even so early as Webster's time, the intransigent Loyalists of what Schele de Vere calls "Boston and the Boston dependencies" imitated the latest English fashions in pronunciation, and how this imitation continues to our own day. New York is but little behind, and with the affectation of what is regarded as English pronunciation there goes a constant borrowing of new English words and phrases,

[18] The curious who desire to pursue this subject will find it discussed at greater length in the essay, The National Letters, in my Prejudices: Second Series; New York, 1920, and in my preface to The American Credo, by George Jean Nathan and me; New York, 1920.

[19] Sometimes this colonialism goes to amusing lengths. During the Summer of 1921 a reviewer in the London *Times* was troubled by the word *hick*, used in a book by my associate, George Jean Nathan. At once an American woman novelist, Roof by name, dispatched a long letter to the *Times*, denouncing this *hick* as "middle class" slang from the West, hinting that such barbarisms were deliberately given circulation by "the German-speaking Jewish population of New York," assuring the editor that her own ancestors "came to America in 1620," and offering him a pledge that she would never cease to "adhere to the King's English." This letter, which appeared in the *Times* on July 14, was quoted with approbation by the *Christian Science Monitor*, the organ of New England *Kultur*, on Aug. 14. But already on July 21 the *Times* had printed a letter from William Archer showing that *hick* was actually perfectly sound English, and that it could be found in Steele's comedy, "The Funeral." Two weeks later, a Norwegian philologist, S. N. Baral, followed with a letter showing that *hick* was connected with the Anglo-Saxon *haeg*, indicating a menial or lout, and that it had cognates in all the ancient Teutonic languages, and even in Sanskrit!

particularly of the sort currently heard in the West End of London. The small stores in the vicinity of Fifth avenue, for some years past, have all been turning themselves into *shops*. Shoes for the persons who shop in that region are no longer *shoes*, but *boots*, and they are sold by *bootmakers* in *bootshops*. One encounters, too, in Fifth avenue and the streets adjacent, a multitude of *gift-shops*, *tea-shops*, *haberdashery-shops*, *book-shops*, *luggage-shops*, *hat-shops* and *print-shops*. Every apartment-house in New York has a *tradesmen's entrance*. *To Let* signs have become almost as common, at least in the East, as *For Rent* signs. *Railway* has begun to displace *railroad*.[20] *Charwoman* has been adopted all over the country, and we have begun to forget our native modification of *char*, to wit, *chore*. Long ago *drawing-room* was borrowed by the *haut ton* to take the place of *parlor*, and *hired girls* began to be *maids*. *Whip* for *driver*, *stick* for *cane*, *top-hat* for *high-hat*, and *to tub* for *to bathe* came in long ago, and *guard* has been making a struggle against *conductor* in New York for years. In August, 1917, signs appeared in the New York surface cars in which the conductors were referred to as *guards*; all of them are *guards* on the elevated lines and in the subways save the forward men, who remain *conductors* officially. In Charles street in Baltimore, some time ago, the proprietor of a fashionable stationery store directed me, not to the elevator but to the *lift*. During the war even the government seemed inclined to substitute the English *hoarding* for the American *billboard*.[21] In the Federal Reserve Act it actually borrowed the English *governor* to designate the head of a bank.

The influence of the stage is largely responsible for the introduction and propagation of such Briticisms. Of plays dealing with fashionable life, most of those seen in the United States are of English origin, and many of them are played by English companies. Thus the social aspirants of the towns become familiar with the standard English pronunciation of the moment and with the current English phrases. It was by this route, I suppose, that *old top* and

---

[20] Evacustes A. Phipson, an Englishman, says in *Dialect Notes*, vol. i, p. 432, that *railway* "appears to be a concession to Anglomania."

[21] See p. 58 of The United States at War, a pamphlet issued by the Library of Congress, 1917. The compiler of this pamphlet was a savant bearing the fine old British name of Herman H. B. Meyer.

its analogues got in. The American actors, having no court to imitate, content themselves by imitating their English colleagues. Thus an American of fashionable pretensions, say in Altoona, Pa., or Athens, Ga., shakes hands, eats soup, greets his friends, enters a drawing-room and pronounces the words *path, secretary, melancholy* and *necessarily* in a manner that is an imitation of some American actor's imitation of an English actor's imitation of what is done in Mayfair—in brief, an imitation in the fourth degree. No wonder it is sometimes rather crude. This crudity is especially visible in speech habits. The American actor does his best to imitate the pronunciation and intonation of the English, but inasmuch as his name, before he became Gerald Cecil, was probably Rudolph Goetz or Terence Googan, he frequently runs aground upon laryngeal impossibilities. Here we have an explanation of the awful fist that society folk in Des Moines and Little Rock make of pronouncing the test words in the authentic English manner. All such words are filtered through Gaelic or Teutonic or Semitic gullets before they reach the ultimate consumer.

The influence of the Protestant Episcopal Church is also to be taken into account. It was the center of Loyalism during the Revolution, and it has fostered a passionate and often excessive Anglomania ever since. In the larger American cities entrance into it is the aim of all social pushers—including, of late, even the Jews [22] —and once they get in they adopt, in so far as they are able, the terminology of its clergy, whose eagerness to appear English is traditional. The fashionable preparatory schools for boys and finishing schools for girls, many of which are directly controlled by this sect, are also very active centers of Anglomania, and have firmly established such Briticisms as *headmaster, varsity, chapel* (for the service as well as the building), *house-master, old boy, monitor, honors, prefect* and *form*, at least in fashionable circles. The late Woodrow Wilson, during his term as president of Princeton, gave currency to various other English academic terms, including *preceptor* and

---

[22] Jews desiring to abandon Moses formerly embraced Christian Science, but of late the more wealthy of them have been taking bold headers into the Anglican communion, especially in New York. I am informed that one of the most fashionable Episcopal churches there has several Jews in its vestry. When I asked for a list of its vestrymen the rector refused it.

quad, but the words died with his reforms. At such schools as Groton and Lawrenceville the classes are called *forms,* and elaborate efforts are made in other ways to imitate the speech of Eton and Harrow. Dr. J. Milnor Coit, while rector of the fashionable St. Paul's School, at Concord, N. H., gave a great impetus to this imitation of English manners. Says a leading authority on American private schools: "Dr. Coit encouraged cricket rather than baseball. The English schoolroom nomenclature, too, was here introduced to the American boy. St. Paul's still has *forms,* but the *removes, evensong* and *matins,* and even the cricket of Dr. Coit's time are now forgotten. Most boys of the three upper forms have separate rooms. The younger boys have *alcoves* in the dormitories similar to the *cubicles* of many of the English public schools." [23]

Occasionally some uncompromising patriot raises his voice against such importations, but he seldom shows the vigorous indignation of the English purists. White, in 1870, warned Americans against the figurative use of *nasty* as a synonym for *disagreeable.* The use of the word was then relatively new in England, though, according to White, the *Saturday Review* and the *Spectator* had already succumbed. His objections to it were unavailing; *nasty* quickly got into American and has been there ever since. In 1883 Gilbert M. Tucker protested against *good-form, traffic* (in the sense of travel), *to bargain* and *to tub* as Briticisms that we might well do without, but all of them took root and are perfectly sound American today. The locutions that are more obviously merely fashionable slang have a harder time of it, and seldom gain lodgment. When certain advertisers in New York sought to appeal to snobs by using such Briticisms as *swagger* and *topping* in their advertisements, the town wits, led by the watchful Franklin P. Adams (though he serves the *Tribune,* which Clement K. Shorter once called "more English than we are English"), fell upon them, and quickly routed them. To the average American of the plain people, indeed, any word or phrase of an obviously English flavor appears to be subtly offensive. To call him *old dear* would be almost as hazardous as to call him

[23] Porter E. Sargent: American Private Schools; Boston, 1920. It is curious to note that Dr. Coit, despite his Anglomania, was born in Harrisburg, Pa., began life as manager of a tube works at Cleveland, and retired to Munich on resigning the rectorate of St. Paul's.

Claude or *Clarence*. He associates all such terms, and the English broad *a* no less, with the grotesque Britons he sees in burlesque shows. Perhaps this feeling entered into the reluctance of the American soldier to borrow British war slang.

I incline to think that both the grand dialects of English would be the better for a somewhat freer interchange, and fully endorse the doctrine laid down by Prof. Gordon Hall Gerould, of Princeton, who argues that it would be a sensible thing for Americans to adopt the English *lift* and *tram* in place of the more cumbersome *elevator* and *trolley-car*, and that the English, in their turn, would find the communication of ideas easier if they borrowed some of our American neologisms.[24] "Logophobia," he says, "has usually been a sign, in men of our race, of a certain thinness of blood. The man of imagination and the man with something to say have never been afraid of words, even words that have rung strangely on the ear. It has been the finicking person, not very sure of himself, who has trod delicately between alternatives, and used the accepted and time-worn word in preference to the newer coinage, out of his abhorrence born of fear. . . . I do not wish to urge . . . the wiping out of those peculiarities of vocabulary by which one region of the English-speaking world is made to seem slightly exotic to the visitor from another. Without such differences of idiom, the common speech of the race would be the poorer, as the waters from many rivulets are needed to feed the river. Let him who says naturally a *pail* of water say so still, and him to whom a *bucket* is more familiar rejoice in his locution. Let my English friend call for his *jug,* while I demand my *pitcher;* for he will—if he be not afflicted with logophobia—enjoy what seems to him the fine archaic flavor of my word. What I would commend is a generous reciprocity in vocabulary, as between section and section, commonwealth and commonwealth, country and country. If it should become convenient for us Americans to use a word now peculiar to Great Britain, I hope we should not be so silly as to stop it at the tongue's end out of national pride or

[24] In Reciprocity in Words, *Literary Review* of the New York *Evening Post*, Feb. 21, 1921. Dr. Gerould incidentally accuses me of attempting to drive a wedge between English and American, and hints that I indulge in "special pleading based on special interests." What those special interests may be he does not say. Probably he has in mind the interests of the Wilhelmstrasse. If so, I am glad to oblige him by seconding him again.

chauvinistic delicacy. It is evident that any 'American' language which might be evolved by the sedulous fostering on our part of native idioms would still retain a good deal of the original English language. Why, then, should we shut ourselves off from the good things in words that have been invented or popularized in Great Britain since the Pilgrims sailed? And why, on the other hand, should the Englishman disdain the ingenious locutions that have come to light on this side the Atlantic?"

A correspondent makes the suggestion that such exchanges, if they were more numerous, would greatly enrich each language's stock of fine distinctions. A loan-word, he says, does not usually completely displace the corresponding native word, but simply puts a new distinction beside it. Unquestionably, this often happens. Consider, for example, the case of *shop*. As it is now used in the American cities it affords a convenient means of distinguishing between a large store offering various lines of merchandise and a small establishment specializing in one line. The old-fashioned country store remains a *store* and so does the department-store. To call either a *shop* would seem absurd. *Shop* is applied exclusively to smaller establishments, and almost always in combination with some word designating the sort of stock they carry. *Shop,* indeed, has always been good American, though its current application is borrowed from England. We have used *shop-worn, shoplifter, shopping, pawn-shop, shopper, shop-girl* and *to shop* for years. In the same way the word *penny* continues to flourish among us, despite the fact that there has been no American coin of that name for more than 125 years. We have *nickel-in-the-slot* machines, but when they take a cent we call them *penny-in-the-slot* machines. We have *penny-arcades* and *penny-whistles.* We do not play *cent*-ante, but *penny*-ante. We still "turn an honest *penny*" and say "a *penny* for your thoughts." The pound and the shilling became extinct legally a century ago,[25] but the penny still binds us to the mother-tongue. But an American knows nothing of *pence.* To him two pennies are always *pennies.*

Exchanges in spelling, some of them very important, are discussed in Chapter VIII.

[25] A correspondent assures me, however, that the York shilling, worth 12½ cents, survived in New York City until 1865.

VI.

TENDENCIES IN AMERICAN

1.

General Characters

The elements that enter into the special character of American have been rehearsed in the first chapter: a general impatience of rule and restraint, a democratic enmity to all authority, an extravagant and often grotesque humor, an extraordinary capacity for metaphor [1] — in brief, all the natural marks of what Van Wyck Brooks calls "a popular life which bubbles with energy and spreads and grows and slips away ever more and more from the control of tested ideas, a popular life with the lid off." [2] This is the spirit of America, and from it the American language is nourished. "The wish to see things afresh and for himself," says Dr. Harry Morgan Ayres,[3] "is so characteristic of the American that neither in his speech nor his most considered writing does he need any urging to seek out ways of his own. He refuses to carry on his verbal traffic with the well-worn counters; he will always be new-writing them. He is on the lookout for words that say something; he has a sort of remorseless and scientific efficiency in the choice of epithets! ... The American ... has an Elizabethan love of exuberant language." Brooks, perhaps, generalizes a bit too lavishly; Ayres calls attention to the fact that below the surface there is also a curious conservatism, even a sort of timorousness. In a land of manumitted peasants the primary trait of the peasant is bound to show itself now and then; as Wendell Phillips once said, "more

[1] An interesting note on this characteristic is in College Words and Phrases, by Eugene H. Babbitt, *Dialect Notes*, vol. ii, pt. i, p. 11.
[2] America's Coming of Age; p. 15.
[3] *Art.* The English Language in America, Cambridge History of American Literature, vol. iv, p. 570.

than any other people, we Americans are afraid of one another"—that is, afraid of isolation, of derision, of all the consequences of singularity. But in the field of language, as in that of politics, this suspicion of the new is often transformed into a suspicion of the merely unfamiliar, and so its natural tendency toward conservatism is overcome. It is of the essence of democracy that it remain a government by amateurs, and under a government by amateurs it is precisely the expert who is most questioned—and it is the expert who commonly stresses the experience of the past. And in a democratic society it is not the iconoclast who seems most revolutionary, but the purist. The derisive designation of *highbrow* is thoroughly American in more ways than one. It is a word put together in an unmistakably American fashion, it reflects an habitual American attitude of mind, and its potency in debate is peculiarly national too.

I daresay it is largely a fear of the weapon in it—and there are many others of like effect in the arsenal—which accounts for the far greater prevalence of idioms from below in the formal speech of America than in the formal speech of England. There is surely no English novelist of equal rank whose prose shows so much of colloquial looseness and ease as one finds in the prose of Howells: to find a match for it one must go to the prose of the neo-Celts, professedly modelled upon the speech of peasants, and almost proudly defiant of English grammar and syntax, and to the prose of the English themselves before the Restoration. Nor is it imaginable that an Englishman of comparable education and position would ever employ such locutions as those I have hitherto quoted from the public addresses of Dr. Wilson—that is, innocently, seriously, as a matter of course. The Englishman, when he makes use of coinages of that sort, does so in conscious relaxation, and usually with a somewhat heavy sense of doggishness. They are proper to the paddock or even to the dinner table, but scarcely to serious scenes and occasions. But in the Unitel States their use is the rule rather than the exception; it is not the man who uses them, but the man who doesn't use them, who is marked off. Their employment, if high example counts for anything, is a standard habit of the language, as their diligent avoidance is a standard habit of English.

A glance through the *Congressional Record* is sufficient to show how small is the minority of purists among the chosen leaders of the nation. Within half an hour, turning at random the pages of the war issues, when all Washington was on its best behavior, I find scores of locutions that would paralyze the stenographers in the House of Commons, and they are in the speeches, not of wild mavericks from the West, but of some of the chief men of the two Houses. Surely no Senator occupied a more conspicuous position during the first year of the war than "Hon." Lee S. Overman, of North Carolina, chairman of the Committee on Rules, and commander of the administration forces on the floor. Well, I find Senator Overman using *to enthuse* in a speech of the utmost seriousness and importance, and not once, but over and over again.[4] I turn back a few pages and encounter it again—this time in the mouth of General Sherwood, of Ohio. A few more, and I find a fit match for it, to wit, *to biograph*.[5] The speaker here is Senator L. Y. Sherman, of Illinois. In the same speech he uses *to resolute*.[6] A few more, and various other characteristic verbs are unearthed; *to demagogue,*[7] *to dope out,*[8] *to fall down*[9] (in the sense of to fail), *to jack up,*[10] *to phone,*[11] *to peeve,*[12] *to come across,*[13] *to hike, to butt in,*[14] *to back pedal, to get solid with, to hospitalize,*[15] *to hooverize, to propaganda,*[16] *to trustify, to feature, to insurge, to haze, to reminisce, to camouflage, to play for a sucker,* and so on, almost *ad infinitum*. And with them, a large number of highly American nouns, chiefly compounds, all pressing upward for recognition: *tin-Lizzie, brain-storm, come-down, pin-head, trustification,*

---

[4] March 26, 1918, pp. 4376-7.
[5] Jan. 14, 1918, p. 903.
[6] It is used again by Mr. Walsh, *Congressional Record*, May 16, 1921, p. 1468, col. 2.
[7] Mr. Campbell, of Kansas, in the House, Jan. 19, 1918, p. 1134.
[8] Mr. Hamlin, of Missouri, in the House, Jan. 19, 1918, p. 1154.
[9] Mr. Kirby, of Arkansas, in the Senate, Jan. 24, 1918, p. 1291; Mr. Lewis, of Illinois, in the Senate, June 6, 1918, p. 8024.
[10] Mr. Weeks, of Massachusetts, in the Senate, Jan. 17, 1918, p. 988.
[11] Mr. Smith, of South Carolina, in the Senate, Jan. 17, 1918, p. 991.
[12] Mr. Borland, of Missouri, in the House, Jan. 29, 1918, p. 1501.
[13] May 4, 1917, p. 1853.
[14] Mr. Snyder, of New York, Dec. 11, 1917.
[15] Senator Walsh, of Massachusetts, May 27, 1921, p. 1835.
[16] Used in the form of *propagandaed* by Mr. Bland, of Indiana, in the House, May 16, 1921, p. 1481, col. 1.

pork-barrel, buck-private, dough-boy, cow-country. And adjectives: *jitney, bush* (for rural), *balled-up,*[17] *dolled-up, phoney, pussy-footed, tax-paid.*[18] And picturesque phrases: *dollars to doughnuts, on the job, that gets me, one best bet.* And back-formations: *ad, movie, photo.* And various substitutions and Americanized inflections: *over* for *more than, gotten* for *got* in the present perfect,[19] *rile* for *roil, bust* for *burst.* This last, in truth, has come into a dignity that even grammarians will soon hesitate to question. Who, in America, would dare to speak of *bursting* a broncho, or of a *trustburster?*[20]

Turn to any issue of the *Congressional Record* and you will find examples of American quite as startling as those I have exhumed—and some a good deal more startling. I open the file for 1919 at random, and at once discover "they had put it on the market in a condition in which it could be *drank* as a beverage." [21] A moment later I find, from the same lips, "The evidence disclosed that Jacobs had *drank* 28 bottles of lemon extract." A few pages further on, and I come to "It will *not* take but a few minutes to dispose of it." [22] I take up another volume and find the following curious letter written by a Senator and inserted in the *Record* at his request:

Hon. Edgar E. Clark,
    Chairman Interstate Commerce Commission,
        Washington, D. C.
My dear Mr. Chairman: It has been brought to my attention by many people in Georgia and those whom I see here that the present high passenger and freight rates are doing more to decrease the amount of income received by the railroads than if a lower rate was in effect, which would cause more freight

---

[17] *Balled-up* and its verb, *to ball up,* were once improper, no doubt on account of the slang significance of *ball,* but of late they have made steady progress toward polite acceptance.
[18] After the passage of the first War Revenue Act cigar-boxes began to bear this inscription: "The contents of this box have been *taxed paid* as cigars of Class B as indicated by the Internal Revenue stamp affixed." Even *tax-paid,* which was later substituted, is obviously better than this clumsy double inflection.
[19] Mr. Bankhead, of Alabama, in the Senate, May 14, 1918, p. 6995.
[20] *Bust* seems to be driving out *burst* completely when used figuratively. Even in a literal sense it creeps into more or less respectable usage. Thus I find "a *busted* tire" in a speech by Gen. Sherwood, of Ohio, in the House, Jan. 24, 1918. The familiar American derivative, *buster,* as in *Buster Brown,* is unknown to the English.
[21] Mr. Tincher, of Kansas, in the House, July 19, 1919, p. 3009.
[22] Mr. Blanton, of Texas, in the House, Aug. 12, 1919, p. 4057.

to move and more people to travel. In other words, the railroads are not carrying an average maximum of freight and passengers since the increase in rates. Of course, the commission doubtless has figures on this question which throw more light than I can by general observations.

It is needless for me to point out to you and the commission that the railroad situation is a problem which has not been solved to any great degree by the transportation act of 1920. The thing which I am greatly interested in is the matter of freight and passenger rates to be placed within reach of the average person, and at the same time give the railroads a reasonable income for their investment. Both the public and the roads deserve an honest living, but I fear that both are now suffering. Because of high freight rates there are products in my State which are now being shipped in such small quantities in comparison with production and demand.

I hope that an adjustment can soon be made which will bring down the rates, and I would thank you to let me have any information on the matter at your convenience which may have been gathered or published by the commission.

With high esteem, I am,

Very sincerely yours,

WM. J. HARRIS [23]

I leave the analysis of the American political style here displayed to grammarians. They will find plenty of further clinical material in the speeches of Mr. Harding—the *one-he* combination in the first sentence of his inaugural address, *illy* in the fourth sentence of his first message to Congress, and many other choice specimens in his subsequent state papers. Nor are politicians the only Americans who practise the flouting of the purists. In a serious book on literature by a former editor of the *Atlantic Monthly*,[24] edited by a committee of Yale professors and published by the university press, I find the *one-he* combination in full flower, and in a book of criticism by Francis Hackett, of the *New Republic,* I find *pinhead* used quite innocently and *to do him proud* topping it.[25] Hackett is relatively conservative. The late Horace Traubel, disciple of Whitman, went much further. All his life he battled valiantly for the use of *dont* (without the apostrophe) with plural subjects!

[23] Of Georgia. *Congressional Record*, Feb. 21, 1921, p. 3755.
[24] The American Spirit in Literature, by Bliss Perry; New Haven, 1918, p. 117. "If *one* habitually prints the words, . . . *one* may do it because *he* is a Carlyle or an Emerson, but the chances are that *he* is neither."
[25] The Invisible Censor; New York, 1921, pp. 6 and 60 respectively. *All by her lonesome* is in Horizons; New York, 1918, by the same author, p. 53.

2.

Lost Distinctions

This general iconoclasm reveals itself especially in a disdain for most of the niceties of modern English. The American, like the Elizabethan Englishman, is usually quite unconscious of them and even when they have been instilled into him by the hard labor of pedagogues he commonly pays little heed to them in his ordinary discourse. The distinction between *each other* and *one another* offers a salient case in point; all the old effort to confine the first to two persons or objects and the latter to more than two seems to be breaking down.[26] So with the very important English distinction between *will* and *shall*. This last, it may be said at once, is far more a confection of the grammarians than a product of the natural forces shaping the language. It has, indeed, little etymological basis, and is but imperfectly justified logically. One finds it disregarded in the Authorized Version of the Bible, in all the plays of Shakespeare, in the essays of the reign of Anne, and in some of the best examples of modern English literature. The theory behind it is so inordinately abstruse that the Fowlers, in "The King's English," [27] require 20 pages to explain it, and even then they come to the resigned conclusion that the task is hopeless. "The idiomatic use [of the two auxiliaries]," they say, "is so complicated that those who are not to the manner born can hardly acquire it." [28] Well, even those who are to the manner born seem to find it difficult, for at once the learned authors cite blunders in the writings of Richardson, Stevenson, Gladstone, Jowett, Oscar Wilde, and even Henry Sweet, author of the best existing grammar of the English language. In American the distinction is almost lost. No ordinary American, save after the most laborious reflection, would

---

[26] "Among the first acquaintances I made was one with Mr. Blackmon. We had offices close to *one another*." Mr. Venable, of Mississippi, in the House, *Congressional Record*, Feb. 20, 1921, p. 3730.
[27] Pp. 133-154.
[28] L. Pearsall Smith, in The English Language, p. 29, says that "the differentiation is . . . so complicated that it can hardly be mastered by those born in parts of the British Islands in which it has not yet been established," *e. g.*, all of Ireland and most of Scotland.

detect anything wrong in this sentence from the *London Times,* denounced as corrupt by the Fowlers: "We must reconcile what we would like to do with what we can do." Nor in this by W. B. Yeats: "The character who delights us may commit murder like Macbeth . . . and yet we will rejoice in every happiness that comes to him." Half a century ago, impatient of the effort to fasten the English distinction upon American, George P. Marsh attacked it as of "no logical value or significance whatever," and predicted that "at no very distant day this verbal quibble will disappear, and one of the auxiliaries will be employed, with all persons of the nominative, exclusively as the sign of the future, and the other only as an expression of purpose or authority." [29] This prophecy has been substantially verified. *Will* is sound American "with all persons of the nominative," and *shall* is almost invariably an "expression of purpose or authority." [30]

And so, though perhaps not to the same extent, with *who* and *whom*. Now and then there arises a sort of panicky feeling that *whom* is being neglected, and so it is trotted out,[31] but in the main the American language tends to dispense with it, at least in its less graceful situations. Noah Webster, always the pragmatic reformer, denounced it so long ago as 1783. Common sense, he argued, was on the side of *"who* did he marry?" Today such a form as *"whom* are you talking to?" would seem somewhat affected in ordinary

[29] Quoted by White, in Words and Their Uses, pp. 264-5. White, however, dissented vigorously and devoted 10 pages to explaining the difference between the two auxiliaries. Most of the other authorities of the time were also against Marsh—for example, Richard Meade Bache (see his Vulgarisms and Other Errors of Speech, p. 92 *et seq.*). Sir Edmund Head, governor-general of Canada from 1854 to 1861, wrote a whole book upon the subject: *Shall* and *Will,* or Two Chapters on Future Auxiliary Verbs; London, 1856. In her Tendencies in Modern American Poetry; New York, 1917, Amy Lowell takes Carl Sandburg and Edgar Lee Masters to task for constantly using *will* for *shall,* and says that they share the habit "with many other modern American writers." See also Text, Type and Style, by George B. Ives; Boston, 1921, p. 289 *ff*.
[30] The probable influence of Irish immigration upon the American usage is not to be overlooked. Joyce says flatly (English As We Speak It in Ireland, p. 77) that, "like many another Irish idiom this is also found in American society chiefly through the influence of the Irish." At all events, the Irish example must have reinforced it. In Ireland "*Will* I light the fire, ma'am?" is colloquially sound.
[31] Often with such amusing results as *"whom* is your father?" and *"whom* spoke to me?" For these, alas, there is eminent authority. *Cf.* Matthew xvi, 13: "When Jesus came into the coasts of Cesarea Philippi, he asked his disciples, saying, *Whom* do men say that I, the Son of Man, *am?"* See also Otto Jespersen: Chapters on English; London, 1918, p. 52.

discourse in America; *"who* are you talking to?" is heard a thousand times oftener, and is doubly American, for it substitutes *who* for *whom* and puts a preposition at the end of a sentence: two crimes that most English purists would seek to avoid. It is among the pronouns that the only remaining case inflections in English are to be found, if we forget the possessive, and even here these survivors of an earlier day begin to grow insecure. Lounsbury's defense of "it is me," [32] as we shall see in the next chapter, has support in the history and natural movement of the language, and that movement is also against the preservation of the distinction between *who* and *whom*. The common speech plays hob with both of the orthodox inflections, despite the protests of grammarians, and in the long run, no doubt, they will be forced to yield to its pressure, as they have always yielded in the past. Between the dative and accusative on one side and the nominative on the other there has been war in the English language for centuries, and it has always tended to become a war of extermination. Our now universal use of *you* for *ye* in the nominative shows the dative and accusative swallowing the nominative, and the practical disappearance of *hither, thither* and *whither,* whose place is now taken by *here, there* and *where,* shows a contrary process. In such wars a *posse comitatus* marches ahead of the disciplined army. American stands to English in the relation of that posse to that army. It is incomparably more enterprising, more contemptuous of precedent and authority, more impatient of rule.

A shadowy line often separates what is currently coming into sound usage from what is still regarded as barbarous. No self-respecting American, I daresay, would defend *ain't* as a substitute for *isn't,* say in "he *ain't* the man," and yet *ain't* is already tolerably respectable in the first person, where English countenances the even more clumsy *aren't*. *Aren't* has never got a foothold in the American first person; when it is used at all, which is very rarely, it is always as a conscious Briticism. Facing the alternative of employing the unwieldy "am I not in this?" the American turns boldly to *"ain't* I in this?" It still grates a bit, perhaps, but *aren't* grates

[32] "It is *I"* is quite as unsound historically. The correct form would be "it *am* I" or "I am it." Compare the German "ich *bin* es," not, "es *ist* ich."

TENDENCIES IN AMERICAN 181

even more.[33] Here, as always, the popular speech is pulling the exacter speech along, and no one familiar with its successes in the past can have much doubt that it will succeed again, soon or late. In the same way it is breaking down the inflectional distinction between adverb and adjective, so that "I feel *bad*" begins to take on the dignity of a national idiom, and *sure, in bad, to go big* and *run slow* [34] become almost respectable. When, on the entrance of the United States into the late war, the Tank Corps chose "Treat 'em *rough*" as its motto, no one thought to raise a grammatical objection, and the clipped adverb was printed upon hundreds of thousands of posters and displayed in every town in the country, always with the imprimatur of the national government. So again, American, in its spoken form, tends to obliterate the distinction between nearly related adjectives, *e. g., healthful* and *healthy, tasteful* and *tasty*. And to challenge the somewhat absurd text-book prohibition of terminal prepositions, so that "where are we *at?*" loses its old raciness. And to dally with the double negative, as in "I have no doubt *but* that." [35]

But these tendencies, or at least the more extravagant of them, belong to the next chapter. How much influence they exert, even indirectly, is shown by the American disdain of the English precision in the use of the indefinite pronoun, already noticed. I turn to the *Saturday Evening Post,* and in two minutes find: "*one* feels like an atom when *he* begins to review *his* own life and deeds." [36] The error is very rare in English; the Fowlers, seeking examples of it, could get them only from the writings of a third-rate woman

---

[33] For an interesting discussion of *aren't* see a letter by H. E. Boot in *English,* June, 1920, p. 376, and one by Daniel Jones in the same periodical, Aug.-Sept., 1920, p. 399.
[34] A common direction to motormen and locomotive engineers. The English form is "slow down." I note, however, that "drive slow*ly*" is in the taxicab shed at the Pennsylvania Station, in New York.
[35] I have already noticed the use of the double negative by a Texas Congressman. Here I quote from a speech made by Senator Sherman, of Illinois, in the Senate on June 20, 1918. *Vide Congressional Record* for that day, p. 8743. Two days later, "There is no question *but* that" appeared in a letter by John Lee Coulter, A.M., Ph.D., dean of West Virginia University. It was read into the *Record* of June 22 by Mr. Ashwell, one of the Louisiana representatives. Even the pedantic Senator Henry Cabot Lodge uses *but that*. *Vide* the *Record* for May 14, 1918, p. 6996. See also Senator Borah's use of it, *Record,* May 14, 1921, p. 1434.
[36] June 15, 1918, p. 62.

novelist, Scotch to boot. But it is so common in American that when Mr. Harding used it in the first sentence of his inaugural address even his Democratic editorial enemies failed to notice it, and when I denounced it in the *Nation* it was vigorously defended. The appearance of a redundant *s* in such words as *towards, downwards, afterwards* and *heavenwards* is equally familiar. In England this *s* is used relatively seldom, and then it usually marks a distinction in meaning, as it does on both sides of the ocean between *beside* and *besides*. "In modern standard English," says Smith,[37] "though not in the English of the United States, a distinction which we feel, but many of us could not define, is made between *forward* and *forwards; forwards* being used in definite contrast to any other direction, as 'if you move at all, you can only move *forwards*,' while *forward* is used where no such contrast is implied, as in the common phrase 'to bring a matter forward.' "[38] This specific distinction, despite Smith, probably retains some force in the United States too, but in general our usage allows the *s* in cases where English usage would certainly be against it. Gould, in the 50's, noted its appearance at the end of such words as *somewhere* and *anyway,* and denounced it as vulgar and illogical. Thornton traces *anyways* back to 1842 and shows that it is an archaism, and to be found in the Book of Common Prayer (*circa* 1560); perhaps it has been preserved by analogy with *sideways*. Henry James, in "The Question of Our Speech," attacked "such forms of impunity as *somewheres else* and *nowheres else, a good ways on* and *a good ways off*" as "vulgarisms with what a great deal of general credit for what we good-naturedly call 'refinement' appears so able to coexist."[39] *Towards* and *afterwards,* though frowned upon in England, are now quite sound in America. I find the former in the title of an article in *Dialect Notes,* which plainly gives it scholastic authority.[40] More (and

---

[37] The English Language, p. 79.
[38] This phrase, of course, is a Briticism, and seldom used in America. The American form is "to take a matter up."
[39] The Question of Our Speech, p. 30. He might have been even more eloquent had he tackled *no place* and *some place,* latter-day substitutes for *nowheres* and *somewheres.* Or the common American habit of treating such plurals as *woods, falls, links, works, yards, grounds,* etc., as singulars. See *Dialect Notes,* vol. iv, pt. i, p. 48 (1913).
[40] A Contribution *Towards,* etc., by Prof. H. Tallichet, vol. i, pt. iv. But the *s* is omitted in the index to *Dialect Notes,* vol. iv, p. 459.

TENDENCIES IN AMERICAN 183

with no little humor), I find it in the deed of a fund given to the American Academy of Arts and Letters to enable the gifted philologs of that sanhedrin "to consider its duty *towards* the conservation of the English language in its beauty and purity." [41] Both *towards* and *afterwards*, finally, are included in the New York *Evening Post's* list of "words no longer disapproved when in their proper places," along with *over* for *more than*, and *during* for *in the course of*.

3.

Processes of Word-Formation

Some of the tendencies visible in American—*e. g.*, toward the facile manufacture of new compounds, toward the transfer of words from one part of speech to another, and toward the free use of suffixes and prefixes and the easy isolation of roots and pseudo-roots—go back to the period of the first growth of a distinct American dialect and are heritages from the English of the time. They are the products of a movement which, reaching its height in the English of Elizabeth, was dammed up at home, so to speak, by the rise of linguistic self-consciousness toward the end of the reign of Anne, but continued almost unobstructed in the colonies.

For example, there is what philologists call the habit of clipping or back-formation—a sort of instinctive search, etymologically unsound, for short roots in long words. This habit, in Restoration days, precipitated a quasi-English word, *mobile,* from the Latin *mobile vulgus,* and in the days of William and Mary it went a step further by precipitating *mob* from *mobile*. *Mob* is now sound English, but in the eighteenth century it was violently attacked by the new sect of purists,[42] and though it survived their onslaught they undoubtedly greatly impeded the formation and adoption of other words of the same category. There are, however, many more such words in standard English, *e. g.*, *patter* from *paternoster*, *van* from

[41] *Yale Review*, April, 1918, p. 545.
[42] *Vide* Lounsbury: The Standard of Usage in English, pp. 65-7.

caravan, *wig* from *periwig*, *cab* from *cabriolet*, *brandy* from *brandy-wine* (= *brandewyn*), *pun* from *pundigrion*, *grog* from *grogram*, *curio* from *curiosity*, *canter* from *Canterbury*, *brig* from *brigantine*, *bus* from *omnibus*, *bant* from *Banting* and *fad* from *fadaise*.[43] In the colonies there was no such opposition to them as came from the purists of the English universities; save for a few feeble protests from Witherspoon and Boucher they went unchallenged. As a result they multiplied enormously. *Rattler* for *rattle-snake*, *pike* for *turnpike*, *draw* for *drawbridge*, *coon* for *raccoon*, *possum* for *opossum*, *cuss* for *customer*, *cute* for *acute*, *squash* for *askutasquash*—these American back-formations are already antique; *Sabbaday* for *Sabbath-day* has actually reached the dignity of an archaism, as has the far later *chromo* for *chromolithograph*. To this day they are formed in great numbers; scarcely a new substantive of more than two syllables comes in without bringing one in its wake. We have thus witnessed, within the past few years, the genesis of scores now in wide use and fast taking on respectability: *phone* for *telephone*, *gas* for *gasoline*, *co-ed* for *co-educational*, *pop* for *populist*, *frat* for *fraternity*, *gym* for *gymnasium*, *movie* for *moving picture*, *plane* for *air-plane*, *prep-school* for *preparatory-school*, *auto* for *automobile*, *aero* for *aeroplane* and *aeronautical*. Some linger on the edge of vulgarity: *pep* for *pepper*, *flu* for *influenza*, *plute* for *plutocrat*, *vamp* for *vampire*, *pen* for *penitentiary*, *con* for *confidence* (as in *con-man*, *con-game* and *to con*), *convict* and *consumption*, *defi* for *defiance*, *beaut* for *beauty*, *rep* for *reputation*, *stenog* for *stenographer*, *ambish* for *ambition*, *vag* for *vagrant*, *champ* for *champion*, *pard* for *partner*, *coke* for *cocaine*, *simp* for *simpleton*, *diff* for *difference*, *grass* for *asparagus*, *mum* for *chrysanthemum*, *mutt* for *muttonhead*,[44] *wiz* for *wizard*, *rube* for *Reuben*, *hon* for *honey*, *barkeep* for *barkeeper*, *divvy* for *dividend* or *division*, *jit* for *jitney*. Others are already in good usage: *smoker* for *smoking-car*, *diner* for *dining-car*, *sleeper* for *sleeping-car*, *oleo* for *oleomar-*

[43] An interesting discussion of such words is in Otto Jespersen's Growth and Structure of the English Language, 3rd ed.; Leipzig, 1919, pp. 170-2. See also Clipped Words, by Elisabeth Wittmann, *Dialect Notes*, vol. iv, pt. ii (1914), pp. 115 *ff.*, and Stunts in Language, by Louise Pound, *English Journal*, vol. ix, no. 2 (Feb., 1920), pp. 88 *ff*.

[44] This etymology for *mutt* is supported by Budd Fisher, creator of Mutt and Jeff. See *Editor and Publisher*, April 17, 1919, p. 21.

TENDENCIES IN AMERICAN 185

garine, hypo for *hyposulphite of soda, Yank* for *Yankee, confab* for *confabulation, memo* for *memorandum, pop-concert* for *popular-concert, gator* for *alligator, foots* for *footlights, ham* for *hamfatter* (actor), *sub* for *substitute, knicker* for *knickerbocker*. Many back-formations originate in college slang, e. g., *prof* for *professor, prom* for *promenade, soph* for *sophomore, grad* for *graduate* (noun), *lab* for *laboratory, dorm* for *dormitory, plebe* for *plebeian*.[45] *Ad* for *advertisement* is struggling hard for general recognition; some of its compounds, e. g., *ad-writer, want-ad, display-ad, ad-card, ad-rate, column-ad* and *ad-man*, are already accepted in technical terminology. *Boob* for *booby* promises to become sound American in a few years; its synonyms are no more respectable than it is. At its heels are *bo* for *hobo*, and *hoak* for *hoakum*, two altogether fit successors to *bum* for *bummer*. *Try* for *trial*, as in "He made a *try* at it," is also making progress but perhaps *try-out*, a characteristically American combination of verb and preposition, will eventually displace it. This production of new words by clipping, back-formation and folk-etymology is quite as active among the verbs as among the nouns. I have already described the appearance of such forms as *to locate* in the earliest days of differentiation and the popularity of such forms as *to enthuse* and *to phone* today. Many more verbs of the same sort have attained to respectability, e. g., *to jell, to auto, to commute, to typewrite, to tiptoe* (for *to walk tiptoe*). Others are still on probation, e. g., *to reminisce, to insurge, to vamp, to peeve, to jubilate, to taxi, to orate, to bach* (i. e., to live in bachelor quarters), *to emote*. Yet others are still unmistakably vulgar or merely waggish, e. g., *to plumb* (from *plumber*), *to barb* (from *barber*), *to chauf* (from *chauffeur*), *to ready* (from *to make ready*), *to elocute, to burgle, to ush, to sculp, to butch, to con* (from *confidence-man*), *to buttle, to barkeep, to dressmake, to housekeep, to boheme, to photo, to divvy*. Such forms seem to make an irresistible appeal to the American; he is constantly experimenting with new ones. "There is a much greater percentage of humorous shortenings among verbs," says Miss Wittmann, "than among other parts of speech. Especially

---

[45] Some of these college forms are very picturesque, e. g., *weir* for *weird* (Dartmouth), *dent* for *dental student* (University of Minnesota), and *psych* for *psychology* (Vassar). See College Words and Phrases, by E. H. Babbitt, *Dialect Notes*, vol. ii, pt. i, p. 3 ff.

is this true of verbs shortened from nouns and adjectives by subtracting what looks like a derivative suffix, *e. g.*, *-er, -or, -ing, -ent* from nouns, or *-y* from adjectives. Many clipped verbs have noun parallels, while some are simply clipped nouns used as verbs."[46] Miss Wittmann calls attention to the curious fact that very few adjectives are clipped in American; there are actually more of them in British English. *Sesech* (from *secessionist*, really a noun, but often used as an adjective) is one of the few familiar examples. Adjectives are made copiously in American, but most of them are made by other processes.

Another popular sort of neologism is the blend- or portmanteau-word. Many such words are in standard English, *e. g.*, Lewis Carroll's *chortle* (from *chuckle* and *snort*), *dumbfound* (from *dumb* and *confound*), *luncheon* (*lunch+nuncheon*), *blurt* (*blare+spurt*). American contributed *gerrymander* (*Gerry+salamander*) so long ago as 1812, and in more recent years has produced many blends that have gone over into standard English, *e. g.*, *cablegram* (*cable+telegram*), *electrocute* (*electricity+execute*), *electrolier* (*electricity+chandelier*, *Amerind* (*American+Indian*), *doggery* (*dog+groggery*), *riffle* (in a stream) (probably from *ripple* and *ruffle*). Perhaps *travelogue* (*travel+monologue*), Luther Burbank's *pomato* (*potato+tomato*), *slanguage* (*slang+language*), and *thon* (*that+one*) [47] will one day follow. *Boost* (*boom+hoist*) is a typical American blend. I have a notion that *blurb* is a blend also. So, perhaps, is *flunk;* Dr. Louise Pound says that it may be from *fail* and *funk*.[48] *Aframerican,* which is now very commonly used in the Negro press, is not American, but was devised by Sir Harry Johnston.[49] Allied with the portmanteau words are many blends of a somewhat different sort, in which long compounds are displaced by forms devised by analogy with existing words. *Printery* (for *printing-office*) appeared very early, and in late years it has been rein-

[46] Clipped Words, *Dialect Notes*, vol. iv, pt. ii, p. 137.
[47] *Thon* was first proposed by C. C. Converse, of Erie, Pa., in 1858, as a substitute for the clumsy *he-and*(or)*-she* and *him-and*(or)*-her*.
[48] Blends; Heidelberg, 1914, p. 25. (*Anglistische Forschungen*, heft 42.) See also her Stunts in Language, *English Journal*, Feb., 1920, p. 91 ff.
[49] "He uses it," writes James W. Johnson, the Negro poet, "in his The Negro in the New World, 1910. He may have used it in some earlier publication also."

TENDENCIES IN AMERICAN 187

forced by many analogues, e. g., *beanery, bootery, boozery, toggery.* *Condensery* is used in the West to indicate a place where milk is condensed. I have encountered *breadery* in Baltimore; Dr. Pound reports *hashery* and *drillery.*[50] Somewhat similar are the words suggested by *cafeteria,* once a California localism.[51] Among other strange forms I have encountered *haberteria* (for *haberdashery*) and *groceriteria* (for *grocery-store*). The wide use of the suffix *-ette* in such terms as *farmerette, conductorette, kitchenette, cellarette, featurette, leatherette, flannelette, crispette, usherette* and *huskerette,* is due to the same effort to make one word do the work of two. In Baltimore, in 1918, the street railways company appealed to the public to drop *conductorette* and go back to *woman conductor,* but the new word survived.[52] I suspect that the popularity of *near-* as a prefix has much the same psychological basis. *Near-beer* is surely simpler than *imitation beer* or *non-alcoholic beer,* and *near-silk* is better than the long phrase that would have to be used to describe it accurately. So with the familiar and numerous terms in *-ee, -ite, -ster, -ist, -er, -dom, -itis, -ism, -ize,* etc., e. g., *draftee, Kreislerite, dopester, chalkologist, soap-boxer, picturedom, golfitis, Palmerism, to hooverize,* and so on. They all represent efforts to condense the meaning of whole phrases into simple and instantly-understandable words. "The great majority of shortened forms," says Miss Wittmann, "are clearly made for convenience; their speakers employ them to save time and trouble."[53] Here, incidentally, the influence of newspaper head-lines is not to be overlooked. The American head-line writer faces peculiar difficulties; he must get clearly explanatory phrases into very small space, and almost always he is handicapped by arbitrary regulations as to typographical arrangement—regulations which do not oppress his English colleague. As a result he is an ardent propa-

[50] Vogue Affixes in Present-Day Word-Coinage, *Dialect Notes,* vol. v, pt. i (1918), p. 10.
[51] A correspondent tells me, however, that the first cafeteria was in Chicago. He says: "A Chicago man was planning to open a new lunchroom in that city with the new feature of the guests serving themselves. He wanted a new and appropriate name for it, and applied to my cousin, who had lived in Buenos Aires. This cousin suggested *cafeteria,* which was adopted. It should be accented on the penultimate, but the patrons immediately moved the accent one place forward. This was about the year 1900."
[52] Baltimore *Trolley News,* June 16, 1918.
[53] Clipped Words, *op. cit.,* p. 116.

gandish for short words, e. g., *probe* (for *investigation*), *grab, steal, haul, wed* (for *wedded*), *hello-girl* (for *telephone-girl*), *soul-mate, love-nest, love-pirate*, and so on. He constantly uses *up* in the *something's up* sense, e. g., "Dry Question *Up* in Legislature." The popularity of *Hun*, during the War, was no doubt largely due to the exigencies of his calling. He never uses a long word when a short one will answer, and he never uses articles when they can be avoided. Possibly the omission of the article in such American phrases as *up street, all year* and *all Sunday* (the Englishman would probably say *all day on Sunday*) is largely due to his influence. Certainly, he is an eager merchant of all such neologisms as *sub-deb, stand-pat, try-out, co-ed, gym, auto, defi* and *phone*.[54]

The same motives show themselves in the great multiplication of common abbreviations in America. "Americans, as a rule," says Farmer, "employ abbreviations to an extent unknown in Europe. . . . This trait of the American character is discernible in every department of the national life and thought." *O. K., C. O. D., N. G., G. O. P.* (get out and push) and *P. D. Q.* are almost national hall-marks; the immigrant learns them immediately after *damn* and *go to hell*. Thornton traces *N. G.* to 1840; *C. O. D.* and *P. D. Q.* are probably almost as old. As for *O. K.*, it was in use so early as 1790. "In colonial days," says a floating newspaper paragraph, "the best rum and tobacco were imported from Aux Cayes, in Santo Domingo. Hence the best of anything came to be known locally as *Aux Cayes*, or *O. K.* The term did not, however, come to be generally used until the Presidential campaign of 1828, when the supposed illiteracy of Andrew Jackson, sometimes known as the founder of Democracy, was the stock in trade of his Whig opponents. Seba Smith, the humorist, writing under the name of 'Major Jack Downing,' started the story that Jackson endorsed his papers *O. K.*, under the impression that they formed the initials of *Oll Korrect*. Possibly the General did use this endorsement, and it was used by other people also. But James Parton has discovered in the records of the Nashville court of which Jackson was a judge, before he became President, numerous documents endorsed *O. R.*, meaning

[54] An amusing article on the influence of headlines upon American speech-habits, by Philip Littell, will be found in the *New Republic*, July 27, 1921.

Order Recorded. He urges, therefore, that it was a record of that court with some belated business which Major Downing saw on the desk of the Presidential candidate. However this may be, the Democrats, in lieu of denying the charge, adopted the letters *O. K.* as a sort of party cry and fastened them upon their banners." There is, however, a rival etymology for *O. K.*, whereby it is derived from an Indian word, *okeh,* signifying "so be it." Dr. Woodrow Wilson supported this derivation, and used *okeh* in approving papers to him as President; it also appears as the name of a popular series of phonograph records. Bartlett says that the figurative use of *A No. 1,* as in an *A No. 1 man,* also originated in America, but this may not be true. There can be little doubt, however, about *T. B.* (for *tuberculosis*), *G. B.* (for *grand bounce*), 23, *on the Q. T., f. o. b., D. & D.* (*drunk and disorderly*) and the army verb, *to a. w. o. l.* (to be absent without leave). The language breeds such short forms of speech prodigiously; every trade and profession has a host of them; they are innumerable in the slang of sport.[55] Often they represent the end-products of terms long in decay, *e. g., elevated railway: elevated: el: L.*

What one sees under all this is a double habit that sufficiently explains the gap which begins to yawn between English and American, particularly on the spoken plane. On the one hand it is a habit of verbal economy—a jealous disinclination to waste two words on what can be put into one, a natural taste for the brilliant and succinct, a disdain of all grammatical and lexicographical daintinesses, born partly, perhaps, of ignorance, but also in part of a sound sense of their imbecility. And on the other hand there is a high relish and talent for metaphor—in Brander Matthews' phrase, "a figurative vigor that the Elizabethans would have realized and understood." Just as the American rebels instinctively against such parliamentary circumlocutions as "I am not prepared to say" and "so much by way of being," [56] just as he would fret under the forms

[55] *Cf.* Semi-Secret Abbreviations, by Percy W. Long, *Dialect Notes*, vol. iv, pt. iii, 1915.
[56] The classical example is in a parliamentary announcement by Sir Robert Peel: "When that question is made to me in a proper time, in a proper place, under proper qualifications, and with proper motives, I will hesitate long before I will refuse to take it into consideration."

of English journalism, with its reporting empty of drama, its third-person smothering of speeches and its complex and unintelligible jargon, just so, in his daily speech and writing he chooses terseness and vividness whenever there is any choice, and seeks to make one when it doesn't exist. There is more than mere humorous contrast between the famous placard in the wash-room of the British Museum: "These Basins Are For Casual Ablutions Only," and the familiar sign at American railroad-crossings: "Stop! Look! Listen!" Between the two lies an abyss separating two cultures, two habits of mind, two diverging tongues. It is almost unimaginable that Englishmen, journeying up and down in elevators, would ever have stricken the teens out of their speech, turning *sixteenth* into simple *six* and *twenty-fourth* into *four;* the clipping is almost as far from their way of doing things as the climbing so high in the air. Nor have they the brilliant facility of Americans for making new words of grotesque but penetrating tropes, as in *corn-fed, tight-wad, bonehead, bleachers* and *juice* (for *electricity*); when they attempt such things the result is often lugubrious; two hundred years of schoolmastering has dried up their inspiration. Nor have they the fine American hand for devising new verbs; *to maffick, to limehouse, to strafe* and *to wangle* are their best specimens in twenty years, and all have an almost pathetic flatness. Their business with the language, indeed, is not in this department. They are not charged with its raids and scoutings, but with the organization of its conquests and the guarding of its accumulated stores.

For the student interested in the biology of language, as opposed to its paleontology, there is endless material in the racy neologisms of American, and particularly in its new compounds and novel verbs. Nothing could exceed the brilliancy of such inventions as *joy-ride, high-brow, road-louse, sob-sister, frame-up, loan-shark, nature-faker, stand-patter, lounge-lizard, hash-foundry, buzz-wagon, has-been, end-seat-hog, shoot-the-chutes* and *grape-juice diplomacy.* They are bold; they are vivid; they have humor; they meet genuine needs. *Joy-ride* is already going over into English, and no wonder. There is absolutely no synonym for it; to convey its idea in orthodox English would take a whole sentence. And so, too, with certain single words of metaphorical origin: *barrel* for large and illicit wealth, *pork* for unnecessary and dishonest appropriations of public money, *joint* for illegal liquor-house, *tenderloin* for gay and dubious neighborhood.[57] Many of these, and of the new compounds with them, belong to the vocabulary of disparagement, e. g., *bone-head, skunk, bug, jay, lobster, boob, mutt, gas* (empty talk), *geezer, piker, baggage-smasher, hash-slinger, clock-watcher, four-flusher, coffin-nail, chin-music, batty* and *one-horse*. Here an essential character of the American shows itself: his tendency to combat the disagreeable with irony, to heap ridicule upon what he is suspicious of or doesn't understand.[58]

The rapidity with which new verbs are made in the United States is really quite amazing. Two days after the first regulations of the Food Administration were announced, *to hooverize* appeared spontaneously in scores of newspapers, and a week later it was employed without any visible sense of its novelty in the debates of Congress and had taken on a respectability equal to that of *to bryanize, to fletcherize* and *to oslerize*. *To electrocute* appeared inevitably in the first public discussion of capital punishment by electricity; *to taxi* came in with the first taxicabs; *to commute* no doubt accompanied the first commutation ticket; *to insurge* attended the birth of the Progressive balderdash. Of late the old affix *-ize*, once fecund of such monsters as *to funeralize*, has come into favor again, and I note, among its other products, *to belgiumize, to vacationize, to picturize, to scenarioize, to cohanize,*[59] *to citizenize* and *to institutionalize*. But often the noun or adjective is used in its original form, without any attempt at explanatory inflection. Thus, I have en-

[57] This use of *tenderloin* is ascribed to Alexander (alias "Clubber") Williams, a New York police captain. *Vide* the *New York Sun*, July 11, 1913. Williams, in 1876, was transferred from an obscure precinct to West Thirtieth Street. "I've been having chuck steak ever since I've been on the force," he said, "and now I'm going to have a bit of tenderloin." "The name," says the *Sun*, "has endured more than a generation, moving with the changed amusement geography of the city, and has been adopted in all parts of the country."
[58] *Cf.* Terms of Disparagement, by Marie Gladys Hayden, *Dialect Notes*, vol. iv, pt. iii, pp. 194 *ff*. Also Terms of Disparagement in the Dialect Speech of High School Pupils in California and New Mexico, by Elsie L. Warnock, *Dialect Notes*, vol. v, pt. ii, pp. 60 *ff*.
[59] Apparently a deliberate invention by George M. Cohan, who uses it in his advertising. It means to embellish a musical piece with the characteristic Cohan touches. In the same way the manufacturers of Neolin, a substitute for leather, have sought to popularize *to neolinize*.

countered *to census,*[60] *to wassermann, to major* (*i. e.,* to make this
or that subject a major study in college), *to debut, to author, to
press-agent, to sacrilege, to house-clean, to reunion,*[61] *to headquarters,
to pendulum, to janitor,*[62] and *to vacation.* Many such verbs are
in the vocabularies of the arts and crafts. American librarians say
that a new book has been *accessioned,* trained nurses speak of *specialing,* firemen use *siamesed* hoses, uplifters report that they have
contacted with cases,[63] dealers in kitchen appliances promise *to
service* them (*i. e.,* to keep them in repair for a definite time), and
the managers of a well-known chain of hotels advertise that they are
Statler-operated. The theatrical magazine, *Variety,* always brilliant with novel Americanisms, uses many such verbs, *e. g., to lobby-
display* (*i. e.,* to display photographs of a performer in a theatre
lobby). A great boldness shows itself in the making of these new
verbs. *To demote,* when it came in during the war, was scarcely
challenged. *To renig,* a few years before, had been fashioned, as a
matter of course, from *renegade* by back-formation. *To knock, to
rattle, to roast* and *to pan,* when they appeared, were accepted without question as quite regular. I have found *to s o s,* in the form
of its gerund.[64] *To loan,* still under the ban in England, has been
long in very respectable use in the United States. I have observed
its employment by a vice-president of the National City Bank of
New York,[65] by the dramatic critic of the *Nation,*[66] and by the
secretary of the Poetry Society of America.[67] Where a verb differs
etymologically from its corresponding noun or is otherwise felt to
be clumsy or pedantic, the tendency seems to be to dispose of the
difference by manufacturing a new verb. Examples are afforded by
to injunct, to steam-roller and *to operate* (transitive). *To injunct,*
I note, has begun to crowd out *to enjoin;* it is obviously more in har-

[60] New International Encyclopedia, vol. xiv, p. 674.
[61] *Freeman,* May 12, 1920, p. 211, col. 1.
[62] Semi-Centennial Anniversary Book, University of Nebraska, Lincoln, Neb., 1919, p. 43.
[63] See a statement by the Interdepartmental Social Hygiene Board, *Congressional Record,* June 28, 1919, p. 2105, col. 1.
[64] New York *Evening Mail,* Feb. 2, 1918, p. 1.
[65] George E. Roberts, *Nation's Business,* Oct., 1920, p. 2, col. 1.
[66] Ludwig Lewisohn, in his translation of Wassermann's The World's Illusion; New York, 1920.
[67] Jessie B. Rittenhouse, *Poetry,* Jan., 1921, p. 229.

TENDENCIES IN AMERICAN 193

mony with its noun, *injunction*. *To steam-roller* early displaced to *steam-roll*.[68] As for *to operate*, the *Journal* of the American Medical Association wars upon it in vain. More and more, surgeons report that they operated a patient, not *on* him.

This last example, however, violates one tendency almost as clearly as it shows another. In general, the English habit of hitching a preposition to a verb is carried to even greater lengths in America than it is in England. The colloquial language is very rich in such compounds, and some of them have come to have special meanings. Compare, for example, *to give* and *to give out, to go back* and *to go back on, to beat* and *to beat it, to light* and *to light out, to butt* and *to butt in, to turn* and *to turn down, to show* and *to show up, to put* and *to put over, to wind* and *to wind up*. Sometimes, however, the addition seems to be merely rhetorical, as in *to start off, to finish up, to open up, to beat up* (or *out*), *to try out, to stop over* (or *off*), and *to hurry up*. *To hurry up* is so commonplace in America that everyone uses it and no one notices it, but it remains rare in England. *Up* seems to be essential to many of these latter-day verbs, e. g., *to pony up, to doll up, to ball up;* without it they are without significance. Sometimes unmistakable adverbs are substituted for prepositions, as in *to stay put* and *to call down*. "Brush your hat *off*" would seem absurd to an Englishman; so would "The Committee reported *out* the bill." Nearly all of these reinforced verbs are supported by corresponding adjectives and nouns, e. g., *cut-up, show-down, kick-in, come-down, hand-out, start-off, wind-up, run-in, balled-up, dolled-up, bang-up, turn-down, frame-up, stop-over, jump-off, call-down, buttinski*.

The rapidity with which words move through the parts of speech must be observed by every student of American. The case of *bum* I have already cited: it is noun, adjective, verb and adverb. The adjective *lonesome*, in "all by her *lonesome*," becomes a sort of pronoun. The verb *to think*, in "he had another *think* coming," becomes a noun. *Jitney* is an old American noun lately revived; a month after its revival it was also an adjective, and before long it will be a verb. *To lift up* was turned tail first and made a substan-

[68] Similarly the agent noun derived from *the New Thought* is not *New Thinker* but *New Thoughter*.

tive, and is now also an adjective and a verb. *Joy-ride* became a verb the day after it was born as a noun. So did *auto* and *phone*. So did the adjective, *a. w. o. l.* Immediately the Workmen's Compensation Act began to appear on the statute-books of the States, the adjective *compensable* was born. Other adjectives are made by the simple process of adding *-y* to nouns, *e. g., classy, tasty, tony.* And what of *livest?* An astounding inflection, indeed—but with quite sound American usage behind it. The *Metropolitan Magazine,* of which Col. Roosevelt was an editor, announces on its letter paper that it is "the *livest* magazine in America," and *Poetry,* the organ of the new poetry movement, used to print at the head of its contents page the following encomium from the *New York Tribune:* "the *livest* art in America today is poetry, and the *livest* expression of that art is in this little Chicago monthly."

We have seen how readily new prefixes and affixes are adopted in America. Often a whole word is thus put to service, and such amalgamations produce many new words. Thus *smith* threatens to breed a long series of new agent nouns, *e. g., ad-smith, joke-smith;* and *fiend* (a characteristic American hyperbole) has already produced a great many, *e. g., movie-fiend, drug-fiend, bridge-fiend, golf-fiend, coke-fiend, kissing-fiend.* Moreover, there is no impediment to their almost infinite multiplication. If some enterprising shoe-repairer began calling himself a *shoe-smith* tomorrow no one would think to protest against the neologism, and if some new game were introduced from abroad, say the German Skat, the corresponding *fiend* would come with it. Always the effort is to dispose of a long explanatory phrase by substituting a succinct and concrete term. This effort is responsible for many whole classes of compounds, *e. g.,* the *hospital* series: *doll-hospital, china-hospital, camera-hospital, pipe-hospital,* etc. It is responsible, too, for many somewhat startling derivatives, *e. g., mixologist* and *tuberculogian.*[69] And it lies behind the invention of many words that are not compounds, but boldly put forth new roots, many of them etymologically unintelligible, *e. g., jazz, jinx, hobo,*[70] *woozy, goo-goo* (eyes), *hoakum, sundae.* A

[69] I encounter this in *The Campaign,* a magazine published by the Health Department of Iowa.
[70] An etymology for *hobo* is suggested by H. R. Jeffrey in *Dialect Notes,* vol. v, pt. iii (1920), p. 86. As for *jazz,* see *English,* May-June, 1919, p. 90.

large number of characteristic Americanisms are deliberate inventions, devised to designate new objects or to clothe old objects with a special character. The American advertiser is an extraordinarily diligent manufacturer of such terms, and many of his coinages, e. g., *kodak, vaseline, listerine, postum, carborundum, klaxon, jap-a-lac, pianola, victrola, dictagraph* and *uneeda* are quite as familiar to all Americans as *tractor* or *soda-mint,* and have come into general acceptance as common nouns. The Eastman Kodak Company, indeed, has sometimes had to call attention to the fact that *kodak* is its legal property, and in the same way the Chesebrough Manufacturing Company has had to protect *vaseline.*[71] Dr. Louise Pound has made an interesting study of these artificial trade-names.[72] They fall, she finds, into a number of well defined classes. There are the terms that are simple derivatives from proper names, e. g., *listerine, postum, klaxon;* the shortenings, e. g., *jell-o, jap-a-lac;* the extensions with common suffixes, e. g., *alabastine, protectograph, dictograph, orangeade, crispette, pearline, electrolier;* the extensions with new or fanciful suffixes, e. g., *resinol, thermos, grafanola, shinola, sapolio, lysol, neolin, crisco;* the diminutives, e. g., *cascaret, wheatlet, chiclet;* the simple compounds, e. g., *palmolive, spearmint, peptomint, autocar;* the blends, e. g., *cuticura, damaskeene, locomobile, mobiloil;* the blends made of proper names, e. g., *Oldsmobile, Hupmobile, Valspar;* the blends made of parts of syllables or simple initials, e. g., *Reo, nabisco;* the terms involving substitution, e. g., *triscut;* and the arbitrary formations, e. g., *kodak, tiz, clysmic, vivil.* Dr. Brander Matthews once published an Horatian ode, of unknown authorship, made up of such inventions.[73] I transcribe it for the joy of connoisseurs:

[71] *Kodak* had even got into the Continental languages. In October, 1917, the Verband Deutscher Amateurphotographen-Vereine was moved to issue the following warning: "Es giebt keine deutschen *Kodaks. Kodak,* als Sammelname für photographische Erzeugnisse, ist falsch und bezeichnet nur die Fabrikate der Eastman-*Kodak*-Company. Wer von einem *Kodak* spricht und nur allgemein eine photographische Kamera meint, bedenkt nicht, dass er mit der Weiterverbreitung dieses Wortes die deutsche Industrie zugunsten der amerikanisch-englischen schädigt." In American there are a number of familiar derivatives, e. g., *to kodak, kodaker, kodak-fiend.*
[72] Word-Coinage and Modern Trade Names, *Dialect Notes*, vol. iv, pt. i (1913), pp. 29-41.
[73] The Advertiser's Artful Aid, *Bookman,* Feb., 1919, p. 659 ff. See also Word-Coinage, by Leon Mead; New York, n. d., and Burgess Unabridged, by Gelett Burgess; New York, 1914.

> Chipeco thermos dioxygen, temco sonora tuxedo
> Resinol fiat bacardi, camera ansco wheatena;
> Antiskid pebeco calox, oleo tyco barometer
>   Postum nabisco!
> Prestolite arco congoleum, karo aluminum kryptok,
> Crisco balopticon lysol, jello bellans, carborundum!
> Ampico clysmic swoboda, pantasote necco britannica
>   Encyclopædia?

One of the words here used is not American, but Italian, *i. e., fiat,* a blend made of the initials of Fabbrica Italiano Automobili Torino; most of the others are quite familiar to all Americans. "But only a few of them," says Dr. Matthews, "would evoke recognition from an Englishman; and what a Frenchman or a German would make out of the eight lines it is beyond human power even to guess. Corresponding words have been devised in France and in Germany, but only infrequently; and apparently the invention of trade-mark names is not a customary procedure on the part of foreign advertisers. The British, although less affluent in this respect than we are, seem to be a little more inclined to employ the device than their competitors on the continent. Every American, traveling on the railways which converge upon London, must have experienced a difficulty in discovering whether the station at which his train has paused is Stoke Pogis or Bovril, Chipping Norton or Mazzawattee. None the less it is safe to say that the concoction of a similar ode by the aid of the trade-mark words invented in the British Isles would be a task of great difficulty on account of the paucity of terms sufficiently artificial to bestow the exotic remoteness which is accountable for the aroma of the American 'ode'."

Of analogous character are artificial words of the *scalawag* and *rambunctious* class, the formation of which constantly goes on. Some of them are telescope forms: *grandificent* (from *grand* and *magnificent*), *sodalicious* (from *soda* and *delicious*) and *warphan* (*age*) (from *war* and *orphan* [*age*]). Others are made up of common roots and grotesque affixes: *swelldoodle, splendiferous* and *peacharino*. Yet others are stretch forms or mere extravagant inventions: *scallywampus, supergobsloptious* and *floozy*.[74] Many of

---

[74] *Cf.* Some English "Stretch Forms," by Louise Pound, *Dialect Notes*, vol. iv pt. i, p. 52. Also Terms of Approbation and Eulogy, by Elsie L. Warnock, *Dialect Notes*, vol. iv, pt. i, p. 13 *ff.*

these are devised by advertisement writers or college students and belong properly to slang, but there is a steady movement of selected specimens into the common vocabulary. The words in -*doodle* hint at German influences, and those in -*ino* owe something to Italian or maybe to Spanish.

4.

Foreign Influences Today

The extent of such influences as those last noted upon the development of American, and particularly spoken American, is often underestimated. In no other large nation of the world are there so many aliens, nor is there any other in which so large a proportion of the resident aliens speak languages incomprehensible to the native. Since 1820 nearly 35,000,000 immigrants have come into this country, and of them probably not 10,000,000 brought any preliminary acquaintance with English with them. The census of 1910 showed that nearly 1,500,000 persons then living permanently on American soil could not speak it at all; that more than 13,000,000 had been born in other countries, chiefly of different language;[75] and that nearly 20,000,000 were the children of such immigrants, and hence under the influence of their speech habits. No other country houses so many aliens. In Great Britain the alien population, for a century past, has never been more than 2 per cent of the total population, and since the passage of the Aliens Act of 1905 it has tended to decline steadily. In Germany, in 1910, there were but 1,259,873 aliens in a population of more than 60,000,000, and of these nearly half were German-speaking Austrians and Swiss. In France, in 1906, there were 1,000,000 foreigners in a population of 39,000,000 and a third of them were French-speaking Belgians, Luxembourgeois and Swiss. In Italy, in 1911, there were but 350,000 in a population of 35,000,000.

This large and constantly reinforced admixture of foreigners has

[75] As I write the 1920 returns are not complete. But a preliminary bulletin shows there were 13,703,987 foreign-born whites in the country that year, of whom less than 3,000,000 came from countries of English speech.

naturally exerted a constant pressure upon the national language, for the majority of them, at least in the first generation, have found it quite impossible to acquire it in any purity, and even their children have grown up with speech habits differing radically from those of correct English. The effects of this pressure are obviously twofold; on the one hand the foreigner, struggling with a strange and difficult tongue, makes efforts to simplify it as much as possible, and so strengthens the native tendency to disregard all niceties and complexities, and on the other hand he corrupts it with words and locutions from the language he has brought with him, and sometimes with whole idioms and grammatical forms. We have seen, in earlier chapters, how the Dutch and French of colonial days enriched the vocabulary of the colonists, how the German immigrants of the first half of the nineteenth century enriched it still further, and how the Irish of the same period influenced its everyday usages. The same process is still going on. The Italians, the Slavs, and above all, the Russian Jews, make steady contributions to the American vocabulary and idiom, and though these contributions are often concealed by quick and complete naturalization their foreignness to English remains none the less obvious. *I should worry,*[76] in its way, is correct English, but in essence it is as completely Yiddish as *kosher, ganof, schadchen, oi-yoi, matzoth* or *mazuma*.[77]

The extent of such influences remains to be studied; in the whole literature I can find but one formal article upon the subject. That article [78] deals specifically with the suffix *-fest,* which came into American from the German and was probably suggested by familiar-

[76] In Yiddish, *ish ka bibble.* The origin and meaning of the phrase have been variously explained. One theory is to the effect that it is a Yiddish corruption of the German *nicht gefiedelt* (=*not fiddled*=*not flustered*). But this seems to me to be fanciful. To the Jews *ish* is probably the first personal pronoun and *ka* appears to be a corruption of *kann.* As for *bibble,* I suspect that it is the offspring of *bedibbert* (=*embarrassed, intimidated*). The phrase thus has an ironical meaning, *I should be embarrassed,* almost precisely equivalent to *I should worry.*

[77] All of which, of course, are coming into American, along with many other Yiddish words. These words tend to spread far beyond the areas actually settled by Jews. Thus I find *mazuma* in a Word-List from Kansas, from the collectanea of Judge J. C. Ruppenthal, of Russell, Kansas, Dialect Notes, vol. iv, pt. v, 1916, p. 322.

[78] Louise Pound: Domestication of the Suffix *-fest,* Dialect Notes, vol. iv, pt. v, 1916. Dr. Pound, it should be mentioned, has also printed a brief note on *-inski.*

TENDENCIES IN AMERICAN 199

ity with *sängerfest*. There is no mention of it in any of the dictionaries of Americanisms, and yet, in such forms as *talkfest, gabfest*,[79] *swatfest* and *hoochfest*, it is met with almost daily. So with *-heimer*, *-inski* and *-bund*. Several years ago *-heimer* had a great vogue in slang, and was rapidly done to death. But *wiseheimer* remains in colloquial use as a facetious synonym for *smart-aleck*, and after awhile it may gradually acquire dignity. Far lowlier words, in fact, have worked their way in. *Buttinski*, perhaps, is going the same route. As for the words in *-bund*, many of them are already almost accepted. *Plunder-bund* is now at least as good as *pork-barrel* and *slush-fund*, and *money-bund* is frequently heard in Congress.[80] Such locutions creep in stealthily, and are secure before they are suspected. Current slang, out of which the more decorous language dredges a large part of its raw materials, is full of them. *Nix* and *nixy*, for *no*, are debased forms of the German *nicht; aber nit*, once as popular as *camouflage*, is obviously *aber nicht*. And a steady flow of nouns, all needed to designate objects introduced by immigrants, enriches the vocabulary. The Hungarians not only brought their national condiment with them; they also brought its name, *paprika*, and that name is now thoroughly American, as is *goulash*.[81] In the same way the Italians brought in *camorra, padrone, spaghetti, chianti,* and other substantives,[82] and the Jews made contributions from Yiddish and Hebrew and greatly reinforced certain old borrowings from German. Once such a loan-word gets in it takes firm root. During the first year of American participation in the World War an effort was made on patriotic grounds to substitute *liberty-cabbage* for *sauer-kraut*, but it quickly failed, for the

---
[79] A writer in *The Editor and Publisher* for Dec. 25, 1919, p. 30, credits the first use of *gabfest* to the late Joseph S. McCullagh, editor of the St. Louis *Globe-Democrat*. He says: "McCullagh coined the word while writing a comment upon an unusually prolonged and empty debate in Congress. No other word in the dictionary or out of it seemed to fit the case so well, and as a great percentage of the readers of the *Globe-Democrat* throughout the Central West were of German birth or origin, *gabfest* was seized upon with hearty zest, and it is today very generally applied to any protracted and particularly loquacious gathering."

[80] For example, see the *Congressional Record* for April 3, 1918, p. 4928.

[81] *Paprika* is in the Standard Dictionary, but I have been unable to find it in any English dictionary. Another such word is *kimono*, from the Japanese.

[82] Including, so Dr. Arthur Livingston tells me, *policy* (the name of the gambling game). Dr. Livingston believes that *policy* is from *polizza*, which is immigrant Italian for the ticket used in a lottery.

name had become as completely Americanized as the thing itself, and so *liberty-cabbage* seemed affected and absurd. In the same way a great many other German words survived the passions of the time. Nor could all the ardor of the professional patriots obliterate that German influence which has fastened upon the American *yes* something of the quality of *ja,* or prevent the constant appearance of such German loan-forms as "it *listens* well" and "I want *out.*" Many American loan-words are of startlingly outlandish origin. *Hooch,* according to a recent writer,[83] is from a northwestern Indian language, and so is *skookum. Cuspidor,* a typical Americanism, is from the Portuguese *cuspador,* one who spits.[84]

Constant familiarity with such immigrants from foreign languages and with the general speech habits of foreign peoples has made American a good deal more hospitable to loan-words than English, even in the absence of special pressure. Let the same word knock at the gates of the two languages, and American will admit it more readily, and give it at once a wider and more intimate currency. Examples are afforded by *café, vaudeville, revue, employé, boulevard, cabaret, exposé, kindergarten, dépôt, fête,* and *menu. Café,* in American, is a word of much larger and more varied meaning than in English and is used much more frequently, and by many more persons. So is *employé,* in the naturalized form of *employee.* So is *toilet:* we have even seen it as a euphemism for native terms that otherwise would be in daily use. So is *kindergarten:* during the war I read of a *kindergarten* for the elementary instruction of conscripts. Such words are not unknown to the Englishman, but when he uses them it is with a plain sense of their foreignness. In American they are completely naturalized, as is shown by the spelling and pronunciation of most of them. An American would no more think of attempting the correct French pronunciation of *depot* (though he always makes the final *t* silent), or of putting the French accents upon it than he would think of spelling *toilet* with the final *te* or of essaying to pronounce *Münchner* in the German manner.

[83] *Writer's Monthly,* March, 1921, p. 251.
[84] A correspondent tells me that it was introduced by James Connolly, of New York, a manufacturer of spittoons.

TENDENCIES IN AMERICAN 201

Often curious battles go on between such loan-words and their English equivalents, and with varying fortunes. In 1895 Weber and Fields tried to establish *music-hall* in New York, but it quickly succumbed to *vaudeville-theatre,* as *variety* had succumbed to *vaudeville* before it. In the same way *lawn-fete* (without the circumflex accent, and sometimes, alas, pronounced *feet*) has elbowed out the English *garden-party*. But now and then, when the competing loan-word happens to violate American speech habits, a native term ousts it. The French *crèche* offers an example; it has been entirely displaced by *day-nursery*.

The English, in this matter, display their greater conservatism very plainly. Even when a loan-word enters both English and American simultaneously a sense of foreignness lingers about it on the other side of the Atlantic much longer than on this side, and it is used with far more self-consciousness. The word *matinée* offers a convenient example. To this day the English commonly print it in italics, give it its French accent, and pronounce it with some attempt at the French manner. But in America it is entirely naturalized, and the most ignorant man uses it without any feeling that it is strange. Often a loan-word loses all signs of its original foreignness. For example, there is *shimmy,* a corruption of both *chemise* and *chemin* (*de fer*), the name of a card game: it has lost both its original forms and, in one sense, its original meaning.[85] The same lack of any sense of linguistic integrity is to be noticed in many other directions—for example, in the freedom with which the Latin *per* is used with native nouns. One constantly sees *per day, per dozen, per hundred, per mile,* etc., in American newspapers, even the most careful, but in England the more seemly *a* is almost always used, or the noun itself is made Latin, as in *per diem*. *Per,* in fact, is fast becoming an everyday American word. Such phrases as "as *per* your letter (or order) of the 15th inst." are met with incessantly in business correspondence. The same greater hospitality is shown by the readiness with which various un-English prefixes and

[85] *Cf.* The Jocularization of French Words and Phrases in Present Day American Speech, by Louise Pound, *Dialect Notes*, vol. v, p. iii, 1920.

affixes come into fashion, for example, *super-* and *-itis*. The English accept them gingerly; the Americans take them in with enthusiasm, and naturalize them instanter.[86]

The pressure of loan-words, of course, is greatest in those areas in which the foreign population is largest. In some of these areas it has given rise to what are almost distinct dialects. Everyone who has ever visited lower Pennsylvania must have observed the wide use of German terms by the natives, and the German intonations in their speech, even when they are most careful with their English.[87] In the same way, the English of everyday life in New Orleans is full of French terms, *e. g., praline, brioche, lagniappe, armoir, kruxingiol* (= *croquignole*), *pooldoo* (= *poule d'eau*),[88] and the common speech of the Southwest is heavy with debased Spanish, *e. g., alamo, arroyo, chaparral, caballero, comino, jornada, frijole, presidio, serape, hombre, quien sabe, vamose*.[89] As in the early days of settlement, there is a constant movement of favored loan-words into the general speech of the country. *Hooch,* from the Chinook, was for long a localism in the Northwest; suddenly it appeared everywhere. So with certain Chinese and Japanese words that have, within late years, entered the general speech from the speech of California. New York has been the port of entry for most of the new Yiddish and Italian loan-words, as it was the port of entry for Irishisms seventy years ago. In Michigan the natives begin to borrow from the Dutch settlers and may later on pass on their borrowings to the rest of the country; in the prairie states many loan-words from the Scandinavian languages are already in use; in Kansas there are even traces of Russian influence.[90]

In the Philippines and in Hawaii American naturally shows even greater hospitality to loan-words; in both places distinct dialects have been developed, quite unintelligible to the newcomer from

---

[86] *Cf.* Vogue Affixes in Present-Day Word-Coinage, by Louise Pound, *Dialect Notes,* vol. v, pt. i, 1918. Dr. Pound ascribes the vogue of *super-* to German influences. See also The Cult of *Super,* Boston *Globe,* Aug. 31, 1921.
[87] See *Dialect Notes,* vol. iv, p. 157; *ibid.,* p. 337.
[88] See *Dialect Notes,* vol. iv, p. 268; *ibid.,* p. 346; *ibid.,* p. 420.
[89] See three articles by the late Prof. H. Tallichet in *Dialect Notes,* vol. i, p. 185, p. 243 and p. 324.
[90] *Cf.* Russian Words in Kansas, *Dialect Notes,* vol. iv, p. 161.

home. Maurice P. Dunlap[91] offers the following specimen of a conversation between two Americans long resident in Manila:

Hola, amigo.
Komusta kayo.
Porque were you *hablaing* with *ese señorita?*
She wanted a job as *lavandera.*
Cuanto?
Ten cents, *conant*, a piece, so I told her *no kerry.*
Have you had *chow?* Well, *spera*, till I sign this *chit* and I'll take a *paseo* with you.

Here we have an example of Philippine American that shows all the tendencies of American Yiddish. It retains the general forms of American, but in the short conversation, embracing but 41 different words, there are eight loan-words from the Spanish (*hola, amigo, porque, ese, señorita, lavandera, cuanto* and *paseo*), two Spanish locutions in a debased form (*spera* for *espera* and *no kerry* for *no quiero*), two loan-words from the Tagalog (*komusta* and *kayo*),[92] two from Pidgin English (*chow* and *chit*), one Philippine-American localism (*conant*), and a Spanish verb with an English inflection (*hablaing*).

The American dialect developed in Hawaii is thus described by a writer in the *Christian Science Monitor:* [93]

Honolulu, despite the score or more of races which intermingle in absolute harmony, is a strictly American community. English is the language which predominates; and yet there are perhaps a hundred or more Hawaiian words which are used by everyone, almost exclusively, in preference to those English words of similar meaning.
"Are you *pau?*" asks the American housekeeper of her Japanese yard man.
"All *pau*," he responds.
The housekeeper has asked if the yard man is through. He has replied that he is. She would not think of asking, "Are you *through?*" *Pau*—pronounced *pow*—as used in Honolulu conveys just as much meaning to the Honolulan as the English[94] word *through*. It is one of the commonest of the Hawaiian words used today.
In Honolulu one does not say "the northwest corner of Fort and Hotel Streets."

[91] What Americans Talk in the Philippines, *American Review of Reviews*, Aug., 1913.
[92] But here *komusta* may be borrowed from the Spanish *como está* (= *how are you?*).
[93] Unluckily, I have been unable to determine the writer's name or the date.
[94] That is, American; *through*, in this sense, is seldom used by the English.

One says "the *makai-ewa* corner." *Makai* means toward the sea. *Ewa* means toward the north or in the direction of the big Ewa plantation which lies toward the north of Honolulu. Thus the *makai-ewa* corner means that corner which is on the seaward side and toward Ewa. Instead of saying *east* or the direction in which the sun rises, Honolulans say *mauka*, which means toward the mountains. To designate south, they say *waikiki*, which means toward Diamond Head or Waikiki Beach.

One often hears a little boy say he has a *puka* in his stocking. The housekeeper directs the yard man to put the rubbish in the *puka*. It is a simple Hawaiian word meaning hole. Another common word is *lanai*. In English it means porch or veranda. One never says, "Come out on the *porch*," but "Come out on the *lanai*."

The two words *pahea oe* are used as a term of greeting. In the States they say, "How do you do?" "How are you?" or "Good day." In Honolulu, "*Pahea oe?*" conveys the same meaning. The response is *Maikai no*, or "Very good," or "All right."

On the mainland the word *aloha* is not new. It is used as a word of greeting or as a word of farewell. "*Aloha oe*" may mean "Farewell to you," "How are you?" or "Good day." The word is not as common among the Americans as some of the others, but is used to a more exclusive extent by the Hawaiians.

A large number of Americans have an entirely wrong interpretation of the word *kanaka*. In its truest and only sense it means *man*. It can be interpreted in no other way. In Hawaiian a man is a *kanaka*, a woman a *wahine*. The word *kane* is also often used as *man*, and coupled with the word *keiki*—*keiki kane*—means *boy*. The Hawaiians have often been referred to as *kanakas*, which on the mainland has developed into more or less of a slang word to designate the people of the Hawaiian race. This, however, is totally incorrect.

The *kamaaina*, or old-timer, usually refers to his hat as his *papale*. His house is his *hale*, and his food is usually designated as *kaukau*, although this is not a Hawaiian word. There are perhaps a hundred other such words which are used daily in preference to those which mean the same in English.

The immigrant in the midst of a large native population, of course, exerts no such pressure upon the national language as that exerted upon an immigrant language by the native, but nevertheless his linguistic habits and limitations have to be reckoned with in dealing with him, and the concessions thus made necessary have a very ponderable influence upon the general speech. Of much importance is the support given to a native tendency by the foreigner's incapacity for employing (or even comprehending) syntax of any complexity, or words not of the simplest. This is the tendency toward succinctness and clarity, at whatever sacrifice of grace. One English observer, Sidney Low, puts the chief blame for the general explosiveness of American upon the immigrant, who must be communicated with in the plainest words available, and is not socially worthy of the suavity of circumlocution anyhow.[95] In his turn the immigrant seizes upon these plainest words as upon a sort of convenient Lingua Franca—his quick adoption of *damn* as a universal adjective is traditional—and throws his influence upon the side of the underlying speech habit when he gets on in the vulgate. Many characteristic Americanisms of the sort to stagger lexicographers— for example, *near-silk*—have come from the Jews, whose progress in business is a good deal faster than their progress in English.

[95] The American People, 2 vols.; New York, 1909-11, vol. ii, pp. 449-50. For a discussion of this effect of contact with foreigners upon a language see also Beach-la-Mar, by William Churchill; Washington, 1911, p. 11 *ff*.

VII.

THE STANDARD AMERICAN PRONUNCIATION

1.

General Characters

"Language," said Sayce, in 1879, "does not consist of letters, but of sounds, and until this fact has been brought home to us our study of it will be little better than an exercise of memory."[1] The theory, at that time, was somewhat strange to English grammarians and etymologists, despite the investigations of A. J. Ellis and the massive lesson of Grimm's law; their labors were largely wasted upon deductions from the written word. But since then, chiefly under the influence of German philologists, they have turned from orthographical futilities to the actual sounds of the tongue, and the latest and best grammar, that of Sweet, is frankly based upon the spoken English of educated Englishmen—not, remember, of conscious purists, but of the general body of cultivated folk. Unluckily, this new method also has its disadvantages. The men of a given race and time usually write a good deal alike, or, at all events, attempt to write alike, but in their oral speech there are wide variations. "No two persons," says a leading contemporary authority upon English phonetics,[2] "pronounce exactly alike." Moreover, "even the best speaker commonly uses more than one style." The result is that it is extremely difficult to determine the prevailing pronunciation of a given combination of letters at any time and place. The persons whose speech is studied pronounce it with minute shades of difference, and admit other differences according as they are conversing naturally or endeavoring to exhibit their pronuncia-

---

[1] The Science of Language, vol. ii, p. 339.
[2] Daniel Jones: The Pronunciation of English, 2nd ed.; Cambridge, 1914, p. 1. Jones is lecturer in phonetics at University College, London.

tion. Worse, it is impossible to represent a great many of these shades in print. Sweet, trying to do it,[3] found himself, in the end, with a preposterous alphabet of 125 letters. Prince L.-L. Bonaparte more than doubled this number, and Ellis brought it to 390.[4] Other phonologists, English and Continental, have gone floundering into the same bog. The dictionary-makers, forced to a far greater economy of means, are brought into obscurity. The difficulties of the enterprise, in fact, are probably unsurmountable. It is, as White says, "almost impossible for one person to express to another by signs the sound of any word." "Only the voice," he goes on, "is capable of that; for the moment a sign is used the question arises, What is the value of that sign? The sounds of words are the most delicate, fleeting and inapprehensible things in nature. . . . Moreover, the question arises as to the capability to apprehend and distinguish sounds on the part of the person whose evidence is given."[5] Certain German orthoëpists, despairing of the printed page, have turned to the phonograph, and there is a Deutsche Grammophon-Gesellschaft in Berlin which offers records of specimen speeches in a great many languages and dialects, including English. The phonograph has also been put to successful use in language teaching by various American correspondence schools.

In view of all this it would be hopeless to attempt to exhibit in print the numerous small differences between English and American pronunciation, for many of them are extremely delicate and subtle, and only their aggregation makes them plain. According to a recent and very careful observer [6] the most important of them do not lie in pronunciation at all, properly so called, but in intonation. In this direction, he says, one must look for the true characters of "the English accent." Despite the opinion of Krapp, a very competent authority, that "the American voice in general starts on a higher plane, is normally pitched higher than the British voice,"[7]

[3] *Vide* his Handbook of Phonetics, p. xv *ff*.
[4] It is given in Ellis' Early English Pronunciations, p. 1293 *ff*. and in Sayce's The Science of Language, vol. i, p. 353 *ff*.
[5] Every-Day English, p. 29.
[6] Robert J. Menner: The Pronunciation of English in America, *Atlantic Monthly*, March, 1915, p. 366.
[7] The Pronunciation of Standard English in America; New York, 1919, p. 50. For White, see Words and Their Uses, p. 58.

I incline to agree with White that the contrary is the case. The nasal twang which Englishmen observe in the *vox Americana,* though it has high overtones, is itself not high pitched, but rather low pitched, as all constrained and muffled tones are apt to be. The causes of that twang have long engaged phonologists, and in the main they agree that there is a physical basis for it—that our generally dry climate and rapid changes of temperature produce an actual thickening of the membranes concerned in the production of sound.[8] We are, in brief, a somewhat snuffling people, and much more given to catarrhs and coryzas than the inhabitants of damp Britain. Perhaps this general impediment to free and easy utterance, subconsciously apprehended, is responsible both for the levelness of tone of American speech, noted by Krapp, and for the American tendency to pronounce the separate syllables of a word with much more care than an Englishman bestows upon them. "To British ears," says Krapp,[9] "American speech often sounds hesitating, monotonous and indecisive, and British speech, on the other hand, is likely to seem to Americans abrupt, explosive and manneristic." The American, in giving *extraordinary* six careful and distinct syllables instead of the Englishman's grudging four, may be seeking to make up for a natural disability. Marsh, in his "Lectures on the English Language," sought two other explanations of the fact. On the one hand, he argued that the Americans of his day read a great deal more than the English, and were thus much more influenced by the spelling of words, and on the other hand he pointed out that "our flora shows that the climate of even our Northern States belongs . . . to a more Southern type than that of England," and that "in Southern latitudes . . . articulation is generally much more distinct than in Northern regions." In support of the latter proposition he cited the pronunciation of Spanish, Italian and Turkish, as compared with that of English, Danish and German—rather unfortunate examples,

---

[8] The following passage from Kipling's American Notes, ch. i, will be recalled: "Oliver Wendell Holmes says that the Yankee schoolmarm, the cider and the salt codfish of the Eastern states are responsible for what he calls a nasal accent. I know better. They stole books from across the water without paying for 'em, and the snort of delight was fixed in their nostrils forever by a just Providence. That is why they talk a foreign tongue today."
[9] The Pronunciation of Standard English in America, p. 50. For Marsh, following, see lecture xxx, The English Language in America.

THE STANDARD AMERICAN PRONUNCIATION 209

for the pronunciation of German is at least as clear as that of Spanish. Swedish would have supported his case far better: the Swedes debase their vowels and slide over their consonants even more markedly than the English. Marsh believed that there was a tendency among Southern peoples to throw the accent toward the ends of words, and that this helped to bring out all the syllables. A superficial examination shows a number of examples of that movement of accent in American: *advertisement, paresis, pianist, primarily, telegrapher, temporarily*. The English invariably accent all of these words on the first syllable; Americans usually accent *primarily* and *telegrapher* on the second, and *temporarily* on the third, and *paresis* and *pianist* on the second. Again there are *frontier* and *harass*. The English accent the first syllables; we accent the second. Yet again there is the verb, *to perfect*. Tucker says [10] that its accentuation on the second syllable, "bringing it into harmony with *perfume, cement, desert, present, produce, progress, project, rebel, record,* and other words which are accented on the final syllable when used as verbs, originated in this country." But when all these examples have been marshalled, the fact remains that there are just as many examples, and perhaps many more, of an exactly contrary tendency. The chief movement in American, in truth, would seem to be toward throwing the accent upon the first syllable. I recall *mamma, papa, inquiry, ally, recess, details, idea, alloy, deficit, armistice* and *adult;* I might add *defect, excess, address, magazine, decoy* and *romance*.

Thus it is unsafe, here as elsewhere, to generalize too facilely, and particularly unsafe to exhibit causes with too much assurance. "Man frage nicht warum," says Philipp Karl Buttmann. "Der Sprachgebrauch lässt sich nur beobachten." [11] But the greater distinctness of American utterance, whatever its genesis and machinery, is palpable enough in many familiar situations. "The typical American accent," says Vizetelly, "is often harsh and unmusical, but it sounds all of the letters to be sounded, and slurs, but does not distort, the rest." [12] An American, for example, almost always sounds the

---
[10] American English, p. 33.
[11] Lexilogus, 2nd ed.; Berlin, 1860, p. 239.
[12] A Desk-Book of 25,000 Words Frequently Mispronounced, p. xvi.

first *l* in *fulfill;* an Englishman makes the first syllable *foo*. An American sounds every syllable in *extraordinary, literary, military, dysentery, temporary, necessarily, secretary* and the other words of the *-ary*-group;[13] an Englishman never pronounces the *a* of the penultimate syllable. *Kindness,* with the *d* silent, would attract notice in the United States; in England, according to Jones,[14] the *d* is "very commonly, if not usually" omitted. *Often,* in America, commonly retains a full *t;* in England it is actually and officially *offen.* Let an American and an Englishman pronounce *program(me).* Though the Englishman retains the long form of the last syllable in writing, he reduces it in speaking to a thick triple consonant, *grm;* the American enunciates it clearly, rhyming it with *damn.* Or try the two with any word ending in *-g,* say *sporting* or *ripping.* Or with any word having *r* before a consonant, say *card, harbor, lord* or *preferred.* "The majority of Englishmen," says Menner, "certainly do not pronounce the *r* . . . ; just as certainly the majority of educated Americans pronounce it distinctly."[15] Henry James, visiting the United States after many years of residence in England, was much harassed by this persistent *r*-sound, which seemed to him to resemble "a sort of morose grinding of the back teeth."[16] So sensitive to it did he become that he began to hear it where it was actually non-existent, save as an occasional barbarism, for example, in *Cuba-r, vanilla-r* and *California-r.* He put the blame for it, and for various other departures from the strict canon of contemporary English, upon "the American school, the American newspaper, and the American Dutchman and Dago." Unluckily for his case, the full sounding of the *r* came into American long before the appearance of any of these influences. The early

---

[13] With the exception of *cemetery;* here the careful pronunciation of the last two syllables is a vulgarism. *Cf.* also the *-oly* and *-ory* groups, *e. g., melancholy* and *laboratory.*

[14] The Pronunciation of English, p. 17.

[15] The Pronunciation of English in America, *op. cit.*, p. 362. See also On English Homophones, by Robert Bridges; Oxford, 1919, and Peetickay, by Wilfrid Perrett; Cambridge, 1920, p. 64 *ff.* Bridges' word-lists show how far the elision of the *r* has gone in England. He gives the following, for example, as homophones: *alms-arms, aunt-aren't, balm-barm, board-bored-bawd, hoar-whore-haw, lorn-lawn, pore-paw, source-sauce, saw-soar-sore, stalk-stork, taut-taught-tort, father-farther, ah-are, ayah-ire, bah-bar-baa, taw-tore, raw-roar, more-maw, floor-flaw.*

[16] The Question of Our Speech, p. 29 *ff.*

THE STANDARD AMERICAN PRONUNCIATION 211

colonists, in fact, brought it with them from England, and it still prevailed there in Dr. Johnson's day, for he protested publicly against the "rough snarling sound" and led the movement which finally resulted in its extinction.[17] Today, extinct, it is mourned by English purists, and the Poet Laureate denounces the clergy of the Established Church for saying "the *sawed* of the *Laud*" instead of "the sword of the Lord."[18]

But even in the matter of elided consonants American is not always the conservator. We cling to the *r*, we preserve the *l* in *almond*, we are relatively careful about the final *g*, we give *nephew* a clear *f*-sound instead of the clouded English *v*-sound, and we boldly nationalize *trait* and pronounce its final *t*, but we drop the second *p* from *pumpkin* and change the *m* to *n*, we change the *ph* ($=f$) sound to plain *p* in *diphtheria, diphthong* and *naphtha*,[19] we relieve *rind* of its final *d*, we begin to neglect the *d* in *landlady, handsome, grandmother*, etc., and, in the complete sentence, we slaughter consonants by assimilation. I have heard Englishmen say *brand-new*, but on American lips it is almost invariably *bran-new*. So nearly universal is this nasalization in the United States that certain American lexicographers have sought to found the term upon *bran* and not upon *brand*. Here the national speech is powerfully influenced by Southern dialectical variations, which in turn probably derive partly from French example and partly from the linguistic limitations of the negro. The latter, even after two hundred years, has great difficulties with our consonants, and often drops them. A familiar anecdote well illustrates his speech habit. On a train stopping at a small station in Georgia a darkey threw up a window and yelled "Wah ee?" The reply from a black on the platform was "Wah oo?" A Northerner aboard the train, puzzled by this inarticulate dialogue, sought light from a Southern passenger, who promptly translated the first question as "Where is he?" and the second as "Where is

[17] *Cf.* The Cambridge History of English Literature, vol. xiv, p. 487.
[18] Robert Bridges: A Tract on the Present State of English Pronunciation; Oxford, 1913.
[19] An interesting discussion of this peculiarity is in Some Variant Pronunciations in the New South, by William A. Read, *Dialect Notes*, vol. iii, pt. vii, 1911, p. 504 *ff.*

who?" A recent viewer with alarm [20] argues that this conspiracy against the consonants is spreading, and that English printed words no longer represent the actual sounds of the American language. "Like the French," he says, "we have a marked *liaison*—the borrowing of a letter from the preceding word. We invite one another to *c'meer* (= *come here*). . . . *Hoo-zat?* (= *who is that?*) has as good a *liaison* as the French *vous avez.*" This critic believes that American tends to abandon *t* for *d*, as in *Sadd'y* (= *Saturday*) and *siddup* (= *sit up*), and to get rid of *h*, as in *ware-zee?* (= *where is he?*). But here we invade the vulgar speech, which belongs to Chapter IX. Even, however, in the standard speech there is a great slaughter of vowels. A correspondent of education, accustomed to observing accurately, sends me the following specimens of his own everyday conversation:

> We mus'n' b'lieve all th'ts said.
> Wh'n y' go t' gi' ch' hat, please bring m' mine.
> Le's go.
> Would'n' stay if ' could.
> Keep on writin' t'll y' c'n do 't right.

But here, of course, we come upon the tendency to depress all vowels to the level of a neutral *e*—a tendency quite as visible in English as in American, though there are differences in detail. The two languages, however, seem to proceed toward phonetic decay on paths that tend to diverge more and more, and the divergences already in effect, though they may seem slight separately, are already of enough importance in the aggregate to put serious impediments between mutual comprehension. Let an Englishman and an American (not of New England) speak a quite ordinary sentence, "My aunt can't answer for my dancing the lancers even passably," and at once the gap separating the two pronunciations will be manifest. Add a dozen everyday words—*military, schedule, trait, hostile, been, lieutenant, patent, laboratory, nephew, secretary, advertisement*, and so on—and the strangeness of one to the other is augmented. "Every Englishman visiting the States for the first time," said an English dramatist some time ago, "has a difficulty in making himself under-

[20] Hugh Mearns: Our Own, Our Native Speech, *McClure's Magazine*, Oct., 1916.

stood. He often has to repeat a remark or a request two or three times to make his meaning clear, especially on railroads, in hotels and at bars. The American visiting England for the first time has the same trouble."[21] Despite the fact that American actors always imitate English pronunciation to the best of their skill, this visiting Englishman asserted that the average American audience is incapable of understanding a genuinely English company, at least "when the speeches are rattled off in conversational style." When he presented one of his own plays with an English company, he said, many American acquaintances, after witnessing the performance, asked him to lend them the manuscript, "that they might visit it again with some understanding of the dialogue."[22] American speech is just as difficult for Englishmen.

2.

The Vowels

In Chapters II and III, I have already discussed historically the pronunciation of *a* in the United States—not, I fear, to much effect, but at all events as illuminatingly as the meagre materials so far amassed permit. The best study of the pronunciation of the letter today is to be found in George Philip Krapp's excellent book, "The Pronunciation of Standard English in America," from which I have already quoted several times. This work is the first adequate treatise upon American phonology to be published, and shows very careful observation and much good sense. Unluckily, Krapp finds it extremely difficult, like all other phonologists, to represent the sounds that he deals with by symbols. He uses, for example, exactly the same symbol to indicate the *a*-sound in *cab* and the *a*-sound in *bad*, though the fact that they differ very greatly must be obvious to everyone. In the same way he grows a bit vague when he tries to represent the compromise *a*-sound which lies somewhere between the *a* of *father* and the *a* of *bad*. "It is heard . . . chiefly," he says,

[21] B. MacDonald Hastings, New York *Tribune*, Jan. 19, 1913.
[22] Various minor differences between English and American pronunciation, not noted here, are discussed in British and American Pronunciation, by Louise Pound, *School Review*, vol. xxiii, No. 6, June, 1915.

"in somewhat conscious and academic speech," as a compromise between the former, "which is rejected as being too broad," and the latter, "which is rejected as being too narrow or flat." This compromise *a*, he says, "is cultivated in words with *a*, sometimes *au*, before a voiceless continuant, or before a nasal followed by a voiceless stop or continuant, as in *grass, half, laugh, path* (also before a voiced continuant, as in *paths, calves, halves, baths*, when the voiced form is a variant, usually the plural, of a head form with a voiceless sound), *aunt, branch, can't, dance, fancy, France, shan't*, etc." Later on he says that this compromise *a*-sound is the same that occurs in *heart, star, large* and *Clarke*, but this, it seems to me, is not quite accurate; there is a perceptible difference. The usual sound of *a* in *heart* is far nearer to that of *a* in *father*.

In any case, as Krapp says, this *a*-sound is commonly an affectation, save in New England, and, as we have seen, it originated as an affectation even there. The flat *a*, on the contrary, is "widely distributed over the whole country," and may be regarded as the normal American *a*, as the *a* of *father* is the normal English *a*. No other difference separates the two dialects more sharply. Krapp notes "the purist tendency to condemn [the flat *a*]" and goes on:

> The result has been to give to [the compromise *a*] extraordinary dictionary and academic prestige in the face of a strongly opposing popular usage. The reasons for this are several: first, that standard British speech and some forms of New England speech have [a broad *a*] in the words in question; second, that New England has exerted, and to some extent continues to exert, a strong influence upon formal instruction and upon notions of cultivation and refinement throughout the country; and third, that [the flat *a*] is often prolonged, or drawled, and nasalized in a way that makes it seem not merely American, but provincially American. To steer between the Scylla of provincialism and the Charybdis of affectation and snobbishness, many conscientious speakers in America cultivate [the compromise *a*]. The writer has tested this sound on many different groups of speakers from various sections of the country, and has never found one who used the sound who did not do so with a certain degree of self-consciousness. If the cult of this sound continues long enough, it may in time come to be a natural and established sound in the language. In the meantime, it seems a pity that so much effort and so much time in instruction should be given to changing a natural habit of speech which is inherently just as good as the one by which the purist would supplant it. Especially in public school instruction it would seem to be wiser to spend time on more important matters in speech than the difference between *half* and *haalf*.[23]

[23] The Pronunciation of Standard English in America, p. 64.

Meanwhile, "the dictionary and academic prestige" of the broad *a*, whatever its precise form, has established it pretty generally in the United States in certain words which formerly had the flat *a*. Those in which it is followed by *lm* offer examples: *psalm, palm, balm* and *calm*. They were once pronounced to rhyme with *ram* and *jam*, but their pronunciation that way has begun to seem provincial and ignorant. Krapp says that the *a* has likewise broadened in *alms, salmon* and *almond*, but it is my own observation that this is not yet generally true. The first syllable of *salmon*, true enough, does not quite rhyme with *ham*, but it is nevertheless still very far from *bomb*. The broad *a*, by a fashionable affectation, has also got into *vase, drama, amen* and *tomato*—in the last case probably helped by the example of Southern speech, in which a few words, notably *master, tomato* and *tassel*, have shown the broad *a* for many years. Its intrusion into *tomato* has been vigorously denounced by an Englishman, Evacustes A. Phipson. "It is really distressing," he says, "to a cultivated Briton visiting America to find people there who . . . follow what they suppose to be the latest London mannerism, regardless of accuracy. Thus we find one literary editress advocating the pedantic British pronunciation *tomahto* in lieu of the good English *tomato*, rhyming with *potato*, saying it sounds so much more 'refined.' I do not know whether she would be of the same opinion if she heard one of our costermongers bawling out: ' 'Ere's yer foine *termarters*, lydy, hownly tuppence a pahnd.' Similarly, we sometimes hear Anglomaniac Americans saying *vahz* for *vase*. Why not also *bahz*, and *cahz?*" [24] Another Englishman calls my attention to an even more curious use of the broad *a* in America, to wit, in *piano*. In England the flat *a* is invariably used in this word. But here, perhaps, a mistaken Anglomania is not to blame. The majority of the better sort of music-teachers in the United States are Continental Europeans, chiefly Germans, and no doubt they teach their pupils to say *piahno* as they teach them the correct Continental pronunciations of such words as *scherzo, lied* and *étude*. The introduction of the broad *a* into *drama* is a pure affectation, and first showed itself, I believe, at the beginning of the heavily self-conscious movement which culminated in the organization of the Drama League of Amer-

[24] *Nation*, Aug. 30, 1919, p. 290.

ica, a society largely composed of college professors and social pushers. *Amen,* with the broad *a,* is a symptom of the movement of social pushers into the Protestant Episcopal Church, which serves, as I have hitherto noted, as the chief center of Anglomania in all parts of the country. E. W. Howe tells a story of a little girl whose mother, on acquiring social aspirations, entered this church from the Methodist Church. The father remaining behind, the little girl had to learn to say *amen* with the flat *a* when she went to church with her father and *amen* with the broad *a* when she went to church with her mother.[25] In Canada, despite the social influence of English usage, the flat *a* has conquered, and along the Canadian-New England border it is actually regarded as a Canadianism, especially in such words as *calm* and *aunt.* The broad *a,* when heard at all, is an affectation, and, as in Boston, is sometimes introduced into words, e. g., *piano* and *amass,* which actually have the flat *a* in England.

A broad *a,* though somewhat shorter than the *a* of *father* (a correspondent compares it aptly to the *a* in the German *mann*) is very widely substituted, in the United States, for the *o* in such words as *got, hot, rob, nobby, prophet, stock* and *chocolate.* The same correspondent suggests that it shows itself clearly in the sentence: *"On top of the log sat a large frog."* To his English ears, this sentence, from American lips, sounds like *"Ann tahp uv thu laug sat a lahrge fraug."* The same *a* is also occasionally heard in *dog, doll, horrid, hog, orange, coffee* and *God,* though it has a rival in the *au*-sound of *audience.*[26] Here, as Krapp observes, there is a considerable variation in usage, even in the same speaker. The man who uses the first *a* in *God* may use the *au*-sound in *dog.* I believe that the former is generally looked upon as more formal. I have often noticed that a speaker who puts the *au*-sound into *God* in his ordinary profane

[25] The Rev. W. G. Polack, of Evansville, Ind., who has made a valuable inquiry into ecclesiastical terminology in America, tells me that among the Lutherans of the Middle West, *amen* has the flat *a* when spoken and the broad *a* when sung. So with the first syllable of *hallelujah,* though the last *a* is always broad.

[26] Krapp says (The Pronunciation of Standard English in America, p. 82) that he also hears this *a*-sound in *project, process, produce* and *provost,* but it is my observation that they are nearly always given a true *o*-sound. *Prohduce* is surely commoner than *prahduce,* and *prohject* is commoner than *prawject.* But *problem, prospect, proverb, product* and *progress* undoubtedly have the *a*-sound of *father.* Henry James denounces *gawd, dawg, sawft, lawft, gawne, lawst* and *frawst* as a "flat-drawling group" in The Question of Our Speech, p. 30, but, as usual, he is somewhat extravagant.

THE STANDARD AMERICAN PRONUNCIATION 217

discourse, will switch to the purer *a*-sound when he wants to show reverence. The broad *a* in *father* seems to have very little influence upon cognate words. Save in New England one never hears it in *gather, lather* and *blather,* and even there it is often abandoned for the flat *a* by speakers who are very careful to avoid the latter in *palm, dance* and *aunt.* Krapp says that the broad *a* is used in "some words of foreign origin," notably *lava, data, errata, bas-relief, spa, mirage* and *garage.* This is certainly not true of the first three, all of which, save exceptionally, have the flat *a.* *Garage,* as one time, threatened to acquire the flat *a,* too, and so became a rhyme for *carriage,* but I believe that a more correct pronunciation is prevailing. In a number of other classes of words the pronunciation of the *a* varies. In *patriot* and its derivatives, for example, the *a* is sometimes that of *hat* and sometimes that of *late.* In *radish* the *a* is sometimes that of *cab* and sometimes a sort of *e,* hard to distinguish from that of *red.* In such proper names as *Alabama, Montana, Nevada* and *Colorado* the flat *a* is commonly heard (especially in the states themselves), but a broad *a* is not unknown. The usual pronunciation of *again* and *against* gives them a second *a* indistinguishable from the *e* of *hen,* but the influence of the schoolmarm has launched a pronunciation employing the *a* of *lane.*

The other vowels present fewer variations from standard English. A spelling pronunciation often appears in *pretty,* making the first syllable rhyme with *set;* it always rhymes with *sit* in standard English. The use of the long *e* in *deaf,* though ardently advocated by Noah Webster, has almost disappeared from cultivated speech; it persists, however, in the vulgate, and is noted in Chapter IX. In the same way the *i*-sound, as in *sit,* has disappeared from *get, yet, chest* and *instead;* even the vulgate is losing it. So, again, the old *ai-sound,* as in *laid,* has vanished from *egg, peg, leg* and their cognates, though here the vulgate preserves it. As Krapp shows, the neutral *e,* toward which all our vowels seem to be tending,[27]

[27] This tendency is not confined to English. The same neutral *e* is encountered in languages as widely differing otherwise as Arabic, French and Swedish. "Its existence," says Sayce, in The Science of Language, vol. i, p. 259, "is a sign of age and decay; meaning has become more important than outward form, and the educated intelligence no longer demands a clear pronunciation in order to understand what is said." Here, of course, decay means phonetic decay; the word has no reference to the general vigor of the language.

shows signs of itself disappearing. This is particularly noticeable, in American, in such words as *moral, quarrel* and *real,* which become *mor'l, quar'l* and *re'l,* each a single syllable. In the vulgar speech this neutral *e* is also dropped from other words, notably *poem, diary, violet* and *diamond,* which become *pome, di'ry, vi'let* and *di'mond.* Even in the standard speech it grows shadowy in the second syllable of *fertile, hostile, servile, fragile, agile, reptile,* etc. In standard English these words are pronounced with the second syllable clearly rhyming with *vile.* The long *e*-sound in *creek* is maintained in standard American, but changed to the short *i*-sound of *sit* in the vulgate. *Sleek* has divided into two words, *slick* and *sleek,* the former signifying cunning and ingratiating and the latter referring especially to appearance. Of late there has been a strong tendency to abandon the old *e*-sound in such terms as *bronchitis* and *appendicitis* for an *ai*-sound, as in *pie* and *buy;* this is a senseless affectation, but it seems to be making progress. A contrary movement to abandon the old *ai*-sound in *iodine, quinine,* etc., for an *e-sound,* as in *sleep,* has better support in etymology, but is apparently less popular. *Chlorine* is always pronounced with the *e*-sound, but *iodine* continues to be *iodyne,* and *kin-een* for *quinine* still sounds strange. In two other familiar words the *ai*-sound has been supplanted in American: in *sliver* by the short *i* of *liver,* and in *farina* by an *e*-sound. Both have the *ai*-sound in standard English. *Been,* in America, almost always is *bin; bean* never appears save as a conscious affectation. But in England *bean* is invariably heard, and in a recent poem an English poet makes it rhyme with *submarine, queen* and *unseen.*[28]

I have already mentioned the displacement of *o* by *ah* or *au* in such words as *dog* and *God.* "Whenever the *o-sound* is fully stressed and long, and especially when it is final, it tends," says Krapp, "to become diphthongal, starting with *o* and closing with [the] *u* [of *bush*], as in *dough, doe, toe, tow, flow, floe, château,* etc." [29] But in British speech a greater variety of diphthongal shadings occur, "some of them familiar in the exaggerated representations of Englishmen

[28] Open Boats, by Alfred Noyes; New York, 1917, pp. 89-91.
[29] The Pronunciation of Standard English in America, p. 81 *ff.*

THE STANDARD AMERICAN PRONUNCIATION 219

and their speech on the American stage. In the speech of many, perhaps of most, Americans there is scarcely any trace of diphthongal quality in the sound." Usage in the pronunciation of *u* still differs widely in the United States. The two sounds, that of *oo* in *goose* and that of *u* in *bush*, are used by different speakers in the same word. The *oo*-sound prevails in *aloof, boot, broom, food, groom, proof, roof, rood, room, rooster, root, soon, spook, spoon* and *woof*, and the *u*-sound in *butcher, cooper, hoof, hoop, nook, rook* and *soot*, but there are educated Americans who employ the *oo*-sound in *coop, hoof* and *hoop*. In *hooves* I have heard both sounds, but in *rooves* only the *oo*-sound. *Rooves* seems to be extinct in the written speech as the plural of *roof*, but it certainly survives in spoken American. In words of the *squirrel, syrup* and *stirrup* class Americans commonly substitute a *u*-sound for the *e*-sound used by Englishmen, and *squirrel* becomes a monosyllable, *squr'l*. In words of the *com* class, save *company*, Americans substitute a broad *a* for the *u* used by Englishmen; even *compass* often shows it. The English are far more careful with the shadowy *y* preceding *u* in words of the *duty* class than Americans. The latter retain it following *m, f, v* and *p*, and usually before *r*, but they are careless about it following *n* and *g*, and drop it following *l, r, d, t, th* and *s*. *Nyew, nyude, dyuke, enthyusiasm* and *syuit* would seem affectations in most parts of the United States, and *ryule* and *blyue* would be impossible.[30] Schoolmasters still battle valiantly for *dyuty*, but in vain. In 1912 the Department of Education of New York City warned all the municipal high-school teachers to combat the *oo*-sound[31] but it is doubtful that one pupil in a hundred was thereby induced to insert the *y* in *induced*. In *figure*, however, Americans retain the *y*-sound, whereas the English drop it. In *courteous* the English insert an *o*-sound, making the first syllable rhyme with *fort;* Americans rhyme it with *hurt*. In *brusque* the English give the first syllable an *oo*-sound; Americans rhyme it with *tusk*. In *clerk*, as everyone knows, the English change the *e* into *a*,

[30] A woman teacher of English, born in Tennessee, tells me that the *y*-sound is much more persistent in the South than in the North. "I have never," she says, "heard a native Southerner fail to retain the sound in *new*. The same is true of *duke, stew, due, duty* and *Tuesday*. But it is not true of *blue* and *true*."
[31] High School Circular No. 17, June 19, 1912.

and make the word rhyme with *lark;* in the United States it rhymes with *lurk.* Finally, there is *lieutenant.* The Englishman pronounces the first syllable *left;* the American invariably makes it *loot.* White says that the prevailing American pronunciation is relatively recent. "I never heard it," he reports, "in my boyhood."[32] He was born in New York in 1821.

[32] Every-Day English, p. 243.

VIII.

AMERICAN SPELLING

1.

The Two Orthographies

The chief changes made in the standard English spelling in the United States may be classified as follows:

1. *The omission of the penultimate* u *in words ending in* -our:

American	English
arbor	arbour
armor	armour
behavior	behaviour
candor	candour
clamor	clamour
clangor	clangour
color	colour
demeanor	demeanour
endeavor	endeavour
favor	favour
fervor	fervour
flavor	flavour
glamor	glamour
harbor	harbour
honor	honour
humor	humour
labor	labour
neighbor	neighbour
odor	odour
parlor	parlour
rancor	rancour
rigor	rigour
rumor	rumour
savor	savour
splendor	splendour
succor	succour
tumor	tumour
valor	valour
vapor	vapour
vigor	vigour

2. *The reduction of duplicate consonants to single consonants:*

American	English
councilor	councillor
counselor	counsellor
fagot	faggot
jewelry	jewellery
net (adj.)	nett
traveler	traveller
wagon	waggon
woolen	woollen

3. *The omission of a redundant* e:

annex (noun)	annexe
asphalt	asphalte
ax	axe
form (printer's)	forme
good-by	goodbye
intern (noun)	interne
peas (plu. of pea)	pease
story (of a house)	storey

4. *The change of terminal* -re *into* -er:

caliber	calibre
center	centre
fiber	fibre
liter	litre
meter	metre
saltpeter	saltpetre
theater	theatre

5. *The omission of unaccented foreign terminations:*

catalog	catalogue
envelop [1]	envelope
epaulet	epaulette
gram	gramme
program	programme
prolog	prologue
toilet	toilette
veranda	verandah

6. *The omission of* u *when combined with* a *or* o:

balk (verb)	baulk
font (printer's)	fount
gantlet (to run the —)	gauntlet
mold	mould
molt	moult
mustache	moustache
stanch	staunch

[1] The English dictionaries make a distinction between the verb, *to envelop*, and the noun, *envelope*. This distinction seems to be disappearing in the United States.

AMERICAN SPELLING

7. *The conversion of decayed diphthongs into simple vowels:*

American	English
anemia	anæmia
anesthetic	anæsthetic
encyclopedia	encyclopædia
diarrhea	diarrhœa
ecology	œcology
ecumenical	œcumenical
edema	œdema
eon	æon
esophagus	œsophagus
esthetic	æsthetic
estival	æstival
etiology	ætiology
hemorrhage	hæmorrhage
medieval	mediæval
septicemia	septicæmia

8. *The change of compound consonants into simple consonants:*

bark (ship)	barque
burden (ship's)	burthen
check (bank)	cheque
draft (ship's)	draught
picket (military)	piquet
plow	plough
vial	phial

9. *The change of o into a:*

naught	nought
pudgy	podgy
slug (verb)	slog
slush	slosh
taffy	toffy (or toffee)

10. *The change of e into i:*

inclose	enclose
indorse	endorse
inquire	enquire
jimmy (burglar's)	jemmy
scimitar	scimetar

11. *The change of y into a, ia or i:*

ataxia	ataxy
baritone	barytone
cachexia	cachexy
cider	cyder
pajamas	pyjamas
siphon	syphon
siren	syren
tire (noun)	tyre

12. *The change of c into s:*

American	English
defense	defence
offense	offence
pretense	pretence
vise (a tool)	vice

13. *The substitution of s for z:*

advertisement	advertizement
fuse	fuze

14. *The substitution of k for c:*

mollusk	mollusc
skeptic	sceptic

15. *The insertion of a supernumerary e:*

forego	forgo
foregather	forgather

16. *The substitution of ct for x:*

connection	connexion
inflection	inflexion

17. *The substitution of y for i:*

dryly	drily
gayety	gaiety
gypsy	gipsy
pygmy	pigmy

18. *Miscellaneous differences:*

alarm (signal)	alarum
behoove	behove
brier	briar
buncombe	bunkum
catsup	ketchup
cloture	closure
cozy	cosy
cutlas	cutlass
czar	tsar
gasoline	gasolene
gray	grey
hostler	ostler
jail	gaol
maneuver	manœuvre
pedler	pedlar
show (verb)	shew
snicker	snigger
stenosis	stegnosis

This list might be very much extended by including compounds and derivatives, *e. g., coloured, colourist, colourless, colour-blind, colour-line, colour-sergeant, colourable, colourably, neighbourhood, neighbourly, neighbourliness, favourite, favourable, slogger, kilogramme, kilometre, amphitheatre, centremost, baulky, anæsthesia, plough-boy, dreadnought, enclosure, endorsement,* and by including forms that are going out of use in England, *e. g., fluxation*[2] for *fluctuation, surprize* for *surprise,* and forms that are still but half established in the United States, *e. g., chlorid, brusk, cigaret, lacrimal, rime, gage, quartet, eolian, dialog, lodgment, niter, sulfite, phenix.* According to a recent writer upon the subject, "there are 812 words in which the prevailing American spelling differs from the English."[3] But enough examples are given here to reveal a number of definite tendencies. American, in general, moves toward simplified forms of spelling more rapidly than English, and has got much further along the road. Redundant and unnecessary letters have been dropped from whole groups of words, simple vowels have been substituted for degenerated diphthongs, simple consonants have displaced compound ones, and vowels have been changed to bring words into harmony with their analogues, as in *tire, cider* and *baritone* (*cf. wire, rider, merriment*). Clarity and simplicity are served by substituting *ct* for *x* in such words as *connection* and *inflection,* and *s* for *c* in words of the *defense* group. The superiority of *jail* to *gaol* is made manifest by the common mispronunciation of the latter by Americans who find it in print, making it rhyme with *coal.* The substitution of *i* for *e* in such words as *indorse, inclose* and *jimmy* is of less patent utility, but even here there is probably a slight gain in euphony. Of more obscure origin is what seems to be a tendency to avoid the *o*-sound, so that the English *slog* becomes *slug, podgy* becomes *pudgy, slosh* becomes *slush, toffee* becomes *taffy,* and so on. Other changes carry their own justification. *Hostler* is obviously better American than *ostler,* though it may be worse English. *Show* is more logical than *shew*.[4] *Cozy* is more nearly

---

[2] I find *"fluxation* of the rate of exchange" in the *New Witness,* Feb. 4, 1921. Cassell marks it obsolete; the Concise Oxford gives only *fluctuation.*
[3] Richard P. Read: The American Language, New York *Sun,* March 7, 1918.
[4] *To shew* has completely disappeared from American, but it still survives in English usage. *Cf.* The *Shewing-Up* of Blanco Posnet, by George Bernard Shaw. The word, of course, is pronounced *show,* not *shoe. Shrew,* a cognate word, still retains the early pronunciation of *shrow* on the English stage, though not in common usage. It is now phonetic in American.

phonetic than *cosy*. *Curb* has analogues in *curtain, curdle, curfew, curl, currant, curry, curve, curtsey, curse, currency, cursory, curtain, cur, curt* and many other common words: *kerb* has very few, and of them only *kerchief* and *kernel* are in general use. Moreover, the English themselves use *curb* as a verb and in all noun senses save that shown in *kerbstone*. Such forms as *monolog* and *dialog* still offend the fastidious, but their merit is not to be gainsaid. Nor would it be easy to argue logically against *gram, toilet, mustache, anesthetic, draft* and *tire*.

But a number of anomalies remain. The American substitution of *a* for *e* in *gray* is not easily explained, nor is the retention of *e* in *forego*, nor the unphonetic substitution of *s* for *z* in *fuse*, nor the persistence of the *y* in *gypsy* and *pygmy*, nor the occasional survival of a foreign form, as in *cloture*.[5] Here we have plain vagaries, surviving in spite of attack by orthographers. Webster, in one of his earlier books, denounced the *k* in *skeptic* as a "mere pedantry," but later on he adopted it. In the same way *pygmy, gray* and *mollusk* have been attacked, but they still remain sound American. The English themselves have many more such illogical forms to account for. They have to write *offensive* and *defensive*, despite their fidelity to the *c* in *offence* and *defence*. They have begun to drop the duplicate consonant from *riveter, leveled* and *biased*, despite their use of *traveller* and *jewellery*.[6] They cling to *programme*, but never think of using *diagramme* or *telegramme*. Worst of all, they are wholly inconsistent in their use of the *-our* ending, the chief hallmark of orthodox English orthography. In American the *u* appears only in *Saviour* and then only when the word is used in the biblical sense. In England it is used in most words of that class, but omitted from a very respectable minority, *e. g., horror, torpor, ambassador*. It is commonly argued in defense of it over there that it serves to dis-

[5] Fowler and Fowler, in The King's English, p. 23, say that "when it was proposed to borrow from France what we [*i. e.*, the English] now know as the *closure*, it seemed certain for some time that with the thing we should borrow the name, *clôture;* a press campaign resulted in *closure*." But in the *Congressional Record* it is still *cloture*, though with the loss of the circumflex accent, and this form is generally retained by American newspapers.
[6] See the preface to the Concise Oxford Dictionary, p. vi.

tinguish French loan-words from words derived directly from the Latin, but Tucker shows[7] that this argument is quite nonsensical, even assuming that the distinction has any practical utility. *Ambassador, ancestor, bachelor, editor, emperor, error, exterior, governor, inferior, metaphor, mirror, progenitor, senator, superior, successor* and *torpor* all came into English from the French, and yet British usage sanctions spelling them without the *u*. On the other hand it is used in *arbour, behaviour, clangour, flavour* and *neighbour*, "which are not French at all." Tucker goes on:

> Even in *ardour, armour, candour, endeavour, favour, honour, labour, odour, parlour, rigour, rumour, saviour, splendour, tumour* and *vapour*, where the *u* has some color of right to appear, it is doubtful whether its insertion has much value as suggesting French derivation, for in the case of twelve of these words the ordinary reader would be quite certain to have in mind only the modern spelling—*ardeur, armure, candeur, faveur, honneur, labeur, odeur, rigneur, rumeur, splendeur, tumeur* and *vapeur*—which have the *u* indeed but no *o* (and why should not one of these letters be dropped as well as the other?)—while *endeavour, parlour* and *saviour* come from old French words that are themselves without the *u*—*devoir, parleor* and *saveor*. The *u* in all these words is therefore either useless or positively misleading. And finally in the case of *colour, clamour, fervour, humour, rancour, valour* and *vigour*, it is to be remarked that the exact American orthography actually occurs in old French! "Finally," I said, but that is not quite the end of British absurdity with these *-our -or* words. Insistent as our transatlantic cousins are on writing *arbour, armour, clamour, clangour, colour, dolour, flavour, honour, humour, labour, odour, rancour, rigour, savour, valour, vapour* and *vigour*, and "most unpleasant" as they find the omission of the excrescent *u* in any of these words, they nevertheless make no scruple of writing the derivatives in the American way—*arboreal, armory, clamorous, clangorous, colorific, dolorous, flavorous, honorary, humorous, laborious, odorous, rancorous, rigorous, savory, valorous, vaporize* and *vigorous*—not inserting the *u* in the second syllable of any one of these words. The British practice is, in short and to speak plainly, a jumble of confusion, without rhyme or reason, logic or consistency; and if anybody finds the American simplification of the whole matter "unpleasant," it can be only because he is a victim of unreasoning prejudice against which no argument can avail.

If the *u* were dropped in *all* derivatives, the confusion would be less, but it is retained in many of them, for example, *colourable, favourite, misdemeanour, coloured* and *labourer*. The derivatives of *honour* exhibit clearly the difficulties of the American who essays to write correct English. *Honorary, honorarium* and *honorific* drop

[7] *American English*; New York, 1921, p. 37.

the *u*, but *honourable* retains it! Furthermore, the English make a distinction between two senses of *rigor*. When used in its pathological sense (not only in the Latin form of *rigor mortis*, but as an English word) it drops the *u*; in all other senses it retains the *u*.

2.

The Influence of Webster

At the time of the first settlement of America the rules of English orthography were beautifully vague, and so we find the early documents full of spellings that seem quite fantastic today. *Aetaernall* (for *eternal*) is in the Acts of the Massachusetts General Court for 1646. But now and then a curious foreshadowing of later American usage is encountered. On July 4, 1631, for example, John Winthrop wrote in his journal that "the governour built a *bark* at Mistick which was launched this day." During the eighteenth century, however, and especially after the publication of Johnson's dictionary, there was a general movement in England toward a more inflexible orthography, and many hard and fast rules, still surviving, were then laid down. It was Johnson himself who established the position of the *u* in the *-our* words. Bailey, Dyche and other lexicographers before him were divided and uncertain; Johnson declared for the *u*, and though his reasons were very shaky [8] and he often neglected his own precept, his authority was sufficient to set up a usage which still defies attack in England. Even in America this usage was not often brought into question until the last quarter of the eighteenth century. True enough, *honor* appears in the Declaration of Independence, but it seems to have got there rather by accident than by design. In Jefferson's original draft it is spelled *honour*. So early as 1768 Benjamin Franklin had published his "Scheme for a New Alphabet and a Reformed Mode of Spelling, with Remarks and

[8] *Cf.* Lounsbury: English Spelling and Spelling Reform; p. 209 *et seq.* Johnson even advocated *translatour, emperour, oratour* and *horrour*. But, like most other lexicographers, he was often inconsistent, and the conflict between *interiour* and *exterior*, and *anteriour* and *posterior*, in his dictionary, laid him open to much criticism.

Examples Concerning the Same, and an Enquiry into its Uses" and induced a Philadelphia typefounder to cut type for it, but this scheme was too extravagant to be adopted anywhere, or to have any appreciable influence upon spelling.[9]

It was Noah Webster who finally achieved the divorce between English example and American practise. He struck the first blow in his "Grammatical Institute of the English Language," published at Hartford in 1783. Attached to this work was an appendix bearing the formidable title of "An Essay on the Necessity, Advantages and Practicability of Reforming the Mode of Spelling, and of Rendering the Orthography of Words Correspondent to the Pronunciation," and during the same year, at Boston, he set forth his ideas a second time in the first edition of his "American Spelling Book." The influence of this spelling-book was immediate and profound. It took the place in the schools of Dilworth's "Aby-sel-pha," the favorite of the generation preceding, and maintained its authority for fully a century. Until Lyman Cobb entered the lists with his "New Spelling Book," in 1842, its innumerable editions scarcely had any rivalry, and even then it held its own. I have a New York edition, dated 1848, which contains an advertisement stating that the annual sale at that time was more than a million copies, and that more than 30,000,000 copies had been sold since 1783. In the late 40's the publishers, George F. Cooledge & Bro., devoted the whole capacity of the fastest steam press in the United States to the printing of it. This press turned out 525 copies an hour, or 5,250 a day. It was "constructed expressly for printing Webster's Elementary Spelling Book [the name had been changed in 1829] at an expense of $5,000." Down to 1889, 62,000,000 copies of the book had been sold.

The appearance of Webster's first dictionary, in 1806, greatly strengthened his influence. The best dictionary available to Americans before this was Johnson's in its various incarnations, but against Johnson's stood a good deal of animosity to its compiler, whose implacable hatred of all things American was well known to the citizens of the new republic. John Walker's dictionary, issued in London in 1791, was also in use, but not extensively. A home-made school

[9] In a letter to Miss Stephenson, Sept. 20, 1768, he exhibited the use of his new alphabet. The letter is to be found in most editions of his writings.

dictionary, issued at New Haven in 1798 or 1799 by one Samuel Johnson, Jr.—apparently no relative of the great Sam—and a larger work published a year later by Johnson and the Rev. John Elliott, pastor in East Guilford, Conn., seem to have made no impression, despite the fact that the latter was commended by Simeon Baldwin, Chauncey Goodrich and other magnificoes of the time and place, and even by Webster himself. The field was thus open to the laborious and truculent Noah. He was already the acknowledged magister of lexicography in America, and there was an active public demand for a dictionary that should be wholly American. The appearance of his first duodecimo, according to Williams,[10] thereby took on something of the character of a national event. It was received, not critically, but patriotically, and its imperfections were swallowed as eagerly as its merits. Later on Webster had to meet formidable critics, at home as well as abroad, but for nearly a quarter of a century he reigned almost unchallenged. Edition after edition of his dictionary was published, each new one showing additions and improvements. Finally, in 1828, he printed his great "*American* Dictionary of the English Language," in two large octavo volumes. It held the field for half a century, not only against Worcester and the other American lexicographers who followed him, but also against the best dictionaries produced in England. Until the appearance of the Concise Oxford in 1914, indeed, America remained far ahead of England in practical dictionary making.

Webster had declared boldly for simpler spellings in his early spelling books; in his dictionary of 1806 he made an assault at all arms upon some of the dearest prejudices of English lexicographers. Grounding his wholesale reforms upon a saying by Franklin, that "those people spell best who do not know how to spell"—*i. e.*, who spell phonetically and logically—he made an almost complete sweep of whole classes of silent letters—the *u* in the -*our* words, the final *e* in *determine* and *requisite,* the silent *a* in *thread, feather* and *steady,* the silent *b* in *thumb,* the *s* in *island,* the *o* in *leopard,* and the redundant consonants in *traveler, wagon, jeweler,* etc. (English: *traveller, waggon, jeweller*). More, he lopped the final *k* from *frolick, physick*

[10] R. O. Williams: Our Dictionaries; New York, 1890, p. 30. See also S. A. Steger: American Dictionaries; Baltimore, 1913.

and their analogues. Yet more, he transposed the *e* and the *r* in many words ending in *re*, such as *theatre, lustre, centre* and *calibre.* Yet more, he changed the *c* in all words of the *defence* class to *s*. Yet more, he changed *ph* to *f* in words of the *phantom* class, *ou* to *oo* in words of the *group* class, *ow* to *ou* in *crowd*, *porpoise* to *porpess*, *acre* to *aker*, *sew* to *soe*, *woe* to *wo*, *soot* to *sut*, *gaol* to *jail*, and *plough* to *plow*. Finally, he antedated the simplified spellers by inventing a long list of boldly phonetic spellings, ranging from *tung* for *tongue* to *wimmen* for *women*, and from *hainous* for *heinous* to *cag* for *keg*.

A good many of these new spellings, of course, were not actually Webster's inventions. For example, the change from *-our* to *-or* in words of the *honor* class was a mere echo of an earlier English uncertainty. In the first three folios of Shakespeare, 1623, 1632 and 1663-6, *honor* and *honour* were used indiscriminately and in almost equal proportions; English spelling was still fluid, and the *-our*-form was not consistently adopted until the fourth folio of 1685. Moreover, John Wesley, the founder of Methodism, is authority for the statement that the *-or*-form was "a fashionable impropriety" in England in 1791. But the great authority of Johnson stood against it, and Webster was surely not one to imitate fashionable improprieties. He deleted the *u* for purely etymological reasons, going back to the Latin *honor, favor* and *odor* without taking account of the intermediate French *honneur, faveur* and *odeur*. And where no etymological reasons presented themselves, he made his changes by analogy and for the sake of uniformity, or for euphony or simplicity, or because it pleased him, one guesses, to stir up the academic animals. Webster, in fact, delighted in controversy, and was anything but free from the national yearning to make a sensation.

A great many of his innovations, of course, failed to take root, and in the course of time he abandoned some of them himself. In his early "Essay on the Necessity, Advantage and Practicability of Reforming the Mode of Spelling" he advocated reforms which were already discarded by the time he published the first edition of his dictionary. Among them were the dropping of the silent letter in such words as *head, give, built* and *realm*, making them *hed, giv, bilt,* and *relm;* the substitution of doubled vowels for decayed diphthongs in such words as *mean, zeal* and *near*, making them *meen, zeel* and *neer;* and the substitution of *sh* for *ch* in such French loan-words as *machine* and *chevalier,* making them *masheen* and *shevaleer.* He also declared for *stile* in place of *style,* and for many other such changes, and then quietly abandoned them. The successive editions of his dictionary show still further concessions. *Croud, fether, groop, gillotin, iland, insted, leperd, soe, sut, steddy, thret, thred, thum* and *wimmen* appear only in the 1806 edition. In 1828 he went back to *crowd, feather, group, island, instead, leopard, sew, soot, steady, thread, threat, thumb* and *women,* and changed *gillotin* to *guillotin.* In addition, he restored the final *e* in *determine, discipline, requisite, imagine,* etc. In 1838, revising his dictionary, he abandoned a good many spellings that had appeared in either the 1806 or the 1828 edition, notably *maiz* for *maize, suveran* [11] for *sovereign* and *guillotin* for *guillotine.* But he stuck manfully to a number that were quite as revolutionary—for example, *aker* for *acre, cag* for *keg, grotesk* for *grotesque, hainous* for *heinous, porpess* for *porpoise* and *tung* for *tongue*—and they did not begin to disappear until the edition of 1854, issued by other hands and eleven years after his death. Three of his favorites, *chimist* for *chemist, neger* for *negro* and *zeber* for *zebra,* are incidentally interesting as showing changes in American pronunciation. He abandoned *zeber* in 1828, but remained faithful to *chimist* and *neger* to the last.

But though he was thus forced to give occasional ground, and in more than one case held out in vain, Webster lived to see the majority of his reforms adopted by his countrymen. He left the ending in *-or* triumphant over the ending in *-our,* he shook the security of the ending in *-re,* he rid American spelling of a great many doubled consonants, he established the *s* in words of the *defense* group, and he gave currency to many characteristic American spellings, notably *jail, wagon, plow, mold* and *ax.* These spellings still survive, and are practically universal in the United States today; their use constitutes one of the most obvious differences between written English and written American. Moreover, they have founded a general tendency, the effects of which reach far beyond the field actually

---

[11] I find *soveran* in the London *Times Literary Supplement* for Aug. 5, 1920, p. 1, *art.* Words for Music, but it seems to have no support elsewhere. Cassell and the Concise Oxford do not list it.

AMERICAN SPELLING 233

traversed by Webster himself. New words, and particularly loanwords, are simplified, and hence naturalized in American much more quickly than in English. *Employé* has long since become *employee* in our newspapers, and *asphalte* has lost its final *e*, and *manœuvre* has become *maneuver*, and *pyjamas* has become *pajamas*. Even the terminology of science is simplified and Americanized. In medicine, for example, the highest American usage countenances many forms which would seem barbarisms to an English medical man if he encountered them in the *Lancet*. In derivatives of the Greek *haima* it is the almost invariable American custom to spell the root syllable *hem*, but the more conservative English make it *hæm*—e. g., in *hæmorrhage* and *hæmiplegia*. In an exhaustive list of diseases issued by the United States Public Health Service [12] the *hæm-* form does not appear once. In the same way American usage prefers *esophagus, diarrhea* and *gonorrhea* to the English *œsophagus, diarrhœa* and *gonorrhœa*. In the style book of the *Journal* of the American Medical Association I find many other spellings that would shock an English medical author, among them *curet* for *curette*, *cocain* for *cocaine*, *gage* for *gauge*, *intern* for *interne*, *lacrimal* for *lachrymal*, and a whole group of words ending in *-er* instead of in *-re*.[13]

Webster's reforms, it goes without saying, have not passed unchallenged by the guardians of tradition. A glance at the literature of the first years of the nineteenth century shows that most of the serious authors of the time ignored his new spellings, though they were quickly adopted by the newspapers. Bancroft's "Life of Washington" contains *-our* endings in all such words as *honor, ardor* and *favor*. Washington Irving also threw his influence against the *-or* ending, and so did Bryant and most of the other literary big-wigs of that day. After the appearance of "An American Dictionary of the English Language," in 1828, a formal battle was joined, with Lyman Cobb and Joseph E. Worcester as the chief opponents of

[11] Nomenclature of Diseases and Conditions, prepared by direction of the Surgeon General; Washington, 1916.
[13] American Medical Association Style Book; Chicago, 1915. At the 1921 session of the American Medical Association in Boston an English gynecologist read a paper and it was printed in the *Journal*. When he received the proofs he objected to a great many of the spellings, e. g., *gonorrheal* for *gonorrhœal*, and *fallopian* for *Falloppian*. The *Journal* refused to agree to his English spellings, but when his paper was reprinted separately they were restored.

the reformer. Cobb and Worcester, in the end, accepted the *-or* ending and so surrendered on the main issue, but various other champions arose to carry on the war. Edward S. Gould, in a once famous essay,[14] denounced the whole Websterian orthography with the utmost fury, and Bryant, reprinting this philippic in the *Evening Post,* said that on account of Webster "the English language has been undergoing a process of corruption for the last quarter of a century," and offered to contribute to a fund to have Gould's denunciation "read twice a year in every school-house in the United States, until every trace of Websterian spelling disappears from the land." But Bryant was forced to admit that, even in 1856, the chief novelties of the Connecticut schoolmaster "who taught millions to read but not one to sin" were "adopted and propagated by the largest publishing house, through the columns of the most widely circulated monthly magazine, and through one of the ablest and most widely circulated newspapers in the United States"—which is to say, the *Tribune* under Greeley. The last academic attack was delivered by Bishop Coxe in 1886, and he contented himself with the resigned statement that "Webster has corrupted our spelling sadly." Lounsbury, with his active interest in spelling reform, ranged himself on the side of Webster, and effectively disposed of the controversy by showing that the great majority of his spellings were supported by precedents quite as respectable as those behind the fashionable English spellings. In Lounsbury's opinion, a good deal of the opposition to them was no more than a symptom of antipathy to all things American among certain Englishmen and of subservience to all things English among certain Americans.[15]

Webster's inconsistencies gave his opponents a formidable weapon for use against him—until it began to be noticed that the orthodox English spelling was quite as inconsistent. He sought to change *acre* to *aker,* but left *lucre* unchanged. He removed the final *f* from *bailiff, mastiff, plaintiff* and *pontiff,* but left it in *distaff.* He changed *c* to *s* in words of the *offense* class, but left the *c* in *fence.* He changed the *ck* in *frolick, physick,* etc., into a simple *c,* but restored it in such derivatives as *frolicksome.* He deleted the silent

[14] *Democratic Review,* March, 1856.
[15] *Vide* English Spelling and Spelling Reform, p. 229.

u in *mould,* but left it in *court.* These slips were made the most of by Cobb in a furious pamphlet in excessively fine print, printed in 1831.[16] He also detected Webster in the frequent *faux pas* of using spellings in his definitions and explanations that conflicted with the spellings he advocated. Various other purists joined in the attack, and it was renewed with great fury after the appearance of Worcester's dictionary, in 1846. Worcester, who had begun his lexicographical labors by editing Johnson's dictionary, was a good deal more conservative than Webster, and so the partisans of conformity rallied around him, and for a while the controversy took on all the rancor of a personal quarrel. Even the editions of Webster printed after his death, though they gave way on many points, were violently arraigned. Gould, in 1867, belabored the editions of 1854 and 1866 [17] and complained that "for the past twenty-five years the Websterian replies have uniformly been bitter in tone, and very free in the imputation of personal motives, or interested or improper motives, on the part of opposing critics." At this time Webster himself had been dead for twenty-two years. Schele de Vere, during the same year, denounced the publishers of the Webster dictionaries for applying "immense capital and a large stock of energy and perseverance" to the propagation of his "new and arbitrarily imposed orthography." [18]

3.

The Advance of American Spelling

The logical superiority of American spelling is well exhibited by its persistent advance in the face of all this hostility at home and abroad. The English objection to our simplifications, as Brander Matthews once pointed out, is not wholly or even chiefly etymological; its roots lie, to borrow James Russell Lowell's phrase, in an esthetic hatred burning "with as fierce a flame as ever did theological

[16] A Critical Review of the Orthography of Dr. Webster's Series of Books . . .; New York, 1831.
[17] Good English; p. 137 *et seq.*
[18] Studies in English; pp. 64-5.

hatred." There is something inordinately offensive to English purists in the very thought of taking lessons from this side of the water, particularly in the mother-tongue. The opposition, transcending the academic, takes on the character of the patriotic. "Any American," said Matthews in 1892, "who chances to note the force and the fervor and the frequency of the objurgations against American spelling in the columns of the *Saturday Review*, for example, and of the *Athenæum*, may find himself wondering as to the date of the papal bull which declared the infallibility of contemporary British orthography, and as to the place where the council of the Church was held at which it was made an article of faith." [19] But that, as I say, was in 1892. Since then there has been an enormous change, and though the editors of the Concise Oxford Dictionary, so recently as 1914, pointedly refrained from listing forms that would "strike every reader as Americanisms," they surrendered in a wholesale manner to forms quite as thoroughly American in origin, among them, *ax, alarm, tire, asphalt, program, toilet, balk, wagon, vial, inquire, advertisement, pygmy* and *czar*. The monumental New English Dictionary upon which the Concise Oxford is chiefly based shows many silent concessions, and quite as many open yieldings—for example, in the case of *ax*, which is admitted to be "better than *axe* on every ground." Moreover, practical English lexicographers tend to march ahead of it, outstripping the liberalism of its editor, Sir James A. H. Murray. In 1914, for example, Sir James was still protesting against dropping the first *e* from *judgement*, a characteristic Americanism, but during the same year the Concise Oxford put *judgment* ahead of *judgement*, and two years earlier the Authors' and Printers' Dictionary, edited by Horace Hart,[20] had dropped *judgement* altogether. Hart is Controller of the Oxford University Press, and the Authors' and Printers' Dictionary is an authority accepted by nearly all of the great English book publishers and newspapers. Its last edition shows a great many American spellings. For example, it recommends the use of *jail* and *jailer* in place of the English *gaol* and *gaoler*, says that *ax* is better than *axe*, drops the

[19] Americanisms and Briticisms; New York, 1892, p. 37.
[20] Authors' & Printers' Dictionary . . . an attempt to codify the best typographical practices of the present day, by F. Howard Collins; 4th ed., revised by Horace Hart; London, 1912.

final *e* from *asphalte* and *forme*, changes the *y* to *i* in *cyder, cypher* and *syren* and advocates the same change in *tyre*, drops the redundant *t* from *nett*, changes *burthen* to *burden*, spells *wagon* with one *g*, prefers *fuse* to *fuze*, and takes the *e* out of *storey*. "Rules for Compositors and Readers at the University Press, Oxford," also edited by Hart (with the advice of Sir James Murray and Dr. Henry Bradley), is another very influential English authority.[21] It gives its imprimatur to *bark* (a ship), *cipher, siren, jail, story, tire* and *wagon*, and even advocates *kilogram* and *omelet*. Cassell's New English Dictionary [22] goes quite as far. Like Hart and the Oxford it clings to the *-our* and *-re* endings and to the diphthongs in such words as *æsthete* and *anæsthesia*, but it prefers *jail* to *gaol*, *net* to *nett*, *story* to *storey*, *asphalt* to *asphalte*, *tire* to *tyre*, *wagon* to *waggon*, *inquiry* to *enquiry*, *vial* to *phial*, *advertise* to *advertize*, *baritone* to *barytone*, and *pygmy* to *pigmy*.

There is, however, much confusion among these authorities; the English are still unable to agree as to which American spellings they will adopt and which they will keep under the ban for a while longer. The Concise Oxford prefers *bark* to *barque* and the Poet Laureate [23] adopts it boldly, but Cassell still clings to *barque*. Cassell favors *baritone;* the Oxford declares for *barytone*. The Oxford is for *czar;* Cassell is for *tsar*. The Oxford admits *program;* Cassell sticks to *programme*. Both have abandoned *enquire* for *inquire*, but they remain faithful to *encumbrance, endorse* and *enclose*, though they list *indorsation* and the Oxford also gives *indorsee*. Hart agrees with them.[24] Both have abandoned *æther* for *ether*, but they cling to *æsthetic* and *ætiology*. Neither gives up *plough, cheque, connexion, mould, pease, mollusc* or *kerb*, and Cassell even adorns the last-named with an astounding compound credited to "American slang," to wit, *kerb-stone broker*. Both favor such forms as *surprise* and *advertisement*, and yet I find *surprized, advertizement* and *to ad-*

[21] Horace Hart: Rules for Compositors and Readers at the University Press, Oxford: 23rd ed.; London, 1914. I am informed by Mr. Humphrey Davy, of the London *Times*, that, with one or two minor exceptions, the *Times* observes the rules laid down in this book.
[22] Edited by Dr. Ernest A. Baker; London, 1919.
[23] English Homophones; Oxford, 1919, p. 7.
[24] Even worse inconsistencies are often encountered. Thus *enquiry* appears on p. 3 of the Dardanelles Commission's First Report; London, 1917; but *inquiring* is on p. 1.

vertize in the prospectus of *English,* a magazine founded to further "the romantic and patriotic study of English," and *advertize* and *advertizing* are in the first number.[25] All the English authorities that I have consulted prefer the *-re* [26] and *-our* endings; nevertheless the London *Nation* adopted the *-or* ending in 1919,[27] and George Bernard Shaw had adopted it years before. The British Board of Trade, in attempting to fix the spelling of various scientific terms, has often come to grief. Thus it detaches the final *-me* from *gramme* in such compounds as *kilogram* and *milligram,* but insists upon *gramme* when the word stands alone. In American usage *gram* is now common, and scarcely challenged. A number of spellings, nearly all American, are trembling on the brink of acceptance in both countries. Among them is *rime* (for *rhyme*). This spelling was correct in England until about 1530, but its recent revival was of American origin. It is accepted by the Concise Oxford and by the editors of the Cambridge History of English Literature, but not by Cassell. It seldom appears in an English journal. The same may be said of *grewsome.* It has got a footing in both countries, but the weight of English opinion is still against it. *Develop* (instead of *develope*) has gone further in both countries. So has *engulf,* for *engulph.*

4.

British Spelling in the United States

American imitation of English orthography has two impulses behind it. First, there is the colonial spirit, the desire to pass as English—in brief, mere affectation. Secondly, there is the wish among printers, chiefly of books, to reach a compromise spelling acceptable in both countries, thus avoiding expensive revisions in

---

[25] London, March, 1919.
[26] *Caliber* is now the official spelling of the United States Army. *Cf.* Description and Rules for the Management of the U. S. Rifle, *Caliber* .30, Model of 1903; Washington, 1915. But *calibre* is still official in England.
[27] *Cf. English,* May-June, 1919, p. 88.

AMERICAN SPELLING 239

case sheets are printed for publication in England.[28] The first influence need not detain us. It is chiefly visible among folk of fashionable pretensions, and is not widespread. At Bar Harbor, in Maine, some of the summer residents are at great pains to put *harbour* instead of *harbor* on their stationery, but the local postmaster still continues to stamp all mail *Bar Harbor*, the legal name of the place. In the same way American haberdashers sometimes advertise *pyjamas* instead of *pajamas*, just as they advertise *braces* instead of *suspenders* and *boots* instead of *shoes*. But this benign folly does not go very far. Beyond occasionally clinging to the *-re* ending in words of the *theatre* group, all American newspapers and magazines employ the native orthography, and it would be quite as startling to encounter *honour* or *traveller* in one of them as it would be to encounter *gaol* or *waggon*. Even the most fashionable jewelers in Fifth avenue still deal in *jewelry*, not in *jewellery*.

The second influence is of more effect and importance. In the days before the copyright treaty between England and the United States, one of the standing arguments against it among the English was based upon the fear that it would flood England with books set up in America, and so work a corruption of English spelling.[29] This fear, as we have seen, had a certain plausibility; there is not the slightest doubt that American books and American magazines have done valiant missionary service for American orthography. But English conservatism still holds out stoutly enough to force American printers to certain compromises. When a book is designed for circulation in both countries it is common for the publisher to instruct the printer to employ "English spelling." This English

[28] Mere stupid copying may perhaps be added. An example of it appears on a map printed with a pamphlet entitled Conquest and Kultur, compiled by two college professors and issued by the Creel press bureau during the Great War. (Washington, 1918.) On this map, borrowed from an English periodical called *New Europe* without correction, *annex* is spelled *annexe*. In the same way English spellings often appear in paragraphs reprinted from the English newspapers. As compensation in the case of *annexe* I find *annex* on pages 11 and 23 of A Report on the Treatment by the Enemy of British Prisoners of War Behind the Firing Lines in France and Belgium; Miscellaneous No. 7 (1918). When used as a verb the English always spell the word *annex*. *Annexe* is only the noun form.
[29] *Vide* Matthews: Americanisms and Briticisms, pp. 33-34.

spelling, at the Riverside Press,[30] embraces all the *-our* endings and the following further forms:

cheque	grey
chequered	inflexion
connexion	jewellery
dreamt	leapt
faggot	premiss (in logic)
forgather	waggon
forgo	

It will be noted that *gaol, tyre, storey, kerb, asphalte, annexe, ostler, mollusc* and *pyjamas* are not listed, nor are the words ending in *-re*. These and their like constitute the English contribution to the compromise. Two other great American book presses, that of the Macmillan Company and that of the J. S. Cushing Company,[31] add *gaol* and *storey* to the list, and also *behove, briar, drily, enquire, gaiety, gipsy, instal, judgement, lacquey, moustache, nought, pygmy, postillion, reflexion, shily, slily, staunch* and *verandah.* Here they go too far, for, as we have seen, the English themselves have begun to abandon *enquire* and *judgement,* and *lacquey* is also going out over there. The Riverside Press, even in books intended only for America, prefers certain English forms, among them, *anæmia, axe, mediæval, mould, plough, programme* and *quartette,* but in compensation it stands by such typical Americanisms as *caliber, calk, center, cozy, defense, foregather, gray, hemorrhage, luster, maneuver, mustache, theater* and *woolen.* The Government Printing Office at Washington follows Webster's New International Dictionary,[32] which supports many of the innovations of Webster himself. This dictionary is the authority in perhaps a majority of American printing offices, with the Standard and the Century supporting it. The latter two also follow Webster, notably in his *-er*

---

[30] Handbook of Style in Use at the Riverside Press, Cambridge, Mass.; Boston, 1913.

[31] Notes for the Guidance of Authors; New York, 1918; Preparation of Manuscript, Proof Reading, and Office Style at J. S. Cushing Company's; Norwood, Mass., n. d.

[32] Style Book, a Compilation of Rules Governing Executive, Congressional and Departmental Printing, Including the *Congressional Record,* ed. of Feb., 1917; Washington, 1917. A copy of this style book is in the proof-room of nearly every American daily newspaper and its rules are generally observed.

endings and in his substitution of *s* for *c* in words of the *defense* class. The Worcester Dictionary is the sole exponent of English spelling in general circulation in the United States. It remains faithful to most of the *-re* endings, and to *manœuvre, gramme, plough, sceptic, woollen, axe* and many other English forms. But even Worcester favors such characteristic American spellings as *behoove, brier, caliber, checkered, dryly, jail* and *wagon*. The *Atlantic Monthly*, which is inclined to be stiff and British, follows Webster, but with certain reservations. Thus it uses the *-re* ending in words of the *center* class, retains the *u* in *mould, moult* and *moustache*, retains the redundant terminal letters in such words as *gramme, programme* and *quartette*, retains the final *e* in *axe* and *adze*, and clings to the double vowels in such words as *mediæval, anæsthesia, homœopathy*, and *diarrhœa*. In addition, it uses the English *plough, whiskey, clue* and *gruesome*, differentiates between the noun *practice* and the verb *to practise*, and makes separate words of *to ensure*, to make certain, and *to insure*, to protect or indemnify. It also prefers *entrust* to *intrust*. It follows the somewhat arbitrary rule laid down by Webster for the doubling of consonants in derivatives bearing such suffixes as *-ed, -ing, -er*, and *-ous*. This rule is that words ending in *l, p, r* and *t*, when this last letter is preceded by a vowel, double the consonant before such suffixes, but only if the words are monosyllables or polysyllables accented on the last syllable. Thus *dispelled* has two *l*'s, but *traveled* has one, *equipped* has two *p*'s but *worshiper* one, *occurred* has two *r*'s but *altered* one, and *petted* has two *t*'s but *trumpeter* one.[33]

There remains a twilight zone in which usage is still uncertain in both England and America. The words in it are chiefly neologisms, *e. g., airplane*. In 1914 or thereabout the London *Times* announced that it had decided to use *airplane* in place of *aëroplane*, but three weeks later it went back to the original form. The Concise Oxford sticks to *aeroplane* (without the dieresis) and so does Cassell's, though it lists *airplane* among war terms. The majority of English newspapers follow these authorities, but in the United States *airplane* is

[33] Text, Type and Style, a Compendium of *Atlantic* Usage, by George B. Ives; Boston, 1921, p. 186 *ff*.

in steadily increasing use. Some confusion is caused by the fact that the French, who originated practically all of our aeronautical terms, use *aeroplane,* but omit the final *e* from *biplan, monoplan,* etc. A correspondent calls my attention to the fact that the two terminations are not the same etymologically. The *plan* of *biplan* is a word meaning "a plane, a plane surface"; while the *plane* of *aeroplane* is a formation taken from the verb *planer,* to soar, to glide. Hence *aeroplane* means "ce qui plane dans l'air," while *biplan* means "ce qui a deux plans." In the United States the current forms are *biplane* and *monoplane.*

In Canada the two orthographies, English and American, flourish side by side. By an Order-in-Council of 1890, all official correspondence must show the English spelling, but practically all of the newspapers use the American spelling and it is also taught in most of the public schools, which are under the jurisdiction, not of the Dominion government, but of the provincial ministers of education. In Australia the English spelling is official, but various American forms are making fast progress. According to the *Triad,* the leading Australian magazine,[34] "horrible American inaccuracies of spelling are coming into common use" in the newspapers out there; worse, the educational authorities of Victoria authorize the use of the American *-er* ending. This last infamy has been roundly denounced by Sir Adrian Knox, Chief Justice of the Commonwealth, and the *Triad* displays a good deal of colonial passion in supporting him. "Unhappily," it says, "we have no English Academy to guard the purity and integrity of the language. Everything is left to the sense and loyalty of decently cultivated people." But even the *Triad* admits that American usage, in some instances, is "correct." It is, however, belligerently faithful to the *-our*-ending. "If it is correct or tolerable in English," it argues somewhat lamely, "to write *labor* for *labour,* why not *boddy* for *body, steddy* for *steady,* and *yot* for *yacht?"* Meanwhile, as in Canada, the daily papers slide into the Yankee orbit.

[34] May 10, 1921, p. 5.

5.

Simplified Spelling

The current movement toward a general reform of English-American spelling is of American origin, and its chief supporters are Americans today. Its actual father was Webster, for it was the long controversy over his simplified spellings that brought the dons of the American Philological Association to a serious investigation of the subject. In 1875 they appointed a committee to inquire into the possibility of reform, and in 1876 this committee reported favorably. During the same year there was an International Convention for the Amendment of English Orthography at Philadelphia, with several delegates from England present, and out of it grew the Spelling Reform Association.[35] In 1878 a committee of American philologists began preparing a list of proposed new spellings, and two years later the Philological Society of England joined in the work. In 1883 a joint manifesto was issued, recommending various general simplifications. Among those enlisted in the movement were Charles Darwin, Lord Tennyson, Sir John Lubbock and Sir J. A. H. Murray. In 1886 the American Philological Association issued independently a list of recommendations affecting about 3,500 words, and falling under ten headings. Practically all of the changes proposed had been put forward 80 years before by Webster, and some of them had entered into unquestioned American usage in the meantime, *e. g.*, the deletion of the *u* from the *-our* words, the substitution of *er* for *re* at the end of words, and the reduction of *traveller* to *traveler*.

The trouble with the others was that they were either too uncouth

[35] Accounts of earlier proposals of reform in English spelling are to be found in Sayce's Introduction to the Science of Language, vol. i, p. 330 *et seq.*, and White's Everyday English, p. 152 *et seq.* The best general treatment of the subject is in Lounsbury's English Spelling and Spelling Reform; New York, 1909. A radical innovation, involving the complete abandonment of the present alphabet and the substitution of a series of symbols with vowel points, is proposed in Peetickay, by Wilfrid Perrett; Cambridge (England), 1920. Mr. Perrett's book is written in a lively style, and includes much curious matter. He criticises the current schemes of spelling reform very acutely. Nearly all of them, he says, suffer from the defect of seeking to represent all the sounds of English by the present alphabet. This he calls "one more reshuffle of a prehistoric pack, one more attempt to deal out 26 cards to some 40 players."

to be adopted without a long struggle or likely to cause errors in pronunciation. To the first class belonged *tung* for *tongue,* *ruf* for *rough,* *batl* for *battle* and *abuv* for *above,* and to the second such forms as *cach* for *catch* and *troble* for *trouble.* The result was that the whole reform received a set-back: the public dismissed the reformers as a pack of dreamers. Twelve years later the National Education Association revived the movement with a proposal that a beginning be made with a very short list of reformed spellings, and nominated the following by way of experiment: *tho, altho, thru, thruout, thoro, thoroly, thorofare, program, prolog, catalog, pedagog* and *decalog.* This scheme of gradual changes was sound in principle, and in a short time at least two of the recommended spellings, *program* and *catalog,* were in general use. Then, in 1906, came the organization of the Simplified Spelling Board, with an endowment of $15,000 a year from Andrew Carnegie, and a formidable list of members and collaborators, including Henry Bradley, F. I. Furnivall, C. H. Grandgent, W. W. Skeat, T. R. Lounsbury and F. A. March. The board at once issued a list of 300 revised spellings, new and old, and in August, 1906, President Roosevelt ordered their adoption by the Government Printing Office. But this unwise effort to hasten matters, combined with the buffoonery characteristically thrown about the matter by Roosevelt, served only to raise up enemies, and since then, though it has prudently gone back to more discreet endeavors and now lays main stress upon the original 12 words of the National Education Association, the Board has not made a great deal of progress. [36] From time to time it issues impressive lists of newspapers and periodicals that are using some, at least, of its revised spellings and of colleges that have made them optional, but an inspection of these lists shows that very few publications of any importance have been converted and that most of the great universities still hesitate. [37] It has, however, greatly reinforced the authority behind many of Webster's spellings, and aided by the Chem-

---

[36] Its second list was published on January 28, 1908, its third on January 25, 1909, and its fourth on March 24, 1913, and since then there have been several others. But most of its literature is devoted to the 12 words and to certain reformed spellings of Webster, already in general use.

[37] In April, 1919, it claimed 556 newspapers and periodicals, with a circulation of 18,000,000, and 460 universities, colleges and normal schools.

AMERICAN SPELLING 245

ical Section of the American Association for the Advancement of Science and the editors of the *Journal* of the American Medical Association, it has done much to reform scientific orthography. Such forms as *gram, cocain, chlorid, anemia* and *anilin* are the products of its influence.[38] Its latest list recommends the following changes:

1. When a word begins with œ or æ substitute *e: esthetic, medieval, subpena.* But retain the diphthong at the end of a word: *alumnæ.*
2. When *bt* is pronounced *t*, drop the silent *b*: *det, dettor, dout.*
3. When *ceed* is final spell it *cede*: *excede, procede, succede.*
4. When *ch* is pronounced like hard *c*, drop the silent *h* except before *e, i* and *y*: *caracter, clorid, corus, cronic, eco, epoc, mecanic, monarc, scolar, scool, stomac, tecnical.* But retain *architect, chemist, monarchy.*
5. When a double consonant appears before a final silent *e* drop the last two letters: *bizar, cigaret, creton, gavot, gazet, giraf, gram, program, quartet, vaudevil.*
6. When a word ends with a double consonant substitute a single consonant: *ad, bil, bluf, buz, clas, dol, dul, eg, glas, les, los, mes, mis, pas, pres, shal, tel, wil.* But retain *ll* after a long vowel: *all, roll.* And retain *ss* when the word has more than one syllable: *needless.*
7. Drop the final silent *e* after a consonant preceded by a short stressed vowel: *giv, hav, liv.*
8. Drop the final silent *e* in the common words *are, gone* and *were: ar, gon, wer.*
9. Drop the final silent *e* in the unstressed final short syllables *ide, ile, ine, ise, ite* and *ive: activ, bromid, definit, determin, practis, hostil.*
10. Drop the silent *e* after *lv* and *rv*: *involv, twelv, carv, deserv.*
11. Drop the silent *e* after *v* or *z* when preceded by a digraph representing a long vowel or a diphthong: *achiev, freez, gauz, sneez.*
12. Drop the *e* in final *oe* when it is pronounced *o*: *fo, ho, ro, to, wo.* But retain it in inflections: *foes, hoed.*
13. When one of the letters in *ea* is silent drop it: *bred, brekfast, hed, hart, harth.*
14. When final *ed* is pronounced *d* drop the *e*: *cald, carrid, employd, marrid, robd, sneezd, struggld, wrongd.* But not when a wrong pronunciation will be suggested: *bribd, cand, fild* (for *filed*), etc.
15. When final *ed* is pronounced *t* substitute *t*: *addrest, shipt, helpt, indorst.*

---

[38] The Standard Dictionary, published in 1906, gave great aid to the movement by listing the 3,500 reformed spellings recommended by the American Philological Association in 1886. The publishers of the Standard are also the publishers of the *Literary Digest*, the only magazine of large circulation to adopt the Simplified Spelling Board's recommendations to any appreciable extent. It substitutes simple vowels for diphthongs in such words as *esthetic* and *fetus*, uses *t* in place of the usual terminal *ed* in *addrest, affixt*, etc., drops the final *me* and *te* in words of the *programme* and *cigarette* classes, and drops the *ue* from words of the *catalogue* class. See Funk & Wagnalls Company Style Card; New York, 1914.

But not when a wrong pronunciation will be suggested: *bakt, fact* (for *faced*), etc.

16. When *ei* is pronounced like *ie* in *brief* substitute *ie: conciet, deciev, wierd*.

17. When a final *ey* is pronounced *y* drop the *e: barly, chimny, donky, mony, vally*.

18. When final *gh* is pronounced *f* substitute *f* and drop the silent letter of the preceding digraph: *enuf, laf, ruf, tuf*.

19. When *gh* is pronounced *g* drop the silent *h: agast, gastly, gost, goul*.

20. When *gm* is final drop the silent *g: apothem, diagram, flem*.

21. When *gue* is final after a consonant, a short vowel or a digraph representing a long vowel or a diphthong drop the silent *ue: tung, catalog, harang, leag, sinagog*. But not when a wrong pronunciation would be suggested: *rog* (for *rogue*), *vag* (for *vague*), etc.

22. When a final *ise* is pronounced *ize* substitute *ize: advertize, advize, franchize, rize, wize*.

23. When *mb* is final after a short vowel drop *b: bom, crum, dum, lam, lim, thum*. But not when a wrong pronunciation would be suggested: *com* (for *comb*), *tom* (for *tomb*), etc.

24. When *ou* before *l* is pronounced *o* drop *u: mold, sholder*. But not *sol* (for *soul*).

25. When *ough* is final spell *o, u, ock* or *up*, according to the pronunciation: *altho, boro, donut, furlo, tho, thoro, thru, hock, hiccup*.

26. When *our* is final and *ou* is pronounced as a short vowel drop *u: color, honor, labor*.

27. When *ph* is pronounced *f* substitute *f: alfabet, emfasis, fantom, fonograf, fotograf, sulfur, telefone, telegraf*.

28. When *re* is final after any consonant save *c* substitute *er: center, fiber, meter, theater*. But not *lucer, mediocer*.

29. When *rh* is initial and the *h* is silent drop it: *retoric, reumatism, rime, rubarb, rithm*.

30. When *sc* is initial and the *c* is silent drop it: *senery, sented, septer, sience, sissors*.

31. When *u* is silent before a vowel drop it: *bild, condit, garantee, gard, ges, gide, gild*.

32. When *y* is between consonants substitute *i: analisis, fisic, gipsy, paralize, rime, silvan, tipe*.

Obviously this list is far ahead of the public inclination. Moreover, it is so long and contains so many exceptions (observe rules 1, 4, 6, 12, 14, 15, 21, 23, 24 and 28) that there is little hope that any considerable number of Americans will adopt it, at least during the lifetime of its proponents. Its extravagance, indeed, has had the effect of alienating the support of the National Education Association, and at the convention held in Des Moines in the Summer of

AMERICAN SPELLING 247

1921 the Association formally withdrew from the campaign.[39] But even so long a list is not enough for the extremists. To it they add various miscellaneous new spellings: *aker, anser, burlesk, buro, campain, catar, counterfit, delite, foren, forfit, frend, grotesk, iland, maskerade, morgage, picturesk, siv, sorgum, sovren, spritely, tuch, yu* and *yung*. The reader will recognize some of these as surviving inventions of Webster. But though all such bizarre forms languish, the twelve spellings adopted by the National Education Association in 1898 are plainly making progress, especially *tho* and *thru*. I read many manuscripts by American authors, and find in them an increasing use of both forms, with the occasional addition of *altho, thoro* and *thoroly*. The spirit of American spelling is on their side. They promise to come in as *honor, bark, check, wagon* and *story* came in many years ago, as *tire*,[40] *esophagus* and *theater* came in later on, and as *program, catalog* and *cyclopedia* came in only yesterday. The advertisement writers seem to be even more hospitable than the authors. Such forms as *vodvil, burlesk, foto, fonograf, kandy, kar, holsum, kumfort, sulfur, arkade, kafeteria* and *segar* are not infrequent in their writings. At least one American professor of English predicts that these forms will eventually prevail. Even *fosfate* and *fotograf*, he says, "are bound to be the spellings of the future." [41] Meanwhile the advertisement writers and authors combine in an attempt to naturalize *alright*, a compound of *all* and *right*, made by analogy with *already* and *almost*. I find it in American manuscripts every day, and it not seldom gets into print.[42] So far no dictionary supports it, but it has already migrated to England and

---

[39] See the *Weekly Review*, July 16, 1921, p. 47.
[40] *Tyre* was still in use in America in the 70's. It will be found on p. 150 of Mark Twain's Roughing It: Hartford, 1872.
[41] Krapp: Modern English, p. 181.
[42] For example, in Teepee Neighbors, by Grace Coolidge; Boston, 1917, p. 220; Duty and Other Irish Comedies, by Seumas O'Brien; New York, 1916, p. 52; Salt, by Charles G. Norris; New York, 1918, p. 135, and The Ideal Guest, by Wyndham Lewis, *Little Review*, May, 1918, p. 3. O'Brien is an Irishman and Lewis an Englishman, but the printer in each case was American. I find *allright*, as one word but with two *l's*, in Diplomatic Correspondence with Belligerent Governments, etc., European War, No. 4; Washington, 1918, p. 214.

has the *imprimatur* of a noble lord.[43] Another vigorous newcomer is *sox* for *socks*. The *White Sox* are known to all Americans; the *White Socks* would seem strange. The new plural has got into the *Congressional Record*.[44]

6.

The Treatment of Loan-Words

In the treatment of loan-words English spelling is very much more conservative than American. This conservatism, in fact, is so marked that it is frequently denounced by English critics of the national speech usages, and it stood first among the "tendencies of modern taste" attacked by the Society for Pure English in its original prospectus in 1913—a prospectus prepared by Henry Bradley, Dr. Robert Bridges, Sir Walter Raleigh and L. Pearsall Smith, and signed by many important men of letters, including Thomas Hardy, A. J. Balfour, Edmund Gosse, Austin Dobson, Maurice Hewlett, Gilbert Murray, George Saintsbury and the professors of English literature at Oxford and London, Sir Arthur Quiller-Couch and W. P. Ker. I quote from this *caveat:*

> Literary taste at the present time, with regard to foreign words recently borrowed from abroad, is on wrong lines, the notions which govern it being scientifically incorrect, tending to impair the national character of our standard speech, and to adapt it to the habits of classical scholars. On account of these alien associations our borrowed terms are now spelt and pronounced, not as English, but as foreign words, instead of being assimilated, as they were in the past, and brought into conformity with the main structure of our speech. And as we more and more rarely assimilate our borrowings, so even words that were once naturalized are being now one by one made un-English, and driven out of the language back into their foreign forms; whence it comes that a paragraph of serious English prose may be sometimes seen as freely sprinkled with italicized French words as a passage of Cicero is often interlarded with Greek. The mere printing of such words in italics is an active force toward degeneration. The Society hopes to discredit this tendency, and it will endeavour to restore to English its old recreative energy; when a choice

[43] *Vide* How to Lengthen Our Ears, by Viscount Harberton; London, 1917, p. 28.
[44] May 16, 1921, p. 1478, col. 2.

is possible we should wish to give an English pronunciation and spelling to useful foreign words, and we would attempt to restore to a good many words the old English forms which they once had, but which are now supplanted by the original foreign forms."

A glance through any English weekly or review, or, indeed, any English newspaper of the slightest intellectual pretension will show how far this tendency has gone. All the foreign words that English must perforce employ for want of native terms of precisely the same import are carefully italicized and accented, e. g., *matinée, café, crêpe, début, portière, éclat, naïveté, régime, rôle, soirée, précis, protégé, élite, gemütlichkeit, mêlée, tête-à-tête, porte-cochère, divorcée, fiancée, weltpolitik, weltschmerz, muzhik, ukase, dénouement.* Even good old English words have been displaced by foreign analogues thought to be more elegant, e. g., *repertory* by *répertoire, sheik* by *shaikh, czar* by *tsar, levee* by *levée, moslem* by *muslim, khalifate* by *khilifat, said* by *seyd, crape* by *crêpe, supper* by *souper, Legion of Honor* by *Légion d'honneur, gormand* by *gourmand, grip* by *la grippe, crown* by *krone.* Proper names also yield to this new pedantry, and the London *Times* frequently delights the *aluminados* by suddenly making such substitutions as that of *Serbia* for *Servia* and that of *Rumania* for *Roumania;* in the course of time, if the warnings of the S. P. E. do not prevail, the English may be writing *München, Kobenhavn, Napoli, Wien, Warszava, Bruxelles* and *s'Gravenhage;* even today they commonly use *Hannover, Habana* and *Leipzig.* Nearly all the English papers are careful about the diacritical marks in proper names, e. g., *Sèvres, Zürich, Bülow, François, Frédéric, Héloise, Bogotá, Orléans, Besançon, Rhône, Côted'Or, Württemberg.* The English dictionaries seldom omit the accents from recent foreign words. Cassell's leaves them off *régime*

[45] S. P. E. Tract No. 1, Preliminary Announcement and List of Members, Oct., 1919; Oxford, 1919, p. 7. The Literary Supplement of the London *Times* supported the Society in a leading article on Jan. 8, 1920. "Of old," it said, "we incorporated foreign words rapidly and altered their spelling ruthlessly. T)day we take them in and go on spelling them and pronouncing them in a foreign way. *Rendezvous* is an example, *régime* is another. They have come to stay; the spelling of the first, and at least the pronunciation of the second, should be altered; and a powerful organization of schoolmasters and journalists could secure changes which the working classes are in process of securing with the words (more familiar to them) *garridge* and *shover.*" See also A Few Practical Suggestions, by Logan Pearsall Smith, S. P. E. Tract No. 3; Oxford, 1920, especially sections i, ii and iii.

and *début*, but preserves them on practically all the other terms listed above; the Concise Oxford always uses them.

In the United States, as everyone knows, there is no such preciosity visible. *Dépôt* became *depot* immediately it entered the language, and the same rapid naturalization has overtaken *employé, matinée, débutante, negligée, tête-à-tête, exposé, résumé, hofbräu,* and scores of other loan-words. *Café* is seldom seen with its accent, nor is *señor* or *divorcée* or *attaché*. In fact, says a recent critic,[46] "the omission of the diacritic is universal. Even the English press of French New Orleans ignores it." This critic lists some rather amazing barbarisms, among them *standchen* for *ständchen* in *Littell's Living Age*, *outre* for *outré* in *Judge*, and *Poincaire, Poincare* and *Poinciarre* for *Poincaré* in an unnamed newspaper. He gives an amusing account of the struggles of American newspapers with *thé dansant*. He says:

> Put this through the hopper of the typesetting machine, and it comes forth, "the *the dansant*"—which even Oshkosh finds intolerable. The thing was, however, often attempted when *thés dansants* came into fashion, and with various results. Generally the proof-reader eliminates one of the *the*'s, making *dansant* a quasi-noun, and to this day one reads of people giving or attending *dansants*. Latterly the public taste seems to favor *dansante*, which doubtless has a Frenchier appearance, provided you are sufficiently ignorant of the Gallic tongue. Two other solutions of the difficulty may be noted:
> Among those present at the *"the dansant"*;
> Among those present at the *the-dansant*;
> that is, either a hyphen or quotation marks set off the exotic phrase.

Even when American newspapers essay to use accents, they commonly use them incorrectly. The same critic reports *Pièrre* for *Pierre, mà* for *ma,* and *bufführ, bufführ, bufführ* and even *buffet* for *buffet*. But they seldom attempt to use them, and in this iconoclasm they are supported by at least one professor, Brander Matthews. In speaking of *naïve* and *naïveté*, which he welcomes because "we have no exact equivalent for either word," he says: "but they will need to shed their accents and to adapt themselves somehow to the traditions of our orthography."[47] He goes on: "After we have decided

---

[46] Charles Fitzhugh Talman: Accents Wild, *Atlantic Monthly*, Dec., 1915, p. 807 ff.
[47] Why Not Speak Your Own Language? *Delineator*, Nov., 1917, p. 12.

AMERICAN SPELLING

that the foreign word we find knocking at the doors of English [he really means American, as the context shows] is likely to be useful, we must fit it for naturalization by insisting that it shall shed its accents, if it has any; that it shall change its spelling, if this is necessary; that it shall modify its pronunciation, if this is not easy for us to compass; and that it shall conform to all our speech-habits, especially in the formation of the plural." This counsel is heeded by the great majority of American printers. I have found *bozart* (for *beaux arts*) on the first page of a leading American newspaper, and a large textile corporation widely advertises *Bozart* rugs. *Exposé* long since lost its accent and is now commonly pronounced to rhyme with *propose*. In the common speech the French word *beau* has been naturalized as *bo,* and is often so spelled. *Schmierkäse* has become *smearkase.* The *sauer,* in *sauer-kraut* and *sauer-braten,* is often spelled *sour. Cole-slaw* has become *cold-slaw. Cañon* is *canyon.* I have even seen *jonteel,* in a trade name, for the French *gentil.*

American newspapers seldom distinguish between the masculine and feminine forms of common loan-words. *Blond* and *blonde* are used indiscriminately. The majority of papers, apparently mistaking *blond* for a simplified form of *blonde,* use it to designate both sexes. So with *employée, divorcée, fiancée, débutante,* etc. Here the feminine form is preferred; no doubt it has been helped into use in the case of the *-ee* words by the analogy of *devotee.* In all cases, of course, the accents are omitted. In the formation of the plural American adopts native forms much more quickly than English. All the English authorities that I have consulted advocate retaining the foreign plurals of most of the loan-words in daily use, *e. g., sanatoria, appendices, indices, virtuosi, formulæ, libretti, media, thésdansants, monsignori.* But American usage favors plurals of native design, and sometimes they take quite fantastic forms. I have observed *delicatessens, monsignors, virtuosos, rathskellers, kindergartens, nucleuses* and *appendixes.* Even the *Journal* of the American Medical Association, a highly scientific authority, goes so far as to approve *curriculums* and *septums. Banditti,* in place of *bandits,* would seem an affectation to an American, and so would *soprani* for *sopranos* and *soli* for *solos,* but the last two, at least, are common in England. Both English and American labor under the lack of native plurals for the two everyday titles, *Mister* and *Missus.* In the written speech, and in the more exact forms of the spoken speech, the French plurals, *Messieurs* and *Mesdames,* are used, but in the ordinary spoken speech, at least in America, they are avoided by circumlocution. When *Messieurs* has to be spoken it is almost invariably pronounced *messers,* and in the same way *Mesdames* becomes *mez-dames,* with the first syllable rhyming with *sez* and the second, which bears the accent, with *games.* In place of *Mesdames* a more natural form, *Madames,* seems to be gaining ground in America. Thus, I have found *Dames du Sacré Cœur* translated as *Madames of the Sacred Heart* in a Catholic paper of wide circulation,[48] and the form is apparently used by American members of the community.

Dr. Louise Pound [49] notes that a number of Latin plurals tend to become singular nouns in colloquial American, notably *curricula, data, dicta, insignia* and *strata,* and with them a few Greek plurals, *e. g., criteria* and *phenomena.* She reports hearing the following uses of them: "The *curricula* of the institution is being changed," "This *data* is very significant," "The *dicta,* 'Go West,' is said to have come from Horace Greeley," "What is that *insignia* on his sleeve?", "This may be called the Renaissance *strata* of loan-words," "That is no *criteria,*" and "What a strange *phenomena!*"—all by speakers presumed to be of some education. The error leads to the creation of double plurals, *e. g., curriculas, insignias, stratas, stimulis, alumnis, bacillis, narcissis.* The Latin names of plants lead to frequent blunders. *Cosmos* and *gladiolus* are felt to be plurals, and from them, by folk-etymology, come the false singulars, *cosma* and *gladiola.* Dr. Pound notes many other barbarous plurals, not mentioned above, *e. g., antennas, cerebras, alumnas, alumnuses, narcissuses, apparatuses, emporiums, opuses, criterions, amœbas, cactuses, phenomenons.*

[48] *Irish World,* June 26, 1918.
[49] The Pluralization of Latin Loan-Words in Present-Day American Speech, *Classical Journal,* vol. xv, no. 3 (Dec., 1919).

AMERICAN SPELLING 253

7.

Minor Differences

In capitalization the English are a good deal more conservative than we are. They invariably capitalize such terms as *Government, Prime Minister* and *Society,* when used as proper nouns; they capitalize *Press, Pulpit, Bar,* etc., almost as often. In America a movement against this use of capitals appeared during the latter part of the eighteenth century. In Jefferson's first draft of the Declaration of Independence *nature* and *creator,* and even *god* are in lower case. During the 20's and 30's of the succeeding century, probably as a result of French influence, the movement against the capitals went so far that the days of the week were often spelled with small initial letters, and even *Mr.* became *mr.* Curiously enough, the most striking exhibition of this tendency of late years is offered by an English work of the highest scholarship, the Cambridge History of English Literature. It uses the lower case for all titles, even *baron* and *colonel* before proper names, and also avoids capitals in such words as *presbyterian, catholic* and *christian,* and in the second parts of such terms as Westminster *abbey* and Atlantic *ocean.*

There are also certain differences in punctuation. The English, as everyone knows, put a comma after the street number of a house, making it, for example, *34, St. James's street.* They usually insert a comma instead of a period after the hour when giving the time in figures, *e. g., 9,27,* and omit the *0* when indicating less than 10 minutes, *e. g.,* 8,7, instead of *8.07.* They do not use the period as the mark of the decimal, but employ a dot at the level of the upper dot of a colon, as in *3·1416.* They cling to the hyphen in such words as *to-day, to-night* and *good-bye;* it begins to disappear in America.

There remains a class of differences that may as well be noticed under spelling, though they are not strictly orthographical. *Specialty, aluminum* and *alarm* offer examples. In English they are *speciality, aluminium* and *alarum,* though *alarm* is also an alternative form. *Specialty,* in America, is always accented on the first syllable; *speciality,* in England, on the third. The result is two distinct words, though their meaning is identical. How *aluminium,* in America, lost its fourth syllable I have been unable to determine, but all American authorities now make it *aluminum* and all English authorities stick to *aluminium.* Perhaps the *boric-boracic* pair also belongs here. In American *boric* is now almost universally preferred, but it is also making progress in England. How the difference between the English *behove* and the American *behoove* arose I do not know. Equally mysterious is the origin of the American *snicker,* apparently a decadent form of the English *snigger.*

IX.

THE COMMON SPEECH

1.

Grammarians and Their Ways

So far, in the main, the language examined has been of a relatively pretentious and self-conscious variety—the speech, if not always of formal discourse, then at least of literate men. Most of the examples of its vocabulary and idiom, in fact, have been drawn from written documents or from written reports of more or less careful utterances, for example, the speeches of members of Congress and of other public men. The whole of Thornton's excellent material is of this character. In his dictionary there is scarcely a locution that is not supported by printed examples.

It must be obvious that such materials, however lavishly set forth, cannot exhibit the methods and tendencies of a living speech with anything approaching completeness, nor even with accuracy. What men put into writing and what they say when they take sober thought are very far from what they utter in everyday conversation. All of us, no matter how careful our speech habits, loosen the belt a bit, so to speak, when we talk familiarly to our fellows, and pay a good deal less heed to precedents and proprieties, perhaps, than we ought to. It was a sure instinct that made Ibsen put "bad grammar" into the mouth of Nora Helmar in "A Doll's House." She is a general's daughter and the wife of a professor, but even professors' wives are not above occasional bogglings of the cases of pronouns and the conjugations of verbs. The professors themselves, in truth, must have the same habit, for sometimes they show plain signs of it in print. More than once, plowing through profound and interminable treatises of grammar and syntax during the writing and revision of the present work, I have encountered the cheering spectacle of one grammarian exposing, with contagious joy, the grammatical lapses of some other grammarian. And nine times out of ten, a few pages further on, I have found the enchanted purist erring himself.[1] The most funereal of the sciences is saved from utter horror by such displays of human malice and fallibility. Speech itself, indeed, would become almost impossible if the grammarians could follow their own rules unfailingly, and were always right.

But here we are among the learned, and their sins, when detected and exposed, are at least punished by conscience. What are of more importance, to those interested in language as a living thing, are the offendings of the millions who are not conscious of any wrong. It is among these millions, ignorant of regulation and eager only to express their ideas clearly and forcefully, that language undergoes its great changes and constantly renews its vitality. These are the genuine makers of grammar, marching miles ahead of the formal grammarians. Like the Emperor Sigismund, each man among them may well say: *"Ego sum . . . supra grammaticam."* It is competent for any individual to offer his contribution—his new word, his better idiom, his novel figure of speech, his short cut in grammar or syntax—and it is by the general vote of the whole body, not by the verdict of a small school, that the fate of the innovation is decided. As Brander Matthews says, there is not even representative government in the matter; the *posse comitatus* decides directly, and despite the sternest protest, finally. The ignorant, the rebellious and the daring come forward with their brilliant barbarisms; the learned and conservative bring up their objections. "And when both sides have been heard, there is a show of hands; and by this the irrevocable decision of the community itself is rendered." [2] Thus it was that the Romance languages were fashioned out of the wreck of Latin, the vast influence of the literate minority to the contrary notwithstanding. Thus it was, too, that English lost its case inflections and many of its old conjugations, and that our *yes* came to be substituted for the *gea-se* (= *so be it*) of an earlier day, and that we

---

[1] Sweet, perhaps the abbot of the order, makes almost indecent haste to sin. See the second paragraph on the very first page of vol. i of his New English Grammar.
[2] *Yale Review*, April, 1918, p. 548.

got rid of *whom* after *man* in *the man I saw,* and that our stark pronoun of the first person was precipitated from the German *ich.* And thus it is that, in our own day, the language faces forces in America which, not content with overhauling and greatly enriching its materials, now threaten to work changes in its very structure.

Where these tendencies run strongest, of course, is on the plane of the vulgar spoken language. Among all classes the everyday speech departs very far from orthodox English, and even very far from any recognized spoken English, but among the lower classes that make up the great body of the people it gets so far from orthodox English that it gives promise, soon or late, of throwing off its old bonds altogether, or, at any rate, all save the loosest of them. Behind it is the gigantic impulse that I have described in earlier chapters: the impulse of an egoistic and iconoclastic people, facing a new order of life in highly self-conscious freedom, to break a relatively stable language, long since emerged from its period of growth, to their novel and multitudinous needs, and, above all, to their experimental and impatient spirit. This impulse, it must be plain, would war fiercely upon any attempt at formal regulation, however prudent and elastic; it is often rebellious for the mere sake of rebellion. But what it comes into conflict with, in America, is nothing so politic, and hence nothing so likely to keep the brakes upon it. What it actually encounters here is a formalism that is artificial, illogical and almost unintelligible—a formalism borrowed from English grammarians, and by them brought into English, against all fact and reason, from the Latin. "In most of our grammars, perhaps in all of those issued earlier than the opening of the twentieth century," says Matthews, "we find linguistic laws laid down which are in blank contradiction with the genius of the language." [3] In brief, the American school-boy, hauled before a pedagogue to be instructed in the structure and organization of the tongue he speaks, is actually instructed in the structure and organization of a tongue that he never hears at all, and seldom reads, and that, in more than one of the characters thus set before him, does not even exist.

[3] *Yale Review, op. cit.,* p. 560. See also Is Grammar Useless? by Walter Guest Kellogg, *North American Review,* July, 1920.

The effects of this are twofold. On the one hand he conceives an antipathy to a subject so lacking in intelligibility and utility. As one teacher puts it, "pupils tire of it; often they see nothing in it, because there *is* nothing in it." [4] And on the other hand, the schoolboy goes entirely without sympathetic guidance in the living language that he actually speaks, in and out of the classroom, and that he will probably speak all the rest of his life. All he hears in relation to it is a series of sneers and prohibitions, most of them grounded, not upon principles deduced from its own nature, but upon its divergences from the theoretical language that he is so unsuccessfully taught. The net result is that all the instruction he receives passes for naught. It is not sufficient to make him a master of orthodox English and it is not sufficient to rid him of the speech-habits of his home and daily life. Thus he is thrown back upon those speech-habits without any helpful restraint or guidance, and they make him a willing ally of the radical and often extravagant tendencies which show themselves in the vulgar tongue. In other words, the very effort to teach him an excessively tight and formal English promotes his use of a loose and rebellious English. And so the grammarians, with the traditional fatuity of their order, labor for the destruction of the grammar they defend, and for the decay of all those refinements of speech that go with it.

The folly of this system, of course, has not failed to attract the attention of the more intelligent teachers, nor have they failed to observe the causes of its failure. "Much of the fruitlessness of the study of English grammar," says Wilcox,[5] "and many of the obstacles encountered in its study are due to 'the difficulties created by the grammarians.' These difficulties arise chiefly from three sources—excessive classification, multiplication of terms for a single conception, and the attempt to treat the English language as if it were highly inflected." Dr. Otto Jespersen puts them a bit differently. "Ordinary grammars," he says, "in laying down their rules, are too apt to forget that the English language is one thing, com-

[4] The Difficulties Created by Grammarians Are to Be Ignored, by W. H. Wilcox, *Atlantic Educational Journal*, Nov., 1912, p. 8. The title of this article is quoted from ministerial instructions of 1909 to the teachers of French *lycées*.
[5] *Op. cit.*, p. 7. Mr. Wilcox is an instructor in the Maryland State Normal School.

mon-sense or logic another thing, and Latin grammar a third, and that these three things have really, in many cases, very little to do with one another. Schoolmasters generally have an astonishing talent for not observing real linguistic facts, and an equally astonishing inclination to stamp everything as faulty that does not agree with their narrow rules." [6] So long ago as the 60's Richard Grant White began an onslaught upon all such punditic stupidities. He saw clearly that "the attempt to treat English as if it were highly inflected" was making its intelligent study almost impossible, and proposed boldly that all English grammar-books be burned.[7] Of late his ideas have begun to gain a certain acceptance, and as the literature of denunciation has grown [8] the grammarians have been constrained to overhaul their texts. When I was a school-boy, during the penultimate decade of the last century, the chief American grammar was "A Practical Grammar of the English Language," by Thomas W. Harvey.[9] This formidable work was almost purely synthetical: it began with a long series of definitions, wholly unintelligible to a child, and proceeded into a maddening maze of pedagogical distinctions, puzzling even to an adult. The latter-day grammars, at least those for the elementary schools, are far more analytical and logical. For example, there is "Longman's Briefer Grammar," by George J. Smith,[10] a text now in very wide use. This book starts off, not with page after page of abstractions, but with a well-devised examination of the complete sentence, and the characters and relations of the parts of speech are very simply and clearly developed. But before the end the author begins to succumb to precedent, and on page 114 I find paragraph after paragraph of such dull, flyblown pedantry as this:

[6] Chapters on English; London, 1918, p. 49.
[7] See especially chapters ix and x of Words and Their Uses and chapters xvii, xviii and xix of Every-Day English; also the preface to the latter, p. xi *et seq.* The study of other languages has been made difficult by the same attempt to force the characters of Greek and Latin grammar upon them. One finds a protest against the process, for example, in E. H. Palmer's Grammar of Hindustani, Persian and Arabic; London, 1906. In all ages, indeed, grammarians appear to have been fatuous. The learned will remember Aristophanes' ridicule of them in The Clouds, 660-690.
[8] The case is well summarized in Simpler English Grammar, by Patterson Wardlaw, *Bull. of the University of S. Carolina,* no. 38, pt. iii, July, 1914.
[9] Cincinnati, 1868; rev. ed., 1878.
[10] New York, 1903; rev. ed., 1915.

Some Intransitive Verbs are used to link the Subject and some Adjective or Noun. These Verbs are called Copulative Verbs, and the Adjective or Noun is called the Attribute.

The Attribute always describes or denotes the person or thing denoted by the Subject.

Verbals are words that are derived from Verbs and express action or being without asserting it. Infinitives and Participles are Verbals.

And so on. Smith, in his preface, says that his book is intended, "not so much to 'cover' the subject of grammar, as to *teach* it," and calls attention to the fact, somewhat proudly, that he has omitted "the rather hard subject of gerunds," all mention of conjunctive adverbs, and even the conjugation of verbs. Nevertheless, he immerses himself in the mythical objective case of nouns on page 108, and does not emerge until the end.[11] "The New-Webster-Cooley Course in English," [12] another popular text, carries reform a step further. The subject of case is approached through the personal pronouns, where it retains its only surviving intelligibility, and the more lucid *object form* is used in place of *objective case*. Moreover, the pupil is plainly informed, later on, that "a noun has in reality but two case-forms: a possessive and a common case-form." This is the best concession to the facts yet made by a text-book grammarian. But no one familiar with the habits of the pedagogical mind need be told that its interior pull is against even such mild and obvious reforms. Defenders of the old order are by no means silent; a fear seems to prevail that grammar, robbed of its imbecile classifications, may collapse entirely. Wilcox records how the Council of English Teachers of New Jersey, but a few years ago, spoke out boldly for the recognition of no less than five cases in English. "Why five?" asks Wilcox. "Why not eight, or ten, or even thirteen? Undoubtedly because there are five cases in Latin." [13] Most of the current efforts at improvement, in fact, tend toward a mere revision and multiplication of classifications; the pedant is eternally

---

[11] Even Sweet, though he bases his New English Grammar upon the spoken language and thus sets the purists at defiance, quickly succumbs to the labelling mania. Thus his classification of tenses includes such fabulous monsters as these: continuous, recurrent, neutral, definite, indefinite, secondary, incomplete, inchoate, short and long.

[12] By W. F. Webster and Alice Woodworth Cooley; Boston, 1903; rev. eds., 1905 and 1909. The authors are Minneapolis teachers.

[13] *Op. cit.*, p. 8.

THE COMMON SPEECH 261

convinced that pigeon-holing and relabelling are contributions to knowledge. A curious proof in point is offered by a pamphlet entitled "Reorganization of English in Secondary Schools," compiled by James Fleming Hosic and issued by the National Bureau of Education.[14] The aim of this pamphlet is to rid the teaching of English, including grammar, of its accumulated formalism and ineffectiveness—to make it genuine instruction instead of a pedantic and meaningless routine. And how is this revolutionary aim set forth? By a meticulous and merciless splitting of hairs, a gigantic manufacture of classifications and sub-classifications, a colossal display of professorial bombast and flatulence!

I could cite many other examples. Perhaps, after all, the disease is incurable. What such laborious stupidity shows at bottom is simply this: that the sort of man who is willing to devote his life to teaching grammar to children, or to training schoolmarms to do it, is not often the sort of man who is intelligent enough to do it competently. In particular, he is not often intelligent enough to deal with the fluent and ever-amazing permutations of a living and rebellious speech. The only way he can grapple with it at all is by first reducing it to a fixed and formal organization—in brief, by first killing it and embalming it. The difference in the resultant proceedings is not unlike that between a gross dissection and a surgical operation. The difficulties of the former are quickly mastered by any student of normal sense, but even the most casual of laparotomies calls for a man of special skill and address. Thus the elementary study of the national language, at least in America, is almost monopolized by dullards. Children are taught it by men and women who observe it inaccurately and expound it ignorantly. In most other fields the pedagogue meets a certain corrective competition and criticism. The teacher of any branch of applied mechanics or mathematics, for example, has practical engineers at his elbow and they quickly expose and denounce his defects; the college teacher of chemistry, however limited his equipment, at least has the aid of text-books written by actual chemists. But English, even in its most formal shapes, is chiefly taught by those who cannot write it decently and get no aid from those who can. One wades through

[14] Bulletin No. 2; Washington, 1917.

treatise after treatise on English style by pedagogues whose own style is atrocious. A Huxley or a Macaulay might have written one of high merit and utility—but Huxley and Macaulay had other fish to fry, and so the business was left to Prof. Balderdash. Consider the standard texts on prosody—vast piles of meaningless words—hollow babble about spondees, iambics, trochees and so on—idiotic borrowings from dead languages. Two poets, Poe and Lanier, blew blasts of fresh air through the fog, but they had no successors, and it has apparently closed in again. In the department of prose it lies wholly unbroken; no first-rate writer of English prose has ever written a text-book upon the art of writing it.

2.

Spoken American As It Is

But here I wander afield. The art of prose has little to do with the stiff and pedantic English taught in grammar-schools and a great deal less to do with the loose and lively English spoken by the average American in his daily traffic. The thing of importance is that the two differ from each other even more than they differ from the English of a Huxley or a Stevenson. The school-marm, directed by grammarians, labors heroically, but all her effort goes for naught. The young American, like the youngster of any other race, inclines irresistibly toward the dialect that he hears at home, and that dialect, with its piquant neologisms, its high disdain of precedent, its complete lack of self-consciousness, is almost the antithesis of the hard and stiff speech that is expounded out of books. It derives its principles, not from the subtle logic of learned and stupid men, but from the rough-and-ready logic of every day. It has a vocabulary of its own, a syntax of its own, even a grammar of its own. Its verbs are conjugated in a way that defies all the injunctions of the grammar books; it has its contumacious rules of tense, number and case; it has boldly re-established the double negative, once sound in English; it admits double comparatives, confusions in person, clipped infinitives; it lays hands on the vowels, changing them to fit its obscure but powerful spirit; it repudiates all the finer distinctions between the parts of speech.

This highly virile and defiant dialect, and not the fossilized English of the school-marm and her books, is the speech of the Middle American of Joseph Jacobs' composite picture—the mill-hand in a small city of Indiana, with his five years of common schooling behind him, his diligent reading of newspapers, and his proud membership in the Order of Foresters and the Knights of the Maccabees.[15] Go into any part of the country, North, East, South or West, and you will find multitudes of his brothers, car conductors in Philadelphia, immigrants of the second generation in the East Side of New York, iron-workers in the Pittsburgh region, corner grocers in St. Louis, holders of petty political jobs in Atlanta and New Orleans, small farmers in Kansas or Kentucky, house carpenters in Ohio, tinners and plumbers in Chicago—genuine Americans all, bawling patriots, hot for the home team, marchers in parades, readers of the yellow newspapers, fathers of families, sheep on election day, undistinguished norms of the *Homo Americanus*. Such typical Americans, after a fashion, know English. They read it—all save the "hard" words, *i. e.,* all save about 90 per cent of the words of Greek and Latin origin.[16] They can understand perhaps two-thirds of it as it comes from the lips of a political orator or clergyman. They have a feeling that it is, in some recondite sense, superior to the common speech of their kind. They recognize a fluent command of it as the salient mark of a "smart" and "educated" man, one with "the gift of gab." But they themselves never speak it or try to speak it, nor do they look with approbation on efforts in that direction by their fellows.

In no other way, indeed, is the failure of popular education made more vividly manifest. Despite a gigantic effort to enforce certain speech habits, universally in operation from end to end of the country, the masses of people turn almost unanimously to very different speech habits, nowhere advocated and seldom so much as even accurately observed. The literary critic, Francis Hackett, somewhere

---

[15] The Middle American, *American Magazine*, March, 1907.
[16] *Cf.* White: Every-Day English, p. 367 *ff.*

speaks of "the enormous gap between the literate and unliterate American." He is apparently the first to call attention to it. It is the national assumption that no such gap exists—that all Americans, at least if they be white, are so outfitted with sagacity in the public schools that they are competent to consider any public question intelligently and to follow its discussion with understanding. But the truth is, of course, that the public school accomplishes no such magic. The inferior man, in America as elsewhere, remains an inferior man despite the hard effort made to improve him, and his thoughts seldom if ever rise above the most elemental concerns. What lies above not only does not interest him; it actually excites his derision, and he has coined a unique word, *high-brow,* to express his view of it. Especially in speech is he suspicious of superior pretension. The school-boy of the lower orders would bring down ridicule upon himself, and perhaps criticism still more devastating, if he essayed to speak what his teachers conceive to be correct English, or even correct American, outside the school-room. On the one hand his companions would laugh at him as a prig, and on the other hand his parents would probably cane him as an impertinent critic of their own speech. Once he has made his farewell to the schoolmarm, all her diligence in this department goes for nothing.[17] The boys with whom he plays baseball speak a tongue that is not the one taught in school, and so do the youths with whom he will begin learning a trade tomorrow, and the girl he will marry later on, and the saloon-keepers, star pitchers, vaudeville comedians, business sharpers and political mountebanks he will look up to and try to imitate all the rest of his life.

So far as I can discover, there has been but one attempt by a competent authority to determine the special characters of this general tongue of the *mobile vulgus.* That authority is Dr. W. W. Charters, now Professor of Education at the Carnegie Institute of Technology, Pittsburgh. In 1914 Dr. Charters was dean of the faculty of education and professor of the theory of teaching in the University of Missouri, and one of the problems he was engaged upon was that of the teaching of grammar. In the course of this study he encountered the theory that such instruction should be confined to the

[17] *Cf.* Sweet: New English Grammar, vol. i, p. 5.

rules habitually violated—that the one aim of teaching grammar was to correct the speech of the pupils, and that it was useless to harass them with principles which they already instinctively observed. Apparently inclining to this somewhat dubious notion, Dr. Charters applied to the School Board of Kansas City for permission to undertake an examination of the language actually used by the children in the elementary schools of that city, and this permission was granted. The materials thereupon gathered were of two classes. First, the teachers of grades III to VII inclusive in all the Kansas City public schools were instructed to turn over to Dr. Charters all the written work of their pupils, "ordinarily done in the regular order of school work" during a period of four weeks. Secondly, the teachers of grades II to VII inclusive were instructed to make note of "all oral errors in grammar made in the school-rooms and around the school-buildings" during the five school-days of one week, by children of any age, and to dispatch these notes to Dr. Charters also. The result was an accumulation of material so huge that it was unworkable with the means at hand, and so the investigator and his assistants reduced it. Of the oral reports, two studies were made, the first of those from grades III and VII and the second of those from grades VI and VII. Of the written reports, only those from grades VI and VII of twelve typical schools were examined.

The ages thus covered ran from nine or ten to fourteen or fifteen, and perhaps five-sixths of the material studied came from children above twelve. Its examination threw a brilliant light upon the speech actually employed by children near the end of their schooling in a typical American city, and *per corollary*, upon the speech employed by their parents and other older associates. If anything, the grammatical and syntactical habits revealed were a bit less loose than those of the authentic *Volkssprache*, for practically all of the written evidence was gathered under conditions which naturally caused the writers to try to write what they conceived to be correct English, and even the oral evidence was conditioned by the admonitory presence of the teacher. Moreover, it must be obvious that a child of the lower classes, during the period of its actual study of grammar, probably speaks better English than at any time before or afterward, for it is only then that any positive pressure is exerted upon it to that end. But even so, the departures from standard usage that were unearthed were numerous and striking, and their tendency to accumulate in definite groups showed plainly the working of general laws.[18]

Thus, no less than 57 per cent of the oral errors reported by the teachers of grades III and VII involved the use of the verb, and nearly half of these, or 24 per cent of the total, involved a confusion of the past tense form and the perfect participle. Again, double negatives constituted 11 per cent of the errors, and the misuse of adjectives or of adjectival forms for adverbs ran to 4 per cent. Finally, the difficulties of the objective case among the pronouns, the last stronghold of that case in English, were responsible for 7 per cent, thus demonstrating a clear tendency to get rid of it altogether. Now compare the errors of these children, half of whom, as I have just said, were in grade III, and hence wholly uninstructed in formal grammar, with the errors made by children of the second oral group—that is, children of grades VI and VII, in both of which grammar is studied. Dr. Charters' tabulations show scarcely any difference in the character and relative rank of the errors discovered. Those in the use of the verb drop from 57 per cent of the total to 52 per cent, but the double negatives remain at 7 per cent and the errors in the cases of pronouns at 11 per cent.

In the written work of grades VI and VII, however, certain changes appear, no doubt because of the special pedagogical effort against the more salient oral errors. The child, pen in hand, has in mind the cautions oftenest heard, and so reveals something of that greater exactness which all of us show when we do any writing that must bear critical inspection. Thus, the relative frequency of confusion between the past tense forms of verbs and the perfect participles drops from 24 per cent to 5 per cent, and errors based on double negatives drop to 1 per cent. But this improvement in one direction merely serves to unearth new barbarisms in other directions, concealed in the oral tables by the flood of errors now remedied. It is among the verbs that they are still most numerous;

[18] Dr. Charters' report appears as Vol. XVI, No. 2, *University of Missouri Bulletin*, Education Series No. 9, Jan., 1915. He was aided in his inquiry by Edith Miller, teacher of English in one of the St. Louis high-schools.

altogether the errors here amount to exactly 50 per cent of the total. Such locutions as *I had went* and *he seen* diminish relatively and absolutely, but in all other situations the verb is treated with the lavish freedom that is so characteristic of the American common speech. Confusions of the past and present tenses jump relatively from 2 per cent to 19 per cent, thus eloquently demonstrating the tenacity of the error. And mistakes in the forms of nouns and pronouns increase from 2 per cent to 19: a shining proof of a shakiness which follows the slightest effort to augment the vocabulary of everyday.

The materials collected by Dr. Charters and his associates are not, of course, presented in full, but his numerous specimens must strike familiar chords in every ear that is alert to the sounds and ways of the *sermo vulgaris*. What he gathered in Kansas City might have been gathered just as well in San Francisco, or New Orleans, or Chicago, or New York, or in Youngstown, O., or Little Rock, Ark., or Waterloo, Iowa. In each of these places, large or small, a few localisms might have been noted—*oi* substituted for *ur* in New York, *you-all* in the South, a few Germanisms in Pennsylvania and in the upper Mississippi Valley, a few Spanish locutions in the Southwest, certain peculiar vowel-forms in New England—but in the main the report would have been identical with the report he makes. "Relatively few Americans," says Krapp,[19] "spend all their lives in one locality, and even if they do, they cannot possibly escape coming into contact with Americans from other localities. . . . We can distinguish with some certainty Eastern and Western and Southern speech, but beyond this the author has little confidence in those confident experts who think they can tell infallibly, by the test of speech, a native of Hartford from a native of Providence, or a native of Philadelphia from a native of Atlanta, or even, if one insist on infallibility, a native of Chicago from a native of Boston." Krapp is discussing the so-called "standard" speech; on the plane of the vulgate the levelling is quite as apparent. That vast uniformity which marks the people of the United States, in political doctrine, in social habit, in general information, in reaction to ideas, in prejudices and enthusiasms, in the veriest details of domestic cus-

[19] The Pronunciation of Standard English in America; New York, 1919, p. viii.

tom and dress, is nowhere more marked, in truth, than in their speech habits. The incessant neologisms of the national dialect sweep the whole country almost instantly, and the iconoclastic changes which its popular spoken form is constantly undergoing show themselves from coast to coast. "He hurt *hisself*," cited by Dr. Charters, is surely anything but a Missouri localism; one hears it everywhere. And so, too, one hears "she invited *him* and *I*," and "it hurt *terrible*," and "I *set* there," and "this *here* man," and "no, I *never, neither*," and "he *ain't* here," and "where is he *at?*" and "it seems *like* I remember," and "if I *was* you," and "*us* fellows," and "he *give* her hell." And "he *taken* and kissed her," and "he *loaned* me a dollar," and "the man was *found* two dollars," and "the bee *stang* him," and "I *wouldda* thought," and "*can* I have one?" and "he got *hisn*," and "the boss *left* him off," and "the baby *et* the soap," and "*them* are the kind I like," and "he *don't* care," and "no one has *their* ticket," and "how *is* the folks?" and "if you *would of gotten* in the car you could *of rode* down."

Curiously enough, this widely dispersed and highly savory dialect —already, as I shall show, come to a certain grammatical regularity —has attracted the professional writers of the country almost as little as it has attracted the philologists. There are foreshadowings of it in "Huckleberry Finn," in "The Biglow Papers" and even in the rough humor of the period that began with J. C. Neal and company and ended with Artemus Ward and Josh Billings, but in those early days it had not yet come to full flower; it wanted the influence of the later immigrations to take on its present character. The enormous dialect literature of twenty years ago left it almost untouched. Localisms were explored diligently, but the general dialect went virtually unobserved. It is not in "Chimmie Fadden"; it is not in "David Harum"; it is not even in the pre-fable stories of George Ade, perhaps the most acute observer of average, undistinguished American types, urban and rustic, that American literature has yet produced. The business of reducing it to print had to wait for Ring W. Lardner, a Chicago newspaper reporter. In his grotesque tales of base-ball players, so immediately and so

THE COMMON SPEECH 269

deservedly successful,[20] Lardner reports the common speech not only with humor, but also with the utmost accuracy. The observations of Charters and his associates are here reinforced by the sharp ear of one especially competent, and the result is a mine of authentic American. In a single story by Lardner, in truth, it is usually possible to discover examples of almost every logical and grammatical peculiarity of the emerging language, and he always resists very stoutly the temptation to overdo the thing. Here, for example, are a few typical sentences from "The Busher's Honeymoon": [21]

> I and Florrie *was* married the day before yesterday just *like* I told you we *was* going to be. . . . You *was* to get married in Bedford, where *not nothing* is nearly half so dear. . . . The sum of what I have *wrote* down is $29.40. . . . Allen told me I *should ought* to give the priest $5. . . . I never *seen* him before. . . . I didn't used to eat *no* lunch in the playing season except when I *knowed* I was not going to work. . . . I guess the meals *has* cost me all together about $1.50, and I have *eat* very little myself. . . .
> I was willing to tell her all about *them* two poor girls. . . . They must not be *no* mistake about who is the boss in my house. Some men *lets* their *wife* run all over them. . . . Allen has *went* to a college foot-ball game. One of the reporters *give* him a pass. . . . He called up and said he *hadn't* only the one pass, but he was not hurting my feelings *none*. . . . The flat across the hall from this *here* one is for rent. . . . If we should *of boughten* furniture it would cost us in the neighborhood of $100, even without *no* piano. . . . I consider myself lucky to *of* found out about this before it was too late and somebody else had *of* gotten the tip. . . . It will always be *ourn*, even when we move away. . . . Maybe you could *of did* better if you had *of went* at it in a different way. . . . Both *her* and you *is* welcome at my house. . . . I never *seen* so much wine *drank* in my life. . . .

Here are specimens to fit into most of Charters' categories—verbs confused as to tense, pronouns confused as to case, double and even triple negatives, nouns and verbs disagreeing in number, *have* softened to *of*, *n* marking the possessive instead of *s*, *like* used in place of *as*, and the personal pronoun substituted for the demonstrative adjective. A study of the whole story would probably unearth all the remaining errors noted in Kansas City. Lardner's baseball player, though he has pen in hand and is on his guard, and is thus

[20] You Know Me Al; New York, 1916.
[21] *Saturday Evening Post*, July 11, 1914.

very careful to write *would not* instead of *wouldn't* and even *am not* instead of *ain't,* offers a comprehensive and highly instructive panorama of popular speech habits. To him the forms of the subjunctive mood have no existence, and *will* and *shall* are identical, and adjectives and adverbs are indistinguishable, and the objective case is merely a variorum form of the nominative. His past tense is, more often than not, the orthodox present tense. All fine distinctions are obliterated in his speech. He uses invariably the word that is simplest, the grammatical form that is handiest. And so he moves toward the philological millennium dreamed of by George T. Lanigan, when "the singular verb shall lie down with the plural noun, and a little conjunction shall lead them."

Lardner, as I say, is a very accurate observer. More, despite the grotesqueness of the fables that he uses as skeletons for his reports, he is a man of sound philological knowledge, and approaches his business quite seriously. As yet the academic critics have failed to discover him, but soon or late such things as "The Busher's Honeymoon" are bound to find a secure place in the new literature of the United States. His influence, indeed, is already considerable, and one sees it plainly in such things as Sinclair Lewis' "Main Street." [22] Much of the dialogue in "Main Street" is in vulgar American, and Mr. Lewis reports it very accurately. Other writers of fiction turn to the same gorgeous and glowing speech, among them Caroline Lockhart.[23] It even penetrates to more or less serious writing. For example, in a recent treatise on angling by an eminent American authority I find such sentences as "You *gotta* give him credit for being on the job" and "For an accommodating cuss we *gotta* tip the kelly to the wall-eyed pike." [24] Finally, there are the experiments in verse by John V. A. Weaver [25]—still a bit uncertain, but perhaps showing the way to a new American poetry tomorrow.

[22] New York, 1920.
[23] See, for example, Blase Cody Gives Cold Eye to Jeraldine Farrar Troupe, Denver *Post,* Aug. 18, 1918.
[24] Fishing, Tackle and Kits, by Dixie Carroll, editor of *The National Sportsman;* Cincinnati, 1919.
[25] See Appendix II; also, the end of the chapter on The Future of the Language.

3.

The Verb

A study of the materials amassed by Charters and Lardner, if it be reinforced by observation of what is heard on the streets every day, will show that the chief grammatical peculiarities of spoken American lie among the verbs and pronouns. The nouns in common use, in the overwhelming main, are quite sound in form. Very often, of course, they do not belong to the vocabulary of English, but they at least belong to the vocabulary of American: the proletariat, setting aside transient slang, calls things by their proper names, and pronounces those names more or less correctly. The adjectives, too, are treated rather politely, and the adverbs, though commonly transformed into adjectives, are not further mutilated. But the verbs and pronouns undergo changes which set off the common speech very sharply from both correct English and correct American. Their grammatical relationships are thoroughly overhauled and sometimes they are radically modified in form.

This process is natural and inevitable, for it is among the verbs and pronouns, as we have seen, that the only remaining grammatical inflections in English, at least of any force or consequence, are to be found, and so they must bear the chief pressure of the influences that have been warring upon all inflections since the earliest days. The primitive Indo-European language, it is probable, had eight cases of the noun; the oldest known Teutonic dialect reduced them to six; in Anglo-Saxon they fell to four, with a weak and moribund instrumental hanging in the air; in Middle English the dative and accusative began to decay; in Modern English they have disappeared altogether, save as ghosts to haunt grammarians. But we still have two plainly defined conjugations of the verb, and we still inflect it for number, and, in part, at least, for person. And we yet retain an objective case of the pronoun, and inflect it for person, number and gender.

Some of the more familiar conjugations of verbs in the American common speech, as recorded by Charters or Lardner or derived from my own collectanea, are here set down:

Present	Preterite	Perfect Participle
Am	was	bin (or ben) [26]
Attack	attackted	attackted
(Be) [27]	was	bin (or ben) [26]
Beat	beaten	beat
Become [28]	become	became
Begin	begun	began
Bend	bent	bent
Bet	bet	bet
Bind	bound	bound
Bite	bitten	bit
Bleed	bled	bled
Blow	blowed (or blew)	blowed (or blew)
Break	broken	broke
Bring	brought (or brung, or brang)	brung
Broke (passive)	broke	broke
Build	built	built
Burn	burnt [29]	burnt
Burst [30]		
Bust	busted	busted
Buy	bought (or boughten)	bought (or boughten)
Can	could	could
Catch	caught [31]	caught
Choose	chose	choose
Climb	clum	clum
Cling (to hold fast)	clung	clung
Cling (to ring)	clang	clang
Come	come	came
Creep	crep (or crope)	crep
Crow	crowed (or crew)	crowed
Cut	cut	cut
Dare	dared (or dast) [32]	dared
Deal	dole [33]	dealt
Dig	dug	dug

[26] *Bin* is the correct American pronunciation. *Bean*, as we have seen, is the English. But I have often found *ben*, rhyming with *pen*, in such phrases as "I *ben* there."
[27] *Be*, in the subjunctive, is practically extinct.
[28] Seldom used. *Get* is used in the place of it, as in "I am *getting* old" and "he *got* sick."
[29] *Burned* with a distinct *d*-sound is almost unknown in American.
[30] Not used. *Bust* has quite displaced it.
[31] *Cotched* is heard only in the South, and mainly among negroes. *Catch*, of course, is usually pronounced *ketch*. Even *catcher* is *ketcher*.
[32] *Dast* is more common in the negative, as in "He *dasn't* do it."
[33] *Dole*, of course, is supported by the noun.

THE COMMON SPEECH

Present	Preterite	Perfect Participle
Dive	dove [34]	dived
Do	done	done (or did)
Drag	drug	dragged
Draw	drawed	drawed (or drew)
Dream	drempt	drempt
Drink	drank (or drunk)	drank
Drive	drove	drove
Drown	drownded	drownded
Eat	et (or eat)	ate (or et)
Fall	fell (or fallen)	fell
Feed	fed	fed
Feel	felt	felt
Fetch	fetched [35]	fetch
Fight	fought [36]	fought
Find	found	found
Fine	found	found
Fling	flang	flung
Flow	flew	flowed
Fly	flew	flew
Forget	forgot (or forgotten)	forgotten
Forsake	forsaken	forsook
Freeze	frozen (or froze) [37]	frozen
Get	got (or gotten)	gotten
Give	give	give
Glide	glode [38]	glode
Go	went	went
Grow	growed	growed
Hang	hung [39]	hung
Have	had	had (or hadden)
Hear	heerd	heerd (or heern)
Heat	het [40]	het
Heave	hove	hove
Hide	hidden	hid
H'ist [41]	h'isted	h'isted
Hit	hit	hit

[34] *Dove* seems to be making its way into standard American. I constantly encounter it in manuscripts. It is used by Amy Lowell in Legends; Boston, 1921, p. 4.
[35] *Fotch* is also heard, but it is not general.
[36] *Fit* and *fitten*, unless my observation errs, are heard only in dialect. *Fit* is archaic English. *Cf.* Thornton, vol. i, p. 322.
[37] *Friz* is used only humorously.
[38] *Glode* once enjoyed a certain respectability in America. It occurs in the *Knickerbocker Magazine* for April, 1856.
[39] *Hanged* is never heard.
[40] *Het* is incomplete without the addition of *up*. "He was *het up*" is always heard, not "he was *het*."
[41] Always so pronounced.

Present	Preterite	Perfect Participle
Hold	helt	held (or helt)
Holler	hollered	hollered
Hurt	hurt	hurt
Keep	kep	kep
Kneel	knelt	knelt
Know	knowed	knew
Lay	laid (or lain)	laid
Lead	led	led
Lean	lent	lent
Leap	lep	lep
Learn	learnt	learnt
Lend	loaned	loaned
Lie (to falsify)	lied	lied
Lie (to recline)	laid (or lain)	laid
Light	lit	lit
Loose [42]	———	———
Lose	lost	lost
Make	made	made
May	———	might'a
Mean	meant	meant
Meet	met	met
Mow	mown	mowed
Pay	paid	paid
Plead	pled	pled
Prove	proved (or proven)	proven
Put	put	put
Quit	quit	quit
Raise	raised	raised
Read	read	read
Rench [43]	renched	renched
Rid	rid	rid
Ride	ridden	rode
Rile [44]	riled	riled
Ring	rung	rang
Rise	riz (or rose)	riz
Run	run	ran
Say	sez	said
See	seen	saw
Sell	sold	sold
Send	sent	sent
Set	set [45]	sat
Shake	shaken (or shuck)	shook
Shave	shaved	shaved

[42] *To loose* is never used; *to unloosen* has displaced it.
[43] Always used in place of *rinse*.
[44] Always used in place of *roil*.
[45] *Sot* is heard as a localism only.

THE COMMON SPEECH

Present	*Preterite*	*Perfect Participle*
Shed	shed	shed
Shine (to polish)	shined	shined
Shoe	shoed	shoed
Shoot	shot	shot
Show	shown	showed
Sing	sung	sang
Sink	sunk	sank
Sit [46]		
Skin	skun	skun
Sleep	slep	slep
Slide	slid	slid
Sling	slang	slung
Slit	slitted	slitted
Smell	smelt	smelt
Sneak	snuck	snuck
Speed	speeded	speeded
Spell	spelt	spelt
Spill	spilt	spilt
Spin	span	span
Spit	spit	spit
Spoil	spoilt	spoilt
Spring	sprung	sprang
Steal	stole	stole
Sting	stang	stang
Stink	stank	stunk
Strike	struck	struck
Swear	swore	swore
Sweep	swep	swep
Swell	swole (or swelled)	swollen
Swim	swum	swam
Swing	swang	swung
Take	taken	took
Teach	taught	taught
Tear	tore	torn
Tell	tole	tole
Thin [47]		
Think	thought [48]	thought
Thrive	throve	throve
Throw	throwed	threw
Tread	tread	tread
Unloosen	unloosened	unloosened
Wake	woke	woken
Wear	wore	wore

[46] See *set*, which is used almost invariably in place of *sit*.
[47] *To thin* is never used; *to thinnen* takes its place.
[48] *Thunk* is never used seriously; it always shows humorous intent.

Present	Preterite	Perfect Participle
Weep	wep	wep
Wet	wet	wet
Win	won (or wan) [49]	won (or wan)
Wind	wound	wound
Wish (wisht)	wisht	wisht
Wring	wrung	wrang
Write	written	wrote

A glance at these conjugations is sufficient to show several general tendencies, some of them going back, in their essence, to the earliest days of the English language. The most obvious is that leading to the transfer of verbs from the so-called strong conjugation to the weak—a change already in operation before the Norman Conquest, and very marked during the Middle English period. Chaucer used *growed* for *grew* in the prologue to "The Wife of Bath's Tale," and *rised* for *rose* and *smited* for *smote* are in John Purvey's edition of the Bible, circa 1385. Many of these transformations were afterward abandoned, but a large number survived, for example, *climbed* for *clomb* as a preterite of *to climb,* and *melted* for *molt* as the preterite of *to melt.* Others showed themselves during the early part of the Modern English period. *Comed* as the perfect participle of *to come* and *digged* as the preterite of *to dig* are both in Shakespeare, and the latter is also in Milton and in the Authorized Version of the Bible. This tendency went furthest, of course, in the vulgar speech, and it has been embalmed in the English dialects. *I seen* and *I knowed,* for example, are common to many of them. But during the seventeenth century it seems to have been arrested, and even to have given way to a contrary tendency—that is, toward strong conjugations. The English of Ireland, which preserves many seventeenth century forms, shows this plainly. *Ped* for *paid, gother* for *gathered,* and *ruz* for *raised* are still in use there, and Joyce says flatly that the Irish, "retaining the old English custom (*i. e.,* the custom of the period of Cromwell's invasion, *circa* 1650), have a leaning toward the strong inflection." [50] Certain verb forms of the American colonial period, now reduced to the estate of localisms, are also probably survivors of the seventeenth century.

[49] Lardner tells me that he believes *win* is supplanting both *won* and *wan* in the past tense.
[50] English As We Speak It in Ireland, p. 77.

"The three great causes of change in language," says Sayce, "may be briefly described as (1) imitation or analogy, (2) a wish to be clear and emphatic, and (3) laziness. Indeed, if we choose to go deep enough we might reduce all three causes to the general one of laziness, since it is easier to imitate than to say something new."[51] This tendency to take well-worn paths, paradoxically enough, is responsible both for the transfer of verbs from the strong to the weak declension, and for the transfer of certain others from the weak to the strong. A verb in everyday use tends almost inevitably to pull less familiar verbs with it, whether it be strong or weak. Thus *fed* as the preterite of *to feed* and *led* as the preterite of *to lead* paved the way for *pled* as the preterite of *to plead*, and *rode* as plainly performed the same office for *glode*, and *rung* for *brung*, and *drove* for *dove* and *hove*, and *stole* for *dole*, and *won* for *skun*. Moreover, a familiar verb, itself acquiring a faulty inflection, may fasten a similar inflection upon another verb of like sound. Thus *het*, as the preterite of *to heat*, no doubt owes its existence to the example of *et*, the vulgar preterite of *to eat*.[52] So far the irregular verbs. The same combination of laziness and imitativeness works toward the regularization of certain verbs that are historically irregular. In addition, of course, there is the fact that regularization is itself intrinsically simplification—that it makes the language easier. One sees the antagonistic pull of the two influences in the case of verbs ending in *-ow*. The analogy of *knew* suggests *snew* as the preterite of *to snow*, and it is sometimes encountered in the American vulgate. But the analogy of *snowed* also suggests *knowed*, and the superior regularity of the form is enough to overcome the greater influence of *knew* as a more familiar word than *snowed*. Thus *snew* grows rare and is in decay, but *knowed* shows vigor, and so do *growed* and *throwed*. The substitution of *heerd* for *heard* also presents a case of logic and convenience supporting

[51] The Science of Language, vol. i, p. 166.
[52] The use of *eat* as its own preterite was formerly sound in English and still survives more or less. I find it on p. 24 of On Human Bondage, by W. Somerset Maugham; New York, 1915. A correspondent informs me that it occurs in Much Ado About Nothing, act iv, sc. i, in A Midsummer Night's Dream, act ii, sc. ii, in As You Like It, act i, sc. iii, in The Taming of the Shrew, act iv, sc. i, in Macbeth, act ii, sc. iv, and in King Lear, act i, sc. iv. How the preterite was pronounced in Shakespeare's day I do not know.

analogy. The form is suggested by *steered, feared* and *cheered,* but its main advantage lies in the fact that it gets rid of a vowel change, always an impediment to easy speech. Here, as in the contrary direction, one barbarism breeds another. Thus *taken,* as the preterite of *to take,* has undoubtedly helped to make preterites of two other perfects, *shaken* and *forsaken.*

But in the presence of two exactly contrary tendencies, the one in accordance with the general movement of the language since the Norman Conquest and the other opposed to it, it is unsafe, of course, to attempt any very positive generalizations. All one may exhibit with safety is a general habit of treating the verb conveniently. Now and then, disregarding grammatical tendencies, it is possible to discern what appear to be logical causes for verb phenomena. That *lit* is preferred to *lighted* and *hung* to *hanged* is probably the result of an aversion to fine distinctions, and perhaps, more fundamentally, to the passive. Again, the use of *found* as the preterite of *to fine* is obviously due to an ignorant confusion of *fine* and *find,* due to the wearing off of *-d* in *find,* and that of *lit* as the preterite of *to alight* to a confusion of *alight* and *light.* Yet again, the use of *tread* as its own preterite in place of *trod* is probably the consequence of a vague feeling that a verb ending with *d* is already of preterite form. *Shed* exhibits the same process. Both are given a logical standing by such preterites as *bled, fed, led, read, dead* and *spread.* But here, once more, it is hazardous to lay down laws, for *shredded, headed, dreaded, threaded* and *breaded* at once come to mind. In other cases it is still more difficult to account for preterites in common use. In my first edition I called attention to the cases of *drug, clum* and *friz.* On this point, a correspondent has since sent me the following interesting observations:

> True enough, these forms may not adhere closely to the rules of umlaut; but are they not born of the *spirit* of umlaut which pervades the English verb? Thus: the most obvious form of strong verb is
>
> | ring | rang | rung |
> | stink | stank | stunk |
> | begin | began | begun |
> | sing | sang | sung |

THE COMMON SPEECH

spin   span [53]   spun
speak   spake   spoke [54]
spit   spat   spot

(I feel in my bones that *spot* is a derivative of *spit*. *Spot* is the name of the mark made by spitting, which is obviously one of the most primary of human acts.)

swim   swam   swum
spring   sprang   sprung

I imagine that more irregular verbs conform to this one succession than to any one of the others. But all of them, including this one, have been interrupted and obscured by the collision of such independent words as *think* and *thank*, i.e.,

think   (thank)   (thunk)

Thank is forced out to avoid collision with

thank   thanked   thanked

Now, if *freeze* had been *regularly* irregular, it would have been

friz   fraz   frozen

but the present being *freeze* instead of *friz*, the procession would normally be

freeze   frez   frozen

I don't know whether I have made my idea plain: it is not based on visible law so much as on innate feeling. Its validity depends on whether, when I state it to you, you too feel instinctively that amid the clash of strong tenses your own mind would select these forms, in obedience to an overmastering impulse of euphony. The proper jury to render the verdict would be one of poets. I do not suppose anyone will deny that a man reacts to the genius of his mother tongue, without knowing why. There are, and must have been, even deeper depths of reaction than these strong verbs, to account for the choice of vowel sounds in different words, which process in early ages was entirely unconscious.

This, of course, is only to intimate that there must have been "method in the madness" of *friz*. As for *clum*, it seems to me that it is visibly *clomb* descended to the next lower level, and then denuded of its final *b*, probably by analogy with *thumb*. Indeed, it is difficult to pronounce that *b* unless one says *clommmb, thummmb!* And will you not agree with me that these are inevitable:

(drig)   drag   drog (descended to drug)
drag   (drog)   drug
(dreeg)   (dreg)   (droge)
(drogg)   (drug)   (droog)

[53] *Span*, of course, is now archaic in standard English, but it survives in vulgar American and in many other English dialects.
[54] *Spoke* replaces the earlier *spak*.

i.e., it scarcely matters what vowel marked the present tense of *dr-g*, for with *any* vowel this combination of consonants *demands*, in any English-speaking mind which is functioning naturally, and not biased by conscious thought, that its past participle be something very close to *drug*.

Some of the verbs of the vulgate show the end and products of language movements that go back to the Anglo-Saxon period, and even beyond. There is, for example, the disappearance of the final *t* in such words as *crep, slep, lep, swep* and *wep*. Most of these, in Anglo-Saxon, were strong verbs. The preterite of *to sleep* (*slœpan*), for example, was *slep,* and of *to weep* was *weop*. But in the course of time both *to sleep* and *to weep* acquired weak preterite endings, the first becoming *slœpte* and the second *wepte*. This weak conjugation was itself degenerated. Originally, the inflectional suffix had been *-de* or *-ede* and in some cases *-ode,* and the vowels were always pronounced. The wearing down process that set in in the twelfth century disposed of the final *e,* but in certain words the other vowel survived for a good while, and we still observe it in such archaisms as *learned* and *beloved*. Finally, however, it became silent in other preterites, and *loved,* for example, began to be pronounced (and often written) as a word of one syllable: *lov'd*.[55] This final *d*-sound now fell upon difficulties of its own. After certain consonants it was hard to pronounce clearly, and so the sonant was changed into the easier surd, and such words as *pushed* and *clipped* became, in ordinary conversation, *pusht* and *clipt*. In other verbs, the *t*-sound had come in long before, with the degenerated weak ending, and when the final *e* was dropped their stem vowels tended to change. Thus arose such forms as *slept*. In vulgar American another step is taken, and the suffix is dropped altogether. Thus, by a circuitous route, verbs originally strong, and for many centuries hovering between the two conjugations, have eventually become strong again.

The case of *helt* is probably an example of change by false analogy.

[55] The last stand of the distinct *-ed* was made in Addison's day. He was in favor of retaining it, and in the *Spectator* for Aug. 4, 1711, he protested against obliterating the syllable in the termination "of our præter perfect tense, as in these words, *drown'd, walk'd, arriv'd,* for *drowned, walked, arrived,* which has very much disfigured the tongue, and turned a tenth part of our smoothest words into so many clusters of consonants."

During the thirteenth century, according to Sweet,[56] "*d* was changed to *t* in the weak preterites of verbs (ending) in *rd, ld, nd.*" Before that time the preterite of *sende* (*send*) had been *sende;* now it became *sente*. It survives in our modern *sent*, and the same process is also revealed in *built, girt, lent, rent* and *bent*. The popular speech, disregarding the fact that *to hold* is a strong verb, arrives at *helt* by imitation.[57] In the case of *tole*, which I almost always hear in place of *told*, there is a leaping of steps. The *d* is got rid of without any transitional use of *t*. So also, perhaps, in *swole*, which is fast displacing *swelled*. *Attackted* and *drownded* seem to be examples of an effort to dispose of harsh combinations by a contrary process. Both are very old in English. *Boughten* and *dreampt* present greater difficulties. Lounsbury says that *boughten* probably originated in the Northern (*i. e.*, Lowland Scotch) dialect of English, "which . . . inclined to retain the full form of the past participle," and even to add its termination "to words to which it did not properly belong."[58] The *p*-sound in *dreampt* follows a phonetic law that is also seen in *warm*(*p*)*th*, *com*(*p*)*fort*, and *some*(*p*)*thing*, and that has actually inserted a *p* in *Thompson* (=*Tom's son*).

The general tendency toward regularization is well exhibited by the new verbs that come into the language constantly. Practically all of them show the weak conjugation, for example, *to phone*, *to bluff*, *to rubber-neck*, *to ante*, *to bunt*, *to wireless*, *to insurge* and *to loop-the-loop*. Even when a compound has as its last member a verb ordinarily strong, it remains weak itself. Thus the preterite of *to joy-ride* is not *joy-rode*, nor even *joy-ridden*, but *joy-rided*. And thus *bust*, from *burst*, is regular and its preterite is *busted*, though *burst* is irregular and its preterite is the verb itself unchanged. The same tendency toward regularity is shown by the verbs of the *kneel*-class. They are strong in English, but tend to become weak in colloquial American. Thus the preterite of *to kneel*, despite the example of *to sleep* and its analogues, is not *knel'*, nor even *knelt*, but *kneeled*. I have even heard *feeled* as the preterite of *to feel*, as in "I *feeled* my way," though here *felt* still persists. *To spread* also

[56] A New English Grammar, pt. i, p. 380.
[57] The noun is commonly made *holt*, as in, "I got a-*holt* of it."
[58] History of the English Language, p. 398.

tends to become weak, as in "he *spreaded* a piece of bread." And *to peep* remains so, despite the example of *to leap*. The confusion between the inflections of *to lie* and those of *to lay* extends to the higher reaches of spoken American, and so does that between *lend* and *loan*. The proper inflections of *to lend* are often given to *to lean*, and so *leaned* becomes *lent*, as in "I *lent* on the counter." In the same way *to set* has almost completely superseded *to sit*, and the preterite of the former, *set*, is used in place of *sat*. But the perfect participle (which is also the disused preterite) of *to sit* has survived, as in "I have *sat* there." *To speed* and *to shoe* have become regular, not only because of the general tendency toward the weak conjugation, but also for logical reasons. The prevalence of speed contests of various sorts, always to the intense interest of the proletariat, has brought such words as *speeder, speeding, speed-mania, speed-maniac* and *speed-limit* into daily use, and *speeded* harmonizes with them better than the stronger *sped*. As for *shoed*, it merely reveals the virtual disappearance of the verb in its passive form. An American would never say that his wife was well *shod;* he would say that she wore good shoes. *To shoe* suggests to him only the shoeing of animals, and so, by way of *shoeing* and *horse-shoer,* he comes to *shoed*. His misuse of *to learn* for *to teach* is common to most of the English dialects. More peculiar to his speech is the use of *to leave* for *to let*. Charters records it in "Washington *left* them have it," and there are many examples of it in Lardner. *Spit,* in American, has become invariable; the old preterite, *spat,* has completely disappeared. But *slit,* which is now invariable in English (though it was strong in Old English and had both strong and weak preterites in Middle English), has become regular in American, as in "she *slitted* her skirt."

In studying the American verb, of course, it is necessary to remember always that it is in a state of transition, and that in many cases the manner of using it is not yet fixed. "The history of language," says Lounsbury, "when looked at from the purely grammatical point of view, is little else than the history of corruptions." What we have before us is a series of corruptions in active process, and while some of them have gone very far, others are just beginning. Thus it is not uncommon to find corrupt forms side by side

THE COMMON SPEECH 283

with orthodox forms, or even two corrupt forms battling with each other. Lardner, in the case of *to throw*, hears "if he had *throwed*"; my own observation is that *threw* is more often used in that situation. Again, he uses "the rottenest I ever seen *gave*"; my own belief is that *give* is far more commonly used. The conjugation of *to give*, however, is yet very uncertain, and so Lardner may report accurately. I have heard "I *given*" and "I would of *gave*," but "I *give*" seems to be prevailing, and "I would of *give*" with it, thus reducing *to give* to one invariable form, like those of *to cut, to hit, to put, to cost, to hurt* and *to spit*. My table of verbs shows various other uncertainties and confusions. The preterite of *to hear* is *heerd*; the perfect may be either *heerd* or *heern*. That of *to do* may be either *done* or *did*, with the former apparently prevailing; that of *to draw* is *drew* if the verb indicates to attract or to abstract and *drawed* if it indicates to draw with a pencil. Similarly, the preterite of *to blow* may be either *blowed* or *blew*, and that of *to drink* oscillates between *drank* and *drunk*, and that of *to fall* is still usually *fell*, though *fallen* has appeared, and that of *to shake* may be either *shaken* or *shuck*. The conjugation of *to win* is yet far from fixed. The correct English preterite, *won*, is still in use, but against it are arrayed *wan* and *winned*, and Lardner, as I have noted, believes that the plain form of the present is ousting all of them. *Wan* seems to show some kinship, by ignorant analogy, with *ran* and *began*. It is often used as the perfect participle, as in "I have *wan* $4." This uncertainty shows itself in many of the communications that I have received since my first edition was published. Practically every one of my conjugations has been questioned by at least one correspondent; nevertheless, the weight of observation has supported all save a few of them, and I have made no more than half a dozen changes.

The misuse of the perfect participle for the preterite, now almost the invariable rule in vulgar American, is common to many other dialects of English, and seems to be a symptom of a general decay of the perfect tenses. That decay has been going on for a long time, and in American, the most vigorous and advanced of all the dialects of the language, it is particularly well marked. Even in the most pretentious written American it shows itself. The English, in their writing, still use the future perfect, albeit somewhat laboriously and self-consciously, but in America it has virtually disappeared: one often reads whole books without encountering a single example of it. Even the present perfect and past perfect seem to be instinctively avoided. The Englishman says "I *have* dined," but the American says "I *am through* dinner"; the Englishman says "I *had* slept," but the American often says "I *was done* sleeping." Thus the perfect tenses are forsaken for the simple present and the past. In the vulgate a further step is taken, and "I have been there" becomes "I *been* there." Even in such phrases as "he *hasn't* been here," *ain't* (= *am not*) is commonly substituted for *have not,* thus giving the present perfect a flavor of the simple present. The step from "I *have taken*" to "I *taken*" was therefore neither difficult nor unnatural, and once it had been made the resulting locution was supported by the greater apparent regularity of its verb. Moreover, this perfect participle, thus put in place of the preterite, was further reinforced by the fact that it was the adjectival form of the verb, and hence collaterally familiar. Finally, it was also the authentic preterite in the passive voice, and although this influence, in view of the decay of the passive, may not have been of much consequence, nevertheless it is not to be dismissed as of no consequence at all.

The contrary substitution of the preterite for the perfect participle, as in "I have *went*" and "he has *did,*" apparently has a double influence behind it. In the first place, there is the effect of the confused and blundering effort, by an ignorant and unanalytical speaker, to give the perfect some grammatical differentiation when he finds himself getting into it—an excursion not infrequently made necessary by logical exigencies, despite his inclination to keep out. The nearest indicator at hand is the disused preterite, and so it is put to use. Sometimes a sense of its uncouthness seems to linger, and there is a tendency to give it an *en*-suffix, thus bringing it into greater harmony with its tense. I find that *boughten,* just discussed, is used much oftener in the perfect than in the simple past tense;[59] for the latter *bought* usually suffices. The quick ear of Lardner detects various other coinages of the same sort, among

[59] And still more often as an adjective, as in "it was a *boughten* dress."

them *tooken,* as in "little Al might of *tooken sick.*"⁶⁰ *Hadden* is also met with, as in "I would of *hadden.*" But the majority of preterites remain unchanged. Lardner's baseball player never writes "I have *written*" or "I have *wroten,*" but always "I have *wrote.*" And in the same way he always writes, "I have *did, ate, went, drank, rode, ran, saw, sang, woke* and *stole.*" Sometimes the simple form of the verb persists through all tenses. This is usually the case, for example, with *to give.* I have noted "I *give*" both as present and as preterite, and "I have *give,*" and even "I had *give.*" But even here "I have *gave*" offers rivalry to "I have *give,*" and usage is not settled. So, too, with *to come.* "I have *come*" and "I have *came*" seem to be almost equally favored, with the former supported by pedagogical admonition and the latter by the spirit of the language.

Whatever the true cause of the substitution of the preterite for the perfect participle, it seems to be a tendency inherent in English, and during the age of Elizabeth it showed itself even in the most formal speech. An examination of any play of Shakespeare's will show many such forms as "I have *wrote,*" "I am *mistook*" and "he has *rode.*" In several cases this transfer for the preterite has survived. "I have *stood,*" for example, is now perfectly correct English, but before 1550 the form was "I have *stonden.*" *To hold* and *to sit* belong to the same class; their original perfect participles were not *held* and *sat,* but *holden* and *sitten.* These survived the movement toward the formalization of the language which began with the eighteenth century, but scores of other such misplaced preterites were driven out. One of the last to go was *wrote,* which persisted until near the end of the century.⁶¹ Paradoxically enough, the very purists who performed the purging showed a preference for *got* (though not *forgot*), and it survives in correct English today in the preterite-present form, as in "I have *got,*" whereas in American, both vulgar and polite, the elder and more regular *gotten* is often used. In the polite speech *gotten* indicates a distinction between a completed action and a continuing action—between obtaining and possessing. "I have *gotten* what I came for" is correct, and so is "I have *got* a house." In the vulgar speech much the same distinc-

⁶⁰ You Know Me Al, p. 180; see also p. 122.
⁶¹ *Cf.* Lounsbury: History of the English Language, pp. 393 *ff.*

tion exists, but the perfect becomes a sort of simple tense by the elision of *have*. Thus the two sentences change to "I *gotten* what I come for" and "I *got* a house," the latter being understood, not as past, but as present.⁶²

In "I have *got* a house" *got* is historically a sort of auxiliary of *have,* and in colloquial American, as we have seen in the examples just given, the auxiliary has obliterated the verb. *To have,* as an auxiliary, probably because of its intimate relationship with the perfect tenses, is under heavy pressure, and promises to disappear from the situations in which it is still used. I have heard *was* used in place of it, as in "before the Elks *was* come here." ⁶³ Sometimes it is confused ignorantly with a distinct *of,* as in "she would *of* drove," and "I would *of* gave." ⁶⁴ More often it is shaded to a sort of particle, attached to the verb as an inflection, as in "he would *'a* tole you," and "who could *'a* took it?" But this is not all. Having degenerated to such forms, it is now employed as a sort of auxiliary to itself, in the subjunctive, as in "if you had *of* went," "if it had *of* been hard," and "if I had *of* had." ⁶⁵ I have encountered some rather astonishing examples of this doubling of the auxiliary. One appears in "I wouldn't had *'a* went"; another in "I'd *'a* had *'a* saved more money." Here, however, the *a* may belong partly to *had* and partly to the verb; such forms as *a-going* are very common in American. But in the other cases, and in such forms as "I had *'a* wanted," it clearly belongs to *had*. Sometimes for syntactical reasons the degenerated form of *have* is put before *had* instead of after it, as in "I could *of* had her if I had *of* wanted to." ⁶⁶ Meanwhile, *to have,* ceasing to be an auxiliary, becomes a general verb indicating compulsion. Here it promises to displace

---

⁶² *Got,* of course, also has a compulsive sense, as in "I have *got* to go." It is also used in the general sense of becoming, as in "I *got* scared."
⁶³ Remark of a policeman talking to another. What he actually said was "before the Elks was *c'm 'ere."* *Come* and *here* were one word, approximately *cmear.* The context showed that he meant to use the past perfect tense.
⁶⁴ The following curious example, sent to me by Dr. Morris Fishbein of the *Journal* of the American Medical Association, is from a letter received by a California physician: "If I *had of* waited a day longer before I wrote to you I *would not of had* to write that letter to you." Here the author plainly mistakes *have* for *of*.
⁶⁵ These examples are from Lardner's story, A New Busher Breaks In, in You Know Me Al, pp. 122 *et seq.*
⁶⁶ You Know Me Al, *op. cit.,* p. 124.

THE COMMON SPEECH 287

must. The American seldom says "I *must* go"; he almost invariably says "I *have* to go," [67] or "I *have got* to go," in which last case, as we have seen, *got* is the auxiliary.

The most common inflections of the verb for mode and voice are shown in the following paradigm of *to bite:*

ACTIVE VOICE
Indicative Mode

Present	I bite	*Past Perfect*	I had of bit
Present Perfect	I have bit	*Future*	I will bite
Past	I bitten	*Future Perfect*	(wanting)

Subjunctive Mode

Present	If I bite	*Past Perfect*	If I had of bit
Past	If I bitten		

Potential Mode

Present	I can bite	*Past*	I could bite
Present Perfect	(wanting)	*Past Perfect*	I could of bit

Imperative (or *Optative*) *Mode*

Future	I shall (or will) bite

Infinitive Mode

(wanting)

PASSIVE VOICE
Indicative Mode

Present	I am bit	*Past Perfect*	I had been bit
Present Perfect	I been bit	*Future*	I will be bit
Past	I was bit	*Future Perfect*	(wanting)

Subjunctive Mode

Present	If I am bit	*Past Perfect*	If I had of been bit
Past	If I was bit		

Potential Mode

Present	I can be bit	*Past*	I could be bit
Present Perfect	(wanting)	*Past Perfect*	I could of been bit

Imperative Mode

(wanting)

Infinitive Mode

(wanting)

[67] Almost always pronounced *haf to,* or, in the past tense, *hat to.* Sometimes *hat to* undergoes composition and the *d* is restored; it then becomes *hadda. Haf to* similarly changes to *hafta.*

A study of this paradigm reveals several plain tendencies. One has just been discussed: the addition of a degenerated form of *have* to the preterite of the auxiliary, and its use in place of the auxiliary itself. Another is the use of *will* instead of *shall* in the first person future. *Shall* is confined to a sort of optative, indicating much more than mere intention, and even here it is yielding to *will*. Yet another is the consistent use of the transferred preterite in the passive. Here the rule in correct English is followed faithfully, though the perfect participle employed is not the English participle. "I am *broke*" is a good example. Finally, there is the substitution of *was* for *were* and of *am* for *be* in the past and present of the subjunctive. In this last case American is in accord with the general movement of English, though somewhat more advanced. *Be,* in the Shakespearean form of "where *be* thy brothers?" was expelled from the present indicative two hundred years ago, and survives today only in dialect. And as it thus yielded to *are* in the indicative, it now seems destined to yield to *am* and *is* in the subjunctive. It remains, of course, in the future indicative: "I will *be*." In American its conjugation coalesces with that of *am* in the following manner:

Present	I am	*Past Perfect*	I had of ben
Present Perfect	I bin (or ben)	*Future*	I will be
Past	I was	*Future Perfect*	(wanting)

And in the subjunctive:

Present	If I am	*Past Perfect*	If I had of ben
Past	If I was		

All signs of the subjunctive, indeed, seem to be disappearing from vulgar American. One never hears "if I *were* you," but always "if I *was* you"; "*was* you going to the dance?" is a very common form. In the third person the *-s* is not dropped from the verb. One hears, not "if she *go*," but always "if she *goes*." "If he *be* the man" is never heard; it is always "if he *is*." Such a sentence as "Had I wished her, I had had her" would be unintelligible to most Americans; even "I had rather" is fast disappearing. This war upon the forms of the subjunctive, of course, extends to the

THE COMMON SPEECH 289

most formal English. "In Old English," says Bradley,[68] "the subjunctive played as important a part as in modern German, and was used in much the same way. Its inflection differed in several respects from that of the indicative. But the only formal trace of the old subjunctive still remaining, except the use of *be* and *were*, is the omission of the final *s* in the third person singular. And even this is rapidly dropping out of use. . . . Perhaps in another generation the subjunctive forms will have ceased to exist except in the single instance of *were*, which serves a useful function, although we manage to dispense with a corresponding form in other verbs." Here, as elsewhere, unlettered American usage simply proceeds in advance of the general movement. *Be* and the omitted *s* are already dispensed with, and even *were* has been discarded.

In the same way the distinction between *will* and *shall*, preserved in correct English but already breaking down in the most correct American, has been lost entirely in the American common speech. *Will* has displaced *shall* completely, save in the imperative. This preference extends to the inflections of both. *Sha'n't* is very seldom heard; almost always *won't* is used instead. As for *should*, it is displaced by *ought to* (degenerated to *oughter* or *ought'a*), and in its negative form by *hadn't ought'a*, as in "he *hadn't oughter* said that," reported by Charters. Lardner gives various redundant combinations of *should* and *ought*, as in "I don't feel as if I *should ought* to leave" and "they *should not ought to* of had." I have encountered the same form, but I don't think it is as common as the simple *ought'a* forms.[69] In the main, *should* is avoided, sometimes at considerable pains. Often its place is taken by the more positive *don't*. Thus "I *don't* mind" is used instead of "I *shouldn't* mind." *Don't* has also completely displaced *doesn't*, which is very seldom heard. "He *don't*" and "they *don't*" are practically universal. In the same way *ain't* has displaced *is not, am not, isn't* and *aren't*, and even *have not* and *haven't*. One recalls a famous speech in a naval melodrama of twenty years ago: "We *ain't* got no manners, but we can fight like hell." Such forms as "he *ain't* here," "I *ain't* the

[68] The Making of English, p. 53.
[69] In the negative, *ought not* has degenerated to *oughten*, as in "you *oughten* do that."

man," "*ain't* it the truth?", "you been there, *ain't* you?", "you *ain't* drank much," "them *ain't* what I want" and "I *ain't* heerd of it" are common.

This extensive use of *ain't,* of course, is merely a single symptom of a general disregard of number, obvious throughout the verbs, and also among the pronouns, as we shall see. Charters gives many examples, among them, "how *is* Uncle Wallace and Aunt Clara?", "you *was,*" "there *is* six" and the incomparable "it *ain't* right to say, 'He *ain't* here today.'" In Lardner there are many more, for instance, "them Giants *is* not such rotten hitters, *is* they?", "the people *has* all wanted to shake hands with Matthewson and I" and "some of the men *has* brung their wife along." *Sez* (= *says*), used as the preterite of *to say,* shows the same confusion. One observes it again in such forms as "then I *goes* up to him." Here the decay of number helps in what threatens to become a decay of tense. A gambler of the humbler sort seldom says "I *won* \$2," or even "I *wan* \$2," but almost always "I *win* \$2." And in the same way he says "I *see* him come in," not "I *saw* him come in" or "*seen* him." Lardner, as we have seen, believes that *win* is displacing both *won, winned* and *wan.* Charters' materials offer other specimens, among them "we *help* distributed the fruit," "she *recognize, hug,* and *kiss* him" and "her father *ask* her if she intended doing what he *ask.*" Perhaps the occasional use of *eat* as the preterite of *to eat,* as in "I *eat* breakfast as soon as I got up," is an example of the same flattening out of distinctions. Lardner has many specimens, among them "if Weaver and them had not of *begin* kicking" and "they would of *knock* down the fence." I notice that *used,* in *used to be,* is almost always reduced to simple *use,* as in "it *use* to be the rule," with the *s* very much like that of *hiss.* One seldom, if ever, hears a clear *d* at the end. Here, of course, the elision of the *d* is due primarily to assimilation with the *t* of *to*—a second example of one form of decay aiding another form. But the tenses apparently tend to crumble without help. I frequently hear whole narratives in a sort of debased historical present: "I *says* to him. . . . Then he *ups* and *says.* . . . I *land* him one on the ear. . . . He *goes* down and out, . . . " and so on.[70] Still under the spell of our disintegrating inflections, we

[70] *Cf. Dialect Notes,* vol. iii, pt. i, p. 59; *ibid.,* vol. iii, pt. iv, p. 283.

are prone to regard the tense inflections of the verb as absolutely essential, but there are plenty of languages that get on without them, and even in our own language children and foreigners often reduce them to a few simple forms. Some time ago an Italian contractor said to me, "I have *go* there often." Here one of our few surviving inflections was displaced by an analytical device, and yet the man's meaning was quite clear, and it would be absurd to say that his sentence violated the inner spirit of English. That inner spirit, in fact, has inclined steadily toward "I have *go*" for a thousand years.

4.

The Pronoun

The following paradigm shows the inflections of the personal pronoun in the American common speech:

FIRST PERSON
Common Gender

		Singular	Plural
Nominative		I	we
Possessive	{ Conjoint	my	our
	{ Absolute	mine	ourn
Objective		me	us

SECOND PERSON
Common Gender

Nominative		you	yous
Possessive	{ Conjoint	your	your
	{ Absolute	yourn	yourn
Objective		you	yous

THIRD PERSON
Masculine Gender

Nominative		he	they
Possessive	{ Conjoint	his	their
	{ Absolute	hisn	theirn
Objective		him	them

Feminine Gender

Nominative		she	they
Possessive	{ Conjoint	her	their
	{ Absolute	hern	theirn
Objective		her	them

		Neuter Gender	
Nominative		it	they
Possessive	{ Conjoint	its	their
	{ Absolute	its	theirn
Objective		it	them

These inflections, as we shall see, are often disregarded in use, but nevertheless it is profitable to glance at them as they stand. The only variations that they show from standard English are the substitution of *n* for *s* as the distinguishing mark of the absolute form of the possessive, and the attempt to differentiate between the logical and the merely polite plurals in the second person by adding the usual sign of the plural to the former. The use of *n* in place of *s* is not an American innovation. It is found in many of the dialects of English, and is, in fact, historically quite as sound as the use of *s*. In John Wycliffe's translation of the Bible (*circa* 1380) the first sentence of the Sermon on the Mount (Mark v, 3) is made: "Blessed be the pore in spirit, for the kyngdam in hevenes is *heren.*" And in his version of Luke xxiv, 24, is this: "And some of *ouren* wentin to the grave." Here *heren* (or *herun*) represents, of course, not the modern *hers,* but *theirs.* In Anglo-Saxon the word was *heora,* and down to Chaucer's day a modified form of it, *here,* was still used in the possessive plural in place of the modern *their,* though *they* had already displaced *hie* in the nominative.[70] But in John Purvey's revision of the Wycliffe Bible, made a few years later, *hern* actually occurs in II Kings vii, 6, thus: "Restore thou to hir alle things that ben *hern.*" In Anglo-Saxon there had been no distinction between the conjoint and absolute forms of the possessive pronoun; the simple genitive sufficed for both uses. But with the decay of that language the surviving remnants of its grammar began to be put to service somewhat recklessly, and so there arose a genitive inflection of this genitive—a true double inflection. In the Northern dialects of English that inflection was made by simply adding *s,* the sign of the possessive. In the Southern dialects the old *n*-declen-

[70] Henry Bradley, in The Making of English, pp. 54-5: "In the parts of England which were largely inhabited by Danes the native pronouns (*i. e., heo, hie, heom* and *heora*) were supplanted by the Scandinavian pronouns which are represented by the modern *she, they, them* and *their.*" This substitution, at first dialectical, gradually spread to the whole language.

sion was applied, and so there arose such forms as *minum* and *eowrum* (= *mine* and *yours*), from *min* and *eower* (= *my* and *your*).⁷¹ Meanwhile, the original simple genitive, now become *youre*, also survived, and so the literature of the fourteenth century shows the three forms flourishing side by side: *youre, youres* and *youren*. All of them are in Chaucer.

Thus, *yourn, hern, hisn, ourn* and *theirn*, whatever their present offense to grammarians, are of a genealogy quite as respectable as that of *yours, hers, his, ours* and *theirs*. Both forms represent a doubling of inflections, and hence grammatical debasement. On the side of the *yours*-form is the standard usage of the past five hundred years, but on the side of the *yourn*-form there is no little force of analogy and logic, as appears on turning to *mine* and *thine*. In Anglo-Saxon, as we have seen, *my* was *min;* in the same way *thy* was *thin*. During the decadence of the language the final *n* was dropped in both cases before nouns—that is, in the conjoint form —but it was retained in the absolute form. This usage survives to our own day. One says *"my* book," but "the book is *mine";* "*thy* faith," but "I am *thine."* ⁷² Also, one says *"no* matter," but "I have *none."* Without question this retention of the *n* in these pronouns had something to do with the appearance of the *n*-declension in the treatment of *your, her, his* and *our*, and, after *their* had displaced *here* in the third person plural, in *their*. And equally without question it supports the vulgar American usage today.⁷³ What that usage shows is simply the strong popular tendency to make language as simple and as regular as possible—to abolish subtleties and exceptions. The difference between *"his* book" and "the book is *his'n"* is exactly that between *my* and *mine, thy* and *thine,* in the examples just given. "Perhaps it would have been better," says Bradley, "if the literary language had accepted *hisn,* but from some cause it did not do so." ⁷⁴

As for the addition of *s* to *you* in the nominative and objective

---

⁷¹ *Cf.* Sweet: A New English Grammar, pt. i, p. 344, § 1096.
⁷² Before a noun beginning with a vowel *thine* and *mine* are commonly substituted for *thy* and *my*, as in *"thine* eyes" and *"mine* infirmity." But this is solely for the sake of euphony. There is no compensatory use of *my* and *thy* in the absolute.
⁷³ I am not forgetting, of course, the possible aid of *his own, her own,* etc.
⁷⁴ The Making of English, p. 58.

of the second person plural, it exhibits no more than an effort to give clarity to the logical difference between the true plural and the mere polite plural. In several other dialects of English the same desire has given rise to cognate forms, and there are even secondary devices in American. In the South, for example, the true plural is commonly indicated by *you-all,* which, despite a Northern belief to the contrary, is seldom used in the singular by any save the most ignorant.[75] *You-all,* like *yous,* simply means *you-jointly* as opposed to the *you* that means *thou.* Again, there is the form observed in "you can *all of you* go to hell"—another plain effort to differentiate between singular and plural. The substitution of *you* for *thou* goes back to the end of the thirteenth century. It appeared in late Latin and in the other Continental languages as well as in English, and at about the same time. In these languages the true singular survives alongside the transplanted plural, but English has dropped it entirely, save in its poetical and liturgical forms and in a few dialects. It passed out of ordinary polite speech before Elizabeth's day. By that time, indeed, its use had acquired an air of the offensive, such as it has today, save between intimates or to children, in Germany. Thus, at the trial of Sir Walter Raleigh in 1603, Sir Edward Coke, then attorney-general, displayed his animosity to Raleigh by addressing him as *thou,* and finally burst into the contemptuous "I *thou* thee, *thou* traitor!" And in "Twelfth Night" Sir Toby Belch urges Sir Andrew Aguecheek to provoke the disguised Viola to combat by *thouing* her. In our own time, with *thou* passed out entirely, even as a pronoun of contempt, the confusion between *you* in the plural and *you* in the singular presents plain difficulties to a man of limited linguistic resources. He gets around them by setting up a distinction that is well supported by logic and analogy. "I seen *yous*" is clearly separated from "I seen *you.*" And in the conjoint position *"yous* guys" is separated from *"you* liar."

Let us now glance at the demonstrative and relative pronouns. Of the former there are but two in English, *this* and *that,* with

[75] *Cf.* The Dialect of Southeastern Missouri, by D. S. Crumb, *Dialect Notes,* vol. ii, pt. iv, 1903, p. 337. It may be due to the influence of the French *vous autres.*

their plural forms, *these* and *those*. To them, American adds a third, *them*, which is also the personal pronoun of the third person, objective case.[76] In addition it had adopted certain adverbial pronouns, *this-here, these-here, that-there, those-there* and *them-there*, and set up inflections of the original demonstratives by analogy with *mine, hisn* and *yourn*, to wit, *thisn, thesen, thatn* and *thosen*. I present some examples of everyday use:

> *Them* are the kind I like.
> *Them* men all work here.
> Who is *this-here* Smith I hear about?
> *These-here* are mine.
> *That-there* medicine ain't no good.
> *Those-there* wops has all took to the woods.
> I wisht I had one of *them-there* Fords.
> *Thisn* is better'n *thatn*.
> I like *thesen* better'n *thosen*.

The origin of the demonstratives of the *thisn*-group is plain: they are degenerate forms of *this-one, that-one*, etc., just as *none* is a degenerate composition form of *no(t)-one*. In every case of their use that I have observed the simple demonstratives might have been set free and *one* actually substituted for the terminal *n*. But it must be equally obvious that they have been reinforced very greatly by the absolutes of the *hisn*-group, for in their relation to the original demonstratives they play the part of just such absolutes and are never used conjointly. Thus, one says, in American, "I take *thisn*" or "*thisn* is mine," but one never says "I take *thisn* hat" or "*thisn* dog is mine." In this conjoint situation plain *this* is always used, and the same rule applies to *these, those* and *that*. *Them,* being a newcomer among the demonstratives, has not yet acquired an inflection in the absolute. I have never heard *them'n*, and it will probably never come in, for it is forbiddingly clumsy. One says, in American, both "*them* are mine" and "*them* collars are mine."

[76] It occurs, too, of course, in other dialects of English, though by no means in all. The Irish influence probably had something to do with its prosperity in vulgar American. At all events, the Irish use it in the American manner. Joyce, in English As We Speak It in Ireland, pp. 34-5, argues that this usage was suggested by Gaelic. In Gaelic the accusative pronouns, *e, i* and *iad* (= *him, her* and *them*) are often used in place of the nominatives, *se, si* and *siad* (= *he, she* and *they*), as in "is iad sin na buachaillidhe" (=*them* are the boys). This is "good grammar" in Gaelic, and the Irish, when they began to learn English, translated the locution literally. The familiar Irish "John is dead and *him* always so hearty" shows the same influence.

This-here, these-here, that-there, those-there and *them-there* are plainly combinations of pronouns and adverbs, and their function is to support the distinction between proximity, as embodied in *this* and *these,* and remoteness, as embodied in *that, those* and *them.* "*This-here* coat is mine" simply means "this coat *here,* or this *present* coat, is mine." But the adverb promises to coalesce with the pronoun so completely as to obliterate all sense of its distinct existence, even as a false noun or adjective. As commonly pronounced, *this-here* becomes a single word, somewhat like *thish-yur,* and *these-here* becomes *these-yur,* and *that-there* and *them-there* become *that-ere* and *them-ere. Those-there,* if I observe accurately, is still pronounced more distinctly, but it, too, may succumb to composition in time. The adverb will then sink to the estate of a mere inflectional particle, as *one* has done in the absolutes of the *thisn-*group. *Them,* as a personal pronoun in the absolute, of course, is commonly pronounced *em,* as in "I seen *em,*" and sometimes its vowel is almost lost, but this is also the case in all save the most exact spoken English. Sweet and Lounsbury, following the German grammarians, argue that this *em* is not really a debased form of *them,* but the offspring of *hem,* which survived as the regular plural of the third person in the objective case down to the beginning of the fifteenth century. But in American *them* is clearly pronounced as a demonstrative. I have never heard *"em* men" or *"em* are the kind I like," but always *"them* men" and *"them* are the kind I like."

The relative pronouns, so far as I have been able to make out, are declined as follows:

Nominative	who	which	what	that
Possessive	{ whose { whosen	whose whosen		
Objective	who	which	what	that

Two things will be noted in this paradigm. First there is the disappearance of *whom* as the objective form of *who,* and secondly there is the appearance of an inflected form of *whose* in the absolute, by analogy with *mine, hisn* and *thesen. Whom,* as we have seen, is fast disappearing from standard spoken American; [77] in the vulgar

[77] Chapter VI, Section 2.

language it is already virtually extinct. Not only is *who* used in such constructions as *"who* did you find there?" where even standard spoken English would tolerate it, but also in such constructions as "the man *who* I saw," "them *who* I trust in" and "to *who?"* Krapp explains this use of *who* on the ground that there is a "general feeling," due to the normal word-order in English, that "the word which precedes the verb is the subject word, or at least the subject form." [78] But this explanation is probably fanciful. Among the plain people no such "general feeling" for case exists. Their only "general feeling" is a prejudice against case inflections in any form whatsoever. They use *who* in place of *whom* simply because they can discern no logical difference between the significance of the one and the significance of the other.

Whosen, which is still relatively rare, is obviously the offspring of the other absolutes in *n.* In the conjoint relation plain *whose* is always used, as in *"whose* hat is that?" and "the man *whose* dog bit me." But in the absolute *whosen* is sometimes substituted, as in "if it ain't *hisn,* then *whosen* is it?" The imitation is obvious. There is an analogous form of *which,* to wit, *whichn,* resting heavily on *which one.* Thus, *"whichn* do you like?" and "I didn't say *whichn"* are plainly variations of *"which one* do you like?" and "I didn't say *which one."* *That,* as we have seen, has a like form, *thatn,* but never, of course, in the relative situation. "I like *thatn"* is familiar, but "the one *thatn* I like" is never heard. If *that,* as a relative, could be used absolutely, I have no doubt that it would change to *thatn,* as it does as a demonstrative. So with *what.* As things stand, it is sometimes substituted for *that,* as in "them's the kind *what* I like." Joined to *but* it can also take the place of *that* in other situations, as in "I don't know *but what."*

The substitution of *who* for *whom* in the objective case, just noticed, is typical of a general movement toward breaking down all case distinctions among the pronouns, where they make their last stand in English and its dialects. This movement, of course, is not peculiar to vulgar American; nor is it of recent beginning. So long

---

[78] Modern English, p. 300.

ago as the fifteenth century the old clear distinction between *ye*, nominative, and *you*, objective, disappeared, and today the latter is used in both cases. Sweet says that the phonetic similarity between *ye* and *thee*, the objective form of the true second singular, was responsible for this confusion.[79] In modern spoken English, indeed, *you* in the objective often has a sound far more like that of *ye* than like that of *you*, as, for example, in "how do *y'* do?" and in American its vowel takes the neutral form of the *e* in the definite article, and the word becomes a sort of shortened *yuh*. But whenever emphasis is laid upon it, *you* becomes quite distinct, even in American. In "I mean *you*," for example, there is never any chance of mistaking it for *ye*. In Shakespeare's time the other personal pronouns of the objective case threatened to follow *you* into the nominative, and there was a compensatory movement of the nominative pronouns toward the objective. Lounsbury has collected many examples.[80] Marlowe used "is it *him* you seek?", "'tis *her* I esteem" and "nor *thee* nor *them* shall want"; Fletcher used "'tis *her* I admire"; Shakespeare himself used "that's *me*." Contrariwise, Webster used "what difference is between the duke and *I?*" and Green used "nor earth nor heaven shall part my love and *I*." Krapp has unearthed many similar examples from the Restoration dramatists.[81] Etheredge used "'tis *them*," "it may be *him*," "let you and *I*" and "nor is it *me*"; Matthew Prior, in a famous couplet, achieved this:

> For thou art a girl as much brighter than *her*
> As he was a poet sublimer than *me*.

The free exchange continued, in fact, until the eighteenth century was well advanced; there are examples of it in Addison. Moreover, it survived, at least in part, even the attack that was then made upon it by the professors of the new-born science of English grammar, and to this day "it is *me*" is still in more or less good colloquial use. Sweet thinks that it is supported in such use, though not, of course, grammatically, by the analogy of the correct "it is *he*" and "it is *she*." Lounsbury, following Dean Alford, says it came into English in imitation of the French *c'est moi*, and defends it as

[79] A New English Grammar, pt. i, p. 339.
[80] History of the English Language, pp. 274-5.
[81] Modern English, pp. 288-9.

THE COMMON SPEECH

at least as good as "it is *I*." [82] The contrary form, "between you and *I*," has no defenders, and is apparently going out. But in the shape of "between my wife and *I*" it is seldom challenged, at least in spoken English.

All these liberties with the personal pronouns, however, fade to insignificance when put beside the thoroughgoing confusion of the case forms in vulgar American. "*Us* fellas" is so far established in the language that "*we* fellas" from the mouth of a car conductor would seem almost an affectation. So, too, is "*me* and *her* are friends." So, again, are "*her* and *I* set down together," "*him* and his wife," and "I knowed it was *her*." Here are some other characteristic examples of the use of the objective forms in the nominative from Charters, Lardner and other writers:

> *Me* and *her* was both late.
> His brother is taller than *him*.
> That little boy was *me*.
> *Us* girls went home.
> They were John and *him*.
> *Her* and little Al is to stay here.
> She says she thinks *us* and the Allens.
> If Weaver and *them* had not of begin kicking.
> *Us* two'll walk, me and him.
> But not *me*.
> *Him* and I are friends.
> *Me* and *them* are friends.

Less numerous, but still varied and plentiful, are the substitutions of nominative forms for objective forms:

> She gave it to mother and *I*.
> She took all of *we* children.
> I want you to meet *he* and *I* at 29th street.
> It is going to cost me $6 a week for a room for *she* and the baby.
> Anything she has is O. K. for *I* and Florrie.[83]

---

[82] Every now and then it is furiously debated in the American newspapers. When, early in 1921, Edward J. Tobin, superintendent of the schools of Cook county, Ill. (*i. e.*, of Chicago), decided that the pupils might use it, the decision was discussed all over the country, and for weeks. See the New York *World*, Feb. 23, 1921; the New York Evening *World*, March 1, and the New York *Times* (a letter from Frank H. Vizetelly), Feb. 24. See also Jespersen: Chapters on English, p. 101 and p. 142. Mr. Tobin is also said to have given his imprimatur to *he don't*.
[83] Sometimes the two errors are combined, as in a speech heard by a correspondent from the lips of a Wyoming hotel-keeper: "Between *I* and *you*, *him* and *her* drinks too much."

Here are some grotesque confusions, indeed. Perhaps the best way to get at the principles underlying them is to examine first, not the cases of their occurrence, but the cases of their non-occurrence. Let us begin with the transfer of the objective form to the nominative in the subject relation. *"Me* and *her* was both late" is obviously sound American; one hears it, or something like it, on the streets every day. But one never hears *"me* was late" or *"her* was late" or *"us* was late" or *"him* was late" or *"them* was late." Again, one hears *"us* girls was there" but never *"us* was there." Yet again, one hears *"her* and John was married," but never *"her* was married." The distinction here set up should be immediately plain. It exactly parallels that between *her* and *hern, our* and *ourn, their* and *theirn:* the tendency, as Sweet says, is "to merge the distinction of nominative and objective in that of conjoint and absolute." [84] The nominative, in the subject relation, takes the usual nominative form only when it is in immediate contact with its verb. If it be separated from its verb by a conjunction or any other part of speech, even including another pronoun, it takes the objective form. Thus *"me* went home" would strike even the most ignorant shopgirl as "bad grammar," but she would use *"me* and my friend went," or *"me* and *him,"* or *"he* and *her,"* or *"me* and *them"* without the slightest hesitation. What is more, if the separation be effected by a conjunction and another pronoun, the other pronoun also changes to the objective form, even though its contact with the verb may be immediate. Thus one hears *"me* and *her* was there," not *"me* and *she"; "her* and *him* kissed," not *"her* and *he."* Still more, this second pronoun commonly undergoes the same inflection even when the first member of the group is not another pronoun, but a noun. Thus one hears "John and *her* was married," not *"John* and *she."* To this rule there is but one exception, and that is in the case of the first person pronoun, especially in the singular. *"Him* and *me* are friends" is heard often, but *"him* and *I* are friends" is also heard. *I* seems to suggest the subject very powerfully; it is actually the subject of perhaps a majority of the sentences uttered by an ignorant man. At all events, it resists the rule, at least partially, and may even do so when actually separated from the verb by another pronoun,

[84] A New English Grammar, pt. i, p. 341.

itself in the objective form, as, for example, in "*I* and *him* were there."

In the predicate relation the pronouns respond to a more complex regulation. When they follow any form of the simple verb of being they take the objective form, as in "it's *me*," "it ain't *him*," and "I am *him*," probably because the transitiveness of this verb exerts a greater pull than its function as a mere copula, and perhaps, too, because the passive naturally tends to put the speaker in the place of the object. "I seen *he*" or "he kissed *she*" or "he struck *I*" would seem as ridiculous to an ignorant American as to the Archbishop of Canterbury, and his instinct for simplicity and regularity naturally tends to make him reduce all similar expressions, or what seem to him to be similar expressions, to coincidence with the more seemly "I seen *him*." After all, the verb of being is fundamentally transitive, and, in some ways, the most transitive of all verbs, and so it is not illogical to bring its powers over the pronoun into accord with the powers exerted by the others. I incline to think that it is some such subconscious logic, and not the analogy of "it is *he*," as Sweet argues, that has brought "it is *me*" to conversational respectability, even among rather careful speakers of English.[85]

But against this use of the objective form in the nominative position after the verb of being there also occurs in American a use of the nominative form in the objective position, as in "she gave it to mother and *I*" and "she took all of *we* children." What lies at the bottom of it seems to be a feeling somewhat resembling that which causes the use of the objective form before the verb, but exactly contrary in its effects. That is to say, the nominative form is used when the pronoun is separated from its governing verb, whether by a noun, a noun-phrase or another pronoun, as in "she gave it to mother and *I*," "she took all of *we* children" and "he paid her and *I*," respectively. But here usage is far from fixed, and one observes variations in both directions—that is, toward using the correct objective when the pronoun is detached from the verb, and toward using

[85] It may be worth noting here that the misuse of *me* for *my*, as in "I lit *me* pipe," is almost unknown in American, either standard or vulgar, though a correspondent in Philadelphia tells me that it is a localism in that city, and it is sometimes used by elderly persons of Irish birth. Even "*me* own" is seldom heard. This boggling of the cases is very common in spoken English. The most correct barristers usually say "*me* lud" in addressing the court.

the nominative even when it directly follows the verb. "She gave it to mother and *me,*" "she took all of *us* children" and "he paid her and *me*" would probably sound quite as correct, to a Knight of Pythias, as the forms just given. And at the other end Charters and Lardner report such forms as "I want you to meet *he* and *I*" and "it is going to cost me $6 a week for a room for *she* and the baby." I have noticed, however, that the use of the nominative is chiefly confined to the pronoun of the first person, and particularly to its singular. Here again we have an example of the powerful way in which *I* asserts itself. And superimposed upon that influence is a cause mentioned by Sweet in discussing "between you and *I.*"[86] It is a sort of by-product of the pedagogical war upon "it is *me.*" "As such expressions," he says, "are still denounced by the grammars, many people try to avoid them in speech as well as in writing. The result of this reaction is that the *me* in such constructions as 'between John and *me*' and 'he saw John and *me*' sounds vulgar and ungrammatical, and is consequently corrected into *I.*" Here the pedagogues, seeking to impose an inelastic and illogical grammar upon a living speech, succeed only in corrupting it still more.

Following *than* and *as* the American uses the objective form of the pronoun, as in "he is taller than *me*" and "such as *her.*" He also uses it following *like,* but not when, as often happens, he uses the word in place of *as* or *as if.* Thus he says "do it like *him,*" but "do it like *he* does" and "she looks like *she* was sick." What appears here is an instinctive feeling that these words, followed by a pronoun only, are not adverbs, but prepositions, and that they should have the same power to put the pronoun into an oblique case that other prepositions have. Just as "the taller of *we*" would sound absurd to all of us, so "taller than *he,*" to the unschooled American, sounds absurd. This feeling has a good deal of respectable support. "As *her*" was used by Swift, "than *me*" by Burke, and "than *whom*" by Milton. The brothers Fowler show that, in some cases, "than *him*" is grammatically correct and logically necessary.[87] For example, compare "I love you more than *him*" and "I love you more than

[86] A New English Grammar, pt. i, p. 341.
[87] The King's English, p. 63.

he." The first means "I love you more than (I love) *him*"; the second, "I love you more than *he* (loves you)." In the first *him* does not refer to *I*, which is nominative, but to *you,* which is objective, and so it is properly objective also. But the American, of course, uses *him* even when the preceding noun is in the nominative, save only when another verb follows the pronoun. Thus, he says, "I love you better than *him,*" but "I love you better than *he* does."

In the matter of the reflexive pronouns the American vulgate exhibits forms which plainly show that it is the spirit of the language to regard *self,* not as an adjective, which it is historically, but as a noun. This confusion goes back to Anglo-Saxon days; it originated at a time when both the adjectives and the nouns were losing their old inflections. Such forms as *Petrussylf* (= *Peter's self*), *Cristsylf* (= *Christ's self*) and *Icsylf* (= *I, self*) then came into use, and along with them came combinations of *self* and the genitive, still surviving in *hisself* and *theirselves* (or *theirself*). Down to the sixteenth century these forms remained in perfectly good usage. "Each for *hisself,*" for example, was written by Sir Philip Sidney, and is to be found in the dramatists of the time, though modern editors always change it to *himself.* How the dative pronoun got itself fastened upon *self* in the third person masculine and neuter is one of the mysteries of language, but there it is, and so, against all logic, history and grammatical regularity, *himself, themselves* and *itself* (not *its-self*) are in favor today. But the American, as usual, inclines against these illogical exceptions to the rule set by *myself.* I constantly hear *hisself* and *theirselves,* as in "he done it *hisself*" and "they know *theirselves.*" Also, the emphatic *own* is often inserted between the pronoun and the noun, as in "let every man save his *own* self." In general the American vulgate makes very extensive use of the reflexive. It is constantly thrown in for good measure, as in "I overeat *myself*" and it is as constantly used singly, as in "*self* and wife."

The American pronoun does not necessarily agree with its noun in number. I find "I can tell each one what *they* make," "each fellow put *their* foot on the line," "nobody can do what *they* like" and "she was one of *these* kind [88] of people" in Charters, and "I am not the kind of man that is always thinking about *their* record," "if he was to hit a man in the head . . . *they* would think *their* nose tickled" in Lardner. At the bottom of this error there is a real difficulty: the lack of a pronoun of the true common gender in English, corresponding to the French *soi* and *son*.[89] *His*, after a noun or pronoun connoting both sexes, often sounds inept, and *his-or-her* is intolerably clumsy. Thus the inaccurate plural is often substituted. The brothers Fowler have discovered "anybody else who have only *themselves* in view" in Richardson and "everybody is discontented with *their* lot" in Disraeli, and Ruskin once wrote "if a customer wishes you to injure *their* foot." In spoken American, even the most careful, *they* and *their* often appear; I turn to the *Congressional Record* at random and in two minutes find "if anyone will look at the bank statements *they* will see." [90] In the lower reaches of the language the plural seems to get into every sentence of any complexity, even when the preceding noun or pronoun is plainly singular. Such forms as "every man knows *their* way," and "nobody oughter never take what ain't *theirn*" are quite common.

In demotic American the pedantry which preserves such forms as *someone's else* is always disregarded; *someone else's* is invariably used. I have heard "who *else's* wife was there?" and "if it ain't his'n, it ain't nobody here *else's*." Finally, I note that *he's* seems to be assimilating with *his*. In such sentences as "I hear *he's* coming here to work," the sound of *he's* is precisely that of *his*.

5.

The Adverb

All the adverbial endings in English, save *-ly,* have gradually fallen into decay; it is the only one that is ever used to form new adverbs. At earlier stages of the language various other endings

---

[88] Here, of course, *kind* is probably felt to be plural. *Those* is used in the same way, as in *"those* are the kind."

[89] *Thon*, as we have seen, was proposed so long ago as 1858, but it has never established itself.

[90] "Hon." Edward E. Browne, of Wisconsin, in the House of Representatives, July 18, 1918, p. 9965.

were used, and some of them survive in a few old words, though they are no longer employed in making new words. The Anglo-Saxon endings were -e and -lice. The latter was, at first, merely an -e-ending to adjectives in -lic, but after a time it attained to independence and was attached to adjectives not ending in -lic. In early Middle English this -lice changed to -like, and later on to -li and -ly. Meanwhile, the -e-ending, following the -e-endings of the nouns, adjectives and verbs, ceased to be pronounced, and so it gradually fell away. Thus a good many adverbs came to be indistinguishable from their ancestral adjectives, for example, *hard* in *to pull hard*, *loud* in *to speak loud*, and *deep* in *to bury deep* (= Anglo-Saxon, *deop-e*). Worse, not a few adverbs actually became adjectives, for example, *wide*, which was originally the Anglo-Saxon adjective *wid* (= *wide*) with the adverbial -e-ending, and *late*, which was originally the Anglo-Saxon adjective *læt* (= *slow*) with the same ending.

The result of this movement toward identity in form was a confusion between the two classes of words, and from the time of Chaucer down to the eighteenth century one finds innumerable instances of the use of the simple adjective as an adverb. "He will answer *trewe*" is in Sir Thomas More; "and *soft* unto himself he sayd" in Chaucer; "the singers sang *loud*" in the Authorized Version of the Bible (Nehemiah xii, 42), and *"indifferent* well" in Shakespeare. Even after the purists of the eighteenth century began their corrective work this confusion continued. Thus one finds "the people are *miserable* poor" in Hume, "how *unworthy* you treated mankind" in the *Spectator*, and *"wonderful* silly" in Joseph Butler. To this day the grammarians battle against the amalgamation, still without complete success; every new volume of rules and regulations for those who would speak by the book is full of warnings against it. Among the great masses of the plain people, it goes without saying, it flourishes unimpeded. The cautions of the school-marm, in a matter so subtle and so plainly lacking in logic or necessity, are forgotten as quickly as her prohibition of the double negative, and thereafter the adjective and the adverb tend more and more to coalesce in a part of speech which serves the purposes of both, and is simple and intelligible and satisfying.

Charters gives a number of characteristic examples of its use:

"wounded very *bad*," "I *sure* was stiff," "drank out of a cup *easy*," "he looked up *quick*." Many more are in Lardner: "a chance to see me work *regular*," "I am glad I was lucky enough to marry *happy*," "I beat them *easy*," and so on. And others fall upon the ear every day: "he done it *proper*," "he done himself *proud*," "she was dressed *neat*," "she was *awful* ugly," "the horse ran *O. K.*," "it *near* finished him," "it sells *quick*," "I like it *fine*," "he et *hoggish*," "she acted *mean*," "he loved her something *fierce*," "they keep company *steady*." The bob-tailed adverb, indeed, enters into a large number of the commonest coins of vulgar speech. *Near-silk*, I daresay, is properly *nearly-silk*. The grammarians protest that "run *slow*" should be "run *slowly*." But *near-silk* and "run *slow*" remain, and so do "to be in *bad*," "it *sure* will help," "to play it up *strong*" and their brothers. What we have here is simply an incapacity to distinguish any ponderable difference between adverb and adjective, and beneath it, perhaps, is the incapacity, already noticed in dealing with "it is *me*," to distinguish between the common verb of being and any other verb. If "it *is* bad" is correct, then why should "it *leaks* bad" be incorrect? It is just this disdain of purely grammatical reasons that is at the bottom of most of the phenomena visible in vulgar American, and the same impulse is observable in all other languages during periods of inflectional decay. During the highly inflected stage of a language the parts of speech are sharply distinct but when inflections fall off they tend to disappear. The adverb, being at best the step-child of grammar—as the old Latin grammarians used to say, *"Omnis pars orationis migrat in adverbium"*—is one of the chief victims of this anarchy. John Horne Tooke, despairing of bringing it to any order, even in the most careful English, called it, in his "Diversions of Purley," "the common sink and repository of all heterogeneous and unknown corruptions."

Where an obvious logical or lexical distinction has grown up between an adverb and its primary adjective the unschooled American is very careful to give it its terminal *-ly*. For example, he seldom confuses *hard* and *hardly*, *scarce* and *scarcely*, *real* and *really*. These words convey different ideas. *Hard* means unyielding; *hardly* means barely. *Scarce* means present only in small numbers; *scarcely* is substantially synonymous with *hardly*. *Real* means genu-

THE COMMON SPEECH 307

ine; *really* is an assurance of veracity. So, again, with *late* and *lately*. Thus, an American says "I don't know, *scarcely*," not "I don't know, *scarce*"; "he died *lately*," not "he died *late*." [91] But in nearly all such cases syntax is the preservative, not grammar. These adverbs seem to keep their tails largely because they are commonly put before and not after verbs, as in, for example, "I *hardly* (or *scarcely*) know," and "I *really* mean it." Many other adverbs that take that position habitually are saved as well, for example, *generally, usually, surely, certainly*. But when they follow verbs they often succumb, as in "I'll do it *sure*" and "I seen him *recent*." And when they modify adjectives they sometimes succumb, too, as in "it was *sure* hot." Practically all the adverbs made of adjectives in -*y* lose the terminal -*ly* and thus become identical with their adjectives. I have never heard *mightily* used; it is always *mighty*, as in "he hit him *mighty* hard." So with *filthy, dirty, nasty, lowly, naughty* and their cognates. One hears "he acted *dirty*," "he spoke *nasty*," "the child behaved *naughty*," and so on. Here even standard English has had to make concessions to euphony. *Cleanlily* is seldom used; *cleanly* nearly always takes its place. And the use of *illy* and *thusly* is confined to ignoramuses.

Vulgar American, like all the higher forms of American and all save the most precise form of written English, has abandoned the old inflections of *here, there* and *where*, to wit, *hither* and *hence, thither* and *thence, whither* and *whence*. These fossil remains of dead cases are fast disappearing from the language. In the case of *hither* (= *to here*) even the preposition has been abandoned. One says, not "I came *to here*," but simply "I came *here*." In the case of *hence*, however, *from here* is still used, and so with *from there* and *from where*. Finally, it goes without saying that the common American tendency to add -*s* to such adverbs as *towards* is carried to full length in the vulgar language. One constantly hears, not only *somewheres* and *forwards*, but even *noways* and *anyways, where'bouts* and *here'bouts*. Here we have but one more example of the movement toward uniformity and simplicity. *Anyways* is obviously fully supported by *sideways* and *always*.

[91] I have, however, noted "here *late*" for "here *lately*." But it is obviously derived from "here *of late*."

6.

The Noun

The only inflections of the noun remaining in English are those for number and for the genitive, and so it is in these two regions that the few variations to be noted in vulgar American occur. The rule that, in forming the plurals of compound nouns or noun-phrases, the *-s* shall be attached to the principal noun is commonly disregarded, and it goes at the end. Thus, "I have two *sons-in-law*" is never heard among the plain people; one always hears "I have two *son-in-laws.*" So with the genitive. I once overheard this: "that umbrella is the *young lady I go with's.*" Often a false singular is formed from a singular ending in *s*, the latter being mistaken for a plural. *Chinee, Portugee* and *Japanee* are familiar; I have also noted *trapee, specie,*[92] *tactic* and *summon* (from *trapeze, species, tactics* and *summons*).[93] Paradoxically, the word *incidence* is commonly misused for *incident*, as in "he told an *incidence.*" Here *incidence* (or *incident*) seems to be regarded as a synonym, not for *happening*, but for *story*. I have never heard "he told *of* an *incidence.*" The *of* is always omitted. The general disregard of number often shows itself when the noun is used as object. I have already quoted Lardner's "some of the men has brung their *wife* along"; in a popular magazine I lately encountered "those book ethnologists . . . can't see what is before their *nose.*" Many similar examples might be brought forward.

7.

The Adjective

The adjectives in English are inflected only for comparison, and the American commonly uses them correctly, with now and then a double comparative or superlative to ease his soul. *More better* is

---

[92] This occasionally gets into print, along with *tactic*. See South American Travels, by Henry Stephens; New York, 1915, p. 114.
[93] It is possible that *hoakum*, the verb of which is *to hoak*, is a similar back-formation from *hoax*.

the commonest of these. It has a good deal of support in logic. A sick man is reported today to be *better*. Tomorrow he is further improved. Is he to be reported *better* again, or *best?* The standard language gets around the difficulty by using *still better*. The American vulgate boldly employs *more better*. In the case of *worse, worser* is used, as Charters shows. He also reports *baddest, more queerer* and *beautifullest*. *Littler,* which he notes, is still outlawed from standard English, but it has, with *littlest,* a respectable place in American. The late Richard Harding Davis wrote a play called "The *Littlest* Girl." The American freely compares adjectives that are incapable of the inflection logically. Charters reports *most principal,* and I myself have heard *uniquer* and even *more uniquer,* as in "I have never saw nothing *more uniquer.*" I have also heard *more ultra, more worse, idealer, liver* (that is, *more alive*), and *wellest,* as in "he was the *wellest* man you ever seen." In general, the *-er* and *-est* terminations are used instead of the *more* and *most* prefixes, as in *beautiful, beautifuller, beautifullest*. The fact that the comparative relates to two and the superlative to more than two is almost always forgotten. I have never heard "the *better* of the two," in the popular speech, but always "the *best* of the two." Charters also reports "the *hardest* of the two" and "my brother and I measured and he was the *tallest*." I have frequently heard "it ain't so *worse,*" but here a humorous effect seems to have been intended.

Adjectives are made much less rapidly in American than either substantives or verbs. The only suffix that seems to be in general use for that purpose is *-y,* as in *tony, classy, daffy, nutty, dinky, leery,* etc. The use of the adjectival prefix *super-* is confined to the more sophisticated classes; the plain people seem to be unaware of it.[94] This relative paucity of adjectives appears to be common to the more primitive varieties of speech. E. J. Hills, in his elaborate study of the vocabulary of a child of two,[95] found that it contained but 23 descriptive adjectives, of which six were the names of colors, as against 59 verbs and 173 common nouns. Moreover, most of the 23 minus six were adjectives of all work, such as *nasty,*

[94] *Cf.* Vogue Affixes in Present-Day Word-Coinage, by Louise Pound, *Dialect Notes,* vol. v, pt. i, 1918.
[95] The Speech of a Child Two Years of Age, *Dialect Notes,* vol. iv, pt. ii, 1914.

funny and *nice*. Colloquial American uses the same rubber-stamps of speech. *Funny* connotes the whole range of the unusual; *hard* indicates every shade of difficulty; *nice* is everything satisfactory; *wonderful* is a superlative of almost limitless scope.

The decay of *one* to a vague *n*-sound, as in *this'n,* is matched by a decay of *than* after comparatives. *Earlier than* is seldom if ever heard; composition reduces the two words to *earlier'n.* So with *better'n, faster'n, hotter'n, deader'n,* etc. Once I overheard the following dialogue: "I like a belt *more looser'n* what this one is." "Well, then, why don't you *unloosen* it *more'n* you got it *unloosened?*"

The almost universal confusion of *liable* and *likely* is to be noted. The former is nearly always used, as in, "he's *liable* to be there" and "it ain't *liable* to happen." *Likely* is reserved for the sense of attractive, as in "a *likely* candidate."

8.

The Double Negative

Syntactically, perhaps the chief characteristic of vulgar American is its sturdy fidelity to the double negative. So freely is it used, indeed, that the simple negative appears to be almost abandoned. Such phrases as "I see nobody," "I could hardly walk," "I know nothing about it" are heard so seldom among the masses of the people that they appear to be affectations when encountered; the well-nigh universal forms are "I *don't* see nobody," "I *couldn't* hardly walk," and "I *don't* know nothing about it." Charters lists some very typical examples, among them, "he ain't *never* coming back *no* more," "you *don't* care for nobody but yourself," "couldn't be *no* more happier" and "I *can't* see nothing." In Lardner there are innumerable examples: "they was *not* no team," "I have *not* never thought of that," "I can't write *no* more," "no chance to get *no* money from *nowhere,*" "we *can't* have nothing to do," and so on. Some of his specimens show a considerable complexity, for example, "Matthewson was *not* only going as far as the coast," meaning, as the context shows, that he was going as far as the coast and no further. *Only* gets into many other examples, *e. g.,* "he hadn't *only* the one pass," "I can't stay *only* a minute," and "I don't work nights no more, *only* except Sunday nights." This last I got from a car conductor. Many other curious specimens are in my collectanea, among them: "one swaller don't make *no* summer," "I *never* seen nothing I would of rather saw," and "once a child gets burnt once it *won't* never stick its hand in *no* fire *no* more," and so on. The last embodies a triple negative. In "You *don't* know *nobody* what *don't* want *nobody* to do *nothing* for 'em, do you?" there is a quadruplet. And in "the more faster you go, the sooner you *don't* get there," there is a muddling that almost defies analysis.

Like most other examples of "bad grammar" encountered in American the compound negative is of great antiquity and was once quite respectable. The student of Anglo-Saxon encounters it constantly. In that language the negative of the verb was formed by prefixing a particle, *ne*. Thus, *singan* (= *to sing*) became *ne singan* (= *not to sing*). In case the verb began with a vowel the *ne* dropped its *e* and was combined with the verb, as in *næfre* (never), from *ne-æfre* (= *not ever*). In case the verb began with an *h* or a *w* followed by a vowel, the *h* or *w* of the verb and the *e* of *ne* were both dropped, as in *næfth* (= has *not*), from *ne-hæfth* (= *not has*), and *nolde* (= *would not*), from *ne-wolde*. Finally, in case the vowel following a *w* was an *i*, it changed to *y*, as in *nyste* (= *knew not*), from *ne-wiste*. But inasmuch as Anglo-Saxon was a fully inflected language the inflections for the negative did not stop with the verbs; the indefinite article, the indefinite pronoun and even some of the nouns were also inflected, and survivors of those forms appear to this day in such words as *none* and *nothing*. Moreover, when an actual inflection was impossible it was the practise to insert this *ne* before a word, in the sense of our *no* or *not*. Still more, it came to be the practise to reinforce *ne*, before a vowel, with *na* (= *not*) or *naht* (= *nothing*), which later degenerated to *nat* and *not*. As a result, there were fearful and wonderful combinations of negatives, some of them fully matching the best efforts of Lardner's baseball players. Sweet gives several curious examples.[96] "Nan ne dorste

[96] A New English Grammar, pt. i, pp. 437-8.

nan thing ascian," translated literally, becomes *"no* one dares *not* ask *nothing."* "Thæt hus na ne feoll" becomes "the house did *not* fall *not."* As for the Middle English "he *never* nadde *nothing,"* it has too modern and familiar a ring to need translating at all. Chaucer, at the beginning of the period of transition to Modern English, used the double negative with the utmost freedom. In "The Knight's Tale" is this:

> He *nevere* yet *no* vileynye *ne* sayde
> In al his lyf unto *no* maner wight.

By the time of Shakespeare this license was already much restricted, but a good many double negatives are nevertheless to be found in his plays, and he was particularly shaky in the use of *nor*. In "Richard III" one finds "I never was *nor never* will be"; in "Measure for Measure," "harp not on that *nor* do *not* banish treason," and in "Romeo and Juliet," "thou expectedst not, *nor* I looked *not* for." This misuse of *nor* is still very frequent. In other directions, too, the older forms show a tendency to survive all the assaults of grammarians. *"No,* it *doesn't,"* heard every day and by no means from the ignorant only, is a sort of double negative. The insertion of *but* before *that,* as in "I doubt *but* that" and "there is no question *but* that," makes a double negative that is probably full-blown. Nevertheless, as we have seen, it is heard on the floor of Congress every day, and the Fowlers show that it is also common in England.[97] Even worse forms get into the *Congressional Record.* Not long ago, for example, I encountered "without *hardly* an exception" in a public paper of the utmost importance.[98] There are, indeed, situations in which the double negative leaps to the lips or from the pen almost irresistibly; even such careful writers as Huxley, Robert Louis Stevenson and Leslie Stephen have occasionally dallied with it.[99] It is perfectly allowable in the Romance languages, and, as we have seen, is almost the rule in the American vulgate. Now and then some anarchistic student of the language boldly defends and even

---

[97] The King's English, p. 322. See especially the quotation from Frederick Greenwood, the distinguished English journalist.
[98] Report of Edward J. Brundage, attorney-general of Illinois, on the East St. Louis massacre, *Congressional Record,* Jan. 7, 1918, p. 661.
[99] The King's English, *op. cit.*

THE COMMON SPEECH 313

advocates it. "The double negative," said a writer in the *London Review* a long time ago,[100] "has been abandoned to the great injury of strength of expression." Surely "I won't take nothing" is stronger than either "I will take nothing" or "I won't take anything."

9.

Other Syntactical Peculiarities

"Language begins," says Sayce, "with sentences, not with single words." In a speech in process of rapid development, unrestrained by critical analysis, the tendency to sacrifice the integrity of words to the needs of the complete sentence is especially marked. One finds it clearly in American. Already we have examined various assimilation and composition forms: *that'n, use'to, would'a, them'ere* and so on. Many others are observable. *Off'n* is a good example; it comes from *off of* and shows a preposition decaying to the form of a mere inflectional particle. One constantly hears "I bought it *off'n* John." *Sort'a, kind'a* and their like follow in the footsteps of *would'a*. *Usen't* follows the analogy of *don't* and *wouldn't*, as in "I didn't *usen't* to be." *Would've* and *should've* are widely used; Lardner commonly hears them as *would of* and *should of*. The neutral *a*-particle also appears in other situations, especially before *way*, as in *that-a way* and *this-a way*. It is found again in *a tall*, a liaison form of *at all*.[101]

Various minor syntactical peculiarities may be noticed; an exhaustive study of them would afford materials for a whole volume. The use of *all the further*, as in, "it was *all the further* I could go," seems to be American. It has bred many analogues, *e. g.*, "is that *all the later* it is?" Another curious formation employs *there* with various negatives in an unusual way; it is illustrated in "there can't anyone break me." Again, there is the use of *in* in such constructions as "he caught *in* back of the plate," apparently sug-

[100] Oct. 1, 1864.
[101] *At all*, by the way, is often displaced by *any* or *none*, as in "he don't love her *any*" and "it didn't hurt me *none*."

gested by *in front.* Yet again, there is the use of *too* and *so* as intensives, as in "You are, *too*" and "You are, *so.*" Yet again, there is the growing tendency to omit the verb of action in phrases indicating desire or intent, as in, "he *wants out*" for "he *wants to go out.*" This last, I believe, originated as a Pennsylvania localism, and probably owes its genesis to Pennsylvania German, but of late it has begun to travel, and I have received specimens from all parts of the country. In the form of "Belgium *wants in* this protective arrangement" it has even got into a leading editorial in the Chicago *Tribune,* "the world's greatest newspaper." [102]

10.

Vulgar Pronunciation

Before anything approaching a thorough and profitable study of the sounds of the American common speech is possible, there must be a careful assembling of the materials, and this, unfortunately, still awaits a phonologist of sufficient enterprise and equipment. Dr. William A. Read, of the State University of Louisiana, has made some excellent examinations of vowel and consonant sounds in the South, Dr. Louise Pound has done capital work of the same sort in the Middle West, and there have been other regional studies of merit. But most of these become misleading by reason of their lack of scope; forms practically universal in the nation are discussed as dialectical variations. This is a central defect in the work of the American Dialect Society, otherwise very industrious and meritorious. It is essaying to study localisms before having first platted the characteristics of the general speech. The dictionaries of Americanisms deal with pronunciation only casually, and often very inaccurately; the remaining literature is meagre and unsatisfactory. Until the matter is gone into at length it will be impossible to discuss any phase of it with exactness. No single investigator can examine the speech of the whole country; for that business a pooling

[102] Nov. 10, 1919, p. 8.

THE COMMON SPEECH 315

of forces is necessary. But meanwhile it may be of interest to set forth a few provisional ideas.

At the start two streams of influence upon vulgar American pronunciation may be noted, the one an inheritance from the English of the colonists, and the other arising spontaneously within the country, and apparently much colored by immigration. The first influence, it goes without saying, is gradually dying out. Consider, for example, the pronunciation of the diphthong *oi*. In Middle English it was as in *boy*, but during the early Modern English period it was assimilated with that of the *i* in *wine*, and this usage prevailed at the time of the settlement of America. The colonists thus brought it with them, and at the same time it lodged in Ireland, where it still prevails. But in England, during the pedantic eighteenth century, this *i*-sound was displaced by the original *oi*-sound, not by historical research but by mere deduction from the spelling, and the new pronunciation soon extended to the polite speech of America. In the common speech, however, the *i*-sound persisted, and down to the time of the Civil War it was constantly heard in such words as *boil, hoist, oil, join, poison* and *roil*, which thus became *bile, hist, ile, jine, pisen* and *rile*. Since then the school-marm has combated it with such vigor that it has begun to disappear, and such forms as *pisen, jine, bile* and *ile* are now very seldom heard, save as dialectic variations. But in certain other words, perhaps supported by Irish influence, the *i*-sound still persists. Chief among them are *hoist* and *roil*.[103] An unlearned American, wishing to say that he was enraged, never says that he was *roiled*, but always that he was *riled*. Desiring to examine the hoof of his horse, he never orders the animal to *hoist* but always to *hist*. In the form of *booze-hister*, the latter is almost in good usage. I have seen *booze-hister* thus spelled and obviously to be thus pronounced, in an editorial article in the *American Issue*, organ of the Anti-Saloon League of America.[104]

Various similar misplaced vowels were brought from England by the colonists and have persisted in America, while dying out of good

[103] *Roil* is obsolete in standard English. Krapp says that "in conventional cultivated use in America" a spelling pronunciation has arisen, making the word rhyme with *oil*. I have never encountered this pronunciation. All Americans, when they use *roiled* at all, seem to make it *riled*.
[104] Maryland edition, July 18, 1914, p. 1.

English usage. There is, for example, short *i* in place of long *e*, as in *critter* for *creature*. *Critter* is common to almost all the dialects of English, but American has embedded the vowel in a word that is met with nowhere else and has thus become characteristic, to wit, *crick* for *creek*. Nor does any other dialect make such extensive use of *slick* for *sleek*. Again, there is the substitution of the flat *a* for the broad *a*, as in *sassy* and apple-*sass*. England has gone back to the broad *a*, but in America the flat *a* persists, and many Americans who use *sassy* every day would scarcely recognize *saucy* if they heard it. Yet again, there is *quoit*. Originally, the English pronounced it *quate*, but now they pronounce the diphthong as in *doily*. In the United States the *quate* pronunciation remains. Finally, there is *deaf*. Its proper pronunciation, in the England that the colonists left, was *deef*, but it now rhymes with *Jeff*. That new pronunciation has been adopted by polite American, despite the protests of Noah Webster, but in the common speech the word is still *deef*.

However, a good many of the vowels of the early days have succumbed to pedagogy. The American proletarian may still use *skeer* for *scare*, but in most of the other words of that class he now uses the vowel approved by correct English usage. Thus he seldom permits himself such old forms as *dreen* for *drain*, *keer* for *care*, *skeerce* for *scarce* or even *cheer* for *chair*. The Irish influence supported them for a while, but now they are fast going out. So, too, are *kivver* for *cover*, *crap* for *crop*, and *chist* for *chest*. But *kittle* for *kettle* still shows a certain vitality, *rench* is still used in place of *rinse*, and *squinch* in place of *squint*, and a flat *a* continues to displace various *e*-sounds in such words as *rare* for *rear* (e. g., as a horse), *thrash* for *thresh*,[105] and *wrassle* for *wrestle*. Contrariwise, *e* displaces *a* in *catch* and *radish*, which are commonly pronounced *ketch* and *reddish*. This *e*-sound was once accepted in standard English; when it got into spoken American it was perfectly sound; one still hears it from the most pedantic lips in *any*.[106] There are also certain other ancients that show equally unbroken vitality among

[105] Here a distinction shows itself: a farmer *thrashes* his boy, but *threshes* his wheat.
[106] *Cf.* Lounsbury: The Standard of Pronunciation in English, p. 172 *ff*.

THE COMMON SPEECH 317

us, for example, *stomp* for *stamp*,[107] *snoot* for *snout, guardeen* for *guardian, janders* for *jaundice, muss* for *mess*, and *champeen* for *champion*.

But all these vowels, whether approved or disapproved, have been under the pressure, for the past century, of a movement toward a general vowel neutralization, and in the long run it promises to dispose of many of them. The same movement also affects standard English, as appears by Robert Bridges' "Tract on the Present State of English Pronunciation," but I believe that it is stronger in America, and will go farther, at least with the common speech, if only because of our unparalleled immigration. Standard English has 19 separate vowel sounds. No other living tongue of Europe, save Portuguese, has so many; most of the others have a good many less; Modern Greek has but five. The immigrant, facing all these vowels, finds some of them quite impossible; the Russian Jew, for example, cannot manage *ur*. As a result, he tends to employ a neutralized vowel in the situations which present difficulties, and this neutralized vowel, supported by the slip-shod speech-habits of the native proletariat, makes steady progress. It appears in many of the forms that we have been examining—in the final *a* of *would-a*, vaguely before the *n* in *this'n* and *off'n*, in place of the original *d* in *use' to*, and in the common pronunciation of such words as *been, come* and *have*, particularly when they are sacrificed to sentence exigencies, as in "I *b'n* thinking," "*c'm 'ere*," and "he would've saw you."

Here we are upon a wearing down process that shows many other symptoms. One finds, not only vowels disorganized, but also consonants. Some are displaced by other consonants, measurably more facile; others are dropped altogether. *D* becomes the unvoiced *t*, as in *holt*, or is dropped, as in *tole, han'kerchief, bran-new, di'nt* (= *didn't*) and *fine* (for *find*). In *ast* (for *ask*) *t* replaces *k;* when the same word is used in place of *asked*, as often happens, e. g., in "I *ast* him his name," it shoulders out *ked*. It is itself

[107] *Stomp* is used only in the sense of to stamp with the foot. One always *stamps* a letter. An analogue of *stomp*, accepted in correct English, is *strop* (e. g., *razor-strop*), from *strap*. In American *champ* (*chomp*) and *tramp* (*tromp*) tend to diverge in the same way. A horse *chomps* its bit, but *champ* (= *champion*) retains the flat *a*. A cow *tromps* her fodder, but a *tramp* remains a *tramp*.

lopped off in *bankrup, quan'ity, crep, slep, wep, kep, gris'-mill* and *les* (= *let's* = *let us*), and is replaced by *d* in *kindergarden* and *pardner*. *L* disappears, as in *a'ready* and *gent'man*. The *s*-sound becomes *tsh*, as in *pincers*. The same *tsh* replaces *ct*, as in *pitcher* for *picture*, and *t*, as in *amachoor*. *G* disappears from the ends of words,[108] and sometimes, too, in the middle, as in *stren'th* and *reco'nize*. *R*, though it is better preserved in American than in English, is also under pressure, as appears by *bust, Febuary, stuck on* (for *struck on*), *cuss* (for *curse*), *yestiddy, sa's'parella, pa'tridge, ca'tridge, they is* (for *there is*) and *Sadd'y* (for *Saturday*). An excrescent *t* survives in a number of words, *e. g., onc't, twic't, clos't, wisht* (for *wish*) and *chanc't;* it is an heirloom from the English of two centuries ago. So is the final *h* in *heighth*. An excrescent *b*, as in *chimbley* and *fambly*, seems to be native. Whole syllables are dropped out of words, paralleling the English butchery of *extraordinary;* for example, in *bound'ry, pro'bition, tarnal* (= *eternal*), *complected, hist'ry, lib'ry* and *prob'ly. Ordinary*, like *extraordinary*, is commonly enunciated clearly, but it has bred a degenerated form, *onry* or *onery*, differentiated in meaning.[109] Consonants are misplaced by metathesis, as in *prespiration, hunderd, brethern, childern, libery, interduce, apern, calvary, govrenment, modren* and *wosterd* (for *worsted*). *Ow* is changed to *er*, as in *piller, swaller, yeller, beller* and *holler*, or to *a*, as in *fella*, or to *i*, as in *minni* (= *minnow*); *ice* is changed to *ers* in *janders*. Words are given new syllables, as in *ellum, fillum, lozenger, athaletic, mischievious, mayorality* and *municipial*, or new consonants, as in *overhalls* and *idear*.

In the complete sentence, assimilation makes this disorganization much more obvious. Mearns, in a brief article,[110] gives many

[108] But not *all* words in *-g*. Lardner calls my attention to the fact that *anything* and *everything* are almost always excepted. He says: "I used, occasionally, to sit on the players' bench at baseball games, and it was there that I noted the exceptions made in favor of these two words. A player, returning to the bench after batting, would be asked, 'Has he got *anything* in there?' ('He—in there' always means the pitcher). The answer would be 'He's got *everything*.' On the other hand, the player might return and (usually after striking out) say, 'He hasn't got *nothin'*.' And the manager: 'Looks like he must have *somethin'*.' "

[109] This word, when written, often appears as *ornery*, but it is almost always pronounced *on'ry*, with the first syllable rhyming with *don*.

[110] Our Own, Our Native Speech, *McClure's Magazine*, Oct., 1916.

examples of the extent to which it is carried. He hears "wah zee say?" for "what does he say?", "ware zee?" for "where is he?", "ast 'er in" for "ask her in," "itt'm owd" for "hit them out," "sry" for "that is right," and "c' meer" for "come here." He believes that the voiceless *t* is gradually succumbing to the voiced *d*, and cites "ass bedder" (for "that's better"), "wen juh ged din?" (for "when did you get in?"), and "siddup" (for "sit up"). One hears countless other such decayed forms on the street every day. *Let's* is *le's*. The neutral vowel replaces the *oo* of *good* in *g'by*. "What did you say?" reduces itself to "wuz ay?" *Maybe* is *mebby*, *perhaps* is *p'raps*, *so long* is *s'long*, *excuse me* is *skus me*; the common salutation, "how are you?" is so dismembered that it finally emerges as a word almost indistinguishable from *high*. Here there is room for inquiry, and that inquiry deserves the best effort of American phonologists, for the language is undergoing rapid changes under their very eyes, or, perhaps more accurately, under their very ears, and a study of those changes should yield a great deal of interesting matter. How did the word *stint*, on American lips, first convert itself into *stent* and then into *stunt?* By what process was *baulk* changed into *buck?*

A by-way that is yet to be so much as entered is that of naturalized loan-words in the common speech. A very characteristic word of that sort is *sashay*. Its relationship to the French *chassé* seems to be plain, and yet it has acquired meanings in American that differ very widely from the meaning of *chassé*. How widely it is dispersed may be seen by the fact that it is reported in popular use, as a verb signifying to prance or to walk consciously, in Southeastern Missouri, Nebraska, Northwestern Arkansas, Michigan, Eastern Alabama and Western Indiana, and, with slightly different meaning, on Cape Cod. The travels of *café* in America would repay investigation; particularly its variations in pronunciation. I believe that it is fast becoming *kaif*. *Plaza, boulevard, vaudeville, menu* and *rathskeller* have entered into the common speech of the land, and are pronounced as American words. Such words, when they come in verbally, by actual contact with immigrants, commonly retain some measure of their correct native pronunciation. *Spiel, kosher, ganof* and *matzoth* are examples; their vowels remain un-American. But words that come in visually, say through street-signs and the newspapers, are immediately overhauled and have thoroughly Americanized vowels and consonants thereafter. School-teachers have been trying to establish various pseudo-French pronunciations of *vase* for fifty years past, but it still rhymes with *face* in the vulgate. *Vaudeville* is *vawd-vill;* *boulevard* has three syllables and a hard *d* at the end; *plaza* has a flat *a;* the first syllable of *menu* rhymes with *bee;* the first of *rathskeller* with *cats;* *fiancée* is *fy-ance-y;* *née* rhymes with *see;* *décolleté* is *de-coll-ty;* *hofbräu* is *huffbrow;* the German *w* has lost its *v*-sound and becomes an American *w*. I have, in my day, heard *proteege* for *protégé,* *habichoo* for *habitué,* *connisoor* for *connoisseur,* *shirtso* for *scherzo,* *premeer* for *première,* *dee tour* for *détour,* *eetood* for *étude* and *prelood* for *prélude*. I once heard a burlesque show manager, in announcing a French dancing act, pronounce *M.* and *Mlle.* as *Em* and *Milly*. *Divorcée* is *divorcey,* and has all the rakishness of the adjectives in -*y*. The first syllable of *mayonnaise* rhymes with *hay*. *Crème de menthe* is *cream de mint*. *Schweizer* is *swite-ser*. *Roquefort* is *roke-fort*. I have heard *début* with the last syllable rhyming with *nut*. I have heard *minoot* for *minuet*. I have heard *tchefdoover* for *chef-d'œuvre*. And who doesn't remember

>As I walked along the *Boys Boo-long*
>With an independent air

and

>Say *aw re-vore,*
>But not good-by!

Charles James Fox, it is said, called the red wine of France *Bordox* to the end of his days. He had an American heart; his great speeches for the revolting colonies were more than mere oratory. John Bright, another kind friend in troubled days, had one too. He always said *Bordox* and *Calass*.

X.

PROPER NAMES IN AMERICA

1.

Surnames

On October 20, 1919, Mr. Mondell, of Wyoming, the majority leader, arose in the House of Representatives and called the attention of the House to the presence in the gallery of a detachment of 27 soldiers, "popularly known by the appropriate title and designation of 'Americans all.' " A few moments later Mr. Wilson, of Connecticut, had the names of these soldiers spread upon the record for the day. Here they are:

Pedro Araez	Frank Kristopoulos
Sylvester Balchunas	Johannes Lenferink
Arezio Aurechio	Fidel Martin
Jules Boutin	Attilio Marzi
Oasge Christiansen	Gurt Mistrioty
Kusti Franti	Michael Myatowych
Odilian Gosselin	Francisco Pungi
Walter Hucko	Joseph Rossignol
Argele Intili	Ichae Semos
Henry Jurk	Joe Shestak
David King	George Strong
John Klok	Hendrix Svennigsen
Norman Kerman	Fritz Wold
Eugene Kristiansen	

This was no unusual group of Americans, though it was deliberately assembled to convince Congress of the existence of a "melting pot that really melts." I turn to the list of promotions in the army sent in to the Senate on the first day of the Harding administration, and find *Lanza, Huguet, Shaffer, Brambila, Straat, Knabenshue, De Armond, Meyer, Wiezorek* and *Stahl* among the new colonels and lieutenant-colonels, and *Ver, Lorch, von Deesten, Violland* and *Armat* among the new majors. I proceed to the roll of the Sixty-sixth Congress and find *Babka, Bacharach, Baer, Chindblom, Crago, Dupré, Esch, Focht, Goldfogel, Goodykoontz, Hernandez, Hoch, Juul, Kahn, Keller, Kiess, Kleczka, Knutson, Kraus, Larsen, Lazaro, Lehlbach, Rodenberg, Romjue, Siegel, Steenerson, Volk, Volstead, Voigt* and *Zihlman* in the House. I go on to the list of members of the National Institute of Arts and Letters (1919) and find *Cortissoz, de Kay, Gummere, Lefevre, Schelling, van Dyke* and *Wister* among the writers, and *Ballin, Betts, Brunner, Carlsen, De Camp, Dielman, Du Mond, Guerin, Henri, Jaegers, La Farge, Niehaus, Ochtman, Roth, Volk* and *Weinman* among the painters and sculptors. I conclude with a glance through "Who's Who in America." There are *Aasgaard, Abbé, Abt, Ackerman, Adler, Agassiz, Agee, Allaire, Alsberg, Alschuler, Althoff, Althouse, Ament, Amstutz, Amweg, Andrus, Angellotti, Anshutz, Anspacher, Anstadt, App, Arndt, Auer, Auerbach, Ault* and *Auman,* to go no further than the A's—all "notable living men and women of the United States" and all native-born.

Practically any other list of Americans would show many names of the same sort. Indeed, every American telephone directory offers plenty of evidence that, despite the continued political and cultural preponderance of the original English strain, the American people have quite ceased to be authentically English in race, or even, as a London weekly has said, "predominantly of British stock."[1] The blood in their arteries is inordinately various and inextricably mixed, but yet not mixed enough to run a clear stream. A touch of foreignness still lingers about millions of them, even in the country of their birth. They show their alien origin in their speech, in their domestic customs, in their habits of mind, and in their very names. Just as the Scotch and the Welsh have invaded England, elbowing out the actual English to make room for themselves, so the Irish, the Germans, the Italians, the Scandinavians and the Jews of Eastern Europe, and in some areas, the French, the Slavs and the hybrid-Spaniards have elbowed out the descendants of the first colonists. It is no exaggeration, indeed, to say that wherever the old stock comes into

[1] *Nation,* March 12, 1912.

PROPER NAMES IN AMERICA 323

direct and unrestrained conflict with one of these new stocks, it tends to succumb, or, at all events, to give up the battle. The Irish, in the big cities of the East, attained to a truly impressive political power long before the first native-born generation of them had grown up.[2] The Germans, following the limestone belt of the Alleghany foothills, pre-empted the best lands East of the mountains before the new republic was born. And so in our own time we have seen the Swedes and Norwegians shouldering the native from the wheat lands of the Northwest, and the Italians driving the decadent New Englanders from their farms, and the Jews gobbling New York, and the Slavs getting a firm foothold in the mining regions, and the French Canadians penetrating New Hampshire and Vermont, and the Japanese and Portuguese menacing Hawaii, and the awakened negroes gradually ousting the whites from the farms of the South.[3] The birth-rate among all these foreign stocks is enormously greater than among the older stock, and though the death-rate is also high, the net increase remains relatively formidable. Even without the aid of immigration it is probable that they would continue to rise in numbers faster than the original English and so-called Scotch-Irish.[4]

Turn to the letter *z* in the New York telephone directory and you will find a truly astonishing array of foreign names, some of them in process of anglicization, but many of them still arrestingly outlandish. The only Anglo-Saxon surname beginning with *z* is *Zacharias*[5] and even that was originally borrowed from the Greek. To this the Norman invasion seems to have added only *Zouchy*. But in Manhattan and the Bronx, even among the necessarily limited class of telephone subscribers, there are nearly 1500 persons whose names begin with the letter, and among them one finds fully 150 different surnames. The German *Zimmermann*, with either one *n* or two, is naturally the most numerous single name, and following close upon it are its relatives, *Zimmer* and *Zimmern*. With them are many more German names, *Zahn, Zechendorf, Zeffert, Zeitler,*

[2] The great Irish famine, which launched the chief emigration to America, extended from 1845 to 1847. The Know Nothing movement, which was chiefly aimed at the Irish, extended from 1852 to 1860.
[3] Richard T. Ely: Outlines of Economics, 3rd rev. ed.; New York, 1916, p. 68.
[4] *Cf.* Seth K. Humphrey: Mankind; New York, 1917, p. 45.
[5] *Cf.* William G. Searle: Onomasticon Anglo-Saxonicum; Cambridge, 1897.

Zeller, Zellner, Zeltmacher, Zepp, Ziegfeld, Zabel, Zucker, Zuckermann, Ziegler, Zillman, Zinser and so on. They are all represented heavily, but they indicate neither the earliest nor the most formidable accretion, for underlying them are many Dutch names, e. g., *Zeeman,* and over them are a large number of Slavic, Italian and Jewish names. Among the first I note *Zabludosky, Zachczynski, Zapinkow, Zaretsky, Zechnowitz, Zenzalsky* and *Zywachevsky;* among the second, *Zaccardi, Zaccarini, Zaccaro, Zapparano, Zanelli, Zicarelli* and *Zucca;* among the third, *Zukor, Zipkin* and *Ziskind.* There are, too, various Spanish names: *Zalaya, Zingaro,* etc. And Greek: *Zapeion, Zarvakos* and *Zouvelekis.* And Armenian: *Zaloom, Zaron* and *Zatmajian.* And Hungarian: *Zadek, Zagor* and *Zichy.* And Swedish: *Zetterholm* and *Zetterlund.* And a number that defy placing: *Zrike, Zvan,*[6] *Zwipf, Zula, Zur* and *Zeve.*

In the New York city directory the fourth most common name is now *Murphy,* an Irish name, and the fifth most common is *Meyer,* which is German and often Jewish. The *Meyers* are the *Smiths* of Austria, and of most of Germany. They outnumber all other clans. After them come the *Schultzes* and *Krauses,* just as the *Joneses* and *Williamses* follow the *Smiths* in Great Britain. *Schultze* and *Kraus* do not seem to be very common names in New York, but *Schmidt, Muller, Schneider* and *Klein* appear among the fifty commonest.[7] *Cohen* and *Levy* rank eighth and ninth, and are both ahead of *Jones,* which is second in England, and *Williams,* which is third. *Taylor,* a highly typical British name, ranking fourth in England and Wales, is twenty-third in New York. Ahead of it, beside *Murphy, Meyer, Cohen* and *Levy,* are *Schmidt, Ryan, O'Brien, Kelly* and *Sullivan. Robinson,* which is twelfth in England, is thirty-ninth in New York; even *Schneider* and *Muller* are ahead of it. In Chicago *Olson, Schmidt, Meyer, Hansen* and *Larsen* are ahead of *Taylor,* and *Hoffman* and *Becker* are ahead of *Ward;* in Boston *Sullivan* and *Murphy* are ahead of any English name save *Smith;* in Philadelphia *Myers* is just below *Robinson.* Nor, as I have said, is this great proliferation of foreign surnames confined to the large cities. There are whole

---

[6] A correspondent suggests that *Zvan* may be a misprint for *Ivan.* But what of the other strange names in the group?
[7] *World* Almanac, 1914, p. 668.

regions in the Southwest in which *López* and *Gonzales* are far commoner names than *Smith, Brown* or *Jones,* and whole regions in the Middle West wherein *Olson* is commoner than either *Taylor* or *Williams,* and places both North and South where *Duval* is at least as common as *Brown.*

Moreover, the true proportions of this admixture of foreign blood are partly concealed by a wholesale anglicization of surnames, sometimes deliberate and sometimes the fruit of mere confusion. That *Smith, Brown* and *Miller* remain in first, second and third places among the surnames of New York is surely no sound evidence of Anglo-Saxon survival. The German and Scandinavian *Schmidt* has undoubtedly contributed many a *Smith,* and *Braun* many a *Brown,* and *Müller* many a *Miller.* In the same way *Johnson,* which holds first place among Chicago surnames, and *Anderson,* which holds third, are plainly reinforced from Scandinavian sources, and the former may also owe something to the Russian *Ivanof. Miller* is a relatively rare name in England; it is not among the fifty most common. But it stands thirtieth in Boston, third in New York, fourth in Baltimore, and second in Philadelphia.[8] In the last-named city the influence of *Müller,* probably borrowed from the Pennsylvania German, is plainly indicated, and in Chicago it is likely that there are also contributions from the Scandinavian *Möller,* the Polish *Jannszewski* and the Bohemian *Mlinár. Myers,* as we have seen, is a common surname in Philadelphia. So are *Fox* and *Snyder.* In some part, at least, they have been reinforced by the Pennsylvania German *Myer, Fuchs* and *Schneider.* Sometimes *Müller* changes to *Miller,* sometimes to *Muller,* and sometimes it remains unchanged, but with the spelling made *Mueller. Muller* and *Mueller* do not appear among the commoner names in Philadelphia; nearly all the *Müllers* seem to have become *Millers,* thus putting *Miller* in second place. But in Chicago, with *Miller* in fourth place, there is also *Mueller* in thirty-first place, and in New York, with *Miller* in third place, there is also *Muller* in twenty-fourth place.

Such changes, chiefly based upon transliterations, are met with in

[8] It was announced by the Bureau of War Risk Insurance on March 30, 1918, that there were then 15,000 *Millers* in the United States Army. On the same day there were 262 *John J. O'Briens,* of whom 50 had wives named Mary.

all countries. The name of *Taaffe*, familiar in Austrian history, had an Irish prototype, probably *Taft*. General *Demikof*, one of the Russian commanders at the battle of Zorndorf, in 1758, was a Swede born *Themicoud*, and no doubt the founder of the house in Sweden was born a Frenchman. Franz Maria von *Thugut*, the Austrian diplomatist, was a member of an Italian Tyrolese family named *Tunicotto*. This became *Thunichgut* ($=$ *do no good*) in Austria, and was changed to *Thugut* ($=$ *do good*) to bring it into greater accord with its possessor's deserts.[9] In *Bonaparte* the Italian *buon(o)* became the French *bon*. Many English surnames are decayed forms of Norman-French names, for example, *Sidney* from *St. Denis, Divver* from *De Vere, Bridgewater* from *Burgh de Walter, Montgomery* from *de Mungumeri, Garnett* from *Guarinot,* and *Seymour* from *Saint-Maure*. A large number of so-called Irish names are the products of rough-and-ready transliterations of Gaelic patronymics, for example, *Findlay* from *Fionnlagh, Dermott* from *Diarmuid,* and *McLane* from *Mac Illeathiain*. In the same way the name of *Phœnix* Park, in Dublin, came from *Fion Uisg* ($=$ *fine water*). Of late some of the more ardent Irish authors and politicians have sought to return to the originals. Thus, *O'Sullivan* has become *O Suilleabháin, Pearse* has become *Piarais, Shields* has become *O'Sheel, Mac Sweeney* has become *Mac Suibhne,* and *Patrick* has suffered a widespread transformation to *Padraic*. But in America, with a language of peculiar vowel-sounds and even consonant-sounds struggling against a foreign invasion unmatched for strength and variety, such changes have been far more numerous than across the ocean, and the legal rule of *idem sonans* is of much wider utility than anywhere else in the world. If it were not for that rule there would be endless difficulties for the *Wises* whose grandfathers were *Weisses,* and the *Leonards* born *Leonhards, Leonhardts* or *Lehnerts,* and the *Manneys* who descend and inherit from *Le Maines*.

"A crude popular etymology," says a leading authority on surnames,[10] "often begins to play upon a name that is no longer significant to the many. So the *Thurgods* have become *Thoroughgoods,* and the *Todenackers* have become the Pennsylvania Dutch *Tooth-*

[9] *Cf.* Carlyle's Frederick the Great, bk. xxi, ch. vi.
[10] S. Grant Oliphant, in the Baltimore *Sun*, Dec. 2, 1906.

akers, much as *asparagus* has become *sparrow-grass*." So, too, the *Wittenachts* of Boyle county, Kentucky, descendants of a Hollander, have become *Whitenecks*, and the *Lehns* of lower Pennsylvania, descendants of some far-off German, have become *Lanes*.[11] The original *Herkimer* in New York was a *Herchheimer;* the original *Waldo* in New England was a German named *Waldow*. Edgar Allan *Poe* was a member of a family long settled in Western Maryland, the founder being one *Poh* or *Pfau*, a native of the Palatinate. Major George *Armistead*, who defended Fort McHenry in 1814, when Francis Scott Key wrote "The Star-Spangled Banner," was the descendant of an *Armstädt* who came to Virginia from Hesse-Darmstadt. General George A. *Custer*, the Indian fighter, was the great-grandson of one *Küster*, a Hessian soldier paroled after Burgoyne's surrender. William *Wirt*, anti-Masonic candidate for the presidency in 1832, was the son of one *Wörth*. William *Paca*, a signer of the Declaration of Independence, was the great-grandson of a Bohemian named *Paka*. General J. J. *Pershing* is the descendant of an Alsatian named *Pfoersching*, who immigrated to America in the eighteenth century; the name was at first debased to *Pershin;* in 1838 the final *g* was restored. General W. S. *Rosecrans* was really a *Rosenkrantz*. Even the surname of Abraham *Lincoln*, according to some authorities, was an anglicized form of the German *Linkhorn*.[12]

Such changes, in fact, are almost innumerable; every work upon American genealogy is full of examples. The first foreign names to undergo the process were Dutch and French. Among the former, *Reiger* was debased to *Riker*, *Van de Veer* to *Vandiver*, *Van Huys* to *Vannice*, *Van Siegel* to *Van Sickel*, *Van Arsdale* to *Vannersdale*, and *Haerlen* (or *Haerlem*) to *Harlan;*[13] among the latter, *Petit* became *Poteet*, *Caillé* changed to *Kyle*, *De la Haye* to *Dillehay*, *Dejean* to *Deshong*, *Guizor* to *Gossett*, *Guereant* to *Caron*, *Soulé* to *Sewell*, *Gervaise* to *Jarvis*, *Bayle* to *Bailey*, *Fontaine* to *Fountain*,

[11] Harriet *Lane* Johnston was of this family. Many other examples are to be found in the pages of the *Pennsylvania-German Magazine*, especially in the "Meaning of Names" department conducted by Dr. Leonard Felix Fuld.
[12] *Cf.* Faust, *op. cit.*, vol. ii, pp. 183-4. See also A Few Bausman Letters, by Lottie M. Bausman, *Pennsylvania-German Magazine*, April, 1910, p. 229.
[13] A Tragedy of Surnames, by Fayette Dunlap, *Dialect Notes*, vol. iv, pt. 1, 1913, pp. 7-8.

Denis to *Denny*, *Pebaudière* to *Peabody*, *Bon Pas* to *Bumpus* and *de l'Hôtel* to *Doolittle*. "Frenchmen and French Canadians who came to New England," says Schele de Vere, "had to pay for such hospitality as they there received by the sacrifice of their names. The brave *Bon Cœur*, Captain Marryatt tells us in his Diary, became Mr. *Bunker*, and gave his name to Bunker's Hill." [14] But it was the German immigration that provoked the first really wholesale slaughter. A number of characteristic German sounds—for example, that of *ü* and the guttural in *ch* and *g*—are almost impossible to the Anglo-Saxon pharynx, and so they had to go. Thus, *Bloch* was changed to *Block* or *Black*, *Ochs* to *Oakes*, *Hoch* to *Hoke*, *Fischbach* to *Fishback*, *Albrecht* to *Albert* or *Albright*, and *Steinweg* to *Steinway*, and the *Grundwort, bach,* was almost universally changed to *baugh* or *paugh*, as in *Brumbaugh* and *Fishpaugh* (or *Fishpaw*). The *ü* met the same fate: *Grün* was changed to *Green*, *Sänger* to *Sanger* or *Singer*, *Glück* to *Gluck*, *Führ* to *Fear* or *Fuhr*, *Wärner* to *Warner*, *Düring* to *Deering*, and *Schnäbele* to *Snabely*, *Snavely* or *Snively*. In many other cases there were changes in spelling to preserve vowel sounds differently represented in German and English. Thus, *Blum* was changed to *Bloom*,[15] *Reuss* to *Royce*, *Koester* to *Kester*, *Kuehle* to *Keeley*, *Schroeder* to *Schrader*, *Stehli* to *Staley*, *Weymann* to *Wayman*, *Klein* to *Kline* or *Cline*, *Federlein* to *Federline*, *Friedmann* to *Freedman*, *Bauman* to *Bowman*, *Braun* to *Brown*, and *Lang* (as the best compromise possible) to *Long*. The change of *Oehm* to *Ames* belongs to the same category; the addition of the final *s* represents a typical effort to substitute the nearest related Anglo-Saxon name or name so sounding. Other examples of that effort are to be found in *Michaels* for *Michaelis*, *Bowers* for *Bauer*, *Johnson* for *Johannsen*, *Ford* for *Furth*, *Hines* for *Heintz*, *Kemp* for *Kempf*, *Foreman* for *Führmann*, *Kuhns* or *Coons* for *Kuntz*, *Hoover* for *Huber*, *Levering* for *Liebering*, *Jones* for *Jonas*, *Redwood* for *Rothholz*, *Grosscup* for *Grosskopf*, *Westfall* for *Westphal*, *Kerngood* for *Kerngut*, *Collenberg* for *Kaltenberg*, *Cronkhite* for *Krankheit*, *Betts* for *Betz*, *Penny-*

---

[14] Americanisms, p. 112.
[15] Henry Harrison, in his Dictionary of the Surnames of the United Kingdom; London, 1912, shows that such names as *Bloom*, *Cline*, etc., always represent transliterations of German names. They are unknown to genuinely British nomenclature.

packer for *Pfannenbecker*, *Crile* for *Kreil*,[16] *Swope* for *Schwab*, *Hite* or *Hyde* for *Heid*, *Andrews* for *André*, *Young* for *Jung* and *Pence* for *Pentz*.[17]

The American antipathy to accented letters, mentioned in the chapter on spelling, is particularly noticeable among surnames. An immigrant named *Fürst* inevitably becomes plain *Furst* in the United States, and if not the man, then surely his son. *Löwe*, in the same way, is transformed into *Lowe* (pro. *low*),[18] *Lürmann* into *Lurman*, *Schön* into *Schon* or *Shane*, *Günther* into *Ginter*, *Suplée* into *Suplee* or *Supplee*, *Lüders* into *Luders*, and *Brühl* into *Brill*. Even when no accent betrays it, the foreign diphthong is under hard pressure. Thus the German *oe* disappears and *Loeb* is changed to *Lobe* or *Laib*, *Oehler* to *Ohler*, *Loeser* to *Leser*, and *Schoen* to *Schon* or *Shane*. In the same way the *au* in such names as *Rosenau* changes to *aw*. So too, the French *oi*-sound is disposed of, and *Dubois* is pronounced *Doo-bóys* and *Boileau* acquires a first syllable rhyming with *toil*. So with the *kn* in the German names of the *Knapp* class; they are nearly all pronounced, probably by analogy with *Knight*, as if they began with *n*. So with *sch*; *Schneider* becomes *Snyder*, *Schlegel* becomes *Slagel*, and *Schluter* becomes *Sluter*. If a foreigner clings to the original spelling of his name he must usually expect to hear it mispronounced. *Roth*, in American, quickly becomes *Rawth*, *Ranft* is pronounced *Ranf*; *Frémont*, losing both accent and the French *e*, becomes *Freemont*; the names in *-thal* take the English *th* sound; *Blum* begins to rhyme with *dumb*; *Mann* rhymes with *van*, and *Lang* with *hang*; *Krantz*, *Lantz* and their cognates with *chance*; *Kurtz* with *shirts*; the first syllable of *Gutmann* with *but*; the first of *Kahler* with *bay*; the first

---

[16] I suggest that the eminent American surgeon, George W. *Crile*, may be a descendant of some early *Kreil*. His mother's name was *Deeds*. During the World War, when an American officer named *Deeds* was under attack, it was alleged that the original form of his name was *Dietz*.

[17] A great many more such transliterations and modifications are listed by Faust, *op. cit.*, particularly in his first volume. Others are in Pennsylvania Dutch, by S. S. Haldemann; London, 1872, p. 60 *et seq.*, and in The Origin of Pennsylvania Surnames, by L. Oscar Kuhns, *Lippincott's Magazine*, March, 1897, p. 395.

[18] I lately encountered the following sign in front of an automobile repair shop:
    For puncture or blow
    Bring it to *Lowe*.

of *Werner* with *turn;* the first of *Wagner* with *nag.* *Uhler,* in America, is always *Youler.* *Berg* loses its German *e*-sound for an English *u*-sound, and its German hard *g* for an English *g;* it becomes identical with the *berg* of *iceberg.* The same change in the vowel occurs in *Erdmann.* In *König* the German diphthong succumbs to a long *o,* and the hard *g* becomes *k;* the common pronunciation is *Cone-ik.* Often, in *Berger,* the *g* becomes soft, and the name rhymes with *verger.* It becomes soft, too, in *Bittinger.* In *Wilstach* and *Welsbach* the *ch* becomes a *k.* In *Anheuser* the *eu* changes to *ow.* The final *e,* important in German, is nearly always silenced; *Dohme* rhymes with *foam;* *Kühne* becomes *keen.* In the collectanea of Judge J. C. Ruppenthal, of Russell, Kansas, a very careful observer, are many curious specimens. He finds *Viereck* transformed into *Fearhake,* *Vogelgesang* into *Fogelsong,* *Pfannenstiel* into *Fanestil,* *Pflüger* into *Phlegar,* *Pfeil* into *Feil,* and *Steinmetz* into *Stimits.* The Bohemian *Hrdlicka* becomes *Herdlichka.* The Dutch *Broywer* (in Michigan, where there are many Hollanders of relatively recent immigration) becomes *Brower,* *Pelgrim* becomes *Pilgrim,* *Pyp* becomes *Pipe,* *Londen* becomes *London,* *Roos* becomes *Rose,* and *Wijngaarden* becomes *Winegar.*

In addition to these transliterations, there are constant translations of foreign proper names. "Many a Pennsylvania *Carpenter,*" says Dr. Oliphant,[19] "bearing a surname that is English, from the French, from the Latin, and there a Celtic loan-word in origin, is neither English, nor French, nor Latin, nor Celt, but an original German *Zimmermann.*"[20] A great many other such translations are under everyday observation. *Pfund* becomes *Pound;* *Becker,* *Baker;* *Schumacher,* *Shoemaker;* *König,* *King;* *Weissberg,* *Whitehill;* *Koch,* *Cook;*[21] *Neumann,* *Newman;* *Schaefer,* *Shepherd* or *Sheppard;* *Gutmann,* *Goodman;* *Goldschmidt,* *Goldsmith;* *Edelstein,* *Nobelstone;* *Steiner,* *Stoner;* *Meister,* *Master(s)*; *Schwartz,* *Black;* *Weiss,* *White;* *Kurtz,* *Short;* *Stern,* *Starr;* *Morgenstern,* *Morningstar;*

[19] Baltimore *Sun,* March 17, 1907.
[20] *Cf.* The Origin of Pennsylvania Surnames, *op. cit.*
[21] *Koch,* a common German name, has very hard sledding in America. Its correct pronunciation is almost impossible to Americans; at best it becomes *Coke.* Hence it is often changed, not only to *Cook,* but to *Cox, Koke* or even *Cockey.*

PROPER NAMES IN AMERICA 331

Weber, Weaver; Bucher, Booker; Vogelgesang, Birdsong; Sonntag, Sunday, and so on. It is not unusual for some members of a family to translate the patronymic while others leave it unchanged. Thus in Pennsylvania (and no doubt elsewhere) there are *Carpenters* and *Zimmermans* of the same blood. A Frenchman named *LeRoi* settled in the Mohawk Valley in the early eighteenth century; today his descendants are variously named *Leroy, Larraway* and *King.* Partial translations are also encountered, e. g., *Studebaker* from *Studebecker,* and *Reindollar* from *Rheinthaler,* and radical shortenings, e. g., *Swiler* from *Lebenschweiler, Kirk* from *Kirkeslager,* and *Castle* (somewhat fantastically) from *Katzenellenbogen.* The same processes show themselves in the changes undergone by the names of the newer immigrants. The Hollanders in Michigan often have to submit to translations of their surnames. Thus *Hoogsteen* becomes *Highstone, Veldhuis* becomes *Fieldhouse, Huisman* becomes *Houseman, Prins* becomes *Prince, Kuiper* becomes *Cooper, Dykhuis* becomes *Dykehouse, Konig* becomes *King, Werkman* becomes *Workman, Nieuwhuis* becomes *Newhouse,* and *Christiaanse* becomes *Christians.* Similarly the Greek *Triantafyllopoulos* (signifying *rose*) is often turned into the English *Rose, Giannopoulos* becomes *Johnson,* and *Demetriades* becomes *Jameson.* So, too, *Constantinopoulos* is shortened to *Constant* or *Constantine, Athanasios* to *Nathan* or *Athan, Pappadakis, Pappadopoulos* or *Pappademetriou* to *Pappas.* Transliteration also enters into the matter, as in the change from *Mylonas* to *Miller,* from *Demopoulos* to *DeMoss,* and from *Christides* to *Christie.*[22] And so, by one route or another, the Polish *Wilkiewicz* becomes *Wilson,* the Scandinavian *Knutson* becomes *Newton,* the Bohemian *Bohumil* becomes *Godfrey,* and the Bohemian *Kovár* and the Russian *Kuznetzov* become *Smith.* Some curious examples are occasionally encountered, particularly among the Italians of the big cities. The late James E. *March,* Republican leader of the Third Assembly District in New York, was originally *Antonio Maggio.* Paul *Kelly,* leader of the Longshoremen's Union, was *Paolo Vaccarelli.* One *Alessandro Smiraglia* has become *Sandy Smash, Francesco Napoli* is

[22] For the Dutch examples, I am indebted to Prof. Henry J. G. Van Andel, of Calvin College, Grand Rapids, Mich., and to Prof. B. K. Kuiper, of the same city. The Greek examples come from Mr. S. S. Lontos, editor of *Atlantis,* the Greek daily newspaper in New York.

Frank Knapp, Francesco Tomasini is *Frank Thomas,* and *Luigi Zampariello* is *Louis Smith.* Henry *Woodhouse,* a gentleman prominent in aeronautical affairs, came to the United States from Italy as Mario Terenzio Enrico *Casalegno;* his new surname is simply a translation of his old one. The *Belmonts,* unable to find a euphonious English equivalent for their German patronymic of *Schönberg,* chose a French one that Americans could pronounce. Edmund Burke *Fairfield,* once chancellor of the University of Nebraska, was the descendant of a Frenchman named *Beauchamp,* who came to America in 1639.

In part, as I have said, these changes in surname are enforced by the sheer inability of Americans to pronounce certain Continental consonants, and their disinclination to remember the Continental vowel sounds. Many an immigrant, finding his name constantly mispronounced, changes its vowels or drops some of its consonants; many another shortens it, or translates it, or changes it entirely for the same reason. Just as a well-known Greek-French poet changed his Greek name of *Papadiamantopoulos* to *Moréas* because *Papadiamantopoulos* was too much for Frenchmen, and as an eminent Polish-English novelist changed his Polish name of *Karzeniowski* to *Conrad* because few Englishmen could pronounce *owski* correctly, so the Italian or Greek or Slav immigrant, coming up for naturalization, very often sheds his family name with his old allegiance, and emerges as *Taylor, Jackson* or *Wilson.* I once encountered a firm of Polish Jews, showing the name of *Robinson & Jones* on its sign-board, whose partners were born *Rubinowitz* and *Jonas.* I lately heard of a German named *Knoche*—a name doubly difficult to Americans, what with the *kn* and the *ch*—who changed it boldly to *Knox* to avoid being called *Nokky.* A Greek named *Papademetracopoulos, Harzidakis, Papalhesdoros, Sakorrhaphos, Jouphexes* or *Oikonomakes* would find it practically impossible to carry on amicable business with Americans; his name would arouse their mirth, if not their downright ire. And the same burden would lie upon a Hungarian named *Beniczkyné,* or *Gyalui,* or *Szilagyi,* or *Vezercsillagok.* Or a Finn named *Kyyhkysen,* or *Jääskelainen,* or *Tuulensuu,* or *Uotinen,* —all honorable Finnish patronymics. Or a Swede named *Sjogren,* or *Leijonhufvud.* Or a Bohemian named *Srb,* or *Hrubka.* Or a

PROPER NAMES IN AMERICA 333

Hollander named *Zylstra,* or *Pyp,* or *Hoogsteen.* Or, for that matter, a German named *Kannengiesser,* or *Schnapaupf,* or *Pfannenbecker.*

But more important than this purely linguistic hostility, there is a deeper social enmity, and it urges the immigrant to change his name with even greater force. For a hundred years past all the heaviest and most degrading labor of the United States has been done by successive armies of foreigners, and so a concept of inferiority has come to be attached to mere foreignness. In addition, these newcomers, pressing upward steadily in the manner already described, have offered the native a formidable, and considering their lower standards of living, what has appeared to him to be an unfair competition on his own plane, and as a result a hatred born of disastrous rivalry has been added to contempt. Our unmatchable vocabulary of derisive names for foreigners reveals the national attitude. The French *boche,* the German *hunyadi* (for Hungarian),[23] and the old English *frog* or *froggy* (for Frenchman) seem lone and feeble beside our great repertoire: *dago, wop, guinea, kike, goose, mick, harp,*[24] *bohick, bohee, bohunk, heinie, square-head, greaser, canuck, spiggoty,*[25] *spick, chink, polack, dutchie, skibby,*[26] *scowegian, hunkie* and *yellow-belly.* This disdain tends to pursue an immigrant with

[23] This is army slang, but promises to survive. The Germans, during the war, had no opprobrious nicknames for their foes. The French were usually simply *die Franzosen,* the English were *die Engländer,* and so on, even when most violently abused. Even *der Yankee* was rare. *Teufelhunde* (devil-dogs), for the American marines, was invented by an American correspondent; the Germans never used it. *Cf.* Wie der Feldgraue spricht, by Karl Bergmann; Giessen, 1916, p. 23.
[24] *Cf.* Some Current Substitutes for *Irish,* by W. A. McLaughlin, *Dialect Notes,* vol. iv, pt. ii.
[25] *Spiggoty,* of which *spick* is a variant, originated at Panama and now means a native of any Latin-American region under American protection, and in general any Latin-American. It is navy slang, but has come into extensive civilian use. It is a derisive daughter of "No *spik* Inglese."
[26] This designates a Japanese and is apparently used only on the Pacific Coast. It originally meant a Japanese loose woman, but is now applied to all persons of the race. Tucker says that *dago* goes back to 1832. It is probably a corruption of *Diego;* it was first applied to Mexicans. The etymologies of *wop, guinea* and *kike* are uncertain, and frequently disputed. Often efforts are made to discourage the use of these nicknames. Dr. P. P. Claxton, United States Commissioner of Education, devised in 1919 a Code of Honorable Names to be subscribed to by the Boy Scouts, whereby they agreed to avoid them. But Dr. Claxton omitted all the opprobrious names for the negroes, and the fact brought forth a protest from them. See Offensive Nicknames, by James W. Johnson, New York *Age,* Feb. 1, 1919.

extraordinary rancor when he bears a name that is unmistakably foreign and hence difficult to the native, and open to his crude burlesque. Moreover, the general feeling penetrates the man himself, particularly if he be ignorant, and he comes to believe that his name is not only a handicap, but also intrinsically discreditable—that it wars subtly upon his worth and integrity.[27] This feeling, perhaps, accounted for a good many changes of surnames among Germans and Jews of German name upon the entrance of the United States into the war. But in the majority of cases, of course, the changes so copiously reported—e. g., from *Bielefelder* to *Benson,* and from *Pulvermacher* to *Pullman*—were merely efforts at protective coloration. The immigrant, in a time of extraordinary suspicion and difficulty, tried to get rid of at least one handicap.[28]

This motive constantly appears among the Jews, who face an anti-Semitism that is imperfectly concealed and may be expected to grow stronger hereafter. Once they have lost the faith of their fathers, a phenomenon almost inevitable in the first native-born generation, they shrink from all the disadvantages that go with Jewishness, and seek to conceal their origin, or, at all events, to avoid

[27] *Cf.* Reaction to Personal Names, by Dr. C. P. Oberndorf, *Psychoanalytic Review,* vol. v, no. 1, January, 1918, p. 47 *et seq.* This, so far as I know, is the only article in English which deals with the psychological effects of surnames upon their bearers. Abraham, Silberer and other German psychoanalysts have made contributions to the subject. Dr. Oberndorf alludes, incidentally, to the positive social prestige which goes with an English air or a French air in America. He tells of an Italian who changed his patronymic of *Dipucci* into *de Pucci* to make it more "aristocratic." And of a German bearing the genuinely aristocratic name of *von Landsschaffshausen* who changed it to "a typically English name" because the latter seemed more distinguished to his neighbors. Why is a French surname regarded as aristocratic in America? The question has never been investigated.

[28] The effects of race antagonism upon language are still to be investigated. The etymology of *slave* indicates that the inquiry might yield interesting results. The word *French,* in English, is largely used to suggest sexual perversion. In German anything *Russian* is barbarous, and *English* education hints at flagellation. The French, for many years, called a certain contraband appliance a *capote Anglaise,* but after the *entente cordiale* they changed the name to *capote Allemande.* The common English name to this day is *French letter. Cf.* The Criminal, by Havelock Ellis; London, 1910, p. 208. In France a sharper is called a *Greek, as drunk as a Pole* is a common phrase, and one of the mainstays of low comedy is *le truc du brésilien.* See Xenophobia, by Rufino Blanco-Fombona, in his La Lámpara de Aladino, pp. 431-440. In most of the non-Prussian parts of Germany cockroaches are called *Preussen;* in Prussia they are *Franzosen;* in some places they are *Schwaben.*

making it unnecessarily noticeable.[29] To this end they modify the spelling of the more familiar Jewish surnames, turning *Levy* into *Lewy, Lewyt, Levitt, Levin, Levine, Levey, Levie* [30] and even *Lever;* *Cohen* into *Cohn, Cahn, Kahn, Kann, Coyne* and *Conn; Aarons* into *Arens* and *Ahrens,* and *Solomon* into *Salmon, Salomon* and *Solmson*.[31] In the same way they shorten their long names, changing *Wolfsheimer* to *Wolf, Goldschmidt* to *Gold,* and *Rosenblatt, Rosenthal, Rosenbaum, Rosenau, Rosenberg, Rosenbusch, Rosenblum, Rosenstein, Rosengarten, Rosenheim* and *Rosenfeldt* to *Rose* or *Ross*.[32] Like the Germans, they also seek refuge in translations more or less literal. Thus, on the East Side of New York, *Blumenthal* is often changed to *Bloomingdale, Schneider* to *Taylor, Reichman* to *Richman,* and *Schlachtfeld* to *Warfield.* One *Lobenstine (i. e., Lobenstein)* had his name changed to *Preston* during the war, and announced that this was "the English version" of his patronymic. A *Wolfsohn* similarly became a *Wilson,* though without attempting any such fantastic philological justification for the change.[33] *Fiedler,* a common Jewish name, often becomes *Harper* in New York; so does *Pikler,* which is Yiddish for *drummer.* *Stolar,* which is a Yiddish word borrowed from the Russian, signifying *carpenter,* is changed to *Carpenter.* *Lichtman* and *Lichtenstein* become *Chandler.* *Meilach,* which is Hebrew for *king,* becomes *King,* and so does *Meilachson.* The strong tendency to seek English-sounding equivalents for names of noticeably foreign origin changes *Sher* into *Sherman, Michel* into

[29] *Cf.* The Jews, by Maurice Fishberg; New York, 1911, ch. xxii, and especially p. 485 *ff.*
[30] The English Jews usually change *Levy* to *Lewis,* a substitution almost unknown in America. They also change *Abraham* to *Braham* and *Moses* to *Moss.* Vide Surnames, Their Origin and Nationality, by L. B. McKenna; Quincy (Ill.), 1913, pp. 13-14. *Taylor* is another common name among them.
[31] I lately encountered *Openhym* in New York, *Dalsemer* (for *Dalsheimer*) in Philadelphia, and *Thalhimer* in Richmond, Va. *Slessinger* and *Slazenger* are common variants of *Schlesinger* in New York.
[32] See A Cycle of Manhattan, by Thyra Samter Winslow, Smart Set, March, 1919. In New York I have encountered *Schönes* transformed into *Shainess.*
[33] I take the following from Dr. Pepys' Diary in the *Journal* of the American Medical Association: "Today in ye clinic a tale told of Dr. *Levy* who hath had his name changed to *Sullivan.* A month after he cometh again to ye court, this time wishing to become *Kilpatrick.* On request for ye reason, he telleth ye court that ye patients continually ask of him, 'What was your name before?' If granted ye change he shall then tell them *'Sullivan.'* "

Mitchell,[34] *Rogowsky* into *Rogers*, *Kolinsky* into *Collins*, *Rabinovitch* into *Robbins*, *Davidovitch* into *Davis*, *Moiseyev* into *Macy* or *Mason*, and *Jacobson*, *Jacobovitch* and *Jacobovsky* into *Jackson*. This last change proceeds by way of a transient change to *Jake* or *Jack* as a nickname. *Jacob* is always abbreviated to one or the other on the East Side. *Yankelevitch* also becomes Jackson, for *Yankel* is Yiddish for *Jacob*.[35] The Jews go further with such changes than any other people. They struggle very hard for position, and try to rid themselves of every unnecessary handicap. Moreover, they are supported by the historical name-shedding of a very eminent Jew, the *Saul* of Tarsus who became *Paul*. In precisely the same way, on attaining to 100 per cent Americanism, the *Itzik Kolinsky* of today becomes *Sidney Collins*.

Among the immigrants of other stocks some extraordinarily radical changes in name are also to be observed. Greek names of five, and even eight syllables shrink to *Smith;* Hungarian names that seem to be all consonants are reborn in such euphonious forms as *Martin* and *Lacy*. I have encountered a *Gregory* who was born *Grgurevich* in Serbia; a *Uhler* who was born *Uhlyarik;* a *Beresford* who was born *Bilkovski;* a *Graves* who descends from the fine old Dutch family of *'sGravesande*. I once knew a man named *Lawton* whose grandfather had been a *Lautenberger*. First he shed the *berger* and then he changed the spelling of *Lauten* to make it fit the inevitable American mispronunciation. There is, again, a family of *Dicks* in the South whose ancestor was a *Schwettendieck*—apparently a Dutch or Low German name. There is, yet again, a celebrated American artist, of the Bohemian patronymic of *Hrubka,* who has abandoned it for a surname which is common to all the Teutonic languages, and is hence easy for Americans. The Italians, probably because of the relations established by the Catholic church, often take Irish names, as they marry Irish girls; it is common to hear of an Italian pugilist or politician named *Kelly* or *O'Brien*. The process of change is often informal, but even legally it is quite facile. The Naturalization

---

[34] I once encountered a *Mitchell Judge* whose original name was *Moses Richter*.

[35] For these observations of name changes among the Jews I am indebted to Mr. Abraham Cahan.

Act of June 29, 1906, authorizes the court, as a part of the naturalization of any alien, to make an order changing his name. This is frequently done when he receives his last papers; sometimes, if the newspapers are to be believed, without his solicitation, and even against his protest. If the matter is overlooked at the time, he may change his name later on, like any other citizen, by simple application to a court of record or even without any legal process whatever.

Among names of Anglo-Saxon origin and names naturalized long before the earliest colonization, one notes certain American peculiarities, setting off the nomenclature of the United States from that of the mother country. The relative infrequency of hyphenated names in America is familiar; when they appear at all it is almost always in response to direct English influences.[36] Again, a number of English family names have undergone modification in the New World. *Venable* may serve as a specimen. The form in England is almost inevitably *Venables,* but in America the final *s* has been lost, and every example of the name that I have been able to find in the leading American reference-books is without it. And where spellings have remained unchanged, pronunciations have been frequently modified. This is particularly noticeable in the South.[37] *Callowhill,* down there, is commonly pronounced *Carrol; Crenshawe* is *Granger; Hawthorne, Horton; Heyward, Howard; Norsworthy, Nazary; Ironmonger, Munger; Farinholt, Fernall; Camp, Kemp; Buchanan, Bohannan; Drewry, Droit; Enroughty, Darby;*[38] and *Taliaferro, Tolliver.* The English *Crowninshields* commonly make it *Crunshel. Van Schaick,* an old New York Dutch name, is pro-

---

[36] They arose in England through the custom of requiring an heir by the female line to adopt the family name on inheriting the family property. Formerly the heir dropped his own surname. Thus the ancestor of the present Duke of Northumberland, born *Smithson,* took the ancient name of *Percy* on succeeding to the underlying earldom in the eighteenth century. But about a hundred years ago, heirs in like case began to join the two names by hyphenation, and such names are now very common in the British peerage. Thus the surname of Lord Barrymore is *Smith-Barry,* that of Lord Vernon is *Venables-Vernon,* and that of the Earl of Wharncliffe is *Montagu-Stuart-Wortley-Mackenzie.*

[37] B. W. Green: Word-Book of Virginia Folk-Speech; Richmond, 1899, pp. 13-16.

[38] A correspondent writes in explanation of this amazing pronunciation: "The family, having rather unwillingly had to change their name to *Enroughty* to secure an inheritance, balanced up by continuing to *pronounce* their original name—*Darby.*"

nounced *Von Scoik,* though the hard Dutch *sh*-sound in other New York names, *e. g., Schurman,* has been softened. A good many American Jews, aiming at a somewhat laborious refinement, change the pronunciation of the terminal *stein* in their names so that it rhymes, not with *line,* but with *bean.* Thus, in fashionable Jewish circles, there are no longer any *Epsteins, Goldsteins* and *Hammersteins* but only *Epsteens, Goldsteens* and *Hammersteens.* The American Jews differ further from the English in pronouncing *Levy* to make the first syllable rhyme with *tea;* the English Jews always make the name *Lev-vy,* to rhyme with *heavy.* In general there is a tendency in America to throw the accents back, *i. e.,* in such names as *Cassels, Brennan, Gerard, Doran, Burnett, Maurice,* etc. In England the first syllable is commonly accented; in the United States, the second.

To match such American prodigies as *Darby* for *Enroughty,* the English themselves have *Hools* for *Howells, Sillinger* for *St. Leger, Sinjin* for *St. John, Weems* for *Wemyss, Luson-Gore* for *Leveson-Gower, Stubbs* for *St. Aubyn, Vane* for *Veheyne, Kerduggen* for *Cadogen, Moboro* or *Mobrer* for *Marlborough, Key* for *Caius, Marchbanks* for *Marjoribanks, Beecham* for *Beauchamp, Chumley* for *Cholmondeley, Trosley* for *Trotterscliffe,* and *Darby* for *Derby.*[39]

2.

Given Names

The non-Anglo-Saxon American's willingness to anglicize his patronymic is far exceeded by his eagerness to give "American" baptismal names to his children. The favorite given names of the old country almost disappear in the first native-born generation. The Irish immigrants quickly dropped such names as *Terence, Dennis* and *Patrick,* and adopted in their places the less conspicuous *John, George* and *William.* The Germans, in the same way, abandoned *Otto, August, Hermann, Ludwig, Heinrich, Wolfgang, Al-*

[39] *Vide* Who's Who Year Book for 1917, pp. 74-82.

brecht, *Wilhelm, Kurt, Hans, Rudolf, Gottlieb, Johann* and *Franz.* For some of these they substituted the English equivalents: *Charles, Lewis, Henry, William, John, Frank,* and so on. In the room of others they began afflicting their offspring with more fanciful native names: *Milton* and *Raymond* were their chief favorites thirty or forty years ago.[40] The Jews carry the thing to great lengths. At present they seem to take most delight in *Sidney, Irving, Milton, Roy, Stanley* and *Monroe,* but they also call their sons *John, Charles, Henry, Harold, William, Richard, James, Albert, Edward, Alfred, Frederick, Thomas,* and even *Mark, Luke,* and *Matthew,*[41] and their daughters *Mary, Gertrude, Estelle, Pauline, Alice* and *Edith.* As a boy I went to school with many Jewish boys. The commonest given names among them were *Isidore, Samuel, Jonas, Isaac* and *Israel.* These are seldom bestowed by the rabbis of today. In the same school were a good many German pupils, boy and girl. Some of the girls bore such fine old German given names as *Katharina, Wilhelmina, Elsa, Lotta, Ermentrude* and *Franziska.* All these have begun to disappear. The Jews have lately shown a great liking for *Lee,* a Southern given name. It has almost displaced *Leon* and *Leopold,* just as it has been substituted for *Li* among the Chinese.

The newer immigrants, indeed, do not wait for the birth of children to demonstrate their naturalization; they change their own given names immediately they land. I am told by Abraham Cahan that this is done almost universally on the East Side of New York.

[40] The one given name that they have clung to is *Karl.* This, in fact, has been adopted by Americans of other stocks, nearly always, however, spelled *Carl.* Such combinations as *Carl* Gray, *Carl* Williams and even *Carl* Murphy are common. Here intermarriage has doubtless had its effect. A variant, *Karle,* has appeared, and I suspect that *Carl* has helped to popularize *Carlo, Carlyle* and *Carleton.* Simon Newton (see the *World* Almanac for 1921, p. 150) lately sought to determine the most popular American given names by examining 100,000 names in biographical dictionaries, Army and Navy registers, Masonic rosters and the Detroit City Directory. He found that *John, William, James, George* and *Charles* were the most popular, in the order named, but that *Carl* was thirty-eighth, and ahead of *Ernest, Michael, Lewis* and *Hugh,* all of which would have been far above it on an English list.
[41] One recalls Montague Glass' DeWitt C. Feinberg and Kent J. Goldstein. In the New York Telephone Directory I find the following given names borne by gentlemen of the name of Cohen: Alexander, Archie, Arthur, Bert, Clarence, Davis, De Witt, Edgar, Edward, Edwin, Eliot, Frank, Godfrey, Harold, Harvey, Herbert, Irving, Jacques, James, Jerome, John, Julian, Lawrence, Mark, Martin, Matthew, Maxwell, Milton, Murry, Nathaniel, Noel, Norman, Oscar, Paul, Philip, Ralph, Robert, Sanford, Sidney, Thomas, Victor, Walter, William.

"Even the most old-fashioned Jews immigrating to this country," he says, "change *Yosel* to *Joseph*, *Yankel* to *Jacob*, *Liebel* to *Louis*, *Feivel* to *Philip*, *Itzik* to *Isaac*, *Ruven* to *Robert*, and *Moise* or *Motel* to *Morris*." Moreover, the spelling of *Morris*, as the position of its bearer improves, commonly changes to *Maurice*, though the pronunciation may remain *Mawruss*, as in the case of Mr. Perlmutter. The immigrants of other stocks follow the same habit. The Italian *Giuseppe* quickly becomes *Joseph* and his brother *Francesco* is as quickly transformed into *Frank*. The Greek *Athanasios* is changed to *Nathan* or *Tom*, *Panagiotis* to *Peter*, *Constantine* to *Gus*, *Demetrios* to *James*, *Chasalambos* to *Charles* and *Vasilios* (*Basil*) to *Bill*. The Dutch *Dirk* becomes *Dick*, *Klaas* becomes *Clarence* or *Claude*, *Gerrit* becomes *Garrett* or *Garritt*, *Mina* becomes *Minnie*, *Neeltje* becomes *Nellie*, *Barend* becomes *Barney*, *Maarten* becomes *Martin*, *Arie* becomes *Arthur*, and *Douwe* becomes *Dewey*.[42] The Polish *Stanislav* is changed to *Stanley*, *Czeslan* to *Chester*, and *Kazimierz* to *Casey*.[43] Every Bohemian *Jaroslav* becomes *Jerry*, every *Bronislav* a *Barney*, every *Stanislav* a *Stanley* and every *Vaclav* or *Vojtech* a *William*.[44] The Hungarians and the Balkan peoples run to *Frank*, *John* and *Joe;* the Russians quickly drop their national system of nomenclature and give their children names according to the American plan. Even the Chinese laundrymen of the big cities become *John*, *George*, *Charlie* and *Frank;* I once encountered one boasting the name of *Emil*.

The Puritan influence, in names as in ideas, has remained a good deal more potent in America than in England. The given name of the celebrated *Praise-God* Barebone marked a fashion which died out in England very quickly, but one still finds traces of it in America, *e. g.*, in such women's names as *Faith*, *Hope*, *Prudence*, *Charity* and *Mercy*, and in such men's names as *Peregrine*.[45] The

---

[42] Here I am again indebted to Mr. S. S. Lontos and to Profs. Van Andel and Kuiper.
[43] Kindly communicated by Dr. C. H. Wachtel, editor of the Polish *Dziennick Chicagoski*.
[44] But I am informed by Judge J. C. Ruppenthal that the Bohemians of Central Kansas change *Vaclav* into *James*.
[45] *Cf.* Curiosities of Puritan Nomenclature, by Charles W. Bardsley; London, 1880. Such names, of course, were not peculiar to the English Puritans. *Cf.* the German *Gottlob*, *Gottlieb*, etc.

religious obsession of the New England colonists is also kept in
mind by the persistence of Biblical names: *Ezra, Hiram, Ezekiel,
Zechariah, Elijah, Elihu,* and so on. These names excite the derision
of the English; an American comic character, in an English play or
novel, always bears one of them. Again, the fashion of using surnames as given names is far more widespread in America than in
England. In this country, indeed, it takes on the character of a
national habit; fully three out of four eldest sons, in families of
any consideration, bear their mothers' surnames as middle names.
This fashion arose in England during the seventeenth century, and
one of its fruits was the adoption of such well-known surnames as
Stanley, Cecil, Howard, Douglas and *Duncan* as common given
names.[46] It died out over there during the eighteenth century, and
today the great majority of Englishmen bear such simple given
names as *John, Charles* and *William*—often four or five of them—
but in America it has persisted. A glance at a roster of the presidents of the United States will show how firmly it has taken root.
Of the eleven that have had middle names at all, six have had
middle names that were family surnames, and two of the six have
dropped their other given names and used these surnames. This
custom, perhaps, has paved the way for another: that of making
given names of any proper nouns that happen to strike the fancy.
Thus General Sherman was named after an Indian chief, *Tecumseh,*
and a Chicago judge was baptized *Kenesaw Mountain* [47] in memory
of the battle that General Sherman fought there. A late candidate
for governor of New York had the curious given name of *D-Cady,*
and a late American ethnologist, McGee, always insisted that his
first name was simply *W J,* and that these letters were not initials
and should not be followed by periods.[48] Various familiar American
given names, originally surnames, are almost unknown in England,
among them, *Washington, Jefferson, Jackson, Lincoln, Columbus*
and *Lee. Chauncey* forms a curious addition to the list. It was

[46] *Cf.* Bardsley, *op. cit.,* p. 205 *ff.*
[47] The Geographic Board has lately decided that *Kenesaw* should be *Kennesaw,* but the learned jurist sticks to one *n.*
[49] Thornton reprints a paragraph from the *Congressional Globe* of June 15, 1854, alleging that in 1846, during the row over the Oregon boundary, when "Fifty-four forty or fight" was a political slogan, many "canal-boats, and even some of the babies, . . . were christened *54° 40'.*"

the surname of the second president of Harvard College, and was bestowed upon their offspring by numbers of his graduates. It then got into general use and acquired a typically American pronunciation, with the *a* of the first syllable flat. It is never encountered in England.

Americans, in general, manifest a much freer spirit in the invention of new given names than the English, who remain faithful, in the main, to the biblical and historical names. Dr. Louise Pound, that most alert observer of American speech-habits, lists some very curious coinages,[49] among them the blends, *Olouise* (from *Olive* and *Louise*), *Marjette* (*Marjorie* + *Henrietta*), *Maybeth* (*May* + *Elizabeth*), *Lunette* (*Luna* + *Nettie*), *Leilabeth* (*Leila* + *Elizabeth*), *Rosella* (*Rose* + *Bella*), *Adrielle* (*Adrienne* + *Belle*), *Birdene* (*Birdie* + *Pauline*), *Bethene* (*Elizabeth* + *Christine*), *Olabelle* (*Ola* + *Isabel*), and *Armina* (*Ardelia* + *Wilhelmina*). Even surnames and men's given names are employed in these feminine blends, as in *Romiette* (*Romeo* + *Juliette*), *Adnelle* (*Addison* + *Nellie*), *Adelloyd* (*Addie* + *Lloyd*), and *Charline* (*Charles* + *Pauline*). A woman professor in the Middle West has the given name of *Eldarema*, coined from those of her grandparents, *Elkanah, Daniel, Rebecca* and *Mary*. In some parts of the United States, particularly south of the Potomac, men's given names are quite as fantastic. *Hoke, Ollie* and *Champ* are familiar to students of latter-day political history In the mountains of Tennessee one encounters such prodigies as *Lute, Bink, Ott* and *Gin*. The negroes, like the white immigrants, have a great liking for fancy given names. The old-time *Janes, 'Lizas* and *Jinnies* have almost disappeared. Among the ladies of color who have passed through my kitchen in Baltimore during the past twenty years have been *Geneva, Nicholine, Leah, Celeste, Evelyn, Olivia, Blanche, Isabelle, Dellott, Irene* and *Violet*.

In the pronunciation of various given names, as in that of many surnames, English and American usages differ. *Evelyn*, in England, is given two syllables instead of three, and the first is made to rhyme with *leave*. *Irene* is given three syllables, making it *Irene-y*. *Ralph* is pronounced *Rafe*. *Jerome* is accented on the first syllable; in

---

[49] Stunts in Language, *English Journal*, Feb., 1920, p. 92; Blends, *Anglistische Forschungen*, heft 42, p. 16.

PROPER NAMES IN AMERICA 343

America it is always accented on the second.[50] In diminutives there are several differences. The English *Jem* is almost unknown in the United States and so are *Hal* and *Alf*. The English, on the other hand, seldom use *Peggy, Teddy* or *Beth*. In general there has been a tendency to drop diminutives. When I was a boy it was rare, at least in the South, to hear such names as *Charles, William, Elizabeth, Frederick, Margaret* and *Lillian* used in full, but now it is very common. This new custom, I believe, owes something to English example.[51]

3.

Geographical Names

"There is no part of the world," said Robert Louis Stevenson, "where nomenclature is so rich, poetical, humorous and picturesque as in the United States of America." A glance at the latest United States Official Postal Guide [52] or report of the United States Geographic Board [53] quite bears out this opinion. The map of the country is besprinkled with place names from at least half a hundred languages, living and dead, and among them one finds examples of the most daring and elaborate fancy. There are Spanish, French and Indian names as melodious and charming as running water; there are names out of the histories and mythologies of all the great races of man; there are names grotesque and names almost sublime. "Mississippi!" rhapsodized Walt Whitman; "the word winds with chutes—it rolls a stream three thousand miles long. . . . Mononga-

[50] The Irish present some curious variants. Thus, they divide *Charles* into two syllables. The man who founded the St. Louis *Republic*, in 1808, was an Irishman named *Charles*. He pronounced his name in two syllables. But his neighbors would not, so he added another *s*. Then he was known as *Charless*.
[51] A rather curious device, apparently confined to Maryland, is that of distinguishing between two relatives (usually cousins) of the same surname and given name by adding the initials of their fathers' given names. Thus, if two cousins are both named *John Brown*, the one being the son of Richard and the other of Thomas, the first becomes John Brown *of R.* and the second John Brown *of T.*
[52] Issued annually in July, with monthly supplements.
[53] The report here used is the fourth, covering the period 1890-1916; Washington, 1916. The fifth was published in 1921.

hela! it rolls with venison richness upon the palate." No other country can match our geographical names for interest and variety. When there arises among us a philologist who will study them as thoroughly and intelligently as the Swiss, Johann Jakob Egli, studied the place names of Central Europe, his work will be an invaluable contribution to the history of the nation, and no less to an understanding of the psychology of its people.[54]

The original English settlers, it would appear, displayed little imagination in naming the new settlements and natural features of the land that they came to. Their almost invariable tendency, at the start, was to make use of names familiar at home, or to invent banal compounds. *Plymouth Rock* at the North and *Jamestown* at the South are examples of their poverty of fancy; they filled the narrow tract along the coast with new *Bostons, Cambridges, Bristols* and *Londons,* and often used the adjective as a prefix. But this was only in the days of beginning. Once they had begun to move back from the coast and to come into contact with the aborigines and with the widely dispersed settlers of other races, they encountered rivers, mountains, lakes and even towns that bore far more engaging names, and these, after some resistance, they perforce adopted. The native names of such rivers as the *James,* the *York* and the *Charles* succumbed, but those of the *Potomac,* the *Patapsco,* the *Merrimac* and the *Penobscot* survived, and they were gradually reinforced as the country was penetrated. Most of these Indian names, in getting upon the early maps, suffered somewhat severe simplifications. *Potowanmeac* was reduced to *Potomack* and then to *Potomac; Unéaukara* became *Niagara; Reckawackes,* by the law of Hobson-Jobson, was turned into *Rockaway,* and *Pentapang* into *Port Tobacco.*[55] But, despite such elisions and transformations, the charm of thousands of them remained, and today they are responsible for much of the characteristic color of American geographical nomenclature. Such names as *Tallahassee, Susquehanna, Mississippi, Allegheny,*

[54] No such general investigation has been attempted, though a good deal of material for it is assembled in the Origin of Certain Place Names in the United States, by Henry Gannett, 2nd ed.; Washington, 1905, and in A History of the Origin of the Place Names in Nine Northwestern States, 2nd ed.; Chicago, 1908.

[55] The authority here is River and Lake Names in the United States, by Edmund T. Ker; New York, 1911. Stephen G. Boyd, in Indian Local Names; York (Pa.), 1885, says that the original Indian name was *Pootuppag.*

Chicago, Kennebec, Patuxent and Kalamazoo give a barbaric brilliancy to the American map. Only the map of Australia can match it. The settlement of the American continent, once the eastern coast ranges were crossed, proceeded with unparalleled speed, and so the naming of the new rivers, lakes, peaks and valleys, and of the new towns and districts no less, strained the inventiveness of the pioneers. The result is the vast duplication of names that shows itself in the Postal Guide. No less than eighteen imitative *Bostons* and *New Bostons* still appear, and there are nineteen *Bristols*, twenty-eight *Newports*, and twenty-two *Londons* and *New Londons*. Argonauts starting out from an older settlement on the coast would take its name with them, and so we find *Philadelphias* in Illinois, Mississippi, Missouri and Tennessee, *Richmonds* in Iowa, Kansas and nine other western states, and *Princetons* in fifteen. Even when a new name was hit upon it seems to have been hit upon simultaneously by scores of scattered bands of settlers; thus we find the whole land bespattered with *Washingtons, Lafayettes, Jeffersons* and *Jacksons,* and with names suggested by common and obvious natural objects, e. g., *Bear Creek, Bald Knob* and *Buffalo*. The Geographic Board, in its fourth report, made a belated protest against this excessive duplication. "The names *Elk, Beaver, Cottonwood* and *Bald,*" it said, "are altogether too numerous." Of postoffices alone there are fully a hundred embodying *Elk;* counting in rivers, lakes, creeks, mountains and valleys, the map of the United States probably shows at least twice as many such names.

A study of American geographical and place names reveals eight general classes, as follows: (a) those embodying personal names, chiefly the surnames of pioneers or of national heroes; (b) those transferred from other and older places, either in the eastern states or in Europe; (c) Indian names; (d) Dutch, Spanish, French, German and Scandinavian names; (e) Biblical and mythological names; (f) names descriptive of localities; (g) names suggested by the local flora, fauna or geology; (h) purely fanciful names. The names of the first class are perhaps the most numerous. Some consist of surnames standing alone, as *Washington, Cleveland, Bismarck, Lafayette, Taylor* and *Randolph;* others consist of surnames in combination with various old and new *Grundwörter,* as *Pittsburgh, Knoxville, Bailey's Switch, Hagerstown, Franklinton, Dodge City, Fort Riley, Wayne Junction* and *McKeesport;* and yet others are contrived of given names, either alone or in combination, as *Louisville, St. Paul, Elizabeth, Johnstown, Charlotte, Williamsburg* and *Marysville.* All our great cities are surrounded by grotesque *Bensonhursts, Bryn Joneses, Smithvales* and *Krauswoods.* The number of towns in the United States bearing women's given names is enormous. I find, for example, eleven postoffices called *Charlotte,* ten called *Ada* and no less than nineteen called *Alma.* Most of these places are small, but there is an *Elizabeth* with 75,000 population, an *Elmira* with 40,000, and an *Augusta* with nearly 45,000.

The names of the second class we have already briefly observed. They are betrayed in many cases by the prefix *New;* more than 600 such postoffices are recorded, ranging from *New Albany* to *New Windsor.* Others bear such prefixes as *West, North* and *South,* or various distinguishing affixes, e. g., *Bostonia, Pittsburgh Landing, Yorktown* and *Hartford City.* One often finds eastern county names applied to western towns and eastern town names applied to western rivers and mountains. Thus, *Cambria,* which is the name of a county but not of a postoffice in Pennsylvania, is a town in seven western states; *Baltimore* is the name of a glacier in Alaska, and *Princeton* is the name of a peak in Colorado. In the same way the names of the more easterly states often reappear in the west, e. g., in *Mount Ohio,* Colo., *Delaware,* Okla., and *Virginia City,* Nev. The tendency to name small American towns after the great capitals of antiquity has excited the derision of the English since the earliest days; there is scarcely an English book upon the states without some fling at it. Of late it has fallen into abeyance, though sixteen *Athenses* still remain, and there are yet many *Carthages, Uticas, Syracuses, Romes, Alexandrias, Ninevehs* and *Troys.* The third city of the nation, *Philadelphia,* got its name from the ancient stronghold of Philadelphus of Pergamon. To make up for the falling off of this old and flamboyant custom, the more recent immigrants have brought with them the names of the capitals and other great cities of their fatherlands. Thus the American map bristles with *Berlins, Bremens, Hamburgs, Warsaws* and *Leipzigs,* and is

PROPER NAMES IN AMERICA 347

beginning to show *Stockholms, Venices, Belgrades* and *Christianias*.[56] The influence of Indian names upon American nomenclature is quickly shown by a glance at the map. No fewer than 26 of the states have names borrowed from the aborigines,[57] and the same thing is true of most of our rivers and mountains, and of large numbers of our towns and counties.[58] There was an effort, at one time, to get rid of these Indian names. Thus the early Virginians changed the name of the *Powhatan* to the *James*, and the first settlers in New York changed the name of *Horicon* to *Lake George*. In the same way the present name of the *White* Mountains displaced *Agiochook*, and *New Amsterdam*, and later *New York*, displaced *Manhattan*, which has been recently revived. The law of Hobson-Jobson made changes in other Indian names, sometimes complete and some-

[56] *Cf.* Amerikanska Ortnamn af Svenskt Ursprung, by V. Berger; New York, 1915. The Swedish names listed by Mr. Berger are chiefly to be found in Minnesota, Iowa, Kansas, Nebraska and the Dakotas.
[57] In most of the states local antiquaries have investigated the state names. Vide, for example, The Origin and Meaning of the Name California, by George Davidson; San Francisco, 1910; California, the Name, by Ruth Putnam; Berkeley, 1917; Arizona, Its Derivation and Origin, by Merrill P. Freeman; Tucson, 1913; Ohio, 1803-1903, by Maria Ewing Martin; New Straitsville, 1903; The Naming of Indiana, by Cyrus W. Hodgin; Richmond (Ind.), 1903; Idaho, Its Meaning, Origin and Application, by John E. Rees; Portland (Ore.), 1917.
[58] The student interested in the subject will find useful information in The History and Geography of Texas as Told in County Names, by Z. T. Fulmore; Austin, 1915; Spanish and Indian Place Names of California, by Nellie van de Grift Sanchez; San Francisco, 1914; The Powhatan Name for Virginia, by W. W. Tooker, *American Anthropologist*, vol. viii, no. 1, 1906; Chicago: Origin of the Name of Our City, by J. F. Steward; Chicago, 1904; Some More About Virginia Names, by W. W. Tooker, *American Anthropologist*, vol. vii, no. 3, 1905; The Origin of the Name of Buffalo, by Wm. Ketchum, *Pub. Buffalo Hist. Society*, vol. i, p. 17, 1879; The Origin of the Name Manhattan, by W. W. Tooker; New York, 1901; British Columbia Coast Names, by John D. Walbran; Ottawa, 1909; Place-Names in the Thousand Islands, by James White; Ottawa, 1910; Minnesota Geographic Names, by Warren Upham, *Collections of the Minnesota Hist. Society*, vol. xvii, 1920; Indian Names of Water Courses in the State of Indiana, by H. W. Beckwith (in Annual Report, Dept. of Geology and Natural History; Indianapolis, 1883); Origin of Ohio Place-Names, by Maria E. Martin, *Ohio Archæological and Historical Quarterly*, vol. xiv, p. 272; Origin and Meaning of Wisconsin Place-Names, by Henry E. Legler, *Tr. of the Wisconsin Academy of Sciences, Arts and Letters*, vol. xiv, pt. i, 1903; Geographical Names on the Coast of Maine, by Edward Ballard (in Report of the Coast Survey; Washington, 1868); Baraboo and Other Place-Names in Sauk County, Wisconsin, by H. E. Cole; Baraboo, 1912; Names of Places of Interest on Mackinac Island, by Frank A. O'Brien; Lansing (Mich.), 1916; The Niagara Frontier, by Orsamus H. Marshall; Buffalo, 1881; How Missouri Counties, Towns and Streams Were Named, by David W. Eaton; Columbia (Mo.), 1917; Indian Place-Names, by Moses Greenleaf; Bangor (Me.), 1903; The Composition of Indian Geographical Names, by J. Hammond Trumbull, *Collections of the Connecticut Hist. Society*, vol. ii, p. 1, 1870; The Indian Place-Names on Long

times only partial. Thus, *Mauwauwaming* became *Wyoming*, *Maucwachoong* became *Mauch Chunk*, *Ouabache* became *Wabash*, *Asingsing* became *Sing-Sing*, and *Machihiganing* became *Michigan*. But this vandalism did not go far enough to take away the brilliant color of the aboriginal nomenclature.[59] The second city of the United States bears an Indian name, and so do the largest American river, and the greatest American water-fall, and four of the five Great Lakes, and the scene of the most important military decision ever reached on American soil.

The Dutch place-names of the United States are chiefly confined to the vicinity of New York, and a good many of them have become greatly corrupted. *Brooklyn*, *Wallabout* and *Gramercy* offer examples. The first-named was originally *Breuckelen*, the second was *Waale Bobht*, and the third was *De Kromme Zee*. *Hell-Gate* is a crude translation of the Dutch *Helle-Gat*. During the early part of the last century the more delicate New Yorkers transformed the term into *Hurlgate*, but the change was vigorously opposed by Washington Irving, and so *Hell-Gate* was revived. The law of Hobson-Jobson early converted the Dutch *hoek* into *hook*, and it survives in various place-names, *e. g., Kinderhook* and *Sandy Hook*. The Dutch *kill* is a *Grundwort* in many other names, *e. g., Catskill, Schuylkill, Peeks-*

Island, by W. W. Tooker; New York, 1911; Indian Names of Places in ... Massachusetts, by Lincoln N. Kinnicutt; Worcester, 1909; Indian Names of Places in and on the Borders of Connecticut, by J. Hammond Trumbull; Hartford, 1881; Dictionary of American-Indian Place and Proper Names in New England, by R. A. Douglas-Lithgow; Salem (Mass.), 1909; California Place-Names of Indian Origin, by A. L. Kroeber; Berkeley, 1916; Indian Names of Places in Rhode Island, by Usher Parsons; Providence, 1861; Indian Geographic Names of Indian Origin, by A. L. Kroeber; Berkeley, 1916; Indian Names of Places Near the Great Lakes, by Dwight H. Kelton; Detroit, 1888; The Indian Names of Boston, by Eben N. Horsford; Cambridge, 1886; Footprints of the Red Men, by E. M. Ruttenber; Newburgh (N. Y.), 1906; Indian Names of Places in Worcester County, Mass., by Lincoln N. Kinnicutt; Worcester, 1905; Indian Names and History of the Sault Ste. Marie Canal, by Dwight H. Kelton; Detroit, 1889; Proper Names from the Muskhogean Languages, by Noxon Toomey; St. Louis, 1917; Report of the Aboriginal Names and Geographical Terminology of the State of New York, by Henry R. Schoolcraft, pt. i; New York, 1845. Other works are listed in the Bibliography.

[59] Walt Whitman bitterly opposed such changes. He even demanded that Indian names be substituted for names of other origin. "California," he said, "is sown thick with the names of big and little saints. Chase them away and substitute aboriginal names. ... No country can have its own poems without having its own names. The name of *Niagara* should be substituted for *St. Lawrence*. Among the places that stand in need of fresh, appropriate names are the great cities of *St. Louis, New Orleans, St. Paul*."

kill, Fishkill and *Kill van Kull;* it is the equivalent of the American *creek.* Many other Dutch place-names will come familiarly to mind: *Harlem, Staten, Flushing, Cortlandt, Calver, Plaat, Nassau, Coenties, Spuyten Duyvel, Yonkers, Barnegat, Bowery* (from *Bouvery*).[60] *Block* Island was originally *Blok,* and *Cape May,* according to Schele de Vere, was *Mey,* both Dutch. A large number of New York street and neighborhood names come down from Knickerbocker days, often greatly changed in pronunciation. *Desbrosses* offers an example. The Dutch called it *de Broose,* but in New York today it is commonly spoken of as *Des-bros-sez.*

French place-names have suffered almost as severely. Few persons would recognize *Smackover,* the name of a small town in Arkansas, as French, and yet in its original form it was *Chemin Couvert.*[61] Schele de Vere, in 1871, recorded the degeneration of the name to *Smack Cover;* the Postoffice, always eager to shorten and simplify names, has since made one word of it and got rid of the redundant *c.* In the same way *Bob Ruly,* a Missouri name, descends from *Bois Brulé; Glazypool,* the name of an Arkansas mountain, from *Glaise à Paul; Low Freight,* the name of an Arkansas river, from *L'Eau Froid,* and *Baraboo* from *Baribault.* "The American tongue," says W. W. Crane, "seems to lend itself reluctantly to the words of alien languages." [62] A large number of French place-names, *e. g., Lac Supérieur,* were translated into English at an early day, and most of those that remain are now pronounced as if they were English. Thus *Des Moines* is *dee-moyns, Terre Haute* is *terry-hut, Beaufort* is *byu-fort* in South Carolina (but *bo-fort* in North Carolina!). *New Orleans* is *or-leens, Bonne Terre,* an old town near St. Louis, is *bonnie tar, Lafayette* has a flat *a, Havre de Grace* has another, and *Versailles* is *ver-sales.* The pronunciation of *sault,* as in *Sault Ste. Marie,* is commonly more or less correct; the Minneapolis, St. Paul and Sault Ste. Marie Railroad is popularly called the *Soo.* This may be due to Canadian example, or to some confusion between *Sault* and *Sioux.* The French *Louis,* in *Louisville,* is usually pro-

[60] *Cf.* Dutch Contributions to the Vocabulary of English in America, by W. H. Carpenter, *Modern Philology,* July, 1908.
[61] *Cf.* Some Old French Place-Names in the State of Arkansas, by John C. Branner, *Modern Language Notes,* vol. xiv, no. 2, 1899.
[62] Our Naturalized Names, *Lippincott's Magazine,* April, 1899.

nounced correctly, but in *St. Louis* it is almost always converted into *Lewis*. The *rouge* in *Baton Rouge* is correctly pronuonced, though the *baton* is commonly boggled. The local pronunciation of *Illinois* is *Illinoy,* an attempt to improve upon the vulgar *Illin-i*.

For a number of years the Geographic Board has been seeking vainly to reëstablish the correct pronunciation of the name of the *Purgatoire* river in Colorado. Originally named the *Rio de las Animas* by the Spaniards, it was renamed the *Rivière du Purgatoire* by their French successors. The American pioneers changed this to *Picketwire,* and that remains the local name of the stream to this day, despite the effort of the Geographic Board to compromise on *Purgatoire* river. Many other French names are being anglicized with its aid and consent. Already half a dozen *Bellevues* have been changed to *Belleviews* and *Bellviews,* and the spelling of nearly all the *Belvédères* has been changed to *Belvidere*. *Belair,* La., represents the end-product of a process of decay which began with *Belle Aire,* and then proceeded to *Bellaire* and *Bellair*. All these forms are still to be found, together with *Bel Air*. The Geographic Board's antipathy to accented letters and to names of more than one word [63] has converted *Isle Ste. Thérèse,* in the St. Lawrence river, to *Isle Ste. Therese,* a truly abominable barbarism, and *La Cygne,* in Kansas, to *Lacygne,* which is even worse.[64] *Lamoine, Labelle, Lagrange* and *Lamonte* are among its other improvements; *Lafayette,* for *La Fayette,* long antedates the beginning of its labors.

The Spanish names of the Southwest are undergoing a like process of corruption, though without official aid. *San Antonio* has changed to *San Antone* in popular pronunciation and seems likely to go to *San Tone; El Paso* has acquired a flat American *a* and a *z*-sound in place of the Spanish *s; Los Angeles* presents such difficulties that no two of its inhabitants agree upon the proper pronunciation, and many compromise on simple *Los,* as the folks of *Jacksonville* com-

[63] *Vide* its fourth report (1890-1916), p. 15.
[64] A correspondent writes: "The river on which the town is located was named by French explorers, late in the 18th century, *Marais des Cygnes*. When the town site was bought from the Miami Indians, about 1868, the town was named *La Cygne*. The railroad, built soon after, put the name in its time tables as *Les Cygnes*. My father started the *Journal* there in 1870. He persuaded the railroad people to change their spelling. The Postal Guide still gives it as *La Cygne*. It is usually pronounced *Lay Seen*."

monly call their town *Jax*. Some of the most mellifluous of American place-names are in the areas once held by the Spaniards. It would be hard to match the beauty of *Santa Margarita, San Anselmo, Alamogordo, Terra Amarilla, Sabinoso, Las Palomas, Ensenada, Nogales, San Patricio* and *Bernalillo*. But they are under a severe and double assault. Not only do the present lords of the soil debase them in speaking them; in many cases they are formally displaced by native names of the utmost harshness and banality. Thus, one finds in New Mexico such absurdly-named towns as *Sugarite, Shoemaker, Newhope, Lordsburg, Eastview* and *Central;* in Arizona such places as *Old Glory, Springville, Wickenburg* and *Congress Junction,* and even in California such abominations as *Oakhurst, Ben Hur, Drytown, Skidoo, Susanville, Uno* and *Ono.*

The early Spaniards were prodigal with place-names testifying to their piety, but these names, in the overwhelming main, were those of saints. Add *Salvador, Trinidad* and *Concepcion,* and their repertoire is almost exhausted. If they ever named a town *Jesus* the name has been obliterated by Anglo-Saxon prudery; even their use of the name as a personal appellation violates American notions of the fitting. The names of the Jewish patriarchs and those of the holy places in Palestine do not appear among their place-names; their Christianity seems to have been exclusively of the New Testament. But the Americans who displaced them were intimately familiar with both books of the Bible, and one finds copious proofs of it on the map of the United States. There are no less than eleven *Beulahs,* nine *Canaans,* eleven *Jordans* and twenty-one *Sharons. Adam* is sponsor for a town in West Virginia and an island in the Chesapeake, and *Eve* for a village in Kentucky. There are five postoffices named *Aaron,* two named *Abraham,* two named *Job,* and a town and a lake names *Moses.* Most of the *St. Pauls* and *St. Josephs* of the country were inherited from the French, but the two *St. Patricks* show a later influence. Eight *Wesleys* and *Wesleyvilles,* eight *Asburys* and twelve names embodying *Luther* indicate the general theological trend of the plain people. There is a village in Maryland, too small to have a postoffice, named *Gott,* and I find *Gotts Island* in Maine (in the French days, *Petite Plaisance*) and *Gottville* in California, but no doubt these were named after German settlers of that awful name, and not after the Lord God directly. There are four *Trinities*, to say nothing of the inherited *Trinidads*.

Names wholly or partly descriptive of localities are very numerous throughout the country, and among the *Grundwörter* embodied in them are terms highly characteristic of American and almost unknown to the English vocabulary. *Bald Knob* would puzzle an Englishman, but the name is so common in the United States that the Geographic Board has had to take measures against it. Others of that sort are *Council Bluffs, Patapsco Neck, Delaware Water Gap, Curtis Creek, Walden Pond, Sandy Hook, Key West, Bull Run, Portage, French Lick, Jones Gulch, Watkins Gully, Cedar Bayou, Keams Canyon, Parker Notch, Sucker Branch, Fraziers Bottom* and *Eagle Pass. Butte Creek*, in Montana, is a name made up of two Americanisms. There are thirty-five postoffices whose names embody the word *prairie*, several of them, *e. g., Prairie du Chien*, Wis., inherited from the French. There are seven *Divides*, eight *Buttes*, eight town-names embodying the word *burnt*, innumerable names embodying *grove, barren, plain, fork, center, cross-roads, courthouse, cove* and *ferry*, and a great swarm of *Cold Springs, Coldwaters, Summits, Middletowns* and *Highlands*. The flora and fauna of the land are enormously represented. There are twenty-two *Buffalos* beside the city in New York, and scores of *Buffalo Creeks, Ridges, Springs* and *Wallows*. The *Elks*, in various forms, are still more numerous, and there are dozens of towns, mountains, lakes, creeks and country districts named after the *beaver, martin, coyote, moose* and *otter*, and as many more named after such characteristic flora as the *paw-paw*, the *sycamore*, the *cottonwood*, the *locust* and the *sunflower*. There is an *Alligator* in Mississippi, a *Crawfish* in Kentucky and a *Rat Lake* on the Canadian border of Minnesota. The endless search for mineral wealth has besprinkled the map with such names as *Bromide, Oil City, Anthracite, Chrome, Chloride, Coal Run, Goldfield, Telluride, Leadville* and *Cement*.

There was a time, particularly during the gold rush to California, when the rough humor of the country showed itself in the invention of extravagant and often highly felicitous place-names, but with the growth of population and the rise of civic spirit they have tended to be replaced by more seemly coinages. *Catfish* creek, in Wisconsin,

PROPER NAMES IN AMERICA 353

is now the *Yakara* river; the *Bulldog* mountains, in Arizona, have become the *Harosomas;* the *Picketwire* river, as we have seen, has resumed its old French name of *Purgatoire*. As with natural features of the landscape, so with towns. Nearly all the old *Boozevilles, Jackass Flats, Three Fingers, Hell-For-Sartains, Undershirt Hills, Razzle-Dazzles, Cow-Tails, Yellow Dogs, Jim-Jamses, Jump-Offs, Poker Citys* and *Skunktowns* have yielded to the growth of delicacy, but *Tombstone* still stands in Arizona, *Goose Bill* remains a postoffice in Montana, and the Geographic Board gives its imprimatur to the *Horsethief* trail in Colorado, to *Burning Bear* in the same state, and to *Pig Eye* lake in Minnesota. Various other survivors of a more lively and innocent day linger on the map: *Blue Ball*, Pa., *Cowhide*, W. Va., *Dollarville*, Mich., *Oven Fork*, Ky., *Social Circle*, Ga., *Sleepy Eye*, Minn., *Bubble*, Ark., *Shy Beaver*, Pa., *Shin Pond*, Me., *Rough-and-Ready*, Calif., *Non Intervention*, Va., *Noodle*, Tex., *Number Four*, N. Y., *Oblong*, Ill., *Stock Yards*, Neb., *Stout*, Iowa, and so on. West Virginia, the wildest of the eastern states, is full of such place-names. Among them I find *Affinity, Annamoriah (Anna Maria?), Bee, Bias, Big Chimney, Billie, Blue Jay, Bulltown, Caress, Cinderella, Cyclone, Czar, Cornstalk, Duck, Halcyon, Jingo, Left Hand, Ravens Eye, Six, Skull Run, Three Churches, Uneeda, Wide Mouth, War Eagle* and *Stumptown*. The Postal Guide shows two *Ben Hurs*, five *St. Elmos* and ten *Ivanhoes*, but only one *Middlemarch*. There are seventeen *Roosevelts*, six *Codys* and six *Barnums*, but no *Shakespeare*. *Washington*, of course, is the most popular of American place-names. But among names of postoffices it is hard pushed by *Clinton, Centerville, Liberty, Canton, Marion* and *Madison*, and even by *Springfield, Warren* and *Bismarck*.

Many American place-names are purely arbitrary coinages. Towns on the border between two states, or near the border, are often given names made of parts of the names of the two states, *e. g.*, *Pen-Mar* (*Pennsylvania+Maryland*), *Mar-Del* (*Maryland+Delaware*), *Texarkana* (*Texas+Arkansas*), *Kanorado* (*Kansas+Colorado*), *Texhoma* (*Texas+Oklahoma*), *Dakoming* (*Dakota+Wyoming*), *Texico* (*Texas+New Mexico*), *Calexico* (*California+Mexico*). *Norlina* is a telescope form of *North Carolina*. *Ohiowa* (Neb.) was named by settlers who came partly from Ohio and partly from Iowa. *Penn Yan*

(N. Y.) was named by Pennsylvanians and New Englanders, *i. e.*, Yankees. *Colwich* (Kansas) is a telescope form of the name of the Colorado and Wichita Railroad. There are two *Delmars* in the United States. The name of one is a blend of *Delaware* and *Maryland;* the name of the other (in Iowa) was "made by using the names (*i. e.*, the initials of the names) of six women who accompanied an excursion that opened the railroad from Clinton, Iowa." [65] In the same state *Le Mars* got its name in exactly the same way. *Benld* (Ill.) is a collision form of *Benjamin L. Dorsey,* the name of a local magnifico; *Cadams* (Neb.) is a collision form of *C. Adams; Wascott* (Wis.) derives from *W. A. Scott; Eleroy* (Ill.) from *E. Leroy; Bucoda* (Wash.) is a blend of *Buckley, Collier* and *Davis; Gilsum* (N. H.) is a blend of *Gilbert* and *Sumner; Paragould* (Ark.) is a blend of *W. J. Paramore* and *Jay Gould; Marenisco* (Mich.) is named after *Mary Relief Niles Scott; Miloma* (Minn.) derives its name from the first syllable of *Milwaukee,* in the name of the Milwaukee, Chicago, Minneapolis & St. Paul Railroad, and the first two syllables of *Omaha,* in the name of the Chicago, Minneapolis & Omaha Railroad; *Gerled* (Iowa) is a blend of *Germanic* and *Ledyard,* the names of two nearby townships; *Rolyat* (Ore.) is simply *Taylor* spelled backward; *Biltmore* (N. C.) is the last syllable of *Vanderbilt* plus the Gaelic *Grundwort, more.*

The Geographic Board, in its laudable effort to simplify American nomenclature, has played ducks and drakes with some of the most picturesque names on the national map. Now and then, as in the case of *Purgatoire,* it has temporarily departed from this policy, but in the main its influence has been thrown against the fine old French and Spanish names, and against the more piquant native names no less. Thus, I find it deciding against *Portage des Flacons* and in favor of the hideous *Bottle portage,* against *Cañada del Burro* and in favor of *Burro canyon,* against *Cañons y Ylas de la Cruz* and in favor of the barbarous *Cruz island.*[66] In *Boug re* landing and *Cañon City* it has deleted the accents. The name of the *De Grasse* river it has changed to *Grass. De Laux* it has changed to the intolerable *Dlo.*

[65] Louise Pound: Blends, *Anglistische Forschungen,* heft 42, p. 10.
[66] Canada goes the United States one better, with *Ste. Anne de la Boundary Line!*

And, as we have seen, it has steadily amalgamated French and Spanish articles with their nouns, thus achieving such barbarous forms as *Duchesne, Eldorado, Deleon* and *Laharpe.* But here its policy is fortunately inconsistent, and so a number of fine old names have escaped. Thus, it has decided in favor of *Bon Secours* and against *Bonsecours,* and in favor of *De Soto, La Crosse* and *La Moure,* and against *Desoto, Lacrosse* and *Lamoure.* Here its decisions are confused and often unintelligible. Why *Laporte,* Pa., and *La Porte,* Iowa? Why *Lagrange,* Ind., and *La Grange,* Ky.? Here it would seem to be yielding a great deal too much to local usage.

The Board proceeds to the shortening and simplification of native names by various devices. It deletes such suffixes as *town, city* and *courthouse;* it removes the apostrophe and often the genitive *s* from such names as *St. Mary's;* it shortens *burgh* to *burg* and *borough* to *boro;* and it combines separate and often highly discreet words. The last habit often produces grotesque forms, *e. g., Newberlin, Boxelder, Sabbathday lake, Fallentimber, Bluemountain, Westtown, Threepines* and *Missionhill.* It apparently cherishes a hope of eventually regularizing the spelling of *Allegany.* This is now *Allegany* for the Maryland county, the Pennsylvania township and the New York and Oregon towns, *Alleghany* for the mountains, the Colorado town and the Virginia town and springs, and *Allegheny* for the Pittsburgh borough and the Pennsylvania county, college and river. The Board inclines to *Allegheny* for all. Other Indian names give it constant concern. Its struggles to set up *Chemquasabamticook* as the name of a Maine lake in place of *Chemquasabamtic* and *Chemquassabamticook,* and *Chatahospee* as the name of an Alabama creek in place of *Chattahospee, Hoolethlocco, Hoolethloces, Hoolethloco* and *Hoolethlocco* are worthy of its learning and authority.[67]

The American tendency to pronounce all the syllables of a word

[67] The Geographic Board is composed of representatives of the Coast and Geodetic Survey, the Geological Survey, the General Land Office, the Post Office, the Forest Service, the Smithsonian Institution, the Biological Survey, the Government Printing Office, the Census and Lighthouse Bureaus, the General Staff of the Army, the Hydrographic Office, the Library and War Records Office of the Navy, the Treasury and the Department of State. It was created by executive order Sept. 4, 1890, and its decisions are binding upon all federal officials. It has made, to date, more than 25,000 decisions. They are recorded in reports issued at irregular intervals and in more frequent bulletins.

more distinctly than the English shows itself in geographical names. White, in 1880, [68] recorded the increasing habit of giving full value to the syllables of such borrowed English names as *Worcester* and *Warwick*. I have frequently noted the same thing. In *Worcester* county, Maryland, the name is usually pronounced *Wooster*, but on the Western Shore of the state one hears *Worcest-'r*. *Norwich* is another such name; one hears *Nor-wich* quite as often as *Norrich*. Another is *Delhi;* one often hears *Del-high*. Another is *Warwick*. Yet another is *Birmingham;* it is pronounced as spelled in the United States, and never in the English manner. White said that in his youth the name of the *Shawangunk* mountains, in New York, was pronounced *Shongo,* but that the custom of pronouncing it as spelled had arisen during his manhood. [69] So with *Winnipiseogee,* the name of a lake; once *Winipisaukie,* it gradually came to be pronounced as spelled. There is frequently a considerable difference between the pronunciation of a name by natives of a place and its pronunciation by those who are familiar with it only in print. *Baltimore* offers an example. The natives always drop the medial *i* and so reduce the name to two syllables; in addition, they substitute a neutral vowel, very short, for the *o*. *Anne Arundel,* the name of a county in Maryland, is usually pronounced *Ann'ran'l* by its people. *Arkansas,* as everyone knows, is pronounced *Arkansaw* by the Arkansans. [70] The local pronunciation of *Illinois* is *Illinoy.* *Iowa,* at home, is *Ioway*.[71] Many American geographical names offer great difficulty to Englishmen. One of my English acquaintances tells me that he was taught at school to accent *Massachusetts* on the second syllable, to rhyme the second

---

[68] Every-Day English, p. 100. See also Tucker: American English, p. 33.

[69] This pedantry seems to have disappeared. The local pronunciation today is *Shongum*. I have often noted that Americans, in speaking of the familiar *Worcestershire* sauce, commonly pronounce every syllable and enunciate *shire* distinctly. In England it is always *Woostersh'r*. The English have a great number of decayed pronunciations, *e. g., Maudlin* for *Magdalen College, Sister* for *Cirencester, Merrybone* for *Marylebone*. Their geographical nomenclature shows many corruptions due to faulty pronunciation and the law of Hobson-Jobson, *e. g., Leighton Buzzard* for the Norman *Leiton Beau Desart*.

[70] *Vide* Proceedings of the Legislature and of the Historical Society of the State of Arkansas, and the Eclectic Society, of Little Rock, Ark., Fixing the Pronunciation of the Name Arkansas; Little Rock, 1881.

[71] Curiously enough, Americans always use the broad *a* in the first syllable of *Albany,* whereas Englishmen rhyme the syllable with *pal*. The Londoners pronounce *Pall Mall* as if it were spelled *pell-mell*. Americans commonly give it two broad *a*'s.

syllable of *Ohio* with *tea,* and to sound the second *c* in *Connecticut.* In Maryland the name of *Calvert* county is given a broad *a,* whereas the name of *Calvert* street, in Baltimore, has a flat *a.* This curious distinction is almost always kept up. A Scotchman, coming to America, would give the *ch* in such names as *Loch Raven* and *Lochvale* the guttural Scotch (and German) sound, but locally it is always pronounced as if it were *k.*

Finally, there is a curious difference between English and American usage in the use of the word *river.* The English invariably put it before the proper name, whereas we almost as invariably put it after. *The Thames River* would seem quite as strange to an Englishman as *the river Chicago* would seem to us. This difference arose more than a century ago and was noticed by Pickering. But in his day the American usage was still somewhat uncertain, and such forms as *the river Mississippi* were yet in use. Today *river* almost always goes after the proper name.

4.

Street Names

"Such a locality as 'the *corner of Avenue H and Twenty-third street,*'" says W. W. Crane, "is about as distinctly American as Algonquin and Iroquois names like *Mississippi* and *Saratoga.*" [72] Kipling, in his "American Notes," [73] gives testimony to the strangeness with which the number-names, the phrase "the corner of," and the custom of omitting *street* fall upon the ear of a Britisher. He quotes with amazement certain directions given to him on his arrival in San Francisco from India: "Go six blocks north to [the] corner of Geary and Markey [Market?]; then walk around till you strike [the] corner of Sutter and Sixteenth." The English always add the word *street* (or *road* or *place* or *avenue*) when speaking of a thoroughfare; such a phrase as *"Oxford* and *New Bond"* would strike them as in-

[72] Our Street Names, *Lippincott's Magazine,* Aug., 1897, p. 264.
[73] Ch. i.

congruous. The American custom of numbering and lettering streets is almost always ascribed by English writers who discuss it, not to a desire to make finding them easy, but to sheer poverty of invention. The English apparently have an inexhaustible fund of names for streets; they often give one street more than one name. Thus, *Oxford* street, London, becomes the *Bayswater* road, *High* street, *Holland Park* avenue, *Goldhawke* road and finally the *Oxford* road to the westward, and *High Holborn, Holborn* viaduct, *Newgate* street, *Cheapside,* the *Poultry, Cornhill* and *Leadenhall* street to the eastward. The *Strand,* in the same way, becomes *Fleet* street, *Ludgate* hill and *Cannon* street. Nevertheless, there is a *First* avenue in Queen's Park, London, and parallel to it are *Second, Third, Fourth, Fifth* and *Sixth* avenues—all small streets leading northward from the Harrow road, just east of Kensal Green cemetery. I have observed that few Londoners have ever heard of them. There is also a *First* street in Chelsea—a very modest thoroughfare near Lennox Gardens and not far from the Brompton Oratory.

Next to the numbering and lettering of streets, a fashion apparently set up by Major Pierre-Charles L'Enfant's plans for Washington, the most noticeable feature of American street nomenclature, as opposed to that of England, is the extensive use of such designations as *avenue, boulevard, drive* and *speedway. Avenue* is used in England, but only rather sparingly; it is seldom applied to a mean street, or to one in a warehouse district. In America the word is scarcely distinguished in meaning from *street.*[74] *Boulevard, drive* and *speedway* are almost unknown to the English, but they use *road* for urban thoroughfares, which is very seldom done in America, and they also make free use of *place, walk, passage, lane* and *circus,* all of which are obsolescent on this side of the ocean. Some of the older American cities, such as Boston and Baltimore, have surviving certain ancient English designations of streets, *e. g., Cheapside* and *Cornhill;* these are unknown in the newer American towns. *Broadway,* which is also

[74] There are, of course, local exceptions. In Baltimore, for example, *avenue* used to be reserved for wide streets in the suburbs. Thus Charles *street*, on passing the old city boundary, became Charles *street-avenue.* Further out it became Charles *street-avenue-road*—probably a unique triplication. But that was years ago. Of late many fifth-rate streets in Baltimore have been changed into avenues.

English, is more common. Many American towns now have *plazas,* which are unknown in England. Nearly all have *City Hall parks, squares* or *places; City Hall* is also unknown over there. The principal street of a small town, in America, is almost always *Main* street; in England it is as invariably *High* street, usually with the definite article before *High.*

I have mentioned the corruption of old Dutch street and neighborhood names in New York. Spanish names are corrupted in the same way in the Southwest and French names in the Great Lakes region and in Louisiana. In New Orleans the street names, many of them strikingly beautiful, are pronounced so barbarously by the people that a Frenchman would have difficulty recognizing them. Thus, *Bourbon* has become *Bur-bun, Dauphine* is *Daw-fin, Foucher* is *Foosh'r, Enghien* is *En-gine,* and *Felicity* (originally *F licité*) is *Fill-a-city.* The French, in their day, bestowed the names of the Muses upon certain of the city streets. They are now pronounced *Cal-y-ope, Terp-si-chore, Mel-po-mean, You-terp,* and so on. *Bons Enfants,* apparently too difficult for the native, has been translated into *Good Children.* Only *Esplanade* and *Bagatelle,* among the French street names of the city, seem to be commonly pronounced with any approach to correctness. Worse, there is a growing tendency to translate the old names. Thus, the *rue Royale* is now usually called *Royal street.*

The use of *at* in the phrase, "Fifth avenue *at* 48th street," seems to be an Americanism. It indicates that the house designated is near the corner, but not actually at it. I have never observed this use of *at* in England.

XI.

AMERICAN SLANG

1.

Its Origin and Nature

There is but one work, so far as I can discover, formally devoted to American slang,[1] and that work is extremely superficial. Moreover, it has been long out of date, and hence is of little save historical value. There are at least a dozen careful treatises on French slang, half as many on English slang,[2] and a good many on German slang, but American slang, which is probably quite as rich as that of France and a good deal richer than that of any other country, is yet to be studied at length. Nor is there much discussion of it, of any interest or value, in the general philological literature. Fowler and all the other early native students of the language dismissed it with lofty gestures; down to the time of Whitney it was scarcely regarded as a seemly subject for the notice of a man of learning. Lounsbury, less pedantic, viewed its phenomena more hospitably, and even defined it as "the source from which the decaying energies of speech are constantly refreshed," and Brander Matthews, following him, has described its function as that of providing "substitutes for the good words and true which are worn out by hard service."[3] But that is about as far as the investigation has got. Krapp has some judicious paragraphs upon the matter in his "Modern English,"[4] there are a few scattered essays upon the

---

[1] James Maitland: The American Slang Dictionary; Chicago, 1891.
[2] The best of these, of course, is Farmer and Henley's monumental Slang and Its Analogues, in seven volumes.
[3] Matthews' essay, The Function of Slang, is reprinted in Clapin's Dictionary of Americanisms, pp. 565-581.
[4] P. 199 *ff.*

underlying psychology,[5] and various superficial magazine articles, but that is all. The practising authors of the country, like its philologians, have always shown a gingery and suspicious attitude. "The use of slang," said Oliver Wendell Holmes, "is at once a sign and a cause of mental atrophy." "Slang," said Ambrose Bierce fifty years later, "is the speech of him who robs the literary garbage cans on their way to the dumps." Literature in America, as we have seen, remains aloof from the vulgate. Despite the contrary examples of Mark Twain and Howells, all of the more pretentious American authors try to write chastely and elegantly; the typical literary product of the country is still a refined essay in the *Atlantic Monthly* manner, perhaps gently jocose but never rough—by Emerson, so to speak, out of Charles Lamb—the sort of thing one might look to be done by a somewhat advanced English curate. George Ade, undoubtedly one of the most adept anatomists of the American character and painters of the American scene that the national literature has yet developed, is neglected because his work is grounded firmly upon the national speech—not that he reports it literally, like Lardner and the hacks trailing after Lardner, but that he gets at and exhibits its very essence. It would stagger a candidate for a doctorate in philology, I daresay, to be told off by his professor to investigate the slang of Ade in the way that Bosson,[6] the Swede, has investigated that of Jerome K. Jerome, and yet, until something of the sort is undertaken, American philology will remain out of contact with the American language.

Most of the existing discussions of slang spend themselves upon efforts to define it, and, in particular, upon efforts to differentiate it from idiomatic neologisms of a more legitimate type. This effort is largely in vain; the border-line is too vague and wavering to be accurately mapped; words and phrases are constantly crossing it, and in both directions. There was a time, perhaps, when the familiar American counter-word, *proposition,* was slang; its use seems to have originated in the world of business, and it was soon afterward adopted

[5] For example, The Psychology of Unconventional Language, by Frank K. Sechrist, *Pedagogical Seminary,* vol. xx, p. 413, Dec., 1913, and The Philosophy of Slang, by E. B. Taylor, reprinted in Clapin's Dictionary of Americanisms, pp. 541-563.

[6] Olaf E. Bosson: Slang and Cant in Jerome K. Jerome's Works; Cambridge, 1911.

by the sporting fraternity. But today it is employed without much feeling that it needs apology, and surely without any feeling that it is low. *Nice,* as an adjective of all work, was once in slang use only; today no one would question "a *nice* day," or "a *nice* time," or "a *nice* hotel." *Awful* seems to be going the same route. "*Awful* sweet" and "*awfully* dear" still seem slangy and school-girlish, but "*awful* children" and "*awful* job" have entirely sound support, and no one save a pedant would hesitate to use them. Such insidious purifications and consecrations of slang are going on under our noses all the time. The use of *some* as a general adjective-adverb seems likely to make its way in the same manner, and so does the use of *kick* as verb and noun. It is constantly forgotten by purists of defective philological equipment that a great many of our respectable words and phrases originated in the plainest sort of slang. Thus, *quandary,* despite a fanciful etymology which would identify it with *wandreth* (= *evil*), is probably simply a composition form of the French phrase, *qu'en dirai-je?* Again, to turn to French itself, there is *tête,* a sound name for the human head for many centuries, though its origin was in the Latin *testa* (= *pot*), a favorite slang word of the soldiers of the decaying empire, analogous to our own *block, nut* and *conch.* The word *slacker,* recently come into good usage in the United States as a designation for a successful shirker of conscription, is a substantive derived from the English verb *to slack,* which was born as university slang and remains so to this day. Brander Matthews, so recently as 1901, thought *to hold up* slang; it is now perfectly good American.

The contrary movement of words from the legitimate vocabulary into slang is constantly witnessed. Some one devises a new and arresting trope or makes use of an old one under circumstances arresting the public attention, and at once it is adopted into slang, given a host of remote significances, and ding-donged *ad nauseam.* The Rooseveltian phrases, *muck-raker, Ananias Club, short and ugly word, nature-faker* and *big-stick,* offer examples. Not one of them was new and not one of them was of much pungency, but Roosevelt's vast talent for delighting the yokelry threw about them a charming air, and so they entered into current slang and were mouthed idiotically for months. Another example is to be found in *steam-roller.*

It was first heard of in American politics in June, 1908, when it was applied by Oswald F. Schuette, of the Chicago *Inter-Ocean,* to the methods employed by the Roosevelt-Taft majority in the Republican National Committee in over-riding the protests against seating Taft delegates from Alabama and Arkansas. At once it struck the popular fancy and was soon in general use. All the usual derivatives appeared, *to steam-roller, steam-rollered,* and so on. Since then the term has gradually forced its way back into good usage, and even gone over to England. In the early days of the World War it actually appeared in the most solemn English reviews, and once or twice, I believe, in state papers.

Much of the discussion of slang by popular etymologists is devoted to proofs that this or that locution is not really slang at all— that it is to be found in Shakespeare, in Milton, or in the Authorized Version. These scientists, of course, overlook the plain fact that slang, like the folk-song, is not the creation of people in the mass, but of definite individuals,[7] and that its character *as* slang depends entirely upon its adoption by the ignorant, who use its novelties too assiduously and with too little imagination, and so debase them to the estate of worn-out coins, smooth and valueless. It is this error, often shared by philologists of sounder information, that lies under the doctrine that the plays of Shakespeare are full of slang, and that the Bard showed but a feeble taste in language. Nothing could be more absurd. The business of writing English, in his day, was unharassed by the proscriptions of purists, and so the vocabulary could be enriched more facilely than today, but though Shakespeare and his fellow-dramatists quickly adopted such neologisms as *to bustle, to huddle, bump, hubbub* and *pat,* it goes without saying that they exercised a sound discretion and that the slang of the Bankside was full of words and phrases which they were never tempted to use. In our own day the same discrimination is exercised by all writers of sound taste. On the one hand they disregard the senseless prohibitions of schoolmasters, and on the other hand they draw the line with more or less watchfulness, according as they are of conservative or liberal habit. I find *the best of the bunch* and

[7] *Cf.* Poetic Origins and the Ballad, by Louise Pound; New York, 1921.

joke-smith in Saintsbury;[8] one could scarcely imagine either in Walter Pater. But by the same token one could not imagine *chicken* (for young girl),[9] *aber nit, to come across* or *to camouflage* in Saintsbury.

What slang actually consists of doesn't depend, in truth, upon intrinsic qualities, but upon the surrounding circumstances. It is the user that determines the matter, and particularly the user's habitual way of thinking. If he chooses words carefully, with a full understanding of their meaning and savor, then no word that he uses seriously will belong to slang, but if his speech is made up chiefly of terms poll-parroted, and he has no sense of their shades and limitations, then slang will bulk largely in his vocabulary. In its origin it is nearly always respectable; it is devised, not by the stupid populace, but by individuals of wit and ingenuity; as Whitney says, it is a product of an "exuberance of mental activity, and the natural delight of language-making." But when its inventions happen to strike the popular fancy and are adopted by the mob, they are soon worn thread-bare and so lose all piquancy and significance, and, in Whitney's words, become "incapable of expressing anything that is real."[10] This is the history of such slang phrases, often interrogative, as "How'd you like to be the ice-man?" "How's your poor feet?" "Merci pour la langouste," "Have a heart," "This is the life," "Where did you get that hat?" "Would you for fifty cents?" "Let her go, Gallagher," "Shoo-fly, don't bother me," "Don't wake him up" and "Let George do it." The last well exhibits the process. It originated in France, as "Laissez faire à Georges," during the fifteenth century, and at the start had satirical reference to the multiform activities of Cardinal Georges d'Amboise, prime minister to Louis XII.[11] It later became common slang, was trans-

---

[8] Cambridge History of English Literature, vol. xii, p. 144.

[9] Curiously enough, the American language, usually so fertile in words to express shades of meaning, has no respectable synonym for *chicken*. In English there is *flapper*, in French there is *ingénue*, and in German there is *backfisch*. Usually either the English or the French word is borrowed.

[10] The Life and Growth of Language; New York, 1897, p. 113.

[11] *Cf.* Two Children in Old Paris, by Gertrude Slaughter; New York, 1918, p. 233. Another American popular saying, once embodied in a coon song, may be traced to a sentence in the prayer of the Old Dessauer before the battle of Kesseldorf, Dec. 15, 1745: "Or if Thou wilt not help me, don't help those Hundvögte."

lated into English, had a revival during the early days of David Lloyd George's career, was adopted into American without any comprehension of either its first or its latest significance, and enjoyed the brief popularity of a year.

Krapp attempts to distinguish between slang and sound idiom by setting up the doctrine that the former is "more expressive than the situation demands." "It is," he says, "a kind of hyperesthesia in the use of language. *To laugh in your sleeve* is idiom because it arises out of a natural situation; it is a metaphor derived from the picture of one raising his sleeve to his face to hide a smile, a metaphor which arose naturally enough in early periods when sleeves were long and flowing; but *to talk through your hat* is slang, not only because it is new, but also because it is a grotesque exaggeration of the truth." [12] The theory, unluckily, is combated by many plain facts. *To hand it to him, to get away with it* and even *to hand him a lemon* are certainly not metaphors that transcend the practicable and probable, and yet all are undoubtedly slang. On the other hand, there is palpable exaggeration in such phrases as "he is not worth the powder it would take to kill him," in such adjectives as *breakbone* (fever), and in such compounds as *fire-eater,* and yet it would be absurd to dismiss them as slang. Between *block-head* and *bonehead* there is little to choose, but the former is sound English, whereas the latter is American slang. So with many familiar similes, *e. g., like greased lightning, as scarce as hen's teeth;* they are grotesque hyperboles, but surely not slang.

The true distinction between slang and more seemly idiom, in so far as any distinction exists at all, is that indicated by Whitney. Slang originates in an effort, always by ingenious individuals, to make the language more vivid and expressive. When in the form of single words it may appear as new metaphors, *e. g., bird* and *peach;* as back formations, *e. g., beaut* and *flu;* as composition-forms, *e. g., whatdyecallem* and *attaboy;* as picturesque compounds, *e. g., booze-foundry;* as onomatopes, *e. g., biff* and *zowie;* or in any other of the shapes that new terms take. If, by the chances that condition language-making, it acquires a special and limited meaning, not served by any existing locution, it enters into sound idiom

[12] Modern English, p. 211.

and is presently wholly legitimatized; if, on the contrary, it is adopted by the populace as a counter-word and employed with such banal imitativeness that it soon loses any definite significance whatever, then it remains slang and is avoided by the finical. An example of the former process is afforded by *tommy-rot*. It first appeared as English school-boy slang, but its obvious utility soon brought it into good usage. In one of Jerome K. Jerome's books, "Paul Kelver," there is the following dialogue:

"The wonderful songs that nobody ever sings, the wonderful pictures that nobody ever paints, and all the rest of it. It's *tommy-rot!*"
"I wish you wouldn't use slang."
"Well, you know what I mean. What is the proper word? Give it to me."
"I suppose you mean *cant.*"
"No, I don't. *Cant* is something that you don't believe in yourself. It's *tommy-rot;* there isn't any other word."

Nor was there any other word for *hubbub* and *to dwindle* in Shakespeare's time; he adopted and dignified them because they met genuine needs. Nor was there any other satisfactory word for *graft* when it came in, nor for *rowdy,* nor for *boom,* nor for *joy-ride,* nor for *omnibus-bill,* nor for *slacker,* nor for *trust-buster.* Such words often retain a humorous quality; they are used satirically and hence appear but seldom in wholly serious discourse. But they have standing in the language nevertheless, and only a prig would hesitate to use them as Saintsbury used *the best of the bunch* and *joke-smith.*

On the other hand, many an apt and ingenious neologism, by falling too quickly into the gaping maw of the proletariat, is spoiled forthwith. Once it becomes, in Oliver Wendell Holmes' phrase, "a cheap generic term, a substitute for differentiated specific expressions," it quickly acquires such flatness that the fastidious flee it as a plague. One recalls many capital verb-phrases, thus ruined by unintelligent appreciation, *e. g., to hand him a lemon, to freeze on to, to have the goods, to cut no ice, to give him the glad hand, to fall for it,* and *to get by.* One recalls, too, some excellent substantives, *e. g., dope* and *dub,* and compounds, *e. g., come-on* and *easy-mark,* and verbs, *e. g., to vamp.* These are all quite as sound in structure as the great majority of our most familiar words and phrases *to cut no ice,* for example, is certainly as good as *to butter no parsnips*—but their adoption by the ignorant and their endless use and misuse in all sorts of situations have left them tattered and obnoxious, and they will probably go the way, as Matthews says, of all the other "temporary phrases which spring up, one scarcely knows how, and flourish unaccountably for a few months, and then disappear forever, leaving no sign." Matthews is wrong in two particulars here. They do not arise by any mysterious parthenogenesis, but come from sources which, in many cases, may be determined. And they last, alas, a good deal more than a month. *Shoo-fly* afflicted the American people for at least two years, and "I *don't* think" and *aber nit* quite as long. Even *"good-night"* lasted a whole year.

A very large part of our current slang is propagated by the newspapers, and much of it is invented by newspaper writers. One need but turn to the slang of baseball to find numerous examples. Such phrases as *to clout the sphere, the initial sack, to slam the pill* and *the dexter meadow* are obviously not of bleachers manufacture. There is not enough imagination in that depressing army to devise such things; more often than not, there is not even enough intelligence to comprehend them. The true place of their origin is the perch of the newspaper reporters, whose competence and compensation is largely estimated, at least on papers of wide circulation, by their capacity for inventing novelties. The supply is so large that connoisseurship has grown up; an extra-fecund slang-maker on the press has his following. During the summer of 1913 the Chicago *Record-Herald*, somewhat alarmed by the extravagant fancy of its baseball reporters, asked its readers if they would prefer a return to plain English. Such of them as were literate enough to send in their votes were almost unanimously against a change. As one of them said, "one is nearer the park when Schulte *slams the pills* than when he merely *hits the ball."* In all other fields the newspapers originate and propagate slang, particularly in politics. Most of our political slang-terms since the Civil War, from *pork-barrel* to *steam-roller,* have been their inventions. The English newspapers, with the exception of a few anomalies such as *Pink-Un,* lean in the other direction; their fault is not slanginess, but an otiose ponderosity—in Dean Alford's words, "the insisting on calling common things by uncommon names; changing our ordinary short Saxon nouns and verbs for long words derived from the Latin." [13] The American newspapers, years ago, passed through such a stage of bombast, but since the invention of yellow journalism by the elder James Gordon Bennett—that is, the invention of journalism for the frankly ignorant and vulgar—they have gone to the other extreme. Edmund Clarence Stedman noted the change soon after the Civil War. "The whole country," he wrote to Bayard Taylor in 1873, "owing to the contagion of our newspaper 'exchange' system, is flooded, deluged, swamped beneath a muddy tide of slang." [14] A thousand alarmed watchmen have sought to stay it since, but in vain. The great majority of our newspapers, including all those of large circulation, are chiefly written, as one observer says, "not in English, but in a strange jargon of words that would have made Addison or Milton shudder in despair." [15]

2.

War Slang

"During the war," says a writer in the New York *Tribune,* "our army was slow in manufacturing words. . . . The English army invented not only more war slang than the American, but much more expressive slang. In fact, we took over a number of their words, such as *dud, cootie* and *bus* (for *aeroplane*). . . . During the first year of [American participation in] the war the Americans had no slang word for *German. Hun* was used sparingly, but only by officers. *Fritzie* was rare. *Boche* was tried, but proved to be ill adapted to Americans. They seemed afraid of it, and, indeed, it was often pronounced *botch*. Finally, after a year all these foreign substitutes were abandoned by the enlisted men, and the German became *Jerry*. Curiously enough, the word was almost

[13] A Plea for the Queen's English, p. 244.
[14] Life and Letters of E. C. Stedman, ed. by Laura Stedman and George M. Gould; New York, 1910, vol. i, p. 477.
[15] Governor M. R. Patterson, of Tennessee, in an address before the National Anti-Saloon League, Washington, Dec. 13, 1917.

invariably used in the singular. We heard a soldier telling about a patrol encounter in which he and twenty companions had driven a slightly larger German force out of an abandoned farmhouse, and he said: 'When we came over the top of the hill we found *Jerry.*' He stuck to that usage all through the story. In the last year of the war the American army began to find names for various things, but the slang list of the first year was short. The French army was the most prolific of all in language, and several large dictionaries of French trench slang have already been published."

The chief cause of this American backwardness is not far to seek. During the first year of American participation in the war few Americans got to France, and those who did found an enormous army of Britishers already in the field. These Britishers, in their three years of service, had developed a vast vocabulary of slang, and it stood ready for use. Naturally enough, some of it was borrowed forthwith, though not much. When the main American army followed in 1918 there was little need to make extensive additions to it. *Frog,* for *Frenchman,* was entirely satisfactory; why substitute anything else? So was *cootie.* So was *bus.* So was *Holy Joe,* for *chaplain.* So were *blimp, Jack Johnson, whizz-bang, to strafe* and *pill-box.* Whatever was needed further was adapted from the everyday slang of the United States. Thus, *handshaker* came to mean a soldier sycophantic to officers, *to bust* got the new meaning of *to demote,* and the cowboy *outfit* was borrowed for general military use. Most of the remaining slang that developed among the troops was derisory, e. g., *Sears-Roebuck* for a new lieutenant, *loot* for *lieutenant, Jewish cavalry* for the Quartermaster's force, *belly-robber* for the mess-sergeant, *punk* for bread, *canned-monkey* for the French canned beef, *gold-fish* for canned salmon. Much that remained was obscene, and had its origin in the simple application of obscene verbs and adjectives, long familiar, to special military uses. In the "Vocabulary of the A. E. F." compiled by E. A. Hecker and Edmund Wilson, Jr.,[16] fully 25 per cent. of the terms listed show more or less indecency; the everyday speech of the troops was extraordinarily dirty. But in this department, as I say, there were

---

[16] It remains unpublished, but the compilers have kindly placed it at my disposal.

very few new coinages. In all departments, in truth, the favorite phrases were not invented in the field but brought from home, e. g., *corp* for *corporal,* *sarge* for *sergeant,* *to salvage* for *to steal,* *chow* for *food.* Even *gob, doughboy* and *leatherneck* were not new. *Gob* and *leatherneck* had been in use in the navy for a long while, though the common civilian designation for a sailor had been *jackie.* The origin of the terms is much disputed. *Gob* is variously explained as a derivative from the Chinese (?) word *gobshite,* and as the old word *gob,* signifying a large, irregular mass, applied to a new use. The original meaning of *gobshite* I don't know. One correspondent suggests that *gob* was first used to designate sailors because of their somewhat voracious and noisy habits of feeding. He tells a story of an old master-at-arms who happened into a land aëro-station and found a party of sailors solemnly at table. "My Gawd," he exclaimed, "lookit the *gobs,* usin' forks an' all!" *Doughboy* was originally applied to the infantry only. It originated in the fact that infantrymen, on practise marches, were served rations of flour, and that they made crude biscuits of this flour when they halted. *Leatherneck* needs no explanation. It obviously refers to the sunburn suffered by marines in the tropics. *Hard-boiled* seems to have originated among the Americans in France. It is one of the few specimens of army slang that shows any sign of surviving in the general speech. The only others that I can think of are *cootie, gob, leatherneck, doughboy, frog,* and *buck-private. Hand-shaker,* since the war ended, has resumed its old meaning of an excessively affable man. *Top-sergeant,* during the war, suffered an interesting philological change, like that already noticed in *buncombe.* First it degenerated to *top-sarge* and then to plain *top.* *To a. w. o. l.* is already almost forgotten. So is *bevo officer.* So are such charming inventions as *submarine* for *bed-pan.* The favorite affirmations of the army, "I'll say so," "I'll tell the world," "You said it," etc., are also passing out. From the French, save for a few grotesque mispronunciations of common French phrases, e. g., *boocoop,* the doughboys seem to have borrowed nothing whatsoever. *To camouflage* was already in use in the United States long before the country entered the war, and such aviation terms as *ace, chandelle, vrille* and *glissade* were seldom heard outside the air-force.

The war-slang of the English, the French and the Germans was enormously richer, and a great deal more of it has survived. One need but glance at the vocabulary in the last edition of Cassell's Dictionary [17] or at such works as Gaston Esnault's "Le Poilu Tel Qu'il se Parle" [18] or Karl Bergmann's "Wie der Feldgraue Spricht" [19] to note the great difference. The only work which pretends to cover the subject of American war-slang is "New Words Self-Defined," by Prof. C. Alphonso Smith, of the Naval Academy.[20] It is pieced out with much English slang, and not a little French slang.

[17] London, 1919.
[18] Paris, 1919.
[19] Giessen, 1916.
[20] New York, 1919.

XII.

THE FUTURE OF THE LANGUAGE

1.

English as a World Language

The great Jakob Grimm, the founder of comparative philology, hazarded the guess more than three-quarters of a century ago that English would one day become the chief language of the world, and perhaps crowd out several of the then principal idioms altogether. "In wealth, wisdom and strict economy," he said, "none of the other living languages can vie with it." At that time the guess was bold, for English was still in fifth place, with not only French and German ahead of it, but also Spanish and Russian. In 1801, according to Michael George Mulhall, the relative standing of the five, in the number of persons using them, was as follows:

French	31,450,000
Russian	30,770,000
German	30,320,000
Spanish	26,190,000
English	20,520,000 [1]

[1] Jespersen, in his Growth and Structure of the English Language, p. 244, lists a number of estimates for previous periods. At the beginning of the sixteenth century English was variously estimated to be spoken by from four to five millions of persons, German by ten, Russian by three, French by from ten to twelve, Spanish by eight and a half and Italian by nine and a half. French was thus in first place, closely followed by German, with English fifth. In the year 1600 English was spoken by six millions, German by ten, Russian by three, French by fourteen, Spanish by eight and a half, and Italian by nine and a half. The six languages thus ranked exactly as they had ranked a century before, but with French showing a greatly increased lead, and English slowly spreading. In the year 1700 the various estimates were: English, eight and a half millions; German, ten; Russian, from three to fifteen; French, twenty; Spanish, eight and a half; Italian, from nine and a half to eleven. Jespersen shows that Mulhall's estimate, given above, differed a good deal from that of other statisticians. The guesses made in the year 1800 and thereabout ranged as follows: English, twenty to forty; German, thirty to thirty-three; Russian, twenty-five to thirty-one; French, twenty-seven to thirty-one; Spanish, twenty-six; Italian, fourteen to fifteen. Mulhall did not list Italian.

THE FUTURE OF THE LANGUAGE 373

The population of the United States was then but little more than 5,000,000, but in twenty years it had nearly doubled, and thereafter it increased steadily and enormously, and by 1860 it was greater than that of the United Kingdom. Since that time the majority of English-speaking persons in the world have lived on this side of the water; today there are nearly three times as many as in the United Kingdom and nearly twice as many as in the whole British Empire. This enormous increase in the American population, beginning with the great immigrations of the 30's and 40's, quickly lifted English to fourth place among the languages, and then to third, to second and to first. When it took the lead the attention of philologists was actively directed to the matter, and in 1868 one of them, a German named Brackebusch, first seriously raised the question whether English was destined to obliterate certain of the older tongues.[2] Brackebusch decided against it on various philological grounds, none of them particularly sound. Hi own figures, as the following table from his dissertation shows,[1] were rather against him:

English 60,000,000
German 52,000,000
Russian 45,000,000
French 45,000,000
Spanish 40,000,000

This is 1868. Before another generation had passed the lead of English, still because of the great growth of the United States, and yet more impressive, as the following figures for 1890 show:

English 111,100,000
German 75,200,000
Russian 75,000,000

---

[1] Long before this the general question of the relative superiority of various languages had been debated in Germany. In 1796 the Berlin Academy offered a prize for the best essay on The Ideal of a Perfect Language. It was won by one Jenisch with a treatise bearing the sonorous title of A Philosophical-Critical Comparison and Estimate of Fourteen of the Ancient and Modern Languages of Europe, viz., Greek, Latin, Italian, Spanish, Portuguese, French, German, Dutch, English, Danish, Swedish, Polish, Russian and Lithuanian.

[2] Is English Destined to Become the Universal Language? by W. Brackebusch; Göttingen, 1868.

French	51,200,000
Spanish	42,800,000
Italian	33,400,000
Portuguese	13,000,000 [4]

The next estimates, for the year 1900, I take from Jespersen. The statisticians responsible for them I do not know:

English	from	116,000,000	to	123,000,000
German	from	75,000,000	to	80,000,000
Russian	from	70,000,000	to	85,000,000
French	from	45,000,000	to	52,000,000
Spanish	from	44,000,000	to	58,000,000
Italian	from	34,000,000	to	54,000,000

Now comes an estimate as of 1911:[5]

English	160,000,000
German	130,000,000
Russian	100,000,000
French	70,000,000
Spanish	50,000,000
Italian	50,000,000
Portuguese	25,000,000

And now one, somewhat more moderate, as of 1912:

English	150,000,000
German	90,000,000
Russian	106,000,000
French	47,000,000
Spanish	52,000,000
Italian	37,000,000 [6]

If we accept the 1911 estimate, we find English spoken by two and a half times as many persons as spoke it at the close of the Civil War, and by nearly eight times as many as spoke it at the beginning of the nineteenth century. No other language spread to any such extent during the century. German made a fourfold gain, but that was just half the gain made by English. Russian, despite the vast extension of the Russian Empire during the century, barely

---

[4] I take these figures from A Modern English Grammar, by H. G. Buehler; New York, 1900, p. 3.

[5] *World* Almanac, 1914, p. 63. See also *English*, March, 1919, p. 20.

[6] Hickmann's Geographisch-Statistischer Universal-Atlas.

more than tripled its users, and French barely doubled them. Perhaps all of the figures in the table are excessive; that is almost certainly true of German, and probably also true of English and French. The same authority, in 1921, modified them as follows:

```
English ............................. 150,000,000
German .............................. 120,000,000
Russian ..............................  90,000,000
French ...............................  60,000,000
Spanish ..............................  55,000,000
Italian ..............................  40,000,000
Portuguese ...........................  30,000,000 ⁷
```

I am inclined to think that the German estimate is still far too high; probably even Hickmann's 90,000,000 is too liberal. The number of Germans in Germany is about 60,000,000, and in German Austria not more than 6,000,000 or 7,000,000. Add the German-speaking inhabitants of Holstein, Alsace-Lorraine, the lost portions of Silesia and the Dantzig territory: perhaps 3,000,000 more. Then the German-speaking peoples of the Baltic region, of Transylvania and of Russia: at most, 2,000,000. Then the German-speaking colonists in North and South America: 2,000,000 or 3,000,000 more. Altogether, I put the number of living users of German at less than 75,000,000, which is probably no more than half of the number of living users of English. Japanese, I daresay, should follow French: it is spoken by at least 60,000,000 persons. But it seems to be making very little progress, and its difficulties put it out of consideration as a world language. Chinese, too, may be disregarded, for though it is spoken by more than 300,000,000 persons, it is split into half a dozen mutually unintelligible dialects, and shows no sign of spreading beyond the limits of China; in fact, it is yielding to other languages along the borders, especially to English in the seaports. The same may be said of Hindustani, which is the language of 100,000,000 inhabitants of British India; it shows wide dialectical variations and the people who speak it are not likely to spread. But English is the possession of a race that is still pushing in all directions, and wherever that race settles the existing languages tend to succumb. Thus French, despite the passionate re-

⁷ *World* Almanac, 1921, p. 145.

sistance of the French-Canadians, is gradually decaying in Canada; in all newly-settled regions English is universal. And thus Spanish is dying out in our own Southwest, and promises to meet with severe competition in some of the nearer parts of Latin-America. The English control of the sea has likewise carried the language into far places. There is scarcely a merchant ship-captain on deep water, of whatever nationality, who does not find some acquaintance with it necessary, and it has become, in debased forms, the *lingua franca* of Oceanica and the Far East generally. "Three-fourths of the world's mail matter," says E. H. Babbitt, "is now addressed in English," and "more than half of the world's newspapers are printed in English." [8]

Brackebusch, in the speculative paper just mentioned, came to the conclusion that the future domination of English would be prevented by its unphonetic spelling, its grammatical decay and the general difficulties that a foreigner encounters in seeking to master it. "The simplification of its grammar," he said, with true philological fatuity, "is the commencement of dissolution, the beginning of the end, and its extraordinary tendency to degenerate into slang of every kind is the foreshadowing of its approaching dismemberment." But in the same breath he was forced to admit that "the greater development it has obtained" was the result of this very simplification of grammar, and an inspection of the rest of his reasoning quickly shows its unsoundness, even without an appeal to the plain facts. The spelling of a language, whether it be phonetic or not, has little to do with its spread. Very few men learn it by studying books; they learn it by hearing it spoken. As for grammatical decay, it is not a sign of dissolution, but a sign of active life and constantly renewed strength. To the professional philologist, perhaps it may sometimes appear otherwise. He is apt to estimate languages by looking at their complexity; the Greek aorist elicits his admiration because it presents enormous difficulties and is inordinately subtle. But the object of language is not to bemuse grammarians, but to convey ideas, and the more simply it accom-

[8] The Geography of Great Languages, *World's Work*, Feb., 1908, p. 9907. Babbitt predicts that by the year 2000 English will be spoken by 1,100,000,000 persons, as against 500,000,000 speakers of Russian, 300,000,000 of Spanish, 160,000,000 of German and 60,000,000 of French.

plishes that object the more effectively it meets the needs of an energetic and practical people and the larger its inherent vitality. The history of every language of Europe, since the earliest days of which we have record, is a history of simplifications. Even such languages as German, which still cling to a great many exasperating inflections, including the absurd inflection of the article for gender, are less highly inflected than they used to be, and are proceeding slowly but surely toward analysis. The fact that English has gone further along that road than any other civilized tongue is not a proof of its decrepitude, but a proof of its continued strength. Brought into free competition with another language, say German or French or Spanish, it is almost certain to prevail, if only because it is vastly easier—that is, as a spoken language—to learn. The foreigner essaying it, indeed, finds his chief difficulty, not in mastering its forms, but in grasping its lack of forms. He doesn't have to learn a new and complex grammar; what he has to do is to forget grammar.

Once he has done so, the rest is a mere matter of acquiring a vocabulary. He can make himself understood, given a few nouns, pronouns, verbs and numerals, without troubling himself in the slightest about accidence. "Me see she" is bad English, perhaps, but it would be absurd to say that it is obscure—and on some not too distant tomorrow it may be very fair American. Essaying an inflected language, the beginner must go into the matter far more deeply before he may hope to be understood. Bradley, in "The Making of English," [9] shows clearly how German and English differ in this respect, and how great is the advantage of English. In the latter the verb *sing* has but eight forms, and of these three are entirely obsolete, one is obsolescent, and two more may be dropped out without damage to comprehension. In German the corresponding verb, *singen,* has no fewer than sixteen forms. How far English has proceeded toward the complete obliteration of inflections is shown by such barbarous forms of it as Pidgin English and Beach-la-Mar, in which the final step is taken without appreciable loss of clarity. The Pidgin English verb is identical in all tenses. *Go* stands for both *went* and *gone; makee* is both *make* and *made.* In the same

[9] New York, 1915, p. 5 *ff.*

way there is no declension of the pronoun for case. *My* is thus *I, me, mine* and our own *my*. "No belong *my*" is "it is not *mine*," a crude construction, of course, but still clearly intelligible. Chinamen learn Pidgin English in a few months, and savages in the South Seas master Beach-la-Mar almost as quickly. And a white man, once he has accustomed himself to either, finds it strangely fluent and expressive. He cannot argue politics in it, nor dispute upon transubstantiation, but for all the business of every day it is perfectly satisfactory.

This capacity of English for clear and succinct utterance is frequently remarked by Continental philologists, many of whom seem inclined to agree with Grimm that it will eventually supersede all of the varying dialects now spoken in Europe, at least for commercial purposes. Jespersen, in the first chapter of his "Growth and Structure of the English Language,"[10] discusses the matter very penetratingly and at great length. "There is one impression," he says, "that continually comes to my mind whenever I think of the English language and compare it with others: it seems to me positively and expressively *masculine;* it is the language of a grown-up man and has very little childish or feminine about it. A great many things go together to produce and to confirm that impression, things phonetical, grammatical, and lexical, words and turns that are found, and words and turns that are not found, in the language." He then goes on to explain the origin and nature of the "masculine" air: it is grounded chiefly upon clarity, directness and force. He says:

> The English consonants are well defined; voiced and voiceless consonants stand over against each other in neat symmetry, and they are, as a rule, clearly and precisely pronounced. You have none of those indistinct or half-slurred consonants that abound in Danish, for instance (such as those in ha*d*e, ha*g*e, li*v*lig), where you hardly know whether it is a consonant or a vowel-glide that meets the ear. The only thing that might be compared to this in English is the *r* when not followed by a vowel, but then this has really given up definitely all pretensions to the rank of a consonant, and is (in the pronunciation of the South of England)[11] either frankly a vowel (as in *here*) or else nothing at all (in *hart*, etc.). Each English consonant belongs distinctly to its own type, a *t*

[10] Third ed., rev.; Leipzig, 1919.
[11] But certainly not in that of the United States, save maybe in the South.

THE FUTURE OF THE LANGUAGE 379

is a *t*, and a *k* is a *k*, and there is an end. There is much less modification of a consonant by the surrounding vowels than in some other languages; thus none of that palatalization of consonants which gives an insinuating grace to such languages as Russian. The vowel sounds, too, are comparatively independent of their surroundings; and in this respect the language now has deviated widely from the character of Old English, and has become more clear-cut and distinct in its phonetic structure, although, to be sure, the diphthongization of most long vowels (in *ale, whole, eel, who,* phonetically *eil, houl, ijl, huw*) counteracts in some degree this impression of neatness and evenness.

Jespersen then proceeds to consider certain peculiarities of English grammar and syntax, and to point out the simplicity and forcefulness of the everyday English vocabulary. The grammatical baldness of the language, he argues (against the old tradition in philology), is one of the chief sources of its vigor. He says:

> Where German has, for instance, *alle diejenigen wilden tiere, die dort leben,* so that the plural idea is expressed in each word separately (apart, of course, from the adverb), English has *all the wild animals that live there,* where *all,* the article, the adjective, and the relative pronoun are alike incapable of receiving any mark of the plural number; the sense is expressed with the greatest clearness imaginable, and all the unstressed endings *-e* and *-en,* which make most German sentences so drawling, are avoided.

The prevalence of very short words in English, and the syntactical law which enables it to dispense with the definite article in many constructions "where other languages think it indispensable, *e.g.,* 'life is short,' 'dinner is ready' "—these are further marks of vigor and clarity, according to Dr. Jespersen. " 'First come, first served,' " he says, "is much more vigorous than the French 'Premier venu, premier moulu' or 'Le Premier venu engrène,' the German 'Wer zuerst kommt, mahlt zuerst,' and especially than the Danish 'Den der kommer forst til molle, far forst malet' " Again, there is the superior logical sense of English—the arrangement of words, not according to grammatical rules, but according to their meaning. "In English," says Dr. Jespersen, "an auxiliary verb does not stand far from its main verb, and a negative will be found in the immediate neighborhood of the word it negatives, generally the verb (auxiliary). An adjective nearly always stands before its noun; the only really important exception is when there are qualifications added to it which draw it after the noun so that the whole complex serves the purpose of a relative clause." In English, the subject almost invariably precedes the verb and the object follows after. Once Dr. Jespersen had his pupils determine the percentage of sentences in various authors in which this order was observed. They found that even in English poetry it was seldom violated; the percentage of observances in Tennyson's poetry ran to 88. But in the poetry of Holger Drachmann, the Dane, it fell to 61, in Anatole France's prose to 66, in Gabriele d'Annunzio to 49, and in the poetry of Goethe to 30. All these things make English clearer and more logical than other tongues. It is, says Dr. Jespersen, "a methodical, energetic, business-like and sober language, that does not care much for finery and elegance, but does care for logical consistency and is opposed to any attempt to narrow-in life by police regulations and strict rules either of grammar or of lexicon." In these judgments another distinguished Danish philologist, Prof. Thomsen, agrees fully.

There is, of course, something to be said on the other side. "Besides a certain ungainliness [Dr. Jespersen's *masculine* quality]," said a recent writer in *English*,[12] "English labors under other grave disadvantages. The five vowels of our alphabet have to do duty for some twenty sounds, and, to the foreigner, there are no simple rules by which the correct vowel sounds may be gauged from the way a word is written; our orthography also reflects the chaotic period before our language was formed, and the spelling of a particular word is often unconnected with either its present pronunciation or correct derivation. And although our literature contains more great poetry than any other, and though our language was made by poets rather than by prose writers, English is not musical in the sense that Greek was, or that Italian is when sung." But these objections have very little genuine force. The average foreigner does not learn English in order to sing it, but in order to speak it. And, as I have said, he does not learn it from books, but by word of mouth. To write it correctly, and particularly to spell it correctly, is a herculean undertaking, but very few foreigners find any need to do either. If our spelling were reformed, most of the difficulties now encountered would vanish.

[12] Feb., 1921, p. 450.

THE FUTURE OF THE LANGUAGE 381

Meanwhile, it remains a plain fact that, if only because of the grammatical simplicity, it is easier to obtain an intelligible working knowledge of English than of any other living tongue. This superior simplicity, added to the commercial utility of knowing the language, will probably more than counterbalance the nationalistic objections to acquiring it. In point of fact, they are already grown feeble. All over the Continent English is being studied by men of every European race, including especially the German. "During my recent stay in Berlin," says a post-war English traveler,[13] "nothing annoyed me more than the frequency with which my inquiries of the man in the street for direction, made in atrocious German, elicited replies in perfect English." This writer accounts for what he observed by the fact that "the English-speaking nations own half the world," and asks, "what language should they study but English?" But the spread of the language was already marked before the war. Another Englishman, writing in 1910,[14] thus described its extension in the Far East, as observed during a trip to Japan:

It was only on reaching Italy that I began fully to realize this wonderful thing, that for nearly six weeks, on a German ship, in a journey of nearly ten thousand miles, we had heard little of any language but English!

It is an amazing thing when one thinks of it.

In Japan most of the tradespeople spoke English. At Shanghai, at Hong Kong, at Singapore, at Penang, at Colombo, at Suez, at Port Said—all the way home to the Italian ports, the language of all the ship's traffic, the language of such discourse as the passengers held with natives, most of the language on board ship itself, was English.

The German captain of our ship spoke English more often than German. All his officers spoke English.

The Chinese man-o'-war's men who conveyed the Chinese prince on board at Shanghai, received commands and exchanged commands with our German sailors in English. The Chinese mandarins in their conversations with the ships' officers invariably spoke English. They use the same ideographs in writing as the Japanese, but to talk to our Japanese passengers they had to speak English. Nay, coming as they did from various provinces of the Empire, where the language greatly differs, they found it most convenient in conversation among themselves to speak English!

If, as some aver, the greatest hindrances to peaceful international intercourse

---

[13] John Cournos: English as Esperanto: Its Extraordinary Popularity in Central Europe, *English*, Feb., 1921, p. 451.

[14] Alexander M. Thompson: Japan for a Week; Britain Forever!; London, 1910.

are the misunderstandings due to diversity of tongues, the wide prevalence of the English tongue must be the greatest unifying bond the world has ever known.

And it grows—it grows unceasingly. At the beginning of last century English was the native speech of little more than twenty million people. At the end of the century it was spoken by 130 millions. Before the year 2000 it will probably be spoken by 250 to 500 millions.

In the most high and palmy state of Rome, the population of the Empire was less than 100 millions. To-day 350 millions own the sway of rulers who speak English.

2.

English or American?

Because of the fact that the American form of English is now spoken by three times as many persons as all the British forms taken together, and by at least twenty times as many as the standard Southern English, and because, no less, of the greater resilience it shows, and the greater capacity for grammatical and lexical growth, and the far greater tendency to accommodate itself to the linguistic needs and limitations of foreigners—because of all this it seems to me very likely that it will determine the final form of the language. For the old control of English over American to be reasserted is now quite unthinkable; if the two dialects are not to drift apart entirely English must follow in American's tracks. This yielding seems to have begun; the exchanges from American into English, as we have seen, grow steadily larger and more important than the exchanges from English into American. John Richard Green, the historian, discerning the inevitable half a century ago, expressed the opinion, amazing and unpalatable then, that the Americans were already "the main branch of the English people." It is not yet wholly true; a cultural timorousness yet shows itself; there is still a class, chiefly of pedagogues and of social aspirants, which looks to England as the Romans long looked to Greece. But it is not the class that is shaping the national language, and it is not the class that is carrying it beyond the national borders. The Americanisms that flood the English of Canada are not borrowed from the dialects of New England Loyalists and fashionable New

Yorkers, but from the common speech that has its sources in the native and immigrant proletariat and that displays its gaudiest freightage in the newspapers.

The impact of this flood is naturally most apparent in Canada, whose geographical proximity and common interests completely obliterate the effects of English political and social dominance. The American flat *a* has swept the whole country, and American slang is everywhere used; turn to any essay on Canadianisms,[15] and you will find that nine-tenths of them are simply Americanisms. No doubt this is chiefly due to the fact that the Canadian newspapers are all supplied with news by the American press associations, and thus fall inevitably into the habit of discussing it in American terms. "The great factor that makes us write and speak alike," says a recent writer on American speech habits,[16] "is the indefinite multiplication of the instantaneous uniformity of the American daily, ... due to a non-sectional, continental exchange of news through the agency of the various press associations." In this exchange Canada shares fully. Its people may think as Britons, but they must perforce think in American.

More remarkable is the influence that American has exerted upon the speech of Australia and upon the crude dialects of Oceanica and the Far East. One finds such obvious Americanisms as *tomahawk, boss, bush, go finish* (= *to die*) and *pickaninny* in Beach-la-Mar [17] and more of them in Pidgin English. The common trade speech of the whole Pacific, indeed, tends to become American rather than English. An American correspondent at Oxford sends me some curious testimony to the fact. Among the Britishers he met there was one student who showed an amazing familiarity with American words and phrases. The American, asking him where he had lived in the United States, was surprised to hear that he had never been here at all. All his Americanisms had been picked up during his youth in a Chinese sea-port, where his father was the British Consul.

[15] For example, Geikie's or Lighthall's. See the Bibliography.
[16] Harvey M. Watts: Need of Good English Growing as World Turns to Its Use, New York *Sun*, Nov. 19, 1919.
[17] *Cf.* Beach-la-Mar, by William Churchill, former United States consul-general in Samoa and Tonga. The pamphlet is published by the Carnegie Institution of Washington.

The English of Australia, though it is Cockney in pronunciation and intonation,[18] becomes increasingly American in vocabulary. In a glossary of Australianisms compiled by the Australian author, C. T. Dennis,[19] I find the familiar verbs and verb-phrases, *to beef, to biff, to bluff, to boss, to break away, to chase one's self, to chew the rag, to chip in, to fade away, to get it in the neck, to back and fill, to plug along, to get sore, to turn down* and *to get wise;* the substantives, *dope, boss, fake, creek, knockout-drops* and *push* (in the sense of *crowd*); the adjectives, *hitched* (in the sense of *married*) and *tough* (as before *luck*), and the adverbial phrases, *for keeps* and *going strong*. Here, in direct competition with English locutions, and with all the advantages on the side of the latter, American is making steady progress. Moreover, the Australians,[20] following the Americans, have completely obliterated several old niceties of speech that survive in England—for example, the distinction between *will* and *shall*. "An Australian," says a recent writer,[21] "uses the phrase *I shall* about as often as he uses the accusative *whom*. Usually he says *I will* or *I'll;* and the expectant *we shall see* is the only ordinary *shall* locution which I can call to mind." But perhaps it is Irish influence that is visible here, and not American.

"This American language," says a recent observer, "seems to be much more of a pusher than the English. For instance, after eight years' occupancy of the Philippines it was spoken by 800,000, or 10 per cent, of the natives, while after an occupancy of 150 years of India by the British, 3,000,000, or one per cent, of the natives speak English."[22] I do not vouch for the figures. They may be inaccurate, in detail, but they at least state what seems to be a fact.

[18] *Cf.* The Australian Accent, *Triad* (Sydney), Nov. 10. 1920, p. 37.
[19] It is in Doreen and the Sentimental Bloke; New York, 1916.
[20] It is a pity that American has not borrowed the Australian invention *wowser*. Says a writer in the Manchester *Guardian:* "*Wowser*, whether used as an adjective or a substantive, covers everyone and everything that is out of sympathy with what some people consider *la joie de vivre*. A *wowser*, as a person, is one who desires to close public-houses, prevent *shouting* (Australese for treating), and so on—in short, one who intends to limit the opportunities 'of all professions that go the primrose way to the everlasting bonfire.'" In the United States fully 99 per cent of all the world's *wowsers* rage and roar, and yet we have no simple word to designate them.
[21] *English*, Sept., 1919, p. 167.
[22] The American Language, by J. F. Healy; Pittsburgh, 1910, p. 6.

Behind that fact are phenomena which certainly deserve careful study, and, above all, study divested of unintelligent prejudice. The attempt to make American uniform with English has failed ingloriously; the neglect of its investigation is an evidence of snobbishness that is a folly of the same sort. It is useless to dismiss the growing peculiarities of the American vocabulary and of grammar and syntax in the common speech as vulgarisms beneath serious notice. Such vulgarisms have a way of intrenching themselves, and gathering dignity as they grow familiar. "There are but few forms in use," says Lounsbury, "which, judged by a standard previously existing, would not be regarded as gross barbarisms." [23] Each language, in such matters, is a law unto itself, and each vigorous dialect, particularly if it be spoken by millions, is a law no less. "It would be as wrong," says Sayce, "to use *thou* for the nominative *thee* in the Somersetshire dialect as it is to say *thee art* instead of *you are* in the Queen's English." American has suffered severely from the effort to impose an impossible artificiality upon it, but it has survived the process, and soon or late there must be a formal abandonment of the pedagogical effort to bring it into agreement with Southern English. "It has had held up to it," says Prof. Ayres, "silly ideals, impossible ideals, ignorant dogmatisms, and for the most part it wisely repudiates them all." [24] The American Academy of Arts and Letters still pleads for these silly ideals and ignorant dogmatisms, and the more stupid sort of schoolmasters echo the plea, but meanwhile American goes its way. In England its progress is not unmarked. Dr. Robert Bridges and the Society for Pure English seek to bring about the precise change in standard English that American shows spontaneously. Maybe the end will be two dialects —standard English for pedants, and American for the world.

As yet, American suffers from the lack of a poet bold enough to venture into it, as Chaucer ventured into the despised English of his day, and Dante into the Tuscan dialect, and Luther, in his translation of the Bible, into peasant German. Walt Whitman made a half attempt and then drew back; Lowell, perhaps, also

[23] History of the English Language, p. 476.
[24] Cambridge History of American Literature, vol. iv, p. 566.

heard the call, but too soon; in our own time, young Mr. Weaver has shown what may be done tomorrow, and Carl Sandburg has also made experiments. The Irish dialect of English, vastly less important than the American, has already had its interpreters—Douglas Hyde, John Millington Synge and Augusta Gregory—with what extraordinary results we all know.[25] Here we have writing that is still indubitably English, but English rid of its artificial restraints and broken to the less self-conscious grammar and syntax of a simple and untutored folk. Synge, in his preface to "The Playboy of the Western World," tells us how he got his gipsy phrases "through a chink in the floor of the old Wicklow house where I was staying, that let me hear what was being said by the servant girls in the kitchen." There is no doubt, he goes on, that "in the happy ages of literature striking and beautiful phrases were as ready to the story-teller's or the playwright's hand as the rich cloaks and dresses of his time. It is probable that when the Elizabethan dramatist took his ink-horn and sat down to his work he used many phrases that he had just heard, as he sat at dinner, from his mother or his children."

The result, in the case of the neo-Celts, is a dialect that stands incomparably above the tight English of the grammarians—a dialect so naïve, so pliant, so expressive, and, adeptly managed, so beautiful that even purists have begun to succumb to it, and it promises to leave lasting marks upon English style. The American dialect has not yet come to that stage. In so far as it is apprehended at all it is only in the sense that Irish-English was apprehended a generation ago—that is, as something uncouth and comic. But that is the way that new dialects always come in—through a drum-fire of cackles. Given the poet, there may suddenly come a day when our *theirns* and *would'a hads* will take on the barbaric stateliness of the peasant locutions of old Maurya in "Riders to the Sea." They seem grotesque and absurd today because the folks who use them seem grotesque and absurd. But that is a too facile logic and under it

---

[25] The Sicilian dialect of Italian has been brought to dignity in the same way by Giovanni Verga, author of the well-known Cavalleria Rusticana. See Giovanni Verga and the Sicilian Novel, by Carlo Linati, *Dial*, Aug., 1921, p. 150 *ff*.

THE FUTURE OF THE LANGUAGE

is a false assumption. In all human beings, if only understanding be brought to the business, dignity will be found, and that dignity cannot fail to reveal itself, soon or late, in the words and phrases with which they make known their high hopes and aspirations and cry out against the intolerable meaninglessness of life.

APPENDIX

I.

Specimens of the American Vulgate

1.

The Declaration of Independence in American

[The following is my own translation, but I have had the aid of suggestions from various other scholars. It must be obvious that more than one section of the original is now quite unintelligible to the average American of the sort using the Common Speech. What would he make, for example, of such a sentence as this one: "He has called together legislative bodies at places unusual, uncomfortable, and distant from the depository of their public records, for the sole purpose of fatiguing them into compliance with his measures"? Or of this: "He has refused for a long time, after such dissolutions, to cause others to be elected, whereby the legislative powers, incapable of annihilation, have returned to the people at large for their exercise." Such Johnsonian periods are quite beyond his comprehension, and no doubt the fact is at least partly to blame for the neglect upon which the Declaration has fallen in recent years. When, during the Wilson-Palmer saturnalia of oppressions, specialists in liberty began protesting that the Declaration plainly gave the people the right to alter the government under which they lived and even to abolish it altogether, they encountered the utmost incredulity. On more than one occasion, in fact, such an exegete was tarred and feathered by the shocked members of the American Legion, even after the Declaration had been read to them. What ailed them was that they could not understand its eighteenth century English. I make the suggestion that its circulation among such patriotic men, translated into the language they use every day, would serve to prevent, or, at all events, to diminish that sort of terrorism.]

When things get so balled up that the people of a country have to cut loose from some other country, and go it on their own hook, without asking no permission from nobody, excepting maybe God Almighty, then they ought to let everybody know why they done it, so that everybody can see they are on the level, and not trying to put nothing over on nobody.

All we got to say on this proposition is this: first, you and me is as good as anybody else, and maybe a damn sight better; second, nobody ain't got no right to take away none of our rights; third, every man has got a right to live, to come and go as he pleases, and to have a good time however he likes, so long as he don't interfere with nobody else. That any government that don't give a man these rights ain't worth a damn; also, people ought to choose the kind of government they want themselves, and nobody else ought to have no say in the matter. That whenever any government don't do this, then the people have got a right to can it and put in one that will take care of their interests. Of course, that don't mean having a revolution every day like them South American coons and yellow-bellies and Bolsheviki, or every time some job-holder does something he ain't got no business to do. It is better to stand a little graft, etc., than to have revolutions all the time, like them coons and Bolsheviki, and any man that wasn't a anarchist or one of them I. W. W.'s would say the same. But when things get so bad that a man ain't hardly got no rights at all no more, but you might almost call him a slave, then everybody ought to get together and throw the grafters out, and put in new ones who won't carry on so high and steal so much, and then watch them. This is the proposition the people of these Colonies is up against, and they have got tired of it, and won't stand it no more. The administration of the present King, George III, has been rotten from the start, and when anybody kicked about it he always tried to get away with it by strong-arm work. Here is some of the rough stuff he has pulled:

He vetoed bills in the Legislature that everybody was in favor of, and hardly nobody was against.

He wouldn't allow no law to be passed without it was first put up to him, and then he stuck it in his pocket and let on he forgot about it, and didn't pay no attention to no kicks.

When people went to work and gone to him and asked him to put through a law about this or that, he give them their choice: either they had to shut down the Legislature and let him pass it all by himself, or they couldn't have it at all.

He made the Legislature meet at one-horse tank-towns out in the alfalfa belt, so that hardly nobody could get there and most of the leaders would stay home and let him go to work and do things as he pleased.

He give the Legislature the air, and sent the members home every time they stood up to him and give him a call-down.

When a Legislature was busted up he wouldn't allow no new one to be elected, so that there wasn't nobody left to run things, but anybody could walk in and do whatever they pleased.

He tried to scare people outen moving into these States, and made it so hard for a wop or one of them poor kikes to get his papers that he would rather stay home and not try it, and then, when he come in, he wouldn't let him have no land, and so he either went home again or never come.

He monkeyed with the courts, and didn't hire enough judges to do the work, and so a person had to wait so long for his case to come up that he got sick of waiting, and went home, and so never got what was coming to him.

He got the judges under his thumb by turning them out when they done anything he didn't like, or holding up their salaries, so that they had to cough up or not get no money.

He made a lot of new jobs, and give them to loafers that nobody knowed nothing about, and the poor people had to pay the bill, whether they wanted to or not.

Without no war going on, he kept an army loafing around the country, no matter how much people kicked about it.

He let the army run things to suit theirself and never paid no attention whatsoever to nobody which didn't wear no uniform.

He let grafters run loose, from God knows where, and give them the say in everything, and let them put over such things as the following:

Making poor people board and lodge a lot of soldiers they ain't got no use for, and don't want to see loafing around.

When the soldiers kill a man, framing it up so that they would get off.

Interfering with business.

Making us pay taxes without asking us whether we thought the things we had to pay taxes for was something that was worth paying taxes for or not.

When a man was arrested and asked for a jury trial, not letting him have no jury trial.

Chasing men out of the country, without being guilty of nothing, and trying them somewheres else for what they done here.

In countries that border on us, he put in bum governments, and then tried to spread them out, so that by and by they would take in this country too, or make our own government as bum as they was. He never paid no attention whatever to the Constitution, but he went to work and repealed laws that everybody was satisfied with and hardly nobody was against, and tried to fix the government so that he could do whatever he pleased.

He busted up the Legislatures and let on he could do all the work better by himself.

Now he washes his hands of us and even declares war on us, so we don't owe him nothing, and whatever authority he ever had he ain't got no more.

He has burned down towns, shot down people like dogs, and raised hell against us out on the ocean.

He hired whole regiments of Dutch, etc., to fight us, and told them they could have anything they wanted if they could take it away from us, and sicked these Dutch, etc., on us without paying no attention whatever to international law.

He grabbed our own people when he found them in ships on the ocean, and shoved guns into their hands, and made them fight against us, no matter how much they didn't want to.

He stirred up the Indians, and give them arms and ammunition, and told them to go to it, and they have killed men, women and children, and don't care which.

Every time he has went to work and pulled any of these things, we have went to work and put in a kick, but every time we have went to work and put in a kick he has went to work and did it again. When a man keeps on handing out such rough stuff all the time, all you can say is that he ain't got no class and ain't fitten to have no authority over people who have got any rights, and he ought to be kicked out.

When we complained to the English we didn't get no more satisfaction. Almost every day we warned them that the politicians over there was doing things to us that they didn't have no right to do. We kept on reminding them who we were, and what we was doing here, and how we come to come here. We asked them to get us a square deal, and told them that if this thing kept on we'd have to do something about it and maybe they wouldn't like it. But the more we talked, the more they didn't pay no attention to us. Therefore, if they ain't for us they must be agin us, and we are ready to give them the fight of their lives, or to shake hands when it is over.

Therefore be it resolved, That we, the representatives of the people of the United States of America, in Congress assembled, hereby declare as follows: That the United States, which was the United Colonies in former times, is now free and independent, and ought to be; that we have throwed out the English King and don't want to have nothing to do with him no more, and are not in England no more; and that, being as we are now free and independent, we can do anything that free and independent parties can do, especially declare war, make peace, sign treaties, go into business, etc. And we swear on the Bible on this proposition, one and all, and agree to stick to it no matter what happens, whether we win or we lose, and whether we get away with it or get the worst of it, no matter whether we lose all our property by it or even get hung for it.

2.

Baseball-American

[I am indebted to Mr. Ring W. Lardner, author of "You Know Me, Al," for the following. It combines the common language with the special argot of the professional baseball-players, a class of men whose speech Mr. Lardner has studied with great diligence.]

[*Plot: The enemy has fallen on our pitcher and scored five runs. The side is finally retired and our men come in to the bench, where the manager awaits them.*]

MANAGER—*What the hell!* [1]

[1] Or, more likely, *the Jesus!*

PITCHER (*indicating the catcher*)—Ask him!

CATCHER—Ask yourself, you yella bum! (*To the manager*) He's been shakin' me off all day.

MANAGER—What was it Peck hit?

PITCHER—I was tryin' to waste it.

CATCHER—Waste it! You dinked it up there chest high.[2] He couldn't of got a better cut at it if he'd of tooken the ball in his hand.

PITCHER (*to the catcher*)—You could of got Shawkey at the plate if you'd of left Jack's peg hop. He never even hit the dirt.

CATCHER—It would of been a short hop and I couldn't take no chance. You wasn't backin' up. You was standin' over in back of third base, posin' for a pitcher (=picture) or somethin'.

MANAGER (*to the catcher*)—What the hell happened on that ball on Bodie?

CATCHER—He (*referring to the pitcher*) crossed me up. I ast him for a hook and he yessed me and then throwed a fast one.

PITCHER—It was a curve ball, just like you ast me, only it didn't break good.

MANAGER (*to the pitcher*)—And what about Ruth? Is that all the more sense you got, groovin' one for that big ape! You'd of did better to roll it up there.

PITCHER—The ball he hit was outside.

MANAGER—You mean after he hit it. For God's sakes, use your head in there! This ain't Fort Worth!

PITCHER—I wisht to hell it was!

MANAGER—And you're li'ble to get your wish!

Glossary

In there: In the pitcher's position.
Up there: In the batter's position.
Shakin' me off: Refusing to pitch the kind of ball I signalled for.
Waste: To pitch a ball so high or so far outside that the batsman cannot reach it.
Dink: To throw a slow ball.
Hook: A curve ball.
Peg: A throw.
Hop: To bound.
Hit the dirt: To slide.

[2] *Chest-high* is a euphemism; the more usual form is *titty-high*.

3.

Ham-American

[Mr. Lardner also very kindly wrote the following for the present work. A *ham*, of course, means a fifth-rate actor. The scene is the sidewalk in front of the Lambs' Club. The two hams, meeting, stop for a chat.]

First Ham—Have you seen Craven?

Second Ham—Yes, I was *in* Thursday.

First Ham—It's a great troupe.[3]

Second Ham—I give him the notion. I says to him last summer, I says, "Frank, I got a great notion for you." He says, "What is it, Charley?" So then I give him the notion.

First Ham—It's a great troupe. I enjoyed every minute, if you know what I mean.

Second Ham—I give him the notion.

First Ham—He's wrote himself a great part, if you know what I mean.

Second Ham—I give him the notion.

First Ham—He's a duke in that kind of a part.

Second Ham—How'd you like the gal?

First Ham—Just fair, if you know what I mean. But What's-his-name was lousy the day I was in, if you know what I mean.

Second Ham—I don't think they cast it very good.

First Ham—No, and when you come right down to it, they's nothin' to the troupe, only the notion.

Second Ham—I give him the notion.

First Ham—It'd be a flop without Craven.

Second Ham—That's the way I figured when I had the notion, and I tol' Craven, I says, "Frank, I got a notion that'd make a play for you, but it'd be a flop for anybody else."

First Ham—They's really nothin' to it but hoakum, if you know what I mean. But they eat it up.

Second Ham—Too bad they ain't got a bigger theater.

---

[3] *Troupe* here means the entire production.

FIRST HAM—You can't tell. It might flop in a bigger house. It's just a little every-day family troupe, if you know what I mean. Nothin' to it but Craven and the notion.
SECOND HAM—I give him the notion.

4.

Vers Américain

[The following "Élégie Américaine," by John V. A. Weaver, of Chicago,[4] marks the first appearance of the American vulgate, I believe, in serious verse. It has been attempted often enough by comic poets, though seldom with the accuracy shown by Mr. Lardner's prose. But it was Mr. Weaver who first directed attention to the obvious fact that the American proletarian is not comic to himself but quite serious, and that he carries on his most lofty and sentimental thoughts in the same tongue he uses in discussing baseball.]

I wished I'd took the ring, not the Victrola.
You get so tired of records, hearin' an' hearin' 'em,
And when a person don't have much to spend
They feel they shouldn't ought to be so wasteful.
And then these warm nights makes it slow inside,
And sittin's lovely down there by the lake
Where him and me would always use ta go.

He thought the Vic'd make it easier
Without him; and it did at first. I'd play
Some jazz-band music and I'd almost feel
His arms around me, dancin'; after that
I'd turn out all the lights, and set there quiet
Whiles Alma Gluck was singin' "Home, Sweet Home",
And almost know his hand was strokin' my hand.

"If I was you, I'd take the Vic," he says,
"It's somethin' you can use; you can't a ring.
Wisht I had ways ta make a record for you,
So's I could be right with you, even though

[4] From *In American*; New York, 1921.

Uncle Sam had me" . . . Now I'm glad he didn't;
It would be lots too much like seein' ghosts
Now that I'm sure he never won't come back. . . .

Oh, God! I don't see how I ever stand it!
He was so big and strong! He was a darb!
The swellest dresser, with them nifty shirts
That fold down, and them lovely nobby shoes,
And always all his clothes would be one color,
Like green socks with green ties, and a green hat,
And everything. . . . We never had no words
Or hardly none. . . .

    And now to think that mouth
I useta kiss is bitin' into dirt,
And through them curls I useta smooth a bullet
Has went. . . .
    I wisht it would of killed me, too. . . .

Oh, well . . . about the Vic. . . . I guess I'll sell it
And get a small ring anyways. (I won't
Get but half as good a one as if
He spent it all on that when he first ast me.)

It don't seem right to play jazz tunes no more
With him gone. And it ain't a likely chanst
I'd find nobody ever else again
Would suit me, or I'd suit. And so a little
Quarter of a carat, maybe, but a real one
That could sparkle, sometimes, and remember
The home I should of had. . . .

    And still, you know,
The Vic was his idear, and so . . .
                  I wonder. . . .

II.

Non-English Dialects in America

1.

German

The German dialect spoken by the so-called Pennsylvania Dutch of lower Pennsylvania is the oldest immigrant language to remain in daily use in the United States, and so it shows very extensive English influences. The fact that it survives at all is due to the extreme clannishness of the people using it—a clannishness chiefly based upon religious separatism. The first Germans came to Pennsylvania toward the end of the seventeenth century and settled in the lower tier of counties, running from Philadelphia westward to the mountains; a few continued into Maryland and then down the Valley of Virginia. They came, in the main, from the Palatinate; the minority hailed from Württemberg, Bavaria, the lower Rhine, Alsace, Saxony and German Switzerland. The language they brought with them was thus High German; it came to be called Dutch by the American colonists of the time because the immigrants themselves called it *Deitsch* (= *Deutsch*), and because *Dutch* was then (and has remained, to some extent, ever since) a generic American term to designate all the Germanic peoples and languages. This misuse of *Dutch* is frequently ascribed to the fact that the colonists were very familiar with the true Dutch in New York, but as a matter of fact *Dutch* was commonly used in place of *German* by the English of the seventeenth century and the colonists simply brought the term with them and preserved it as they preserved many other English archaisms. The Pennsylvania Germans themselves often used *Pennsylvania Dutch* in place of *Pennsylvania German*.

Their dialect has produced an extensive literature and has been studied and described at length by competent philologians; in consequence there is no need to deal with it here at any length.[5] Excel-

[5] See the Bibliography, p. 447, and especially the works of Haldeman, Horne, Learned, Lins, Miller and Rauch.

lent specimens of it are to be found in "Harbaugh's Harfe: Gedichte in Pennsylvanisch-Deutscher Mundart." [6] That part of it which remains genuinely German shows a change of *a* to *o*, as in *jor* for *jahr;* of the diphthong *ö* to a long *e*, as in *bees* for *böse*, and of the diphthongs *ei* and *äu* to the neutral *e*, as in *bem* for *bäume*. Most of the German compound consonants are changed to simple consonants, and there is a general decay of inflections. But the chief mark of the dialect is its very extensive adoption of English loan words. Harbaugh, in his vocabulary, lists some characteristic examples, *e. g., affis* from *office, altfäschen* from *old-fashioned, beseid* from *beside, boghie* from *buggy, bortsch* from *porch, diehlings* from *dealings, Dschäck* from *Jack, dscheneral-'leckschen* from *general-election, dschent'lleit* (= *gentle leut*) from *gentlemen, Dschim* from *Jim, dschuryman* from *juryman, ebaut* from *about, ennihau* from *anyhow, gehm* from *game, kunschtabler* from *constable, lofletters* from *love-letters, tornpeik* from *turnpike* and *'xäktly* from *exactly*. Many English words have been taken in and inflected in the German manner, *e.g., gedscheest* (= *ge* + *chased*), *gedschumpt* (*ge* + *jumped*) and *gepliescht* (= *ge* + *pleased*). The vulgar American pronunciation often shows itself, as in *heist* for *hoist* and *krick* for *creek*. An illuminating brief specimen of the language is to be found in the sub-title of E. H. Rauch's "Pennsylvania Dutch Handbook":[7] *"En booch for inschtructa."* Here we see the German indefinite article decayed to *en*, the spelling of *buch* made to conform to English usage, *für* abandoned for *for*, and a purely English word, *instruction*, boldly adopted and naturalized. Some astounding examples of Pennsylvania German are to be found in the copious humorous literature of the dialect; *e.g.,* "Mein *stallion* hat über die *fenz geschumpt* and dem nachbar sein *whiet* abscheulich *gedämätscht.*" (My stallion jumped over the fence, and horribly damaged my neighbor's wheat.) Such phrases as "Es giebt gar kein *use*" and "Ich kann es nicht *ständen*" are very common on Pennsylvania German lips. Of late, with the improvement in communications, the dialect shows signs of disappearing. The younger Pennsylvania Germans learn English in school, read English newspapers,

[6] Philadelphia, 1874; rev. ed., 1902.
[7] Mauch Chunk, Pa., 1879.

and soon forget their native patois. But so recently as the eighties of the last century, two hundred years after the coming of the first German settlers, there were thousands of their descendants in Pennsylvania who could scarcely speak English at all. An interesting variant dialect is to be found in the Valley of Virginia, though it is fast dying out. It is an offshoot of Pennsylvania German, and shows even greater philological decay. The genitive ending has been dropped and possession is expressed by various syntactical devices, *e.g., der mann sei buch, dem mann sei buch* or *am mann sei buch*. The cases of the nouns do not vary in form, adjectives are seldom inflected, and only two tenses of the verbs remain, the present and the perfect, *e.g., ich geh* and *ich bin gange*. The indefinite article, *en* in Pennsylvania German, has been worn away to a simple *'n*. The definite article has been preserved, but *das* has changed to *des*. It is declined as follows:

Nom.	der	die	des-'s	die
Dat.	dem-'m	der	dem-'m	dene
Acc.	den-der	die	des-'s	die

In brief, this Valley German is a language in the last stages of decay. The only persons speaking it are a few remote countryfolk and they have reduced it to its elements: even the use of polite pronouns, preserved in Pennsylvania German and so important in true German, has been abandoned. It has been competently investigated and described by H. M. Hays,[8] from whom I borrow the following specimen of it:

'S war wimol ei Mätel, wu ihr Liebling fat in der Grieg is, un' is dot gmacht wure. Sie hut sich so arg gedrauert un' hut ksat: "O wann ich ihn just noch eimol sehne könnt!" Ei Ovet is sie an 'n Partie gange, aver es war ken Freud dat für sie. Sie hut gwünscht, ihre Lieve war dat au. Wie freundlich sie sei hätt könne! Sie is 'naus in den Garde gange, un' war allei im Monlicht khockt. Kschwind hut sie 'n Reiter höre komme. 'S war ihre Lieve ufm weisse Gaul. Er hut ken Wat ksat, aver hut sie uf den Gaul hinner sich gnomme, un' is fatgritte. . . .

The German spoken elsewhere in the United States is much less decayed. The hard effort of German schoolmasters and the exten-

[8] On the German Dialect Spoken in the Valley of Virginia, *Dialect Notes*, vol. iii, p. 263.

sive literature that it has produced [9] tend to keep it relatively pure, even from English influences. But a great many loan-words have nevertheless got into it, and it shows some phenomena that instantly arrest the attention of a German arriving from Germany, for example, the use of *gleiche* for *to like,* by false analogy from *gleich* (= *like, similar*). The German encountered in German newspapers printed in the United States is often very bad, but this is simply due to the fact that much of it is written by uneducated men. Nothing approaching a general decay is visible in it; in intent, at least, it is always good High German.

2.

French

The French spoken in Canada has been so extensively studied and literature is so accessible that it is scarcely necessary to describe it at any length. A very extensive investigation of it was undertaken by the late Dr. A. M. Elliott, of the Johns Hopkins University; his conclusions may be found in the *American Journal of Philology*.[10] Since then researches into its history, phonology and morphology have been made by James Geddes, Jr.,[11] A. F. Chamberlain [12] and other competent philologists, and there has grown up an extensive literature by native, French-speaking Canadians.[13] Dr. Elliott says that alarmed purists predicted so long ago as 1817 that the French of Canada would be completely obliterated by English, and this fear still shows itself in all discussions of the subject by French-

[9] *Cf.* Non-English Writings: I, German, by A. B. Faust, in the Cambridge History of American Literature, vol. iv, p. 572 *ff.* There is a valuable bibliography appended, p. 813 *ff.*
[10] Vol. vi, p. 135; vol. vii, p. 141; vol. vii, p. 135 and p. 338; vol. x, p. 133.
[11] Mr. Geddes' studies have been chiefly published in Germany. His Study of an Acadian-French Dialect Spoken on the North Shore of the Baie-des-Chaleurs; Halle, 1908, contains an exhaustive bibliography.
[12] He printed an article on Dialect Research in Canada in *Dialect Notes,* vol. i, p. 43. A bibliography is added.
[13] For example: La Langue Française au Canada, by Louvigny de Montigny; Ottawa, 1916, and Le Parler Populaire des Canadiens Français; by N. E. Dionne; Quebec, 1909. The latter is a lexicon running to 671 pages.

Canadians. But the language continues as the daily speech of perhaps 1,500,000 persons, and still has an official status, and is often heard in the Dominion Parliament. "The effect of English on the French," says Elliott, "has been immeasurably greater than that of French on the English. . . . The French has made use of all the productive means—suffixes, prefixes—at its disposal to incorporate the English vocables in its word-supply, . . . and to adapt them by a skilful use of its inflectional apparatus to all the requirements of a rigid grammatical system." On one page of N. E. Dionne's lexicon I find the following loan-words from English: *barkeeper, bargaine* (used in place of *marché*), *bar-room, bull's-eye, buckwheat, buggy, buck-board, bugle, bully, bum, business, bus.* As will be observed, a large proportion of them are not really English at all, but American. Many other Americanisms have got into the language, e. g., *gang* (in the political sense), *greenback, ice-cream, elevateur, knickerbockers, trolley-car, sweater, swell* (as an adjective of all work), *caucus, lofeur* ($=$ *loafer,* a loan-word originally German) and *lager,* another. "Comme tu es *swell* ce matin, vas-tu aux noces?" —this is now excellent Canadian French. So is *gologne* ($=$ *go 'long*). Louvigny de Montigny, in "La Langue Française au Canada," complains bitterly that American words and phrases are relentlessly driving out French words and phrases, even when the latter are quite as clear and convenient. Thus, *un patron,* throughout French Canada, is now *un boss, pétrole* is *l'huile de charbon* ($=$ *coal-oil*), *une bonne à tout faire* is *une servante générale,* and *un article d'occasion* is *un article de seconde main!*

The French dialect spoken by the Creoles and their colored retainers in Louisiana has been extensively studied,[14] as has the dialect of the French West Indies. Its principal characters must be familiar to every reader of the stories of Lafcadio Hearn, George W. Cable, Kate Chopin and Grace Elizabeth King. It produced a large oral literature, chiefly in the form of songs, during the days of actual

[14] For example, by J. A. Harrison, in The Creole Patois of Louisiana, *American Journal of Philology,* vol. iii, p. 285 ff.; by Alcée Fortier, in The French Language in Louisiana and the Negro French Dialect; New Orleans, n. d.; Acadians of Louisiana and Their Dialect; New Orleans, 1891, and A Few Words About the Creoles of Louisiana; Baton Rouge, 1892; and by H. Schuchardt, in Beiträge zur Kenntniss des Englischen Kreolisch, *Englische Studien,* vol. xii, p. 470; vol. xiii, p. 158, and vol. xv, p. 286.

French rule in Louisiana, and some of this literature is still preserved, though the French-speaking population of the state is rapidly diminishing, and New Orleans is now a thoroughly American city. But the written literature of the Creoles was almost wholly in standard French. Curiously enough, nearly the whole of it was produced, not during the days of French rule, but after the American occupation in 1803. "It was not until after the War of 1812," says a recent historian of it,[15] "that letters really flourished in French Louisiana. The contentment and prosperity that filled the forty years between 1820 and 1860 encouraged the growth of a vigorous and in some respects a native literature, comprising plays, novels, and poems." The chief dramatists of the period were Placide Canonge, A. Lussan, Oscar Dugué, Le Blanc de Villeneufve, P. Pérennes and Charles Testut; today all their works are dead, and they themselves are but names. Testut was also a poet and novelist; other novelists were Canonge, Alfred Mercier, Alexandre Barde, Adrien Rouquette, Jacques de Roquigny and Charles Lemaître. The principal poets were Dominique Rouquette, Tullius Saint-Céran, Constant Lepouzé, Felix de Courmont, Alexandre Latil, A. Lussan, and Armand Lanusse. But the most competent of all the Creole authors was Charles E. A. Gayerré (1805-95), who was at once historian, dramatist and novelist. Today the Creole literature is practically extinct. A few poets and essayists are still at work, but they are of no importance.

3.

Spanish

The mutations of Spanish in Spanish-America have been very extensively studied by Spanish-American philologists, and there are separate monographs on Cubanisms, Mexicanisms, Porto Ricanisms, Venezuelanisms, Argentinisms, Peruanisms, Chileanisms, Costa Ricanisms and Honduranisms, and even extensive discussions

[15] Edward J. Fortier, in the Cambridge History of American Literature, vol. iv, p. 591. A bibliography is appended, p. 820 *ff*.

APPENDIX 403

of the dialects of single cities, notably Buenos Ayres and the City of Mexico.[16] The influence of the Indian language has been especially studied.[17] But the only extensive treatise upon the Spanish spoken in the United States is a series of four papers by Dr. Aurelio M. Espinosa, of Leland Stanford, Jr., University, in the *Revue de Dialectologie Romane* under the general title of "Studies in New Mexican Spanish."[18] These papers, however, are of such excellence that they almost exhaust the subject. The first two deal with the phonology of the dialect and the last two with its morphology. Dr. Espinosa, who was a professor in the University of New Mexico for eight years, reports that the Spanish of the Southwest, in its general characters, shows a curious parallel with American English. There is the same decay of grammatical niceties —the conjugations of the verb, for example, are reduced to two—the same great hospitality to loan-words, the same leaning toward a picturesque vividness, and the same preservation of words and phrases that have become archaic in the standard language. "It is a source of delight to the student of Spanish philology," he says, "to hear daily from the mouths of New Mexicans such words as *agora, ansi, naidien, trujo, escrebir, adrede*"—all archaic Castilian forms, and corresponding exactly to the *fox-fire, homespun, andiron, ragamuffin, fall* (for *autumn*), *flapjack* and *cesspool* that are preserved in American. They are survivors, in the main, of the Castilian Spanish of the fifteenth and sixteenth centuries, though some of them come from other Spanish dialects. Castilian has changed very much since that time, as standard English has changed; it is probable, indeed, that a Castilian of the year 1525, coming back to life today, would understand a New Mexican far more readily than he would understand a Spaniard, just as an Englishman of 1630 would understand a Kentucky mountaineer more readily than he would understand a Londoner.

New Mexico has been in the possession of the United States since

[16] See the Bibliography—Non-English Languages in America: Spanish—under Abeille, Arons, Ferraz, Maspero, Armengal y Valenzuela, Malaret, Calanno, Pichardo, Rincón, Ramos y Duarte, Sanchez, Sanz and Toro y Gisbert.
[17] See Ferraz, Armengal y Valenzuela, Robelo, Sanchez and Espinosa in the Bibliography.
[18] Tome i, p. 157 and p. 269; tome iii, p. 251; tome iv, p. 241.

1846, and so it is natural to find its Spanish corrupted by American influences, especially in the vocabulary. Of the 1,400 words that Dr. Espinosa chooses for remark, 300 are English, 75 are Nahuatl, 10 come from the Indian languages of the Southwest, and 15 are of doubtful or unknown origin; the rest are pure Spanish, chiefly archaic. As in the case of the Pennsylvania Germans, the French Canadians and the Scandinavians of the Northwest, the Spanish-speaking people of New Mexico have borrowed the American names of all objects of peculiarly American character, e. g., *besbol* (= *baseball*), *grimbaque* (= *greenback*), *aiscrim* (= *ice-cream*), *quiande* (= *candy*), *fayaman* (= *fireman*), *otemil* (= *oatmeal*), *piquenic* (= *picnic*), *lonchi* (= *lunch*). Most of them have been modified to bring them into accord with Spanish speech-habits. For example, all explosive endings are toned down by suffixes, e. g., *lonchi* for *lunch*. So with many r-endings, e. g., *blofero* for *bluffer*. And sibilants at the beginning of words are shaded by prefixes, e. g., *esteque* for *steak* and *espechi* for *speech*. Not only words have been taken in, but also many phrases, though most of the latter are converted into simple words, e. g., *olraite* (= *all right*), *jaitun* (= *hightoned*), *jamachi* (= *how much*), *sarape* (= *shut up*), *enejau* (= *anyhow*). Dr. Espinosa's study is a model of what such an inquiry should be. I cordially commend it to all students of dialect.

English has also greatly influenced the Spanish spoken in Spanish-America proper, especially in Mexico, Cuba, Porto Rico and in the seaports of South America. *Sandwich* and *club,* though they are not used by the Spaniards, are quite good Mexican. *Bluffer* is quite as familiar in Cuban Spanish as it is in New Mexican Spanish, though in Cuba it has become *blofista* instead of *blofero*. I take the following from *El Mundo,* one of the Havana newspapers, of June 28, 1920:

<small>New York, junio 27.—Por un sensacional *batting rally,* en el octavo *inning* en el que los Yankees dieron seis *hits* incluyendo un *triple* de Ruth y tubeyes de Ward y Meusel, gano el New York el *match* de esta tarde, pues hizo cinco carreras en ese episodio, venciendo 7 a 5. Mays el *pitcher* de los *locales* autuó bien, con excepcion del cuarto *round,* cuando Vitt le dió un *home run* con dos en *bases*.</small>

Nor are such words any longer exotic; the Cubans have adopted the terminology with the game, and begin to use it figuratively as the Americans use it. Along the east coast of South America the everyday speech of the people is full of Americanisms, and they enter very largely into the fashionable slang of the upper classes. *Cocktail, dinner-dance, one-step, fox-trot, sweater, kimono, high-ball, ginger-ale* and *sundae* are in constant use, and most of them are pronounced correctly, though *sundae* is transformed into *soondáe*. *Bombo* (= *boom*) is used by all the politicians, and so are *plataforma* (= *platform*), *mitin* (= *meeting*), *alarmista, big-stick, damphool* and various forms of *to bluff*. The American *auto* has been naturalized, and so has *ice-cream,* but in the form of *milkcream,* pronounced *milclee* by the lower orders. The boss of a train down there is the *conductor del tren;* a commuter is a *commutador; switch* is used both in its American railroad sense and to indicate the electrical device; *slip, dock* and *wharf* (the last pronounced *guáfay*) are in daily use; so is *socket* (electrical), though it is pronounced *sokáytay;* so are *poker* and many of the terms appertaining to the game. The South Americans use *just* in the American way, as in *justamente a* (or *en*) *tiempo* (= *just in time*). They are very fond of *good-bye* and *go to hell*. They have translated the verb phrase, *to water stocks,* into *aguar las acciones*. The American *white elephant* has become *el elefanto blanco*. In Cuba the *watermelon— patilla* or *sandía,* in Spanish—is the *mélon-de-agua*. Just as French-Canadian has borrowed Americanisms that are loan-words from other immigrant tongues, e. g., *bum* and *loafer* from the German, so some of the South American dialects have borrowed *rapidas* (= *rapids*), and *kimono,* the first brought into American from the French and the second from the Japanese.[19]

4.

Yiddish

Yiddish, even more than American, is a lady of easy virtue among the languages. Basically, a medieval High German, it has become so overladen with Hebrew, Russian, Polish, Lithuanian and even

[19] For most of these observations I am indebted to Dr. A. Z. López-Penha, the distinguished Colombian poet and critic.

Hungarian words that it is unintelligible to Germans.[20] Transported to the United States, it has taken in so many English words and phrases, and particularly so many Americanisms, that it is now nearly unintelligible, as spoken in the big cities of the East, to recent arrivals from Russia and Poland. Such typical Americanisms as *sky-scraper, loan-shark, graft, bluffer, faker, boodler, gangster, crook, guy, kike, piker, squealer, bum, cadet, boom, bunch, pants, vest, loafer, jumper, stoop, saleslady, ice-box,* and *raise* are quite as good Yiddish as they are American. For all the objects and acts of everyday life the East Side Jews commonly use English terms, e. g., *boy, chair, window, carpet, floor, dress, hat, watch, ceiling, consumption, property, trouble, bother, match, change, party, birthday, picture, paper* (only in the sense of *newspaper*), *gambler, show, hall, kitchen, store, bedroom, key, mantelpiece, closet, lounge, broom, table-cloth, paint, landlord, fellow, tenant, bargain, sale, haircut, razor, basket, school, scholar, teacher, baby, mustache, butcher, grocery, dinner, street* and *walk*. In the factories there is the same universal use of *shop, wages, foreman, boss, sleeve, collar, cuff, button, cotton, thimble, needle, machine, pocket, remnant, sample,* etc., even by the most recent immigrants. Many of these words have quite crowded out the corresponding Yiddish terms, so that the latter are seldom heard. For example, *ingle*, meaning *boy* (= Ger. *jüngling*), has been wholly obliterated by the English word. A Jewish immigrant almost invariably refers to his son as his *boy*, though strangely enough he calls his daughter his *meidel*. "Die *boys* mit die *meidlach* haben a good time" is excellent American Yiddish. In the same way *fenster* has been completely displaced by *window*, though *tür* (= *door*) has been left intact. *Tisch* (= *table*) also remains, but *chair* is always used, probably because few of the Jews had chairs in the old country. There the *beinkel*, a bench without a back, was in use; chairs were only for the well-to-do. *Floor* has apparently prevailed because no invariable corresponding word was

---

[20] During the war I visited Lithuania and Livonia while they were occupied by the Germans. The latter could not understand the Yiddish of the native Jews, but there were in almost every town a few Jews who had been to the United States and could speak English, and these were employed as interpreters. Among the Germans, of course, there were many English-speaking officers.

employed at home: in various parts of Russia and Poland a floor is a *dill,* a *podlogé,* or a *bricke.* So with *ceiling.* There were six different words for it.

Yiddish inflections have been fastened upon most of these loanwords. Thus, "er hat ihm *abgefaked"* is "he cheated him," *zubumt* is the American *gone to the bad, fix'n* is *to fix, usen* is *to use,* and so on. The feminine and diminutive suffix *-ké* is often added to nouns. Thus *bluffer* gives rise to *blufferké* (= *hypocrite*), and one also notes *dresské, hatké, watchké* and *bummerké.* "Oi! is sie a *blufferké!"* is good American Yiddish for "isn't she a hypocrite!" The suffix *-nick,* signifying agency, is also freely applied. *Allrightnick* means an upstart, an offensive boaster, one of whom his fellows would say "He is all right" with a sneer. Similarly, *consumptionick* means a victim of tuberculosis. Other suffixes are *-chick* and *-ige,* the first exemplified in *boychick,* a diminutive of *boy,* and the second in *next-doorige,* meaning the woman next-door, an important person in ghetto social life. Some of the loan-words, of course, undergo changes on Yiddish-speaking lips. Thus *landlord* becomes *lendler, certificate* (a pretty case of Hobson-Jobson!) becomes *stiff-ticket, lounge* becomes *lunch, tenant* becomes *tenner,* and *whiskers* loses its final *s.* "Wie gefällt dir sein *whisker?"* (= how do you like his beard?) is good Yiddish, ironically intended. *Fellow,* of course, changes to the American *fella* or *feller,* as in "Rosie hat schon a *fella"* (= Rosie has got a *fella, i. e.,* a sweetheart). *Show,* in the sense of *chance,* is used constantly, as in "git ihm a *show"* (= give him a *chance*). *Bad boy* is adopted bodily, as in "er is a *bad boy."* *To shut up* is inflected as one word, as in "er hat nit gewolt *shutup'n"* (= he wouldn't shut up). *To catch* is used in the sense of to obtain, as in *"catch'n* a gmilath chesed" (= to raise a loan). Here, by the way, *gmilath chesed* is excellent Biblical Hebrew. *To bluff,* unchanged in form, takes on the new meaning of to lie: a *bluffer* is a liar. Scores of American phrases are in constant use, among them, *all right, never mind, I bet you, no sir* and *I'll fix you.* It is curious to note that *sure Mike,* borrowed by the American vulgate from Irish English, has gone over into American Yiddish. Finally, to make an end, here are two complete American Yiddish sentences: "Sie wet *clean'n* die *rooms, scrub'n* dem *floor, wash'n* die *windows,* *dress'n* dem *boy* und gehn in *butcher-store* und in *grocery*. Dernoch vet sie machen *dinner* und gehn in *street* für a *walk.*" [21]

For some time past there has been an active movement among the New York Jews for the purification of Yiddish. This movement is an offshoot of Zionism, and has resulted in the establishment of a number of Yiddish schools. Its adherents do not propose, of course, that English be abandoned, but simply that the two languages be kept separate, and that Jewish children be taught Yiddish as well as English. The Yiddishists insist that it is more dignified to say *a gooten tog* than *good-bye,* and *billet* instead of *ticket.* But the movement makes very poor progress. "The Americanisms absorbed by the Yiddish of this country," says Abraham Cahan, "have come to stay. To hear one say 'Ich hob a *billet* für heitige vorschtellung' would be as jarring to the average East Side woman, no matter how illiterate and ignorant she might be, as the intrusion of a bit of Chinese in her daily speech."

Yiddish, as everyone knows, has produced a very extensive literature during the past two generations; it is, indeed, so large and so important that I can do no more than refer to it here.[22] Much of it has come from Jewish authors living in New York. In their work, and particularly their work for the stage, there is extensive and brilliant evidence of the extent to which American English has influenced the language.

5.

Italian

Rémy de Gourmont, the French critic, was the first to call attention to the picturesqueness of the Americanized Italian spoken by Italians in the United States;[23] unluckily his appreciation of its qualities has not been shared by American Romance scholars.

[21] I am indebted throughout this section to Mr. Abraham Cahan, editor of the leading Yiddish daily in New York, and a distinguished writer in both Yiddish and English.
[22] *Cf.* the article on Yiddish, by Nathaniel Buchwald, in the Cambridge History of American Literature, vol. iv, p. 598, and the bibliography following, p. 822 *ff.*
[23] In L'Esthétique de la Langue Française; Paris, 1899.

APPENDIX 409

The literature dealing with it, in fact, is confined to one capital study by Dr. Arthur Livingston,[24] formerly of Columbia University, who says that other "American philologists have curiously disdained it." Meanwhile, it has begun to produce, like Yiddish, an extensive literature, ranging in character and quality from such eloquent pieces as Giovanni Pascoli's "Italy" to the Rabelaisian trifles of Carlo Ferrazzano. Ferrazzano shines in the composition of *macchiette coloniali* for the cheap Italian theatres in New York. The *macchietta coloniale* is an Americanized variety of the Neapolitan *macchietta*, which Dr. Livingston describes as "a character-sketch—etymologically, a character-'daub'—most often constructed on rigorous canons of 'ingenuity': there must be a literal meaning, accompanied by a double sense, which in the nature of the tradition, inclines to be pornographic." The *macchietta* was brought to New York by Edoardo Migliacci (Farfariello), purged of its purely Neapolitan materials, and so adapted to the comprehension of Italians from other parts of Italy. Farfariello wrote fully five hundred *macchiette* and Ferrazzano has probably written as many more; many of the latter have been printed. They are commonly in verse, with now and then a descent to prose. I take from Dr. Livingston's study a specimen of the latter:

Ne sera dentro na *barra* americana dove il patrone era americano, lo *visco* era americano, la birra era americana, ce steva na ghenga de *loffari* tutti americani: solo io non ero americano; quanno a tutto nu mumento me mettono mmezzo e me dicettono: *Alò spaghetti; iu mericano men?* No! no! *mi Italy men! Iu blacco enze.* No, no! *Iu laico chistu contrì.* No, no! *Mi laico mio contry! Mi laico Italy!* A questa punto me chiavaieno lo primo *fait!* "Dice: *Orrè for America!*" Io tuosto: *Orrè for Italy!* Un ato *fait.* "Dice: *Orrè for America!*" *Orrè for Italy! N'ato fait* e *n ato fait,* fino a che me facetteno addurmentare; ma però, *orrè for America* nun o dicette!

Quanno me scietaie, me trovaie ncoppa lu marciepiedi cu nu *pulizio* vicino che diceva; *Ghiroppe bomma!* Io ancora stunato alluccaie: *America nun gudde! Orrè for Italy!* Sapete li *pulizio* che facette? Mi arrestò!

Quanno fu la mattina, lu *giorge* mi dicette: *Wazzo maro laste naite?* Io risponette: *No tocche nglese!* "No? *Tenne dollari.*" E quello porco dello *giorge* nun scherzava, perchè le diece pezze se le pigliaie! . . .

Most of the Americanisms are obvious: *barra* for *bar, visco* for *whisky, blacco enze* for *black-hand, laico* for *like, chistu* for *this,*

[24] La Merica Sanemagogna, *Romanic Review,* vol. ix, no. 2, p. 206 *ff.*

contri for *country,* *fait* for *fight* (it is also used for *punch,* as in *chiaver nu fair,* give a punch, and *nato fait,* another punch), *loffari* for *loafers,* *ghiroppe* for *get up,* *bomma* for *bum,* *pulizio* for *police,* *nun gudde* for *no good,* *orré* for *hurray,* *giorge* for *judge,* *wazzo maro* for *what's the matter,* *laste* for *last,* *naite* for *night,* *toccho* for *talk,* *tenne* for *ten,* *dollari* for *dollars.* All of the *macchiette coloniali* are gaudy with the same sort of loan-words; one of the best of them, says Dr. Livingston, is Farfariello's "A lingua 'nglese," which is devoted almost wholly to humorous attempts to represent English words as ignorant Italians hear and use them.

As in the case of Yiddish, there is a movement among Italian intellectuals in America, and especially in New York, for the restoration of a purer Italian. These purists are careful to use the *sotterraneo* to take them *nell bassa città.* But the great majority prefer *il subway* or the *tonno* ($=$ *tunnel*) to take them *tantane* ($=$ *downtown*). All the common objects of life tend similarly to acquire names borrowed from American English, sometimes bodily and sometimes by translation. In the main, these loan-words are given Italianized forms and inflected in a more or less correct Italian manner. Dr. Livingston presents a number of interesting examples from the advertising columns of an Italian newspaper in New York. *Pressers* are *pressatori,* operators are *operatori,* machines are *mascine,* carpenters are *carpentieri,* presser's helpers are *sottopressatori,* a store is a *storo,* board is *bordo,* boarders are *abbordato,* bushelmen are *buscellatori,* customs-coats are *cotti da costume,* men's coats are *cotti da uomo.* "Originally," he says, "the policy of this paper was to translate, in correct form, the Italian copy. The practice had to be abandoned because poorer results were obtained from advertisements restored to the literary tongue." In other words, the average Italian in New York now understands American-Italian better than he understands the standard language of his country.

The newly arrived Italian quickly picks up the Americanized vocabulary. Almost at once he calls the man in charge of his *ghenga* ($=$ *gang*) his *bosso,* and talks of his work in the *indiccio* ($=$ *ditch*) and with the *sciabola* ($=$ *shovel*), *picco* ($=$ *pick*) and *stim-sciabola* ($=$ *steam-shovel*). He buys *sechenze* ($=$ *second-hand*) clothes, works on the *tracca* ($=$ *track*), buys food at the *grosseria* ($=$ *gro-*

APPENDIX 411

cery) or *marchetto* (= *market*), eats *pinozze* (= *peanuts*), rides on the *livetta* (= *elevated*), rushes a *grollo* (= *growler*) for near-beer, gets on good terms with the *barritenne* (= *bartender*), and speaks of the *auschieppe* (= *housekeeper*) of his boarding-house, denounces idlers as *loffari* (= *loafers*), joins a *globbo* (= *club*), gets himself a *ghella* (= *girl*), and is her *falò* (= *fellow*). Some of the new words he acquires are extremely curious, e. g., *canabuldogga* (= *bulldog*), *pipe del gasso* (= *gas-pipe*), *coppetane* (= *'ncuop* + *town* = *uptown*), *fruttistenne* (= *fruit-stand*), *sanemagogna* (= *son-of-a-gun*), *mezzo-barrista* (= *half-time bartender*). Several quite new words, unknown to Americans, have been made of American materials and added to the vocabulary. An example is afforded by *temeniollo,* signifying a very large glass of beer. Dr. Livingston says that it comes from *Tammany Hall!* Another Italian-American invention is *flabussce,* used as an interjection to indicate the extreme of pessimism. It comes from *Flatbush,* where the principal Italian cemetery is situated.

The large emigration of Italians during the past half dozen years has transported a number of Americanisms to Italy. *Bomma* (= *bum*) is now a familiar word in Naples: a strange wandering, indeed, for the original *bum* was German. So is *schidù* (= *skiddoo*). So is *briccoliere* (= *bricklayer*).[25]

6.

Dano-Norwegian

Here are some characteristic specimens of the Dano-Norwegian spoken by Norwegian settlers in Minnesota, as given by Dr. Nils Flaten, of Northfield, Minn.:[26]

[25] In addition to my indebtedness to Dr. Livingston, I owe thanks for assistance to Prof. A. Arbib Costa, of the College of the City of New York, and to Mr. Alfred Boni, editor of *Il Progresso Italo-Americano.*
[26] Notes on American-Norwegian, with a Vocabulary, *Dialect Notes,* vol. ii, p. 115 *ff.*

Mrs. Olsen va *aafel bisi* idag; hun maatte *béke kék*. (Mrs. Olsen was awfully busy today; she had to bake cake.)
Den *spattute stiren* braekka sig ut av *pastre* aa *rönna* langt ind i *fila* aa je va ikke *aebel* te aa *kaetsche'n;* men saa *sigga* je *doggen* min paa'n. (The spotted steer broke out of the pasture and ran far into the field before I was able to catch him; but then I sicked my dog at him.)
Reileaaden ha *muva schappa* sine. (The railroad has moved its shops.)
Je kunde ikke faa *resa* saa mye *kaes* at je fik betalt *morgesen* i *farmen* min. (I couldn't raise enough cash to pay the mortgage on my farm.)
Det *meka* ingen *difrens.* (That makes no difference.)
Det *kötta* ingen *figger.* (That cuts no figure.)
Hos'n *fila* du? *Puddi gud.* (How do you feel? Pretty good.)

The words in italics would be unintelligible to a recent arrival from Norway; they are all American loan-words. "Such words," says Dr. Flaten, "are often mutilated beyond recognition by an American. . . . In the case of many words the younger generation cannot tell whether they are English or Norse. I was ten years old before I found that such words as *paatikkel* (= *particular*), *staebel* (= *stable*), *fens* (= *fence*) were not Norse, but mutilated English. I had often wondered that *poleit, trubbel, söperéter* were so much like the English words *polite, trouble, separator.* So common is this practise of borrowing that no English word is refused admittance into this vocabulary provided it can stand the treatment it is apt to get. Some words, indeed, are used without any appreciable difference in pronunciation, but more generally the root, or stem, is taken and Norse inflections are added as required by the rules of the language." Sometimes the English loan-word and a corresponding Norwegian word exist side by side, but in such cases, according to Dr. George T. Flom,[27] "there is a prevalent and growing tendency" to drop the latter, save in the event that it acquires a special meaning. "Very often in such cases," continues Dr. Flom, "the English word is shorter and easier to pronounce or the Norse equivalent is a purely literary word—that is, does not actually exist in the dialect of the settlers. . . . In the considerable number of cases where the loan-word has an exact equivalent in the Norse dialect it is often very difficult to determine the reason for the loan, though it would be safe to say that it is frequently due simply to a

---

[27] English Elements in the Norse Dialects of Utica, Wisconsin, *Dialect Notes*, vol. ii, p. 257 *ff.*

desire on the part of the speaker to use English words, a thing that becomes very pronounced in the jargon that is sometimes heard." Dr. Flaten exhibits the following declension of a typical loanword, *swindler*. In Dano-Norwegian there is no letter *w*, and the suffix of agency is not -*er* but -*ar;* so the word becomes *svindlar*. It is regarded as masculine and declined thus:

	Singular	
	Indefinite	Definite
Nom.	ein svindlar	svindlarn
Gen.	aat svindlar	aat svindlaré
Dat.	(te) ein svindlar	(te) svindlaré
Acc.	ein svindlar	svindlarn
	Plural	
Nom.	noko svindlara	svindlaradn
Gen.	aat noko svindlara	aat svindlaro
Dat.	(te) noko svindlara	(te) svindlaro
Acc.	noko svindlara	svindlaradn

The vocabularies of Drs. Flaten and Flom show a large number of such substitutions of English (including some thoroughly American) words. The Dano-Norwegian *øl* is abandoned for the English *beer*, which becomes *bir*. *Tonde* succumbs to *baerel, barel* or *baril* (= *barrel*), *frokost* to *brekkfaest* (= *breakfast*), *forsikring* to *inschurings* (= *insurance*),[28] *stald* to *staebel* (= *stable*), *skat* to *taex* (=*tax*), and so on. The verbs yield in the same way: *vaeljuéte* (= *valuate*), *titsche* (*teach*), *katte* (*cut*), *klém* (*claim*), *savére* (*survey*), *refjuse* (*refuse*). And the adjectives: *plén* (*plain*), *jelös* (*jealous*), *kjokfuldt* (*chock-full*), *krésé* (*crazy*), *aebel* (*able*), *klir* (*clear*), *pjur* (*pure*), *pur* (*poor*). And the adverbs and adverbial phrases: *isé* (*easy*), *reit evé* (*right away*), *aept to* (*apt to*), *allreit* (*all right*). Dr. Flaten lists some extremely grotesque compound words, e. g., *nekk-töi* (*necktie*), *kjaens-bogg* (*chinch-bug*), *hospaar* (*horse-power*), *gitte long* (*get along*), *hardvaer-staar* (*hardware-store*), *staets-praessen* (*state's-prison*), *traevling-maen* (*traveling-man*), *uxe-jogg* (*yoke of oxen*), *stim-baat* (*steamboat*). Pure Americanisms are not infrequent, e. g., *bösta*

---

[28] Connoisseurs will recall Abe Potash's *insurings*. What we have here is the substitution of a familiar suffix for one of somewhat similar sound but much less familiar—a frequent cause of phonetic decay.

(*busted*), *bés-baal* (*baseball*), *boggé* (*buggy*), *dipo* (*depot*), *fraimhus* (*frame-house*), *jukre* (*to euchre*), *kaemp-mid'n* (*camp-meeting*), *kjors* (*chores*), *magis* (*moccasin*), *malasi* (*molasses*), *munke-rins* (*monkey-wrench*), *raad-bas* (*road-boss*), *sjante* (*shanty*), *sörpreisparti* (*surprise-party*), *strit-kar* (*street-car*), *tru trin* (*through train*). The decayed American adverb is boldly absorbed, as in *han file baed* (= *he feels bad*). "That this lingo," says Dr. Flaten, "will ever become a dialect of like importance with the Pennsylvania Dutch is hardly possible. . . . The Norwegians are among those of our foreign-born citizens most willing to part with their mother tongue." But meanwhile it is spoken by probably half a million of them, and it will linger in isolated farming regions for years.

7.

Swedish

A useful study of American-Swedish is to be found in "Vårt Språk," by Vilhelm Berger,[29] editor of the Swedish semi-weekly, *Nordstjernan,* published in New York. In his preface to his little book Mr. Berger mentions two previous essays upon the same subject: "Det Svenske Språket in Amerika," by Rector Gustav Andreen, of Rock Island, Ill., and "Engelskans Inflytande på Svenska Språket in Amerika," by Dr. E. A. Zetterstrand, but I have been unable to gain access to either. Mr. Berger says that the Swedes who come to America quickly purge their speech of the Swedish terms indicating the ordinary political, social and business relations and adopt the American terms bodily. Thus, *borgmästere* is displaced by *mayor, länsman* by *sheriff, häradsskrifvare* by *county-clerk, centraluppvärmning med ånga* by *steam-heat,* and *ananas* by *pineapple,* the Swedish measurements give way to *mile, inch, pound, acre,* etc., and there is an immediate adoption of such characteristic Americanisms as *graft, trust, ring, janitor, surprise-party, bay-window, bluff, commencement* (college), *homestead, buggy* and *pull.* Loan-words taken into American from other immigrant languages

[29] Rock Island, Ill., 1912.

APPENDIX 415

go with the purely English terms, *e. g., luffa* (= to *loaf*, from the German) and *vigilans* (= *vigilantes*, from the Spanish). Many of these borrowings are adapted to Swedish spelling, and so *sidewalk* becomes *sajdoak, street* becomes *strit, fight* becomes *fajt, business* becomes *bissness,* and *housecleaning* becomes *husklining*. But even more important is the influence that American English has upon the vocabulary that remains genuinely Swedish; when words are not borrowed bodily they often change the form of familiar Swedish words. Thus *sängkammare* (= *bedroom*) is abandoned for *bäddrum, husållsgöromål* (= *housework*) gives way to *husarbete, kabeltelegram* to *kabelgram, brandsoldat* (=*fireman*) to *brandman, regnby* (=*rainstorm*) to *regnstorm, brekfort* (=*postcard*) to *postkort,* and *beställa* (=*order*) to *ordra*. The Swedish-American no longer speaks of *frihet;* instead he uses *fridom,* an obvious offspring of *freedom.* His wife abandons the *hattnål* for the *hattpinne*. He acquires a *hemadress* (=*home address*) in place of his former *bostadsadress*. Instead of *kyrkogård* (= *churchyard*) he uses *grafgård* (= *graveyard*). For *godståg* (= *goods-train*) he substitutes *frakttåg* (= *freight-train*). In place of words with roots that are Teutonic he devises words with roots that have been taken into English from the Latin, the Greek or the French, *e.g., investigera, krusad, minoritetsrapport, officerare, audiens, affär, exkursion, evangelist, hospital, liga* (= *league*), *residens, sympati*.

This influence of American extends to grammar and syntax. The inflections of Swedish tend to fall off in the United States, as the inflections of German have fallen off among the Pennsylvania Germans. And the Americanized Swede gradually acquires a habit of putting his sentences together English-fashion. At home he would say *Bröderna Anderson,* just as the German would say *Gebrüder Anderson,* but in America he says *Anderson Bröderna*. In Sweden *all over* is *öfverallt;* in America, following the American construction, it becomes *allt öfver*. *Mina vänner* (= *my friend*) is Americanized into *en vän af mina* (= *a friend of mine*). *Tid efter annan* (literally, *time after another*) becomes *från tid till tid* (= *from time to time*). The American verb *to take* drags its Swedish relative, *taga,* into strange places, as in *taga kallt* (=*to take cold*), *taga nöje i* (=*to take pleasure in*), *taga fördel af* (=*to take advantage of*), and *taga tåget* (=*to take a train*). The thoroughly American use of *right* is imitated by a similar use of its equivalent, *rätt*, as in *rätt af* (=*right off*), *rätt iväg* (=*right away*) and *rätt intill* (=*right next to*). The Swede at home says *här i landet* (=*here in this country*); in America he says *i det här landet* (= *in this here country*). *All right, well* and other such American counter-words he adopts instantly, just as he adopts *hell* and *damn*. He exiles the preposition, imitating the American vulgate, to the end of the sentence. He begins to use the Swedish *af* precisely as if it were the English *of*, and *i* as if it were *in*. After a few years his Swedish is so heavy with American loan-words and American idioms that it is almost unintelligible to his brother recently arrived from home.

8.

Dutch

The Dutch language exists in two forms in the United States, both differentiated from the original Dutch of Holland by the influence of American-English. The first is the so-called Jersey, or Bergen County Dutch, which is spoken by the descendants of seventeenth century Dutch settlers in Bergen and Passaic counties, New Jersey. In New York, as everyone knows, Dutch completely disappeared many years ago, but in these Jersey counties it still survives, though apparently obsolescent, and is spoken by many persons who are not of Dutch blood, including a few negroes. The second variety of Americanized Dutch is spoken by more recent immigrants, chiefly in Michigan. There is little if any communication between the two dialects.

An excellent short study of Jersey Dutch was published by Dr. J. Dyneley Prince in 1910;[30] it remains the only one in print. The dialect, says Dr. Prince, "was originally the South Holland or Flemish language, which, in the course of centuries (*ca.* 1630-1880), became mixed with and partially influenced by English, having bor-

[30] The Jersey Dutch Dialect, *Dialect Notes*, vol. iii, pp. 459 *ff.*

rowed also from the Mindi (Lenâpe-Delaware) Indian language a few animal and plant names. This Dutch has suffered little or nothing from modern Holland or Flemish immigration, although Paterson (the county seat of Passaic County) has at present a large Netherlands population. The old county people hold themselves strictly aloof from these foreigners, and say, when they are questioned as to the difference between the idioms: 'Onze tal äz lex däuts en hoelliz äs Holläns; kwait dääfrent' (our language is low Dutch and theirs is Holland Dutch; quite different). An intelligent Fleming or South Hollander with a knowledge of English can make shift at following a conversation in this Americanized Dutch, but the converse is not true."

As usual, contact with English has worn off the original inflections, and the definite and indefinite articles, *de* and *en,* are uniform for all genders. The case-endings have nearly all disappeared, in the comparison of adjectives the superlative affix has decayed from *-st* to *-s,* the person-endings in the conjugation of verbs have fallen off, and the pronouns have been much simplified. The vocabulary shows many signs of English influence. A large number of words in daily use have been borrowed bodily, *e. g., bottle, town, railroad, cider, smoke, potato, match, good-bye.* Others have been borrowed with changes, *e.g., säns (since), määm (ma'm), belange (belong), boddere (bother), bääznäs (business), orek (earache).* In still other cases the drag of English is apparent, as in *blaubääse,* a literal translation of *blueberry* (the standard Dutch word is *heidebes*), in *mep'lbom* (= *mapletree;* Dutch, *ahoornboom*), and in *njeuspampir* (= *newspaper;* Dutch, *nieuwsblad*). A few English archaisms are preserved in the dialect; for example, the use of *gentry* as a plural for *gentleman.*

The Dutch spoken by the colonists from Holland in Michigan has been very extensively modified by American influences, both in vocabulary and in grammar. As in Jersey Dutch and in South African Dutch there has been a decay of inflections, and the neuter article *het* has been absorbed by the masculine-feminine article *de.* Says Prof. Henry J. G. Van Andel, of the chair of Dutch history, literature and art in Calvin College at Grand Rapids: "Almost all the American names of common objects, *e. g., stove, mail, carpet, bookcase, kitchen, store, post-office, hose, dress, pantry, porch, buggy, picture, newspaper, ad, road, headline,* particularly when they differ considerably from the Dutch terms, have been taken into the everyday vocabulary. This is also true of a great many verbs and adjectives, e. g., to move (*moeven*), to dig (*diggen*), to shop (*shoppen*), to drive (*dryven:* a meaning different from the standard Dutch one), *slow, fast, easy, pink,* etc. The religious language has remained pure, but even here purity has only a relative meaning, for the constructions employed are often English." This corrupted vulgate is called Yankee-Dutch by the Hollanders of Michigan, and, like Pennsylvania German, it has begun to produce a literature, chiefly humorous in character. A little book of sketches by Dirk Nieland, called "Yankee-Dutch," [31] contains some amusing specimens, e. g., *piezelmietje* (= pleased to meet you), and *"You want 'n ander kop koffie."* From an anonymous piece kindly supplied by Dr. John J. Hiemenga, president of Calvin College, I extract the following:

't Had tamelijk ferm gesneeuwd de laatste twee dagen, zoodat de *farmers* toch nog een *sleeride* konden krijgen in het bijna vervlogen jaar. Vooral de *young folks* hunkerden naar een *cutter-ride.* Bijna allerwege in den omtrek van de Star Corners waren de *cutters* dan ook voor den dag gehaald en nagezien, want alles moest natuurlijk in *running-order* zijn. De *dust* moest er afgeveegd, hier en daar een bur wat *aangetight,* de *kussens* een weinig *opgefixt,* en de *bells* vooral nauwkeurig onderzocht.

Dit was hedenmiddag ook Frits zijn *job* geweest, met het doel hedenavond zijn eerste *ride* in de mooie *cutter* can Klaas Ekkel, biji wien hij als winterknecht diende, te nemen. Hij begon dan ook al vroeg met de *chores,* molk in a *hurry* en was daarmee dus tijdig klaar. 't *Supper* werd even vlug verorberd, *zoodat* Frits om *half-zeven* al in de *barn was,* om Florie *op te hichen.*

Trotsch op haar nieuw *harness* en schallende *bellen,* draaft Florie gezwind en fier daarheen. Hier en daar waar een oude *railfence* de *sneeuw* opving, *zoodat* de *road* bijna geheel *opgeblokt* is, gaat of rakelings langs de andere *fence* of over de *fields.* Wel zijn er van daag een paar *teams* langs gegaan, doch de *sneeuw* en de wind hebben hun *tracks* geheel *opgecoverd, zoodat* Frits zijn eigen pad maar moet maken.

Dat 't vinnig koud is voelt hij niet, dank zij zijn dikke *furcoat.* Voelt hij de koude echter niet, hooren deed hij haar wel. War knarst en giert die *sneeuw* onder de *runners!* Ook de milliarden fonkelende sneeuwkelkjes, die met evenveel kleuren het licht der halve maan weerkaatsen, getuigen van de koude.

[31] Yankee-Dutch, humoristische schetsen uit het Hollandsch-Amerikaansche volksleven; Grand Rapids, Mich., 1919.

APPENDIX 419

Frits geniet dit schoone kleurenspel en verzinkt weldra in diep gepeins. Plotseling schrikt hij op.

"Hello, Frits, *going to the store?*"

"Ja, Henry, als je er in *jumpen* wilt, kan je zoover meerijden, maar 't is haast te veel *troebel* voor 't geld."

Henry wil ook kunnen zeggen, dat hij van avond een *cutter-ride gehad* heeft en stapt dus in. Nog enkele rods en ze zijn bij de *stables* achter de kerk, waar ze 't paard *stallen* en nu naar de *store*. Zoo 'n *country-store* is de lievelingsplek van de meeste jongens uit den omtrek, als 's avonds het werk aan kant is. Enkele *loafers* maken zoo'n *store* hun *home*. Heel gezellig is men 's avonds soms bij elkaar. Is her een onnoozele bloed aanwezig, dan heeft men *wat fun* met hem. *Stories* hoort men er *bij de wholesale*. Twijfelt Jan er aan of Piet wel een *barrel* met *salt* kan tillen, dan noopt een "*I'll bet you the cigars*" hem om te zwijgen of te wedden. Voor *cigars, peanuts* en *candy* wordt er dan ook heel wat geld gespend. . . .

This curious dialect promises to be short of life. On the one hand the leaders among the colonists strive to make them use a purer Dutch and on the other hand the younger members, particularly those born in America, abandon both good and bad Dutch for English. I am informed by various observers in Grand Rapids and its vicinity that there seems to be but small prospect that Yankee-Dutch will survive as long as Pennsylvania German.[32]

9.

Icelandic

The only study that I have been able to find of the changes undergone by Icelandic in America is a brief but informative note on the inflection of loan-nouns by Vilhjálmer Stefánsson,[33] the well-known arctic explorer, who was born of Icelandic parents in Canada. There are relatively few Icelanders in the United States and most of them are concentrated in a few North Dakota and Minnesota counties. There are many more in Manitoba. Their language, philologically,

[32] I am indebted to Prof. B. K. Kuiper, to Mr. H. H. D. Langereis, to Mr. D. J. Van Riemsdyck, of the Eerdmans-Sevensma Co., the Dutch publishers of Grand Rapids, and to Dr. Paul H. De Kruif, of the Rockefeller Institute, for aid and suggestions.

[33] English Loan-Nouns Used in the Icelandic Colony of North Dakota, *Dialect Notes*, vol. ii, pp. 354 ff.

is one of the most ancient of Europe, for the remote situation and poor communications of Iceland have served to preserve many early Teutonic characters that have long since vanished from the related languages. It is, of course, highly inflected, and the most interesting thing about its relations with American English in the United States is the sturdy way in which it fastens inflections upon loan-words from the latter. "No word," says Mr. Stefánsson, "can be used in Icelandic without being assigned a gender-form distinguished by the post-positive article." This law produces some curious effects when English nouns are taken in. The very American *baseball, buggy, candy, cyclone* and *corn-starch* are all neuter, but *beer, boss, cowboy, cowcatcher, nickel* and *populist* are masculine, and *tie* (railroad), *prohibition* and *siding* are feminine. In the case of many words usage varies. Thus *caucus* has no fixed gender; different speakers make it masculine, feminine or neuter. *Crackers* and *automobile* are other such words. *Banjo* may be either feminine or neuter, *bicycle* may be either masculine or neuter, and *broncho* may be either masculine or feminine. The gender of such loan-words tends to be logical, but it is not always so. *Farmer* is always masculine and so is *engineer*, and *nurse* is always feminine, but *dressmaker* is given the masculine post-positive article, becoming *dressmakerinn*. However, when the pronoun is substituted, *hún*, which is feminine, is commonly used. Words ending in *-l* or *-ll* are usually considered neuter, e. g., *baseball, corral, hotel, hall*. "A striking example," says Mr. Stefánsson, "is the term *constable*. The natural gender is evidently masculine and the Icelandic equivalent, *lögreglumathur*, is masculine; yet *constable* is usually employed as a neuter, though occasionally as a masculine." Words in *-er* fall under the influence of the Icelandic masculine nouns in *-ari*, denoting agency, and so usually become masculine, e. g., *director, ginger, mower, parlor, peddler, reaper, separator*. *Republican* and *socialist* are masculine, but *democrat* is neuter. Why *cashbook, clique, contract, election* and *grape* should be feminine it is hard to understand. Of the 467 loan-nouns listed by Mr. Stefánsson, 176 are neuters and 137 are masculines. There are but 44 clear feminines, though 80 others are sometimes feminine.

On the syntax of American-Icelandic I can find nothing. The literature of the dialect is not extensive, and it has produced very

APPENDIX 421

few writers of any ability. Nearly all the Icelandic periodicals of the New World are published in Canada, chiefly at Winnipeg.[34] They are conducted, in the main, by natives of Iceland, and hence endeavor to preserve the purity of the language. But the Icelander born in America prefers to speak English, and even when he essays Icelandic he fills it with English words and phrases.

10.

Greek

I am informed by Mr. S. S. Lontos, editor of *Atlantis,* the Greek newspaper published in New York, that Greek journalists and other writers working in the United States try to avoid the use of Americanisms in their writing, and that the same care is observed by educated Greeks in conversation. But the masses of Greek immigrants imitate the newcomers of all other races by adopting Americanisms wholesale. In most cases the loan-words, as in Italian, undergo changes. Thus, *bill-of-fare* becomes *biloferi, pie* changes to *pya, sign* and *shine* to *saina* (there is no *sh*-sound in Greek), *cream* to *creamy, fruit-store* to *fruitaria, clams* to *clammess,* steak to *stecky, polish* to *policy, hotel* to *otelli,* stand to *stanza,* lease to *lista,* depot to *depos,* car to *carron* (= Modern Greek, *karron,* a cart), *picture* to *pitsa,* elevator and elevated to *elevata,* and so on. The Greeks suffer linguistic confusion immediately they attempt English, for in Modern Greek *nay* (spelled *nai*) means *yes,* P. M. indicates the hours *before* noon, and the letter *N* stands for *South.* To make things even worse, the Greek *papoose* means grandfather and *mammie* means grandmother.

So far as I know, no philological study of American Greek has been made. Undoubtedly all the processes of decay that have been going on in Greece itself for centuries will be hastened in this country. Whenever English begins to influence another language it plays havoc with the inflections.

[34] Icelandic-American Periodicals, by Halldór Hermannsson, *Pub. Soc. for the Advancement of Scandinavian Study,* vol. iii, no. 2; Urbana, Ill., July, 1916.

11.

The Slavic Languages

So far as I have been able to discover there is no literature in English upon the philological results of transplanting the Slavic languages, Polish, Czech, Serbian and Bulgarian, to America. Dr. C. H. Wachtel, editor of the *Dziennik Chicagoski,* the Polish daily newspaper published in Chicago, informs me that the Polish spoken in the United States has "taken over a great multitude of English words and phrases," and says that the Rev. B. E. Goral, a priest of Milwaukee, has written several articles in Polish upon the subject and collected a vocabulary. But I have been unable to get into communication with Father Goral. I am likewise informed by the editor of the *Svornost,* the Bohemian daily of Chicago, that a study of the changes undergone by Czech in the United States has been published by Dr. J. Salaba Vojan, of Chicago, but my inquiries of Dr. Vojan are unanswered. Regarding Serbian and Bulgarian I have been unable to obtain any information whatever. Of late years several chairs of Slavic languages and literatures have been set up in American universities. It is to be hoped that among the students they attract there will be some who will devote themselves to the transplanted living tongues as the scholars of the Middle West have devoted themselves to Dano-Norwegian.

III.

Proverb and Platitude

No people, save perhaps the Spaniards, have a richer store of proverbial wisdom than the Americans, and surely none other makes more diligent and deliberate efforts to augment its riches. The American literature of "inspirational" platitude is enormous and almost unique. There are half a dozen authors, *e. g.,* Dr. Orison Swett Marden and Dr. Frank Crane, who devote themselves almost exclusively, and to vast profit, to the composition of arresting and uplifting apothegms, and the fruits of their fancy are not only sold in books but also displayed upon an infinite variety of calendars, banners and wall-cards. It is rarely that one enters the office of an American business man without encountering at least one of these wall-cards. It may, on the one hand, show nothing save a succinct caution that time is money, say, "Do It Now," or "This Is My Busy Day"; on the other hand, it may embody a long and complex sentiment, ornately set forth. The taste for such canned sagacity seems to have arisen in America at a very early day. Benjamin Franklin's "Poor Richard's Almanac," begun in 1732, remained a great success for twenty-five years, and the annual sales reached 10,000. It had many imitators, and founded an aphoristic style of writing which culminated in the essays of Emerson, often mere strings of sonorous certainties, defectively articulated. The "Proverbial Philosophy" of Martin Farquhar Tupper, dawning upon the American public in the early 40's, was welcomed with enthusiasm; as Saintsbury says,[35] its success on this side of the Atlantic even exceeded its success on the other. But that was the last and perhaps the only importation of the sage and mellifluous in bulk. In late years the American production of such merchandise has grown so large that the balance of trade now flows in the other direction. Every traveling American must have observed the translations of the chief works of Dr. Marden that are on sale in all the countries of Europe, and with them the masterpieces of such other apostles of the New Thought as Ralph Waldo Trine and Elizabeth Towne. No other American books are half so well displayed.

The note of all such literature, and of the maxims that precipitate themselves from it, is optimism. They "inspire" by voicing and revoicing the New Thought doctrine that all things are possible to the man who thinks the right sort of thoughts—in the national phrase, to the *right-thinker*. This right-thinker is indistinguishable from the *forward-looker*, whose belief in the continuity and benignity of the evolutionary process takes on the virulence of a religious faith. Out of his confidence come the innumerable saws, axioms and *geflügelte Worte* in the national arsenal, ranging from the "It won't hurt none

[35] Cambridge History of English Literature, vol. xiii, p. 167.

to try" of the great masses of the plain people to such exhilarating confections of the wall-card virtuosi as "The elevator to success is not running; take the stairs." Naturally enough, a grotesque humor plays about this literature of hope; the folk, though it moves them, prefer it with a dash of salt. "Smile, damn you, smile!" is a typical specimen of this seasoned optimism. Many examples of it go back to the early part of the last century, for instance, "Don't monkey with the buzz-saw," "The silent hog eats the swill," and "It will never get well if you pick it." Others are patently modern, e. g., "The Lord is my shepherd; I should worry" and "Roll over; you're on your back." The national talent for extravagant and pungent humor is well displayed in many of these maxims. It would be difficult to match, in any other folk-literature, such examples as "I'd rather have them say 'There he goes' than 'Here he lies,'" or "Don't spit: remember the Johnstown flood," or "Shoot it in the leg; your arm's full," or "Foolishness is next to happiness," or "Work is the curse of the drinking classes," or "It's better to be a has-been than a never-was," or "Cheer up; there ain't no hell," or "If you want to cure homesickness, go back home." Many very popular phrases and proverbs are borrowings from above. "Few die and none resign" originated with Thomas Jefferson; Bret Harte, I believe, was the author of "No check-ee, no shirt-ee," General W. T. Sherman is commonly credited with "War is hell," and Mark Twain with "Life is one damn thing after another." An elaborate and highly characteristic proverb of the uplifting variety—"So live that you can look any man in the eye and tell him to go to hell"—was first given currency by one of the engineers of the Panama Canal, a gentleman later retired, it would seem, for attempting to execute his own counsel. From humor the transition to cynicism is easy, and so many of the current sayings are at war with the optimism of the majority. "Kick him again; he's down" is a depressing example. "What's the use?" is another. The same spirit is visible in "Tell your troubles to a policeman," "How'd you like to be the ice-man?" "Some say she do and some say she don't," "Nobody loves a fat man," "Ain't it hell to be poor!", "Have a heart!", "I love my wife, but O you kid," and "Would you for fifty cents?" The last originated in the ingenious mind of an advertisement writer and was immediately adopted. In the course of time it acquired a naughty significance, and helped to give a start to the amazing button craze of the first years of the century—a saturnalia of proverb and phrase making which finally aroused the guardians of the public morals and was put down by the *Polizei*.

The war, as we have seen in the chapter on Slang, produced very little new slang, but the doughboys showed all the national talent for manufacturing proverbs and proverbial expressions, chiefly derisive. "Our American visitors," said an English writer at the end of the war, "are startling London with vivid phrases. Some of them are well known by now. 'Hurry up and get born' is one of them. Others are coming on, such as 'Put crape on your nose; your brains are dead,' and 'Snow again, kid, I've lost your drift.' " [36] Perhaps the favorite in the army was "It's a great life if you don't weaken," though "They say the first hundred years are the hardest" offered it active rivalry. No study of these military witticisms has been made. The whole subject of American proverbs, in fact, has been grossly neglected; there is not even a collection of them. The English publisher, Frank Palmer, prints an excellent series of little volumes presenting the favorite proverbs of all civilized races, including the Chinese and Japanese, but there is no American volume among them. Nor is there one in the similar series issued by the *Appeal to Reason*. Even such exhaustive collections as that of Robert Christy [37] contain no American specimens—not even "Don't monkey with the buzz-saw" or "Root, hog, or die."

[36] *English*, March, 1919, p. 6.
[37] Proverbs, Maxims and Phrases of All Ages; New York, 1905. This work extends to 1267 pages and contains about 30,000 proverbs, admirably arranged.

BIBLIOGRAPHY

[A few duplications will be found here. I have thought it better to make them than to use cross-references. In three or four cases works listed are marked "not published." I have examined all of these; they will be published later on.]

1.

GENERAL

A. F. L.: English As She Is Spoke, *Baltimore Evening Sun*, Nov. 18, 1920.
Aldington, Richard: English and American, *Poetry*, May, 1920.
Alford, Henry: A Plea for the Queen's English; London, 1863.
Allen, Grant: Americanisms (in Chambers' Encyclopædia, new ed.; Phila., 1906, vol. i).
Anon.: American English (in America From a French Point of View; London, 1897).
——: *Art.* Americanisms, Everyman Encyclopædia, ed. by Andrew Boyle; London, n. d.
——: *Art.* Americanisms, New International Encyclopædia, 2nd ed., ed. by F. M. Colby and Talcott Williams; New York, 1917.
——: Americanisms, a Study of Words and Manners, *Southern Review*, vol. ix, p. 290 and p. 529.
——: Americanisms, *Academy*, March 2, 1889.
——: Americanisms, *Southern Literary Messenger*, Oct., 1848.
——: British Struggles With Our Speech, *Literary Digest*, June 19, 1915.
——: I Speak United States, *Saturday Review*, Sept. 22, 1894.
——: Our Strange New Language, *Literary Digest*, Sept. 16, 1916.
——: Progress of Refinement, *New York Organ*, May 29, 1847.
——: Some So-called Americanisms, *All the Year Round*, vol. lxxvi, p. 38.
——: The American English, *Critic*, vol. xiii, p. 115.
——: The American Language, *Putnam's Magazine*, Nov., 1870.
——: The Great American Language, *Cornhill Magazine*, vol. lviii, p. 363.
——: They Spake With Diverse Tongues, *Atlantic Monthly*, July, 1909.
——: To Teach the American Tongue in Britain, *Literary Digest*, Aug. 9, 1913.
——: Triumphant Americanisms, *New York Evening Post*, June 11, 1921.
Archer, William: America and the English Language, *Pall Mall Magazine*, Oct., 1898.
——: The American Language (in America To-day; New York, 1899).
Ayres, Harry Morgan: The English Language in America (in The Cambridge History of American Literature; New York, 1921, vol. iv).
Bache, Richard Meade: Vulgarisms and Other Errors of Speech, 2nd ed.; Phila., 1869.
Baker, Franklin T.: The Vernacular (in Munro's Principles of Secondary Education; New York, 1915, ch. ix).

Barentz, A. E.: Woordenboek der Engelsche Spreektaal . . . and Americanisms . . . ; Amsterdam, 1894.
Barringer, G. A.: Étude sur l'Anglais parlé aux États Unis (la Langue Américaine), *Actes de la Société Philologique de Paris*, March, 1874.
Bendelari, George: Curiosities of American Speech, *New York Sun*, Nov., 1895.
Benet, W. C.: Americanisms: English as Spoken and Written in the United States; Abbeville (S. C.), 1880.
Bicknall, Frank N.: The Yankee in British Fiction, *Outlook*, vol. xcvi, 1910.
Bowen, Edwin W.: Briticisms vs. Americanisms, *Popular Science Monthly*, vol. lxix, p. 324.
——: Questions at Issue in Our English Speech; New York, 1914.
Bradley, W. A.: In Shakespeare's America, *Harper's Magazine*, Aug., 1915.
Bristed, Charles A.: The English Language in America (in Cambridge Essays; London, 1855).
Bryant, William Cullen: Index Expurgatorius (reprinted in Helpful Hints in Writing and Reading, by Grenville Kleiser; New York, 1911, p. 15).
Burton, Richard: American English (in Literary Likings; Boston, 1899).
Carter, Alice P.: American English, *Critic*, vol. xii, p. 97.
Channing, William Ellery: The American Language and Literature, *North American Review*, Sept., 1815.
Charters, W. W. (and Edith Miller): A Course of Study in Grammar Based Upon the Grammatical Errors of School Children of Kansas City, Mo., *University of Missouri Bulletin*, vol. xvi, No. 2, Jan., 1915.
Chesterton, Cecil: British Struggles With Our Speech (summary of art. in *New Witness*), *Literary Digest*, June 19, 1915.
Chubb, Percival: The Menace of Pedantry in the Teaching of English, *School Review*, vol. xx, Jan., 1912.
Clemens, Samuel L. (Mark Twain): Concerning the American Language (in The Stolen White Elephant; New York, 1888).
Coxe, A. Cleveland: Americanisms in England, *Forum*, Oct., 1886.
Crane, W. W.: The American Language, *Putnam's Monthly*, vol. xvi, p. 519.
Crosland, T. W.: The Abounding American; London, 1907.
Darling, Gertrude: Standards in English, *Education*, vol. xvii, p. 331.
Dilnot, Frank: The Written and Spoken Word (in The New America; New York, 1919).
Eggleston, Edward: Wild Flowers of English Speech in America, *Century Magazine*, April, 1894.
Field, Eugene: London letter in *Chicago News*, March 10, 1890.
Flügel, Felix: Die Englische Philologie in Nordamerika, *Gersdorf's Repertorium*, 1852.
——: Die Englische Sprache in Nordamerika, *Archiv für das Studium der neueren Sprachen und Literaturen*, band iv, heft i; Braunschweig, 1848.
Fowler, H. W. (and F. G. Fowler): The King's English, 2nd ed.; Oxford, 1908.
Fowler, Wm. C.: The English Language, . . . 2nd ed.; New York, 1855.
Freeman, Edward A.: Some Points in American Speech and Customs, *Longmans' Magazine*, Nov., 1882.

BIBLIOGRAPHY

Gerek, William (and others): Is There Really Such a Thing as the American Language? *New York Sun*, March 10, 1918.

Gould, Edward S.: Good English . . . ; New York, 1867.

Grandgent, C. H.: English in America, *Die Neueren Sprachen*, vol. ii, p. 243 and p. 520.

Hall, Fitzward: Sundry "Americanisms," *Nation*, vol. lvii, p. 484.

——: Americanisms Again, *Academy*, vol. xlvii, p. 278.

——: The American Dialect, *Academy*, vol. xliii, p. 265.

——: English, Rational and Irrational, *Nineteenth Century*, Sept., 1880.

——: Modern English; New York, 1873.

——: Recent Exemplifications of False Philology; New York, 1872.

Hartt, Irene Widdemar: Americanisms, *Education*, vol. xiii, p. 367.

Hastings, Basil MacDonald: More Americanisms (interview), *New York Tribune*, Jan. 19, 1913.

Healy, J. F.: The American Language; Pittsburgh, 1910.

Hempl, George: The Study of American English, *Chautauquan*, vol. xxii, p. 436.

Herrig, Ludwig: Die Englische Sprache und Literatur in Nord-Amerika, *Archiv für das Studium der Neueren Sprachen und Literaturen*, vol. xii, p. 241; vol. xiii, p. 76 and p. 241; vol. xiv, p. 1.

Higginson, Thomas Wentworth: English and American Phrases, *Independent*, vol. lii, p. 410.

——: English and American Speech, *Harper's Bazar*, vol. xxx, p. 958.

Hill, Adams Sherman: Our English; New York, 1889.

Hodgins, Joseph L.: Our Common Speech, *New York Sun*, March 1, 1918.

Holliday, Robert Cortes: Caun't Speak the Language (in Walking-Stick Papers; New York, 1918, p. 201).

Howells, William Dean: The Editor's Study, *Harper's Magazine*, Jan., 1886.

Hughes, Rupert: Our Statish Language, *Harper's Magazine*, May, 1920.

Hurd, Seth T.: A Grammatical Corrector or Vocabulary of the Common Errors of Speech . . . ; Phila., 1847.

J. D. J.: American Conversation, *English Journal*, April, 1913.

James, Henry: The Question of Our Speech; Boston, 1905.

Kartzke, Georg: Die Amerikanische Sprache, *Archiv für das Studium der Neueren Sprachen und Literaturen*, 1921, p. 181.

Knortz, Karl: Amerikanische Redensarten und Volksgebräuche, Leipzig, 1907.

Krapp, George Philip: Modern English; New York, 1910.

Lang, Andrew: Americanisms, *London Academy*, March 2, 1895.

Lienemann, Oskar: Eigentümlichkeiten des Engl. d. Vereinigten Staaten Nebst Wenig Bekannten Amerikanismen; Zittau, 1886.

Lloyd, R. J.: Northern English; Leipzig, 1908.

Lodge, Henry Cabot: The Origin of Certain Americanisms, *Scribner's Magazine*, June, 1907.

——: Shakespeare's Americanisms (in Certain Accepted Heroes; New York, 1897).

Lounsbury, Thomas R.: Americanisms Real or Reputed, *Harper's Magazine*, Sept., 1913.

Lounsbury, Thomas R.: Differences in English and American Usage, *Harper's Magazine*, July, 1913.
———: The English of America, *International Review*, vol. viii, p. 472.
———: A History of the English Language, revised ed.; New York, 1907.
———: Linguistic Causes of Americanisms, *Harper's Magazine*, June, 1913.
———: Scotticisms and Americanisms, *Harper's Magazine*, Feb., 1913.
———: The Standard of Usage in English; New York and London, n. d.
———: What Americanisms Are Not, *Harper's Magazine*, March, 1913.
Low, Sidney: Ought American to be Taught in Our Schools? *Westminster Gazette*, July 18, 1913.
Lowell, James Russell: prefaces to The Biglow Papers, 1st and 2nd series; Cambridge, 1848-66.
Mackay, Charles: The Ascertainment of English, *Nineteenth Century*, Jan., 1890.
Mackintosh, Duncan: Essai Raisonné sur la Grammaire et la Prononciation Anglaise . . . ; Boston, 1797.
Marshall, Archibald: American English and the English Language, *North American Review*, Nov., 1921.
Matthews, Brander: Americanisms and Briticisms . . . ; New York, 1892.
———: American English and British English (in Essays on English, New York, 1921.)
———: Outskirts of the English Language, *Munsey's Magazine*, Nov., 1913.
———: Parts of Speech; New York, 1901.
———: Why Not Speak Your Own Language? *Delineator*, Nov., 1917.
Mead, Theo. H.: Our Mother Tongue; New York, 1890.
Mencken, H. L.: The American: His Language, *Smart Set*, Aug., 1913.
———: The American Language Again, *New York Evening Mail*, Nov. 22, 1917.
———: American Pronouns, *Baltimore Evening Sun*, Oct. 25, 1910.
———: How They Say It "Over There," *New York Evening Mail*, Oct. 25, 1917.
———: More American, *Baltimore Evening Sun*, Oct. 20, 1910.
———: Moulding Our Speech, *Chicago Tribune*, Nov. 18, 1917.
———: Notes on the American Language, *Baltimore Evening Sun*, Sept. 7, 1916.
———: The Two Englishes, *Baltimore Evening Sun*, Sept. 15, 1910.
Molee, Elias: Nu Tutonish, an International Union Language; Tacoma, 1906.
———: Plea for an American Language . . . ; Chicago, 1888.
———: Pure Saxon English; or, Americans to the Front; Chicago, 1890.
———: Tutonish; Tacoma (Wash.), n. d.
———: Tutonish, or, Anglo-German Union Tongue; Chicago, 1902.
Moon, G. Washington: The Dean's English, 7th ed.; New York, 1884.
Newcomen, George: Americanisms and Archaisms, *Academy*, vol. xlvii, p. 317.
Phipson, Evacustes A.: British vs. American English, *Dialect Notes*, vol. i, pt. i, 1889.
Proctor, Richard A.: Americanisms, *Knowledge*, vol. vii, p. 171.
———: English and American-English, *New York Tribune*, Aug. 14, 1881.
———: "English As She is Spoke" in America, *Knowledge*, vol. vi, p. 319.
Rambeau, A.: Amerikanisches, *Die Neueren Sprachen*, vol. ii, p. 53.
Read, Richard P.: The American Language, *New York Sun*, March 7, 1918.

BIBLIOGRAPHY 431

Read, Richard P.: The American Tongue, *New York Sun*, Feb. 26, 1918.
Russell, T. Baron: Current Americanisms; London, 1893.
Schele de Vere, M.: Americanisms: the English of the New World; New York, 1872.
———: Studies in English; New York, 1867.
Schulz, Carl B.: The King's English at Home, *New York Evening Mail*, Oct. 29, 1917.
Shipman, Carolyn: The American Language, *Critic*, new series, vol. xxxvi, p. 81.
Smith, Chas. Forster: Americanisms, *Southern Methodist Quarterly*, Jan., 1891.
Spies, Heinrich: Die Englische Sprache und das Neue England; Langensalza, 1921.
Stearns, Charles W.: Americanisms in Shakespeare's Plays (in Shakespeare Treasury of Wisdom; New York, 1869).
Swinton, William: English in America (in Rambles Among Words; New York, 1872).
Sykes, Fred H.: American Speech and Standard English, *Our Language*, vol. ii, p. 52.
Trench, Richard C.: English Past and Present; London, 1855; rev. ed., 1905.
———: On the Study of Words; London, 1851; rev. ed., 1904.
Tucker, Gilbert M.: American English; New York, 1921.
———: American English (in Our Common Speech; New York, 1895).
———: American English, *North American Review*, April, 1883.
———: American English, a Paper Read Before the Albany Institute, July 6, 1882, With Revision and Additions; Albany, 1883.
Tuttle, R. M.: Americanisms, *Athenæum*, vol. i, p. 209.
Untermeyer, Louis: Whitman and the American Language, *New York Evening Post*, May 31, 1919.
Van der Voort, J. H.: Hedendaagsche Amerikanismen; Gouda (Holland), 1894.
Wardlaw, Patterson: Simpler English, *Bulletin of the University of South Carolina*, no. 38, pt. iii, July, 1914.
Warren, Arthur: Real Americanisms, *Boston Herald*, Nov. 20, 1892.
Watts, Harvey M.: Prof. Lounsbury and His Rout of the Dons on Americanisms, *Philadelphia Public Ledger*, April 16, 1915.
Wetherill, George N.: The American Language, *Anglo-Continental*, Jan., 1894.
Wheeler, Benjamin Ide: Americanisms (in Johnson's Cyclopedia, new ed.; New York, 1893).
Whibley, Charles: The American Language, *Bookman*, Jan., 1908.
White, Richard Grant: American Speech (in Every-Day English; Boston, 1880).
———: Americanisms, parts i-viii, *Atlantic Monthly*, April, May, July, Sept., Nov., 1878; Jan., March, May, 1879.
———: British Americanisms, *Atlantic Monthly*, May, 1880.
———: Every-Day English . . . ; Boston, 1880.
———: Some Alleged Americanisms, *Atlantic Monthly*, Dec., 1883.
———: British-English and American-English (in Words and Their Uses; New York, 1870; rev. ed., New York, 1876).
Whitman, Walt: An American Primer; Boston, 1904.

Williams, Ralph O.: Some Peculiarities, Real and Supposed, in American English (in Our Dictionaries and Other English Language Topics; New York, 1890).
Witherspoon, John: various notes on Americanisms in vol. iv of his Works; Phila., 1801.

2.

DICTIONARIES OF AMERICANISMS

Bartlett, John Russell: A Glossary of Words and Phrases Usually Regarded as Peculiar to the United States; New York, 1848; 2nd ed., enlarged, Boston, 1859; 3rd ed., 1860; 4th ed., 1877.
Beck, T. Romeyn: Notes on Mr. Pickering's Vocabulary, . . . *Transactions of the Albany Institute*, vol. i, 1830.
Clapin, Sylva: A New Dictionary of Americanisms . . . ; New York, 1902.
Elwyn, A. L.: A Glossary of Supposed Americanisms . . . ; Phila., 1859.
Fallows, Samuel: Dictionary of Americanisms, Briticisms, etc. (in Synonyms and Antonyms; New York, 1886).
———: Handbook of Briticisms, Americanisms, Colloquial and Provincial Words and Phrases; Chicago, 1883.
Farmer, John S.: Americanisms Old and New . . . ; London, 1889.
Hagar, George J. (ed.): Dictionary of Americanisms (in New Universities Dictionary; New York, 1915).
Halliwell-Phillips, J. O.: A Dictionary of Archaisms and Provincialisms, Containing Words Now Obsolete in England, All of Which Are Familiar and in Common Use in America; 2nd ed.; London, 1850.
Keijzer, M.: Woordenboek van Amerikanismen . . . ; Gorinchem (Holland), 1854.
Koehler, F.: Wörterbuch der Amerikanismen . . . ; Leipzig, 1866.
Pickering, John: A Vocabulary or Collection of Words and Phrases Which Have Been Supposed to be Peculiar to the United States of America . . . ; Boston, 1816.
Thornton, Richard H.: An American Glossary, . . . 2 vols.; Phila. and London, 1912.

3.

THE PROCESS OF LANGUAGE GROWTH

A. H. N.: Some New "American Words," *Dial*, vol. xiv, p. 302.
Anon.: Political Americanisms, *Saturday Review*, vol. lx, p. 709.
———: The Decay of Syntax, *London Times Supplement*, May 8, 1919, p. 1.
———: Words Popularized by the Bicycle, *New York Times Saturday Review*, Aug. 7, 1897.
Bergen, Fanny D.: Folk-Names of Animals, *Jour. Am. Folk-Lore*, vol. xii, p. 291.
———: Popular American Plant-Names, *Jour. Am. Folk-Lore*, vol. v, p. 89.
Bergström, G. A.: On Blendings of Synonyms or Cognate Expressions in English; Lund (Sweden), 1906.
Bradley, Henry: The Making of English; London, 1904.

BIBLIOGRAPHY 433

Brandenburg, George C.: Psychological Aspects of Language, *Journal of Educational Psychology*, June, 1918.
Buck, Gertrude: Make-Believe Grammar, *School Review*, vol. xxii, Jan., 1909.
Buehler, H. G.: A Modern English Grammar; New York, 1900.
Davis, W. M.: New Terms in Geology, *Science*, new series, vol. vi, p. 24.
Earle, John: The Philology of the English Tongue; London, 1866; 5th ed., 1892.
——: A Simple Grammar of English Now in Use; London, 1898.
Ernst, C. W.: Words Coined in Boston, *New England Magazine*, vol. xv, p. 337.
Fehr, Bernhard: Zur Agglutination in der Englischen Sprache; Zurich, 1910.
Fiske, John: The Genesis of Language, *North American Review*, Oct., 1869, p. 20.
Franzmeyer, F.: Studien über den Konsonantismus und Vokalismus der Neuenglischen Dialekte; Strassburg, 1906.
Greenough, James B. (and George L. Kittredge): Words and Their Ways in English Speech; New York, 1902.
Hayward, S.: Popular Names of American Plants, *Jour. Am. Folk-Lore*, vol. iv, p. 147.
Helfenstein, James: A Comparative Grammar of the Teutonic Languages . . . ; London, 1870.
Horn, W.: Historische Neuenglische Grammatik; Strassburg, 1908.
——: Untersuchungen zur Neuenglischen Lautgeschichte; Strassburg, 1905.
Kaluza, Max: Historische Grammatik der Englischen Sprache, 2 vols. Berlin, 1900-1.
Jespersen, Otto: Chapters on English; London, 1918.
——: Growth and Structure of the English Language; Leipzig, 1905; 2nd ed., 1912; 3rd ed., rev., 1919.
——: Language: Its Nature, Development and Origin; London, 1921.
——: A Modern English Grammar on Historical Principles, 2 vols.; Heidelberg, 1909-14.
Kellner, Leon: Historical Outlines of English Syntax; London, 1892.
Kellog, Walter Guest: Is Grammar Useless? *North American Review*, July, 1920.
Klein, E.: Die Verdunkelten Wortzusammensetzungen im Neuenglischen; Königsberg, 1911.
Marsh, George P.: Lectures on the English Language; New York, 1859; 4th ed., enlarged, 1870.
——: The Origin and History of the English Language; New York, 1862; rev. ed., 1885.
Matthews, Brander: Essays on English; New York, 1921.
Mead, Leon: Word Coinages; New York, 1902.
Micholson, G. A.: English Words with Native Roots and with Greek, Latin, or Romance Suffixes; Chicago, 1916.
Morris, Richard: Historical Outlines of English Accidence; London, 1872; 2nd ed., rev., 1895.
Murison, W.: Changes in the Language Since Shakespeare's Time (in The Cambridge History of English Literature, vol. xiv; New York, 1917).
Norton, Chas. Ledyard: Political Americanisms . . . ; New York and London, 1890.

Pope, Michael: Words on Trial, *English*, Sept., 1919, p. 150.
Pound, Louise: Backward Spellings, *Dialect Notes*, vol. iv, p. 303.
———: Blends: Their Relation to English Word Formation; Heidelberg, 1914.
———: Indefinite Composites and Word-Coinage, *Modern Language Review*, 1913.
———: Intrusive Nasals in Present-Day English, *Englische Studien*, vol. xlv, 1912.
———: Some English "Stretch-Forms," *Dialect Notes*, vol. iv, p. 52.
———: Some Plural-Singular Forms, *Dialect Notes*, vol. iv, p. 48.
———: "Stunts" in Language, *English Journal*, vol. ix, p. 88.
———: Transposition of Syllables in English, *Dialect Notes*, vol. iv, p. 51.
———: Vogue Affixes in Present-Day Word-Coinage, *Dialect Notes*, vol. v, p. 1.
———: Word-Coinage and Modern Trade-Names, *Dialect Notes*, vol. iv, p. 29.
Poutsma, H.: A Grammar of Late Modern English, 2 vols.; Groningen, 1904-5.
Sayce, A. H.: Introduction to the Science of Language, 2 vols.; 4th ed., London, 1900.
Schröder, H.: Streckformen, ein Beitrag zur Lehre von der Wortenstehung und der Germanischen Wortbetonung; Heidelberg, 1906.
Sturtevant, E. H.: Linguistic Change; Chicago, 1917.
Sunden, Karl: Contributions to the Study of Elliptical Words in Modern English; Upsala (Sweden), 1904.
Tweedle, W. M.: Popular Etymology, *Modern Language Notes*, vol. vii, p. 377.
Whitney, William D.: The Life and Growth of Language; New York, 1875.
———: Language and the Study of Language; New York, 1867.
Wilcox, W. H.: The Difficulties Created by the Grammarians Are to Be Ignored, *Atlantic Educational Journal*, Nov., 1912.
Wittmann, Elisabeth: Clipped Words: A Study of Back-Formations and Curtailments in Present-Day English, *Dialect Notes*, vol. iv, p. 115.
Wood, F. A.: Iteratives, Blends and "Streckformen," *Modern Philology*, Oct., 1911.
———: Language and Nonce-Words, *Dialect Notes*, vol. iv, p. 42.
Wyld, H. C. K.: The Growth of English; London, 1907.
———: The Historical Study of the Mother Tongue; New York, 1906.

4.

LOAN-WORDS

Ben Aryah, Israel: The Hebrew Element in English, *English*, April, 1920, p. 331; May, p. 351.
Blackmar, F. W.: Spanish-American Words, *Modern Language Notes*, vol. vi, p. 91.
Bowen, Edwin W.: The English Speech on Irish Lips, *Atlantic Monthly*, vol. lxxviii, p. 575.
———: Some Disputed Hibernicisms, *Dial*, vol. xxii, p. 43.
Burke, William: The Anglo-Irish Dialect, *Irish Ecclesiastical Record*, 1896.
Carpenter, W. H.: Dutch Contributions to the Vocabulary of English in America, *Modern Philology*, July, 1908.
Chamberlain, A. F.: Algonquin Words in American English, *Jour. Am. Folk-Lore*, vol. xv, p. 240.

BIBLIOGRAPHY 435

Chapin, Florence A.: Spanish Words That Have Become Westernisms, *Editor*, July 25, 1917.
English, Thomas Dunn: Irish in America, *New York Times Saturday Review*, Nov. 5, 1898.
G. D. C.: Russian Words in Kansas, *Dialect Notes*, vol. iv, p. 161.
Gerard, W. R.: Dictionary of Words Introduced into English from American Indian Languages (*not published*).
Griffis, William Elliot: The Dutch Influence in New England, *Harper's Magazine*, vol. lxxxviii, p. 213.
Hayden, Mary (and Marcus Hartog): The Irish Dialect of English: Its Origins and Vocabulary, *Fortnightly Review*, April and May, 1909.
Hempl, George: Language-Rivalry and Speech-Differentiation in the Case of Race-Mixture, *Trans. Am. Philological Assoc.*, vol. xxix, p. 31.
Joyce, P. W.: English as We Speak It in Ireland, 2nd ed.; London, 1910.
Matthews, Brander: On the Naturalization of Foreign Words, *Bookman*, vol. iv, p. 433.
——: What is Pure English? (in Essays on English; New York, 1921).
Navarino, James: The Slavonic Element in English, *English*, March, 1921, p. 468.
Pound, Louise: Domestication of a Suffix (*-ski*), *Dialect Notes*, vol. iv, p. 304.
——: The Jocularization of French Words and Phrases in Present-Day American Speech, *Dialect Notes*, vol. v, p. 77.
——: Domestication of the Suffix *-fest*, *Dialect Notes*, vol. iv, p. 353.
Scott, Fred N.: Pronunciation of Spanish-American Words, *Modern Language Notes*, vol. vi, p. 435.
Sproull, Wm. O.: Hebrew and Rabbinical Words in Present Use, *Hebraica*, Oct., 1890.
Tallichet, H.: A Contribution Towards a Vocabulary of Spanish and Mexican Words Used in Texas, *Dialect Notes*, vol. i, p. 185, p. 243 and p. 324.
Vizetelly, Frank H.: The Foreign Element in English, *New Age*, Oct., 1913.

5.

PRONUNCIATION

Andrews, Eliza Frances: Common Sense in the Pronunciation of English, *Chautauquan*, vol. xxii, p. 595.
Anon.: Standard Pronunciation, *Journal of Education*, vol. xliv, p. 48.
Bell, Alexander Graham: The "Nasal Twang," *Modern Language Notes*, vol. v, p. 150.
Bridges, Robert: A Tract on the Present State of English Pronunciation; Oxford, 1913.
——: On English Homophones (in Tract No. II, Society for Pure English; Oxford, 1919).
Burch, G. J.: The Pronunciation of English by Foreigners; Oxford, 1911.
Crowley, Mary C.: Miss Anderson and Her "Moybid" Friend, *Critic*, vol. xiii, p. 233.
Dunstan, A. C.: Englische Phonetik; Berlin, 1912.

Elliott, John (and Samuel Johnson, Jr.): A Selected Pronouncing and Accented Dictionary . . . ; Suffield (Conn.), 1800.
Ellis, Alexander J.: On Early English Pronunciation, 4 vols.; London, 1869-89.
Emerson, Oliver F.: Sweet's Phonetics and American English, *Modern Language Notes*, vol. v, p. 404.
Grandgent, C. H.: American Pronunciation, *Le Maître Phonétique*, June, 1891, p. 75.
———: American Pronunciation Again, *Modern Language Notes*, vol. viii, p. 273.
———: English Sentences in American Mouths, *Dialect Notes*, vol. i, p. 198.
———: Fashion and the Broad *A* (in Old and New; Cambridge, Mass., 1920).
———: From Franklin to Lowell: A Century of New England Pronunciation, *Pub. Modern Language Assoc.*, vol. ii.
———: *Haf* and *Haef*, *Dialect Notes*, vol. i, p. 269.
———: More Notes on American Pronunciation, *Modern Language Notes*, vol. vi, p. 458.
———: The Dog's Letter (in Old and New; Cambridge, Mass., 1920).
———: Notes on American Pronunciation, *Modern Language Notes*, vol. vi, p. 82.
James, Henry: The Question of Our Speech; Boston, 1905.
Jones, Daniel: The Pronunciation of English; Cambridge, 1909.
Koeppel, Emil: Spelling-Pronunciation: Bemerkungen über den Einfluss des Schriftbildes auf den Laut im Englischen, *Quellen und Forschungen zur Sprach- und Culturgeschichte der Germanischen Völker*, lxxxix; Strassburg, 1901.
Krapp, George P.: The Pronunciation of Standard English in America; New York, 1919.
Lewis, Calvin L.: A Handbook of American Speech; Chicago, 1916.
Lounsbury, Thomas R.: The Standard of Pronunciation in English; New York, 1904.
March, F. A.: Standard English: Its Pronunciation, *Trans. Am. Philological Assoc.*, vol. xix, p. 70.
Matthews, Brander: A Standard of Spoken English (in Essays on English; New York, 1921).
Mearns, Hugh: Our Own, Our Native Speech, *McClure's Magazine*, Oct., 1916; reprinted, *Literary Digest*, Sept. 30, 1916.
Mencken, H. L.: Spoken American, *Baltimore Evening Sun*, Oct. 19, 1910.
Menger, L. E.: A Note on American Pronunciation, *Le Maître Phonétique*, Dec., 1893, p. 168.
Menner, Robert J.: Common Sense in Pronunciation, *Atlantic Monthly*, Aug., 1913.
———: The Pronunciation of English in America, *Atlantic Monthly*, March, 1915.
Montgomery, M.: Types of Standard Spoken English; Strassburg, 1910.
Pound, Louise: British and American Pronunciation, *School Review*, June, 1915.
Rippmann, W.: The Sounds of Spoken English; London, 1906.
Root, E.: American and British Enunciation, *Lippincott's*, Sept., 1911.
Sargeaunt, John: The Pronunciation of English Words Derived from the Latin (in Tract No. IV, Society for Pure English; Oxford, 1920).

BIBLIOGRAPHY 437

Scott, Fred. N.: The Pronunciation of Spanish-American Words, *Modern Language Notes*, vol. vi.
Smalley, D. S.: American Phonetic Dictionary of the English Language; Cincinnati, 1855.
Smart, B. H.: A Practical Grammar of English Pronunciations; London, 1810.
Stearns, Edward J.: A Practical Guide to English Pronunciation for the Use of Schools; Boston, 1857.
Stratton, Clarence: Are You Uhmurican or American? *New York Times*, July 22, 1917.
——: The New Emphasis of Oral English, *English Journal*, Sept., 1917.
Sweet, Henry: A Handbook of Phonetics; London, 1877.
——: A History of English Sounds; London, 1876; Oxford, 1888.
——: A Primer of Spoken English; Oxford, 1900.
——: The Sounds of English; Oxford, 1908.
Vizetelly, Frank H.: A Desk-book of 25,000 Words Frequently Mispronounced; New York and London, 1917.
Wheeler, D. H.: Our Spoken English (in By-Ways of Literature; New York, 1883).
White, D. S.: American Pronunciation, *Journal of Education*, July 13, 1916.

6.

REGIONAL VARIATIONS

a. General Discussions

Bondurant, Alexander L.: Dialect in the United States, *Dial*, vol. xviii, p. 104.
Carpenter, W. H.: The Philosophy of Dialect, *Modern Language Notes*, vol. i, p. 64.
Combs, J. H.: Dialect of the Folk-Song, *Dialect Notes*, vol. iv, p. 311.
Eggleston, Edward: Folk-speech in America, *Century*, vol. xlviii, p. 867.
Emerson, Oliver F.: American Dialects, *Modern Language Notes*, vol. xii, p. 254.
——: The American Dialects, *Providence* (R. I.) *Sunday Journal*, Oct. 16, 1892.
Hempl, George: American Dialects, *Modern Language Notes*, vol. ix, p. 124 and p. 310.
——: Local Usage in American Speech, *Dial*, vol. xiv, p. 172.
——: American Speech Maps, *Dialect Notes*, vol. iv, p. 315.
Mead, W. E.: The American Dialect Dictionary, *Dialect Notes*, vol. iii, p. 168.
Sheldon, E. S.: What Is a Dialect? *Dialect Notes*, vol. i, p. 286.
Skeat, W. W.: English Dialects from the Eighth Century to the Present Day; Cambridge, 1911.
Wright, Joseph: An English Dialect Dictionary, 6 vols.; London, 1896-1905.
——: The English Dialect Grammar; Oxford, 1905.
Wyld, H. C. K.: The Study of Living Popular Dialects and Its Place in the Modern Science of Language; London, 1904.

b. New England

Allen, Frederic D.: Contributions to the New England Vocabulary, *Dialect Notes*, vol. i, p. 18.
Babbitt, E. H.: The Dialect of Western Connecticut, *Dialect Notes*, vol. i, p. 339.

Babbitt, E. H.: List of Verbs From Western Connecticut, *Dialect Notes*, vol. i, p. 276.
Carr, J. W.: A Word-List From Aristook, *Dialect Notes*, vol. iii, p. 407.
——: A Word-List From Eastern Maine, *Dialect Notes*, vol. iii, p. 239.
——: A Word-List From Hampstead, N. H., *Dialect Notes*, vol. iii, p. 179.
Chase, George Davis: Cape Cod Dialect, *Dialect Notes*, vol. ii, p. 289 and p. 433; vol. iii, p. 419.
Choate, I. B.: New England Notes, *Dialect Notes*, vol. i, p. 213.
Daniell, M. Grant: New England Notes, *Dialect Notes*, vol. i, p. 213.
England, George Allan: Rural Locutions of Maine and Northern New Hampshire, *Dialect Notes*, vol. iv, p. 67.
Ernst, C. W.: Words Coined in Boston, *New England Magazine*, vol. xv, p. 337.
Grandgent, C. H.: New England Pronunciation (in Old and New; Cambridge, Mass., 1920).
——: From Franklin to Lowell: a Century of New England Pronunciation, *Pub. Modern Language Assoc.*, vol. ii.
Griffis, William Elliott: The Dutch Influence in New England, *Harper's Magazine*, vol. lxxxviii, p. 213.
Leonard, Arthur N.: Lists From Maine, *Dialect Notes*, vol. iv, p. 1.
Macy, William F. (and Roland B. Hussey): Nantucket Word-List, *Dialect Notes*, vol. iv, p. 332.
Mead, William E. (and George D. Chase): A Central Connecticut Word-List, *Dialect Notes*, vol. iii, p. 1.
Rees, Byron: Word-List From Chilmark, Martha's Vineyard, 1917, *Dialect Notes*, vol. v, p. 15.
Sheldon, E. S.: A New Englander's English and the English of London, *Dialect Notes*, vol. i, p. 33.
——: The New England Pronunciation of O, *Proc. Am. Philological Assoc.* for 1883, p. xix.
Wadleigh, Frances E.: New England Dialect, *Boston Evening Transcript*, March 8, 1893.

c. The Middle States

Allen, W. H.: Pennsylvania Word-List, *Dialect Notes*, vol. iv, p. 157.
Babbitt, E. H.: The English of the Lower Classes in New York City and Vicinity, *Dialect Notes*, vol. i, p. 457.
Bowen, B. L.: A Word-List From Western New York, *Dialect Notes*, vol. iii, p. 435.
Child, Clarence Griffin: The Diphthong *oi* in New England, *Modern Language Notes*, vol. xv, p. 123.
Crowley, Mary C.: Miss Anderson and Her "Moybid" Friend, *Critic*, vol. xiii, p. 233.
Emerson, Oliver F.: The Ithaca Dialect, *Dialect Notes*, vol. i, p. 85.
Grumbine, Lee L.: Provincialisms of the "Dutch" Districts of Pennsylvania, *Proc. Am. Philological Assoc.* for 1886, p. xii.
Heydrick, B. A.: Pennsylvania Word-List, *Dialect Notes*, vol. iv, p. 337.
Lee, Francis B.: Jerseyisms, *Dialect Notes*, vol. i, p. 327.

BIBLIOGRAPHY 439

Lee, Francis B.: Jerseyisms; Trenton, 1889.
Ralph, Julian: The Language of the Tenement Folk, *Harper's Weekly*, vol. xli, p. 90.
White, Henry Adelbert: A Word-List From Central New York, *Dialect Notes*, vol. iii, p. 565.
Zimmermann, H. E.: Maryland Word-List, *Dialect Notes*, vol. iv, p. 343.

d. The South

Allen, F. Sturges: Florida Word-List, *Dialect Notes*, vol. iv, p. 344.
Andrews, Eliza Frances: Cracker English, *Chautauquan*, vol. xxiii, p. 85.
Bolton, Henry Carrington: The Pronunciation of Folk-Names in South Carolina, *Jour. Am. Folk-Lore*, vol. iv, p. 270.
Bourke, Henry M.: Language and Folk Usage of the Rio Grande Valley, *Jour. Am. Folk-Lore*, vol. ix, p. 81.
Brown, Calvin S., Jr.: Dialectical Survivals in Tennessee, *Modern Language Notes*, vol. iv, p. 409.
——: Other Dialectical Forms in Tennessee, *Pub. Modern Language Assoc.*, vol. vi, p. 171.
——: Tennessee Word-List, *Dialect Notes*, vol. iv, p. 345.
Carr, J. W.: A List of Words from Northwest Arkansas, *Dialect Notes*, vol. ii, p. 416; vol. iii, p. 68 and p. 124; vol. iii, p. 205 and p. 392.
Combs, J. H.: A Word List From the South, *Dialect Notes*, vol. v, p. 31.
——: Old, Early and Elizabethan English in the Southern Mountains, *Dialect Notes*, vol. iv, p. 283.
Crow, C. L.: Texas Word-List, *Dialect Notes*, vol. iv, p. 347.
Crumb, D. S.: The Dialect of Southeastern Missouri, *Dialect Notes*, vol. ii, p. 304.
Dingus, L. R.: A Word-List From Virginia, *Dialect Notes*, vol. iv, p. 177.
Edson, H. A. (and others): Tennessee Mountain Word-List, *Dialect Notes*, vol. i, p. 370.
Fruit, John P.: Kentucky Words, *Dialect Notes*, vol. i, p. 229.
——: Kentucky Words and Phrases, *Dialect Notes*, vol. i, p. 63.
Green, B. W.: Word-book of Virginia Folk-speech; Richmond, 1899.
Hancock, Elizabeth H.: Southern Speech, *Neale's Monthly*, Nov., 1913.
Kephart, Horace: The Mountain Dialect (in Our Southern Highlanders; New York, 1913).
——: A Word-List From the Mountains of Western North Carolina, *Dialect Notes*, vol. iv, p. 407.
Lang, Henry R.: Zu den Charleston Provincialisms, *Phonetische Studien*, vol. ii, p. 185.
Lloyd, John Uri: The Language of the Kentucky Negro, *Dialect Notes*, vol. ii, p. 179.
Man, A. P., Jr.: Virginia Word-List, *Dialect Notes*, vol. iv, p. 158.
Morley, Margaret W.: The Speech of the Mountains (in The Carolina Mountains; Boston, 1913).
Payne, L. W., Jr.: A Word-List From East Alabama, *Dialect Notes*, vol. iii, p. 279.
——: A Word-List From Alabama; Austin (Texas), 1909.

BIBLIOGRAPHY

Pearce, J. W.: Notes From Louisiana, *Dialect Notes*, vol. i, p. 69.
Primer, Sylvester: Charleston Provincialisms, *Phonetische Studien*, vol. i, p. 227.
———: Dialectical Studies in West Virginia, *Colorado College Studies* for 1891.
———: The Huguenot Element in Charleston's Provincialisms, *Phonetische Studien*, vol. iii, p. 139.
———: The Pronunciation of Fredericksburg, Va., *Pub. Modern Language Assoc.*, vol. v, p. 185.
———: The Pronunciation Near Fredericksburg, Va., *Proc. Am. Philological Assoc.* for 1889, p. xxv.
Read, William A.: The Southern *R*, *Louisiana State University Bulletin*, Feb., 1910.
———: Some Variant Pronunciations in the New South, *Dialect Notes*, vol. iii, p. 497.
Riedel, E.: New Orleans Word-List, *Dialect Notes*, vol. iv, p. 268.
Rollins, Hyder E.: A West Texas Word-List, *Dialect Notes*, vol. iv, p. 224.
Routh, James: Louisiana Word-List, *Dialect Notes*, vol. iv, p. 346.
——— (and others): Terms From Louisiana, *Dialect Notes*, vol. iv, p. 420.
Shands, H. A.: Some Peculiarities of Speech in Mississippi; n. p., 1893.
Shearin, Hubert G.: An Eastern Kentucky Dialect Word-List, *Dialect Notes*, vol. iii, p. 537.
Sherwood, Adiel: Southern Glossary (in Gazetteer of Georgia; Charleston, 1827).
Smith, Charles Forster: On Southernisms, *Trans. Am. Philological Assoc.*, vol. xiv, p. 42; vol. xvii, p. 34.
———: Southern Dialect in Life and Literature, *Southern Bivouac*, Nov., 1885.
Southem, A.: The Vowel System of the Southern United States, *Englische Studien*, vol. xli.
Steadman, J. M., Jr.: A North Carolina Word-List, *Dialect Notes*, vol. v, p. 18.
Tallichet, H.: A Contribution Towards a Vocabulary of Spanish and Mexican Words Used in Texas, *Dialect Notes*, vol. i, p. 185, p. 243.
Weeks, Abigail E.: A Word-List From Barbourville, Ky., *Dialect Notes*, vol. iii, p. 456.

e. The Middle West

Brown, Rollo Walter: A Word-List From Western Indiana, *Dialect Notes*, vol. iii, p. 570.
Carruth, W. H.: Dialect Word List (of Kansas), *Kansas University Quarterly*, vol. i, p. 95 and p. 133; vol. vi, p. 51 and p. 85.
G. D. C.: Russian Words in Kansas, *Dialect Notes*, vol. iv, p. 161.
Hanley, O. W.: Dialect Words From Southern Indiana, *Dialect Notes*, vol. ii, p. 113.
Hart, J. M. (and others): Notes from Cincinnati, *Dialect Notes*, vol. i, p. 60.
Kenyon, John S.: Western Reserve Word-List, *Dialect Notes*, vol. iv, p. 386.
Parry, W. H.: Dialect Peculiarities in Southeastern Ohio, *Dialect Notes*, vol. iv, p. 339.
Pound, Louise: A Second Word-List From Nebraska, *Dialect Notes*, vol. iii, p. 541; vol. iv, p. 271.
———: Dialect Speech in Nebraska, *Dialect Notes*, vol. iii, p. 55.

BIBLIOGRAPHY 441

Rice, William O.: The Pioneer Dialect of Southern Illinois, *Dialect Notes*, vol. ii, p. 225.
Ruppenthal, J. C.: A Word-List From Kansas, *Dialect Notes*, vol. iv, p. 101 and p. 319.
Weeks, R. L.: Notes From Missouri, *Dialect Notes*, vol. i, p. 235.

f. The Far West

Bruner, Helen (and Frances Francis): A Short Word-List From Wyoming, *Dialect Notes*, vol. iii, p. 550.
Chapin, Florence A.: Spanish Words That Have Become Westernisms, *Editor*, July 25, 1917.
Garrett, R. M.: A Word-List From the Northwest, *Dialect Notes*, vol. v, p. 54 and p. 80.
Harvey, Bartlett: A Word-List From the Northwest, *Dialect Notes*, vol. iv, p. 26 and p. 162.
Hayden, Marie Gladys: A Word-List From Montana, *Dialect Notes*, vol. iv, p. 243.
Lehman, Benjamin H.: A Word-List From the Northwestern United States, *Dialect Notes*, vol. v, p. 22.
McLean, John: Western Americanisms (in The Indians: Their Manners and Customs; Toronto, 1889).
Man, A. P., Jr.: Arizona Word-List, *Dialect Notes*, vol. iv, p. 164.

g. The Colonies

Dunlap, Maurice P.: What Americans Talk in the Philippines, *American Review of Reviews*, Aug., 1913.

h. Negro-English

Fruit, J. P. (and C. H. Grandgent): Uncle Remus in Phonetic Spelling, *Dialect Notes*, vol. iv, p. 196.
Grade, P.: Das Neger-Englisch, *Anglia*, vol. xiv, p. 362.
Harrison, James A.: Negro-English, *Modern Language Notes*, vol. vii, p. 123.
———: Negro English, *Proc. American Philological Association*, 1885.
Lloyd, John Uri: The Language of the Kentucky Negro, *Dialect Notes*, vol. ii, p. 179.
Thom, William Taylor: Some Parallelisms Between Shakespeare's English and the Negro-English of the United States, *Shakespeariana*, vol. i, p. 129.

7.

SPELLING

Allen, F. Sturges: Principles of Spelling Reform; New York, 1907.
Anderson, William W.: The Craze for Wrong Spelling, *Dial*, vol. xix, p. 173.
Anon.: Another Spelling Standard, *Journal of Education*, vol. xlii, p. 436.
———: English Spelling and the Movement to Improve It (Part 1 of Handbook of Simplified Spelling, Simplified Spelling Board); New York, 1919.
———: The Case for Simplified Spelling (Part 2 of Handbook of Simplified Spelling, Simplified Spelling Board); New York, 1920.

BIBLIOGRAPHY

Anon.: Rules and Dictionary List (Part 3 of Handbook of Simplified Spelling, Simplified Spelling Board); New York, n. d.

——: Rules for Simplified Spelling Adopted by the Simplified Spelling Board; New York, 1919.

——: The Future of English Spelling, *Dial*, vol. xxi, p. 273.

——: Revised Spellings, *Educational Review*, vol. xvi, p. 402.

——: Suggestions to Medical Authors: American Medical Association Style Book; Chicago, 1919.

Ayres, Leonard P.: The Spelling Vocabularies of Personal and Business Letters (Circular E126, Division of Education, Russell Sage Foundation); New York, n. d.

Benton, Joel: The Webster Spelling-Book, . . . *Magazine of American History*, Oct., 1883.

Century Magazine: Style-sheet; New York, 1915.

Chicago Daily News: Style-book . . . ; Chicago, 1908.

Chicago, University of: Manual of Style . . . 3rd ed.; Chicago, 1911.

Cobb, Lyman: A Critical Review of the Orthography of Dr. Webster's Series of Books . . . ; New York, 1831.

——: New Spelling Book . . . ; New York, 1842.

Collins, F. Howard: Authors' & Printers' Dictionary, 4th ed., rev. by Horace Hart; London, 1912.

Cushing, J. S. Company: Preparation of Manuscript, Proof Reading, and Office Style at J. S. Cushing Company's; Norwood (Mass.), n. d.

Drummond, H.: Simplified Spelling, *English*, March, 1920, p. 315.

——: Spelling Reform Forty Years Ago, *English*, June, 1920, p. 375.

Ellis, Alexander: On Glosik, a Neu Sistem ov Inglish Spelling; London, 1870.

Fernald, F. A.: Ingglish az She iz Spelt; New York, 1885.

Ford, Henry A.: The Capitalization of English Words, *Journal of Education*, vol. xli, p. 104.

Franklin, Benjamin: Scheme for a New Alphabet and a Reformed Mode of Spelling; Phila., 1768.

Funk & Wagnalls Company: Style-card; New York, 1914.

Gladstone, J. H.: Spelling Reform; London, 1878.

Grattan, J. H. G.: "Peetickay," *English*, Oct., 1920, p. 408.

Hart, Horace: Rules for Compositors and Readers at the University Press, Oxford; 23rd ed.; London, 1914.

Ives, George B.: Text, Type and Style: a Compendium of *Atlantic* Usage; Boston, 1921.

Johnson, Samuel, Jr.: A School Dictionary . . . ; New Haven (1798?).

Lounsbury, Thomas R.: English Spelling and Spelling Reform; New York, 1909.

Macmillan Co.: Notes for the Guidance of Authors; New York, 1918.

March, Francis A.: Spelling Reform; Washington, 1893.

Matthews, Brander: American Spelling, *Harper's Magazine*, vol. lxxxv, p. 277.

Mencken, H. L.: The Curse of Spelling, *New York Evening Mail*, April 11, 1918.

Müller, Max: Spelling, *Fortnightly Review*, April, 1876.

Payne, James E. (and others): Style Book: a Compilation of Rules Governing Executive, Congressional and Departmental Printing, Including the *Congressional Record;* Washington, 1917.
Peck, Harry Thurston: The Collapse of Simplified Spelling, *Bookman*, vol. xxiv, p. 459.
——: The Progress of "Fonetic Refawrm," *Bookman*, vol. vi, p. 196.
Perrett, Wilfrid: Peetickay: an Essay Toward the Abolition of Spelling; Cambridge (England), 1920.
Riverside Press: Handbook of Style in Use at the Riverside Press, Cambridge, Mass.; Boston and New York, 1913.
Skeat, W. W.: Modern English Spelling, *National Review*, vol. xlviii, p. 301.
——: On the History of Spelling; London, 1908.
Smith, Benjamin E.: The Future of Spelling Reform, *Forum*, vol. xxii, p. 367.
Smith, Logan Pearsall: A Few Practical Suggestions (in Tract No. III, Society for Pure English; Oxford, 1920).
Talman, Charles Fitzhugh: Accents Wild, *Atlantic Monthly*, Dec., 1915.
Vaile, E. O.: Our Accursed Spelling; Oak Park, Ill., 1901.
Webster, Noah: An American Dictionary of the English Language . . . 2 vols.; New York, 1828.
——: The American Spelling Book . . . Being the First Part of a Grammatical Institute of the English Language . . . ; Boston, 1783.
——: The American Spelling Book . . . revised ed.; Sandbornton (N. H.), 1835.
——: A Compendious Dictionary of the English Language; Hartford, 1806.
——: A Dictionary of the English Language Compiled for the Use of Common Schools in the United States; Boston, 1807.
——: A Dictionary of the English Language . . . for Common Schools . . . ; Hartford, 1817.
——: Dissertations on the English Language . . . ; Boston, 1789.
——: The Elementary Spelling Book . . . ; Phila., 1829.
——: The Elementary Spelling Book . . . revised ed.; New York, 1848.
——: A Grammatical Institute of the English Language . . . in Three Parts; Hartford, 1783.
——: A Letter to the Hon. John Pickering on the Subject of His Vocabulary; Boston, 1817.
——: The New American Spelling Book . . . ; New Haven, 1833.

8.

GEOGRAPHICAL NAMES

Ackerman, William K.: Origin of Names of Stations on the Illinois Central Railroad (in Early Illinois Railroads; Chicago, 1884).
Ames, Evelyn: English Place-Names in English Speech, *English*, Nov., 1920, p. 422.
Anon.: A History of the Origin of the Place-Names in Nine Northwestern States; Chicago, 1908.
——: Nicknames of the States, *Current Literature*, vol. xxiv, p. 41.

BIBLIOGRAPHY

Baker, Marcus: Alaskan Geographic Names; Washington, 1900.
Battle, Kemp P.: The Names of the Counties of North Carolina; Winston, N. C., 1888.
Beauchamp, Wm. M.: Aboriginal Place-Names of New York; Albany, 1907.
———: Indian Names in New York; Fayetteville (N. Y.), 1893.
Beckwith, H. W.: Indian Names of Water-Courses in the State of Indiana (in Annual Report of the Indiana Dept. of Geology and Natural History; Indianapolis, 1883).
Berger, V.: Amerikanska Ortnamn af Svenskt Ursprung; n. p., n. d.
Bonnell, J. W.: Etymological Derivation of the Names of the States, *Journal of Education*, vol. xlvii, p. 378.
Boyd, Stephen G.: Indiân Local Names; York (Pa.), 1885.
Brainerd, E.: The Significance of Some Familiar Names of Persons and Places, *Education*, vol. xix, p. 140.
Branner, John Casper: Some Old French Place-Names in the State of Arkansas, *Modern Language Notes*, vol. xiv, p. 65.
Clarke, James Freeman: On Giving Names to Towns and Streets; Boston, 1880.
Cowan, John F.: The Origin of Familiar Names, *Education*, vol. xix, p. 640.
Coxe, A. C.: American Geographical Names, *Forum*, vol. iv, p. 67.
Davis, William T.: Staten Island Names; New Brighton, N. Y., 1896.
Douglas-Lithgow, R. A.: Dictionary of American Indian Place and Proper Names in New England; Salem (Mass.), 1909.
Drake, C. M.: California Names and Their Literal Meanings; Los Angeles, 1893.
Egli, Johann J.: Nomina Geographica, 2nd ed.; Zurich, 1893.
———: Der Völkergeist in den geographischen Namen; Zurich, 1894.
Feipel, Louis N.: The Lure of American Place-Names (*unpublished*).
Fulmore, Z. T.: The History and Geography of Texas as Told in County Names; Austin, Tex., 1915.
Gannett, Henry: The Origin of Certain Place-Names in the United States, 2nd ed.; Washington, 1905.
Ganzemüller, Konrad: Definitions of Geographical Names; New York, 1894.
Greenleaf, Moses: Indian Place-Names; Bangor, Me., 1903.
Hagner, Alexander B.: Street Nomenclature of Washington City, *Records Columbia Historical Society*, vol. vii, p. 237.
Haywood, Edward F.: The Names of New England Places, *New England Magazine*, new series, vol. xiii, p. 345.
Hempl, George: The Stress of German and English Compound Geographical Names, *Modern Language Notes*, vol. xi, p. 232.
Horsford, Eben N.: The Indian Names of Boston; Cambridge, Mass., 1886.
Hubbard, Lucius L.: Some Indian Place-Names and Their Meanings (in Woods and Lakes of Maine; Boston, 1884).
Kellogg, Louise Phelps: Organization, Boundaries and Names of Wisconsin Counties, *Proc. State Historical Society of Wisconsin* for 1909, p. 184.
Kelton, Dwight H.: Indian Names of Places Near the Great Lakes; Detroit, 1888.
Ker, Edmund T.: River and Lake Names in the United States; New York, 1911.
Kinnicutt, Lincoln N.: Indian Names of Places in . . . Massachusetts; Worcester, Mass., 1909.

BIBLIOGRAPHY 445

Knox, Alexander: Glossary of Geographical and Topographical Terms; London, 1904.
Kroeber, A. L.: California Place-Names of Indian Origin; Berkeley, Calif., 1916.
Lange, F. W. T.: Geographical Names, *English*, Feb., 1920, p. 287.
Legler, Henry E.: Origin and Meaning of Wisconsin Place-Names; Madison, Wis., 1903.
Long, Charles M.: Virginia County Names; New York, 1908.
McAdoo, W. G.: American Geographical Nomenclature; Milledgeville, Ga., 1871.
Martin, Maria Ewing: Origin of Ohio Place-Names, *Ohio Archæological and Historical Quarterly*, vol. xiv, p. 272.
Meany, Edmond S.: Indian Geographic Names of Washington; Seattle, 1908.
Mooney, James, ed.: Geographic Nomenclature of the District of Columbia, *American Anthropologist*, Jan., 1893.
Moreno, H. M.: Dictionary of Spanish-Named California Cities and Towns; Chicago, 1916.
Olaguibel, Manuel de: Onomatologia del Estaso de Mexico; Roluca (Mexico), 1893.
Parsons, Usher: Indian Names of Places in Rhode Island; Providence, R. I., 1861.
Peñafiel, Antonio: Nombres Geográficos de Mexico; Mexico, 1885.
Perkins, Franklin: Geographical Names, *Journal of Education*, vol. xlv, p. 367 and p. 403.
Renault, Raoul: Some Old French Place-Names in the State of Arkansas, *Modern Language Notes*, vol. xiv, p. 191.
Rouillard, Eugène: Noms Géographiques de la Province de Québec et des Provinces Maritimes; Quebec, 1906.
Salverte, Eusèbe: History of the Names of Men, Nations and Places, tr. by L. H. Mordacque, 2 vols.; London, 1862-4.
Sanchez, Nellie van de Grift: Spanish and Indian Place-Names of California; San Francisco, 1914.
Skinner, Charles M.: Some Odd Names of Places Across the Border, *Current Literature*, vol. xxv, p. 41.
Thomas, George Francis: The Meaning and Derivation of Names of Rivers, Lakes, Towns, etc., of the Northwest (in Legends of the Land of Lakes; Chicago, 1884).
Tooker, William W.: Indian Names of Places in the Borough of Brooklyn; New York, 1901.
———: The Indian Names for Long Island; New York, 1901.
———: The Indian Place-Names on Long Island; New York, 1911.
Trumbull, J. Hammond: The Composition of Indian Geographical Names, *Collection of the Conn. Historical Society*, vol. ii.
———: Indian Names of Places, etc., in and on the Borders of Connecticut; Hartford, 1881.
Upham, Warren: Minnesota Geographical Names; St. Paul, Minn., 1920.
U. S. Geographic Board: Fourth Report, 1890 to 1916; Washington, 1916.
———: Fifth Report, 1890 to 1920; Washington, 1921.
———: Correct Orthography of Geographic Names, rev. to Jan., 1911; Washington, 1911.

U. S. Geographic Board: Decisions of the Board; Washington, v. d.
White, James: Place-Names in the Thousand Islands; Ottawa, 1910.
Whitmore, William Henry: An Essay on the Origin of the Names of Towns in Massachusetts; Boston, 1873.

9.

SURNAMES AND GIVEN NAMES

Anjou, Gustave: List of Dutch and Frisian Baptismal Names With Their English Equivalents (in Ulster County, N. Y., Probate Records; New York, 1906).
Anon.: A List of Christian Names, Their Derivatives, Nicknames and Equivalents in Several Foreign Languages, For Use in the Adjutant General's Office, War Department; Washington, 1920.
——: Guide to Similar Surnames, For Use in the Adjutant General's Office, War Department; Washington, 1920.
——: List of Persons Whose Names Have Been Changed in Massachusetts, 1780-1892; Boston, 1893.
Arthur, William: An Etymological Dictionary of Family and Christian Names; New York, 1857.
Bardsley, Charles W.: Curiosities of Puritan Nomenclature; London, 1880.
Baring-Gould, S.: Family Names and Their Story; London, 1910.
Barker, Henry: British Family Names; London, 1894.
Bradley, Charles William: Patronomatology; Baltimore, 1842.
Burnham, Sarah Maria: Our Names: Their Origin and Significance; Boston, 1900.
Charnock, Richard S.: Prænomina; London, 1882.
Crane, W. W.: Our Naturalized Names, *Lippincott's Magazine*, vol. lxiii, p. 575.
Daniel, James Walter: A Ramble Among Surnames; Nashville, Tenn., 1893.
Dixon, B. Homer: Surnames; Boston, 1855.
Dubbs, Joseph H.: A Study of Surnames; Lancaster (Pa.), 1886.
Dunlap, Fayette: A Tragedy of Surnames, *Dialect Notes*, vol. iv, pt. i, 1913.
Ferguson, Robert: English Surnames; London, 1858.
——: Surnames as a Science; London, 1883.
Fernow, Berthold: New Amsterdam Family Names and Their Origin; New York, 1898.
Flom, George F.: Norwegian Surnames, *Scandinavian Studies and Notes*, vol. v, p. 139.
Gardner, J. E.: List of Chinese Family Names; Washington, 1909.
Gentry, Thomas G.: Family Names of the Irish, Anglo-Saxon, Anglo-Norman and Scotch; Phila., 1892.
Harrison, Henry: A Dictionary of the Surnames of the United Kingdom; London, 1912.
Hill, Geoffry: Christian Names in England (in Some Consequences of the Norman Conquest; London, 1904).
Howell, George Rogers: The Origin and Meaning of English and Dutch Surnames of New York State Families; Albany, 1894.
Ingraham, E. D.: Singular Surnames; Phila., 1873.
Inman, Thomas: On the Origin of Certain Christian and Other Names; Liverpool, 1866.

Jones, David D.: The Surnames of the Chinese in America; San Francisco, 1904.
Judson, Amos M.: A Grammar of American Surnames; Washington, 1898.
King, Marquis Fayette: Changes in Names By Special Acts of the Legislature of Maine, 1820-1895; Portland, Me., 1901.
Kuhns, L. Oscar: The Origin of Pennsylvania Surnames, *Lippincott's Magazine*, vol. lix, p. 395, March, 1897.
——: Studies in Pennsylvania German Family Names; New York, 1902.
Latham, Edward: A Dictionary of Names, Nicknames and Surnames; London, 1904.
Lower, M. A.: Patronymica Britannica; London, 1860.
McKenna, L. B.: Surnames, Their Origin and Nationality; Quincy (Ill.), 1913.
Oliphant, Samuel Grant: The Clan of Fire and Forge, or, The Ancient and Honorable Smiths; Olivet (Mich.), 1910.
——: Surnames in Baltimore, *Baltimore Sunday Sun*, 62 weekly articles, Dec. 2, 1906-Jan. 26, 1908, inc.; index, Feb. 2, 9, 16, 23, 1908.
Pearson, T. R.: The Origin of Surnames, *Good Words*, June, 1897.
Quigley, Hugh: A Vocabulary of Ancient and Modern Irish Family Names (in The Irish Race in California; San Francisco, 1878).
Rupp, Israel D.: A Collection of . . . Names of German, Swiss, Dutch, French and Other Immigrants in Pennsylvania from 1727 to 1776, 2nd rev. ed.; Phila., 1876.
——: General Remarks on the Origin of Surnames; Harrisburg, Pa., 1856.
Saurusaitis, Peter: List of Lithuanian Family Names; Shenandoah, Pa., 1908.
Schele de Vere, Maximilian: A Few Virginia Names, *Modern Language Notes*, vol. ii, p. 145 and p. 193.
Searle, William G.: Onomasticon Anglo-Saxonicum; Cambridge, 1897.
Tolman, A. H.: English Surnames (in The Views About Hamlet; Boston, 1904).
Weekley, Ernest: Surnames; London, 1916.

10.

NON-ENGLISH LANGUAGES IN AMERICA

a. German

Aurand, Ammon M.: Aurand's Collection of Pennsylvania German Stories and Poems; Beaver Springs, Pa., 1916.
Beidelman, William: The Story of the Pennsylvania Germans, . . . Their Origin, Their History and Their Dialect; Easton, Pa., 1898.
Bonneheur, Armin de: Pennsylvania Dutch, *Nation*, vol. lxvii, p. 482.
Faust, A. B.: Non-English Writings: I. German (in Cambridge History of American Literature, vol. iv, p. 572; New York, 1921).
Fischer, H. L.: Kurzweil and Zeitfertreib; York, Pa., 1882.
Fogel, Edwin Miller: Beliefs and Superstitions of the Pennsylvania Germans; Philadelphia, 1915.
Fuchs, Meik, *pseud.*: Dreiguds un Noschens; Milwaukee, 1898.
Haldeman, S. S.: Pennsylvania Dutch . . . ; Phila., 1872.
Harbaugh, H.: Harbaugh's Harfe, rev. ed.; Phila., 1902.

Hays, H. M.: On the German Dialect Spoken in the Valley of Virginia, *Dialect Notes*, vol. iii, p. 263.
Horne, Abraham R.: Horne's Pennsylvania German Manual, 3rd ed.; Allentown, Pa., 1905.
Learned, M. D.: Application of the Phonetic System of the American Dialect Society to Pennsylvania German, *Modern Language Notes*, vol. v, p. 237.
——: The Pennsylvania German Dialect, Part I; Baltimore, 1889.
Lins, James C.: Common Sense Pennsylvania German Dictionary; Reading, Pa., 1895.
Miller, Daniel: Pennsylvania German, 2 vols.; Reading, Pa., 1903-11.
Miller, Harvey M.: Pennsylvania-German Stories, Prose and Poetry; Elizabethville, Pa., 1911.
Pennsylvania-German, Jan., 1900——. (Quarterly, 1903-05; bimonthly, Jan.-July, 1906; monthly, Sept., 1906——. Edited by P. C. Croll, H. A. Schuler, H. W. Kriebel, at Lebanon, East Greenville, Lititz, Cleona, Pa.)
Rauch, E.: Rauch's Pennsylvania Dutch Hand-Book; Mauch Chunk, Pa., 1879.
Stein, Thomas S.: 'Uf'm Oewerste Speicher; Annville, Pa., 1900.
Stoudt, John Baer: The Folklore of the Pennsylvania-German; Lancaster, Pa., 1915.
Wollenweber, L. A.: Gemälde aus dem Pennsylvanischen Volksleben; Phila., 1869.
Womer, William A.: Physician's German Interpreter; n. p., 1904.

b. French

Bibaud, Maximilien: Le Mémorial des Vicissitudes et des Progrès de la Langue Française en Canada; Montreal, 1879.
Bonny, H. P.: Anglicisms in Lower Canadian French, *Jour. and Proc. Hamilton Assoc.* for 1891, p. 101.
Brandon, Edgar Z.: A French Colony in Michigan, *Modern Language Notes*, vol. xiii, p. 242.
Buies, Arthur: Anglicismes et Canadianismes; Quebec, 1888.
Caron, M. N.: Petit Vocabulaire à l'Usage des Canadiens Français; Trois-Rivières, 1880.
Chamberlain, A. F.: Bibliography of the Franco-Canadian Dialect, *Dialect Notes*, vol. i, p. 53.
——: Dialect Research in Canada, *Dialect Notes*, vol. i, p. 43.
——: Notes on the Canadian French Dialect of Granby, P. Q., *Modern Language Notes*, vol. vii, p. 12; vol. viii, p. 16.
——: The Life and Growth of Words in the French Dialect of Quebec, *Modern Language Notes*, vol. ix, p. 78 and p. 135.
Clapin, Sylva: Dictionnaire Canadien-Français; Montreal, 1894.
Dionne, N. E.: Le Parler Populaire des Canadiens Français; Quebec, 1909.
Dunn, Oscar: Glossaire Franco-Canadien et Vocabulaire de Locutions Vicieuses Usitées au Canada; Quebec, 1880.
Elliott, A. M.: Contributions to a History of the French Language of Canada, *Am. Jour. of Philology*, vol. vi, p. 135; vol. vii, p. 141; vol. viii, p. 135 and p. 338; vol. x, p. 133.

BIBLIOGRAPHY 449

Fortier, Alcée: Acadians of Louisiana and Their Dialect; New Orleans, 1891.
——: French Language in Louisiana and the Negro French Dialect; New Orleans, n. d.
——: Louisiana Studies; New Orleans, 1894.
——: Louisiana Folk-Tales, in French Dialect and English Translation; Boston, 1895.
Fortier, Edward J.: Non-English Writings: II. French (in Cambridge History of American Literature, vol. iv, p. 590; New York, 1921).
Geddes, James, Jr.: Canadian-French, 1890-1900, *Kritischer Jahresbericht über die Fortschritte der Romanischen Philologie*, bd. v, p. 294; bd. vi, p. 408; bd. viii, p. 217.
——: Comparison of Two Acadian French Dialects Spoken in the Northeast of North America With the Franco-Canadian Dialect Spoken at Ste. Anne de Beaupré, Province of Quebec, *Modern Language Notes*, vol. viii, p. 449; vol. ix, p. 1 and p. 99.
——: Study of an Acadian-French Dialect Spoken on the North Shore of the Baie-des-Chaleurs; Halle, 1908.
Harrison, J. A.: The Creole Patois of Louisiana, *Am. Jour. Philology*, vol. iii, p. 285.
Lacasse, R. P. Z.: Ces Jeunes-là on ne les Comprend Plus (in Une Mine Produisant l'Or et l'Argent; Quebec, 1880, pp. 252-6).
Legendre, Napoléon: La Langue Que Nous Parlons, *Mémoires et Comptes-Rendus de la Société Royale de Canada* for 1887, p. 129.
——: La Langue Française au Canada; Quebec, 1890.
Montigny, Louvigny de: La Langue Française au Canada; Ottawa, 1916.
Northrup, Clark S.: A Bibliography of the English and French Languages in America From 1894 to 1900, *Dialect Notes*, vol. ii, p. 151.
Réveillaud, Eugène: La Langue et la Littérature Françaises au Canada, *Revue Suisse*, Aug., 1883, p. 311.
Rivard, Adjutor: Étude sur les Parlers de France au Canada; Quebec, 1914.
Schuchardt, H.: Beiträge zur Kenntniss des Englischen Kreolisch, *Englische Studien*, vol. xii, p. 470; vol. xiii, p. 158; vol. xv, p. 286.
Sheldon, E. S.: Some Specimens of a French-Canadian Dialect Spoken in Maine, *Trans. Modern Language Assoc.*, vol. iii, p. 210.
Squair, John: A Contribution to the Study of the Franco-Canadian Dialect, *Proc. Canadian Institute*, series iii, vol. vi, p. 161.
Tardivel, J. P.: L'Anglicisme: Voilà l'Ennemi; Quebec, 1880.
——: La Langue Française au Canada; Montreal, 1901.

c. Dano-Norwegian

Flaten, Nils: Notes on American-Norwegian, With a Vocabulary, *Dialect Notes*, vol. ii, p. 115.
Flom, George T.: A Grammar of the Song Dialect of Norwegian, *Dialect Notes*, vol. iii, p. 25.
——: English Elements in Norse Dialects of Utica, Wisconsin, *Dialect Notes*, vol. ii, p. 257.

d. Dutch

Nieland, Dirk: Yankee-Dutch; Grand Rapids, Mich., 1919.
Prince, J. Dyneley: The Jersey Dutch Dialect, *Dialect Notes*, vol. iii, p. 459.

e. Swedish

Berger, V.: Vart Språk; Rock Island, Ill., 1912.

f. Spanish

Abeille, Luciano: El Idioma Nacional de los Argentinos; Paris, 1900.
Armengal y Valenzuela, P.: Glossario Etimológico de Nombres de Hombres, Animales, Plantas, Ríos y Lugares, y de Vocablos Incorporados en el Lenguaje Vulgar; Aborígenes de Chile y de Algún Otro País Americano; Santiago de Chile, vol. i, 1918; vol. ii, 1919.
Arona, Juan de: Diccionario de Peruanismos; Lima, 1882.
Batres y Jáuregni, Antonio: Vicios del Lenguaje y Provincialismos de Guatemala; Guatemala, 1892.
Bayo, Ciro: Vocabulario Criollo-Español Sud-Americano; Madrid, 1910.
——: Vocabulario de Provincialismos Argentinos y Bolivianos, *Rev. Hispanique*, vol. xiv, p. 241.
Blanco-Fombona, R.: Letras y Letrados de Hispano-América; Paris, 1908.
Buitre Gryngo, El, *pseud.*: Pidgin-Spanish, *Nation*, vol. lxii, p. 323.
Calcaño, Julian: El Castellano en Venezuela; Caracas, 1897.
Cisneros, Jeremias: Hondureñismos, *Revista del Archivo y de la Biblioteca Nacional de Honduras*, vol. iii, p. 154, p. 181, p. 212, p. 250, p. 282, p. 289 and p. 313.
Cuervo, Rufino J.: Apuntaciones Criticas Sobre el Lenguaje Bogotano, 6th ed.; Paris, 1914.
Dihigo, Juan M.: El Hablar Popular al Través de la Literatura Cubana, *Rev. de la Facultad de Letras y Ciencias de la Universidad de la Habana*, vol. xx, p. 53.
Espinosa, Aurelio M.: Cuentitos Populares Nuevo-Mejicanos y su Transcripción Fonética, *Bulletin de Dialectologie Romane*, tome iv, p. 97.
——: Studies in New Mexican Spanish, *Revue de Dialectologie Romane*, tome i, p. 157 and p. 269; tome iii, p. 251; tome iv, p. 241; tome v, p. 142.
Ferraz, Juan Fernándes: Nahuatlismos de Costa Rica; San José de Costa Rica, 1892.
Gagini, C.: Diccionario de Barbarismos y Provincialismos de Costa Rica; San José de Costa Rica, 1893.
Hills, E. C.: New Mexican Spanish, *Pub. Modern Language Assoc.*, vol. xxi, p. 706.
Lamao, M. E.: Apuntaciones Críticas el Idioma Castellano; Santa Marta (Colombia), 1920.
Macías, José Miguel: Diccionario Cubano; Vera Cruz, 1885.
Malaret, Augusto: Diccionario de Provincialismos de Puerto Rico; San Juan, 1917.
Marden, C. C.: The Phonology of the Spanish Dialect of Mexico City; Baltimore, 1896.

BIBLIOGRAPHY 451

Maspero, G.: Sobre Algunas Particularidades Fonéticas del Español Hablado por los Campesinos de Buenos Aires y de Montevideo; Halle, 1862.

Maspero, J.: Singularidades del Español de Buenos Ayres, *Memorias de la Sociedad de Lingüistica de Paris*, tome ii.

Membreño, Alberto: Hondureñismos; Tegucigalpa, 1897.

Mendoza, Eufemio: Apuntes Para un Catalogo Razonado de las Palabras Mexicanas Introducidas al Castellano; Mexico, 1872.

Montori, Arturo: Modificaciones Populares del Idioma Castellano en Cuba; Havana, 1916.

Pichardo, Estében: Diccionario Provincial Casi-Razonado de Vozes y Frases Cubanas, 4th ed.; Havana, 1875.

Prada, M. G.: Pájinas Libres; Paris, 1894.

Ramos y Duarte, Félix: Diccionario de Mejicanismos, . . . 2nd ed.; Mexico, 1898.

Retana, W. E.: Diccionario de Filipinismos; Madrid, 1921.

Rincón, Pedro Antonio de: Gramática y Vocabulario Mejicanos; Mexico, 1885.

Robelo, Cecilio A.: Diccionario de Aztequismos; Mexico, 1906.

Román, Manuel Antonio: Diccionario de Chilenismos, *Revista Católica* (Santiago de Chile), vols. i-v, 1901-18.

Sanchez, Jesus: Glossario de Voces Castellanas Derivadas Nahüatl ó Mexicano; n. p., n. d.

Sandoval, Rafael: Arte de la Lengue Mexicana; Mexico, 1888.

Sanz, S. Monner: Notas al Castellano en America; Buenos Ayres, 1903.

Starr, Frederick: Recent Mexican Study of the Native Languages of Mexico; Chicago, 1900.

Toro y Gisbert, Miguel de: Americanismos, Paris, n. d.

———: Revindicación de Americanismos, *Bol. Real Academia Española*, tome vii, p. 290 and p. 443.

Zayas y Alfonso, Alfredo: Lexicografia Antillana; Havana, 1914.

g. Icelandic

Stefánsson, V.: English Loan-Nouns Used in the Icelandic Colony of North Dakota, *Dialect Notes*, vol. ii, p. 354.

h. Italian

Livingston, Arthur: La Merica Sanemagogna, *Romanic Review*, vol. ix, p. 206.

i. Yiddish

Abelson, Paul: English-Yiddish Encyclopedic Dictionary; New York, 1915.

Bassein, Leon: Di Jidishe Shprach; New York, 1914.

Buchwald, Nathaniel: Non-English Writings: III. Yiddish (in Cambridge History of American Literature, vol. iv; New York, 1921, p. 598).

Grolman, F. L. A. von: Die Teutsche Gauner-Jenische- oder Kochemer-Sprache, mit Besonderer Rücksicht auf die Ebräisch-Teutsche Judensprache (in Wörterbuch der in Teutschland üblichen Spitzbubensprachen; Giessen, 1822).

Harkavy, Alexander: Harkavy's Yiddish-American School; New York, 1900.

———: A Dictionary of the Yiddish Language; New York, 1898.

Harkavy, Alexander: English-Jewish Pocket Dictionary; New York, 1900.
Levin, J. L.: Di Naie Yidishe Shul; New York, 1916.
Meyer, Raphael: Jiddisch; Copenhagen, 1918.

j. Portuguese

Amaral, Amadeus: O Dialecto Caipira; São Paulo, 1920.
Cintro, Assis: Questoes de Portuguez; São Paulo, 1921.
Nobiling, O.: Brasileirismos e Crioulismos, *Revue de Dialectologie Romane*, tome iii, p. 189.
Ribeiro, João: A Lingua Nacional; São Paulo, 1921.
Roméro, Sylvio: Historia de Litteratura Brasileira, 2nd ed.; Rio de Janeiro, 1902.
Verissimo, José: Estudos de Litteratura Brasileira, 6ta serie; Rio de Janeiro. 1907.

k. General

Smith, L. Pearsall: The English Element in Foreign Languages, *English*, March, April, July, Aug., Sept., Oct., Nov., 1919.
Talbot, Winthrop: Teaching English to Aliens, a Bibliography of Text-books, Dictionaries and Glossaries, and Aids to Librarians; Washington, 1918.

11.

OTHER COLONIAL DIALECTS OF ENGLISH

a. Australian

Anon.: The Australian Accent, *Triad* (Sydney), Nov. 10, 1920.
Dennis, C. J.: Glossary (in Doreen and the Sentimental Bloke; New York, 1916).
Lentzer, Karl: Wörterbuch der Englischen Volkssprache Australiens und der Englischen Mischsprachen; Halle, 1891.
——: Colonial English; London, 1891.
Morris, Edward E.: Austral English . . . ; London, 1898.

b. Beach-la-Mar

Church, William: Beach-la-Mar: the Jargon or Trade Speech of the Western Pacific; Washington, 1911.

c. South African

Pettman, Charles: Africanderisms: a Glossary of South African Colloquial Words and Phrases; London, 1913.

d. Canadian

Chamberlain, A. F.: List of Articles on "Canadian English," *Dialect Notes*, vol. i, p. 53.
Geikie, A. S.: Canadian English, *Canadian Journal*, vol. ii, p. 344.
Lighthall, W. D.: Canadian English, *Week* (Toronto), Aug. 16, 1889.

BIBLIOGRAPHY 453

McLean, John: Western Americanisms (in The Indians: Their Manners and Customs; Toronto, 1889, pp. 197-201).
Mott, L. F.: Canada Word-List, *Dialect Notes*, vol. iv, p. 332.
Tweedie, W. M.: British Maritime Provinces Word-List, *Dialect Notes*, vol. i, p. 377.

e. East Indian

Yule, Henry (and A. C. Burnell): Hobson-Jobson: a Glossary of Anglo-Indian Words and Phrases, and of Kindred Terms, Etymological, Historical, Geographical and Discursive; new ed., ed. by Wm. Crooke; London, 1903.

f. Pidgin-English

C. P. A.: Pigeon English ou Bichelamar, *Revue de Linguistique*, tome xlvi, p. 109 and p. 184.
Dobson, William F.: Pidgin-English, *Argosy*, vol. lxxiii, p. 105.
Lentzer, Karl: Wörterbuch der Englischen Volkssprache Australiens und der Mischsprachen; Halle, 1891.

12.

SLANG

A. F. L.: English As She Is Spoke, *Baltimore Evening Sun*, Nov. 18, 1920.
Allen, E. A.: The Origin in Literature of Vulgarisms, *Chautauquan*, Nov., 1890.
Andrews, Eliza Frances: Slang and Metaphor, *Chautauquan*, vol. xxiii, p. 462.
Anon.: Dictionnaire des Termes Militaires et de l'Argot Poilu; Paris, 1916.
——: French Soldier Slang, *Times Literary Supplement*, Aug. 28, 1919.
——: L'Argot Poilu, *Times Literary Supplement*, July 27, 1916.
——: The Philosophy of Slang, *Littell's Living Age*, vol. ccxxiii, p. 324.
——: Quick Lunch Lingo, *Literary Digest*, March 18, 1916.
——: Slang in Our Colleges, *Bookman*, vol. v, p. 448.
——: Supplement Comprising Words Coined, Introduced or Brought Into Popular Use During the Great War (in Cassell's New English Dictionary; London, 1919).
——: War and the Language, *Times Literary Supplement*, Aug. 6, 1919.
——: The War's Verbal Bequest, *Philadelphia Public Ledger*, Oct. 20, 1919.
——: Word-Coining and Slang, *Living Age*, July 13, 1907.
Babbitt, E. H.: College Words and Phrases, *Dialect Notes*, vol. ii, p. 3.
Barrère, Albert (and Chas. G. Leland): A Dictionary of Slang, Jargon and Cant, 2 vols.; New York, 1889.
Baumann, H.: Londonismen (Slang and Cant), 2nd ed.; Berlin, 1902.
Bergmann, Karl: Wie der Feldgraue Spricht; Giessen, 1916.
Bolwell, Robert: College Slang Words and Phrases, *Dialect Notes*, vol. iv, p. 231.
Bosson, Olaf E.: Slang and Cant in Jerome K. Jerome's Works; Cambridge, England, 1911.
Bowen, Edwin W.: What is Slang? *Popular Science Monthly*, vol. lxviii, p. 127.
Conant, R. W.: Classic Slang, *Dial*, vol. xx, p. 63.

BIBLIOGRAPHY

Cook, Edward: Words and the War (in Literary Recreations; London, 1919).
Crofton, A. F. B.: The Language of Crime, *Popular Science Monthly*, vol. i, p. 831.
Dauzet, Albert: L'Argot de la Guerre; Paris, 1918.
Dawson, A. H.: A Dictionary of English Slang and Colloquialisms; New York, 1913.
Déchelette, François: L'Argot des Poilus; Paris, 1918.
Delcourt, René: Expressions d'Argot Allemand et Autrichien; Paris, 1917.
Delesalle, Georges: Dictionnaire Argot-Français et Français-Argot; Paris, 1896.
Esnault, Gaston: Le Poilu tel qu'il se Parle; Paris, 1919.
Farmer, John S. (and W. E. Henley): Slang and its Analogues, 7 vols.; London, 1890-1904.
Garver, Milton: French Army Slang, *Modern Language Notes*, vol. xxxii, p. 151; vol. xxxv, p. 508.
Giles, Richard: Slang and Vulgar Phrases; New York, 1913.
Gore, Willard C.: Notes on Slang, *Modern Language Notes*, vol. xi, p. 385.
Graham, G. F.: Slang Words and Americanisms (in A Book About Words; London, 1869).
Grasserie, Raoul de la: Étude Scientifique sur l'Argot et le Parler Populaire; Paris, 1907.
———: La Psychologie de l'Argot, *Revue Philosophique*, vol. lx, p. 260.
Grose, Francis: A Classical Dictionary of the Vulgar Tongue; London, 1785.
[Hall, B. H.]: A Collection of College Words and Customs; Cambridge (Mass.), 1851; 2nd ed., 1856.
Hamdorf, Adolf: Ueber die Bestandtheile des Modernen Pariser Argots; Berlin, 1886.
Harvey, B. T.: Navy Slang, *Dialect Notes*, vol. iv, p. 150.
Hecker, E. A. (and Edmund Wilson, Jr.): The Vocabulary of the A. E. F. (*not published*).
Higginson, T. W.: American Flash Language in 1798, *Science*, May, 1885.
Hochstetter, Gustav: Der Feldgraue Büchmann; Berlin, 1916.
Horn, Paul: Die Deutsche Soldatensprache, 2nd ed.; Giessen, 1905.
Hotten, John Camden: A Dictionary of Modern Slang, Cant and Vulgar Words . . . ; London, 1859.
Kildare, Owen: The Jargon of Low Literature, *Independent*, vol. lxi, p. 139.
King, R. W.: Slang in War-Time, *Athenæum*, Aug. 8, 1919.
Krueger, G.: Was ist Slang, Bezüglich Argot? (in Festschrift Adolf Taber; Braunschweig, 1905).
Lambert, Claude: Le Langage des Poilus; Bordeaux, 1915.
Littman, Enno: 23 and Other Numerical Expressions, *Open Court*, vol. xxii, 1908.
Long, Percy W.: Semi-Secret Abbreviations, *Dialect Notes*, vol. iv, p. 245 and p. 357.
Lynch, Arthur: Some Thoughts on Slang, *English*, July, 1919, p. 109.
McCutcheon, Roger P.: A Note on Cant, *Modern Language Notes*, vol. xxxvi, p. 22.
Maitland, James: The American Slang Dictionary . . . ; Chicago, 1891.
Masson, Thomas L.: Do You "Get Me"? *Boston Evening Transcript*, Sept. 7, 1921.

Matthews, Brander: The Function of Slang, *Harper's Magazine*, vol. lxxxviii, p. 304.
Melville, A. H.: An Investigation of the Function and Use of Slang, *Pedagogical Seminary*, vol. xix, p. 94, 1912.
Niceforo, Alfredo: Le Génie de l'Argot; Paris, 1912.
Prévot, Georges: Essai sur l'Emploi Figuré des Termes de Guerre dans le Langage Contemporain, *Mercure de France*, Jan. 16, 1919.
Reusch, J.: Die Alten Syntaktischen Reste im Modernen Slang; Münster, 1893.
Saineanu, Lazar: L'Argot des Tranchées; Paris, 1915.
Schröder, Georg: Ueber den Einfluss der Volksetymologie auf den Londoner Slang-Dialekt; Rostock, 1893.
Sechrist, Frank K.: The Psychology of Unconventional Language, *Pedagogical Seminary*, vol. xx, p. 413.
Sherman, E. B.: A Study in Current Slanguage, *Critic*, new series, vol. xxvii, p. 153.
Sidney, F. H.: Hobo Cant, *Dialect Notes*, vol. v, p. 41.
Smith, C. Alphonso: New Words Self-Defined; New York, 1919.
Sparke, Archibald: Slang in War-Time, *Athenæum*, Aug. 1, 1919.
Thérive, André: L'Argot et la Langue Populaire, *Revue Critique des Idées et des Livres* (Paris), tome xxxii, p. 272.
Whitman, Walt: Slang in America, *North American Review*, vol. cxli, p. 431.
Wilson, A. J.: A Glossary of Colloquial Slang and Technical Terms in Use in the Stock Exchange and in the Money Market; London, 1895.
Wilson, Charles B.: Dialect and Slang, *Athenæum*, vol. ii, p. 291.

13.

EUPHEMISMS, NICKNAMES, AND FORBIDDEN WORDS

Anon.: American Nicknames, *Chambers Journal*, March 31, 1875.
——: Note on the Word "Jew," n. p., n. d.
——: The Slang of Venery and Its Analogues (*unpublished*).
Hayden, Marie Gladys: Terms of Disparagement in American Dialect Speech, *Dialect Notes*, vol. iv, p. 194.
Johnson, Burges: The Everyday Profanity of Our Best People, *Century Magazine*, June, 1916.
McLaughlin, W. A.: Some Current Substitutes for "Irish," *Dialect Notes*, vol. iv, p. 146.
MacMichael, J. Holden: National Nicknames, *Notes and Queries*, 9th series, vol. iv, p. 212.
Scott, Fred N.: Verbal Taboos, *School Review*, vol. xx, 1912, pp. 366-78.
Sechrist, Frank K.: The Psychology of Unconventional Language, *Pedagogical Seminary*, vol. xx, Dec., 1913.
Warnock, Elsie L.: Terms of Approbation and Eulogy in American Dialect Speech, *Dialect Notes*, vol. iv, p. 13.
——: Terms of Disparagement in the Dialect Speech of High School Pupils in California and New Mexico, *Dialect Notes*, vol. v, p. 60.

14.

RUDIMENTARY SPEECH

Bolton, Henry Carrington: The Language Used in Talking to Domestic Animals, *American Anthropologist*, vol. x, p. 65 and p. 97.
Carruth, W. H.: The Language Used to Domestic Animals, *Dialect Notes*, vol. i, p. 263.
Crew, Lena: Words and the Child, *English*, July, 1920, p. 379.
Hall, G. Stanley: Children's Pet Names, *Amer. Jour. Psychology*, vol. ix, p. 368.
Hills, Elijah Clarence: The Speech of a Child Two Years of Age, *Dialect Notes*, vol. iv, p. 84.
Lukens, Herman T.: The Speech of Children, *Jour. Am. Folk-Lore*, vol. viii, p. 158.
Molesworth-Roberts, H.: Inarticulate Sounds (animals), *English*, Dec., 1920, p. 434.
Peters, A. H.: Man's Speech to the Brutes, *Chautauquan*, vol. xxi, p. 67.

15.

THE FUTURE OF THE LANGUAGE

Babbitt, Eugene H.: The Geography of the Great Languages, *World's Work*, Feb., 1908.
Bather, F. A. (and others): Will English Become the World Language? *English*, Feb., 1921, p. 451.
Brackebusch, W.: Is English Destined to Become the Universal Language of the World? Göttingen, 1868.
Emerson, Oliver F.: The Future of American Speech, *Dial*, vol. xiv, p. 270.
Long, Bernard (and others): English vs. Esperanto As A World Language, *English*, March, 1919, p. 19.
Matthews, Brander: Is the English Language Degenerating? (in Essays on English; New York, 1921).
———: One World-Language or Two? (in Essays on English; New York, 1921).
Porter, D. G.: English as a Universal Language, *Jour. Society of Science*, vol. xxxii, p. 117.
Read, Richard P.: The American Tongue, *New York Sun*, Feb. 26, 1918.
Watts, Harvey M.: Need of Good English Growing as World Turns to Its Use, *New York Sun*, Nov. 9, 1919.
Weaver, John V. A.: Serious Uses of the American Language, *Double-Dealer* (New Orleans), Oct., 1921, p. 143.

16.

BIBLIOGRAPHIES OF AMERICAN ENGLISH

Anon.: Bibliography of Books and Articles on American English (supplementary to the bibliography published by Gilbert M. Tucker, *q. v.*, in *Tr. Albany Institute*, 1883), *Dialect Notes*, vol. i, p. 13.
Babbitt, E. H. (and others): Bibliography of Books and Articles on American English, *Dialect Notes*, vol. i, p. 344.

BIBLIOGRAPHY 457

Chamberlain, A. F.: List of Articles on "Canadian English," *Dialect Notes*, vol. i, p. 53.

Mencken, H. L.: Bibliography of American English (in The American Language, 1st ed.; New York, 1919).

Northrup, Clark S.: A Bibliography of the English and French Languages in America From 1894 to 1900, *Dialect Notes*, vol. ii, p. 151.

Sheldon, Edward S. (and others): Bibliography of American English, *Dialect Notes*, vol. i, p. 254.

Tucker, Gilbert M.: Bibliography of American English, *Tr. Albany Institute* for 1883, p. 358.

——: The Bibliography of the Subject (in American English; New York, 1921).

——(and others): Bibliography of American English, *Dialect Notes*, vol. i, p. 80.

LIST OF WORDS AND PHRASES

The parts of speech are indicated only when it is desirable for clearness. The following abbreviations are used:

a. adjective	n. noun	pro. pronoun	v. verb
adj. adverb	pref. prefix	suf. suffix	vp. verb-phrase
art. article	p. pronunciation		

a, p., 69ff, 110, 213, 316, 350
abbordato, 410
aber nit, 199, 367, 384
abgefaked, 407
abolitionist, 98
above, 244
absquatulate, 96
a, art., 73
a, p., 11, 69, 70, 110, 111, 117
abuv, 244
accommodation-train, 97
accouchement, 150
ace, 370
ace-high, 128
aceptress, 88
accessioned, 192
achiev. 245
ach Louie, 104
achtel, 132
acre, 231, 232, 234
activ, 245
acy, suf., 91
ad, 176, 185, 418, 245
adamic, 88
ad-card, 185
addition, 88
address, 209
addrest, 245
ad-man, 185
administration, 124
admitted to the bar, vp., 125
adobe, 101
ad-rate, 185
ad-smith, 194
ad-writer, 185
adult, 209
advertise, 237
advertisement, 209, 212, 224, 236, 237
advertising-agent, 145
advertize, 237, 238, 246
advertizement, 224, 237
advertizing, 238
advize, 246
advocate, v., 36, 59, 61
adze, 67, 241
aeon, 223
aero, 184
aeroplane, 241
aesophagus, 233
aesthete, 237
aesthetic, 223, 237
aestival, 223
aetaernall, 228
aether, 237
aetiology, 237

aetiology, 223
affetuoso, 88
affiliate, 92
affis, 398
Aframerican, 186
African golf, 130
afterwards, 182
again, 217
against, 217
agast, 246
agenda, 115, 130n
ag'in, 106
aggravate, 92, 162
agile, 218
a good ways off, 182
a good ways on, 182
ai, p., 218
ain't, 21, 180, 284, 289
air-line, 97, 122
airplane, 241
aiscrim, 404
aisle manager, 144
aker, 231, 232, 234, 247
Alabama, 111, 217
alabastine, 195
alamo, 202
alarm, n., 224, 236, 253
alarmist, 42
alarmista, 405
alarum, 224, 253
alcove, 170
alderman, 57
alfabet, 246
alfalfa, 126
all by her lonesome, 177n, 193
all-fired, 153
allot upon, vp., 39
allow, 41
alloy, 209
allreit, 413
all right, 404, 407, 413, 416
allrightnick, 407
all Sunday, 188
all the further, 313
all the later, 313
ally, 209
all year, 188
almoner, 130
almond, 211, 215
alms, 215
aloha, 204
aloof, 219
alright, 36, 247
alter, 149
altered, 241
altfäschen, 398
altho, 244, 246, 247

aluminium, 253, 254
aluminum, 196, 253, 254
alumnae, 245
alumnas, 252
alumnis, 252
alumnuses, 252
am, 272, 288
amachoor, 318
amass, 110, 216
amateur, 141
ambassador, 226, 227
ambish, 184
amen, 215, 216
Americanize, 92
Amerind, 186
amigo, 203
am not, 289
amoebas, 252
amphitheatre, 225
ampico, 196
an, 73
anaemia, 223, 240
anaesthesia, 225, 237, 241
anaesthetic, 223
analisis, 246
Ananias Club, 362
ancestor, 227
andiron, 67
anemia, 223, 245
anesthetic, 223, 226
angry, 115
anilin, 245
annex, n., 222, 239n; annex, v., 239n
annexe, n., 222, 239n, 240
announce, 130n
A No. 1, 189
ansco, 196
anser, 247
ant, 111
antagonize, 59, 162
ante, v., 101, 281
antennas, 252
anteriour, 228n
ante up, vp., 101, 128
anti-fogmatic, 99
antiskid, 196
antmire, 149
anxious-bench, 98
anxious-seat, 98
anyhow, 404
anything, 318n
anyway, 182
anyways, 182, 307
apartment, 127
apern, 318
apothem, 246
apple, 110
apparatuses, 252

459

LIST OF WORDS AND PHRASES

appendices, 251
appendicitis, 218
appendixes, 251
apple-butter, 57
apple-jack, 100
apple-pie, 26
apple-sass, 316
appreciate, 59
approbate, 68
ar, 245
arbor, 221
Arbor Day, 133
arboreal, 227
arbour, 221, 227
architect, 245
arco, 196
ardor, 233
ardour, 227
aren't, 180, 181n, 289
are you there?, 118
arkade, 247
armistice, 209
armoir, 202
armor, 221
armory, 227
armour, 221, 227
arroyo, 202
arse, 154
ary, *suf.*, 210
as, 302
as drunk as a Pole, 334n
ask, 110
ash-can, 57, 113, 117
ash-cart, 113
ash-man, 113, 117
ask, 70
asphalt, 222, 236, 237
asphalte, 222, 237, 240
ass, 154
as scarce as hen's teeth, 365
assistant-master, 121
assistant-treasurer, 145
associate-editor, *a.*, 145
associational, 39
assurance policy, 126
ast, 317
a tall, 313
ataxia, 223
ataxy, 223
ate, *suf.*, 91
ate, 273
athaletic, 318
attaboy, 365
attaché, 250
attack, *v.*, 272
attackted, 272, 281
au, *p.*, 329
aunt, 70, 110, 111, 214, 216, 217
auschieppe, 411
author, *v.*, 192
auto, *n.*, 127, 184, 188, 405; auto, *v.*, 127, 185, 194
auto-car, 195
automobile, 420
autumn, 10, 67
avenue, 358
away, 165
awful, 306, 362
a. w. o. l., *v.*, 189, 370, 194
aw re-vore, 320
awry-eyed, 100
ax, 222, 232, 236
axe, 222, 236, 240, 241

baby-carriage, 164
baby's-class, 120
bacardi, 196
baccalaurate, 144
bach, *suf.*, 328
bach, *v.*, 185
bachelor, 227
bacillis, 252
back and fill, *vp.*, 93, 384
back and forth, 39
back-country, 57
back-log, 57
back-number, 95, 163
back pedal, *vp.*, 175
back-settlements, 57
back-settlers, 57
back-talk, 10, 95
back-taxes, 95
back water, *vp.*, 93
backwoods, *a.*, 59; backwoods, *n.*, 57, 59
backwoodsman, 50, 57, 59, 160
back-yard, 113, 127, 163, 164
bad, 306
baddest, 309
bag, 152
baggage, 26, 40, 43, 113
baggage-car, 113
baggage-check, 97, 134
baggage-master, 97
baggage-room, 97
baggage-smasher, 97, 191
bagman, 114
bailiff, 234
Bakerloo, 129
balance, *n.*, 61
balk, *n.*, 236; balk, *v.*, 222
ballast, 113
balled-up, 176n
ballot, *n.*, 124
ballot-box stuffer, 124
ball up, *vp.*, 176n, 193
ballyhoo, 107
ballyhoo-man, 107
balm, 70, 111, 215
balopticon, 196
bandits, 251
banditti, 251
band-wagon, 15
bang-up, 193
banjo, 54, 420
bank-account, 123
bank-bill, 39
bank-holiday, 114, 132
banking-account, 123
bank-note, 39
bankrup, 318
banner-state, 98
bant, 184
barb, *v.*, 185
barbecue, 50, 54
barber-shop, 113, 144
barber's-shop, 113, 114
bargain, *v.*, 170
bargaine, 401
baritone, 223, 225, 237
bark, *n.*, 223, 237, 247
barkeep, *n.*, 184; barkeep, *v.*, 185
barkeeper, 401
bark up the wrong tree, *pp.*, 41, 93
barly, 246
barmaid, 122
barman, 122
barn, 62
barometer, 196
barque, 223, 237
barra, 409
barrel, 190
barrel-house, 100
barrens, 56, 352
barrister, 125
barritenne, 411
bar-room, 401
bartender, 14, 100, 122, 411
barytone, 223, 237
baseball, 414, 420
basket, 70
bas-relief, 217
bat, *n.*, 100
bath, 70, 113
bathe, 168
bath-robe, 113
bath-tub, 113
batl, 244
batteau, 53, 58, 101, 128
batting-average, 128
battle, 244
batty, 191
baulk, *v.*, 222, 319
baulky, 225
bay, 64
bayberry, 64
bayou, 39, 101, 352
bay-window, 67, 163, 414
be, 272
bean, *v.*, 272n
beanery, 187
beat, *v.*, 272
beaten, 272
beastly, 24
beat, 193
beat it, *v.*, 193
beat up (or out), *vp.*, 193
beau, 251
beaupré, 52
beaut, 184, 365
beautiful, 309
beautifuller, 309
beautifulest, 309
became, 272
become, 272
beef, *n.*, 67; beef, *v.*, 384
bee-line, 57
been, 212, 218
beer, 420
beet, 113, 118
beet-root, 113, 118
began, 272, 278
begin, 272, 278
begob, 105
begorry, 105
begun, 272, 278
behavior, 221
behaviour, 221, 227
behoove, 224, 241, 254
behove, 224, 240, 254
bellans, 196
beinkel, 406
bejabers, 154
be left at the post, *vp.*, 93
Belgian hare, 64
belgiumize, 191
belittle, 41, 59, 161
bell-hop, 95-96
belly-robber, 369
ben, *v.*, 272, 288
bend, *v.*, 272
benefice, 130
bent, 272
bent, *v.*, 280
bés-baal, 414
besbol, 404
beseid, 398
beside, 182
best of the bunch, 363
bet, *v.*, 272

LIST OF WORDS AND PHRASES 461

betray, 150
be treated good, vp., 136
betterment, 96
betterments, 39
bet your life, vp., 107
bevo officer, 370
bhoy, 107
biased, 226
bid, n., 113
biff, v., 365, 384
big-bug, 95
big-chief, 52
big-stick, 362, 405
bild, 246
bile, v., 42, 100, 315
bill-board, 35, 113, 117, 168
billion, 95
biloferi, 421
bilt, 231
bin, v., 272, 288
bind, 272
bindery, 59
bingle, 129
biograph, v., 174
biplan, 242
biplane, 242
bir, 413
bird, 365
biscuit, 64, 114
bishop, 99
bit, 287
bitch, 148, 149
bite, v., 272, 287
bitten, 272, 287
bizar, 245
blacco enze, 409
black-country, 126
black-hand, 409
black-stripe, 99
blast, 70
blather, 217
bleachers, 122, 128, 190
bled, 272
bleed, 272
bleeding, 156
blew, 272, 283
blighter, 153
blimp, 369
blind-baggage, 97n
blind-pig, 100
blind tiger, 41
blizzard, 95, 125, 162
block, 126, 127, 362
block-head, 365
blofero, 404
blofista, 161, 404
blond, 251
blonde, 251
blooded, 61
blood-poison, 150
bloody, 24, 155
bloomer, 95
blouse, 116, 118
blow, v., 60, 272, 283
blowed, 272, 283
blow-out, 95
blue-blazer, 99
blue-grass, 56, 126
bluff, n., 56, 407, 414, 245, 352; bluff, v., 161, 384, 405, 281
bluffer, 404, 406, 407
blufferké, 407
blurb, 186
blurt, 186
blutwurst, 103
bo, 185, 251
boar, 149

boarder, 113, 117
board-school, 115, 120
board-walk, 113
bob-sled, 57
bobby, 122
boche, 333, 368
bock-beer, 103
bog, 57, 125
boggé, 414
boghie, 398
bogie, 97, 116
bogus, 53, 61, 93
bohee, 333
boheme, 185
bohick, 333
bohunk, 333
boil, n., v., 106, 315
boiled-shirt, 95
bolt, vp., 98
bolter, 98
bom, 246
bombo, 405
bomma, 411, 410
bonanza, 101
bonehead, 154, 190, 191, 365
bonnet, 114
boob, 14, 154, 159, 185, 191
booch, 398
boocoop, 370
boodle, 98, 158
boodler, 98, 406
book, v., 123
booking-office, 97, 116
bookseller's shop, 39
book-shop, 168
book-store, 39
boom, n., 366, 405, 406; boom, v., 32, 92, 163
boomer, 92
boom-town, 92
boost, n., 151, 158, 186; boost, v., 92, 159, 163
boot, 26n, 63, 113, 116, 122, 127, 168, 219, 239
bootery, 187
boot-lace, 116
boot-legger, 16, 100
boot-maker, 63, 116, 168
boot-polish, 116
boots, 26
boot-shop, 63, 168
boot-tree, 116
booze-hister, 315
boozery, 187
booze-foundry, 365
boracic, 254
bordo, 410
Bordox, 320
boric, 254
boro, 246, 355
borough, suf., 355
bortsch, 398
bosom, 149
boss, n., 15, 39, 54, 81, 124, 159, 383, 384, 401, 420, 406; boss, v., 92, 163, 384
bosso, 410
bösta, 413
bottom, n., 352; bottom, v., 49
bottom dollar, 95
bottom-land, 39, 56
bottoms, 56
bought, 272
boughten, 269, 272, 281, 284

boulevard, 200, 319, 320, 358
bouncer, 92, 100
bound, v., 272
bourgeois, 132
bower, 104
bowler, 114, 118, 164
box, n., 122
box-car, 97
box-office clerk, 145
box-office junior clerk, 145
boy, 406
boychick, 407
bozart, 251
braces, 26n, 116, 118, 239
bracken, 57, 114
brain-storm, 175
brainy, 94
brakeman, 113
brakesman, 113
branch, n., 56, 70, 214, 352
brand-new, 211
brandy, 184
brandy-champarelle, 99
brandy-crusta, 99
brand-new, 211, 317
brang, 272
brash, 94
braten, 103n
brave, n., 101
breaded, 278
breadery, 187
breadstuffs, 50, 61, 63
break away, vp., 384
break, v., 272
break-bone, 365
breakdown, 54
breakfast, 119
bred, n., 245
brekfast, 245
brethern, 318
breve, 132
brevier, 132
brevis, 132
briar, 224, 240
briccoliere, 411
bridal couple, 147
bridge-fiend, 194
brief, v., 125
brier, 224, 241
brig, 184
brilliant, 132
bring, 272
brioche, 202
Briticism, 12
broad-gauge man, 97n
broiler, 119
broke, 272
broken, 272
broker, 123
bromid, 245
bronchitis, 218
broncho, 101, 420
broncho-buster, 101
broom, 219
brought, 272
brown-shoes, 127
brung, 272, 277
brusk, 225
brusque, 219
bryanize, 191
bub, 67
buck, n., 149; buck, v., 319
buck-board, 401
bucket, 171
bucket-shop, 161
Buckeye, 41

462 LIST OF WORDS AND PHRASES

buck-private, 176, 370
buckra, 39
buck the tiger, *vp.*, 93
buckwheat, 26, 401
buffalo, 352
buffer, 113
buffet, *n.*, 144, 250
bug, 148, 191
bugaboo, 95
buggy, 401, 414, 418, 420
bugle, 401
build, 272
built, 231, 272, 280
bull, 149
bulldoze, 92, 98
bull-frog, 55, 56
bull's-eye, 401
bully, 401
bum, *a.*, 32; bum, *adv.*, 32; bum, *n.*, 32, 103, 148, 185, 193, 401, 405, 406, 410, 411; bum, *v.*, 32, 103
bummer, 103
bummery, 103
bumper, 113
bumpers, 97
bunch, 406
bunco, *n.*, 15n, 31
buncombe, 31, 95, 98, 161, 224
bunco-steerer, 15
bund, *suf.*, 199
bungalow, 119
bung-starter, 100
bunk, 31
bunkum, 161, 224
bunned, 100
bunt, *v.*, 281
burden, *n.*, 223, 237
bureau, 41, 53, 113
burg, *suf.*, 355
burgh, *suf.*, 355
burglarize, 32
burgle, 92, 185
burgoo-picnic, 126
burlesk, 247
burly, 68
burn, *v.*, 272
burned, 272n
burnt, 272
buro, 247
burro, 101
burst, 176, 272, 281
burthen, 223, 237
bury, 147
bus, 184, 368, 369, 401
buscellatori, 410
bush, *a.*, 176; bush, *n.*, 54, 219, 383
busher, 128
bush-town, 54
bushwhacker, 54
business, 401
business-block, 126
bust, *n.*, 32, 100, 318; *v.*, 42, 176, 272, 281, 369
busted, 272, 281, 414
buster, 42
butch, 185
butcher, 219
butt, 193
butte, 101, 352
butterine, 144
butter no parsnips, *vp.*, 367
butter-nut, 56
but that, 181, 312
butt in, *vp.*, 175, 193

buttinski, 44, 193, 199
buttle, 185
buy, 272
buz, 245
buzz-saw, 95
buzz-wagon, 190
B. V. D.'s, 144
by God, 153
by gosh, 153
by-law, 113
byre, 57
by way of being, 164

cab, 184
caballero, 202
cabaret, 200
cablegram, 186
caboose, 53
cach, 244
cache, *n.*, 39, 53
cachexia, 223
cachexy, 223
cactuses, 252
cadet, 150, 406
café, 144, 200, 319, 250, 249
cafeteria, 187
cag, 231, 232
cake-walk, 95, 163
calaboose, 39, 54
calamity-howler, 95
calculate, 39, 81
cald, 245
calendar, 113
caliber, 222, 240, 241
calibre, 222, 231
calico, 118
call a bluff, *vp.*, 128
call down, *vp.*, 193
called to the bar, 125
calm, 70, 215, 216
calox, 196
calumet, 52
calvary, 318
came, 272
camera, 196
camerado, 88
camera-hospital, 194
camorra, 199
camouflage, *n.*, 199; camouflage, *v.*, 161, 175, 364, 370
campain, 247
campaign, *n.*, 113, 124
camp-meeting, 57, 414
campus, 95, 122
can, *n.*, 113, 117, 122; can, *v.*, 117, 272
canabuldogga, 411
candidacy, 98
candor, 221
candour, 221, 227
candy, 113, 118, 404, 420
candy-store, 15
cane, 113, 127, 168
cane-brake, 57
canned-goods, 113, 117
canned-monkey, 369
cannon-ball, 144
canoe, 52, 58, 103, 128
canon, 130, 251
can't, 117, 214
can't come it, *vp.*, 40
canter, 184
canuck, 333
canvas-back, 56
canvass, *n.*, 113, 124
canyon, 251, 352
capitalize, 42

capote Allemande, 334n
capote Anglaise, 334n
captain, 138
cap the climax, *vp.*, 93
car, 26, 70, 113
caracter, 245
carborundum, 195, 196
card, 41
card up his sleeve, 128, 160
care, *v.*, 316
caretaker, 114, 127
caribou, 51, 53
carnival, 96
carpentieri, 410
carpet-bagger, 95, 98
carriage, 26, 113, 217n
carriage-paid, 115, 118
carrid, 245
carrier, 97
carry-all, 53, 59
carry on, *vp.*, 137, 166
cars, 52n
carv, 245
cascaret, 195
cash in, *vp.*, 128
casket, 147
castle, 70
castrate, 149
catalogue, 222
catalog, 222, 244, 246, 247
catalpa, 51
catar, 247
cat-bird, 56
cat-boat, 58
catch, *v.*, 272, 244, 316
catcher, 272n
catnip, 126
ca'tridge, 318
catsup, 224
catty-cornered, 68
caucus, *n.*, 39, 43, 50, 157, 161, 401, 420; caucus, *v.*, 58
caucusdom, 158
caucuser, 158
caught, 272
cause-list, 113
cavalleress, 42
cave in, *vp.*, 39
cavort, 60
cellarette, 187
cemetery, 210n
census, *v.*, 192
cent, 58
center, 222, 240, 241, 246
centre, 222, 231
centremost, 225
cerebras, 252
certain dangerous disease, 151
certainly, 307
cesspool, 67
ch, *p.*, 328, 330, 332
chain-gang, 95
chair, 149, 316
chair-car, 97
chairman, 123
chair-warmer, 10, 96
chalkologist, 187
chambers, 127
champ, *n.*, 184, 317n
champeen, 317
champion, 317
chancellor, 121
chandelle, 370
change cars, *vp.*, 52n
channel, 125
chaparral, 202

LIST OF WORDS AND PHRASES 463

chapel, 131, 169
chapparal, 39
chapter, 130
char, n., 67, 168
charge it, vp., 118
Charley-horse, 128
charwoman, 67, 168
chase, n., 57
chase one's self, vp., 384
chaser, 100
chauf, 185
chautauqua, 132, 166
chautauquan, 166
château, 218
check, 123, 223, 247
cheap, 144
checkered, 241
checkers, 113
cheer, n., 316
chef d'oeuvre, 320
chemist, 114, 232, 245
chemist's shop, 114
cheque, 123, 223, 237, 240
chequered, 240
chest, 217, 316
chest of drawers, 113
chevalier, 232
chew the rag, vp., 384
chianti, 199
chick, suf., 407
chicken, 119, 364
chicken-yard, 113
chiclet, 195
chicory, 119
chief-clerk, 113
chief constable, 113, 121
chief lithographer, 145
chief of police, 113, 121
chief of the ushers, 145
chief-reporter, 113
childern, 318
chimbley, 318
chimist, 232
chimney-piece, 115
chimny, 246
china-hospital, 194
chinch, 67
Chinee, 308
chink, v., 32, 92
chink, n., 333
chinkapin, 51
chin-music, 191
chipeco, 196
chip in, vp., 128, 384
chipmunk, 51
chipped-beef, 95
chist, 316
chistu, 409
chit, 203
chlorid, 245, 225
chlorine, 218
chocolate, 216
chomp, v., 317n
choo-choo, 119n
choose, 272
chore, 68, 122, 168, 414
chortle, 186
chose, 272
chow, 203, 370
chowder, 53
Christ, 154
Christer, 155
chromo, 184
chunky, 61
church, 131
churchman, 131
chute, 39
cider, 223, 225
cigaret, 225, 245

cinch, n., 15
cinema, 15, 35, 115
cipher, 237
circuit-rider, 131
circus, 358
citified, 91
City Hall, 359
citizenize, 91, 191
citizen's-clothes, 122
cits, 122
City, 123, 164
City editor, 123
city-editor, 113
City men, 123
city-ordinance, 113
civil-servant, 122
claim-jumper, 95
clam-bake, 126
clam-chowder, 126
clamor, 221
clamorous, 227
clamour, 221, 227
clang, v., 272
clangor, 221
clangorous, 227
clangour, 221, 227
clapboard, 39, 50
Clarke, 214
clas, 245
class, 120
class-day, 121
classy, 32, 194, 309
claw-hammer, 95
cleanlily, 307
cleanly, 307
clean-up, 15
clearing, n., 56
clear the track, vp., 97
clerk, n., 26n, 63, 144, 219;
    clerk, v., 60
clever, 39, 41, 68, 81
climb, 272
climbed, 276
cling-stone, 56
cling, 272
clipping, n., 113, 125
clock-watcher, 191
clodhopper, 67
clomb, 279
clorid, 245
closed-season, 113
closed-shop, 137
close-season, 113
closet, 155
closure, 226n, 224
cloture, 226, 224
cloudburst, 95, 125
clout the sphere, vp., 367
club, 404
club-car, 97
clue, 241
clum, 272, 279, 278
clung, 272
c'meer, 212
clysmic, 195
coal, n., 113
coal-oil, 113
coal-operator, 164
coal-owner, 164
coals, 113
coast, v., 92
coat-and-skirt, 118
coatee, 91
cocain, 233, 245
cocaine, 233
cock, 26n, 115
cocktail, 26, 99, 405
C. O. D., 188
codfish, a., 32, 94

co-ed, 184, 188
co-education, 163
coffee, 216
coffin, 147
coffin-nail, 191
cohanize, 191
coiner, 114
coke, 184
coke-fiend, 194
cold-deck, 128
cold-feet, 166
cold-slaw, 54, 251
cold-snap, 41, 57, 95, 125
cole-slaw, 251
collar-button, 114
collateral, 96
colleen, 105
college, 144
collide, 92, 162
collide head-on, vp., 97n
colonel, 138
color, 26n, 221, 246
Colorado, 217
colorific, 227
colour, 221, 227
colour-blind, 224
colourable, 227, 225
coloured, 227, 224
colourist, 224
colourless, 224
colour-line, 225
colour-sergeant, 225
column-ad, 185
combe, 57
come, 272, 285
come across, vp., 175, 364
comed, 276
come-down, 95, 175, 193
come-on, 159, 366
come out at the little end
    of the horn, vp., 41, 93
comino, 202
command, 70
commencement, 121, 414
commission-agent, 114
commission-merchant, 114
committee, 124
common, n., 57
common-loafer, 103
communicable disease, 151, 152
commutador, 405
commutation-ticket, 114
commute, 97, 185, 191
commuter, 405
company, 124, 219
compass, 219
compensable, 194
complected, 61, 318
compromit, v., 36, 60
con, n., 184; con, v., 185
conant, 203
concertize, 91
conch, 362
conciet, 246
condensery, 187
condit, 246
conduct, v., 40
conductor, 26, 114, 138
conductorette, 187
confab, 185
confessional-address, 130n
confirmand, 130n
conflagrative, 60
congoleum, 196
congressional, 39, 61
connection, 224, 225
connexion, 224, 237, 240
conniption, 95

464　LIST OF WORDS AND PHRASES

cooler, 99
consign to earth, *vp.*, 147
consociational, 39, 89, 91
consols, 123
constable, 115, 122
constituency, 124
consumptionick, 407
contact, *v.*, 192
contri, 410
convict, 184
convocation, 130
cookey, 54
cook-general, 117
coon, 184
cooper, 219
cootie, 368, 369, 370
copious, 68
copper-head, 56
coppetane, 411
cord, *n.*, 127
cord, *v.*, 60
cordwood, 67
corn, 26, 63, 114, 119
corn-cob, 57, 119
corn-crib, 57
corn-dodger, 57
corner, *n.*, 114 ; corner, *v.*, 92, 162
corner-loafer, 103, 165
corn-factor, 114
corn-fed, 190
corn-juice, 100
corn-market, 164
corn-meal, 114
corn-starch, 420
corp, 370
corporation, 123
corpse-reviver, 100
corral, *n.*, 32, 420 ; corral, *v.*, 32
corset, 149
corus, 245
cosma, 252
cosmos, 252
coster(monger), 114
costume, 118
cosy, 224, 226
cotched, 272n
cottage, 119
cotti da costume, 410
cotti da uomo, 410
cottonwood, 345, 352
cougar, 51
could, 272
council, 124
councillor, 222
councilor, 222
council-school, 120
counsellor, 222
counselor, 222
counterfeiter, 114
counterfit, 247
court, *n.*, 235
courteous, 219
court-house, 352, 355
cover, *n.*, 316
cowboy, 420
cow-catcher, 36, 114, 420
cow-country, 176
cow-creature, 149
cowhide, *v.*, 55
coyote, 352
cozy, 225, 240
crab-cocktail, 126
Cracker, 41
cracker, 63, 64, 114, 420
crack up, *vp.*, 93
cranberry-bog, 57n
crank, *n.*, 96

crap, *n.*, 316
crape, 249
crawfish, *n.*, 119 ; crawfish, *v.*, 92, 119n, 352
crayfish, 52, 119
crazy-bone, 114
crazy-quilt, 58
cream, 144
creature, 316
credit-trade, 114, 118
creek, 57, 62, 125, 218, 316, 384, 352
creep, 272
crème de menthe, 320
creole, 54
crep, 272, 318, 352
crêpe, 249
creton, 245
crevasse, 39
crew, *v.*, 272
crick, 316
cricket, 128
crickey, 154
criminal assault, 150
criminal operation, 150
crisco, 195, 196
crispette, 187, 195
criteria, 252
criterions, 252
critter, 316
cronic, 245
crook, *n.*, 15, 159, 406
crook the elbow, *vp.*, 100
crop, 316
crope, 272
crossing, *n.*, 114, 127
crossing-plate, 36, 114
crossing-sweeper, 116, 122
cross-purposes, 67, 162
cross-roads, 352
cross-tie, 114
crotchet, 132
croud, 232
crow, *n.*, 124, 232 ; crow, *v.*, 98, 272
crowd, 231
crowed, 272
crown, *n.*, 58, 249
cruet, 164
cruller, 39, 54
crypt, 130
crystal, 114
ct, *p.*, 318
cuanto, 203
curate, 130
curb, 226
curet, 233
curette, 233
curio, 184
curricula, 252
curriculas, 252
curriculums, 251
curse, 153
cuspador, 200
cuspidor, 144, 200
cuss, *n.*, 318 ; *v.*, 153, 184
cussedness, 96
cussword, 153
customable, 60
cut, *v.*, 272
cut a swath, *vp.*, 93
cute, 61, 184
cuticura, 195
cutlas, 224
cutlass, 224
cut no ice, *vp.*, 366, 367
cut-off, 95
cutting, *n.*, 113, 125
cut-up, 193

cyclone, 125, 420
cyclopedia, 247
cyder, 223, 237
cypher, 237
czar, 224, 236, 237, 249

d, *p.*, 211, 317
daffy, 16, 309
dago, 333n
damaskeene, 195
damfino, 153
damn, 153, 154
damnation, 153
damndest, 153n
damphool, 153, 405
dance, 70, 110, 111, 214, 217
D. & D., 189
dander, 54
dansants, 251
dare, *v.*, 272
dared, 272
darken one's doors, *vp.*, 41, 60
darkey, 61
darn, 153
dast, 272
dasn't, 272n
data, 217, 252
daunt, 111
day-coach, 97, 134
day-nursery, 201
D. D., 138
deacon, *n.*, 144
deacon, *v.*, 91
dead, *a.*, 107
dead-beat, 15, 15n, 95, 159
dead-head, *n.*, 161
dead-head, *v.*, 97
deaf, 70, 71, 111, 217, 316
deal, *v.*, 272
deals, 115
dealt, 272
dean, 121, 130, 145
dear, 142
début, *n.*, 249, 250, 320 ; début, *v.*, 192
débutante, 250, 251
decalog, 244
decent, 152
deciev, 246
deck, 95
decline business, *vp.*, 123
décolletté, 320
Decoration Day, 133
decoy, 209
deed, *v.*, 59
deef, 111, 316
deep, 305
defect, 209
defence, 224, 226, 231
defense, 224, 225, 232, 240, 241
defensive, 226
defi, 184, 188
deficit, 209
definit, 245
deft, 68
degrees of frost, 126
Deitsch, 397
delicate condition, 150
delicatessen, 103, 166
delicatessens, 251
delite, 247
deliveress, 88
dell, 57
demagogue, *v.*, 175
demean, 62, 160, 162
demeanor, 221

LIST OF WORDS AND PHRASES 465

demeanour, 221
demisemiquaver, 132
demoralize, 59
demote, v., 192
dénouement, 249
dent, n., 185n
dental surgeon, 144
dentist, 144, 145
department-store, 114, 118
depos, 421
dépôt, 97, 159, 200, 250, 414, 421
deputize, 60
derange, 59
derby, 114, 118, 163, 164
dern, 153
deserv, 245
desperado, 101
dessert, 127
det, 245
details, 209
determin, 245
determine, 230, 232
dettor, 245
develop, 238
develope, 238
devil-dog, 333n
devilled-crabs, 126
dexter meadow, 367
diagram, 246
dialog, 225, 226
diamond, 132, 218
diarrhea, 223, 233
diarrhœa, 223, 233, 241
diary, 218
dicker, v., 60
dicta, 252
dictograph, 195
did, 273, 283, 284
diehlings, 398
die with one's boots on, vp., 93
diff, 184
different from, 133
different than, 133
different to, 133
dig, 272
digged, 276
diggings, 39, 96
dilatory, 81
dime, 58
dime-novel, 114
diminute, 88
din, 67
diner, 97, 184
dink, 393
dinky, 309
dinner, 119
dinner-dance, 405
di'nt, 317
dioxygen, 196
diphtheria, 211
diphthong, 211
dipo, 414
directly, 24, 133, 135
direct-primary, 124
dirt, 155
dirty, 307
discipline, 232
disorderly-house, 150
dispelled, 241
display-ad, 185
dissenter, 130, 131
distaff, 234
district, 114, 124, 126
dive, n., 15, 15n, 100, 159; dive, v., 273
dived, 273
divide, n., 56, 352

division, 114, 115, 124
divorcée, 249, 250, 251
divvy, n., 98, 128, 184;
   divvy, v., 185
Dixie, 41
do a landoffice business, vp., 93
do, 273, 283
dock, n., 405
docket, 96
doctor, 137, 138n, 145
dodge the issue, vp., 93
do don't, 40
doe, 218
does, 81
dog, 216, 218
dog-gone, 153
doggery, 96, 100, 186
do him proud, vp., 177
do him in, vp., 123
do him up, vp., 123
dol, 245
dole, v., 272, 277
doll, 216
dollar, 58
dollari, 410
dollars to doughnuts, 176
dolled-up, 176, 193
doll-hospital, 194
doll up, vp., 193
dolorous, 227
dom, suf., 187
dominie, 54
don, 121
donate, 36, 62, 162, 163
done, 273, 283
donky, 246
don't, 177
donut, 246
doodle, suf., 197
dope, n., 16, 34, 366, 384
dope out, vp., 109, 175
dopester, 187
dorm, 185
double-header, 128
double pica, 132
dough, 159, 218
dough-boy, 176, 370
do up brown, vp., 93
dout, 245
dove, v., 273, 277
dowager, 147
down-and-out, 32, 96
down-East, 126
downs, 57, 125
down-town, 93
down-train, 126
downwards, 182
doxologize, 36, 89, 91
draft, 111, 223, 226
draftee, 187
drag, v., 273
dragged, 273
drain, v., 316
drains, 116
drama, 215
drank, 176, 269, 273, 283
draper, 122
draper's shop, 114
draught, 223
draughts, 113
draw, n., 61, 184; draw, v., 273, 283
draw a bead, vp., 60
drawed, 273, 283
drawers, 127
drawing-pin, 116
drawing-room, 115, 118, 168

drawing-room car, 42, 43n
dreaded, 278
dreadful, 39
dreadnought, 225
dream, v., 273
dreampt, 281
dreamt, 240
dreen, 316
drempt, 273
dressing-gown, 113
dressmake, 185
drew, 273, 283
drillery, 187
drily, 224, 240
drink, v., 273, 283
drive, v., 358, 273
driver, 168
drove, v., 273, 277
drown, 273
drownded, 106, 273, 281
drug, v., 273, 278
drug-fiend, 194
druggist, 114, 163
drug-store, 114, 163
drummer, 15, 15n, 114
drunk, v., 100, 273, 283
dry-goods, 63, 64
dry-goods-store, 114
dryly, 224, 241
Dschäck, 398
dscheneral-'leckschen, 398
dschent'lleit, 398
Dschim, 398
dschuryman, 398
dub, 15, 166, 366
duck, 100
dud, 166, 368
due, 219n
dug, 272
dug-out, 95
duke, 219n
dul, 245
dum, 246
dumb, 104
dumbfound, 186
dumb-head, 105n
dump, v., 60
Dunkard, 131
during, 183
durn, 153
dust-bin, 113, 117
dust-cart, 113
dustman, 113, 117
Dutch, 397
dutchie, 333
dutiable, 50, 60, 61
duty, 219
dysentery, 210

e, p., 71, 111, 112, 212, 217, 218, 316
each other, 178
eagle, 58
earlier'n, 310
eastbound, 127
East End, 127
East Side, 164
East Side agitators, 147
easy, 306
easy-mark, 366
eat, 273, 277
eat crow, vp., 98
ebaut, 398
eclaircise, 88
éclat, 249
eco, 245
ecology, 223
ecumenical, 223
edema, 223

LIST OF WORDS AND PHRASES

edged, 100
editor, 145, 227
editorial, *n.*, 114, 125
editorial-paragraph, 125
ee, *suf.*, 187
eel-grass, 56
effuse, 88
eg, 245
egad, 154
egg, 217
egg-plant, 56, 126
ei, *p.*, 112
either, 112
el, 189
eldorado, 101
electrocute, 186, 191
electrolier, 186, 195
elevata, 421
elevated, 189, 411, 421
elevated railway, 189
elevateur, 401
elevator, 15, 61, 114, 159, 171, 421
elevator-boy, 114
élite, 249
elk, 345, 352
ellum, 318
elocute, 185
embalming surgeon, 114n
emerald, 132
emfasis, 246
emote, 185
emperor, 227m
emperour, 228n
employd, 245
employé, 144, 200, 250, 233
employee, 251, 233
employment-bureau, 53n
emporiums, 252
enceinte, 150
enclose, 223, 237
enclosure, 225
encumbrance, 237
encyclopædia, 223
encyclopedia, 223
endeavor, 221
endeavour, 221, 227
endive, 119
endorse, 92, 223, 237
endorsement, 225
end-seat-hog, 190
enejau, 404
engine-driver, 115
engineer, *v.*, 32, 92, 162
engineer, *n.*, 97
English, 132, 334n
engulf, 238
engulph, 238
enlisted-man, 114
ennihau, 398
enquire, 223, 237, 240
enquiry, 237
ensure, 241
ent, *suf.*, 186
enter a claim, *vp.*, 93
enteric, 116
enthuse, 92, 175, 185
entrust, 241
enuf, 246
envelop, *n.*, 222; envelop, *v.*, 222n
eolian, 225
eon, 223
eosophagus, 223
epaulet, 222
epaulette, 222
Episcopalian, 131
epoc, 245
equipped, 241

er, *suf.*, 186, 187
errata, 217
error, 129, 227
eruptiveness, 42
ese, 203
esophagus, 223, 247, 233
espechi, 404
Esq., 141
estate-agent, 125
esteque, 404
esthetic, 223, 245
estival, 223
et, 263, 273, 277
eternal, 153, 228
ether, 237
etiology, 223
ette, *suf.*, 187
étude, 320, 215
eu, *p.*, 330
euchre, *n.*, 414; euchre, *v.*, 160
European plan, 134
evensong, 170
eventuate, 59
everything, 318n
evincive, 61
example, 111
excede, 245
excess, 209
exchange, *n.*, 144
excursionist, 114, 162
excurt, 92
excuse me, 319
executive-session, 98
ex-ex-seventh, 120
exfluncticate, 96
expect, 39, 81
exposé, *n.*, 200, 250, 251
express, *v.*, 97
express-car, 97
expressman, 97
express-office, 97
ex-seventh, 120
exterior, 227, 228
extraordinary, 208, 210
eye-opener, 100

face-cloth, 116
face the music, *vp.*, 60
factor, 114
fad, 184
fade away, *vp.*, 384
fagot, 222
faggot, 222, 240
fait, 410
faith-healing, 163
fake, 384
faker, 406
fall, *n.*, 10, 15, 41, 67, 159; fall, *v.*, 273, 283
fall down, *v.*, 175
fallen, 273, 283
fallen woman, 150
fall for it, *vp.*, 366
fallopian, 233n
falloppian, 233n
falls, 182n
falò, 411
fan, *n.*, 128
fancy, 214
fanlight, 116
fan-tan, 108
fantom, 246
far, 111
farina, 218
farmerette, 187
fast, 110
fast-freight, 97
father, 70, 111, 214

Father of Waters, 100
faucet, 116
favor, 221, 233
favorite-son, 98
favour, 221, 227
favourable, 225
favourite, 225, 227
favorite-son, 98
fayaman, 404
feather, 230, 232
feature, *v.*, 15, 163, 175
featurette, 187
feaze, 92
fed, 273, 277
feed, *v.*, 273
feel, *n.*, 273
feel, *v.*, 281
feel good, *vp.*, 136
feeled, 281
fell, 57
fell, *v.*, 273, 283
fella, 318, 407
fellow, 133, 411
fellowship, *v.*, 36, 39, 68
felt, *n.*, 273
felt, *v.*, 281
female, 149, 150
fen, 57
fence, 234
fences, 98
fens, 412
ferns, 114
fertile, 218
fervor, 221
fervour, 221, 227
fest, *suf.*, 198n
fetch, 273
fetched, 273
fête, 200
fether, 232
fiancée, 249, 251
fiat, 196
fiber, 246, 222
fibre, 222
fiddled, 100
fiend, *suf.*, 194
fight, *v.*, 273
figure, 219
filibuster, 98
filing-cabinet, 114
fill, *v.*, 134
fillet, 116, 118
fill the bill, *vp.*, 93
fillum, 318
filthy, 307
finale, 88
find, *v.*, 273
fine, *v.*, 273, 317
finger, 100
finish up, *vp.*, 193
fire, *v.*, 97
fire-brigade, 114, 121
fire-bug, 95
fire-department, 114, 121
fire-eater, 10, 95, 365
fire-laddy, 122
fireman, 404
fire-water, 16, 52
first-floor, 117
first-form, 120
first-standard, 120
first-storey, 117
first-year-man, 121
fish-dealer, 114
fishmonger, 114
fish-plate, 97
fisic, 246
fit, *v.*, 273n
fitten, 273n

LIST OF WORDS AND PHRASES 467

fix, v., 134
fix'n, 407
fizz, n., 99
fizzle, v., 60
fizzle out, vp., 93
flag, v., 97
flagman, 97
flanellette, 187
flabussce, 411
flang, 273
flap-jack, 67
flare up, vp., 39
flat, n., 127
flat-boat, 95
flat-car, 97
flat-footed, 32, 93, 163
flat-house, 127
flavor, 221
flavorous, 227
flavour, 221, 227
flem, 246
fletcherize, 191
flew, 273
flier, 144
fling, v., 273
floater, 98
floe, 218
floor-walker, 114, 144
floozy, 196
flop-flop, 108
flow, v., 273, 218
flowed, 273
flu, 184, 365
fluctuation, 225
flume, 15, 15n
flung, 273
flunk, 186
flunk out, vp., 39
flurry, 96
fluxation, 225
fly, v., 273
fly off the handle, vp., 60
fly-time, 42, 43
f. o. b., 189
foes, 245
fonograf, 246, 247
font, 222
food, 219
foot-hill, 56
footpath, 116, 117
foots, 185
force, n., 42
foregather, 224, 240
forego, 224, 226
foren, 247
forfit, 247
forget, 273
forget it, 16
forgo, 224, 240
forgot, 273
forgotten, 273
fork, n., 41, 56, 352
for keeps, 128, 384
fork over, vp., 39
form, n., 120, 169, 170, 222
forme, 237, 222
formulæ, 251
for rent, 168
forsake, 273
forsaken, 273
forsook, 273
fortnight, 132
forty-rod, 100
forward-looker, 423
forwards, 182, 307
fosfate, 247
fotch, 273n
foto, 247
fotograf, 246, 247

fought, 273
foul, v., 128
found, 263-273, 278
fount, 222
four-flusher, 128, 191
fowl-run, 113
fox-fire, 67
fox-trot, 103, 405
fragile, 218
fraim-hus, 414
frame-house, 57, 414
frame-up, 190, 193
France, 214
franchize, 246
frankfurter, 103
Franzosen, 333n
frat, 121, 184
fraternal-order, 114
fraz, 279
frazzle, n., 160
frazzle, v., 166
frazzled, 100
free-lunch, 26
freez, 245
freeze, v., 273, 279
freeze on to, vp., 93, 366
freight, 114
freight-agent, 114
freight-car, 15, 97, 114
freight-elevator, 114
French, 334n
French letter, 334n
frend, 247
fresher, 121
freshet, 62
freshman, 121
frez, 279
friendly-society, 114
frier, 119
frijole, 202
Fritzie, 368
friz, 273n, 278, 279
frock-coat, 119
frog, 36, 97, 114, 216, 333, 369, 370
froggy, 333
frolick, 230, 234
frolicksome, 234
frontier, 209
froze, 273
frozen, 273, 279
fruitaria, 421
fruit-store, 420
fruttistenne, 411
fulfill, 210
full-house, 128
full-stop, 115
fun, 108
funds, 123
funeral, 147
funeral-director, 144
funeralize, 89, 91, 191
funny, 310
funny-bone, 114
furlo, 246
fuse, n., 224, 226, 237
fuze, 224, 237

g.p., 72, 210, 318, 328, 330
gabfest, 199n
gage, 233
gag-rule, 98, 124
gage, 225
gaiety, 224, 240
galoot, 95
gang, 401
gangster, 406
ganof, 198, 319
gantlet, 222

ganze, 132
ganz gut, 104
gaol, 224, 225, 231, 236, 237, 239, 240
gaoler, 236
garage, 217k
garantee, 246
garbage-man, 117
gard, 246
garden, 113, 127
garden-party, 201
garters, 114
garter-snake, 56
gas, 184, 191
gasolene, 224
gasoline, 114, 224
gastly, 246
gate-money, 128
gather, 217
gator, 185
gauge, 233
gauntlet, 222
gauz, 245
gave, 283
gavot, 245
gayety, 224
gay Quaker, 41
gazet, 245
gazabo, 101
G. B., 189
ge, pref., 96
gedämätscht, 398
gedscheest, 398
gedschumpt, 398
gee-whiz, 153
geezer, 191
geflop, 96
gehm, 398
gemütlichkeit, 249
general, 138
generally, 307
gentil, 251
gentleman, 141
gentleman-author, 141
gentleman-clerk, 141
gentleman-cow, 149
gentleman-player, 141
gentleman-rider, 141
gepliesht, 398
gerrymander, n., 98, 124, 161, 186
ges, 246
gesundheit, 104
get, 71, 217, 272, 273
get ahead of, vp., 93
get a move on, vp., 84
get-away, 15
get away with it, vp., 365
get by, vp., 366
get it in the neck, vp., 384
get-out, 15
get solid with, vp., 93, 175
get sore, vp., 384
get the bulge on, vp., 93
get the deadwood on, vp., 93
get the drop on, vp., 93
get the hang of, vp., 40
get wise, vp., 384
ghella, 411
ghenga, 410
ghetto, 147
ghiroppe, 410
give, 193
give out, vp., 193
gide, 246
gift-shop, 168
gild, 246
gillotin, 232

LIST OF WORDS AND PHRASES

gin-fizz, 99
ginger-ale, 99, 405
ginger-beer, 99n
ginger-pop, 99
ginseng, 108
gink, 163
ginx, 163
giorge, 410
gipsy, 224, 240, 246
giraf, 245
girl for general housework, 117
git, 71
girt, 280
giv, 231, 245
give, 231, 273, 283, 285
give him the glad hand, *vp.*, 366
given, 283
glad-eye, 159
gladiola, 252
gladiolus, 252
glamor, 221
glamour, 221
glas, 245
glass, 110
glass-arm, 128
glebe, 130
gleiche, 400
glide, *v.*, 273
glissade, 370
globbo, 411
glode, 273, 277
gmilath chesed, 407
guillotin, 232
guillotine, 232
go, 273, 377
go-aheadativeness, 36
goatee, 96
gob, 370
go back, *vp.*, 193
go back on, *vp.*, 93, 193
go big, *vp.*, 181
God, 218, 216
God damn, 154
God-damned, 153
go finish, 383
go for, *vp.*, 93
going some, 34, 136
going strong, 384
go into service, *vp.*, 133
go it blind, *vp.*, 93
go it one better, *vp.*, 128
gol darn, 154
goldarned, 153
golden-slipper, 99
gold-fish, 369
golf-fiend, 194
golfitis, 187
gologne, 401
gon, 245
gone coon, 41
goner, 59
gonorrhea, 233
gonorrheal, 233n
gonorrhœa, 151, 233
gonorrhœal, 233n
goober, 54
good, 135
good and hard, 136
good-afternoon, 134
good-by, 222
good-bye, 134, 222, 253, 405
good-day, 134
good-form, 170
good-night, 367
goods, 114, 159
goods-manager, 114
goods-waggon, 97

goods-wagon, 114
goo-goo, 194
go on the war-path, *vp.*, 60
goose, 333, 219
G. O. P., 188
gopher, 53
gormand, 249
gost, 246
got, 133, 273, 216, 286
gother, 276
go the whole hog, *vp.*, 93
go through, *vp.*, 93
gotta, 270
gotten, 41, 133, 176, 273, 285
go to hell, *vp.*, 405
go-to-meeting, 94
goul, 246
goulash, 199
go up Salt River, *vp.*, 98
gourmand, 249
government, 123
governor, 116, 168, 227
grab, *n.*, 98, 188
grab-bag, 95
grade, 114, 120
gradient, 114
gradual, 112
grafonola, 195
graft, *n.*, 15, 161, 366, 406, 414; *v.*, 161
grain, 114
grain-broker, 114
grain-market, 164
gram, 222, 226, 238, 245
gramme, 222, 238, 241
grand, 39
grandificent, 196
grandmother, 211
grand-stand-play, 128
grapefruit, 126
grape-juice-diplomacy, 190
grass, 110, 184, 214
gray, 224, 226, 240
greaser, 41, 95, 333
great-coat, 115
great God, 153
great primer, 132
great Scott, 153
great shakes, 107
Great White Father, 100
Greek, 334n
green, 39
greenback, 401, 404
greenhorn, 67, 162
grewsome, 238
grey, 224, 240
grimbaque, 404
grip, *n.*, 249
grip-sack, 95
gris-mill, 318
groceries, 114, 117
groceriteria, 187
grog, 184
grollo, 411
groom, 219
groop, 232
grosseria, 410
grotesk, 247, 232
grotesque, 232
ground-floor, 117
ground-hog, 41, 56
grounds, 182n
group, 231, 232
grow, 273
growed, 273, 276, 277
growler, 122, 411
grub-stake, 95

gruesome, 241
guard, *n.*, 26, 97, 114, 168
guardeen, 317
guardian, 317
gubernatorial, 36, 37 *n.*, 50, 61, 162
guess, *v.*, 39, 41, 43, 68, 81
guinea, 333
gulch, 95, 352
gully, 95, 352
gumbo, 54, 126
gum-shoe, *n.*, 95; *v.*, 34
guy, *n.*, 153, 166, 406; *v.*, 153
guyascutis, 96
gym, 184, 188
gypsy, 224, 226

h, *p.*, 72
Habana, 249
haberdasher, 122
haberdashery-shop, 168
haberteria, 187
hablaing, 203
hacienda, 39
hack, 126
had, 273
hadda, 287n
hadden, 273, 285
hæmiplegia, 233
hæmorrhage, 223, 233
hafta, 287n
haf to, 287n
hainous, 231, 232
halbe, 132
hale, 204
half, 214
half-breed, 57
hallelujah, 216n
halloo, 92n
ham, 185
hamburger, 103
hammer, 110
hand-car, 97
hand down a decision, *vp.*, 125
hand him a lemon, *vp.*, 365, 366
hand it to him, *vp.*, 365
handle without gloves, *vp.*, 93
hand-me-downs, 42
hand-out, 193
hand out a decision, *vp.*, 125
hand-shaker, 369, 370
handsome, 211
handy, 61
hang, 273
hang-bird, 41
hanged, 273n, 278
hankerchief, 317
Hannover, 249
happify, 36, 60
happy hunting ground, 100
happy pair, 147
harang, 246
harass, 209
harbor, 239
harbour, 239
hard, 111, 305, 306
hard-boiled, 370
hard-cider, 100
have money in the stocks, *vp.*, 123
have the brokers in the house, *vp.*, 123

LIST OF WORDS AND PHRASES 469

hardly, 306.
hardshell, 94
hard-shell Baptists, 131
hardvaer-staar, 413
hardware-dealer, 114
hardware-store, 413
hare, 64, 126
hari-kari, 99
hart, 245
harth, 245
has-been, 32, 190
hashery, 187
hash-foundry, 190
hash-slinger, 191
has went, 21
hath, 70
hat-shop, 168
hat to, 287n
haul, *n.*, 188, *v.*, 63, 64
hausfrau, 103
haut ton, 168
have, 269, 273, 286
have an ax to grind, *vp.*, 93
have not, 289
haven't, 289
have the floor, *vp.*, 93
have the goods, *vp.*, 366
hay-barrack, 54
hay-cock, 57
hay-stack, 57
handsome, 110
harbor, 221
harbour, 221
haze, *v.*, 175
he, 291
head, *n.*, 121-231
head-clerk, 113
headed, 278
head-electrician, 145
head-liner, 114, 123
head-master, 121, 122, 169
head-mistress, 121
headquarter, *v.*, 192
healthful, 181
healthy, 181
hear, *n.*, 283; hear, *v.*, 273
hear, hear! 134
heard, 71
heart, 214
heat, *v.*, 273
heath, 57
heave, 273
heavenwards, 182
Hebrew, 131, 145
hed, 231, 245
heeler, 98
heerd, 273, 277-283
heern, 273, 283
heft, *v.*, 63, 65
hefty, 65
heighth, 106, 318
heimer, *suf.*, 199
heinie, 333
heinous, 231, 232
held, 274
hell, 152n
hell-box, 95
hell-fired, 153
hellion, 91
hello, 92n
hello-girl, 188
hell-roaring, 91
helluva, 153
help, *n.*, 39, 41, 117, 144, 161
Help Wanted, 161-162
helpt, 245
helt, 274, 280

hemidemisemiquaver, 132
hemorrhage, 223, 240
hence, 307
her, 291
herb, 72
here, 180, 307
here'bouts, 307
hern, 291, 292, 293
hers, 293
het, 273, 277
het up, *vp.*, 100, 273n
hiccup, 246
hickory, 51
hid, 273
hidden, 273
hide, 273
high-ball, 405, 99
high-boot, 113
high-brow, 166, 174, 190
highfalutin, 93, 163
high-hat, 168
high-school 120
High street, 359
hike, *v.*, 166, 175
hill-side, 39
him, 291
himself, 303
hired-girl, 57, 118, 168
hired-man, 57
hire-purchase, 118
hire-purchase plan, 114
his, 291, 293
His Excellency, 139, 140
His Highness, 139
His Honor, 140
hisn, 263, 291, 293
hisself, 263, 303
hist, 315
h'ist, 106, 273
h'isted, 273
hit, *v.*, 273
hitched, 16, 384
hither, 180, 307
hit the dirt, *vp.*, 393
hoak, 185
hoakum, 194
hoarding, 35, 113, 117, 168
hobo, 15, 15n, 159, 166, 194
hoch, 104
Hock, 115, 119, 246
Hock-cup, 26n
hod-carrier, 114
Hodge, 134
hodman, 114
hoe-cake, 43, 55, 57
hoed, 245
hog, *v.*, 32
hoggish, 306
hog-pen, 114
hog-wallow, 43, 55
hofbräu, 320, 250
hoist, *n.*, 315, 114, *v.*, 106
hola, 104
hold on, *vp.*, 39, 105
holden, 285
hold, *v.*, 274, 285
hold out, *vp.*, 128
hold-up, 15, 15n, *vp.*, 362
holler, *v.*, 92, 274, 318
hollered, 274
holloa, 92n
holsum, 247
holt, 317
holy gee, 153
holy Jesus, 153
Holy Joe, 369
holy orders, 130
holy-roller, 131

hombre, 202
homely, 68, 127
homœopathy, 241
home-run, 129
homespun, 67, 162
homestead, 414
hominy, 41, 50, 52
homologize, 60
Hon., 139
hon. agent, 141
hon. gentleman, 124
honor, 246, 247, 228-231, 221, 233
honorary, 227
Honorable, 139
honorable friend, 124
honorary, 140
honors, 169
honorarium, 227
honorific, 227
honour, 221, 227, 228, 231, 239
honourable, 228
hooch, 100, 200, 202
hoochfest, 199
hood, 114
hoodlum, 15, 15n, 159
hoodoo, 54, 122
hoof, 219
hook, *n.*, 54, 352, 393
hooligan, 159
hoop, 219
hooverize, 175, 187, 191
hooves, 219
hoo-zat, 212
hop, *v.*, 109, 393
hornswoggle, 92
horse's neck, 99
horrid, 216
horror, 226
horrour, 228n
horse of another colour, 42
horse-sense, 95
horse-shoer, 282
hospital, 72, 114, 194
hospitalize, 175
hospital-nurse, 116, 119
hostil, 245
hostile, 212, 218
hostler, 224, 225
hot, 216
hot-box, 97
hotel, 72, 144
hotel-valet, 145
hot-stuff, 166
hot-tamale, 101
house-clean, *v.*, 192
housekeep, *v.*, 185
house-master, 169
house of ill repute, 150
house of questionable repute, 150
hove, 273, 277
hub, 39
huckleberry, 56
huckster, 114
humble, 72
humbug, *n.*, 40
humor, 221
humorous, 227
humour, 221-227
Hun, 188, 368
hunderd, 318
hung, 273, 278
hunker, 40
hunkie, 333
hunky-dory, 96
hunting, *n.*, 114, 134
hunyadi, 333

LIST OF WORDS AND PHRASES

Hupmobile, 195
hurray, 410
hurricane, 125
hurry up, *vp.*, 193
hurt, 274
huskerette, 187
hustle, *v.*, 68
hypo, 185

I, 291
i, *p.*, 71
ice-box, 406
ice-cream, 67, 401, 404, 405
ice-cream soda, 26
iced-water, 126
ices, 127
ice-water, 126
idea, 209
idealer, 309
idear, 318
ify, *suf.*, 91
ige, *suf.*, 407
iland, 232, 247
ile, 315
ill, 10, 67, 116, 148
illy, 49, 177, 307
imagine, 232
imitation mahogany, 144
immediately, 133
immigrate, 59
imperturbe, 88
in bad, 181
Inc., 123
incidence, 308
incident, 308
inclose, 223, 225
incohonee, 52n
Indian, 114
Indian-corn, 62, 114
Indian-file, 57
Indian-giver, 57
Indian-meal, 114
Indian summer, 57, 114
indices, 251
indiccio, 410
indorsation, 237
indorse, 223, 225, 237
indorst, 245
inferior, 227
inflection, 224, 225
inflexion, 224, 240
influential, 61, 159
in foal, 148
infract, 60
ing, *suf.*, 186
initial sack, 367
initiative and referendum, 124
injunct, 192
ink-slinger, 42
inland-revenue, 114
inn, 64
ino, *suf.*, 197
inquire, 223, 236, 237
inquiry, 209, 237
inschtructa, 398
insect, 148
insignia, 252
insignias, 252
inski, *suf.*, 198n, 199
instal, 240
instalment-business, 114
instalment-plan, 114
instead, 217, 232
insted, 232
institutionalize, 191
instruct, 125
insure, 241
insurge, 175, 185, 191, 281

interduce, 318
interesting condition, 150
interiour, 228n
intern, 222, 233
internal-revenue, 114
interne, 222, 233
interval-land, 39
interview, *n.*, 163; *v.*, 68
in the course of, 183
intrust, 241
inure, 88
invalided home, 147
inverted-commas, 115
in writing, 134
involv, 245
iodin, 218
iodine, 218
iron-horse, 97
ironmonger, 26n, 114
I say, 133
ish ka bibble, 198n
I should worry, 163, 198
island, 230, 232
ism, *suf.*, 187
is not, 289
isn't, 289
ist, *suf.*, 187
it, 292
ite, *suf.*, 187
itemize, 32, 92
itis, *suf.*, 187, 202
it is me, 180, 298
it listens well, 200
its, 292
itself, 303
ize, *suf.*, 91, 187

jackass, 154
Jack Johnson, 369
jack-pot, 128
jack up, *vp.*, 175
jag, 100
jagged, 100
jail, 224, 225, 231, 232, 237, 241
jaitun, 404
jamachi, 404
janders, 317
janitor, *n.*, 114, 414, *v.*, 192
jap-a-lac, 195
Japanee, 308
jaundice, 317
jay, 191
jazz, 166, 194
jeans, 67
jell, *v.*, 32, 185
jell-o, 195, 196
jemmy, 223
jeopardize, 61, 92
jerked-beef, 54
jerk-water, 97
Jerry, 368
jersey, 116
Jesus, 153, 154
Jew, 131, 145
jew, *v.*, 63, 65
jew down, *vp.*, 65
jeweler, 230
jeweller, 230
jewellery, 222, 226, 239, 240
jewelry, 222, 239
Jewish, 146
Jewish cavalry, 369
Jewry, 131, 146
jig's up, 42
jiggered, 100
jimmy, 223, 225

Jimson-weed, 56
jine, 106, 315
jinx, 163, 194
jit, 184
jitney, *a.*, 32, 176, *n.*, 166, 193
Johnny-cake, 57
John-Collins, 26, 99
Johnny jump-up, 56
join, *v.*, 106, 315
joiner, 26n
joint, 115, 191
join up, *vp.*, 133
joke-smith, 194, 363
jolly, 134
jonteel, 251
jornada, 202
joss, 108
journalist, 115, 124
joy-ride, *n.*, 10, 157, 166, 190, 194, 366; *v.*, x, 194, 281
joy-rided, 281
joy-rode, 281
juba, 54
jubilate, 185
judge, *n.*, 145
judgement, 236, 240
judgmatical, 61
judgment, 236
jug, 115, 171
jugged, 100
juice, 190
jukre, 414
julep, 26n, 67
jump a claim, *vp.*, 93
jump the rails, *vp.*, 97n
jumper, 96, 406
jumping-off-place, 95
jump-off, 193
jump on with both feet, *vp.*, 93
June-bug, 56, 126
junior, *n.*, 121
junior school, 120
junk, 159
junket, 124
just, 135, 405

k, *p.*, 317
kaemp-mid'n, 414
kafeteria, 247
kaif, 319
kamaaina, 204
kanaka, 204
kandy, 247
kar, 247
karo, 196
katzenjammer, 103
kaukau, 204
kayo, 203
K. C., 125
ke, *suf.*, 407
ked, *p.*, 317
kedge, 81
keep, *v.*, 274
keep a stiff upper lip, *vp.*, 93
keep company, *vp.*, 133
keep tab, *vp.*, 93
keer, 316
keg, 231, 232
kep, 274, 318
ker, *pref.*, 96
kerb, 226, 237, 240
kerb-stone broker, 237
ker-bang, 96
ker-flop, 96
ker-flummux, 96

LIST OF WORDS AND PHRASES 471

ker-plunk, 96
ker-slam, 96
ker-splash, 96
ker-thump, 96
ketch, 106, 272n, 316
ketchup, 224
kettle, 316
key, 54, 352
keyless-watch, 35, 116
khalifate, 249
khilifat, 249
kick, *n.*, 362, *v.*, 92, 362
kicker, 92
kick-in, 193
kick the bucket, *vp.*, 93
kidding, 14
kiddo, 107
kike, 134, 333, 406
kill, *n.*, 348
kilogram, 237, 238
kilogramme, 225
kilometre, 225
kimona, 199n, 405
kind'a, 313
kindergarden, 318
kindergarten, 103, 120, 200
kindergartens, 251
kindness, 210
King's Counsel, 125
kinky, 61
kissing-fiend, 194
kit, 274
kitchenette, 187
kitchen-fender, 164
kittle, 316
kitty, 128
kivver, 316
kjors, 414
klaxon, 195
kn, *p.*, 329, 332
kneel, 274, 281
kneeled, 281
knelt, 274
knew, 274
knickebein, 26n
knicker, 185
knickerbocker, 401
knife, *v.*, 98
knob, 56, 353
knock, *v.*, 192
knocked up, 152
knock into a cocked hat, *vp.*, 93
knockout-drops, 384
know, 274
knowed, 274, 276, 277
know him like a book, *vp.*, 93
know-nothing, 43, 160
know the ropes, *vp.*, 93
kodak, 195
kodaker, 195n
kodak-fiend, 195n
komusta, 203
kosher, 198, 319
kow-tow, *v.*, 108
Kreisterite, 187
Kriss Kringle, 104
krone, 249
kruller, 39
kruxingiol, 202
kryptok, 196
kumfort, 247
kümmel, 104
kunschtabler, 398

L., 189
lab, 185

lab. monitor, 121
labor, 221, 242, 246
laboratory, 210n, 212
Labor Day, 133
laborer, 114, 144
laborious, 227
labour, 221, 227, 242
labourer, 227
lacquey, 240
lacrimal, 225, 233
lachrymal, 233
ladies' wear, 141
lady, 141, 147n, 149
lady-clerk, 141
lady-champion, 141
Lady Day, 133
lady-doctor, 141
lady-golfer, 141
lady-inspector, 141
lady-secretary, 141
lady-typist, 141
laf, 246
Lafayette, 111n
lager, 401
lager-beer, 103
lagniappe, 101, 202
la grippe, 249
laico, 409
laid, 274
lain, 274
lam, 246
lamb, 144
lame-duck, 32, 98, 124
lanai, 204
landlady, 211
land-office, 57
landslide, 57
land-slide, 98
lane, 358
large, 214
lariat, 101
lasso, *n.*, 101, *v.*, 101
last, 110
laste, 410
late, 305, 307
lately, 307
lather, 217
lauds, 130
laugh, *n.*, 110, 111, 214
laugh in your sleeve, *vp.*, 365
laundry, 111
lava, 217
lavandera, 203
law-abiding, 61
lay, *v.*, 282
lay-readers, 130
lead, *v.*, 274
leader, 114, 125
leaderette, 125
leader of the orchestra, 145
leading-article, 114, 125
leads, *n.*, 116, 117
leag, 246
lean, 274
leap, *v.*, 274
leaped, 106
leapt, 240
learn, 274, 282
learnt, 274
leatherette, 187
leatherneck, 370
leave, *v.*, 282
leberwurst, 103
led, 274, 277
leery, 309
leg, 217
legal-holiday, 114, 133

Légion d'honneur, 249
Legion of Honor, 249
legislate, 60, 61
Leipzig, 249
lend, 274, 282
lengthy, 41, 49, 60, 61, 159
leniency, 62
lent, 274, 280, 282
leopard, 230, 232
lep, 106, 274, 280
leperd, 232
le's, 245, 319
les, 318
let, 168, 282
let it slide, *vp.*, 93
let on, *vp.*, 39
le truc du bresilien, 334n
letter-box, 115
letter-carrier, 26n, 115, 118, 163
levee, 39, 101, 249
leveled, 226
liable, 310
liberty-cabbage, 199, 200
liberty, 318
libretti, 251
licensed-trade, 122
licensed-victualler, 122
lick, *n.*, 352
lickety-split, 55
lie, *v.*, 274, 282
lied, 215, 274
lieutenant, 212
life insurance policy, 126
lift, *n.*, 114, 168, 171
lift-man, 114
lift up, *vp.*, 193
light, *v.*, 193, 274
lighted, 278
lighter, 115
lightning-bug, 56
lightning-rod, 41
light out, *vp.*, 93, 193
like, 269
like greased lightning, 365
likely, 39, 41, 68, 310
lim, 246
limb, 149, 150
limehouse, 190
limited, *n.*, 97, 144
limited liability company, 123
line, 97, 115, 116, 123
lineage-rates, 125
linen-draper, 26n
links, 182n
listerine, 195
lit, 278
liter, 222
literary, 210
literatus, 88
litre, 222
liturgy, 130
Little Mary, 148
littler, 309
littlest, 309
liv, 245
live-oak, 41, 56
live out, *vp.*, 133
liver, *a.*, 309
liverwurst, 103
livest, 194
livetta, 411
live-wire, 15
living, *n.*, 130
living-room, 118
LL. D., 138
loaded, 100

loaf, *n.*, 103; *v.*, 103, 162, 415
loafer, 40, 103, 405, 406, 410, 411
Loaferies, 162
loan, *v.*, 68, 192, 282
loaned, 263, 274
loan-office, 144
loan-shark, 190, 406
lobby, *v.*, 98
lobby-agent, 98
lobbyist, 98
lobby-display, *v.*, 192
lobster, 159, 191
locate, 60, 61, 185
loco, 101
locoed, 94
loco foco, 40
locomobile, 195
locomotive, 99
locomotive engineer, 115
locum-tenens, 130
locust, 41, 56, 352
lodgment, 225
lofeur, 401
loffari, 410, 411
lofletters, 398
log, 216
log-cabin, 57n
log-house, 57
logroll, *v.*, 55
lonchi, 404
longa, 132
long-distance-call, 115
long primer, 132
long-sauce, 41
long-vacation, 133
loophole, 67
loop-the-loop, *v.*, 281
loose, 274n
loot, *n.*, 369
lorry, 116
los, 245
lose, 122, 274
lost, 274
lot, 39, 62
loud, 305
lounge, *n.*, 122
lounge-lizard, 190
lounge-suit, 122
love-nest, 188
loved, 280
love-pirate, 188
low-down, 43
low-flung, 94
lowly, 307
lozenger, 318
Ltd., 123
lucre, 234
luffa, 415
luggage, 26, 43, 113
luggage-shop, 168
luggage-van, 97, 113
lumber, 63, 64, 115
lumberjack, 64
lumberman, 64
lumber-room, 64
lumber-yard, 64, 115
luncheon, 186
luster, 240
lustre, 231
lynch, *v.*, 92, 162
lynch-law, 39
lysol, 195, 196

M., 320
machine, 98, 115, 125, 127, 232
mackinaw, 52

mad, 115
Madame, 147, 252
mad as a hornet, 94
mad as a March hare, 94
mad-dog, 94
made, 274
mad-house, 94
maffick, 190
magazine, 209
magistrate, 145
mail, *n.*, 118; *v.*, 118
magis, 414
mahoganized, 144
maid, 168
make, 274
Maikai no, 204
mail, *n.*, 164
mail-box, 118
mail-clerk, 97
mail-order, 118
mail-train, 118
mail-van, 118
Main street, 359
maiz, 232
maize, 52, 63, 114, 232
major, *v.*, 192
makai-ewa, 204
make a kick, *vp.*, 93
makee, 377
make good, *vp.*, 159, 166
make the fur fly, *vp.*, 93
make tracks, *vp.*, 93
malasi, 414
male-cow, 149
Mamie-Taylor, 99
mamma, 209
managing-director, 123
maneuver, 224, 233, 240
mangel-wurzel, 126
man higher up, 124
manitee, 52
männerchor, 104
manœuvre, 224, 233, 241
mansions, 127
mantelpiece, 115
marchetto, 411
mare, 148, 149
marrid, 245
marsh, 125
mascine, 410
masheen, 232
maskerade, 247
mass, 110, 131n
massive, 110
mass-meeting, 39, 95, 98
master, 110, 215
master of properties, 145
mastiff, 234k
matinée, 201, 249, 250
matins, 130, 170
matron, 145
matter, 110
matzoth, 198, 319
mauka, 204
maverick, 95
may, 274
maybe, 319
mayonnaise, 320
mayorality, 318
mazuma, 198
me, 291
mean, *n.*, 231; *v.*, 274
meant, 274
media, 251
mebby, 319
mecanic, 245
mediæval, 223, 240, 241
medicine-man, 52
medieval, 223, 245

meet, *v.*, 274
meen, 231
meidel, 406
melancholy, 169, 210n
melée, 249
melted, 276
memo, 185
memorandum-book, 127
menhaden, 51
ment, *suf.*, 91
menu, 200, 319, 320
merchant, 144
mercy, 71
mes, 245
mesa, 101
mesdames, 252
mess, *n.*, 317
messieurs, 252
met, 274
metal, 113
metals, 97
metaphor, 227
meter, 222, 246
Methodist, 115, 131
metre, 222
mews, 57
mezzo-barrista, 411
Michaelmas, 133
might, *n.*, 39
mightily, 307
mighty, 307
might'a, 274
mileage, 61
mileage-book, 97
military, 210, 212
milk-shake, 166
mill, 58
milligram, 238
mine, 291, 293
minerals, 116, 99
minim, 132
minima, 132
mining-regions, 126
minion, 132
minion-nonpareil, 182
minister, *n.*, 130
ministry, 124
minnow, 318
minor-leaguer, 128
minuet, 320
minster, 130
mirage, 217
mirror, 227
mis, 245
mischievous, 318
misdemeanour, 227
miss, *v.*, 122
missionate, 39, 89, 91
mission-festival, 130n
missionsfest, 130n
missus, 252
Mister, 138n, 252
mitin, 405
mixologist, 194
Mlle., 320
mob, 183
mobiloil, 195
moccasin, 42, 43, 52, 414
moccasin-snake, 56
molasses, 10, 67, 115, 414
mollusc, 224, 237, 240
mollusk, 224, 226
mold, *n.*, 222, 232, 246
molt, 222, 276
monarc, 245
monarchy, 245
money-bund, 199
money-order, 118
monitor, 169

LIST OF WORDS AND PHRASES 473

monkey-nut, 115, 126
monkey-wrench, 115, 414
monolog, 226
monoplan, 242
monoplane, 242
monsignori, 251
monsignors, 251
Montana, 217
mont-de-piété, 144n
mony, 246
moon, 52
moon-shine, 100
moor, 57, 122, 125
moose, 51, 126, 352
moral, 218
more better, 308
more queerer, 309
more than, 183
more ultra, 309
more uniquer, 309
more worse, 309
morgage, 247
morning-coat, 119
mortgage-shark, 95
mortician, 144
moslem, 249
mossback, 57
Most Hon., 140
motor, 127
motor-car, 127
mould, n., 222, 235, 237, 240, 241
moult, 222, 241
moustache, 222, 240, 241
movie, 35, 166, 176, 184
movie-fiend, 194
moving-picture-theatre, 115
mow, v., 274
mowed, 274
mown, 274
Mr., 141, 145, 253
Mrs., 65
mucker, 43n, 153
muck-raker, 362
mud-hen, 56
mud-scow, 58
muff, 130
mufti, 122
mugwump, 98
mum, 184
municipal, 318
munke-rins, 414
mush, 57
music-hall, 116, 123
mushquash, 160
music-hall, 201
muslin, 249
muss, n., 40, 67, 317
v., 92
mustache, 222, 226, 240
mustang, 101
mutt, 184, 191
muzhik, 249
my, 291, 377
my dear, 142
myself, 303

nabisco, 195, 196
naite, 410
naive, 250
naivete, 249, 250
nameable, 42
naphtha, 211
narcissis, 252
narcissuses, 252
nasty, 170, 307
nature, 71, 112
nature-faker, 190, 362
naught, 223

naughty, 307
navvy, 95, 114
near, 32, 187, 231
near-accident, 44
near-beer, 187
near-silk, 32, 205, 306
necco, 196
necessarily, 169, 210
neck, 56, 352
necktie, 115
née, 320
neer, 232
negative, v., 60
neger, 232
negligée, 250
negro, 232
neighbor, 221
neighbour, 221, 227
neighbourhood, 225
neighbourliness, 225
neighbourly, 225
neither, 112
neolin, 195
neolinize, 191n
nephew, 211, 212
nest-of-drawers, 114
net, adv., 222, 237
nett, adv., 222, 237
Nevada, 217
never mind, 407
new, 219n
news-agent, 115
news-dealer, 115
newspaper-man, 115
next-doorige, 407
N. G., 31, 188
nib, 115
nice, 362
nickel, 420
nice, 310
nick, suf., 407
nickel-in-the-slot, 172
nigger in the woodpile, 124
night-rider, 43
nine-pins, 116, 128
nineteenth hole, 130
niter, 225
nix, 199
nix come eraus, 104
nixy, 199
no-account, 36, 55, 59
nobby, 216
no good, 410
no-how, 55, 59
no kerry, 203
non-committal, 93, 163
nonconformist, 130
nonconformist conscience, 131
none, 311
nonpareil, 132
noodle, 54, 103
nook, 219
no place, 182n
normal income tax, 126
no sir, 407
no-siree, 107
notch, n., 56, 352
nothin', 318n
nothing, 311
notify, v., 63, 133
notions, 115
not nothing, 269
not on your life, 107
nought, 223, 240
noways, 107
nowheres else, 182
nucleuses, 251
nun gidde, 410

nuptial ceremony, 147
nurse the constituency, vp., 124
nursing-home, 114, 119
nursing-sister, 119
nut, 362
nutty, 309

o, p., 218
ö, p., 330
oatmeal, 115, 404
obligate, 39, 59, 91, 162
oblige, 71
obsequies, 147
occurred, 241
ocelot, 52
oclysmic, 196
octoroon, 54
odor, 221
odorous, 227
odour, 221, 227
odsblood, 154
oecology, 223
oecumenical, 223
œdema, 223
of, 286
offal, 67
offence, 224, 226
offense, 224, 234
offensive, 226
office-building, 126
office-holder, 35, 42, 43, 115, 121
offices, 115
office-seeker, 98
offset, 39
off'n, 313, 317
often, 210
oh, oh!, 184
oi, p., 315, 329
oil, 315
oi-yoi, 198
O. K., 31, 188, 306
okeh, 189
old boy, 169
old dear, 170
Oldsmobile, 195
Old-Stick-in-the-Mud, 101
old top, 168
oleo, 184, 196
oleomargarine, 144
olraite, 404
omelet, 237
omnibus-bill, 42, 124, 366
once, 106
oncet, 106
onc't, 318
one another, 178
one, 310
one best bet, 176
one-he, 177
one-horse, 59, 191
onery, 34, 318, 106
one-step, 103, 405
on his legs, vp., 124
onry, 318
on the bench, 128
on the fence, 98
on the Fritz, 104
on the hoof, 95
on the job, 166, 176
on the Q. T., 189
on the rates, 122
on time, 134
on to his curves, 128
ontologist, 144
on top, 216
oo, p., 219

LIST OF WORDS AND PHRASES

open-shop, 137
open up, *vp.*, 193
operate, 192
operatori, 410
opossum, 41, 51
oppose, 59, 61
opuses, 252
or, *suf.*, 186
orange, 216
orangeade, 195
orate, 185
oratory, 81
oratour, 228n
orchestra, 115, 123
ordain, 130
order, *n.*, 125
ordinary, 106, 318
ordinary tax, 126
ornate, 68
orré, 410
oslerize, 191
ossified, 100
ostent, 88
ostler, 224, 225, 240
otemii, 404
ouch, 104
ought'a, 289
oughter, 289
our, 291
ourn, 269, 291, 293
ours, 293
ous, *suf.*, 91
outbuildings, 115
outfit, 369
out-house, 10, 162
outré, 250
over, 176, 183
overcoat, 115
over his signature, 134
overhalls, 318
ow, *p.*, 318
own self, 303
owski, *suf.*, 332
oyster-stew, 126
oyster-supper, 95, 126

paatikkel, 412
package, 115
padrone, 199
pahea oe, 204
paid, 274
pail, 171
paint the town red, *vp.*, 93
pajamas, 223, 233, 239
pale, *n.*, 39
pale-face, 52
palm, 215, 217
Palmerism, 187
palmetto, 54
palmolive, 195
pan, *v.*, 192
panel-house, 43
pan-fish, 57
pan out, *vp.*, 93, 162
pantasote, 196
pantry, 110
pants, 36, 127, 160, 406
papa, 209
papoose, 52, 421
paprika, 199
par, 125
paraffin, 113
paralize, 246
parcel, 115
pard, 184
pardner, 318
paresis, 209
parlor, 115, 118, 122, 168, 221

parlor-car, 43, 115, 221
parlour, 227
parson, 130
partiolist, 88
partridge, 63, 64
pas, 245
pasea, 203
pass, *n.*, 352; pass, v., 111
passage, 43n, 358
passage-way, 43
pass-degree, 121
passenger-coach, 97
pastor, 110
patent, 212
patent-inside, 43n
patent-outside, 43n
path, 70, 127, 169, 111, 214
pa'tridge, 318
patrolman, 43, 115
patter, 183
pau, 203
pavement, 18n, 116, 127
pawn-shop, 144, 172
paw-paw, 51, 52, 352
pay, 274
pay-day, 115, 163
pay-dirt, 41, 43, 95
paying-guest, 113, 117, 144
P. D. Q., 31, 43n, 188
peach, 159, 365
peacharino, 196
peach-pit, 54
pea-nut, 56, 115, 126, 410
peanut-politics, 126
pearl, 132
pearline, 195
peart, 94
peas, 222
pease, 222, 237
pebeco, 196
pecan, 51
ped, 276
pedagog, 244
pedlar, 224
pedler, 224
peep, *v.*, 282
peeve, 175, 185
peewee, 54
peg, 217, 393
pemmican, 52
pen, 184
pence, 172
pennant-winner, 128
penny, 41, 172
penny-ante, 128, 172
penny-arcade, 172
penny-bill, 58
penny-dreadful, 114
penny-in-the-slot, 172
pennyr'yal, 126
penny-whistle, 172
pen-point, 115
peon, 101
peonage, 101
pep, 184
peptomint, 195
perambulator, 164
per, 201
per-diem, 98
perfect, 209
perhaps, 319
period, 115
permanent-official, 122
permanent-way, 97, 115
persimmon, 41, 51, 126
pesky, 94
peter out, *vp.*, 93
petrol, 114, 164
petted, 241

ph., *p.*, 211
phantom, 231
phenix, 225
phenomena, 252
phenomenons, 252
phial, 223, 237
phlegm-cutter, 100
phone, *n.*, 184, 188, 194;
  phone, *v.*, 175, 185, 194,
  281
phoney, 176
photo, *n.*, 176; *v.*, 175, 185
physick, 230, 234
P. I., 150
pianist, 209
piano, 215, 216
pianola, 195
pica, 132
picayune, 94, 101, 122
pickaninny, 54, 383
picket, 223
picco, 410
picturesk, 247
picturedom, 187
picture-palace, 115
picturize, 191
pie, 26, 63, 115, 421
pie-counter, 98
piezelmietje, 418
pifflicated, 100
piffled, 100
piggery, 114
pigmy, 224, 237
pike, 184
piker, 191, 406
pill, 129
pillar-box, 115, 118
pill-box, 369
pimp, 150
pine-knot, 57
pinhead, 154, 175, 177
pinozze, 411
pinocle, 103
pint, 122
pipe del gasso, 411
pipe-hospital, 194
pipe-of-peace, 52
piquenic, 404
piquet, 223
pisen, 315
pismire, 149
pissoir, 150n
pit, 54
pitch-pine, 56
pitcher, 26, 115, 171, 318
placate, 59, 162
place, *n.*, 63, 358
placer, 101
plaguey, 39
plaintiff, 234
plane, 184
planing-machine, 42
plank, 98
plank down, *vp.*, 93
plant, *n.*, 70, 115
planted to corn, 134
plataforma, 405
plate, 116
platform, 98, 163, 405
play ball, *vp.*, 128
played-out, 93
play for a sucker, *vp.*, 175
play 'possum, *vp.*, 93
plaza, 101, 319, 359
plead, 274
pled, 277
plebe, 185
pled, 274

LIST OF WORDS AND PHRASES 475

plough, n., 35, 97, 114, 231, 237, 240, 241
plough-boy, 225
plow, n., 223; plow, v., 231, 232
plug along, vp., 384
plumb, adv., 94; v., 185
plump, 94
plunder, n., 40, 41
plunder-bund, 199
pluralist, 130
plute, 184
Plymouth Brethren, 131
pocketbook, 127
podgy, 223, 225
poem, 218
points, n., 97; v., 116
poison, 315
poker, 109, 405
pokerish, 109
poke-weed, 56
polack, 333
poleit, 412
policy, 199n
pomato, 186
poncho, 101
pond, 56, 62, 352
pone, 41, 52
pooldoo, 202
pony up, vp., 128, 193
poorhouse, 115, 122
pop, n., 184, 99
pop-concert, 185
pop-corn, 26, 57
poppy-cock, 95
popular-priced, 144
populist, 420
porgy, 51
pork, 191
pork-barrel, 98, 124, 176
porpess, 231, 232
porpoise, 231, 232
porque, 203
porridge, 57, 115, 122
portage, 53, 101, 352
port-cochère, 249
porter, 114, 127
portière, 249
Portugee, 308
'possum, 184
post, n., 118, 164; v., 118
postal-card, 118
postal-order, 118
post-card, 118
posterior, 228n
post-free, 115, 118
postillion, 240
postman, 26n, 115, 118
postoffice-order, 118
postpaid, 115, 118
postum, 195, 196
pot, 128
potato-bug, 56
poteen, 105
potpie, 115
powerful, 39
practical, 110
practis, 245
practise, 241
prairie, 50, 53, 101, 352
prairie-schooner, 95
praline, 202
p'raps, 319
prebendary, 130
preceptor, 169
precinct, 98
précis, 249
predicate, v., 92
prefect, 121, 159

prélude, 320
première, 320
premises, 240
prepaid, 115, 118
prep-school, 120, 184
pres, 245
presentation, 130
president, 121, 145
presidential, 39, 61, 162
presidio, 101, 202
prespiration, 318
press, 115
press-agent, n., 144; v., 192
pressatori, 410
pressman, 115, 124
press-representative, 145
prestolite, 196
pretence, 224
pretense, 224
pretty, 217
pretzel, 103
Preussen, 334n
preventable disease, 151
prickly-heat, 57
primarily, 209
primary, n., 98
primate, 130
Prince-Albert, 14, 119
principal, 121
printery, 186
print-shop, 168
private-detective, 127
private enquiry agent, 127
private-soldier, 114
probate, v., 125
probe, n., 188
problem, 216n
procede, 245
process, 216n
procurer, 150
produce, 216n
product, 216n
prof, 185
professor, 41, 137
progenitor, 227
program, 115, 210, 222, 236, 237, 244, 245, 247
programme, 210, 222, 226, 240, 241
progress, v., 49, 59, 61, 81, 92, 210n
prohibition, 420
project, 216n
prolog, 222, 244
prologue, 222
prom, 185
promenade, 113
promulge, 88
pronto, 166
proof, 219
propaganda, n., 42; v., 175
prophet, 216
proposition, 134
prosit, 104
prospect, 216n
prostitute, 150
protectograph, 195
protégé, 249, 320
Protestant Episcopal, 131
prove, v., 125; prove, n., 274
proved, 274
proven, 274
proverb, 216n
provost, 121, 216n
psalm, 215
psych, 185n
pub, 122, 164

public comfort station, 150
public-company, 123
public elementary school, 120
public-house, 115, 122, 144
publicist, 144
public-school, 115, 119
public-servant, 35, 115, 121
publishment, 39, 91
pudgy, 223, 225
puff-puff, 119n
puka, 204
pulizio, 410
pull, n., 98, 124, 414
pull up stakes, vp., 93
pull wool over his eyes, vp., 93
pumpernickel, 103
pumpkin, 211
pun, 184
pung, 58
pungy, 58, 128
punk, 369
punt, 128
purse, 127
purchasing-agent, 145
push, n., 384
pusht, 280
pussy-footed, 176
put, 193, 274
put a bug in his ear, vp., 93
put it down, vp., 118
put on, vp., 123
put over, vp., 193
put up, vp., 123
pygmy, 224, 226, 236, 237, 240
pyjamas, 223, 233, 239, 240

quad, 170
quadroon, 54
quaff, 110
quahaug, 39, 52
quandary, 362
quan'ity, 318
quarantine-flag, 148
quarrel, 218
quarter-day, 132
quarter of, 133
quarter to, 133
quartet, 225, 245
quartette, 240, 241
quaver, 132
questionize, 91
queue, 123
quiande, 404
quick, 306
quien, 202
quinine, 218
quit, 274
quite, 133, 135
quite so, 135
quitter, 15
quoit, 316
quotation-marks, 115

r, p., 71, 72, 210, 318
raad-bas, 414
rabbit, 64
raccoon, 51, 161n
racing-dope, 109
radish, 217, 316
ragamuffin, 67
rail, 97
railroad, n., 115, 168; v., 97
railroad-man, 97, 115
rails, 115

LIST OF WORDS AND PHRASES

railway, 115, 168
railway guard, 97, 138
railway servant, 115
raise, n., 41, 133, 406; v., 274
raised, 274
rake-off, 10
ram, 149
rambunctious, 96, 163
ran, 274
ranch, n., 101; ranch, v., 101
ranchero, 39
ranch-house, 101
ranchman, 101
rancho, 39
rancor, 221
rancorous, 227
rancour, 221, 227
rank, 274, 278
range, n., 96
rapides, 405
rapids, 50, 56, 101, 405
rare, a., 115, 118; rare, v., 316
ratepayer, 116, 121
rates, 116, 121
rather, 111
rathskeller, 103, 251, 319, 320
rattle, v., 192
rattler, 184
rattling, 135n
razor-back, 56
razor-strop, 317n
read, 274
read for holy orders, vp., 130
read law, vp., 119
ready, 185
ready-made, 144
ready-tailored, 144
ready-to-put-on, 144
ready-to-wear, 144
real, 218, 306
real-estate agent, 26, 125, 144
really, 306, 307
realm, 231
realtor, 144
rear, v., 316
recall, n., 124
receipts, 115
recess, 209
reckon, 39, 81
rector, 121, 130, 144
reddish, 316
red-eye, 100
Red Indian, 114
red-light district, 150
reed-bird, 56
reel of cotton, 118
reflexion, 240
refresher, 125
régime, 249n
regular, 98
regular guy, 153
regularity, 98
reit ev, 413
releasement, 39, 91
reliable, 36, 37n, 61, 159
relm, 231
reminisce, 175, 185
remove, n., 121, 170
rendezvous, 249n
renig, 192
rench, 106, 274, 316
renched, 274
rent, v., 280

Reo, 195
rep, 184
repeater, 98, 124
repertoiré, 249
repertory, 249
reptile, 218
requirement, 39
requiset, 230
requisite, 232
resinol, 195, 196
resolute, v., 92, 175
restaurant, 144
résumé, 250
resurrect, 32, 92
retainer, 125
retiracy, 91
retiring-room, 150
retoric, 246
return-ticket, 115, 122
reunion, v., 192
reumatism, 246
Rev., 142
revener, 130n
revenor, 130n
reverend, 130n
reverner, 130n
revernor, 130n
revue, 200
Rhine-wine, 115, 119
Rhine-wine cup, 26n
rhyme, 238
rickey, 99
rid, 274
ride, v., 274
ridden, 274
ridiculosity, 88
riffle, 56, 186
right, 32, 135, 136
right away, 135, 136, 413
right good, 135
right-of-way, 97
Right Honorable, 138
right now, 135
right-o, 24
right-off, 135
right on time, 135
right smart, 136
right there, 136
right-thinker, 423
right well, 136
rigor, 221, 228
rigor mortis, 228
rigorous, 221, 227
rigour, 227
rile, 176, 274, 315
riled, 274, 315
rime, 225, 238, 246
rind, 211
ring, n., 414; v., 274, 278
rinse, 106, 274, 316
ripping, 135n
rise, n., 133; v., 124, 274
rised, 276
rithm, 246
ritualism, 130
riveter, 226
riz, 274
rize, 246
road-agent, 15, 15n
road-bed, 115
road-boss, 414
road-house, 190
road-mender, 115
road-repairer, 115
roast, n., 115; roast, v., 192
roasting-ear, 57
rob, 216
robd, 245

rock, n., 40, 41, 63, 64
rock-pile, 64
rode, 274-277
roil, 176, 274
roil, v., 315
rôle, 249
roll, n., 115
roll-call, 115, 124
roller-coaster, 92
rolling-country, 56
Roman Catholic, 181
romance, 209
romanza, 88
rood, 219
roof, 219
rook, 219
room, n., 219; v., 60
room-clerk, 125
roorback, 98
rooster, 26n, 115, 149, 219
root, 219
rooter, 128
rooves, 219
rope in, vp., 93
Roquefort, 320
rose, v., 274
Rotten Row, 52
rotter, 153
rough, 244
roundsman, 122
round-trip ticket, 122
rough-house, 32
rough-neck, 95
round-trip, 97
round-trip-ticket, 115
round-up, 95
'rous mit 'im, 104
roustabout, 95
row, n., 126
rowdy, 96, 366
royal supreme knight commander, 145
R. S. O., 97
rubarb, 246
rubber-neck, n., 10, 15, 31
v., 281
rube, 15, 134, 184
ruby, 132
ruby-nonpareil, 132
ruf, 244, 246
Rugby, 128
Rugger, 128
Rumania, 249
rumbustious, 163
rum-dumb, 104
rumor, 221
rumour, 221, 227
run, n., 56, 97, 125, 352;
run, v., 98, 124, 135, 274
rung, 274, 277, 278
run-in, 193
run into the ground, vp., 93
run slow, 181
Russian, 334n
rutabaga, 126
ruz, 476

Sabbaday, 184
sabe, 101, 202
sachem, 52
sack, 41
sacrifice, n., 130
sacrilege, v., 192
Sadd'y, 212
sagamore, 39, 52
said, n., 249, 274
salesgirl, 141
saleslady, 141, 406

LIST OF WORDS AND PHRASES 477

saleswoman, 115, 141
saloon, 26, 100, 115
salmon, 215
saloon-carriage, 115
saloon-corner men, 165
saloon-keeper, 100
saloon-loafer, 164
salt-lick, 57, 352
saltpeter, 222
saltpetre, 222
Salt river, 124
saltwater-taffy, 14
salvage, v., 370
samp, 52
sample-room, 100
sanatoria, 251
sandwich, 404
sanemagogna, 411
sang, 275, 278
sängerfest, 104
sank, 275
Santa Claus, 54
sapolio, 195
sarape, 404
sarge, 370
sashay, 319
sa's'parella, 318
sass, 106
sassy, 316
sat, 274
satisfaction, 110
sauce, 106
saucy, 316
sauer-braten, 251
sauerkraut, 39, 54, 103, 199, 251
saunter, 111
savagerous, 91
saviour, 227
savor, 221
savory, 227
savour, 221
saw, v., 274
say, 133, 274
says, 289
scab, 15, 159
scalawag, 96, 163
scallawag, 163
scallywampus, 196
scalp, 160
scant, 68
scarce, 306, 316
scarcely, 306
scarf-pin, 115
scary, 32, 94
scenarioize, 191
sceptic, 224, 241
sch, p., 73, 329
schadchen, 198
schedule, 73, 212
scherzo, 215, 320
schidü, 411
schmierkäse, 251
schnitzel, 103
schooner, 58, 100, 122
schützenfest, 104
Schwaben, 334n
Schweizer, 103, 320
sciabola, 410
scientist, 36, 37n, 157
scimetar, 223
scimitar, 223
scolar, 245
scool, 245
scoon, v., 58
scoot, 92
scow, 50, 54, 58, 115, 128
scowegian, 333
scrap, 160

scrape, 96
scrotum, 152
scrumptious, 96
scullery-maid, 118
sculp, 185
scuppernong, 51
sea-board, 39
seafood dinner, 126
Sears-Roebuck, 369
sea-shore, 39
season-ticket, 114
seat, 149
sechenze, 410
secondary-school, 120
second-floor, 117
second-hand, 144
second wing, 149
second-year-man, 121
secret disease, 150
secretary, 125, 169, 210, 212
section, 126
see, 274
seen, 274, 276
see the elephant, vp., 93
segar, 247
seidel, 104
selectman, 39, 57
self, 303
sell, v., 274
semibreve, 132
semi-brevis, 132
semiminima, 132
semi-occasional, 36, 96, 163
semi-quaver, 132
senator, 227
send, 274
senery, 246
senior, n., 121
senior-prom, 121
señor, 250
señorita, 203
sent, 274
sented, 246
septer, 246
septicæmia, 223
septicemia, 223
septums, 251
serape, 202
Serbia, 249
servant, 117, 144, 161
service, v., 192
services, 130n
servile, 218
sesech, 186
set, v., 274, 282
seven-and-forty, 132
Seventh Day Adventists, 131
sew, 231, 232
sewerage, 116
seyd, 249
sez, 274
shack, 15
shaddock, 126
shaikh, 249
shake, v., 274, 283
shaken, 274, 283
shal, 245
shall, 178, 179, 270, 288, 289, 384
shan't, 214, 289
shanty, 101, 414
share, 123
shareholder, 116, 123
shares, 116
shave, v., 274
shaved, 274
she, 291

shebang, 108
shed, v., 275, 278
sheik, 249
shell, 100
shell-road, 57
sherry-cobbler, 99
shevaleer, 232
shew, 224, 225
shillelah, 105
shily, 240
shimmy, 201
shin, v., 60
shine, v., 275
shined, 275
shingle, n., 57
shingle, v., 58
shinola, 195
shipt, 245
shirt, 149
shirtwaist, 116, 118
shoat, 41
shod, 282
shoe, n., 26n, 63, 116, 127, 168, 239; v., 275, 282
shoed, 275, 282
shoeing, 282
shoemaker, 116
shoe-shine, 116
shoe-smith, 194
shoestring, 116
shoe-tree, 116
sholder, 246
shoo-fly, 367
shook, 274
shoot, v., 275
shooting, n., 114, 134
shoot-the-chutes, 190
shop, n., 63, 122, 168, 172; v., 172
shop-assistant, 115
shop-fittings, 116
shop-girl, 172
shop-walker, 114, 144
shoplifter, 172
shopper, 172
shopping, 172
shop-worn, 172
short and ugly word, 362
shot, v., 275
shot-gun, 95
should, 289
should of, 313
should've, 313
should ought, 269
show, v., 193, 224, 225, 275
show-down, 10, 193
shown, 275
show up, vp., 193
shredded, 278
shrub, 99
shuck, v., 58, 283, 274
shunt, 97, 116
shut out, 128
shut up, vp., 404, 407
showed, 275
shyster, 104
siamese, v., 192
sick, 10, 67, 116, 148
sick at the stomach, 148
sick-bed, 148
sick-flag, 148
sick-leave, 148
sick-list, 148
sick-room, 148
siddup, 212
side-hill, 39
side-stepper, 14
side-swipe, 97
side-track, v., 97

478 LIST OF WORDS AND PHRASES

sidewalk, 15, 18n, 57, 116, 127
sideways, 182
siding, 420
sience, 246
sierra, 101
silk-stocking, 124
silvan, 246
silver, 116
silver-fizz, 26
simp, 184
sinagog, 246
sing, 275, 278
single-track mind, 97n
sink, v., 275
siphon, 223
siren, 223, 237
sissors, 246
sit, 275, 282, 285
sitten, 285
sitting-room, 118
siv, 247
sjante, 414
skeedaddle, 96, 163
skeer, 316
skeerce, 316
skeptic, 224
skibby, 333
skiddoo, 107, 411
skin, n., 99; v. 275
skookum, 200
skun, 275, 277
skunk, 51, 160, 191
sky-scraper, 406
slack, v., 362
slacker, 362, 366
slam the pill, vp., 367
slang, v., 275
slangwhanger, 40
slanguage, 186
slate, 98, 117
sled, 116
sledge, 116
sleek, 316, 218
sleep, v., 32, 275
sleeper, 97, 114, 184
sleep good, vp., 136
sleigh, 50, 116
slep, 318, 275, 280
slick, 81, 316, 218
slid, 275
slide, v., 275
slily, 240
slightly-used, 144
slim, 94
sling, n., 99; v., 99
slip, n., 61, 405
slipper, 63
slipt, 280
slit, v., 282, 275
slitted, 275, 282
sliver, 218
slog, v., 223, 225
slogger, 225
s'long, 319
slopped, 100
slosh, 223, 225
slow, 306
slow down, 181n
slowly, 306
slug, n., 223; v., 225
slumgullion, 96
slung, 275
slush, 223, 225
slush-fund, 199
small, 94
small pearl, 132
small pice, 132
small-potatoes, 41, 95

small-wares, 115
smart, 39
smash, 99
smearcase, 54
smearkase, 251
smell, v., 275
smelt, v., 275
smited, 276
smith, suf., 194
smithereens, 105
smoker, 184
smoke-room, 116
smoking-room, 116
snake, 124
snake-fence, 95
sneak, v., 275
sneez, 245
sneezd, 245
snicker, n., 224; v., 254
snew, 277
snigger, v., 224, 254
snitz, 104
snoop, 60
snoot, 317
snooted, 100
snout, 317
snowed, 277
snow-plow, 57
snuck, 275
so, 314
soap-boxer, 147, 187
S. O. B., 150
sob-sister, 190
soccer, 128
social disease, 150, 151
sockdolager, 96
socket, 405
sock-suspenders, 114, 118
sodalicious, 196
soda-mint, 195
soe, 231, 232
soft-drinks, 99, 116
soirée, 249
sold, 274
soli, 252
solicitor, 125
solid, 61
so long, 319
solos, 252
sombrero, 15, 101
some, 136, 362
someone else's, 304
someone's else, 304
some place, 182n
some pumpkins, 41
somethin', 318n
something's up, 188
somewhere, 182
somewheres, 307
somewheres else, 182
son-in-laws, 308
son-of-a-bitch, 154
son-of-a-gun, 154, 411
sonora, 196
sons-in-law, 308
soon, 219
soondáe, 405
soot, 219, 231, 232
sophomore, 57, 121
süpperéter, 412
soprani, 251
sopranos, 252
sorgum, 247
sörpreis-parti, 414
sort'a, 313
s o s, v., 192
sot, 274n
sotterraneo, 410
sottopressatori, 410

soul-mate, 188
sound, n., 125
souper, 249
sour, n., 99
sour-braten, 103n
soused, 100
soveran, 232n
sovereign, 232
sovren, 247
sow, n., 149
sox, 248
space-rates, 124
spa, 217k
spaghetti, 199
spake, 279
spalpeen, 105
span, n., 54, 279; v., 279, 275
spanner, 115
spat, 279, 282
speak, 279
speak-easy, 100
speaking-tour, 124
spearmint, 195
special, v., 192
speciality, 253, 254
specialty, 253
specie, 308
specific blood-poison, 150
specific stomach, 152
specific ulcer, 152
speck, 104
sped, 282
speed, v., 275, 282
speeded, 275, 282
speeder, 282
speeding, 282
speed-limit, 282
speed-mania, 282
speed-maniac, 282
speedway, 358
spell, v., 275
spelling-bee, 57
spelt, 275
spera, 203
spick, 333n
spiel, 319
spieler, 108
spigot, 116
spiggoty, 333
spill, v., 275
spilt, 275
spin, v., 275, 279
spit, v., 275, 279, 282
spittoon, 144
splendiferous, 196
splendor, 221
splendour, 221, 227
splinter-bar, 116
split one's sides, vp., 107
split-ticket, 98, 124
split a ticket, vp., 98
splurge, n., 92
splurge, v., 92
spoil, v., 275
spoilt, 275
spoke, v., 279
spondulix, 96, 163
sponge, 116
spoof, 153
spook, 219
spool, 115
spool of thread, 118
sporting-house, 150
spot, v., 279
sprang, 275, 279
spread, v., 281
spread-eagle, 95
spreaded, 282

LIST OF WORDS AND PHRASES 479

spread one's self, *vp.*, 93
spring, *v.*, 275, 279
spritely, 247
sprung, 275, 279
spry, 40
spuke, 39
spun, 279
square, *n.*, 127
square-head, 333
square-meal, 95, 163
squash, 51, 52, 184
squat, 60, 62
squatter, 39, 50
squaw, 52, 160
squaw-man, 100
squealer, 406
squinch, 316
squint, 316
squirrel, 219
squirrel-whiskey, 100
squs me, 319
staebel, 412
stag, *a.*, 15, 15n
stage, 40
stage-manager, 145
stag-party, 95, 163
stallion, 149
stalls, 115, 123
stalwart, 98
stamp, *v.*, 111, 317
stampede, 54
stamping-ground, 58
stanch, 222
stand, *v.*, 124
standard, 120
ständchen, 250
standee, 43n
ständen, 398
stand-pat, *a.*, 188; *vp.*, 128
stand-patter, 190
standpoint, 36, 37n, 61, 105, 162
stang, 263, 275
stank, 275, 278
star, 214
start-off, 193
start off, *vp.*, 193
statehouse, 57
Statler-operated, 192
statutory offense, 150
staunch, 222, 240
stave off, *vp.*, 39
stay put, *vp.*, 193
steady, 230, 232
steal, *n.*, 188; *v.*, 188
steam-roller, *n.*, 362; *v.*, 363
stegnosis, 224
stein, *suf.*, 338
steam-roll, *v.*, 193
steam-roller, *n.*, 124; *v.*, x, 192, 193
steam-rollered, 363
steddy, 232
stein, 104
stem-winder, 35, 116
stenog, 184
stenosis, 224
stent, *n.*, 319
ster, *suf.*, 187
stew, *n.*, 219n
steward, 124
stewed, 100
stick, *n.*, 100, 113, 127, 168
stick-work, 129
stiff-ticket, 407
stim-sciabola, 410
stimulis, 252
sting, *v.*, 275

stink, *v.*, 275, 278
stinkibus, 99
stint, *n.*, 319
stirrup, 219
St. Martin's Summer, 114
stock, 67, 123, 216
stock-broker, 123
stockholder, 116
stocking-feet, 95
stocks, 116, 123
stogie, 122
stole, *v.*, 275, 277
stomach, 148, 149, 245
stomp, 317
stone, 132
stone-fence, 99
stone-ginger, 99n
stone-wall, 99
stoop, *n.*, 39, 54, 406
stop, *v.*, 134
stop-over, 97, 193
stop-over (or off), *vp.*, 97, 193
store, *n.*, 63, 172
store-clothes, 95
store-fixtures, 116
storekeeper, 144
stores, 114, 116, 117, 118
storey, 222, 237, 240
storo, 410
story, 222, 237, 247
strafe, 190, 369
straight, 100
straight-ticket, 98, 124
strap, 317n
strata, 252
stratas, 252
street-car, 414
street-cleaner, 116, 122
street-railway, 116
street-walker, 151
stricken out, 125
strike, *v.*, 275
strike it rich, *vp.*, 93
strike out, *vp.*, 125, 128
string, *n.*, 127
strit-kar, 414
stroll, 129
strong-arm-squad, 122
strop, 317n
struck, 275
struggld, 245
stuck on, *vp.*, 318
stud, 114
study for the ministry, *vp.*, 130
study medicine, *vp.*, 119
stump, *v.*, 32, 55, 60, 161
stumping-trip, 124
stump-oratory, 161
stunk, 275, 278
stunning, 135n
stunt, 159, 319
style, 232
sub, 185
subaltern, 122
sub-deb, 188
submarine, 370
subpena, 245
subway, 116, 127
succede, 245
successor, 227
succor, 221
succotash, 39, 41, 52
succour, 221
sucker, 15, 159
suffragan, 130
sugar, 159
sulfite, 225

sulfur, 246, 247
summon, 308
sundae, 43n, 194, 405
sunflower, 352
sung, 278
sunk, 275
sung, 275
supawn, 52
super, *pref.*, 202
supergobsloptious, 196
superior, 227
supertax, 126
supper, 119, 249
sure, 181, 306
surely, 307
sure Mike, 407
surprise, 225, 237
surprise-party, 414
surprize, 225
surprized, 237
surtax, 126
suspenders, 26n, 96, 116, 118, 239
sut, 231, 232
suveran, 232
svindlar, 413
swagger, *a.*, 170
swam, 275, 279
swamp, *n.*, 125
swang, 275
swat, 129
swatfest, 199
swear off, *vp.*, 162
sweater, 116, 401, 405
Swedes, 119
sweep, *v.*, 275
sweetheart, 154
sweet-potato, 56, 126
sweets, 113, 118, 127
swell, *a.*, 401; *v.*, 275
swelled, 275
swelldoodle, 196
swep, 275, 280
swim, *v.*, 275, 279
swing, *v.*, 275
swingle-tree, 67
switch, *n.*, 97, 116, 405; *v.*, 97, 116
switchman, 97
switching-engine, 97
switch-yard, 97
swoboda, 196
swole, 275
swollen, 275
sword, 71
swore, 275
swum, 275, 279
swung, 275
sycamore, 352
syphilis, 150, 151
syphon, 223
syren, 223, 237
syrup, 219

t, *p.*, 318
tabernacle, 131
table, *v.*, 59
table-tapping, 163n
table-turning, 163n
tactic, 308
taffy, 223, 225
tailor, 145
tailor-made suit, 118
take, 275
take a back seat, *vp.*, 93
take in, *vp.*, 118
taken, 275, 278
take on, *vp.*, 39

480 LIST OF WORDS AND PHRASES

take orders, *vp.*, 130
take silk, *vp.*, 125
take to the woods, *vp.*, 60
takings, 115
talented, 39, 159
talkfest, 199
talk through your hat, *vp.*, 365
tamale, 101
tangle-foot, 166
tango, 103n
tanked, 100
tank-town, 97n
tantane, 410
tap, *n.*, 116
tapioca, 52
tariff-reform, 123
tarn, 57
tarnal, 153, 318
tarnation, 153
tart, 154
tassel, 215
tasteful, 181
tasty, 32, 36, 181, 194
taught, 275
tavern, 64
taxes, 116
taxi, *n.*, 191; *v.*, 185
tax-paid, 176
taxpayer, 116
T. B., 189
tea, 119
teach, 275, 282
team, 62
tear, *v.*, 275
tea-shop, 168
technical, 245
teetotaler, 96
tel, 245
telefone, 246
telegraf, 246
telegrapher, 209
telescope, *v.*, 97, 161
tell, 275
temco, 196
temeniollo, 411
temporarily, 209
tender, *n.*, 113
tenderfoot, 95, 163
tenderloin, 116, 118, 191
tenne, 410
ten-pins, 116, 128
tepee, 52
temporary, 210
terminal, 116
terminus, 116
terrapin, 51, 126
tete, 362
tête-à-tête, 249, 250
teufelhunde, 333n
thal, *suf.*, 329
than, 302, 310
thank, 279
thanked, 279
Thanksgiving Day, 133
that, 294, 296
that'n, 313
that-a way, 313
that gets me, 176
that'n, 295, 297
that-there, 295, 296
theater, 222, 231-239, 240, 246-247
thé dansant, 250
thee, 298
theirn, 291, 293, 304, 386
theirs, 293
theirself, 303
theirselves, 303

them, 291, 295
them'ere, 313
themselves, 303
them-there, 295, 296
thence, 307
there, 81, 180, 307
there's no two ways about it, *vp.*, 40
thermos, 195, 196
these, 295
these-here, 295, 296
thesen, 295
These States, 88
they, 291
they is, 318
thin, 275
thine, 293
think, 193, 275, 279
thinnen, 275n
third-degree, 122
this, 294
this'a way, 313
this-here, 263, 295
this'n, 295, 310, 317
thither, 180, 307
tho, 244, 246, 247
thon, 186, 304n
thoro, 244, 246
thorofare, 244
thoroly, 244, 247
thoro, 247
those, 295
thosen, 295
those-there, 295, 296
thou, 294
thought, *v.*, 275
thrash, 316
thread, 230, 232
threaded, 278
threat, 232
thred, 232
three-bagger, 129
three-of-a-kind, 128
three strikes and out, 128
thresh, 316
thret, 232
threw, 275, 283
thrive, 275
through, 133, 203, 284
throve, 275
throw, *v.*, 275, 283
throw a rock, *vp.*, 64
throwed, 275, 277, 283
thru, 244, 246, 247
thruout, 244
thum, 232, 246
thumb, 230, 232
thumb-tack, 116
thunk, 275, 279
thusly, 307
ticket, 41
ticket-office, 97, 116
ticket-scalper, 95, 97
tickler, 96
tie, *n.*, 97, 115, 420
tie-pin, 115
tight-wad, 190
tiles, 117
timber-yard, 115
tin, *n.*, 113, 117; *v.*, 117
tinker, 116
tin-Lizzie, 175
tinned, 117
tinned-goods, 113
tinner, 116
tin-roof, 116
tipe, 246
tip-toe, *v.*, 23, 185

tire, *n.*, 223, 225, 226, 236, 237, 247
titty-high, 393
tiz, 195
toboggan, 52, 160
toccho, 410
to-day, 253
toe, 218
toffee, 225
toffy, 223
toggery, 187
toilet, 150, 200, 222, 226, 236
toilette, 222
tole, 275, 317
tomahawk, *n.*, 52, 383; *v.*, 59
Tom-and-Jerry, 99
tomato, 215
Tom-Collins, 99
tommy-rot, 366
tong, 108
tongue, 231, 232, 244
to-night, 253
tonsorial-parlor, 144
tony, 36, 96, 194, 314
too, 314
took, 275
tooken, 285
top, 370
top-hat, 168
top-liner, 114, 123
topping, 170
top-sarge, 370
top-sergeant, 370
tore, 275
torn, 275
tornado, 101, 125
tornpeik, 398
torpor, 226, 227
tote, 40, 60
tough, *n.*, 159, 384
tow, 218
towards, 182
towerman, 97
tracca, 410
track, 116
track-walker, 97
tractor, 195
tradesman, 144
tradesmen's-entrance, 168
trades-unionist, 137
traffic, 170
trail, *n.*, 57; trail, *v.*, 58
train-boy, 97
trained-nurse, 116, 163
trait, 211, 212
tram, 122
tramcar, 116
tramp, *n.*, 159, 171, 317n
tramway, 116
transom, 116
translatour, 228n
transpire, 160, 162
trapee, 308
traveled, 241
traveler, 222
traveller, 222, 239
trash, 67
traveler, 230, 243
traveller, 226, 230, 243
travelogue, 186
treacle, 10, 115, 122
tread, *n.*, 275; *v.*, 278
treasurer, 145
treat 'em rough, 181
tripos, 121
tripper, 97, 114
triscut, 195

troble, 244
trolley-car, 116, 171, 401
tromp, v., 317n
trouble, 244
troupe, 394n
trousers, 127, 160
trubbel, 412
truck, 97, 116
true-blue, 93
trumpeter, 241
trunk-call, 115
trust, n., 414
trust-burster, 176
trust-buster, 366
trustification, 175
trustify, 175
tru trin, 414
try, 185
try-out, n., 185, 188; vp., 193
tsar, 224, 237, 249
tub, v., 168, 170
tube, 116, 127
tuberculogian, 194
tuch, 247
Tuesday, 219n
tuf, 246
tumor, 221
tumour, 221, 227
tung, 231, 232, 244, 246
turbot, 126
turkey-gobbler, 56
turn-down, 193
turn down, vp., 193, 384
turning, n., 127
turnpike, 40
turn-verein, 104
tuxedo, 196
twelv, 245
twelve-month, 132
twenty-three, 189
twic't, 318
twine, n., 127
twirling, 129
two-fer, 93
2 o'clock, 150
tyco, 196
typist, 116, 118
tyre, 247n
typewrite, 185
typewriter, 116, 118
typhoid-fever, 116
tyre, 223, 237, 240

u, p., 112, 219
ü, p., 328
ugly, 39
ukase, 249
uhrgucker, 105n
under-brush, 56
undercut, n., 116, 118
underdone, 115, 118
underground, n., 116, 127
underground-railroad, 97n
underpinned, 61
underpinning, 67
undershirt, 116, 127
undertaker, 144
under the weather, 95, 125
underwear, 144
uneeda, 195
union, 122
union-man, 137
uniquer, 309
unit, 58
United Brethren, 131
Universal preacher, 40
university, 144
unloosen, 274, 275, 310

unloosened, 275
unwell, 152
up, 124
up against it, 160
up-lift, 10, 132
up-line, 127
up-state, 32, 126
up street, 188
up-train, 127
ur, p., 317
us, 291
used, 144, 289
used to could, vp., 40
usen, 407
usen't, 313
use'to, 313
ush, 185
usher, 121
usherette, 187
usually, 307

vacation, v., 192
vacationize, 191
vag, 184
vally, 246
valor, 221
valorous, 227
valour, 221, 227
Valspar, 195
vamose, 101, 202
vamp, n., 184; v., 185, 366
van, 112, 113, 183
vapor, 221
vaporize, 227
vapour, 221, 227
variate, 39
variety, 201
varsity, 169
vase, 111, 215
vaseline, 195
vaudeville, 200, 201, 319, 320
vaudevil, 245
vaudeville-theatre, 116, 201
venereal, 151
venereal disease, 150, 151
veranda, 222
verandah, 222, 240
verger, 130
Vespasien, 150n
vest, 116, 127, 406
vestry, 124
vial, 223, 236, 237
vicar, n., 130; v., 130
vice, 224
vice-chancellor, 121
vice diseases, 151
vice-president, 145
vice-rector, 121
victrola, 195
viertel, 132
vigilans, 415
vigilante, 101, 415
vigor, 221
vigorous, 227
vigour, 221, 227
villa, 119
violet, 218
virgin, 152
virtuosi, 251
virtuosos, 251
visco, 409
vise, 224
vivil, 195
vodvil, 247
voodoo, 54
voting-paper, 124
voyageur, 53
vrille, 370

w, p., 71
waffle, 54
wage-day, 115
waggon, 113, 222, 230, 237, 239, 240
wagon, 26n, 105, 222, 230, 232, 236, 237, 241-247
waikiki, 204
wain, 57
waistcoat, 116, 127
wake, v., 275
walk, n., 358
walking-stick, 127
walk-out, 158
walk out, vp., 133
walk the ties, vp., 97n
walk-up, n., 127n
walk-up-apartment, 127n
Wall Street, 164
Wall Street broker, 123
wallow, n., 352
wampum, 41, 52
wampum-keeper, 52n
wan, 276, 283
wanderlust, 104
wangle, 166
wan't, 72
want-ad, 185
warden, 116
ward-executive, 122
ward-heeler, 124
wardman, 122
warehouse, 116
ware-zee, 212
war-paint, 52
war-path, 52, 60
warphan, 196
was, 272, 288
wash-basin, 162-163
wash-hand-basin, 163
wash-hand-stand, 116, 163
wash-out, n., 24
wash-rag, 116
wash-stand, 26, 116, 162
wasn't, 72
wassermann, v., 192
waste, 393
waste-basket, 116
waste-paper-basket, 116
watch-glass, 114
water, v., 161
water-closet, 150n, 155
water-gap, 56-352
watermelon, 405
water-pitcher, 26
watershed, 58
water stocks, vp., 405
water-wagon, 32
way, 165
way-bill, 97
wazzo maro, 410
W. C., 150n
we, 291
weald, 57
wear, v., 275
wed, 188
wedding, 147
week-end, 122
weep, 276
weir, 128, 185n
well, expletive, 44, 416
well-fixed, 135
well-heeled, 94
well-posted, 93
weltpolitik, 249
weltschmerz, 249
went, 273, 284
wep, 276, 280, 318
wer, 245

LIST OF WORDS AND PHRASES

weren't, 72
Wesleyan, 115, 131
westbound, 127
West End, 127
wet, 276
whap, 39
wharf, 405
what, 296
whatdyecallem, 365
what 'ell, 153
what the hell, 153
wheatena, 196
wheatlet, 195
wheat-pit, 95
whence, 307
where, 81, 180, 307
where'bouts, 307
whip, *n.*, 168
whippletree, 116
wie gehts, 104
which, 296
whichn, 297
whiskey, 241
whiskey-and-soda, 99
whiskey-daisy, 99
whiskey-sour, 26
white elephant, 405
white-lion, 26n
white-plush, 99
white slave, 150
whitewash, *n.*, 42
whitewash, *v.*, 60
white-wings, 117
whither, 180, 307
whittle, 68
whizz-bang, 369
who, 179, 180, 296
whole-souled, 93
whom, 179, 180, 257-296
whose, 296
whosen, 296, 297
wide, 305
wiener, 103
wienie, 103
wienerwurst, 103
wier, 57
wierd, 246
wife, 150
wig, 184
wigwam, 41, 52
wild-cat, *v.*, 95
will, 178, 179, 270, 288, 289, 384
willn't, 72
willow, 129

wilt, *v.*, 39, 68
wimmen, 231, 232
win, 276, 283
wind, *v.*, 193
windfall, 41
wind-up, 193
wind up, *vp.*, 193
winned, 283
wipe, *n.*, 116
wireless, *v.*, 281
wire-puller, 98
wiseheimer, 199
wish, *v.*, 276
wisht, 276
witness-box, 116
witness-stand, 116
wiz, 184
wize, 246
wo, 231
woe, 231
woke, 275
woken, 275
wold, 57
woman, 149
women, 231, 232
women's singles, 141
women's wear, 141
won, 276, 277, 284
wonderful, 310
won't, 72, 289
woodchuck, 52
woods, 182n
woof, 219
woolen, 222, 240
woollen, 222, 241
woozy, 194
wop, 134, 333
wore, 275
workhouse, 115, 122
workman, 144
works, 115, 182n
worser, 309
worshiper, 241
would-a, 263, 317
would'a, 313
would of, 313
would of gotten, 263
would've, 313
wound, *v.*, 276
wowser, 394n
wrang, 276
wrangle, 190
wrangler, 121
wrassle, 316
wrath, 70

wrecking-crew, 97
wrestle, 316
wring, 276
write, 276
written, 276
wrongd, 245
wrote, 276
wroten, 285
wrung, 276

xaktly, 398

y, *suf.*, 186
yam, 126
Yank, 185
yank, *v.*, 40, 92
Yankee, 333n
yap, 134
yards, 182n
ye, 180
yeller, 318
yellow-back, 160
yellow-belly, 333
yellow-journalism, 163n
yellow-press, 163n
yen, *v.*, 108
yes, 200, 256
yes-indeedy, 107
yestiddy, 318
yet, 217
yodel, 104
yok-a-mi, 108
Yom Kippur, 133
you, 180, 291, 294, 298
you-all, 267, 294
you betcha, 165
you bet your, 165
young man, 133
your, 291
yourn, 291, 293
yours, 293
yous, 291, 294
yu, 247
yung, 247

z, *p.*, 73
zeal, 231
zeber, 232
zebra, 232
zeel, 231
zowie, 365
zubumt, 407
zwei, 104
zwieback, 104

INDEX

Abbreviations, 31, 150, 188
Académie Française, 5
Actes de la Société Philologique de Paris, 26n
Adams, Franklin P., 170
Adams, James Truslow, 65n
Adams, John, 60, 76
Adams, John Quincy, 48, 59
Addison, Joseph, 280n, 298, 368
Ade, George, 19, 268, 361
Adjective, American, 308
Adverb, American, 304*ff*
Aikman, Henry G., 17
Aldington, Richard, 18
Alford, Henry, 90, 91, 160, 298, 367
American Academy of Arts and Letters, 183, 385
American Anthropologist, 347n
American Association for the Advancement of Science, 245
American Dialect Society, vii, xi, 6, 7, 314
Americanism, definitions of, 10, 11, 38, 39, 40, 41, 42, 43, 47
American Issue, 315
American Journal of Philology, 400, 401n
American language, characters of, 17, 19, 22, 28*ff*, 38, 39, 40, 41, 42, 43, 44
American Magazine, 263n
American Mercury, 65
American Philological Association, 243, 245n
American Philosophical Society, 46
American Review of Reviews, 203n
Ames, Nathaniel, 57
Andreen, Gustav, 414
Anglistische Forschungen, 186n, 342n, 354n
Anglomania, ix, x, xv, 12, 63, 75, 110, 112, 167*ff*, 215, 238*ff*
Annual Review, 48, 49
Anti-Jacobin Review, 49n
Appeal to Reason, 425
Archer, William, 13, 17, 18, 37, 167n
Archiv für das Studium der neueren Sprachen und Literaturen, 25
Aristophanes, 259n
Armistead, George, 327

Arnold, Matthew, 3
Arthur, T. S., 149n
Athenæum, 18n, 236
Atlantic Educational Journal, 258n
Atlantic Monthly, 71n, 136, 177, 207n, 241, 250n, 361
Atlantis, 331n
Australian English, 54, 144n, 242, 383, 384
Authors' and Printers' Dictionary, 236
Ayres, Harry Morgan, 3n, 173, 385

Babbitt, Eugene H., 173n, 185n, 376
Bache, Richard Meade, 111n, 154n, 179n
Baedeker, 26
Baker, Ernest A., 237n
Balfour, A. J., 143n, 248
Ballard, Edward, 347n
Baltimore Sun, 326n, 330n
Baltimore Trolley News, 187n
Banche, Henri, 5
Bancroft, Aaron, 49, 233
Bancroft, George, 84
Bankhead, Senator, 176n
Baral, S. N., 167n
Barde, Alexandre, 402
Bardsley, Charles W., 340n, 341n
Barentz, A. E., 25
Barrère, Albert, 54, 109
Barringer, G. A., 26
Bartlett, John Russell, 10, 38, 43, 50, 54 89, 101, 189
Baseball vocabulary, 128, 129
Bausman, Lottie M., 327n
Beach-la-Mar, 377, 383
Beckwith, H. W., 347n
Beecher, Henry Ward, 91
Belknap, Jeremy, 49
Benjamin, Judah P., 131
Bennett, Arnold, 13
Berger, V., 347n, 414
Bergmann, Karl, 333n, 371
Berlin Academy, 373n
Beverley, Robert, 51, 56
Bible, Authorized Version, 67, 178, 276, 305
Bicknell, Frank M., 164
Bierce, Ambrose, 361

483

484 INDEX

Billings, Josh, 268
Black, Mrs. Harry C., ix
Blackwood's Magazine, 79
Bloom, Marion L., ix
Bohemian given names, 340
Bohemian language, 422
Bohemian surnames, 325, 330, 332, 336
Bonaparte, Prince. L.-L., 207
Boni, Alfred, 411n
Bookman, 22n, 153, 195n
Book of Common Prayer, 130, 182
Boot, H. E., 181n
Borah, Senator, 134n, 181n
Bosson, Olaf E., 361
Boston Globe, 202n
Boucher, Jonathan, 47, 61, 184
Boucicault, Dion, 108
Boyd, Stephen G., 344n
Brackebusch, W., 373, 376
Bradford, Gamaliel, 136n
Bradley, Henry, 143n, 237, 244, 248, 289, 292n, 293, 377
Brailsford, H. N., 13, 16
Branner, John C., 349n
Brazilian Portuguese, 6
Bremer, Otto, 5
Bridges, Robert, vii, 143n, 210n, 211, 237, 248, 317, 385
Bright, John, 320
British Critic, 48, 49, 60
Bristed, Charles Astor, 45, 90, 92n, 135n
British Review, 79
Brooke, Rupert, 165
Brooks, John Graham, 82n, 149n
Brooks, Van Wyck, 4, 173
Brownell, W. C., 34
Brundage, Edward J., 312n
Bryant, William Cullen, 36n, 61, 78, 84, 86, 233, 234
Buchwald, Nathaniel, 408n
Buehler, H. G., 374n
Bulgarian language, 422
Bulletin of the University of South Carolina, 259n
Burbank, Luther, 186
Burgess, Gelett, 195n
Burke, Edmund, 302
Burnell, A. C., 51
Burnett, John L., 92n
Burnham, Lord, 131
Burr, Aaron, 98
Burton, Richard, 21
Butler, Samuel, 160
Buttmann, Philipp Karl, 209

Cable, George W., 401
Cahan, Abraham, 336n, 408
Cairns, William B., 49n, 79

California localisms, 108, 187, 202
Cambridge History of American Literature, 66n, 82n, 173, 385n, 400n, 402n, 408n
Cambridge History of English Literature, 13, 37n, 45, 55n, 70n, 160, 211n, 238, 253, 364n, 423n
Canadian dialect, 382, 383
Canadian pronunciation, 216
Canadian spelling, 242
Canning, George, 61
Canonge, Placide, 402
Carlyle, Thomas, 161
Carnegie, Andrew, 244
Carpenter, W. H., 349n
Carroll, Dixie, 270n
Carroll, T. W., 153n
Cassell's New English Dictionary, 37n, 104n, 157, 158n, 159, 161, 162, 163, 166, 225n, 232n, 237, 238, 241, 249, 371
Century Dictionary, 40
Century Magazine, 36n, 37n, 143
Chamberlain, Alex. F., 51n, 57n, 400
Chamberlain, Joseph, 157, 161
Channing, William Ellery, 49, 82, 86
Charters, W. W., ix, xi, 4, 264*ff*, 282, 289, 290, 299, 302, 304, 309, 310
Chaucer, Geoffrey, 68, 111, 276, 292, 293, 305, 312
Chesterfield, Lord, 106n
Chesterton, Cecil, 13, 16
Chesterton, G. K., 13, 153, 164
Chicago Daily News, 36n, 37n
Chicago Inter-Ocean, 363
Chicago Record-Herald, 367
Chicago Tribune, 25, 314
Child, J. J., 6n
Chinese given names, 340
Chinese immigration, 108
Chinese language, 375
Chinese loan-words, 108, 202, 370
Chopin, Kate, 401
Christian Disciple, 91
Christian names, 338*ff*
Christian Science Monitor, 167n, 203
Christian World, 131n
Christy, Robert, 425
Churchill, William, 205n, 383n
Civil War, effects of, 85, 92
Clapin, Sylva, 41, 52, 360n, 361n
Classical Journal, 252n
Claxton, P. P., 333n
Clemenceau, Georges, 27
Clemens, Samuel L., 20, 34, 247n, 361, 424
Cleveland, Grover, 33
Clive, C. J., 119
Cobb, Lyman, 8, 11, 111, 229, 233, 235

INDEX 485

Cohan, George M., 191n
Coit, J. Milnor, 170
Coke, Edward, 294
Cole, H. E., 347n
Collections Connecticut Historical Society, 347n
Collections Minnesota Historical Society, 347n
College slang, 185
Collier, Price, 141
Collins, F. Howard, 236n
Combs, J. H., 69
Comstock Postal Act, 150
Concise Oxford Dictionary, 36, 64, 104n, 136, 157, 158n, 159, 161, 162, 225n, 226n, 230, 232n, 236, 237, 238, 241, 250
Congressional Globe, 89, 91, 341n
Congressional Record, 92n, 94, 126n, 134n, 136, 139, 142, 143n, 175, 176, 177n, 178n, 181n, 192n, 199n, 226n, 240n, 248, 304, 312
Connecticut Code of 1650, 62
Connolly, James, 200n
Conrad, Joseph, 332
Constitution of the United States, 76
Continental Congress, 58
Converse, C. C., 186n
Cooley, Alice W., 260n
Coolidge, Grace, 247n
Cooper, J. F., 34, 80, 82, 84
Costa, A. Arbib, 411n
Coulter, John Lee, 181n
Council of English Teachers of New Jersey, 260
Courmont, Felix de, 402
Cournos, John, 381n
Coxe, A. Cleveland, 61, 159, 234
Crane, Frank, 422
Crane, W. W., 349, 357
Crile, George W., 329n
Critical Review, 48, 49n
Crossen, Wilhelm, 69
Crumb, D. S., 294n
Cuban Spanish, 404, 405
Current Literature, 33n
Custer, George A., 327
Czech, *see* Bohemian

Danish loan-words, 292n
Dano-Norwegian language, 5, 411ff
D'Annunzio, Gabrielle, 380
Darwin, Charles, 243
Davidson, George, 347n
Davis, Richard Harding, 309
Declaration of Independence, 388ff
Deering, Addie B., ix
De Kruif, Paul H., 419n
Delineator, 250n

Dennis, C. T., 384
Denver Post, 270n
Deutsche Grammophon-Gesellschaft, 207
Dewey, John, 34
Dial, 386n
Dialect Notes, 8, 44n, 69n, 168n, 182, 184n, 186n, 187n, 189n, 191n, 194n, 195n, 196n, 198n, 201n, 202n, 211n, 290n, 294n, 309n, 327n, 333n, 400n, 411n, 412n, 416n, 419n
Dickens, Charles, 13, 90, 135, 159
Dickinson, G. Lowes, 33n
Dionne, N. E., 400n, 401
Disraeli, Benjamin, 304
Dobson, Austin, 248
Dooley, Mr., 35
Double negative, 310
Douglas-Lithgow, R. A., 348n
Drachmann, Holger, 380
Dramatic Mirror, 108
Dreiser, Theodore, 94
Drinks, names of, 26, 99
Dryden, John, 106n
Dugué, Oscar, 402
Dunlap, Fayette, 327n
Dunlap, Maurice P., 203
Dutch given names, 340
Dutch language, 416ff
Dutch loan-words, 53, 54, 57, 109
Dutch place-names, 345, 348
Dutch surnames, 324, 327, 331, 336, 337
Dwight, Timothy, 80
Dziennik Chicagoski, 422

Eaton, David W., 347n
Ecclesiastical vocabulary, 130ff
Eclectic Review, 48, 49n
Edinburgh Review, 48, 49n, 66n, 79
Editor and Publisher, 124n, 184n, 199n
Educational vocabulary, 119ff
Egli, Johann Jakob, 344
Elkus, Abram L., 138n
Elliott, A. M., 400, 401
Elliott, John, 230
Ellis, A. J., 206, 207
Ellis, Havelock, 334n
El Mundo, 404
Elwyn, Alfred L., 40
Ely, Richard, 5, 323n
Emerson, Ralph Waldo, 84, 86, 423
Encyclopædia Britannica, 13
Englische Studien, 401
English, vii, 33n, 103n, 155n, 163n, 181n, 194n, 238, 380, 384n, 425n
English criticisms of American, 13ff, 33, 34, 36, 37, 47ff, 60, 79ff
English dialects, 29, 292
English given names, 342, 343
English Journal, 186n, 342n

486 INDEX

English Review, 33n
English spelling, 239
English surnames, 338
Esnault, Gaston, 371
Espinosa, Aurelio M., 403
Euphemisms, 144, 148*ff*
European Magazine and London Review, 48, 49n
Evans, Lewis, 47
Everett, Edward, 80, 84

Farmer, John S., 40, 100, 101, 360n
Faulkner, W. G., 15, 159
Faust, A. B., 327n, 329n, 400n
Ferrazzano, Carlo, 409
Financial vocabulary, 123, 161
Finnish surnames, 332
First Congress, 61, 139
Fishbein, Morris, 152, 286n
Fishberg, Maurice, 335n
Fisher, Budd, 184n
Fisher, Sydney George, 66n
Fiske, John, 21
Flaten, Nils, 411, 413, 414
Fletcher, John, 298
Flom, George T., 412, 413
Flügel, Felix, 25
Fombona, Rufino Blanco, 334n
Foreign Quarterly, 79, 90
Fortier, Alcée, 401n
Fortier, Edward J., 402n
Fortnightly Review, 160
Fowler, N. W. & F. G., 13, 160, 178, 179, 181, 226n, 302, 304, 312
Fowler, William C., 8, 9, 38, 86, 89, 91, 360
Fox, Charles James, 320
France, Anatole, 380
Francis, Alexander, 33n
Franklin, Benjamin, 46, 59, 61, 65, 66, 70, 71, 75, 228, 230, 423
Franklin, James, 66
Freeman, 192n
Freeman, Merrill P., 347n
French language, 5, 364n, 372, 373, 374, 375, 376n, 379, 400*ff*
French loan-words, 53, 56, 101, 161n, 200*ff*, 242, 251, 320, 362, 370
French place-names, 345, 349, 350, 351, 354
French slang, 371
French surnames, 326, 327, 328, 329, 332
Frith, Walter, 165
Frost, Robert, 87
Fuld, Leonard Felix, 327n
Fulmore, Z. T., 347n
Furnivall, F. I., 244

Gannett, Henry, 344n
Garrick, David, 71

Gayerré, Charles E. A., 402
Geddes, James, Jr., 400
Gentlemen's Magazine, 79
Geographical Names, 343*ff*
George, David Lloyd, 365
George, W. L., 13, 144, 164
Gerard, W. R., 53
German given names, 338
German immigration, 54, 102
German language, 5, 58n, 161n, 195n, 209, 364n, 372, 373, 374, 375, 376n, 377, 379, 397*ff*
German loan-words, 54, 96, 102*ff*, 118n, 130n, 135n, 197, 198, 202, 251, 411
German slang, 371
German surnames, 323, 324, 325, 326, 327, 328, 329, 330, 331, 333, 334
Gerould, Gordon Hall, 171
Gifford, William, 45, 46, 79, 83
Gilbert, W. S., 92n
Given names, 338*ff*
Gladstone, W. E., 178
Glass, Montague, 15, 339n
Goddard, Harold, 136n
Goethe, 380
Goral, B. E., 422
Gordon, William, 158n
Gosse, Edmund, 143n, 248
Gould, Edward S., 61, 112, 143, 182, 234, 235
Gourmont, Rémy de, 408
Government Printing Office, 240, 244
Grammar, as taught, vi, 3, 4
Grandgent, Charles H., vii, 6, 11, 70, 71n, 106, 110, 111, 244.
Greek given names, 340
Greek language, 421
Greek surnames, 331, 332
Greeley, Horace, 234, 252
Green, B. W., 337n
Green, John Richard, 382
Greenleaf, Moses, 347n
Greenwood, Frederick, 312n
Gregory, Augusta, 386
Grey, Edward, 35
Grimm, Jakob, 372
Griswold, Rufus Wilmot, 85, 86

Hackett, Francis, 177, 263
Haldmann, S. S., 329n
Haliburton, Thomas C., 91
Hall, Basil, 7, 90, 91
Hall, Fitzedward, 9, 36
Hall, Prescott F., 65, 102n
Halliwell, J. O.; 67
Hamilton, Alexander, 60, 74
Hancock, Elizabeth H., 72n
Harbaugh, Henry, 398
Harberton, Viscount, 248n
Harding, Warren G., 177, 182

INDEX 487

Hardy, Thomas, 248
Harper's Magazine, 10, 20, 22n
Harris, William J., 177
Harrison, Frederic, 159
Harrison, Henry, 328n
Harrison, J. A., 401n
Hart, Horace, 236, 237
Harte, Bret, 35, 424
Harvard University, 57, 66
Harvey, Thomas W., 259
Hastings, B. MacDonald, 213n
Hawaiian-American, 203
Hawthorne, Nathaniel, 34, 66
Hayden, Marie Gladys, 191n
Hays, H. M., 399
Hildreth, Richard, 65n
Hills, E. J., 309n
Hillyard, Anna Branson, 165
Honorifics in Canada, 140
Honorifics in England, 137ff, 252
Hornung, E. W., 165
Horsford, Eben N., 348n
Hosic, James Fleming, 261
Howe, E. W., 216
Howells, William Dean, 4, 20, 86, 94, 174, 361
Hughes, Rupert, 21ff
Hume, David, 305
Humphrey, Seth K., 323n
Hungarian given names, 340
Hungarian loan-words, 199
Hungarian surnames, 324, 332, 336
Hutchinson, Thomas, 63
Huxley, T. H., 138, 262, 312
Hyde, Douglas, 386
Hyne, C. J. Cutcliffe, 165
Head, Edmund, 179n
Healy, J. F., 29n, 384n
Hearn, Lafcadio, 401
Hecker, E. A., 166, 369
Heckwelder, John G. E., 53
Hermannsson, Halldór, 421
Herrig, Ludwig, 18
Hewlett, Maurice, 248
Hickman's Geographisch-Statistischer Universal-Atlas, 374n, 375
Hiemenga, John J., 418
Hobson-Jobson, law of, 51, 53, 54, 348
Hodgin, Cyrus W., 347n
Holmes, O. W., 34, 110, 361, 366

Ibsen, Henrik, 255
Icelandic language, 419ff
Illinoiser Staats-Zeitung, 25
Il Progresso Italo-Americano, 411n
Immigration to the United States, 65, 102, 197ff, 323
Indian loan-words, 52, 100, 404, 417
Indian place-names, 344, 347, 348, 355
International exchanges, 2, 157ff, 369

Irish given names, 338
Irish immigration to America, 102
Irish influence on American, 102, 105ff, 135, 154, 179n, 295n, 315
Irish surnames, 324, 326, 336
Irish World, 252n
Irving, Washington, 78, 80, 82, 83, 84, 86, 99, 233, 348
Italian given names, 340
Italian language, 372n, 374, 375, 408ff
Italian loan-words, 199
Italian surnames, 324, 331, 332, 336
Ives, George B., 73n, 179n, 241n

Jackson, Andrew, 76, 77, 88, 188
Jacobs, Joseph, 263
James, Henry, 71, 182, 210, 216n
Japanese language, 375
Japanese loan-words, 199n, 202, 405
Jargon, English, 33, 189n
Jefferson, Thomas, 1, 48, 59, 60, 61, 66n, 74, 75, 76, 98, 161, 228, 253, 424
Jeffrey, Francis, 66n
Jeffrey, H. R., 194n
Jepson, Edgar, 13, 18n
Jerome, Jerome K., 361, 366
Jersey Dutch, 416
Jespersen, Otto, ix, 3n, 33n, 179n, 184n, 258, 299n, 372n, 374, 378, 379, 380
Jewish given names, 339, 340
Jewish surnames, 324, 332, 334, 335, 336, 338
Jews, 145, 169n, 205, 334
Johnson, James W., 186n, 333n
Johnson, Samuel, 47, 228, 229, 231
Johnson, Samuel, Jr., 230
Johnston, Harriet Lane, 327n
Johnston, Harry, 186
Jones, Daniel, 181n, 206n, 210
Jonson, Ben, xvi
Journal of American Folk-Lore, 51n
Journal of the American Medical Association, 140n, 152, 193, 233, 245, 251, 286n, 335n
Jowett, Benjamin, 178
Joyce, P. W., 105, 106n, 107, 131n, 179n, 276, 295n

Kahn, Otto H., 138n
Kalm, Peter, 65n
Kansas Localisms, 105n, 152
Kartzke, Georg, 25
Kellogg, Walter G., 257n
Kelton, Dwight H., 348n
Kennedy, John P., 84
Kendrick, William, 106n
Ker, Edmund T., 344n
Ker, W. P., 248
Ketchum, William, 347n
King, Grace Elizabeth, 401

Kinnicutt, Lincoln N., 348n
Kipling, Rudyard, 13, 164, 208n, 357
Kirby, Senator, 175n
Knapp, S. L., 82, 83
Knickerbocker Magazine, 58, 273n
Knight, Sarah Kemble, 128n
Knox, Adrian, 242
Koehler, F., 25
Korean language, 3
Krapp, George Philip, viii, 4, 6, 11, 207n, 208, 213, 214, 215, 216, 217, 218, 247n, 267, 297, 298, 315n, 360, 365
Kroeber, A. L., 348n
Kuhns, L. Oscar, 329n
Kuiper, B. K., 331n, 340n

La Follette, Robert, 126n
Lancaster (Pa.) Journal, 99n
Landsmaal, 6n
Langereis, H. H. D., 419n
Lanier, Sidney, 262
Lanusse, Armand, 402
Lardner, Ring W., viii, xi, 44, 268*ff*, 276n, 282, 283, 284, 286n, 290, 299, 302, 304, 306, 310, 311, 318n, 361, 392, 394, 395
Latil, Alexandre, 402
Legler, Henry E., 347n
Leland, Charles G., 54, 109
Lemaître, Charles, 402
Lepouzé, Constant, 402
Les Marges, 27
Lewis, Sinclair, 270
Lewis, Wyndham, 247n
Lewisohn, Ludwig, 192n
Linati, Carlo, 386n
Lincoln, Abraham, 4
Lindsay, Vachel, 87
Lippincott's Magazine, 329n, 349n, 357n
Literary Digest, 17n, 245n
Literary Magazine and British Review, 49n
Literary Review, 18n
Littell, Philip, 188n
Little Review, 17n, 247n
Livingston, Arthur, 199, 409, 410, 411
Lockhart, Caroline, 270
Lodge, Henry Cabot, 75, 82, 181n
London Daily Herald, 16n
London Daily Mail, 15, 159
London Daily News, 15, 37
London Daily Telegraph, 131
London Magazine, 79
London Nation, 238
London New Age, 35
London New Witness, 16, 24, 225n
London Review, 313

London Times, 6n, 33n, 162, 167n, 179, 232n, 241, 249
Long, Percy W., 189n
Longfellow, H. W., 58, 84
Lontos, S. S., 331n, 340n, 421
López-Penha, A. Z., 405n
Lossing, B. J., 34, 75
Lounsbury, Thomas S., 6, 9, 10, 11, 12, 38, 50, 70, 106n, 112, 180, 183n, 228n, 234, 243n, 244, 281, 282, 283n, 296, 298, 316n, 360, 385
Low, Sidney, 13, 204
Lowell, A. Lawrence, 124n
Lowell, Amy, 179n
Lowell, James Russell, 21, 34, 60, 68, 86, 235, 385
Lubbock, John, 243
Lussan, A., 402
Lyell, Charles, 59

M. A. B., 24n
Macaulay, T. B., 86, 262
Mack, Willard, 15
Madison, James, 66n
Mahoney, Charles, 99n
Maitland, James, 360
Manchester Guardian, 17, 384n
March, F. A., 244
Marcy, William L., 84
Marden, Orison Sweet, 422, 423
Marlowe, Christopher, 298
Marryat, Captain, 128n
Marsh, Edward, 165
Marsh, George Perkins, 8, 179, 208
Marshall, Archibald, 72n
Marshall, John, 34, 48, 59, 60
Marshall, Orsamus H., 347n
Martin, Maria Ewing, 347n
Maryland Archives, 57
Massachusetts Spy, 63
Masters, Edgar Lee, 87, 179n
Mather, Cotton, 66
Mather, Increase, 57
Matthews, Brander, 6, 12, 21, 22, 24, 189, 195, 196, 235, 236, 239n, 250, 256, 257, 360n, 362, 367
Maugham, W. Somerset, 277n
McClure's Magazine, 211n, 318n
McCullagh, Joseph S., 199n
McKenna, L. B., 335
McLaughlin, W. A., 333n
Mead, Leon, 195n
Meany, Edmond S., 348n
Mearns, Hugh, 212n, 318
Medical Press, 16
Meloney, W. B., 58n
Menner, Robert J., 11, 71, 207n
Mercier, Alfred, 402
Metropolitan Magazine, 194
Meyer, Herman H. B., 168n

INDEX 489

Michigan Dutch, 417
Michigan localisms, 202
Migliacci, Edoardo, 409
Miller, Edith, 266n
Milton, John, 59, 276, 302, 368
Modern Language Notes, 8, 349n
Modern Philology, 349n
Moore, George, 13
Molee, Elias, 27
Money, names for American, 58, 172
Monthly Mirror, 48
Monthly Review, 48, 49n
Montfort, Eugène, 27
Montigny, Louvigny de, 400n, 401
More, Thomas, 305
Morfill, W. R., 88
Mormon, Book of, 63n
Morris, Gouverneur, 58, 59
Morse, John T., 66n
Moslem Sunrise, 27
Mulhall, Michael George, 372
Murison, W., 37, 70n
Murray, Gilbert, 35, 248
Murray, James A. H., 236, 237, 243
Musical vocabulary, 132
Myers, Gustavus, 98n

Nares, Robert, 70n
Nashe, Thomas, 59
Nathan, George Jean, 167n
Nation, 182, 192, 215n, 322n
National Bureau of Education, 261
National Council of Teachers of English, vii, 11
National Education Association, 244, 246
National Institute of Arts and Letters, 322
Nation's Business, 192n
Naturalization of loan-words, 200*ff*
Neal, J. C., 268
Neal, John, 80
Negro loan-words, 54
New England Courant, 66
New England pronunciation, 28, 69*ff*, 110, 214*ff*
New English Dictionary, 68, 104, 236
New Europe, 239n
New International Encyclopaedia, 29, 127n, 142, 192n
New Jersey Archives, 61
New Mexican Spanish, 403, 404
New Orleans localisms, 202
New Republic, 34n, 177, 188n
Newspaper head-lines, 187
New Thought, 423
Newton, Simon, 339n
New York Age, 333n
New York Evening Mail, 192n

New York Evening Post, 36n, 37n, 87n, 151, 166n, 171n, 183, 234
New York Evening World, 299n
New York Organ, 149n
New York Sun, 68n, 85n, 144n, 160n, 225n, 383n
New York Times, 12, 155, 191n, 299n
New York Tribune, 150n, 170, 194, 213n, 234, 368
New York World, 28, 299n
Nicholas I, of Russia, 85n
Nieland, Dirk, 418
Niles' Register, 98
Norris, Charles G., 247n
Norris, Senator, 134n
North American Review, 28n, 49, 60, 61, 257n
Norton, Charles Ledyard, 98
Notes and Queries, 103n
Noun, American, 308
Noyes, Alfred, 218n
Nursery vocabulary, 119n, 152n

Oberndorf, C. P., 334n
O'Brien, Frank A., 347n
O'Brien, Seumas, 247n
Obsolete Americanisms, 52
Ochs, Adolph S., 12, 21
Ohio Archeological and Historical Quarterly, 347n
Oliphant, S. Grant, 326n, 330
Oppenheim, James, 87
Opprobrium, terms of, 333, 368
O'Sullivan, Vincent, 24
Outlook, 164n
Overman, Lee S., 175

Paca, William, 327
Palma, Ricardo, 6n
Palmer, E. H., 259n
Palmer, Frank, 425
Parsons, Usher, 348n
Parton, James, 188
Pattee, F. L., 30n
Patterson, M. R., 368n
Paulding, J. K., 80, 89
Pedagogical Seminary, 361n
Peel, Robert, 189n
Penn, William, 51
Pennsylvania German, 103, 202, 397*ff*, 419
Pennsylvania localisms, 202
Pep, 151
Perennes, P., 402
Perrett, Wilfrid, 210n, 243
Perry, Bliss, 66, 177n
Pershing, J. J., 327
Philippine localisms, 203
Phillips, Wendell, 173
Philological Society of England, 243

490 INDEX

Phipson, Evacustès A., 168n, 215
Phonetic alphabets, 207
Pickering, John, 8, 29, 38, 50, 59, 72, 78, 94
Pidgin English, 203, 377, 383
Pinkney, William, 61
Poe, Edgar Allan, 34, 86, 149n, 327
Poetry: A Magazine of Verse, 18n, 192n, 194
Polack, W. G., 130n, 216n
Polish given names, 340
Polish language, 422
Polish surnames, 325, 331, 332
Political vocabulary, 98, 124*ff*, 157*ff*
Pomeroy, Samuel C., 85
Pope, Alexander, 106n
Pope, T. Michael, 163n
Portuguese language, 6, 374, 375
Portuguese loan-words, 200
Pory, John, 55
Pound, Louise, vii, ix, 186, 195, 196n, 198n, 201n, 202n, 213n, 252, 309n, 314, 342, 354n, 363n
Prince, J. Dyneley, 416
Printers' vocabulary, 132
Profanity, 153*ff*
Pronunciation, American, 69*ff*, 110*ff*, 206*ff*
Protestant Episcopal Church, 169, 216
Psychoanalytic Review, 334n
Publications Buffalo Historical Society, 347n
Publications Society for the Advancement of Scandinavian Study, 421n
Public Health Reports, 142n
Puritan given names, 340
Pronoun, American, 291
Purvey, John, 276
Putnam, Ruth, 347n

Quarterly Review, 45, 46n, 49n, 79, 80, 83
Quiller-Couch, Arthur, 33, 248

Railroad terms, 97
Raleigh, Walter, 248
Ramos y Duarte, Félix, 101n
Ramsay, David, 78
Rauch, E. H., 398
Read, Richard P., 225n
Read, William A., 211n, 314
Real Academia Española de la Lengua, 6
Red Men, Order of, 52
Reed, Alfred Z., 85n
Rees, John E., 347n
Revue de Dialectologie Romane, 403
Richardson, Samuel, 178, 304
Rittenhouse, Jessie B., 192n
Riverside Press, 240

Roberts, George E., 192n
Robertson, D. M., 5n
Robinson, Andrew, 58
Romanic Review, 409n
Roof, Katharine Metcalf, 167n
Roosevelt, Theodore, 58n, 194, 244, 362, 363
Roquiny, Jacques de, 402
Rosecrans, W. S., 327
Rouquette, Adrien, 402
Rouquette, Dominique, 402
Ruppenthan, J. C., 105n, 198n, 330, 340n
Ruskin, John, 13, 304
Russian language, 372, 373, 374, 375, 376n
Ruttenber, E. M., 348n

Sadig, Mufti Muhammad, 27
Saint-Céran, Tullius, 402
Saintsbury, George, 143, 248, 364, 366
Sala, George Augustus, 13
Sanchez, Nellie van de Grift, 347
Sandburg, Carl, 87, 179n, 386
Sargent, Porter E., 170n
Saturday Evening Post, 181, 269n
Saturday Review, 119, 136n, 170, 236
Sayce, A. H., 13, 31, 37, 206, 207n, 217n, 243n, 277, 313, 385
Scandinavian surnames, 324, 325, 331
Scandinavian Studies and Notes, 5n
Schele de Vere, Maximilian, 6n, 12, 40, 43, 109, 167, 235, 328, 349
Schoolcraft, Henry R., 348n
School Review, 213n
Schuchardt, H., 401n
Schuette, Oswald F., 363
Schwab, Charles M., 138n
Scotch dialect, 102n
Scribner's Magazine, 17n
Seaman, H. W., ix
Searle, William G., 323n
Sechrist, Frank K., 361n
Seeley, J. R., 65n
Serbian language, 422
Sewall, Samuel, 64n
Shakespeare, William, 68, 178, 231, 276, 277n, 283, 298, 312, 363
Shaw, George Bernard, 155, 225n, 238
Sheridan, Thomas, 70
Sherman, L. Y., 175, 181n
Sherman, W. T., 424
Sherwood, General, 175, 176n
Shorter, Clement K., 170
Sidney, Philip, 303
Sigourney, Lydia, 83
Simplified Spelling, 243*ff*
Simplified Spelling Board, 244*ff*
Skeat, W. W., 29n, 244
Sketch, 119

INDEX 491

Slang, American, 16, 156, 360*ff*
Slaughter, Gertrude, 364n
Slavic languages, 422
Slavic surnames, 324
Smart Set, 335n
Smith, C. Alphonso, 371
Smith, George J., 259
Smith, Capt. John, 51
Smith, L. P., 103n, 163, 178, 182, 248, 249n
Smith, Seba, 188
Smith, Senator, of South Carolina, 175n
Smith, Sydney, 79, 160
Snyder, Homer P., 134n, 175
Social Hygiene Bulletin, 152
Société des Parlers de France, 5
Society for Pure English, vii, 137n, 143n, 248, 249, 385
South African Dutch, 417
South African English, 54
South American Spanish, 6, 404, 405
Southern localisms, 138n, 211, 215, 294
Southey, Robert, 59, 80
Southwestern localisms, 202
Spanish language, 6, 161n, 372, 373, 374, 375, 376, 402*ff*
Spanish loan-words, 54, 88, 101, 197, 203
Spanish place-names, 345, 350, 351, 354
Spanish surnames, 325
Spectator, 170
Spelling, American, 48, 221*ff*
Springfield Republican, 151n
Squire, J. C., 13, 18n
Stage, language of the, 169, 219
Standard Dictionary, 64n, 103, 104, 199n, 240, 245n
Stedman, Edmund Clarence, 368
Stefánsson, Vilhjálmer, 419, 420
Steger, S. A., 230n
Stephen, Leslie, 312
Stephens, Henry, 308n
Stephenson, John C., 144n
Sterling, James, 80
Stevenson, R. L., 178, 262, 312
Steward, J. F., 347n
Story, Joseph, 78
Street names, 357*ff*
Sullivan, Raymond E., 99n
Sumner, Wm. Graham, 77n
Sunday, Billy, 24, 138n
Surnames, 321*ff*
Svornost, 422
Swedish language, 5, 414*ff*
Swedish surnames, 332
Sweet, Henry, 3n, 34, 69, 178, 207, 256n, 260, 264n, 281, 293n, 296, 298, 300, 301, 311

Swift, Jonathan, 155n, 302
Symonds, S., 57
Synge, J. M., 386

Taft, William H., 28, 363
Tagalog loan-words, 203
Tallichet, H., 182n, 202n
Talmon, Charles F., 250n
Tammany Hall, 52, 98
Taylor, E. B., 361n
Taylor, Bayard, 36, 84, 368
Temple, William, 111
Tennyson, Alfred, 243
Testut, Charles, 402
Thompson, Alexander M., 381n
Thoreau, Henry, 34
Thornton, R. H., viii, ix, 6n, 15n, 41, 42, 43, 44, 50, 54, 57n, 59, 60, 67, 85, 93 95n, 96, 98, 99n, 101, 103n, 104, 109, 135, 153, 182, 341n
Ticknor, George, 84
Tobin, Edward J., 299n
Tooke, John Horne, 306
Tooker, W. W., 347n
Toomey, Noxon, 348n
Toro y Gisbert, Miguel, 101n
Towne, Elizabeth, 423
Town Topics, 104
Transactions Wisconsin Academy of Sciences, 347n
Traubel, Horace, 87n, 177
Triad, 242, 384n
Trine, Ralph Waldo, 423
Trollope, Mrs., 149
Trumbull, J. Hammond, 347n
Tucker, Gilbert M., viii, ix, 6n, 28, 42, 43, 50, 67n, 153, 170, 209, 227, 356n
Tupper, Martin F., 423

Undersökningen av Svenska Folkmål, 5
United States Geographic Board, 341n, 343, 350, 353, 355n
United States Official Postal Guide, 343
Universities, American, 144n
University of Missouri Bulletin, 266n
Untermeyer, Louis, 87
Upham, Warren, 347n

Van Andel, Henry G., 331n, 340n, 417
Van Buren, Martin, 98, 174n
Van Doren, Carl, 30n, 78n
Van Riemsdyck, D. J., 419n
Variety, 192
Verb, American, 271*ff*
Verga, Giovanni, 386n
Villeneufve, Le Blanc de, 402
Virginia pronunciation, 111
Vizetelly, Frank H., 106n, 111, 112, 209, 299n
Vojan, J. Salaba, 422

Wachtel, C. H., 340n, 422
Walbran, John D., 347n
Walker, John, 70n, 112, 229
Walsh, Robert, 80
Walsh, Senator, of Massachusetts, 175n
Ward, Artemus, 268
Wardlaw, Patterson, 259n
Ware, J. R., 54, 92n, 96, 157, 158, 162
Warnock, Elsie L., 96n, 191n, 196n
War slang, 368*ff*
Washington, George, 59, 66n, 74, 76, 98
Washington, Mrs., 147n
Watson, H. B. Marriott, 165
Watts, Harvey M., 383n
Weaver, John V. A., viii, 270, 386, 395
Weber and Fields, 201
Webster, Daniel, 89
Webster, Noah, 1, 6, 7, 8, 45, 46, 59, 65, 69, 71, 73, 84, 91, 110, 112, 179, 217, 228*ff*, 243, 244, 247, 316
Webster's New International Dictionary, 240n
Webster, W. F., 260n
Weekley, Ernest, xv, 53
Weekly Review, 247n
Weeks, Senator, 175n
Wells, H. G., 13, 24, 161, 163
Wendell, Barrett, 78n
Wesley, John, 231
Westminster Gazette, 13, 18n
Westminster Review, 29n
Wheelock, John Hall, 87
Whewell, William, 36
White, James, 347n
White, Richard Grant, 4n, 6, 9, 10, 11, 36n, 38, 59, 62, 110, 131n, 143, 149n, 150, 162, 163, 170, 179n, 207, 220, 243n, 259, 356

Whitman, Walt, 21, 86, 87, 88, 343, 348n, 385
Whitney, William D., 360, 364
Wilcox, W. H., 258, 260
Williams, Alexander, 191n
Williams, R. O., 83, 84, 136, 230n
Wilson, A. J., 123n
Wilson, Edmund, Jr., 166, 369
Wilson, W. A., 151
Wilson, Woodrow, 16, 34, 76n, 169, 174, 189
Winslow, Thyra Samter, 335n
Winthrop, John, 228
Wirt, William, 327
Witherspoon, John, 8, 47, 94, 184
Wittmann, Elisabeth, 184n, 185, 186, 187
Worcester Dictionary, 241
Worcester, Joseph E., 80, 110, 112, 230, 233, 235
Wordsworth, William, 80
World Almanac, 142, 324n, 339n, 374n, 375n
World's Work, 376n
Wright, Almroth, 138, 161
Writer's Monthly, 200n
Wycliffe, John, 292

Yale Review, 183n, 256n, 257n
Yankee-Dutch, 418, 419
Yeats, W. B., 179
Yiddish language, 405*ff*
Yiddish loan-words, 109, 163, 198
Y. M. C. A., 25
Yule, Henry

Zetterstrand, E. A., 414

www.ingramcontent.com/pod-product-compliance
Lightning Source LLC
Chambersburg PA
CBHW022000100426
42738CB00042B/953